Managerial Economics

Managerial Economics

BARRY KEATING
University of Notre Dame

J. HOLTON WILSON
Central Michigan University

ACADEMIC PRESS COLLEGE DIVISION

(Harcourt Brace Jovanovich, Publishers)
Orlando   San Diego   San Francisco   New York
London   Toronto   Montreal   Sydney   Tokyo   São Paulo

To Maryann, John, Vincent, and Alice
   — B. K.

To Ron and Eva
   — J. H. W.

Academic Press, Inc.
Orlando, Florida 32887

United Kingdom edition published by
Academic Press, Inc. (London) Ltd.
24/28 Oval Road, London NW1 7DX

ISBN: 0-12-402860-8

LIBRARY OF CONGRESS CATALOG
CARD NUMBER: 85-71542

Printed in the United States of America

Contents

6 Forecasting   254

7 Production   335

Preface

Managerial Economics is for use in an *applied* microeconomics course that deals with the economics of the firm. Usually universities that offer managerial economics also offer students a more theoretical course called microeconomic theory. The difference between a course in managerial economics and one in microeconomic theory is largely a matter of emphasis. In managerial economics, applications and tools with which to apply the theory are quite important. In addition, a managerial economics course stresses *practice* in the application of those techniques and tools. *Managerial Economics* was written with an emphasis on the applications of microeconomic theory and also provides numerous examples and opportunities for practicing new economic tools and skills. This text is not only an *applied* microeconomic theory text but also includes tools from statistics, mathematics, operations research, and a few concepts from macroeconomic theory.

The tools and applications we have emphasized were chosen from those that businesses actually use (see Forgionne's list in Chapter 1, page 3). To help students gain an appreciation for how these applications and tools can be usefully applied, we have taken the time to show clearly the relevance of the material included in the text. Students are shown in Chapter 1 the results of studies that illustrate how widely such concepts as elasticity, forecasting, and the analysis of demand, production, and cost are used by corporate decision makers. In Chapters 2–13 many applications are cited, and representative problems are fully developed from formulation through solution and interpretation. Many applied topics are covered in enough detail so that students should feel quite comfortable using these tools in class as well as in real business situations. Consider the forecasting tools covered in Chapter 6. Time series decomposition, for example, is a commonly used technique that is explained in detail with a *completely worked-out example*. Students will feel confident of their ability to use this technique after practicing with problems 4, 9, 13, 14, 15, and 18 in the end-of-chapter problems. Likewise, the extended example presented on sales forecasting in Exhibit 6.2 (Chapter 6, pages 285–302) will further reinforce a student's facility with forecasting tools. The exhibit is actually an article written for business forecasters with an exact description of commonly used forecasting techniques.

Economic theory is *not* sacrificed by our applied approach. We have included complete explanations of those portions of economic theory having immediate applications to business situations. Consider the discussion of price discrimination and its reliance on the economic concept of price elasticity (Chapter 10, pages 513–522). Here we explain the economic concept at length, list some representative examples of its use in the real world (see Table 10.1, page 515), and explain to students precisely how they can apply the concept. Your students will gain valuable experience in applying the concepts of price elasticity of demand and the related technique of price discrimination in the end-of-chapter problems (problems 3, 4, 5, 6, 7, and 12).

Some 208 problems, at varying levels of difficulty and many with multiple parts, are provided to help students verify their ability to apply the concepts they have studied. Many of these problems are really mini-cases based on actual decision-making situations taken from both the private and public sectors. Nearly all of these problems have been used in our own classes over the years, and we have found them to be useful not only in verifying what the students have learned, but also in stimulating their interest in the course. Students enjoy being able to apply what they have been studying to real-life situations.

For some students our appendixes will be helpful in allowing complete mastery of all the material in the book. Appendix A is a review of algebra; Appendix B is an extended treatment of calculus concepts found in Chapter 3 (Optimization); and Appendix C is a list of data sources that we have found invaluable for students completing projects that require real rather than contrived information. Appendixes that add detail and rigor, but which the instructor may choose to skip without loss of continuity, are found directly following Chapters 2, 5, 6, and 8.

Virtually all of the material in the text has been classroom tested, modified, and retested. This process has been helpful in clarifying the presentation of what is often fairly technical information. In addition we, and the text, have benefited a great deal from the thoughtful review of many of our collegues who teach the course. They include Jack Adams, Richard Anderson, Charles Breeden, Jeff Clark, Richard Evans, David Gay, Larry Gianchetta, Harriet Hinck, John McKean, James Moser, Michael Panik, Michael Payne, R. D. Peterson, Edward Sattler, John Snyder, Len Tashman, and Richard Zuber.

A complete instructional package has been produced to augment the textbook and make its use an exciting prospect. Northwest Analytical, which supplies econometrics software to Evans Economics, has written a special microcomputer software package for students that includes all the econometric tools used in the text as well as a linear programming solution routine. In addition, Paul Hemmeter and Barry Keating have prepared lecture demonstration software, which is available for adopters. An excellent student Study Guide has been prepared by Charles Breeden, and a Solutions Manual with complete solutions to all end-of-chapter problems is available for instructors. We believe this package of instructional materials will enhance instructors' enjoyment in teaching the course and students' interest in learning the useful concepts presented in *Managerial Economics*.

Managerial Economics

1

Managerial Economics: An Introduction and Overview

As you begin your study of managerial economics, you may be asking your-self: How does managerial economics differ from the other economics I have studied? The difference is primarily one of emphasis. In this course, the emphasis is on the application of economic concepts to business prob-lems. Managerial economics is a pragmatic course designed to help you apply economic models and economic reasoning in making managerial decisions. As you progress through this course of study, you will see how economic theory and mathematical and statistical tools can be applied to a wide variety of management decisions in both the private and public sec-tors of the economy.

1.1 ECONOMICS, MANAGEMENT, AND DECISION MAKING

Managerial, or business, economists are often employed in staff, or support, positions within a firm. It is important for them to have a good understand-ing of all the basic business functions—accounting, finance, marketing, production, and so on—because managerial economics crosses these func-tional lines, using data from throughout the firm and providing information to managers in many different functional areas.

Most students who take a course in managerial economics will never work as a business economist. However, they may well have the oppor-tunity to work with business economists and/or hire business economics consulting services. Thus, it is worthwhile for every manager to have an understanding of what business economists do and what kinds of tools they have in their tool kits. Such an understanding helps the manager ask the right questions of business economists and helps the manager in using reports, analyses, and forecasts appropriately.

It is important for management to work closely with the firm's busi-ness economists in a cooperative effort. Business economists play an important role in helping to interpret events in the outside world for managers and in putting those events in a perspective that helps management make better operating and planning decisions. Decisions based on the best available information and analysis are likely to lead to the best outcomes for the firm. However, good decisions do not always lead to good outcomes. A decision is good if it is based on a thoughtful evaluation of the best available information. If it turns out that the results are not as positive as were hoped for, that does not mean the decision was bad. For example, if the weather report you hear in the morning while getting dressed calls for sunny skies and warm temperatures, you make appropriate decisions regarding which clothes to wear. If during the day a sudden change brings a rainy, cool afternoon and you get wet going between classes, that does not mean you made a bad decision. You made a good decision based on the available information but happened to incur a bad outcome. Business economists can help managers avoid bad outcomes by providing good information upon which to base decisions. They cannot, however, prevent bad outcomes.

1.2 THE USEFULNESS OF MANAGERIAL ECONOMIC SKILLS

The skills you will learn about and see applied in this course are widely used in the business world. In the early 1980s, Wicander surveyed a sample of members of the National Association of Business Economists (NABE) concerning skills they thought were important for undergraduate business economics students and Master of Business Administration (MBA) students to know.[1] Seventy-five skill areas were identified, and respondents were asked to rate the importance of each.

For both student groups, oral and written communication skills were rated the most important. For undergraduate students, 14 of the 23 next most important skills included topics covered in this course, for example, simple linear regression, time value of money, economic analysis of demand, sales forecasting, and economic analysis of cost. The results for MBA students were similar. Thirteen of the skill areas rated from third to twenty-fifth for that group are included in this course. These ratings represent the thinking of professionals actively engaged in the day-to-day business world.

In 1984, Forgionne reported complementary findings.[2] Over 80 percent of the executives who participated in this study reported that they used regression analysis and econometric skills. Chapter 3 of this text will help

---

[1] Linda C. Wicander, "An Inquiry into the Attitudes of NABE Members Concerning Course and Skill Attributes of Business, Economic and MBA Students," unpublished master's thesis, Central Michigan University, 1981.

[2] Guisseppi A. Forgionne, "Economic Tools Used by Management in Large American Operated Corporations," *Business Economics*, April 1984, pp. 5–17.

you learn to understand and use these skills. In addition, many applications of regression analysis are reported throughout the text, and in chapter-end problems, you will have the opportunity to apply these skills yourself. Statistical decision analysis was reported as being used by nearly 77 percent of the executives in Forgionne's study. Chapter 2 of this text introduces this area of decision making, along with some other tools Forgionne reported as being used frequently (e.g., net present value and risk return analysis).

Optimization tools were also reported as being used relatively frequently by corporate decision makers. Forgionne found that marginal analysis and calculus were used by about 65 percent of the executives in his study. In this text, Chapter 3 and the appendix covering differentiation introduce these concepts, and they are applied frequently throughout the text as appropriate. Linear programing—another optimization tool, developed in Chapter 8—was reported as being used by over 72 percent of the firms in Forgionne's study.

Examples of other economic tools that Forgionne found to be used in marketing, production, cost analysis, financial analysis, and pricing include the following:

Forecasting	93.8%	Cost functions	84.6%
Market share analysis	89.2	Break-even analysis	83.1
Demand curves	69.2	Economies of scale	72.3
Elasticity	66.2	Capital rationing	61.5
Input-output analysis	55.4	Full cost pricing	75.4
Marginal productivity	53.9	Marginal cost pricing	73.8
Production functions	36.9	Price leadership	61.5

The percentages following each economic tool represent the percent of executives who reported using that concept. All of these concepts are covered in this text. Many others that Forgionne also found to be used by business decision makers are included as well.

Some of the benefits of implementing economic concepts in decision making are: (1) the analysis generates useful data, (2) it forces decision makers to define problems clearly and concisely, (3) it highlights relevant policy implications and ramifications, and (4) it provides a useful laboratory for testing various policies.[3] The topics you will study in managerial economics will help you to better understand how economic, statistical, and mathematical skills can be integrated into a wide range of managerial decision making situations even if you never become a practicing business economist. This understanding will enable you to better communicate with economic analysts and will enhance the benefit you receive from managerial economic analysis.

---

[3]Forgionne, p. 11.

1.3   WHAT DO BUSINESS ECONOMISTS DO?

To illustrate further the importance of the tools you will study in this course, let us look at 10 representative job descriptions from a 1983 list of employment opportunities.[4] These job descriptions also provide a brief synopsis of how business economists contribute to the management of modern organizations. We include this set of examples, not because we expect you to look for such jobs, but because, by reading through the list, you will get some sense of the high level of corporate demand for people with business economics skills.

1. *Vice President.* Corporate planning department in major financial institution. Opportunity to use economic analysis, econometric model-based tools, statistical analysis, and financial analysis. Projects are done to advise senior management officers on major decision-making problems. Opportunity for advancement to major business areas is most likely.

2. *Chief Economist.* To advise senior bank management and board of directors on external economic conditions and their impact on corporate and bank activities; support business-unit–level activities such as market research, industry analysis, pricing and portfolio strategy, and interest rate forecasting; participate in asset-liability management; serve as bank's spokesperson on economic matters. Strong verbal and written communication skills essential. Salary commensurate with experience.

3. *Junior Economist.* For New York City investment bank. General business conditions analysis, help to estimate the next month's CPI, auto sales, etc. Some writing. Salary to $30K.

4. *Industry Analyst.* Consumer durables, to do short-term and long-term industry sales forecasts, special market analysis, build and maintain econometric models. Quantitative undergrad with MA in economics, 2 to 5 years' experience. Mid-Atlantic. Salary to $45K.

5. *Senior Product Planning Consultant.* Get involved in strategic marketing department, plotting corporate direction, and recommending allocation of resources into new technologies and products. Requires marketing and planning experience, including one or more of the following: forecasting, market research, pricing, economic analysis, financial, opera-

---

[4]*Employment Opportunities for Business Economists: July 1983* (Cleveland, OH: National Association of Business Economists, 1983).

tions, or product planning. MBA in marketing or a quantitative discipline required plus minimum of two years' experience; must be fluent in APL, Fortran, or BASIC. Central-southern location. Salary commensurate with background and experience.

6.   *Supervisor of Energy Demand and Econometric Forecasting.* Connecticut utility requires minimum of 7 + years' experience in econometric modeling, forecasting, and evaluation of energy demand and economy. Get involved in planning and supervising of all forecasting activities, and supervise two analysts. Should have a strong understanding of macro- and microeconomics, econometrics, probability, and statistics. Must have an MBA or master's in economics. Salary commensurate with experience.

7.   *Economist.* Fortune 500 firm seeks person responsible for assisting in preparation of macroeconomic and vehicle sales forecasts. Prefer PhD in economics with strong background in macroeconomics and several years of related work experience. A broad understanding of quantitative methods is necessary.

8.   *Econometricians.* For major national communications firm. PhD's and MA's to develop econometric models that will assist in the analysis and forecasting of economic developments, industry competition, supply and demand of matters affecting their industry. Excellent communicative skills mandatory.

9.   *Senior Economist.* For investment research and management firm in New York City to do GNP and business cycle forecasting. Small department. Must have solid experience, including total responsibility for GNP forecasts. $100K to $150K.

10.   *Electrical Utility Economist.* To forecast and evaluate economic and consumer energy demand conditions. The individual sought must have a demonstrated ability to plan, establish, and supervise forecasting-oriented activities and complete projects on time. MA or MBA with effective communications skills and proven capabilities in econometrics and probability statistics is particularly desirable. Firm is located in the Northeast. Salary to $40K.

These job descriptions provide evidence of the demand for personnel with the types of skills you will study in your managerial economics course. They also give you a sense of what business economists do in their work. In addition, they reassert the desirability of good communications skills.

The skills of business economists are utilized in many ways by a wide variety of firms in our economy. For example, in 1974, the *New York Times* hired a business economist to work on two specific problems: (1) they were losing market share to radio, television, and suburban daily papers; and (2) they were concerned about the future impact of the economy on their advertising and circulation revenues.[5] An effective econometric model was developed to forecast advertising and circulation revenues and was the basis for reshaping the format, layout, and special sections of the news-paper. The results were very favorable. The success of the business economist in solving these problems also led to the development of a formal planning system at the *New York Times*.

A second example of the use of business economics skills is provided by the automotive industry. Marina Whitman, vice president and chief economist at General Motors, has an economics staff of over 70 people in New York, Detroit, and London.[6] The General Motors economics staff grew out of a social and economic relations section started in 1946. The business economists at GM have three primary functions: (1) economic forecasting, (2) public policy analysis, and (3) strategic planning. They do long-term and short-term forecasting using econometric and judgmental methods; they analyze government actions in areas such as antitrust, labor, taxes, and government spending; they study the energy situation, including demand, supply, prices, and alternative fuels. In addition, they develop alternative future business scenarios and evaluate potential new business ventures.

1.4   THE ROLE OF MODELS IN APPLIED ECONOMIC ANALYSIS

Throughout this text, various models are used to explain business and economic phenomena. A model represents an activity but at the same time simplifies that activity to manageable proportions. The most important factors influencing the activity are included in a model, while less important factors are omitted, allowing us to focus on those with the greatest influence. Students are sometimes frustrated by the use of models because they leave out so many real world influences. But after working with models for awhile, they soon learn to appreciate the essential role of modeling in investigating complex phenomena.

Physicists would not argue that the only factors determining the speed of a falling object are the force of gravity and time. Certainly wind velocity, temperature, relative humidity, and other factors may influence that

---

[5]Thomas H. Naylor, "The Politics of Corporate Economics," *Business Economics*, March 1981, pp. 6–16.

[6]Marina Whitman, "Economics from Three Perspectives," *Business Economics*, January 1983, pp. 20–24.

speed. But, nonetheless, their model involving just time and the force of gravity is *very* effective in explaining the behavior of falling objects. The other variables are omitted because they are less important. The same can be said of modeling complex economic events. Through simplification—that is, through evaluating relationships between the most important factors while omitting less important ones—economic models may allow us to explain complex relationships in a way that helps us make better business decisions.

Physical Models

Models may take a variety of forms, for example, physical, schematic, graphic, and algebraic, or mathematical. For some purposes, a physical model is most useful in representing the essential features of a complex set of relationships. Architects frequently develop small-scale physical models to represent large buildings, urban redevelopment programs, industrial parks, and so on. Physical models are also quite common in the biological sciences as well as in chemistry and physics. A simple plastic model of the human body that includes major skeletal features, important organs, and blood vessels is useful in explaining complex interactions to biology students, even though much is left out of the model (i.e., it is far from human). In organic chemistry, physical models of molecular structures are helpful in explaining various types of chemical bonds. They can give us a visual image of a benzene molecule, for example, even though in the real world such molecules are not discernible by the human eye. But, once again, only the most important features are represented in these molecular models, while other components, such as electron shells, protons, and neutrons, are absent.

Schematic Models

A schematic model represents interrelationships in a diagrammatic manner. Such models are particularly common in the electronics field. A schematic model with which most economics and business students are familiar is the simple circular flow model showing the relationships between households and businesses in our economy, as illustrated in Figure 1.1. By using this diagram, beginning students can grasp some of the most important aspects of the interaction between households and businesses without getting lost in the maze of more complex interactions that also exist in the economy. Schematic models are used extensively in marketing, management, finance, and other areas of concentration within the general realm of business and economic studies.

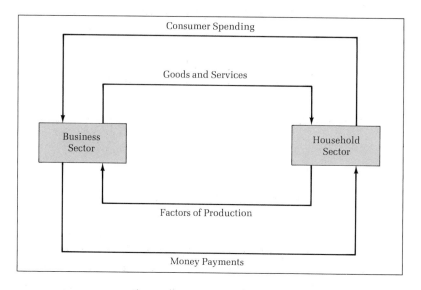

FIGURE 1.1   Simple Schematic Model of the Relationship between Households and Businesses in the Economy   This model shows how money flows in exchange for goods and services (upper loop) and how firms make money payments to people for the use of various factors of production, such as labor (lower loop).

Graphic Models

The most widely used models in the study of economics and business are graphic and algebraic, or mathematical. This is certainly true in managerial economics, as we shall see in subsequent chapters. To illustrate the use of a graphic model, let us suppose that we want to estimate the number of tickets a person might buy for professional football games during a given season. We might suspect that a wide range of variables would influence this decision, such as age, marital status and family size, distance from residence to the site of the games, income, price of tickets, occupation and other reference groups to which the person belongs, educational background, and so on. Some of these variables are difficult to quantify. Others, such as price, are constant for all persons; thus, we could well be led to settle on monthly income as the single most important and readily measured variable influencing the number of tickets a person is likely to purchase in a season.

Although the findings are mixed, we might expect a positive relationship between ticket sales and income. Let us suppose that such a relationship has been discovered and that we want to illustrate it by using a graphic model, as in Figure 1.2. We see from this graph that a person with an income of $500 per month or less is not likely to purchase any tickets; but for every $100 increase in monthly income above $500, a person is likely to buy one

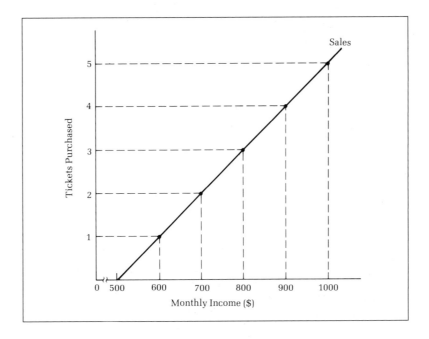

FIGURE 1.2   **Graphic Model of Football Ticket Sales as a Function of Monthly Income**   As personal income rises, so does the number of tickets purchased, as evidenced by the positive slope of the line. The value of the slope (.01 in this case) indicates how fast sales rise as income increases. We see that it takes a $100 increase in income to stimulate a one-unit increase in ticket purchases.

additional ticket during the season. For example, a person with a monthly income of $800 would be expected to purchase 3 tickets.

Mathematical Models

The graphic model depicted in Figure 1.2 may be expressed in mathematical, or algebraic, terms as follows:

$$S = -5 + .01M$$

where S represents ticket sales per person and M is monthly income. From this algebraic representation of the model depicted in Figure 1.2, we can reach the same conclusions. For example, if we want to determine the threshold income level below which a person would not buy a ticket, we could set sales equal to 0 and solve for income. Thus,

$$0 = -5 + .01M$$
$$-.01M = -5$$
$$M = \$500$$

Therefore, we see again that at an income level of $500 or less, ticket sales would be 0 (because negative ticket sales are not meaningful, the relevant range for this function is for $M > \$500$). If we let $M = \$800$, we can once more determine ticket sales at that level of income as

$$S = -5 + .01(\$800)$$
$$S = -5 + 8$$
$$S = 3$$

the same result depicted in the graphic model of this relationship.

You might well ask: Why use the mathematical form when a geometric model can be used to reach the same conclusions? The most important reason is that graphically we are limited in the number of variables that can be incorporated into the model. Furthermore, mathematical models are generally more precise and can also be used for more sophisticated forms of analysis. The importance of using models to explain complex phenomena through simplification and abstractions is common to all forms, whether schematic, physical, graphic, or mathematical in nature.

The Role of Assumptions in Using Models

Because models are abstractions and simplifications of more complex relationships, it is necessary to make various assumptions in constructing models. For example, in the model of personal purchases of football tickets as a function of income, we assume that the relationship is valid as long as the other variables, such as price, do not change. Economists refer to this as the *ceteris paribus* assumption, meaning "other things held constant." Another assumption that economists make, and students often find hard to accept, is that firms attempt to maximize profits. Whether or not firms in fact try to do so is not really as important to the models based on that assumption as whether firms behave as if they tried to maximize profits. That is, if a model built on the profit maximization assumption allows us to make reasonable predictions and explanations about the behavior of firms, then that assumption is useful in economic analysis. In evaluating a model and/or the assumptions on which it is based, one important criterion is the ability of the model to explain observable behavior. It is also important that the set of assumptions underlying any given model be consistent with one another.

Students who learn to use models in their academic work will find that this skill is most valuable in later, on-the-job applications. They may seldom, if ever, use the models in the text without modification to fit the situation at hand. But the ability to work with and develop models is one of the most important assets in a complex and changing economic environment. As you work through this course, keep in mind that the most important result is the ability to use models in a variety of situations and that the particular models used in this text are only representative examples to illustrate the strength of this approach to solving economic decision problems.

1.5   LABOR SUPPLY AND DEMAND AS AN ECONOMIC MODEL

The fundamental concepts of supply and demand analysis are introduced to business and economics students in a principles of economics course. As you learned in that course, every market has two sides: supply and demand. Demand represents the quantities of particular goods or services that consumers are willing and able to buy at various prices. Further, demand curves are described as being negatively sloped, as illustrated in the upper left panel of Figure 1.3. This negative slope is indicative of the observation that consumers buy more of most things at lower prices than at higher prices, *ceteris paribus*. Thus, the familiar demand curve represents a graphic model of consumer behavior. We will investigate this model in considerable detail in Chapter 6.

Supply is defined as the quantities of particular goods or services that producers are willing and able to make available for sale at various prices, *ceteris paribus*. For reasons that are explored later in the text, supply curves are positively sloped, as shown in the upper right-hand graph of Figure 1.3.

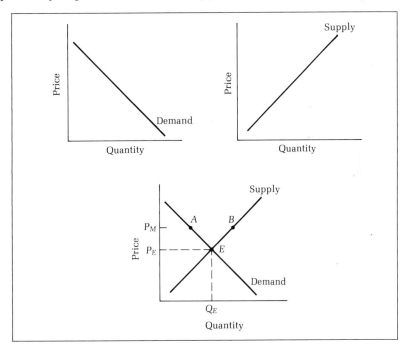

FIGURE 1.3   **Supply and Demand Model**   The demand curve has a negative slope, while the supply curve has a positive slope. Where the two curves cross (E), supply and demand are in balance; there is an equilibrium. If the price is above the equilibrium price (P_E), such as at P_M, the quantity demanded (Q_E) is less than the quantity supplied by an amount equal to the distance between points A and B.

This positive slope indicates that, other things being constant, more units are supplied at higher prices than at lower prices.

Both demand and supply are plotted on the bottom graph in Figure 1.3. Suppose the market represented here is the market for labor. The demand curve represents the quantity of labor that firms are willing and able to employ at various wages (i.e., at various prices per unit of labor service hired). The supply curve shows the amount of labor that people in the economy make available at each wage. You can see in the diagram that free market forces establish an equilibrium wage at P_E and that Q_E units of labor are employed. Supply and demand are in balance at this wage rate and employment level.

You can now use this simple model to see what would result if some well-meaning politicians decided to mandate a minimum wage above the equilibrium wage. Suppose the minimum wage is set at P_M. Draw a horizontal line from P_M through the demand curve at point A and the supply curve at point B. Rather than a balance between supply and demand, you see that at the higher wage, fewer units of labor are demanded than are supplied. The distance between points A and B is one measure of the resulting unemployment.

This model of the labor market is clearly a simplification of the real world of labor markets. But even so, or perhaps because of, this simplification, it helps us to understand and evaluate some of the ramifications of a minimum wage law. You will find that all the models of economic and business behavior discussed in the remainder of the text will help you to better understand and evaluate complex events, and it follows that a better understanding of events should lead to better managerial decisions.

1.6   THE DECISION PROCESS

Decision making is an integral part of our lives. Every day is filled with decisions of one sort or another. These decisions depend to a large extent on one's relative position in life. Students, for example, must make daily decisions on what to wear, whether to go to classes, how much time to spend studying, where to eat, and so on. Some days, more complex decisions arise, such as: What classes should I take next semester? Should I accept a job with company A or company B? Should I go to graduate school, and if so, which school?

Managers are also faced with a wide range of decisions on any given day. There are decisions of a personal nature as well as those related to professional activities. It is the latter with which we are concerned in this book. For a manager, the ability to make the best professional decision is the key to success. It is important, therefore, for students of economics and business administration—tomorrow's managers—to have an appreciation and fundamental understanding of the decision process.

It may well be argued that a course in managerial economics is a study of the decision process in an economic context. As the table of contents indicates, this text deals with topics related to economic decisions: demand, cost, pricing, forecasting, production, and so on. However, as we shall see, the main thrust of managerial economics is toward one phase—albeit it an extremely important one—of the decision process: determining the consequences of alternative actions.

A seven-step "scientific" decision process is applicable to the most simple decisions as well as to the most complex. The simpler the decision, the more automatic many of the steps, and little cognitive attention may be paid to the formal process. However, for more far-reaching business decisions, each of the steps may be broken down into substeps for rigorous evaluation. A schematic diagram of the decision process appears in Figure 1.4.

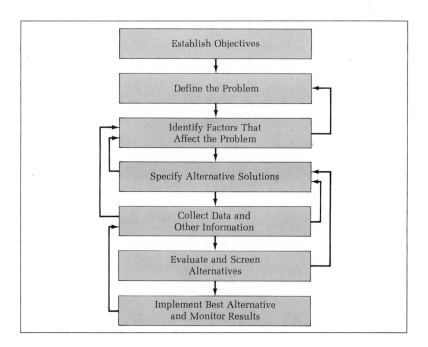

FIGURE 1.4   **Seven-Step Decision Process**   It is important to follow a logical sequence, such as shown here, in making decisions. In simple daily decisions, the process is almost automatic and may be simplified. More complex decisions require greater attention to each phase of the process and may involve recycling through earlier phases as new insights are gained.

Setting Objectives

When we make a decision, we choose from a set of alternative acts the one that we believe will best contribute to some particular result. That is, decisions are made within the context of and are influenced by the objective or set of objectives defined by the decision maker. Thus, the first step in the decision process is to establish objectives or to take account of those that have been previously defined.

Objectives should be defined in a concrete, operational form, since if they are stated in a very general or vague form, it is virtually impossible for us to establish whether a particular decision brings us closer to the stated goal. Consider, for example, the following two ways in which a firm might state one of its objectives:

- Objective A: to increase our share of the market
- Objective B: to increase our market share by at least 2.5% in the next fiscal year

With objective A, the firm has little way to evaluate the effectiveness of various decisions as they relate to this goal. A .001-percent increase in market share satisfies the objective, as does a 1-percent increase or a 5-percent increase. Some people within the company may argue that the firm has successfully met its objective with a particular increase in market share, while others may consider the same result a dismal failure. However, the wording of objective B leaves less room for debate about success or failure. The firm either increases market share by the prescribed amount or it does not. From year to year, the specific amount in objective B might be revised. If the firm consistently achieves a given objective, then the objective might be changed to prevent underachievement.

Problem Definition

Once the objectives have been established, the next phase in the decision process is to *define the particular problem* that gives rise to the need for a decision. The fact that someone must make a decision implies that there is a problem to be solved. In defining a problem, we should be as precise as possible and should state the problem explicitly. Specific questions should be asked: *What* factors are involved? *Who* is affected by or influences the problem area? *Where* are the critical activities? *When* can the situation be best altered? *Why* have situations developed into a problem? *How* are these considerations interrelated? The exact form of the questions we pose depends, of course, on the particular circumstances of the individual decision process.

In defining problems, we should take care not to define a symptom rather than the real problem. Symptoms enable us to recognize the existence of a problem, but they are rarely synonymous with the problem. For example, consider a firm whose executives observe that sales for each month in 1985 exceeded those for each month in 1986. Contrary to the first impression of many, the decline in sales is not the problem—it is a symptom of the real problem or problems. Sales have fallen for some reason. The fact that the firm's prices are out of line with competitors', that product changes have been viewed as undesirable by consumers, that the promotional program is ineffective, or other similar circumstances may be the real problem. By asking the appropriate what, who, where, when, why, and how questions, we can identify the real problems.

Identifying Causal Factors

The identification of the real problems provides a basis for the third phase of the decision process: the *explicit identification of factors* that impinge on the problems that have been identified and their influences on important variables. If sound economic decisions about a problem are to be made, it is absolutely requisite that the decision maker carefully consider the variables that have potential impact on the situation and hypothesize the relationships between or among them. Thus, this phase of the decision process includes some form of model building.

Suppose you are interested in establishing the retail price of a new product. What variables may affect such a decision? The following list is indicative: the price of similar products currently on the market, the projected sales volume at various prices, the warranty or guarantee provisions, the different possible distribution channels, the fixed production costs, the variable production costs, the promotional expense, the price image of the firm's existing product mix, the price of complementary products, the probability that competitors will market a similar product (and if probable, when), production capacity, the income of the target market, the possible changes in input costs, and so on.

Some of the factors or variables recognized as having potential impact on a particular decision are less important than others. Often, the decision maker has reason to believe that potentially influential variables are not critical in the situation being evaluated. In such cases, he or she makes assumptions regarding the behavior and influence of those variables. For example, in the new product pricing decision, it may be known that input prices were relatively stable in the past, and it may be reasonable to assume that they will not change in the period covered by the decision at hand. When any such assumptions are made concerning potentially influential variables, they should be stated explicitly; if they are not, evaluation of the effectiveness of the decision is hampered.

Having identified the variables impinging on the decision, we then hypothesize the relationship among these variables. That is, a tentative explanation of how these factors relate to the problem is developed. This process amounts to building a model or models of the situation. The important factors are included and less important ones deleted. Each model may subsequently be used to evaluate possible courses of action. As we progress further along the decision process, we gain additional insight into the problem. Such insight sometimes leads to changing the original model to incorporate this new information and thus improve the evaluation process.

Alternative Solutions

The fourth phase of the decision process is to *identify possible alternative courses of action*. At first, only the most obvious will be evident. We must be cautious not to stop trying to identify alternatives too quickly. The processes of enumerating possible courses of action should be exhaustive. It is often useful to have several people sit around a table brainstorming to compile a list of alternatives that is as complete as possible. It should be recognized that taking no action may be an important alternative. Some of the suggested actions are later dismissed without comprehensive evaluation because some of their attributes are immediately recognized as counterproductive.

The remaining alternatives should be studied rigorously, using the models developed, to determine their consequences. Obviously, the more alternatives that are fully evaluated, the better the decision is likely to be. However, evaluation is expensive in terms of both time and money. In most cases, the constraints imposed by these resources make it mandatory that fewer alternatives be more closely investigated than the manager desires. Thus, many of the alternatives originally identified may be scrapped without using a model to determine their consequences. It is the unfortunate lot of decision makers that they must usually arrive at a decision with less information than is desirable. Decisions are made in a risk-laden and far less than certain environment. Risk and uncertainty are discussed further in Chapter 2.

Gathering Information

If we are to evaluate alternatives, we must have the necessary information to use the models. Thus, the fifth stage of the decision process is *gathering data* related to the important variables impinging on the decision problem. Some of these data are readily available within the firm. Records kept in the production, marketing, finance, personnel, accounting, quality control, or other departments within the firm are a rich source of data. Often this information is not in the most desirable form or as readily available as might be expected, but with some effort and a spirit of interdepartmental cooperation, it can usually be obtained in usable form. At times, the necessary internal information has not been collected and new data must be generated. Because this process can be very costly and time consuming, we may return to the model to see if some other variable, for which data exists, might be used as a proxy.

In addition to data from within the firm, further information from external sources is often required. Again, some of these data may have been previously assembled and may be available to the firm through published documents, by request from the agency or firm that compiled the data, or by a purchase agreement with such an agency or firm. These sources of secondary data vary depending on the industry, firm, and particular situation involved.

Additional external data can be obtained by direct action of the firm. Surveys of various types can be conducted to obtain new, or primary, data relating to variables of interest to the firm. Collecting such data must be done with great care, especially if samples are used. The sampling design should be carefully developed by persons thoroughly schooled in sampling methods. The sampling process should also be done with meticulous care. The sample selected should be representative of the universe and consistent with the experimental, or sampling, design.

Evaluation of Alternatives

In the sixth phase of the decision process, the information that has been obtained is used to *evaluate and screen the alternatives* previously specified. Some of the original alternatives may be eliminated without formal analysis because they are inconsistent with the objectives established at the outset. Some may clearly be too expensive to implement, even if analysis would show them to be desirable. The remaining alternatives are subject to more comprehensive investigation to determine their consequences as precisely as possible.

This analysis and investigation process is at the core of managerial economics. In the following chapters, methods of analysis are reviewed, and representative models are presented to help you develop a basis for business economic decision making. It is, of course, impossible to provide a model for evaluating the results of every possible decision situation you may eventually face. Even if that were possible, it would not be desirable to allocate time, money, paper, and other resources to such an effort. Throughout the text, our objective is to help develop a way of thinking about business economic problems that will provide a solid basis upon which you can build as your individual careers unfold.

The evaluation of alternatives must be done with the prescribed objectives kept closely in mind. The best alternative is the one that achieves the goals determined by those objectives or brings the firm closest to those goals. This evaluation process should combine quantitive analysis with good judgment by persons thoroughly familiar with the institutional and nonquantifiable factors affecting the decision.

Implementing and Monitoring

Once the alternatives have been evaluated and screened, the seventh and final phase of the decision process is undertaken: to *implement and monitor* the appropriate actions. Even though these actions are expected to lead to satisfying the firm's objectives, those expectations may not be realized. It is, therefore, important to *establish procedures to monitor and evaluate the progress of the implemented solution.* From time to time, adjustments are likely to be desirable to accommodate variations in the firm's environment.

This seven-step decision process is applicable to a wide range of business and economic problems. Every problem has unique characteristics, and the decision process should be appropriate to each particular situation. In making recurring decisions, this may mean omitting some steps in order to simplify the process. In making more complicated decisions, it may mean extending some phases or looping back partway through the process. For example, in the process of gathering information to evaluate alternatives, the decision maker might identify additional variables that may be important or may see a previously neglected alternative. Some other points at which decision loops are likely to be necessary are illustrated in Figure 1.4. It is important to have a framework for decision making and yet to remain flexible within that framework.

1.7   AN OVERVIEW OF THE TEXT

In Chapter 2, the discussion of the decision process is expanded to include risk and uncertainty. Some of the basic statistical concepts you have learned in other courses are applied to the measurement of risk and to the present value concept to illustrate how risk can be accounted for in evaluating a future stream of revenues, costs, or profits.

Chapters 3 and 4 review mathematical and statistical tools that business and economics graduates are expected to have. Calculus and algebra are reviewed in Chapter 3. Most of you have had some exposure to calculus and may need only scan this material to refresh the skills you learned earlier. Students with little or no math background should be able to work through Chapter 3 and Appendixes A and B. This material has been tested over several years with students who have entered an MBA program from a nonquantitative undergraduate curriculum such as music or social work. By carefully working through the problems given as examples and as exercises, such students have learned to apply calculus to solve business economics problems. Thoughtful study of this material will give you sufficient understanding of calculus to use it freely in the rest of this course and in your other studies.

The statistical tool of regression analysis is the topic of Chapter 4. A pragmatic approach is used in presenting this material in an effort to give you a comfortable feeling about using this very powerful technique. Many students who work while going to school find immediate applications for regression analysis in their jobs. At the very least, you should be able to apply these concepts to the topics covered later in this course and to research you may do in other courses.

Chapter 5 is the first of two chapters that focus on the demand side of the marketplace. The determinants of demand are reviewed, and the demand function for Big Sky Foods is estimated from quarterly sales data using regression analysis. The concept of elasticity is covered in detail, with applications given for each of the major types of elasticity. A comprehensive look at the demand for automobiles in the United States is included.

Chapter 6 reviews various approaches to forecasting, including both qualitative and quantitative techniques. The primary emphasis of the chapter is on sales forecasting. However, macroeconomic forecasting is introduced and shown to be an important input into the sales forecast for a firm. Methods of detecting and measuring the effects of seasonality are included and demonstrated by specific examples.

In Chapter 7, attention turns to the supply side of the market. Both short-run and long-run production concepts are covered, including the principle of diminishing marginal productivity and economies of scale. Optimization in production is shown in a graphic form, using isoquant and isocost curves, as well as in a mathematical form, using the Lagrangian multiplier method developed in Chapter 3. Examples of applications of these concepts are shown for both the private and the public sectors.

In Chapter 8, the optimization tool linear programming is introduced. The chapter emphasizes when to use linear programming and the interpretation of results. Several examples are included to illustrate the application of linear programming.

Chapter 9 covers the theory and analysis of costs. Various ways of looking at costs are introduced, and short-run and long-run cost functions are reviewed. The important relationship between production and cost is seen throughout this chapter. Examples of actual cost functions are included to illustrate the usefulness of these concepts.

The demand and supply sides of the marketplace are combined in the last four chapters of the text. In Chapters 10 and 11, the major market structures are reviewed, including perfect competition, monopolistic competition, oligopoly, and monopoly. The role of monopoly power is treated extensively. Some special pricing models for cartels, price leadership, transfer pricing, and limit pricing are developed using both graphic and algebraic models.

In Chapter 12, additional topics related to pricing decisions are covered, including cost-plus pricing, pricing multiple products, peak load pricing, and the use of price discounts. The discussion of pricing leads naturally to the topic of regulation, covered in Chapter 13. That chapter describes the emergence of regulatory agencies and the development of an economic theory of regulation. Examples of regulations and regulatory agencies are included.

Throughout the text, examples are used extensively. In addition, many exercises are provided at the end of the chapters. To maximize your understanding of the concepts covered in this course and to enhance the ease with which you use quantitative forms of analysis, you should work as many of the chapter-end problems as possible.

SUMMARY

This chapter has given you some evidence of the usefulness of the concepts discussed in later chapters of the text. One complaint sometimes heard about economics courses goes something like this: The material is not useful; I want to see applications of economic concepts to real world situations. However, this course emphasizes applications. You will see economic analysis brought to bear on many real world problems with very useful results.

The use of economic models, introduced in this chapter, is extended in subsequent chapters. You will find that by constructing and analyzing models of behavior, you will be better able to understand why and how various systems work. This better understanding will, in turn, help you make better economic and business decisions.

SUGGESTED READINGS

Baumol, William J. "What Can Economic Theory Contribute to Managerial Economics?" *American Economic Review, Papers and Proceedings,* May 1961, pp. 142–146.

Cohen, Kalman J., and Cyert, Richard M. "Some Reasons for Studying Business Behavior," "The Methodology of Model Building," and "Decision Making by Marginal Analysis." In *Theory of the Firm: Resource Allocation in a Market Economy.* Englewood Cliffs, NJ: Prentice-Hall, 1965, Chapters 1, 2, and 3.

Forgionne, Guisseppi A. "Economic Tools Used by Management in Large American Operated Corporations." *Business Economics,* April 1984, pp. 5–17.

Friedman, Milton. "The Methodology of Positive Economics." In *Essays in Positive Economics.* Chicago: University of Chicago Press, 1953, pp. 3–43.

Harris, Robert G. "The Values of Economic Theory in Management Education." *American Economic Review,* May 1984, pp. 122–126.

Hatten, Mary Louise. *Macroeconomics for Management,* 2d ed. Englewood Cliffs, NJ: Prentice-Hall, 1985.

Keating, Barry P., and Keating, Maryann O. *Not-for-Profit.* Glen Ridge, NJ: Thomas Horton and Daughters, 1980.

Machlup, Fritz. "Theories of the Firm: Marginalist, Behavioral, Managerial." *The American Economic Review*, March 1976, pp. 1–33.

Naylor, Thomas H. "The Politics of Corporate Economics." *Business Economics*, March 1981, pp. 6–16.

Whitman, Marina. "Economics from Three Perspectives." *Business Economics*, January 1983, pp. 20–24.

PROBLEMS

1. What is a model? Give examples of a physical model, a graphic model, a schematic model, and a mathematical (or algebraic) model based on your general educational experiences (i.e., not necessarily from business or economics). Explain why each of these fits the definition of a model and how each may be useful in the appropriate field.

2. Explain the seven-step decision process in the context of some specific decision you have made recently. Be as explicit as possible in identifying components of each step. Examples of possible decisions include the decision to buy a calculator, a stereo, a car, or some other item; the decision to interview with a particular firm for employment after graduation; the decision to apply to graduate school; the decision to take a spring-break vacation in the South; and so on.

3. List five not-for-profit organizations and five public sector agencies that could make use of economic analysis in various decisions. Give two examples of such decisions for each of the ten listings.

4. Suppose that the chairperson of your major department asked you for help in the decision regarding potential summer session offerings. How could you apply the seven-step decision process to this problem? Explain each step in the decision carefully. Why are the first two steps particularly important?

5. In the text you read the following statement: "Most students who take a course in managerial economics will never work as a business economist." Could the same thing be said of accounting courses? Marketing courses? Finance courses? Why, then, should you take these courses?

6. Explain the difference between bad decisions and bad outcomes. How can management reduce the risk of bad outcomes? Give some examples of situations in which you have made or observed good decisions that resulted in bad outcomes.

7. Suppose that you were hired by a new firm that makes and sells frozen pizza in the local market. The owner-manager wants you to help in evaluating the firm's progress and in providing information on which better decisions can be based in the future. One area of particular interest is the firm's market share. What factors would you include in a market share model for such a firm? Which of these factors are subject to internal managerial control, and which are external to the firm? How could your model be useful to the owner-manager?

2

Risk and Capital Budgeting

The municipal government of Mishawaka, Indiana, is planning to construct a bypass that will run parallel to the main city street. The municipal planners must choose between an expensive, modern, four-lane bypass, which would be quite expensive, and a cheaper, narrower street of lesser quality. The planners are not certain of the amount of traffic that will be borne by the new bypass, but they have tentative projections to aid their planning. Which choice is the best for Mishawaka?

Allstate Insurance is considering hiring an additional claims adjuster for the coming year. Allstate is unsure, however, precisely how many claims it will have during the coming year, but it does have information on previous years, and there is a reliable forecast of policy sales for next year. Should Allstate hire the additional adjuster?

First Bank and Trust Company is considering the construction of an automated teller facility at its downtown location. The automated tellers are expensive to build, and the bank is unsure of how many such teller windows are needed. How could the bank decide how many teller windows to install?

A "big-eight" auditing team is visiting McLintock Corporation today. In the past, the accounts receivable balances have been in error 2 percent of the time. The auditors can handle 30 accounts per day. Would it be unusual if they found 2 errors in the first day of the audit?

The situations described above have an element in common: in each case there is some risk that must be borne by the decision maker.

2.1 RISK VERSUS UNCERTAINTY

Risk and uncertainty are important in managerial economics because management decisions are almost always made by people who have some doubt about the outcome of their actions. But decisions must be made and must be based on the limited information available. In situations of certainty, the decision maker knows for sure what outcome will follow from each alternative choice. If all situations were certain, decisions would be much easier to make. Suppose, for example, that the municipal planners of Mishawaka knew for certain what would happen if they constructed an expensive, modern, wide bypass and what would happen if they built a cheaper, narrower, lower-quality bypass. In this case, the decision would take place under certainty, and quite clearly the decision process would be greatly simplified.

If the amount of information about the results of the two alternatives open to Mishawaka is less than complete, then the decision about which type of bypass to build must take place under conditions of either risk or uncertainty. This obviously makes the decision process more difficult. The amount of information available to the decision maker determines whether a decision is made in a state of risk or in a state of uncertainty. To the economist, risk and uncertainty are not identical in meaning. Let us look at both more closely.

Risk

If you are to make a decision that can have several outcomes and each outcome occurs with a known probability, then the decision can be said to be made under conditions of risk. Risk requires that you know all the possible outcomes of a decision and, in addition, that you have some idea of how likely each outcome is to actually take place. In a college football game, there are only three possible outcomes (each team may win, lose, or tie), and many people attach probabilities to those outcomes each fall. The precise outcome of a particular game is unknown before the game, but since the range of outcomes and the odds that a particular team will win are commonly published, the situation may be described as one involving risk.

Likewise, if you flip a fair coin—one that has an equal probability of turning up heads or tails—the range of outcomes is known (either heads or tails), and the probability of each of those outcomes is also known. The actual outcome on any given toss, however, is not known with certainty, and so, again, the situation involves risk.

Uncertainty

If the possible outcomes of an action are unknown or the probabilities of the outcomes are unknown, a state of uncertainty exists.

Some board games, such as Dungeons and Dragons, require the use of icosahedron, or 20-sided, dice. If a player new to the game is asked to predict the outcome of the roll of a Dungeons and Dragons die, the player would be at a total loss to venture even a guess. How would a new player know that the die had exactly 20 sides; and how would such a player know that the digits 0 through 9 each appeared on 2 of the die's faces? Asked to make an estimate of the value of the next roll, a new player would be in a state of uncertainty.

If the decision maker lacks information about the precise nature of the outcomes or is unable to assign probabilities to known outcomes, the situation is uncertain. This chapter deals mainly with situations of risk rather than of uncertainty; only the discussion of game theory concerns situations in which the decision maker is unable (or unwilling) to specify the possible outcomes and the probabilities that those outcomes will actually take place.

While very few situations in the real world involve complete information (certainty), there are many situations in which the degree of uncertainty is so small that it would not be worthwhile to use the techniques covered in this chapter. Thus, we do not want to imply that all decisions about which an individual is less than certain require the use of one of the sophisticated tools covered in this chapter to arrive at a "best" decision. Use of these tools must be tempered by the completeness of the information available about a decision and the importance attached to making the correct decision (i.e., the size of the outcome). Whether to wear a raincoat on a cloudy spring day is surely a decision made without complete information, but the importance of the outcome is perhaps so trivial that few individuals would spend more than a moment or two making the decision and very few indeed would engage in a formal analysis of the outcomes.

2.2 SOME PROBABILITY CONCEPTS

An understanding of probability is at the heart of the analysis of risk and uncertainty. *Probability* is defined as the percentage chance that a particular outcome of an event will occur. The key to understanding how economists and businesspeople use probability lies in understanding a related concept: *subjective probability*. Let us consider an event that entails some risk, say, buying a bond issued by General Motors Corporation. The situation involves risk because you cannot be absolutely certain when you purchase the bond what the outcome will be at the bond's maturity. Three possible outcomes are listed in Table 2.1 (we assume that these are the only possible outcomes). The column titled "Subjective Probability" is the decision maker's estimate of the percentage chance of each outcome. It is common to refer to such percentage chances simply as probabilities, but it is important to note that these probability estimates are subject to limited knowledge, feelings, and whatever reasoning the decision maker chooses to apply. It is impossible to give a precise formulation of how subjective probabilities are conceived by individuals in various situations.

TABLE 2.1   **Subjective Probability Distribution of Possible Outcomes of Buying a General Motors Bond**

Outcome	Subjective Probability
General Motors pays principal at maturity and meets all interest payments	.95
General Motors fails to meet at least one interest payment (interest default)	.04
General Motors fails to redeem bonds at maturity (principal default)	.01
Total	1.00

You may feel, for instance, that the Chicago Cubs will ultimately win the World Series next year, and you might even be inclined to estimate a probability of 75 percent for that event. How might you arrive at such a subjective probability? Surely your estimate would be based in part on past performance of the Cubs. If you are a Cubs fan, your estimate may be influenced by a bit of wishful thinking. But regardless of how probabilities are estimated, all are used in the same manner in decision making. The basis on which the probability is determined is unimportant to a decision maker; only the probability itself is relevant.

Any statement of probability concerns a future event involving risk. Choosing to buy a particular stock is risky because you cannot know for sure whether it will rise or fall in value. You may use the services of an investment analyst with 20 years' experience in the market who compares the stock of the firm with every other possible purchase. The analyst's experience and analysis serve only to aid in the formulation of a proxy for the true probability that the stock will rise in value. The probability that the stock will rise in value, as related to you by the analyst, is only a subjective probability estimate based on the wisdom of that analyst.

Whether the investment analyst engages in rather sophisticated financial analysis or uses a hunch, a vague feeling, or a premonition of the future, there is no logical difference in the meaning or use of the probabilities. No technique available allows you or the investment analyst to arrive at an objective probability. These subjective probabilities, then—which are our percentage chance estimates of the outcome of an event—become the inputs for making decisions under risk.

Using whatever method the decision maker chooses, a probability distribution for all the possible outcomes may be developed. Table 2.1 represents such a probability distribution, since we have assumed that the three outcomes listed are the only possible outcomes of purchasing General Motors bonds. The complete set of estimates for the outcome to an event, such as those listed in the table, are referred to as a *probability distribution*. Note that the table indicates that there is a 95-percent chance of the first outcome, a 4-percent chance of the second outcome, and only a 1-percent chance of the final outcome. Probabilities are commonly stated, as they are in the table, as a number between 0 and 1. The fact that the table probabilities sum to 1 is important: it indicates that one of the three outcomes must occur (because the sum of the separate, independent outcomes totals 100 percent). By definition, no other outcome can take place.

Table 2.1 also demonstrates a discrete probability distribution because there are a finite number of possible outcomes. Probability distributions used by statisticians are often continuous distributions. Such distributions have an infinite number of outcomes some of which are more likely than others.

2.3   EXPECTED VALUE

Probability distributions have a characteristic called *expected value* associated with them. An expected value is a single number calculated from the probability distribution that combines some measure of the size of the outcomes (often in dollars) with the probabilities (percentage chances) that the outcomes will take place. Consider Table 2.2, which lists the possible outcomes of an investment and the probabilities with which they are expected to occur. In this simple case, a corporation has three estimates of the outcome of a particular investment. A cash flow of $2000 is the most likely outcome, while a cash flow of $3000 is the least likely. A third and final possibility is that the cash flow will be $1000.

TABLE 2.2   **Probabilities of Possible Outcomes of a Hypothetical Investment**

Possible Net Cash Flows	Probability of Specific Cash Flow (%)
$1000	40
2000	50
3000	10
Total	100

Plotting the information in Table 2.2 as shown in Figure 2.1, we get a probability distribution consisting of three points. If the number of possible cash flows is increased, the probability distribution consists of more points. In fact, if the number of possible cash flows is very large or infinite, the continuous probability distribution shown in Figure 2.2 might result. (The outcomes from many decisions can be estimated by assuming that they are represented by the *normal probability distribution*. This assumption is often correct and greatly simplifies calculations.)

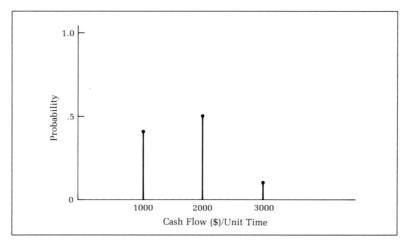

FIGURE 2.1   **Discrete Probability Distribution**   This discrete probability distribution consists of only three possible outcomes. The height of the line associated with each outcome indicates the probability that the outcome will occur.

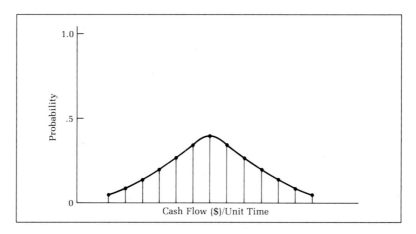

FIGURE 2.2   **Continuous Probability Distribution**   With many outcomes—actually, an infinite number—a probability distribution is continuous. Only 13 representative outcomes are shown by vertical lines here. Each point along the horizontal axis represents a potential outcome with a probability equal to the height of the distribution above it.

From the information in Table 2.2, the expected value of the distribution may be calculated. The expected value is the sum of each outcome multiplied by its probability of occurrence; that is,

$$\text{Expected value} = \overline{x} = \sum_{i=1}^{n} x_i \, P(x_i)$$

where $\overline{x}$ is the expected value, x_i is the ith outcome (where there are n outcomes), and $P(x_i)$ is the probability of the ith outcome. For the project in Table 2.2, the calculation is

$$\overline{x} = (\$1000)(.40) + (\$2000)(.50) + (\$3000)(.10)$$
$$\overline{x} = \$400 + \$1000 + \$300$$
$$\overline{x} = \$1700$$

It is often helpful to think of the expected value $(\overline{x})$ as a weighted average.

The expected value of $1700 should be used as the best estimate of the future cash flow. Note carefully, however, that $1700 was not one of the three possible outcomes of the project. A value of $1700 would not actually occur in any given year. The expected value is a combination of value and probability that may be explained in the following way. Suppose you invested in the project in Table 2.2 this year; next year you again invested in the identical project and, in fact, you continued doing so for many hundreds of years. What would be the average amount you would receive as a net cash flow per year after making the investment perhaps thousands of times? The answer is $1700, or the expected value.

The expected value, then, is not the value you can expect for a single investment but, rather, the value that is expected to occur on the average if a project was invested in a large number of times.

2.4 THE MEASUREMENT OF RISK

In addition to knowing the expected value of a decision, you must also have some measure of risk in order to compare the results of different management decisions. As well as having an expected value, each probability distribution has a characteristic known as a *standard deviation*, which can help in measuring risk. The standard deviation is a statistical measure of the dispersion of a variable about the mean. The standard deviation is used as a measure of the variability, or risk, of the alternative outcomes of a decision. The smaller the standard deviation, the less risky the project is in the sense that the outcome will more likely be close to the expected outcome of the project. The standard deviation is calculated in the following way:

$$\sigma = \sqrt{\sum_{i=1}^{n}(x_i - \overline{x})^2 P(x_i)}$$

where σ is the standard deviation. The standard deviation of the project in Table 2.2 is given by the following calculation:

$$\sigma = \sqrt{(1000 - 1700)^2(.40) + (2000 - 1700)^2(.50) + (3000 - 1700)^2(.10)}$$
$$\sigma = \sqrt{196,000 + 45,000 + 169,000} = \sqrt{410,000}$$

$$\sigma = 640.31$$

A standard deviation of 0 signifies no risk, since the standard deviation is 0 only if all outcomes equal the expected value (in which case all outcomes are the same and hence there is no risk).

However, the use of the standard deviation as a measure of risk has a serious shortcoming. Consider the two projects listed in Table 2.3. Projects A and B are identical except that the possible outcomes of project B are exactly 10 times as large as those of project A. The standard deviation for B is also 10 times that for A, but it would be incorrect to say that project B is 10 times as risky as project A.

TABLE 2.3
Standard Deviations of Two Investments

	Project A			Project B		
Possible Outcomes	300	200	100	3000	2000	1000
Probability	.25	.50	.25	.25	.50	.25

$\bar{x} = 200$

$\sigma = \sqrt{(300 - 200)^2 (.25) +}$
$\overline{(200 - 200)^2 (.50) +}$
$\overline{(100 - 200)^2 (.25)}$

$\sigma = 70.71$

$\bar{x} = 2000$

$\sigma = \sqrt{(3000 - 2000)^2 (.25) +}$
$\overline{(2000 - 2000)^2 (.50) +}$
$\overline{(1000 - 2000)^2 (.25)}$

$\sigma = 707.1$

It is incorrect to compare the standard deviation of A to that of B because the standard point from which variability is measured is different in each case. For project A the standard point is the expected outcome of 200, but for project B the standard point is 2000: its expected value. If you measure variability in A from 200 and in B from 2000, the comparison of the resulting figures is flawed. There is an easy way around this problem, however. We can calculate a measure of risk that is invariant with respect to the unit of measure or size of the outcome. This can be done by dividing the standard deviation by the expected value of outcomes. The resulting measure is called the *coefficient of variation*. The coefficient of variation is then

$$C = \frac{\sigma}{\bar{x}}$$

where C is the coefficient of variation. The coefficient of variation for projects A and B is given by

$$C_A = \frac{70.71}{200} = .354$$

$$C_B = \frac{707.1}{2000} = .354$$

Project A and project B are now seen to be equally risky (since both have a coefficient of variation equal to .354). The use of the coefficient of variation helps a manager to accurately compare the riskiness of projects whose expected values vary widely in magnitude.

The coefficient of variation is interpreted in much the same fashion as the standard deviation: as the coefficient of variation increases, the project is presumed to be more risky. A coefficient of variation of 0 denotes a riskless project.

Having derived a good measure of risk—the coefficient of variation— a manager is still confronted with the task of selecting appropriate courses of action. A number of approaches have been developed for incorporating risk into decision making. Five of them are explicitly covered in the remaining sections of this chapter: risk-adjusted discount rates, certainty equivalent factors, decision trees, simulation, and game theory. These five techniques do not cover all methods available, but there is some evidence that these are the most used of risk-associated techniques.[1] As a preface to looking at how risk can be incorporated into decision making, let us consider how individuals are thought to perceive risk.

2.5   RISK AVERSION AND RISK PREFERENCE

Suppose you are faced with what statisticians call a fair game, such as the situation described in Table 2.4. In particular, you are faced with the decision of drilling or not drilling a well for oil. Based on the information available, your consulting geologist tells you that the chances of finding oil if you drill the well are 20 in 100, or 20 percent. If you do not drill the well, you will not, of course, find any oil.

Now, drilling a well is an expensive proposition, and if you fail to find oil, you will have run up $20,000 in expenses with no positive return for your efforts. If, however, you are lucky and you do find oil, you will be able to pay all your expenses and have $80,000 left over (i.e., you will net $80,000). Of course, if you do not drill, you will have no expenses and no payoff regardless of whether there is oil at the site.

---

[1] R.E. Shannon and W.E. Biles, "The Utility of Certain Curriculum Topics to Operations Research Practitioners," *Operations Research,* July-August 1970, pp. 741–744; E. Turban, "A Sample of Operations Research Activities at the Corporate Level," *Operations Research,* 20(1) 1972, pp. 708–721; and Thomas M. Cook and Robert A. Russell, "A Survey of Industrial OR/MS Activities in the 70's," *Proceedings of the Eighth Annual Conference of the American Institute for Decision Sciences,* November 1976, pp. 122–124.

TABLE 2.4   **Relationship of Expected Value to Strategy Selected in a Fair Game**

| | Outcomes | | Expected |
Strategies	.20 Success	.80 Failure	Values
Drill	$80,000	− $20,000	$0
Do not drill	0	0	0

Statisticians call this a *fair game* because it does not matter which strategy you use (drill or do not drill); the expected value is the same no matter what choice is made. As we have said, the expected value is calculated as a weighted average. Each outcome is weighted by its probability, which is calculated as follows:

Expected value of drilling $= (\$80,000)(.20) + (-\$20,000)(.80) = 0$
Expected value of not drilling $= (\$0)(.20) + (\$0)(.80) = 0$

Based only on the maximization of expected monetary payoff, you would be indifferent as to the two choices. That is, your choice makes no difference in an expected value sense.

But what if we took into account your *utility function*? A utility function measures an individual's level of satisfaction as more of a good or service is received. We commonly assume that individuals (and most corporations as well) exhibit risk aversion in their utility functions. But what does risk aversion mean? And can a person be a risk preferrer? We can imagine three attitudes of individuals toward risk. *Risk aversion* characterizes a person who chooses the least risky investment, all other things being equal. *Risk preference* is exhibited by a person who chooses a riskier investment, all other things being equal. *Risk neutral* describes an individual who is indifferent to the risk of an investment, all other things being equal.

Consider the choices listed in Table 2.4. Clearly the choice to drill is riskier than the choice not to drill. If you do not drill, you are certain of the outcome. You will have a net payoff of 0. If you choose to drill, you will wind up $20,000 in the hole or $80,000 better off; even though the expected value is $0, the actual outcome after drilling a single well must be either $80,000 or − $20,000. If you are like most individuals, you will be unwilling to accept this fair game. That is, you will be unwilling to drill when the expected payoff is no better than the riskless proposition of not drilling. To most people, there does not appear to be anything for them in such a situation. By definition, a person who will not accept a fair bet (i.e., the individual who would choose not to drill) is risk averse.

Now let us consider the same choice—to drill or not to drill—from a utility function perspective. We will assume that an individual seeks to maximize his or her utility. Most persons, however, are subject to *diminishing marginal utility*, which means that they gain less and less satisfaction

TABLE 2.5   **Utility of Money Schedule for a Person with Diminishing Marginal Utility for Money**

Money	Utility
− $20,000	− 5
0	0
+ 20,000	+ 3
+ 40,000	+ 5
+ 60,000	+ 6.4
+ 80,000	+ 7.5

per unit as more and more of something is consumed. Marginal utility is measured as the slope of the utility function. A utility schedule representing a utility function with diminishing marginal utility is given in Table 2.5 and graphed in Figure 2.3. Note that, in Figure 2.3, the slope of the utility function becomes less steep (meaning that marginal utility becomes less) as you move to the right.

Table 2.5 describes a particular person's utility function for money and allows us to view the drilling decision using a different choice crite-

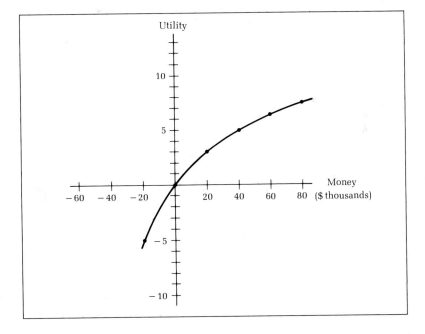

FIGURE 2.3   **Utility Function for a Person with Diminishing Marginal Utility for Money**   Utility increases as more money is received, but the increase in utility becomes smaller as additional increments of $20,000 are received.

rion—maximize utility instead of maximize money. This time the person chooses the option that offers the maximum amount of utility. The utility function described in Table 2.5 and graphed in Figure 2.3 is characterized by decreasing marginal utility of money. In other words, as the person's wealth increases in equal $20,000 installments, the person receives less additional satisfaction from each $20,000 increment to wealth. If we were to calculate the expected values of the two choices based on utility (rather than dollars) they would be:

$$\text{Expected value of drilling} = (+7.5)(.20) + (-5)(.80)$$
$$= 1.5 - 4.0 = -2.5$$
$$\text{Expected value of not drilling} = (0)(.20) + (0)(.80) = 0$$

Therefore, the optimal decision based on the maximization of expected utility is not to drill. The situation remains a fair game, but because of the diminishing marginal utility of money exhibited by the individual, there is an unambiguous preference for not drilling. Because a person making such a choice in a fair game situation must have diminishing marginal utility for money, the terms *risk aversion* and *diminishing marginal utility for money* mean the same thing.

A second, and perhaps less common,[2] individual is represented by the utility schedule in Table 2.6 and its graphic representation in Figure 2.4.

TABLE 2.6   **Utility of Money Schedule for a Person with Increasing Marginal Utility for Money**

Money	Utility
− $20,000	− 2
0	0
+ 20,000	+ 2.5
+ 40,000	+ 5.5
+ 60,000	+ 9
+ 80,000	+ 13

This person is characterized by *increasing marginal utility* for money; as the person's wealth increases, the person receives more additional satisfaction from each $20,000 increment to wealth. Calculating the expected values of the two choices, again based on utility,

$$\text{Expected value of drilling} = (+13)(.20) + (-2)(.80)$$
$$= 2.6 - 1.6 = 1$$
$$\text{Expected value of not drilling} = (0)(.20) + (0)(.80) = 0$$

[2]M. Friedman and L.J. Savage, "The Utility Analysis of Choices Involving Risk," *The Journal of Political Economy*, August 1948, pp. 279–304.

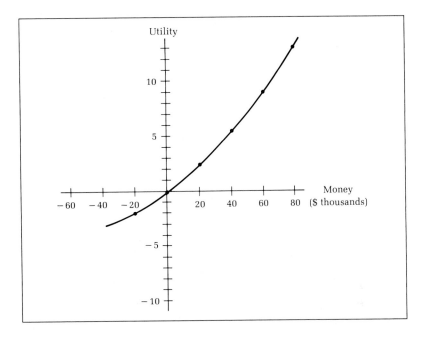

FIGURE 2.4   **Utility Function for a Person with Increasing Marginal Utility for Money**   Utility increases as more money is received, but the increase in utility becomes larger as additional increments of $20,000 are received.

The optimal decision based on utility for a person subject to increasing marginal utility for money is to drill (Table 2.6 and Figure 2.4). The unambiguous choice is to drill because this option has a utility value of 1. A person who makes such a choice is a risk preferrer. A risk preferrer and a person with increasing marginal utility for money are thus the same.

Although not illustrated here, there is possibly a third type of individual who is neither a risk preferrer nor risk averse: the individual who is risk neutral. Such an individual is identified as possessing a constant marginal utility for money and, therefore, even in utility terms, remains indifferent as to the choices in our fair bet example.[3] A risk neutral person can be thought of as being somewhere in between the common risk averse person and the much less common risk preferrer.

Because a person's attitude toward risk affects the shape of his or her utility function for money, it affects the choices the person makes in deci-

---

[3]See problem 11 at the end of this chapter, in which you are asked to demonstrate the calculation of the expected value, in utility terms, of this decision for a risk-neutral person.

sions involving risk. Remember, a risk averter is the most common type of individual or corporation. A risk averter does not accept risk unless compensated, or rewarded, for doing so. In the remainder of this chapter, we will assume that the decision makers under discussion are risk averse.

2.6 RISK AND CAPITAL BUDGETING: RISK-ADJUSTED DISCOUNT RATE

Now let us consider how the concepts of probability and risk can be applied to business decisions. We have indicated that most people are risk averters and that this characteristic is reflected in the manner in which individuals and corporations evaluate investment projects. If a firm considers investing in a risky project, the risk level affects the value of the project to the firm and ultimately the value of the firm itself.

The net present-value capitalization model taught in beginning finance courses assumes certainty in the projection of future cash flows.[4] Certainty is the most restrictive assumption used in these models; all current and future data values are assumed to be known with certainty. Certainty is assumed with respect to all future events. Future payments and future receipts are assumed to be made or received as prescribed. There is no uncertainty about whether payment or receipts will occur. However, very few, if any, of these items are known with certainty in real situations. When a company is evaluating a project, there is often uncertainty about the size and timing of cash flows. Whether some cash flows will even materialize is often in question.

To illustrate the calculation of the net present value of an investment under certainty, let us consider the profitability of investments A and B, given in Table 2.7, assuming that the firm's cost of capital is 10 percent.[5] For investment A, we have the following information:

$$\text{Initial outlay} = CP_0 - CO_0 = \$10,000$$
$$\text{First-year net cash flow} = CP_1 - CO_1 = \$2000$$
$$\text{Second-year net cash flow} = CP_2 - CO_2 = \$8000$$
$$\text{Third-year net cash flow} = CP_3 - CO_3 = \$1000$$
$$\text{Fourth-year net cash flow} = CP_4 - CO_4 = \$1000$$

where

$$CP_i = \text{cash proceeds in year } i$$
$$CO_i = \text{cash outlays in year } i$$

---

[4]See footnote 1.

[5]A review of present value concepts is found in the appendix of this chapter. Readers who have not previously studied present value or feel they may benefit from some review may want to read that appendix at this time.

Therefore, the net present value (NPV) of investment A is

$$NPV_A = -\$10,000 + \frac{\$2000}{(1 + .10)} + \frac{\$8000}{(1 + .10)^2} + \frac{\$1000}{(1 + .10)^3} + \frac{\$1000}{(1 + .10)^4}$$

$$NPV_A = -\$10,000 + \$1818 + \$6612 + \$751 + \$683$$

$$NPV_A = -\$136$$

Since the net present value of investment A is negative, we may conclude that investment in the project would not be in the firm's best interest.

In the same manner, the net present value of investment B can be calculated as

$$NPV_B = -\$10,000 + \frac{\$4000}{(1 + .10)} + \frac{\$4000}{(1 + .10)^2} + \frac{\$4000}{(1 + .10)^3} + \frac{\$4000}{(1 + .10)^4}$$

$$NPV_B = -\$10,000 + \$3636 + \$3306 + \$3005 + \$2732$$

$$NPV_B = \$2679$$

TABLE 2.7   **Yearly Net Cash Flow for Alternative Investments**

Investment	Initial Cash Outlay	Net Cash Flow Per Year			
		Year 1	Year 2	Year 3	Year 4
A	$10,000	$2000	$8000	$1000	$1000
B	10,000	4000	4000	4000	4000

Obviously, investment B should be undertaken because its net present value is greater than 0. As a matter of fact, the firm could pay up to $2679 more for the investment and still at least break even on the project. As noted above, however, investment A should not be undertaken, since it would reduce the profitability of the firm. The firm would have to be paid an initial sum of at least $136 to consider undertaking investment A, or the initial cost would have to be reduced by that amount.

In real situations, cash proceeds and cash outlays are subject to risk for each year of the project's duration. Future net cash flows (the difference between cash proceeds and cash outlays) must be forecast, and risk must be incorporated in the analysis. To illustrate this, consider the following example. Valley Mould must purchase a continuous sand mixer for its foundry operation. There are two pieces of equipment being considered: the dependable Fordath 450 ER and the similar C. E. Cast 1000. Each has an expected life of 3 years, after which it must be replaced. While the two machines have many features in common, they differ with respect to purchase price and expected net cash flows. Table 2.8 contains the relevant information for each machine. We will assume the firm's discount rate is 10 percent.

TABLE 2.8
Expected Net Cash Flow for Alternative Pieces of Equipment

	Fordath 450 ER			C.E. Cast 1000		
Purchase Price	$106,000			$100,000		
Salvage Value after Three Years	0			0		
Possible Net Cash Flow	$85,000	$75,000	$65,000	$74,000	$71,000	$69,000
Probability of Occurrence	.25	.50	.25	.25	.50	.25
Expected Cash Flow in Each of Three Years	($85,000)(.25) + ($75,000)(.50) + ($65,000)(.25) = $21,250 + $37,500 + $16,250 = $75,000			($74,000)(.25) + ($71,000)(.50) + ($69,000)(.25) = $18,500 + $35,500 + $17,250 = $71,250		

The first step in choosing the best machine for Valley Mould is to calculate the expected net cash flows for each of the three years for each machine. In this example, the expected net cash flows are the same for each of the three years for both the Fordath and the C. E. Cast machines. The expected net cash flows for the machines are used in calculating the unadjusted (for risk) net present value for each project as follows:

$$NPV_{Fordath} = -\$106,000 + \frac{\$75,000}{(1 + .10)^1} + \frac{\$75,000}{(1 + .10)^2} + \frac{\$75,000}{(1 + .10)^3}$$
$$= -\$106,000 + \$68,182 + \$61,983 + \$56,349$$
$$= \$80,514$$

$$NPV_{C.\,E.\,Cast} = -\$100,000 + \frac{\$71,250}{(1 + .10)^1} + \frac{\$71,250}{(1 + .10)^2} + \frac{\$71,250}{(1 + .10)^3}$$
$$= -\$100,000 + \$64,773 + \$58,884 + \$53,531$$
$$= \$77,188$$

It would appear that the Fordath machine is the better choice, since its net present value is higher than that of the C. E. Cast machine. But the two projects also differ in degree of risk, and the net present value does not take this into account. In order to adjust the calculation for risk, we must first assign some risk measure to each project. This is done by first calculating the coefficient of variation (C) for each of the two projects as follows:

$$\sigma_{Fordath} = \sqrt{(\$85,000 - \$75,000)^2(.25) + (\$75,000 - \$75,000)^2(.50) + (\$65,000 - \$75,000)^2(.25)}$$
$$= \sqrt{\$25,000,000 + 0 + \$25,000,000}$$
$$= \$7071$$
$$C_{Fordath} = \sigma/EV = \$7071/\$75,000 = .0943$$

$$\sigma_{\text{C. E. Cast}} = \sqrt{\begin{aligned}(\$74,000 - \$71,250)^2(.25) + (\$71,000 - \$71,250)^2(.50) + \\ (\$69,000 - \$71,250)^2(.25)\end{aligned}}$$

$$= \sqrt{(\$1,890,625) + (\$31,250) + (\$1,265,625)}$$

$$= \$1785$$

$$C_{\text{C. E. Cast}} = \sigma/EV = \$1785/\$71,250 = .0251$$

where

σ = standard deviation

EV = expected value

The coefficient of variation for the Fordath machine is higher than that for the C. E. Cast machine. This was to be expected, since the probabilities for payment were identical with the two machines (i.e., 25 percent, 50 percent, and 25 percent) but the range of outcomes was more dispersed with the Fordath machine. As we have said, as measured by the coefficient of variation, risk is adjusted for the size of the project. The Fordath option is, then, the riskier.

In our example, the riskier alternative also promises the greater returns. This relationship often exists in reality. If the less risky alternative promises the greater returns, the choice is obvious. But in our case, a dilemma exists: should we pick the riskier project because it offers higher expected returns, or should we choose the less risky project because it offers less risk? Let us now see how determining the risk-adjusted discount rate can help us make such a decision.

Determination of the Risk-Adjusted Discount Rate

A discount rate is commonly defined as the cost of capital to a firm. However, the cost of capital is subject to, or a function of, the level of risk of the firm, and as projects that the firm undertakes become riskier, so does the existence of the firm itself. Risk-adjusted discount rates assume a trade-off by firms between risk and expected rate of return such as the one shown in Figure 2.5.

The curve in Figure 2.5 is a risk-return trade-off function. The function depicts the preferences of an individual investor or of a particular company. The function is actually an indifference curve showing all the possible situations to which a particular investor is indifferent compared with an investment with 0 risk and a 10-percent expected rate of return, as shown at point A.

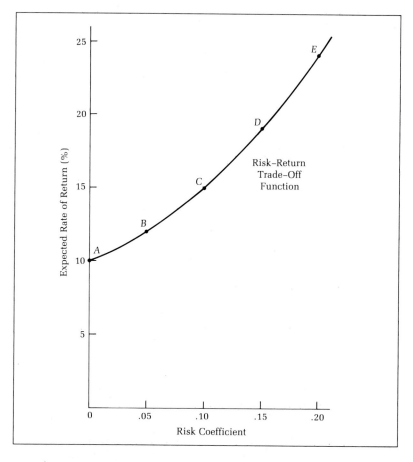

FIGURE 2.5   **Risk-Return Trade-off Function**   The function shows many points of indifference for an individual investor. This investor, for instance, is indifferent between receiving a 12-percent return with a risk of .05 and receiving a 19-percent return with a risk of .15, where risk is measured by the coefficient of variation.

This particular investor is indifferent to the following situations:

Point	Risk	Expected Return (%)
A	0	10
B	.05	12
C	.10	15
D	.15	19
E	.20	24

Note that this investor requires higher and higher expected returns as risk increases. The extra return required because of risk is referred to as the *risk premium*. In this case, a 2-percent risk premium is required to move the investor from a riskless project to one with a coefficient of variation of .05, a 3-percent risk premium is required to move the investor from a project with a .05 coefficient of variation to one with a .10 coefficient of variation, and so on.

If we believe this trade-off function to be representative of actual investors and corporations, we can see how expected rates of return associated with particular investments can modify the net present value equation:

$$NPV^{ra} = \sum_{i=1}^{n} \left(\frac{\text{net cash flows}_i}{(1 + k + r)^i} \right)$$

where

NPV^{ra} = risk-adjusted net present value
n = duration of project
k = discount rate (or cost of capital)
r = risk premium
i = period number

A firm using this approach calculates the coefficient of variation of the various investment projects under consideration. Those projects with the same general degree of risk as the existing assets have a risk premium of 0, while projects of greater risk are assigned risk premiums that increase with magnitude of risk.

Continuing with the Valley Mould example, let us assume the company decision maker decides to use the following risk premiums for the related risk measures:

Risk (Coefficient of Variation)	Risk Premium (%)	Risk–Adjusted Discount Rate (%) ($k + r$)
0–.090	0	10
.091–.190	2	12
.191–.290	5	15

Since the C. E. Cast option has a coefficient of variation of .0251 and thus falls in the first category above, the associated risk premium is 0, and the net present value calculated earlier is also the risk-adjusted net present value (i.e., $NPV = NPV^{ra} = \$77,188$).

The Fordath option, however, has a coefficient of variation of .0943, putting it in the second risk category, with a risk premium of 2 percent. The risk-adjusted net present value for the Fordath machine is

$$NPV^{ra}{}_{Fordath} = -\$106,000 = \frac{\$75,000}{(1 + .12)^1} + \frac{\$75,000}{(1 + .12)^2} + \frac{\$75,000}{(1 + .12)^3}$$

$$= -\$106,000 + \$66,964 + \$59,790 + \$53,384$$

$$= \$74,138$$

The adjusted *NPV* for the Fordath machine has dropped from the original $80,514. This downward adjustment is due to the extra risk involved in the expected return from the project. It is this risk-adjusted value—$74,138—that is correctly compared with the risk-adjusted value for the C. E. Cast machine ($77,188). A choice may now be made between the machines. The one with the highest risk-adjusted net present value is the best choice: the C. E. Cast machine.

It should be noted that a different risk premium could be used for each year during the life of the project. It may be more appropriate to use varying risk premiums, since risk usually increases the further into the future net cash flows are projected. However, as the technique is usually applied, one risk-adjusted discount rate is used for the entire stream of cash flows.

2.7 RISK AND CAPITAL BUDGETING: CERTAIN EQUIVALENT FACTORS

A second method may also be used to adjust for risk in such projects as the Valley Mould example. The basic objective of this technique is to derive a value, called a *certainty equivalent,* such that the firm is indifferent between receiving this net cash flow with certainty and receiving an uncertain net cash flow as represented by the probability distribution of actual outcomes.

For example, Valley Mould has an *expected* cash flow of $75,000 per year from the Fordath machine. However, since there is some uncertainty as to the actual cash flow, the decision maker is asked to state an amount X_i^*, such that he or she would be indifferent between receiving X_i^* with certainty each year and receiving the "lottery" outcome each year with risk (i.e., 25-percent chance of $85,000; 50-percent chance of $75,000; 25-percent chance of $65,000).

If we define the return represented by the probability distribution as X_i, then the certainty equivalent factor is

$$CE = X_i^*/X_i = \text{certain return/risky return}$$

where *CE* is the certainty equivalent factor. If the decision maker at Valley Mould was indifferent between the risky expected $75,000 per year, say, and a certain $72,500 per year, the certainty equivalent factor appropriate to apply to the Fordath machine would be

$$CE = \$72,500/\$75,000 = .9667$$

The certainty equivalent factor is then used in the numerator of the net present value equation to adjust the cash flows, rather than in the denominator, as the risk-adjusted discount rate is used. The calculation for the risk-adjusted net present value of the Fordath machine using a certainty equivalent factor (NPV^{CE}) is as follows:

$$NPV^{CE}_{\text{Fordath}} = -\$106,000 + \frac{(CE)\,(\$75,000)}{(1 + .10)^1} + \frac{(CE)\,(\$75,000)}{(1 + .10)^2} +$$

$$\frac{(CE)\,(\$75,000)}{(1 + .10)^3}$$

$$= -\$106,000 + CE\,(\$68,182) + CE\,(\$61,983) +$$

$$CE\,(\$56,349)$$

$$= -\$106,000 + .9667(\$68,182) + .9667(\$61,983) +$$

$$.9667(\$56,349)$$

$$= -\$106,000 + \$180,303$$

$$= \$74,303$$

Had the decision maker been perfectly consistent in setting the X_i^* and the risk premiums, the risk-adjusted net present value would have been the same regardless of whether a certainty equivalent factor or a risk-adjusted discount rate had been used. The two techniques are simply alternative procedures for making the same adjustment; the choice of technique should not affect the decision. The best choice remains the C. E. Cast machine.

2.8 DECISION TREES

The risk-adjusted net present value calculations discussed above take into account the desire to have a cash flow now rather than later through adjusting the discount factor to account for risk and adjusting the yearly net cash flows to reflect the certainty equivalent of the uncertainty inherent in those cash flows. These techniques form the basis of much useful work, but to capture the full influence of risk and time preferences, it is often helpful to view business decisions in a decison tree format. Decision trees are relatively simple tools but are also flexible enough to apply to most business decisions, including rather complex problems involving risk.

The technique called decision tree analysis is really a method of diagraming and analyzing problems involving risk. The decision tree is composed of branches that show the various possible alternatives that could result from management decision.

For example, consider the following decision facing a firm that manufactures $5\frac{1}{4}$-inch floppy disk drives and sells them to personal computer firms to be included in the final products sold to business and household users. The disk manufacturer, M. C. Drives, must determine the number of read head mounting jigs to purchase for use in producing the disk drives to be sold to its two leading customers. M. C. Drives has obtained a firm contract from one of these buyers, Micro-One, but the contract simply guarantees that all drives will be purchased from M. C. Drives, leaving the actual number of units undetermined. On the basis of information supplied by Micro-One, M. C. Drives has estimated the following probability distribution regarding the sales of disk drives to that one buyer (Micro-One):

Probability (%)	Sales Level to Micro-One
40	35,000 disk drives
40	25,000 disk drives
20	15,000 disk drives

The other major buyer of disk drives, Compu II, has told the vice president for sales at M. C. Drives that there is a 60-percent chance that her company's order will go their way, which would mean the sale of an additional 15,000 drives.

Management of M. C. Drives' production department must make a decision to buy 32 mounting jigs, which would give them a maximum capacity of 55,000 disk drives, or to purchase just 16 of the jigs, with a resulting capacity of 35,000 drives.

In order to decide whether to purchase 32 or 16 jigs, decision tree analysis may be useful in helping M. C. Drives evaluate the various outcomes of this situation. The first two branches of the tree indicate that the firm can purchase either 32 or 16 jigs.

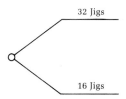

The next set of branches reflects the 50-percent probability that M. C. Drives will receive the order from Compu II for 15,000 drives.

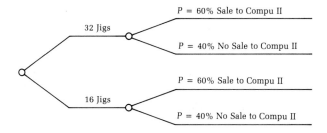

Another set of branches represents the various levels of sales that may result to Micro-One. The final tree diagram is illustrated in Figure 2.6.

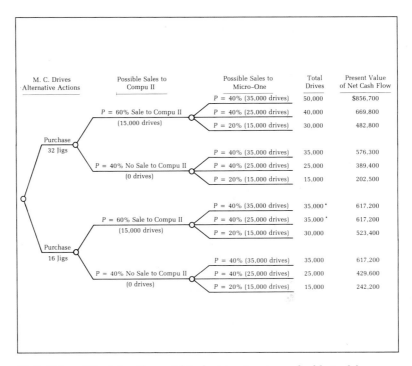

The following table content appears within the figure:

M. C. Drives Alternative Actions	Possible Sales to Compu II	Possible Sales to Micro–One	Total Drives	Present Value of Net Cash Flow
		P = 40% (35,000 drives)	50,000	$856,700
	P = 60% Sale to Compu II (15,000 drives)	P = 40% (25,000 drives)	40,000	669,800
		P = 20% (15,000 drives)	30,000	482,800
Purchase 32 Jigs		P = 40% (35,000 drives)	35,000	576,300
	P = 40% No Sale to Compu II (0 drives)	P = 40% (25,000 drives)	25,000	389,400
		P = 20% (15,000 drives)	15,000	202,500
		P = 40% (35,000 drives)	35,000 *	617,200
	P = 60% Sale to Compu II (15,000 drives)	P = 40% (25,000 drives)	35,000 *	617,200
		P = 20% (15,000 drives)	30,000	523,400
Purchase 16 Jigs		P = 40% (35,000 drives)	35,000	617,200
	P = 40% No Sale to Compu II (0 drives)	P = 40% (25,000 drives)	25,000	429,600
		P = 20% (15,000 drives)	15,000	242,200

FIGURE 2.6   **M. C. Drives' Decision Tree**   This decision tree is a valuable tool for evaluating whether M.C. Drives should buy 32 jigs or 16 jigs to use in installing read heads in the disk drives that are sold to two computer firms (Compu II and Micro-One). (*Note: Even though total demand would be greater than 35,000, only 35,000 could be sold because that is the capacity constraint if only 16 assembly jigs are purchased.)

On the basis of the total number of units that would be sold under the various possible circumstances, the present value of the net cash flows can be calculated based on company cost and revenue data (which is not shown). M. C. Drives can then determine the expected, or mean, present value of the net cash flows by multiplying the joint probability for each of the 12 possible outcomes by the corresponding present value. The joint probabilities are determined by multiplying the individual probabilities because it is assumed that sales to Micro-One and Compu II are independent of one another. These calculations are illustrated for the cases of buying both 32 jigs and 16 jigs in Table 2.9.

Comparing only the expected present values for the decision to purchase 32 jigs versus 16 jigs, it appears that the decision should be to purchase the 32 assembly jigs. However, as you have seen, in addition to the expected net present value, M. C. Drives should also be interested in the risk, or dispersion, of the cash flow around the expected value. As seen in Table 2.10, the coefficient of variation for the investment in 32 jigs is greater than that for the acquisition of 16. At this point, management of M. C. Drives can use either the certainty equivalent or the risk-adjusted discount rate method to further analyze the trade-off between a decision with a higher return but greater risk and one with a somewhat lower return and lower risk.

TABLE 2.9 **Calculation of Expected Net Present Value from Alternative Decisions**

Purchase 32 Assembly Jigs		
(1) Joint Probability	(2) Present Value of Net Cash Flow	(3) Column 1 Times Column 2
.6 × .4 = .24	$856,700	$205,608
.6 × .4 = .24	669,800	160,752
.6 × .2 = .12	482,800	57,936
.4 × .4 = .16	576,300	92,208
.4 × .4 = .16	389,400	62,304
.4 × .2 = .08	202,500	16,200

Expected present value of net cash flows (sum of column 3) = $595,008

Purchase 16 Assembly Jigs		
(1) Joint Probability	(2) Present Value of Net Cash Flow	(3) Column 1 Times Column 2
.6 × .4 = .24	$617,200	$148,128
.6 × .4 = .24	617,200	148,128
.6 × .2 = .12	523,400	62,808
.4 × .4 = .16	617,200	98,752
.4 × .4 = .16	429,600	68,736
.4 × .2 = .08	242,200	19,376

Expected present value of net cash flows (sum of column 3) = $545,928

TABLE 2.10 **Calculation of the Coefficient of Variation for Alternative Decisions**

Purchase 32 Assembly Jigs

$$(\$856,700 - \$595,008)^2 \times .24 = \$1.643584 \text{ E10*}$$
$$(\$669,800 - \$595,008)^2 \times .24 = \$1.342522 \text{ E9}$$
$$(\$482,800 - \$595,008)^2 \times .12 = \$1.510876 \text{ E9}$$
$$(\$576,300 - \$595,008)^2 \times .16 = \$5.599828 \text{ E7}$$
$$(\$389,400 - \$595,008)^2 \times .16 = \$6.763943 \text{ E9}$$
$$(\$202,500 - \$595,008)^2 \times .08 = \$1.232500 \text{ E10}$$

$$C = \frac{\sqrt{\$3.843417 \text{ E10}}}{\$595,008}$$
$$C = \frac{\$196,046}{\$595,008}$$
$$C = .32$$

Purchase 16 Assembly Jigs

$$(\$617,200 - \$545,928)^2 \times .24 = \$1.219127 \text{ E9}$$
$$(\$617,200 - \$545,928)^2 \times .24 = \$1.219127 \text{ E9}$$
$$(\$523,400 - \$545,928)^2 \times .12 = \$6.090129 \text{ E7}$$
$$(\$617,200 - \$545,928)^2 \times .16 = \$8.127517 \text{ E8}$$
$$(\$429,600 - \$545,928)^2 \times .16 = \$2.165152 \text{ E9}$$
$$(\$242,200 - \$545,928)^2 \times .08 = \$7.380055 \text{ E9}$$

$$C = \frac{\sqrt{\$1.285711 \text{ E10}}}{\$545,928}$$
$$C = \frac{\$113,389}{\$545,928}$$
$$C = .21$$

NOTE: The coefficient of variation (C) is calculated as $C = \dfrac{\sqrt{\Sigma(x_i - \overline{x})^2 P(x_i)}}{\overline{x}}$.

*E10 is exponential notation (i.e., 1.64E10 = 1.64 × 10^{10}).

The purpose of this section has been to illustrate how decision tree analysis can be used to diagram the various paths that can result from investment decisions, along with their likelihood. The example presented has been kept relatively simple in order to facilitate illustrating the basic usefulness of the method. In many business situations, however, the decision tree can be quite complex.

2.9 SIMULATION

It is useful for us to think about simulation as a technique that can help us find out more information concerning an event or series of events by conducting an experiment. Experiments are useful because outcomes occur with some risk involved; and the more information we have about the likely outcomes, the better will be the decisions we make. The vehicle for the experiment is a model that mimics the essential features of the real world situation being evaluated. In Chapter 1, several types of models were discussed: graphic models; algebraic, or mathematical, models; and physical models. The latter are often referred to as iconic models and can be quite useful in simulation experiments. Some familiar iconic models are model airplanes, model trains, and dolls. Iconic models look like the real thing; a model airplane looks like its much larger counterpart, but the small model usually lacks movable surfaces (rudder, elevator, etc.), and the model probably has few inner parts, such as the engine, seats, and controls of the full-sized airplane. Iconic models of airplanes can be useful, however, in the simulation of the reactions of a real aircraft in, say, a wind tunnel. Small, inexpensive models are used in a wind tunnel to simulate the real, full-sized airplane for precisely the same reasons businesses use simulation. The two most important reasons are:

1. *Risk.* There is some risk in judging how the real life counterpart of the model will react to various situations.

2. *Cost and Convenience.* It is far less expensive to simulate a new design's reactions than to build the new design and use it.

Using a model—that is, performing a simulation—an experimenter is free to adjust and change various conditions and then observe the simulated results. An aeronautical engineer may change wind speed or direction in a wind tunnel and observe the effect on the model airplane in much the same way a manager might use a business model to portray the demand for a particular product and observe the change in inventory as conditions vary. The models, or simulations, used in business are not iconic models but, rather, numerical and/or mathematical models that portray real situations. Most often, the model is in the form of a computer program that reflects hypothetical conditions specified by the decision maker. The output from the simulation is in the form of numerical results that mimic what would actually happen if the hypothetical conditions occurred in the real world.

To help you see how simulation studies can be set up and run, let us consider some different techniques that could be used to resolve the following situation involving risk. An archer shoots 10 arrows at a target. Having observed this archer for some time, we "know" the probability that she will hit the target each time she shoots. What we would like to know, however, is the probability that she will hit the target exactly 7 times in 10 shots.

There are at least four ways we could approach the problem: (1) the analytical method, (2) experimentation, (3) iconic simulation, and (4) numerical (Monte Carlo) simulation. We will discuss each of these in the context of the problem described above.

Analytical Method

Using the analytical method, we compute the exact solution using the appropriate statistical distributions. In our archery example, the binomial formula fits this simple problem. The solution follows:

$$P(r) = \frac{n!}{r!(n - r)!} \, P^r(1 - p)^{n - r}$$

where

$$P = \text{the probability that any particular shot results in a hit}$$
$$1 - P = \text{the probability that any particular shot results in a miss}$$
$$P(r) = \text{the probability of exactly } r \text{ hits}$$
$$n = \text{the number of shots}$$
$$r = \text{the number of hits}$$

If we assume the archer has a 25-percent probability of hitting the target on each shot, the exact probability that the archer would hit the target 7 times in 10 shots can be calculated as follows:

$$P(7) = \frac{10!}{7! \, (10 - 7)!} \, (.25)^7 (.75)^3$$

$$P(7) = \frac{3,628,800}{5040(6)} \, (.000061)(.421875)$$

$$P(7) = .003088$$

Thus, the archer has about a .003 chance of hitting the target exactly 7 times in 10 shots (that's about a .3% chance).

Often the analytical route is the best to use in solving business problems that fall neatly into a particular statistical problem category (such as the binomial theorem above), but more often the match between real world problems and statistical technique is inexact. Then other methods are called for.

Experimentation

We could answer our question about the archer by running an experiment. Assuming our archer has great stamina, we could ask her to shoot 100,000 arrows at the target (10,000 salvos of 10 shots each). We could then count the number of salvos resulting in exactly 7 hits and divide that by the total number of salvos shot (10,000), and we would have an experimentally determined answer to our question.

Experimentation is a recognized technique in business—marketers are perhaps the most enthusiastic users of real world experiments—however, experiments are usually expensive and time-consuming. Consider, for example, a food processing firm whose decision makers want to evaluate the potential sales of ketchup packaged in a new squeezable plastic container. A common way to facilitate such an evaluation is to offer the new product for sale in a test market. The use of test markets is a form of experimentation designed to simulate what might happen if the product were introduced on a full scale. But think of the costs of test marketing. The following list identifies just some of the cost-generating activities involved:

1. Design the new squeezable container.

2. Have perhaps 10,000 to 15,000 of the containers produced.

3. Develop and/or purchase cases designed to ship the new containers.

4. Modify filling machines to accommodate the new containers.

5. Develop advertising and in-store promotions.

6. Convince retailers to provide shelf space.

7. Fill and ship the sample of new containers.

8. Monitor and analyze results.

In all experimentation, you must be able to limit outside influences that could affect your results. In the case of a test market simulation, factors outside of your control can cause the experiment to fail, and the money spent may generate little useful information. For example, suppose another firm decides to run a special price promotion on their ketchup during your test market experiment. If your new container does not sell well, is it because consumers do not like the new container or because another brand is available at a special lower price?

Even with the high cost and the difficulty of controlling other factors, experimentation is sometimes the best form of simulation available.

The plethora of test marketing that businesses do provides some evidence that this experimental form of simulation is a valuable management tool.

Iconic Simulation Models

An iconic representation of the archer problem can be developed by replacing the archer and the target with a top and a clock, respectively. When a cone-shaped top is flung and its string held, a spinning motion sets it revolving on the pointed end of the cone. As the top spins slower and slower, a wobble develops, and eventually the top falls on its side. The clock we will use has a second hand revolving around the perimeter one time each 60 seconds. We will divide the perimeter into two parts: one part signifying a hit and the other a miss.

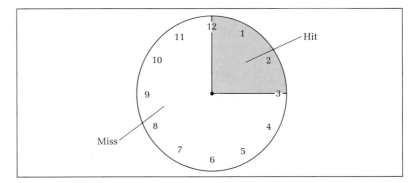

If, for example, the archer's probability of a hit on each individual try is observed to be 25 percent, we designate 25 percent of the clock's perimeter to stand for a hit. The remainder of the perimeter stands for a miss.

We can use this rather unusual iconic model by spinning the top and starting the clock simultaneously. The instant the top falls over on its side, we stop the clock. If the second hand is within the hit area, we score a hit; otherwise, we record a miss. By repeating the simulation many times and then calculating the percentage of "salvos" resulting in exactly 7 hits, we could answer our original question. It would understandably be difficult to find individuals willing to spin a top or pull the plug on a clock 10,000 times.

Monte Carlo Simulations

Because it employs probability distributions, the Monte Carlo simulation was named for the famous gambling capital, where probability rules. To illustrate this type of simulation, let us again find the archer's probability of getting exactly 7 bull's-eyes out of 10 shots, when her probability of hitting that target on any one shot is 25 percent. Our first task is to determine how the simulation will determine if our archer has a hit or a miss on any simulated shot.

Suppose that we have a computer with a random number generator that, when called, returns, say, a 7-digit value drawn at random from the interval of numbers between .0000000 and .9999999. Since we know that the probability of a hit is 25 percent, we can identify any (arbitrarily chosen) segment of the number line over this interval in such a way that 25 percent of the line is included in the subset. Then, if choosing a number from the random number generator returns a value within that subset, the result is interpreted as a hit; otherwise it is a miss. The number line below illustrates the point.

In the long run, the number of simulated shots counted as hits will tend toward 25 percent. The calculation of the probability of exactly 7 hits in 10 tries is the same as for the top-clock simulation. In fact, the only difference between Monte Carlo simulations and iconic simulations is in ease of use; their techniques are identical. You could do this simulation on almost any computer, even the most inexpensive personal computer or microcomputer. Why not try it? Here are some guidelines to help you get started.

First, find out how to generate a random number on your computer. It is usually as simple as LET $X = RND$ or a similar command. Then set up a loop in which a random number is selected 10 times. For each random number, use a counter to tally a hit if the random number is between .0000000 and .2500000. Each time through this loop of 10 random numbers, there will be 0, 1, 2, 3, 4, 5, 6, 7, 8, 9, or 10 hits, depending on how often a random number in the specified interval is selected from your computer's random number generator. Now have the computer run through this loop many, many times (say, 100,000 times, although in testing your program, use just 50 or 100 times). Each time, have a counter tally the number of hits for that series of 10 "shots." At the end, have the computer record the total number of times there were 7 hits and the total number of rounds (100,000 for example). In a trial of this simulation on a personal computer, the following results were obtained:

Number of 7 hits = 315
Number of rounds = 100,000

Dividing the number of 7 hits by the number of rounds, we get the estimate of the probability of having 7 hits in 10 shots (given a probability of .25 for a hit on any one shot) based on a Monte Carlo simulation:

Probability of 7 hits in 10 tries = 315/100,000 = .00315

This compares favorably with the probability of .003088 that we calculated earlier using the binomial distribution.

Are Simulation Models Really Used?

Even though some statisticians view simulation as a last resort in solving problems, it is one of the most widely used techniques of handling risky situations. Practicing decision makers have ranked simulation a more common technique than either linear programming or the use of inventory models.

While the archer example implies the reasons for the popularity of simulation as a decision-making aid, let us summarize them explicity:

1. Operation of the actual system or process might prove to be not only expensive but also disruptive (for example, in comparing two inventory ordering systems for a single firm, the confusion that could result from operating two systems for long enough to obtain valid information might be quite high).

2. Simulation may be the only method available for gathering information because it is difficult or impossible to observe the actual situation under certain controlled conditions.

3. It may not be possible to determine a mathematical solution because some processes are stochastic; that is, they respond to a given input with a range of possible outcomes.

4. Time constraints may prevent a decision maker from allowing a process to continue until sufficient data are gathered. Simulation allows telescoping of time and provides more immediate results.

How do managers actually use simulation to deal with risky situations? An exhaustive list would be far too long to publish here, but the following examples give you an idea of the versatility and usefulness of the technique:

1. The County of Los Angeles simulates its emergency medical operation to estimate the various levels of service needed by varying numbers of medical units assigned to various locations.

2. A timber products firm producing a variety of wood-board products uses a corporate simulation model to reduce working capital, help control raw materials inventories, project cash flows, and fully utilize capital equipment.

3.   A simulation is used by a financial services company to derive optimal financial portfolio holding times and asset mix.

4.   Simulations are used as training devices for new decision makers both in business and technical fields.

5.   Marketing simulations use a representative sample of customers distributed geographically to search for new or optimal marketing strategies that fit particular market segments.

6.   Physical distribution problems are commonly analyzed using simulations to consider such problems as the optimum number of warehouses, the type and frequency of shipments to use, and the determination of distribution charges.

2.10   A SIMULATION OF AUTOMATED TELLER MACHINE USE

Now let us construct and run a realistic simulation that can be calculated manually. Almost all simulations used today have the same essential characteristics but are done on a computer system, often on only a microcomputer.

A bank located in a downtown area is going to place one or more automatic teller machines (ATMs) on its outside wall, facing the street, for the convenience of its customers. Each ATM consists of a keyboard on which customers input the type of transaction they wish to make, a window for displaying the information keyed in, and a drawer that opens to disburse or collect cash. The automated teller window has the advantage of remaining open 24 hours a day, 7 days a week.

The bank, however, is unsure how many of its customers would use such a device and therefore how many units to install. Because the machines are expensive, the bank manager does not want to purchase too many of them. The manager is trying to decide between having one or two machines. The manager feels that customers would be annoyed at waiting longer than three minutes for service at the teller machine and suggests that a simulation of the use of one teller machine might indicate whether the purchase of a second machine was necessary.

An analysis of the arrival pattern of 100 customers at an ATM at a branch of the downtown bank allowed the construction of the interarrival time frequency distribution shown in the top part of Table 2.11. Observation of 100 customers using the automated teller machines at the branch revealed the service time frequency distribution shown in the bottom part of Table 2.11.

TABLE 2.11   **Interarrival Time and Service Time Frequency Distributions for Customers Using Automated Teller Machine**

Interarrival Time Frequency Distribution

(1) Time Between Customer Arrivals (minutes)	(2) Number of Occurrences	(3) Probability Distribution	(4) Assigned Numbers
1	18	.18	0–17
2	17	.17	18–34
3	15	.15	35–49
4	12	.12	50–61
5	10	.10	62–71
6	9	.09	72–80
7	8	.08	81–88
8	5	.05	89–93
9	2	.02	94–95
10	1	.01	96
11	1	.01	97
12	1	.01	98
13	1	.01	99
Totals	100	1.00	

Service Time Frequency Distribution

(1) Service Time (minutes)	(2) Number of Customers	(3) Probability Distribution	(4) Assigned Numbers
1	48	.48	0–47
2	20	.20	48–67
3	16	.16	68–83
4	12	.12	84–95
5	2	.02	96–97
6	2	.02	98–99
Totals	100	1.00	

NOTE: Data are from 100 observations at a branch bank.

Column 4 in each part of Table 2.11 represents the segment of the number line used to represent a particular category. For instance, in the top part of Table 2.11, 18 percent of the digits between 0 and 99 are assigned to represent an arrival interval of 1 minute, 17 percent of the numbers (i.e., 18 through 34) are assigned to represent an arrival interval of 2 minutes, and so on. When a particular random number is drawn in our simulation, we will compare that number with the assigned numbers in column 4 to determine either when the customer arrives (top part of the table) or how long the customer uses the automated teller (bottom part of the table).

The form shown in Table 2.12 was constructed to allow the simulation to be run. The form takes into account that the manager wants to look both at the arrival pattern of customers (which involves risk) and at the service time for each customer (which also involves risk).

To run the simulation, a set of two-digit, random numbers (i.e., 0 to 99) is generated and placed in column 2 of Table 2.12; these numbers are used to determine the arrival pattern of the customers in the simulation. We have generated only 10 numbers corresponding to 10 different customers here, but an actual simulation run might include several thousand numbers representing several thousand customers (many more than any of us would like to calculate by hand).

A second set of 10 random numbers is generated and placed in column 4 to determine service times for each of the customers. These numbers cannot be the same as those used to determine arrival times if we believe arrival times and length of service time to be independent.

By comparing the random numbers in column 2 to the assigned numbers in the top part of Table 2.11, we can generate the interarrival times listed in column 3 of Table 2.12. The random numbers in column 4 of Table 2.12 are used to generate service times based on the assigned numbers in the lower portion of Table 2.11. Thus, column 5 of Table 2.12 is arrived at by comparing the random numbers in column 4 to the assigned numbers in column 4 of the bottom part of Table 2.11. In this way, service times for our 10 simulated customers are generated independently of their arrival times.

TABLE 2.12
Worksheet for Simulating the Use of an Automated Teller Machine

(1) Customer Number	(2) First Random Number	(3) Interarrival Time (minutes)	(4) Second Random Number	(5) Service Time (minutes)	(6) Arrival (minutes into simulation)	(7) Time Service Begins (minutes into simulation)	(8) Departure Time (minutes into simulation)	(9) Customer Waiting Time (minutes)
1	57	4	50	2	04	04	06	0
2	03	1	89	4	05	06	10	1
3	95	9	31	1	14	14	15	0
4	38	3	70	3	17	17	20	0
5	62	5	08	1	22	22	23	0
6	80	6	54	2	28	28	30	0
7	11	1	90	4	29	30	34	1
8	17	1	75	3	30	34	37	4
9	78	6	00	1	36	37	38	1
10	34	2	44	1	38	38	39	0

NOTE: Average waiting time = 0.7 minutes
Maximum waiting time = 4   minutes

In column 6 of Table 2.12, we begin the simulation run. We will assume that the simulation starts at time 00. Row 1, column 3, of Table 2.12

tells us the first customer arrives 4 minutes after the last customer, but since there is no previous customer, we take this to mean 4 minutes after the beginning of the simulation. The customer's arrival time is then written in column 6 as 04 (or 4 minutes into the simulation). Since there are no customers at the ATM, this first customer may begin to be served immediately; thus, service also begins (column 7) at 04.

By consulting "Service Time," in column 5, we see that this customer requires 2 minutes to be served; if service begins at 04 (column 7), the customer is free to leave 2 minutes later, at 06 (column 8). Customer waiting time is recorded in column 9. For the first customer, column 9 reads 0 because this customer did not have to wait after arriving at the ATM.

Row 2 of Table 2.12 represents the second simulated customer. Note that this customer arrives 1 minute after the first customer (column 3, row 2) and so arrives at time 05 (column 6, row 2). Since customer 1 is still at the ATM (because customer 1 does not leave until 06), customer 2 must wait until customer 1 has departed. This means customer 2 must wait 1 minute (column 9, row 2). It is just such instances that we are attempting to observe through simulation. Note that in row 8 of Table 2.12, which represents the eighth customer, a bottleneck develops when three large service times occur consecutively. The eighth customer winds up waiting 4 minutes.

From the bank's simulation, it appears that with one automated teller there will be some waiting time for customers. Whether this waiting time, on the average, is acceptable to the bank is a matter of management's willingness to accept the (seemingly small) risk of a customer's becoming dissatisfied due to waiting longer than three minutes for service. In this abbreviated simulation, only one of the ten customers waited longer than three minutes. Whether management accepts a 10-percent probability that a random customer will wait more than three minutes should be compared with the costs of buying a second automated teller, with a resulting drop in that probability. Some banks might find the extra expense worth the reduced risk of customer dissatisfaction due to waiting longer than three minutes.

It is dangerous to draw solutions from very short simulations. If we had repeated the simulation many times using different sets of random numbers each time, then we could feel more sure of the accuracy of the results. We also assumed that the variables in the simulation (interarrival time and service time) were independent of each other. If this is not true, the simulation will provide poor results. Finally, we used discrete (as opposed to continuous) distributions for both the variables. In practice, when computers are used to make the calculations, continuously distributed random variables would likely provide more accurate results.

2.11   GAME THEORY AND DECISIONS UNDER UNCERTAINTY

Early in this chapter, we noted that decision makers function in three distinct environments: certainty, risk, and uncertainty. These environments differ in the knowledge available to the decision maker concerning possible outcomes. The certain environment is one in which the decision maker enjoys complete certainty about the future. We have said little about this environment because it involves only very routine decisions that in many cases are concerned with inconsequential issues.

Most of our discussion has been devoted to decisions made under conditions of risk. Techniques employing risk-adjusted discount rates, certainty equivalent factors, decision trees, and simulation are all useful in this category of decision making. These are the most widely used of the techniques for handling risk.

Now we turn to the third type of environment: uncertainty. In a situation of uncertainty, more than one outcome exists, and the decision maker has no knowledge about the probabilities of various states or is unwilling to specify the probabilities of occurrence of the various possible outcomes. Business situations of this type arise when there is no past experience for setting the probabilities of occurrence of various outcomes. Problems associated with the introduction of a new product, the floating of a bond issue, and increasing plant capacity are examples that could fall into this category.

Several decision criteria, or decision rules, are used in decision making under uncertainty, and no single criterion can be specified as the best. The two criteria we will examine are the most common in practice: the *minimax* (or Savage) criterion and the *maximin* (or Wald) criterion.

The Maximin Criterion

The maximin decision criterion suggests that the decision maker should always be conservative or perhaps even pessimistic. Consider a company considering the introduction of a new untested product. Suppose that only three strategies are open to the executives of this company:

1. They may choose to introduce the new product, replacing an existing (somewhat similar) product in their line with the new product in a higher price category.

2. They may choose to modify the old product with only a moderate increase in price.

3. They may choose to make no change at all, keeping the existing product at its present price and saving on investment costs.

Let us assume that the decision is to be made against one of three possible economic backdrops: in an economy that may be either booming, stagnant, or contracting. These are called states of nature because they are outside of management's control. Hypothetical expected payoffs under the various strategies and conditions are presented in the payoff matrix shown in Table 2.13. Note that no probability factors are given in Table 2.13 because the company is in a state of uncertainty. The company therefore has no way to calculate an expected payoff for each of the three strategies and no way to calculate the risk associated with each of the three categories. Instead of one possible solution to the problem, there are many, each with its own rationale.

TABLE 2.13
Product Introduction Decision Payoff Matrix for a Decision Using the Maximin Criterion

| | Three Possible States of Nature | | | |
Possible Strategies	(1) Booming Economy	(2) Stagnant Economy	(3) Contracting Economy	Minimum Payoff for Each Strategy
1. Replace old product with new one at a higher price.	$5 million	$1 million	− $.5 million	− $.5 million
2. Modify old product and raise its price.	3 million	2.5 million	.5 million	.5 million
3. Make no product change.	1 million	1.5 million	2 million	1 million*

* One million dollars is the largest of the minimum payoffs for the three strategies. Thus, strategy 3 is the maximin choice because it satisfies the maximin criterion.

Using the maximin criterion, the decision maker views the states of nature pessimistically and chooses the strategy that offers the maximum of the minimum payoffs. In the example in Table 2.13, the minimum payoff of strategy 1 is − .5; the minimum payoff of strategy 2 is .5; and the minimum payoff of strategy 3 is 1. Strategy 3 would be selected as a maximin choice because it is the largest (*maximum*) of the smallest (*minimum*) payoffs.

The Minimax Criterion

The minimax decision criterion suggests that the decision maker may experience regret after the fact because of choosing the incorrect strategy for a given state of nature. The amount of regret associated with a particular strategy is the difference between the best possible payoff and what is actually obtained, given a strategy choice for the state of nature that ultimately occurs. Constructing a *regret matrix* makes the application of the decision rule quite simple.

To construct the regret matrix found in Table 2.14, we take the largest number from each column of the original payoff matrix (Table 2.13) and subtract it from every other number in the column. For example, the highest payoff in column 1 ("Booming Economy") of the payoff matrix is $5 million. Subtracting $5 million from each number in column 1 of Table 2.13 yields column 1 of the regret matrix (Table 2.14). No regret is associated with strategy 1 if the economy is booming, so the regret matrix value for that combination is 0. But if the decision makers choose strategy 2 while the economy is booming, they will feel regret to the extent of − $2 million because if they had chosen strategy 1, they could have been better off by $2 million.

TABLE 2.14
Product Introduction Decision Regret Matrix for a Decision Using the Minimax Criterion

Possible Strategies	Three Possible States of Nature			Minimum Payoff for Each Strategy
	(1) Booming Economy	(2) Stagnant Economy	(3) Contracting Economy	
1. Replace old product with new one at a higher price.	$0	− $1.5 million	− $2.5 million	− $2.5 million
2. Modify old product and raise its price.	− 2 million	0	− 1.5 million	− 2 million*
3. Make no product change.	− 4 million	− 1 million	0	− 4 million

* Minus two million dollars is the smallest of the maximum regrets for the three strategies. Thus, strategy 2 is the minimax choice because it satisfies the minimax criterion.

Once the regret matrix is specified, it is possible to determine the minimax strategy. The rule is to choose that strategy that offers the minimum of the maximum regrets. The right-hand column in Table 2.14 represents the maximum regret for each strategy. Choosing the smallest of these results in strategy 2 as the minimax choice. Note that this is not the same decision we obtained using the maximin strategy.

The choice of the criterion used by a firm must be made by the decision maker, who must match the company's objectives and current condition with the decision criterion.

SUMMARY

In this chapter, you have read that many business decisions are made under conditions that entail some risk. The possible results are known, along with the likelihood that each result will occur, but the decision maker does not know exactly which result will come to pass. In such situations, we can determine the expected value of a decision as the weighted average of the possible outcomes. The weights used are the probabilities associated with the various outcomes. For example, if there is a 30-percent chance of having $10 million in sales and a 70-percent chance of having $20 million in sales, the expected value of sales is (.3) ($10 million) + (.7) ($20 million) = $17 million.

Risk is sometimes measured by the standard deviation of the distribution of possible outcomes. However, the use of the coefficient of variation as a measure of risk is preferable because it eliminates some of the problems of using the standard deviation. In particular, the coefficient of variation is better for comparing the risks of projects of very different magnitudes. The coefficient of variation is the ratio of the standard deviation to the mean, or expected, value of the outcomes (i.e., $C = \sigma/\overline{x}$).

While monetary measures are often used to determine the best decision, it is sometimes desirable to use a utility measure instead. If a person is either risk averse or a risk preferrer, the best decision may be different if utility is used as the measure. Only when the decision maker is risk neutral will there be absolutely no difference between using a money or a utility measure to evaluate decisions.

We can account for risk in evaluating capital budgeting decisions in several ways. A risk measure can be incorporated in the calculation of net present values by adjusting the discount rate to reflect the degree of risk involved in a given return. The greater the risk, the higher the adjusted discount rate. Certainty equivalents can also be used to adjust the net present value to account for risk. Certainty equivalent factors are used in the numerators of net present value calculations to adjust each year's net cash flow to its certainty equivalent.

Decision trees and simulation studies can be useful to decision makers when risk is a factor. Decision trees provide a helpful way of organizing and analyzing complex events. In addition, the graphic nature of decision trees makes them a helpful aid in communicating the analysis to others. Simulation studies can generate additional information for decision makers and thus help them in making better business decisions. Simulations do not necessarily require large computer systems. Some can be done by hand, and many can be done rather easily on modern microcomputers or personal computers.

Game theory is a useful tool in reaching decisions under conditions characterized by uncertainty. Uncertainty exists when the possible outcomes or the probabilities of the outcomes are unknown to the decision maker. Two common decision criteria used under such conditions are the minimax criterion and the maximin criterion. The minimax criterion is evaluated using a regret matrix in which the best strategy choice is the one that provides the smallest of the maximum strategy regrets. The maximin *criterion is evaluated using a payoff matrix in which the payoff for each strategy and each state of nature is identified; the strategy that offers the greatest minimum payoff is selected.*

SUGGESTED READINGS

Brown, Rex. "Do Managers Find Decision Theory Useful." *Harvard Business Review*, May–June 1970, pp. 78–89.

Friedman, D. "Why There Are No Risk Preferers." *Journal of Political Economy*, July 1981, p. 600.

Friedman, J., and Savage, L.J. "The Utility Analysis of Choices Involving Risk." *Journal of Political Economy*, August 1948, pp. 279–304.

Gold, Bela, and Boylan, Myles G. "Capital Budgeting, Industrial Capacity, and Imports." *Quarterly Review of Economics and Business*, Autumn 1975, pp. 17–32.

Hirshleifer, Jack. "Investment Decisions under Uncertainty: Choice-Theoretic Approaches." *Quarterly Journal of Economics*, November 1965, pp. 509–536.

Hurtz, David B. "Risk Analysis in Capital Investment." *Harvard Business Review*, January–February 1974, pp. 32–38.

Luce, R.D., and Raiffa, H. *Games and Decisions.* New York: Wiley, 1957.

Magee, John T. "How to Use Decision Trees in Capital Budgeting." *Harvard Business Review*, September–October 1964, pp. 75–95.

Mas, James C.T. "Survey of Capital Budgeting: Theory and Practice." *Journal of Finance*, May 1970, pp. 349–360.

Raiffa, H. *Decision Analysis: Introductory Lectures on Choices under Uncertainty.* Reading, MA: Addison-Wesley, 1970.

Shubik, M. "A Curmudgeon's Guide to Microeconomics." *Journal of Economic Literature*, June 1970, pp. 405–429.

Simon, H.E. "Theories of Decision Making in Economics and Behavior Science." *American Economic Review*, June 1959, pp. 253–380.

von Neumann, J., and Morgenstern, O. *Theory of Games and Economic Behavior*, 3d ed. Princeton, NJ: Princeton University Press, 1953.

PROBLEMS

1. Demand for computer diskettes at General Microcomputer's warehouse has always been 0, 1, 2, 3, 4, or 5 cases (10 boxes of diskettes per case) per day. During the recent past (360 working days), General Microcomputer has observed the following frequencies of demand:

Quantity of Demanded Cases	Number of Days
0	20
1	80
2	95
3	90
4	50
5	25

What is the subjective probability for each outcome in the future, assuming the past pattern of probabilities applies?

2. The marketing director of St. Joseph Bank informs you that if the stock market reaches the 2000-point level by August, there is a 70-percent chance that the bank's trust portfolio will go up in value. Your own estimate of the probability that the market will reach the 2000-point level by August is 40 percent. Calculate the probability that both the stock market will reach the 2000-point level and the value of the trust portfolio will go up.

3. American National Bank is considering lending Stepan's Sporting Goods money for the purchase of inventory. The bank believes that there is a 90-percent chance that Stepan's will repay the loan according to the loan terms. If this is the case, the bank will earn $2000. If, however, Stepan's defaults on the loan, the net return to American National would be a loss of $500. What is the expected value to American National of granting Stepan's Sporting Goods the loan?

4. LaFortune Toys has been offered a contract of $1,000,000 net for the development and production of a voice-activated module for use with computer games. If there is a sharp downturn in consumer interest in computer games, LaFortune believes it will be able to sell the module to end users at a profit of only $200,000. However, if demand remains strong for computer games, the novel voice-activated module should be worth $2,000,000 in profits. At what probability of a drop in consumer interest would LaFortune Toys be indifferent between their two alternatives?

5. Coast Manufacturing Corporation is a major supplier of accessories to automobile manufacturers. Coast's mainstay has been the production of electrically heated rear windows for automobiles. Because these windows have imbedded heating elements visible to the naked eye, they are used only as rear windows and not as windshields.

    Now Coast has perfected a transparent heated membrane to electrically heat windshields, eliminating the need for a defroster. Truck and school bus manufacturers have expressed interest in the electric windshield, and Coast believes there is a chance the entire automobile industry will purchase the devices.

Coast is investigating three possibilities for producing the electrically heated windshields. They may choose not to develop the product line and to sell the patent rights for an estimated $180,000, which would more or less just cover the costs of development (hence, a net return of 0). The company also has the options of opening and using either a large or a small plant for the heated windshields.

Regardless of which choice the company makes, the marketing department has indicated that the electric windshield will either be a large success or fail to catch on completely and result in a very unfavorable market. If the corporation were to construct the large plant, a favorable market would result in Coast Manufacturing's making a profit of $200,000. If the market were unfavorable, the net loss would be $180,000. The small-plant alternative and a favorable market would result in a net profit of $100,000, but with an unfavorable market, the net loss would be $20,000.

a.   Construct a payoff matrix for Coast Manufacturing including the conditional profits and losses given above.

b.   Assume that the probability of a favorable market is $\frac{1}{2}$, or 50 percent, and that the only other type of market is unfavorable. Calculate the expected value of each alternative open to Coast.

c.   Is the alternative that includes the sale of the patent rights *necessarily* the weakest (least desirable) of the alternatives?

d.   Draw a decision tree representing the decision facing Coast.

6.   Sorin Food Services is trying to decide whether to bid for the concession rights to McCormick Place exhibition center in Chicago next season. Sorin's decision makers believe that the amount of food and drink sold depends on the state of the economy (which affects trade show bookings at McCormick Place). They believe that there is a .20 probability of a booming economy and that the large number of trade shows generated will return $400,000 over the cost of providing services. If the economy were in a recession (.05 subjective probability), the trade shows would generate only $10,000 in net revenues. The only other possibility is that a healthy economy would generate $300,000 in net revenue. Sorin wishes to offer $250,000 for the concession rights. What course of action would you recommend?

7.   Some stocks tend to perform better in relationship to other stocks in bull markets (periods of generally rising stock prices), while other stocks perform relatively well in bear markets (periods of generally falling stock prices). Vincent Aircraft Manufacturing (VAM) stock is widely considered to perform well in relationship to other stocks dur-

ing boom periods, while John's Bargain Stores (JBS) stock tends to do well during recessions. The following information represents your subjective probabilities of various economic conditions next year and the dollar returns (price appreciation or depreciation plus dividends) of the two stocks. Both stocks have current market prices of $100 per share.

Status of Nature	Boom	Moderate Growth	Recession	Depression
VAM STOCK	$150	$125	$100	$60
JBS STOCK	105	120	110	60
Probability	.3	.4	.2	.1

a. Compare the expected returns of investments of (1) $1,000 in JBS stock, (2) $1,000 in VAM stock, (3) $400 in JBS stock and $600 in VAM stock, and (4) $600 in JBS stock and $400 in VAM stock.
b. Evaluate the risk associated with each of the four investment portfolios and explain which you would prefer.
c. Draw a decision tree representing each of the four investment portfolios.

8. Alice's Restaurant is issuing $2 million worth of $1000 (maturity value) revenue bonds (on which the interest and principal are paid solely from earnings) due to mature in 15 years with a coupon rate of 12 percent (the interest rate specified on interest coupons attached to a bond, i.e., the nominal interest rate). Your bank has analyzed the company and has decided either to purchase the entire issue for your trust accounts or to purchase an equal dollar value of treasury bonds with an identical maturity. The treasury bonds have a coupon rate of 11 percent.

Your bank's analysis of Alice's Restaurant has resulted in your belief that there are three possible outcomes if you purchase the bonds: (1) the terms of the bonds are fully met and on time (probability 90 percent); (2) the company encounters some years in which it operates at a loss and is unable to make all interest payments, and your return is 11 percent (probability 5 percent); and (3) all interest payments are on time, but the firm is unable to retire its bonds completely at maturity, giving you a return of 9 percent (probability 5 percent).

After much deliberation, your bank decided to purchase the treasury bonds instead of the Alice's Restaurant bonds. How would you characterize the behavior of the bank's decision makers? Are they operating as risk averters, risk preferrers, or risk neutral decision makers? Is this behavior rational in terms of the chapter's discussion of risk preference?

9. Hurley Manufacturing Company is considering two mutually exclusive investment projects. Each project would cost $175,000 (payable on the first day of the first year of each project). Each of the projects is three years in duration. Annual net cash flows from each project begin one year after the initial investment and have the following probability distributions (i.e., both projects involve risk) in *each* of the three years:

Project	Probability	Net Cash Flow
1	.2	$100,000
	.6	125,000
	.2	130,000
2	.2	0
	.6	125,000
	.2	250,000

Hurley intends to evaluate the riskier project at a 13-percent discount rate and the less risky project at an 11-percent discount rate (both rates include a risk premium). Which project would Hurley choose?

10. Penguin Software produces computer software primarily for use on personal computers in homes. This software is for arcade-type games, microcomputer versions of board games and adventure games. Prices for these games have for the last two years ranged between $30 and $40.

Penguin's executives feel that they and other software manufacturers in this market grossly underestimated the price elasticity of purchasers. That is, they feel the current prices of $30 to $40 are too high and that by cutting their prices, they can increase sales so much that total revenue (and profit) will increase dramatically. Penguin is considering whether to drop the price of each of their software packages by 25 or 50 percent, to $30 or $20 each. They are unsure of exactly what effect this will have on profit and are also unsure of how competitors will react.

Penguin has estimated the first-year effect of their policy in the following way:

First Year

Alternative	Probability	Effect
Drop price by 50%	.8 (success)	$120,000
	.2 (failure)	11,000
Drop price by 25%	.6 (success)	95,000
	.4 (failure)	60,000
Continue present pricing policies	1.0 (success)	70,000

In the second year, the competitors of Penguin may react and, in fact, are quite likely to react if Penguin's first-year profits improve after a price decrease. Penguin has estimated the following probabilities for the possible second-year situations:

Second Year

Alternative	Probability	Reaction	Effect (increased profits)
Drop price by 50%	.6 (given first-year success)	Yes	$125,000
	.4 (given first-year success)	No	130,000
	.1 (given first-year failure)	Yes	10,000
	.9 (given first-year failure)	No	11,000
Drop price by 25%	.8 (given first-year success)	Yes	97,000
	.2 (given first-year success)	No	102,000
	.2 (given first-year failure)	Yes	58,000
	.8 (given first-year failure)	No	60,000
Continue present pricing policies	.5 (given first-year success)	Yes	70,000
	.5 (given first-year success)	No	91,000

a. Produce a decision tree for Penguin outlining each of the first- and second-year outcomes of the three alternatives.
b. For computational ease, assume that all first-year net revenues are received on December 31 of that year and all second-year net revenues are received on December 31 of that year. If the discount rate is 13 percent, what are the net discounted present values of the three alternatives?
c. Rank the three alternatives according to risk and indicate which Penguin should select.

11. Section 2.5 discussed a decision regarding whether to drill for oil. The situations explored in the text were for one person who was risk

averse and another who was a risk preferrer. Suppose that a third person was confronted with this decision and that this person had the following utility schedule for money:

Money	Utility
− $20,000	− 3
0	0
20,000	3
40,000	6
60,000	9
80,000	12

a. How would you describe this person's marginal utility for money?
b. Plot this utility for money function on both Figure 2.4 and Figure 2.5. Explain how it differs from the utility functions already plotted on each of those graphs.
c. Calculate the expected value (in utility terms) of drilling and not drilling the well for this person. Use the following format:

Expected value of drilling = (   ) (.2) + (   ) (.8) =
Expected value of not drilling = (   ) (.2) + (   ) (.8) =

d. Does it make any difference in this case whether the decision is evaluated in money or utility terms? Explain why or why not.

12. A sporting goods store owner must decide whether or not to expand his store. He believes that there is a 60-percent probability that the expansion will increase profits and a 40-percent probability that it will not succeed. If the owner's expansion is successful, profits will increase by $100,000; but if the expansion is not successful, a loss of $80,000 will result.
   a. What kinds of probabilities are the 60-percent chance of success and the 40-percent chance of failure? How are these probabilities computed? Since these two probabilities sum to 100 percent, can anything *other* than either success or failure happen if the owner decides to expand.
   b. Draw a decision tree for this problem, being careful to label each branch.
   c. Use the decision tree in part b to solve the problem, assuming the store owner ignores risk (i.e., is indifferent to risk.).
   d. If the store owner believed the probability of success was only 50 percent, would this alter the decision made in part c?
   e. What probability of success would just make the owner indifferent between expanding and not expanding (assume again that the owner is indifferent to risk)?

13. Knute Kline claims that he is perfectly indifferent to risk. Assume that Knute attaches a total utility of 1 to $10,000 and 2 to $20,000. Assuming Knute is correct about his risk neutrality, what utility would he attach to
    a. $40,000?
    b. $5,000?
    c. −$5,000?

14. How would you characterize the following statements? Are they made under conditions of certainty, uncertainty, or risk?
    a. If the college lowers admissions standards, I would expect a 50-percent chance of increasing enrollments by 2,000 students.
    b. In order to construct a desk, it requires 12 board feet of lumber and 2 hours of skilled labor.
    c. I have no idea whether we will earn any profit next year on this product; it depends totally on business conditions at that time.
    d. This bond pays 12 percent if I hold it until maturity.
    e. Based on past experience, I would say we have a 20-percent chance of increasing sales by 1000 units if we drop the price.

15. Twin Cities Manufacturing is considering purchasing a small company in a neighboring town that manufactures garden tools. Twin Cities believes that there is an even chance that, if they buy the firm, they will be able to make $500,000 by modernizing the firm and reselling it; if Twin Cities cannot modernize the company successfully, it stands to lose $400,000.
    a. Construct a decision tree for the problem.
    b. Use the decision tree to make the decision to purchase or not to purchase, assuming Twin Cities is indifferent to risk.
    c. Which decision (purchase or not purchase) is the riskiest for Twin Cities? What measure of risk could you use to explain your answer?

16. In a particular manufacturing plant, there is a 95-percent chance that no accidents will occur in a week. In this same plant, there is a 3-percent chance that one accident will occur and a 2-percent chance that two accidents will occur.
    a. What is the expected number of accidents per week? Would you characterize this as a risky situation?
    b. What is the expected number of accidents in a year (assume 52 weeks per year)?
    c. What is the standard deviation of the number of accidents in a week?
    d. Assume that safety rules at the plant are modified and the probability of no accidents in a week falls to 90 percent, while the probabil-

ity of one accident rises to 9 percent and the probability of two accidents falls to 1 percent. Has the expected number of accidents in a
week risen or fallen?

  e. Is the situation in part d a riskier or less risky situation than the orig-
     inal situation? Explain.

17. Keenan Tool and Die Company is considering the purchase of a new
     piece of machinery that it expects to reduce costs and thus increase
     profits. The management of Keenan has listed the expected net cash
     flows from the project as the following:

Year	Expected Net Cash Flow
0	– $3000
1	3000
2	3000
3	3000

     The discount rate for Keenan is 7 percent. Your department has
been given the task of calculating the net discounted present value of
the project adjusted for risk. Some of the members of your department
want to use the risk-adjusted discount rate method of analysis, and
they believe that a risk premium of 1 percent is appropriate for analyzing this project. Another faction of your department believes that the
certainty equivalent approach is appropriate for the analysis, and they
suggest that an alpha factor of .982 is consistent with the company's
risk exposure policies.

  a. Calculate the net discounted present value adjusted for risk using
     the risk-adjusted discount rate method.
  b. Calculate the net discounted present value adjusted for risk using
     the certainty equivalent method.
  c. What difference in net discounted present values adjusted for risk
     did the two methods yield? Explain the difference you have found.
  d. Explain under what conditions the two methods would yield
     widely differing results.

18. If an investment manager were buying stocks for a portfolio, she might
     reasonably like to know how each additional stock selected to be pur-
     chased might affect the overall risk of the portfolio. Assume there are
     only three stocks to choose from and that each stock is selling for the
     same price and each stock has the same expected value of dividends
     and standard deviation of dividends. If the manager is concerned only
     with the riskiness of dividends received in the portfolio, would the
     manager purchase only one of the stocks, two of the stocks, or all
     three? Explain.

19.   Consider the utility function of Alice Savage, shown below:

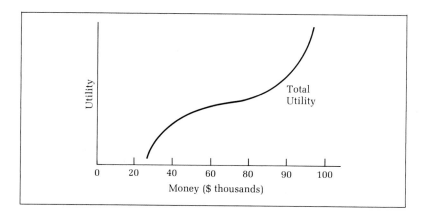

a. Is Alice a risk averter at all levels of money income?
b. Is Alice a risk preferrer at all levels of money income?
c. Would Alice prefer the certainty of getting $60,000 over an uncertain situation (i.e., a gamble) in which there is a 50-percent chance of receiving $40,000 and a 50-percent chance of receiving $60,000? Explain.
d. Would Alice prefer a certain $80,000 of income over an uncertain situation in which there is a 50-percent chance of receiving $100,000 and a 50-percent chance of receiving $60,000? Explain.
e. Would Alice prefer a certain $90,000 of income over an uncertain situation in which there is a 50-percent chance of receiving $120,000 and a 50-percent chance of receiving $60,000? Explain.

APPENDIX   Present Value Concepts

The present value of x dollars to be received in n years with the rate of interest equal to r percent is merely the amount that must be invested (or lent) at r percent to receive x dollars in n years. For example, suppose that a firm can deposit money in a bank at 7 percent and wants to deposit enough so as to receive $2000 at the end of two years. In other words, what is the present value of $2000 to be received two years from today when the interest rate is 7 percent. If we let PV equal the amount we must deposit, then at the end of one year, the principal and interest due the depositor would be given by $PV(1 + .07)$. If this amount is kept on deposit for another year, the principal and interest at the end of the second year, which must equal $2000, according to our problem, would be expressed as $[PV(1 + .07)](1 + .07)$. That is,

$$PV(1 + .07)^2 = \$2000$$

or

$$PV = \frac{\$2000}{(1 + .07)^2}$$

$$PV = \frac{\$2000}{1.1449}$$

$$PV = \$2000(.8734)$$

$$PV = \$1747$$

In other words, if the interest rate is 7 percent, then $1747 received today is equivalent to $2000 received two years from today. The procedure for finding the present value of the $2000 is called discounting, with the rate of discount being 7 percent. Let us look at three other examples to further illustrate this concept.

Example 1.   Find the present value of $550 to be received three years from now if the interest rate is 8 percent. As stated above, the present value of $550 can be thought of as the amount we must deposit (or lend), now at 8 percent interest, to have $550 in principal and interest at the end of three years. If PV represents the amount we deposit, then at the end of one year, the principal and interest at 8 percent would amount to $PV(1 + .08)$. In the same manner, at the end of the second year, the principal and interest would be $[PV(1 + .08)](1 + .08)$, or $PV(1 + .08)^2$, while at the end of the third year, the total amount on deposit would be $[PV(1 + .08)^2](1 + .08) = PV(1 + .08)^3$. According to our problem,

$$PV(1 + .08)^3 = \$550$$

or

$$PV = \frac{\$550}{(1 + .08)^3}$$

$$PV = \frac{\$550}{1.2597}$$

$$PV = \$550(.7938)$$

$$PV = \$436.61$$

Example 2.   The present value of a stream of cash flows can be found by adding the present values of the cash flows for each year. For example, suppose that the problem is to determine the present value of $3000 to be received in two years, $4200 to be received in four years, and $2600 to be received in five years if the interest rate is 7.5 percent. To arrive at the present value for this stream of cash flows, we discount each of the cash flows with a discount rate of 7.5 percent:

$$PV = \frac{\$3000}{(1 + .075)^2} + \frac{\$4200}{(1 + .075)^4} + \frac{\$2600}{(1 + .075)^5}$$

$$PV = \frac{\$3000}{1.1556} + \frac{\$4200}{1.3355} + \frac{\$2600}{1.4356}$$

$$PV = \$2596 + \$3145 + \$1811$$

$$PV = \$7552$$

These calculations indicate that, if the interest rate is 7.5 percent, $7525 now is equivalent to $3000 in two years plus $4200 in four years plus $2600 in five years.

Example 3. Suppose that, as winner of a state lottery, you must make a decision concerning whether to receive $10,000 a year for the next 10 years or $70,000 today. Assume that the interest rate is 6 percent and that the cash flows are tax free. You should calculate the present value of the stream of cash flows and compare it with $70,000. Discounting the stream of cash flows is done as follows:

$$PV = \frac{10,000}{(1 + .06)^1} + \frac{10,000}{(1 + .06)^2} + \cdots + \frac{10,000}{(1 + .06)^{10}}$$

This discounting procedure can be accomplished using present value tables for an annuity. An annuity is a series of equal payments made at regular time intervals, for example, yearly. Obviously, in calculating the present value of this annuity, we are assuming that the interest rate is constant over the 10-year period. Referring to a table that gives the present value of an annuity,[6] we find that the present value of $10 received for 10 years is $7.3601 if the interest rate is 6 percent. Therefore, the present value of $10,000 received for 10 years is

$$PV = \$10,000 \, (\$7.3601) = \$73,601$$

The other procedure that can be used to calculate the present value of this stream of cash flows is to discount the cash flow in each of the 10 years and sum the discounted values:

$$PV = \$10,000(.9434) + \$10,000(.8900) + \$10,000(.8396) +$$
$$\cdots + \$10,000(.5584)$$
$$= \$73,601$$

The discount factors .9434, .8900, .8396, . . . , .5584 are the present value of $1 received 1, 2, 3, . . . , 10 years from now, respectively, with an

---

[6]See, for example, the financial tables in John A. Halloran and Howard P. Lanser, *Introduction to Financial Management* (Glenview, IL: Scott, Foresman and Company, 1985).

interest rate of 6 percent. These discount factors can be extracted from a present value table and are derived as follows:

$$.9434 = \frac{1}{(1.06)}$$

$$.8900 = \frac{1}{(1.06)}$$

$$.8396 = \frac{1}{(1.06)}$$

$$.$$
$$.$$
$$.$$

$$.5584 = \frac{1}{(1.06)^{10}}$$

These numbers sum to 7.3601, which is the value we found in the present value table, which represents the present value of $1 received for 10 years when the interest rate is 6 percent.

By multiplying future dollars by these discount factors, we are taking into consideration that a dollar received in the future is less valuable to us than a dollar received today. Therefore, we are putting the cash flows on a comparable basis into order to evaluate the options facing our lottery winner. Obviously, at an interest rate of 6 percent, the better choice is to receive $10,000 each year for the next 10 years, since the present value ($73,601) of these cash flows exceeds the $70,000 that would have been received immediately.

To summarize, the present value of a stream of cash flows (A_1, A_2, ..., A_n, where A_i is the dollar amount that will be received at the end of the ith period) is calculated by discounting the net payments according to the following procedure:

$$PV = A_0 + \frac{A_1}{(1+r)} \quad \frac{A_2}{(1+r)^2} \quad \frac{A_3}{(1+r)^3} \quad \cdots \quad \frac{A_n}{(1+r)^n}$$

The use of programmable calculators can make such present value calculations simple. In effect, the information in a present value table is programmed into the calculator. You should check the results we have shown with your calculator to be sure you are using it correctly.

3

Optimization

Economic and business decisions involve selecting the best possible alternative, usually from a large number of potential actions. The criteria for determining the best possible alternative depend on the type of activity involved and on the objectives of the decision makers. Some common criteria include (1) the level of output that will maximize sales, (2) the combination of inputs that will produce a given volume of output at the lowest possible cost, and (3) the allocation of the advertising budget among alternative media so that maximum customer exposure is obtained. While these examples are only illustrative, they do show that most decisions are made with the intention of maximizing some positive result (benefit) or minimizing some negative result (cost). In some cases, the desired result is to maximize a net benefit (i.e., the difference between benefits and costs).

You are well aware that our entire society is becoming increasingly quantitative and analytical. This trend has been especially apparent in business and economic affairs. The widespread use of high-speed electronic computers along with the compilation of vast amounts of data related to business and economic activities has enlarged the number of alternatives for decision makers to evaluate. It has also increased the complexity of the decisions by enabling more variables to be considered in the process. The ability to formulate and work with quantitative models of business and economic problems has become an important part of today's academic training in business schools and in economics departments at nearly every college and university.

The widespread use of analytic models has increased the importance of being able to evaluate and work with mathematical statements of business and economic problems. This chapter will involve you in actively using some basic algebraic concepts and a small amount of calculus. Unfortunately, when many students are first exposed to these concepts, there is very little emphasis on applications. When applications are discussed, they usually focus on topics in the physical sciences rather than social science or business situations. The result is that most business and economics students have very little "feel" for the usefulness of mathe-

matical analysis. In fact, you are not alone if you are one of those students who is absolutely frightened by the thought of learning and using such concepts.

It is the purpose of this chapter to help you review some basic mathematical concepts and perhaps learn some new ones. After finishing this chapter, you should have developed the ability and confidence to work with such concepts in solving business and economic problems. We will begin by discussing what is meant by a function and progress through the use of some elementary calculus to find maxima and minima. Graphs will be used to help you get a better picture of what the mathematical statements represent. [1]

3.1 FUNCTIONS AND FUNCTIONAL NOTATION

Mathematical functions are convenient and precise methods of stating relationships between variables in economic and business analysis. In general terms, a function can be defined as follows:

> A *function* shows how one or more independent variables can be transformed into, or associated with, a dependent variable.

We often use the letter Y to represent the dependent variable and X (or X_1, X_2, X_3, etc.) to represent the independent variable (or variables). A function is the mathematical statement or expression that gives us the value of Y for any specified value of X (or X_1, X_2, X_3, etc.).[2] Y is called the dependent variable because its value depends on the values of the independent variables. In terms of cause and effect, changes in the X's are causes, while the resulting change in Y is the effect. Changes in the independent variables bring about, or cause, a change in Y.

In practice, you may use various letters and groups of letters to represent variables. For example, if you wanted to work with the relationship

---

[1]Students who have had a college course in calculus may be able to skip most of this chapter; however, it has been our experience that a review of these topics is beneficial to most students. Since constrained optimization is often not usually covered in the first calculus course, all students should be certain to look over section 3.10. A review of some additional basic algebraic concepts is provided in Appendix A. Some students may also want to look through that material at this time.

[2]Strictly speaking, for any set of values for the independent variables (X's), only one value of the dependent variable (Y) is generated by a function. If more than one value of Y results, the expression is not a function. Thus, $Y = \pm\sqrt{X}$ is not a function, but both $Y = -\sqrt{X}$ and $Y = +\sqrt{X}$ are functions.

between engine size, measured in cubic inch displacement, and the number of miles per gallon that a car gets, you might write the variables as follows:

$$CID = \text{engine size in cubic inch displacement}$$
$$MPG = \text{miles per gallon}$$

This practice is followed frequently throughout the text. For example, quantity will usually be represented by Q, labor by L, and capital by K (K rather than C so that we do not confuse it with various costs for which we might use C).

Ways to State Simple Functions

Functions can be written in a very general form or in a very specific form. At one time or another, you have probably said that one thing was a function of, or dependent on, something else. If you let Y represent the former and X the latter, in mathematical notation you would write:

$$Y = f(X)$$

This is read: Y is a function of X. The letter f is simply the most common notation for a function. Other letters (e.g., g and h) are also sometimes used.

This function, $Y = f(X)$, is a very general function. It tells us only that Y is dependent on the value of X but does not indicate the nature of that dependence. If you know that Y is a linear function of X, you could write the function as

$$Y = a + bX$$

This is one common way of expressing a linear function. It tells us that Y is equal to the value of a plus b times the value of X. Both a and b may have any value. They may be positive or negative, and may be integer or decimal numbers. In this form, the function is more specific. It tells us more about the relationship between Y and X than does $Y = f(X)$.

If you had some empirical evidence, you could express the function in an even more specific form. For example, you might know that the value of Y is equal to 10 plus one-half the value of X. You could then write the function as

$$Y = 10 + .5X$$

This is a very specific function. You now can find a specific value for the dependent variable Y, given some value for X. If X equaled 100, you would find that Y would be 60:

$$Y = 10 + .5(100) = 60$$

You might be able to estimate the functional relationship between the gas mileage of cars and their engine sizes from data collected by the government.[3] The most general function you might state is

$$MPG = f(CID)$$

where *MPG* represents the number of miles per gallon a car gets and *CID* represents the car's engine size measured in cubic inches of displacement. If you expect the function to be linear, you could write the function as

$$MPG = a + b(CID)$$

All the functions we have used as examples so far have had just two variables: *Y* and *X*, or *MPG* and *CID*. Such functions are called bivariate functions because there are just two variables: the dependent variable and one independent variable.

Multivariable Functions

In many situations, the dependent variable is a function of several independent variables, which may be denoted X_1, X_2, X_3, and so on or with other letters more directly related to each variable (e.g., *CID* for cubic inch displacement). When several variables are involved, the most general functional form is

$$Y = f(X_1, X_2, X_3)$$

This function says that *Y* is dependent on the values of the three independent variables X_1, X_2, and X_3. This is a multivariable function. If you thought the relationship between this set of independent variables and *Y* was linear, you could write the function as

$$Y = a + b_1 X_1 + b_2 X_2 + b_3 X_3$$

Where each b_i represents the coefficient for its respective independent variable X_i. This is a more specific function, but the function could be written in an even more specific way as

$$Y = 100 + 2.5X_1 - 10X_2 + 32X_3$$

In this form, we see that *Y* is positively related to X_1 and X_3 (as X_1 or X_3 increase, so does *Y*) and negatively related to X_2 (as X_2 increases, *Y* decreases).

Often functional relationships are not linear. As you continue with the study of managerial economics, you will see many applications of both linear and nonlinear functions. Some representative linear and nonlinear functions are graphed in Figure 3.1. Look at these carefully. Doing so will help you to develop your sense of what various mathematical functions represent.

---

[3]We will discuss the way in which you might estimate such functions in the next chapter, and you will estimate this particular relationship as an example.

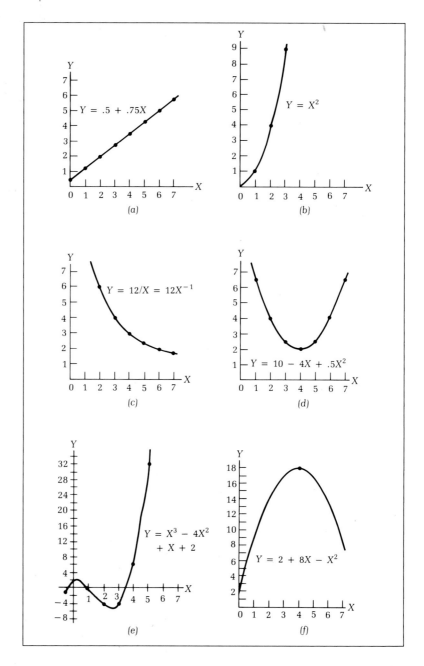

FIGURE 3.1   **Representative Linear and Nonlinear Functions**   These six graphs provide a visual representation of the information contained in the equation accompanying each graph. For each function $Y = f(X)$, there is a graph that depicts that function.

3.2 SLOPE AND THE CONCEPT OF A DERIVATIVE

It is often important to know the way in which changes in the independent variable (X) affect the dependent variable (Y). The rate of change in Y as X changes is the slope of a function. As you will see, this rate of change is the basis of the calculus used in the rest of the text.

A Linear Function

The function $Y = 2X$ is shown in Figure 3.2. Comparing this function to the general linear equation, $Y = a + bX$, you can see that in this case $a = 0$ and $b = 2$.

    Look at Figure 3.2. What is the rate of change between the origin (0) and P_1? Between P_1 and P_2? Between P_2 and P_3? In going from 0 to P_1, Y increases from 0 to 2. We can denote this change in Y as ΔY.[4] Thus, $\Delta Y = 2$. Over the same interval X increases from 0 to 1. This change in X is denoted

---

[4]A Δ is often used to represent a change. Thus, ΔY is read as a "change in Y," while ΔX means a "change in X."

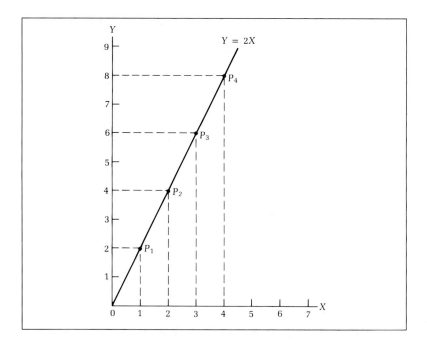

FIGURE 3.2   **Graphic Representation of the Linear Function $Y = 2X$**   The slope of this function is constant; it is always 2.

as ΔX and is equal to 1. The average rate of change in Y per unit change in X is defined as $\Delta Y / \Delta X$.

From 0 to P_1, $\Delta Y / \Delta X = (2 - 0)/(1 - 0) = 2/1 = 2$
From P_1 to P_2, $\Delta Y / \Delta X = (4 - 2)/(2 - 1) = 2$
From P_2 to P_3, $\Delta Y / \Delta X = (6 - 4)/(3 - 2) = 2$

The average rate of change between any pair of adjacent points in this function is a constant (2). This is to be expected since the function is linear. For each unit increase (decrease) in X, there is a two-unit increase (decrease) in Y.

A Nonlinear Function

We can define the average rate of change, $\Delta Y / \Delta X$, similarly for a nonlinear function such as the one illustrated in Figure 3.3. The equation for this function is $Y = X^2$. The *average* rate of change between P_1 and P_2 is $\Delta Y / \Delta X = 3/1 = 3$. This is the slope of the straight line through P_1 and P_2. Similarly, the average rate of change between P_2 and P_3, represented by the slope of the straight line between that pair of points, is $\Delta Y / \Delta X = 5/1 = 5$.

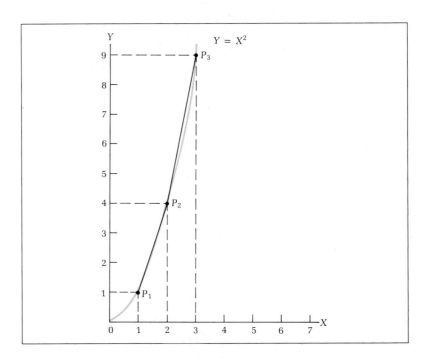

FIGURE 3.3   **Graphic Representation of the Quadratic Equation $Y = X^2$**   The slope of this function increases from P_1 to P_2 to P_3.

If you look closely at the curved line representing the function $Y = X^2$ between P_1 and P_2, you will see that the slope of this line near P_1 is less than the average rate of change between P_1 and P_2, and that the slope near P_2 is greater than that average rate of change (slope of the straight line between P_1 and P_2). There is just one point on the curved line between P_1 and P_2 for which the slope of the curve equals the average slope between those two points. The average rate of change between the two points has been defined as $\Delta Y / \Delta X$. If you allow ΔX to become smaller and smaller, ΔY also becomes smaller and $\Delta Y / \Delta X$ approaches a value that is the slope of the tangent to the function at a point such as P_1. The slope of this tangent is called the derivative of the function.

The Concept of a Derivative

Because the derivative is the slope of a function at a point, it is sometimes called an instantaneous rate of change. It is the rate of change in Y as X changes at some point along the function. In more mathematical terms, the derivative of a function is defined as the rate of change in the function as the change in the independent variable becomes *very* small (as ΔX approaches 0, which is often written as $\Delta X \rightarrow 0$). Thus, the derivative is the value that $\Delta Y / \Delta X$ becomes in the limit as $\Delta X \rightarrow 0$. (See section A.3 in Appendix B.) We then have [5]

$$\begin{bmatrix} \text{rate of } \Delta Y \\ \text{at a point} \end{bmatrix} = \begin{bmatrix} \text{derivative of } Y \\ \text{as } X \text{ changes} \end{bmatrix} = \begin{bmatrix} \lim_{\Delta X \rightarrow 0} \dfrac{\Delta Y}{\Delta X} \end{bmatrix}$$

Note that ΔX never reaches 0, so there is no problem with dividing by 0. The notations y', $f'(X)$, and dY/dX are all frequently used to denote a derivative. So

$$y' = f'(X) = \frac{dY}{dX} = \lim_{\Delta X \rightarrow 0} \frac{\Delta Y}{\Delta X}$$

These notations (e.g., dY/dX) are simply operators instructing you to perform some mathematical operation, much as a plus sign instructs you to add.

As you work with derivatives, keep the following two points in mind:

1.   A derivative is the slope of a function at a point on the function.

---

[5]This approach to the concept of a derivative is developed more fully in Appendix B. It may be helpful in developing your understanding of the concept of a limit to consider the following analogy. Hold your hands out in front of you separated by the width of your shoulders. Now move your hands closer together in steps such that in each step you move them closer by one-half of the existing distance between them. Your hands move closer and closer but never touch. In the limit, the distance between them shrinks toward 0 but never quite becomes 0 even though the remaining distance is continually cut in half.

2. A derivative should always be thought of as a rate of change. Thus, dY/dX is the rate of change in the variable Y as the variable X changes.

If you think back to your introductory economics course, you will recall the frequent use of the term *marginal*. This term always relates to a rate of change. Marginal cost is the rate of change in cost as more output is produced. Marginal utility is the rate of change in total satisfaction as more of a good is consumed. The marginal propensity to consume is the rate of change in consumption as income changes. These and other "marginal" concepts are made operational through the use of derivatives when the changes represent small intervals.

3.3   RULES FOR FINDING DERIVATIVES OF COMMONLY USED FUNCTIONS

Reading the slope of a tangent line from a graph or using the mathematical definition of a derivative can be cumbersome ways of determining the rate of change in a function. Fortunately, a set of rules has been developed to allow us to determine instantaneous rates of change, or derivatives, of various types of functions. Derivatives enable us to describe the properties of the majority of functions encountered in business and economics. In the following discussion, $f'(X)$, dY/dX, and y' notations are all used to designate derivatives to familiarize you with these common forms.

The Constant Rule

If $Y = C$, where C is a constant, Y will not change as X changes, and thus $dY/dX = 0$. Consider the following examples:

a. $Y = 200$
$y' = 0$
b. $Y = 30M$ (M is not a function of X)
$dY/dX = 0$

Note that these results are consistent with the fact that the graph of $Y = C$ (i.e., $Y =$ any constant) is a horizontal line at a height C above the horizontal axis, and the slope of a horizontal line is 0.

The General Power Function Rule

If $Y = f(X) = aX^n$, where a and n can be any numbers, the rate of change in Y as X changes (the derivative of Y with respect to X) is defined as

$$y' = naX^{n-1}$$

For example,

1. $Y = X^2$
$dY/dX = 2X^{2-1} = 2X$

2. $Y = 4X^3$
$y' = (3)(4X^{3-1})$
$y' = 12X^2$

3. $Y = 8.5X^4$
$dY/dX = (4)(8.5X^{4-1})$
$dY/dX = 34X^3$

4. $Y = 2X^{1.5}$
$y' = (1.5)(2X^{1.5-1})$
$y' = 3X^{.5}$

5. $Y = 4X^{.5}$
$f'(X) = (.5)(4X^{.5-1})$
$f'(X) = 2X^{-.5}$

6. $Y = 2X^{-2}$
$y' = (-2)(2X^{-2-1})$
$y' = -4X^{-3}$

This is the general power function rule. It is the basis for most of the derivatives that you will need to find. Remembering the relationships boxed off below will be most helpful in your future work in managerial economics:

For the function
$$Y = aX^n$$
the derivative is
$$dY/dX = naX^{n-1}$$

The Sum or Difference Rule

If $Y = f(X)$ is a polynomial composed of the sums (or differences) of several individual terms, the derivative is the sum (or difference) of the derivatives of each separate term. This statement is really much simpler than it sounds and can be made clear with a few examples. As you will see, it is an extension of the power function rule and the constant rule. Consider these examples:

1.
$$Y = X^2 + 4X^3$$
$$f'(X) = 2X^{2-1} + (3)(4X^{3-1})$$
$$f'(X) = 2X + 12X^2$$

2.
$$Y = 3X^2 - 2X^4 + 5$$
$$y' = (2)(3X^{2-1}) - (4)(2X^{4-1}) + (0)$$
$$y' = 6X - 8X^3 + 0$$
$$y' = 6X - 8X^3$$

3.
$$Y = 12X - 3X^{-2} + 4X^{20}$$
$$y' = (1)(12X^{1-1}) - (-2)(3X^{-2-1}) + (20)(4X^{20-1})$$
$$y' = 12X^0 + 6X^{-3} + 80X^{19}$$
$$y' = 12 + 6X^{-3} + 80X^{19}$$

Note that $X^0 = 1$ (any number raised to the 0 power is equal to 1).

4.
$$Y = 2X^4 + 6X^{4.5}$$
$$dY/dX = (4)(2X^{4-1}) + (4.5)(6X^{4.5-1})$$
$$dY/dX = 8X^3 + 27X^{3.5}$$

Other Rules

You can learn the constant rule, the general power function rule, and the sum or difference rule if you practice finding derivatives of such functions. Working the chapter-end problems will help a great deal. As with most new concepts, learning to use some calculus is not a spectator sport. You have to participate to get the benefit. So work some problems. Practice.

While these rules will see you through this course, you may encounter other types of functions in your reading or in assignments you may get from your instructor. Therefore, we have provided some additional useful rules for finding derivatives in Appendix B. Use that resource as appropriate. Having mastered the three rules discussed above, you will find it easier to work with more complex functions when you run across their use.

3.4 FINDING HIGHER-ORDER DERIVATIVES

The derivatives you have learned about so far are often called *first derivatives* or *first-order derivatives*. It is also possible to find second-, third-, and fourth- (or even higher) order derivatives. A second derivative is the derivative, or rate of change, of a first derivative. A third derivative is the derivative of the second derivative. How would you find a tenth derivative? You are correct if you said that it would be the derivative of the ninth derivative. While such higher-order derivatives are possible, you will rarely need to go beyond a second or third derivative.

Before looking at the process of obtaining higher-order derivatives, let us think a little about what they mean. Recall that a first derivative is the rate of change in some function. It follows, then, that the second derivative is the rate of change in the first derivative. While the first derivative measures the slope of a function, the second derivative describes how fast that slope is changing. Consider, for example, the line graphed in Figure 3.2. Looking at the line, you see that it is a linear function, or a straight line. That line is described by the equation $Y = 2X$. You now know that the slope of this line is the derivative of Y with respect to X. That is, the slope is

$$dY/dX = y' = 2$$

Thus, the slope of the line is the constant 2. This means that the slope of $Y = 2X$ is always equal to 2. The slope never changes. The second derivative was described above as the derivative of the first derivative. Well, what is the derivative of 2? The answer, of course, is 0 (i.e., if $y' = 2$, $dy'/dX = 0$). Since the second derivative describes how fast the slope of the function changes, this means that the *rate of change in the slope* of $Y = 2X$ is 0. The *slope* of $Y = 2X$ does not change. It is, therefore, a linear function.

Let us now show the procedures for finding higher-order derivatives more explicitly. The rule for finding a second derivative can be stated as follows: for $Y = f(X)$, the first derivative is $dY/dX = y' = f'(X)$. The second derivative is $df'(X)/dX$ and is denoted in one of the following ways:

$$d^2Y/dX^2, \text{ or } y'', \text{ or } f''(X)$$

The third derivative is found in a similar way. The third derivative of $Y = f(X)$ is the derivative of the second derivative:

$$df''(X)/dY$$

and can be denoted in the following ways:

$$d^3Y/dX^3, \text{ or } y''', \text{ or } f'''(X)$$

Consider the following examples:

1. Let $Y = f(X) = 80X - 12X^2 + 6X^3$
    The first derivative is $dY/dX = 80 - 24X + 18X^2$
    The second derivative is $d^2Y/dX^2 = -24 + 36X$
    The third derivative is $d^3Y/dX^3 = 36$
    You should be able to see that the fourth derivative in this case is 0.

2. Let $Y = f(X) = -4X^{-1} + 2X$
    The first derivative is $y' = 4X^{-2} + 2$
    The second derivative is $y'' = -8X^{-3}$
    The third derivative is $y''' = 24X^{-4}$
    Try to find the fourth derivative in this case.
    Do you get $y'''' = -96X^{-5}$? You should.

3. Let $Y = f(X) = 100X - 2X^2$
   The first derivative is $f'(X) = 100 - 4X$
   The second derivative is $f''(X) = -4$
   The third derivative is $f'''(X) = 0$
   Would you agree that the fourth and all higher order derivatives are also 0 in this case?

3.5 SOME APPLICATIONS OF DERIVATIVES

Before using derivatives to determine where functions may have maximum or minimum values, let us look at some other applications. Earlier, we related the concept of a derivative to the economic concept of marginal relationships. We will now combine these two concepts.

Consider first the marginal propensity to consume that you studied in macroeconomics. In most cases, C is used to represent consumption and Y is used to represent income. The consumption function is often expressed as follows:

$$C = f(Y)$$
$$C = a + bY$$

The slope of this function, called the marginal propensity to consume (MPC), is

$$dC/dY = b$$

If $b = .8$ and $a = 10$, the consumption function is

$$C = 10 + .8Y$$

and the MPC is

$$MPC = dC/dY = .8$$

This means that for every dollar increase in income, consumption expenditures are expected to rise by 80 cents.

In your microeconomics course, you no doubt talked about total cost functions that increased first at a decreasing rate and then at an increasing rate, such as the one shown in the top portion of Figure 3.4. You also learned that in such cases the marginal cost curve is U shaped, such as the one shown at the bottom of Figure 3.4.

Remember, the marginal cost is the rate of change in total cost as more units of output are produced. Does this sound a lot like the way you would define the slope of the total cost function? It surely does. It follows that the

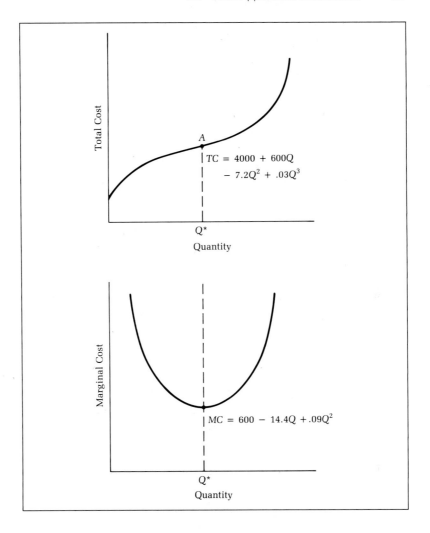

FIGURE 3.4   **Representative Total Cost and Marginal Cost Functions**   Total cost is a cubic function of the level of output (Q), while marginal cost is a quadratic function of Q. The equation for marginal cost is the derivative of the equation for total cost, and thus the value of marginal cost for Q is the measure of the slope of total cost. Note that to the left of Q^*, marginal cost diminishes and to the right of Q^*, marginal cost increases, as does the slope of the total cost curve.

marginal cost curve is the derivative (or slope) of the total cost curve. A representative total cost function might be

$$TC = 4000 + 600Q - 7.2Q^2 + .03Q^3$$

This function would look like the one at the top of Figure 3.4 if you were to graph it. You can now find the equation for the marginal cost curve by finding the derivative of total cost:

$$MC = dTC/dQ = 600 - 14.4Q + .09Q^2$$

If you graph this function, you will see that is has a shape similar to the curve below the total cost curve in Figure 3.4.

You will find that the ability to determine marginal relationships such as this will be very useful. You will be able to use the calculus you have learned to find marginal utility, marginal revenue, and marginal product as well as marginal cost functions.

3.6   MAXIMA AND MINIMA: MARGINAL ANALYSIS IN ACTION

One of the most important uses of the calculus you have been studying is to find where various functions have maxima or minima. Some functions have no maximum or minimum, while others have more than one such point. In this section, we will consider examples that illustrate a variety of cases.

In Figure 3.5, two graphs from Figure 3.1 are reproduced. Look first at the left-hand graph in Figure 3.5. The function graphed there rises at first, but as you follow it from left to right, you see that its slope becomes less steep. Eventually, the curve turns downward and has a negative slope that becomes increasingly steep. As the slope of the curve goes from being positive to negative, the function reaches its highest point. What else happens at this point? The slope of the curve is 0! As long as the slope is positive, Y must increase as X increases. When the slope is negative, Y decreases as X increases. So it makes sense that the function reaches its highest value where the slope changes from being positive to negative (i.e., where the slope is 0).

The First-Order Condition for Extreme Points

At what value of the independent variable X does this maximum occur? We could try to read that value from the horizontal axis, but that is an inexact method. Five people estimating the value might get five different answers. This is especially true when the horizontal axis has fine divisions.

We know from our visual inspection of the function that its maximum is at the point where the slope of the function is 0. How else can you find the value of X where the slope of the function is 0? Remember that the first derivative of a function is the slope of the function. So you can find the first derivative of $Y = 2 + 8X - X^2$ and then find the value of X that will make that derivative (the slope of the function) equal to 0. The derivative is

$$dY/dX = 8 - 2X$$

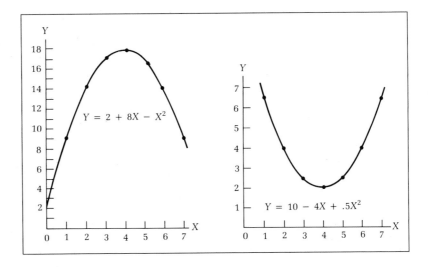

FIGURE 3.5   **Graphs of Functions with a Maximum and a Minimum**   The left-hand graph rises at a decreasing rate until it reaches a maximum and then declines. The right-hand graph decreases at a decreasing rate until it reaches a minimum and then increases. In both cases, extreme points are reached at the point at which the slope of the function is 0.

Keep in mind that this equation is the slope of the original function. Now, if you set that derivative equal to 0 and solve for X, you will have the value of X where the slope is 0:

$$dY/dX = 8 - 2X = 0$$
$$-2X = -8$$
$$X = 4$$

This tells us that the function $Y = 2 + 8X - X^2$ has a slope of 0 at $X = 4$, which is consistent with the graph of the function in Figure 3.5. You can see that the function reaches its highest point when $X = 4$, the point at which its slope is 0.

In the right-hand graph of Figure 3.5, you see that the function $Y = 10 - 4X + .5X^2$ at first falls, reaches a minimum, and then rises. When the slope of this function changes from being negative to positive (i.e., when the slope is 0), the function has its minimum value. The derivative (slope) of the function is

$$dY/dX = -4 + X$$

By setting this equation equal to 0, you can find the value of X where the function's slope is 0 and where it has a minimum:

$$dY/dX = -4 + X = 0$$
$$X = 4$$

You now know that when $X = 4$, the function graphed in the right-hand quadrant of Figure 3.5 has a minimum.

The results you have seen for these examples lead to an important generalization: *a function may have a maximum point or a minimum point when its first derivative is equal to 0.* This is called a *first-order condition* (or *necessary condition*) for a maximum or minimum. Algebraically, this condition is stated as

$$dY/dX = 0$$

That is, you set the equation for the first derivative equal to 0 and solve that equation for the value or values of X that satisfy that condition. These values are called the *critical values* of the function.

The Second-Order Condition

In the examples you have looked at so far, you could tell whether the function had a maximum or a minimum where its slope was 0 because you had a visual aid. The functions were graphed in Figure 3.5. How could you tell whether there was a maximum or a minimum if you did not have such a visual aid? To answer this question, let us look more closely at the two examples.

In the first case, you noted that the slope of the function was at first positive and decreasing, it became 0, and then it became more and more negative. So the slope of $Y = 2 + 8X - X^2$ goes from positive to negative. The slope is a decreasing function of X. As X gets larger, the slope of the function gets smaller. Remember that the slope of $Y = 2 + 8X - X^2$ is

$$dY/dX = 8 - 2X$$

This is an equation representing the slope of the original function, and you can see that as X increases, dY/dX becomes smaller.

What is the slope of the function that represents the slope of the original function? By inspection, you can probably see that in this case the slope is -2. Again, remember that any slope is a derivative. So if you find the derivative of $dY/dX = 8 - 2X$, you have the slope of the dY/dX function. This is a second derivative:

$$d^2Y/dX^2 = -2$$

Note that the second derivative is negative. This is an important result. The function $Y = 2 + 8X - X^2$ has a *maximum* where its *first derivative is 0* ($dY/dX = 0$) and its *second derivative has a negative value* ($d^2Y/dX^2 < 0$).

Now let us turn our attention to the function $Y = 10 - 4X + .5X^2$, which you know reaches a minimum at $X = 4$. You can see from Figure 3.5 that the slope of this function goes from being negative to being positive at

$X = 4$. The slope of this function is itself an increasing function of X. You have found the slope of this original function to be

$$dY/dX = -4 + X$$

By finding the second derivative of the original function, you can find the slope of the function dY/dX:

$$d^2Y/dX^2 = 1$$

Here the second derivative is positive. That is, the slope of the first derivative is positive. This is, again, an important result. The function $Y = 10 - 4X + .5X^2$ has a *minimum* where its *first derivative is 0* ($dY/dX = 0$) and its *second derivative has a positive value* ($d^2Y/dX^2 > 0$).

The extremely useful results obtained above are summarized as follows:

Given a function $Y = f(X)$,

1. *For a Maximum*

First-order condition: $dY/dX = 0$
Second-order condition: $d^2Y/dX^2 < 0$

2. *For a Minimum*

First-order condition: $dY/dX = 0$
Second-order condition: $d^2Y/dX^2 > 0$

Finding Maxima and Minima

Following are a few examples to help you develop a good ability to determine maxima and minima:

1.
$$Y = 600 - 14.4X + .09X^2$$
$$dY/dX = -14.4 + .18X = 0$$
$$.18X = 14.4$$
$$X = 80$$
$$d^2Y/dX^2 = .18 > 0$$

Thus, this function has a minimum at $X = 80$.

2.
$$Y = 84X - .2X^2$$
$$dY/dX = 84 - .4X = 0$$
$$-.4X = -84$$
$$X = 210$$
$$d^2Y/dX^2 = -.4 < 0$$

Thus, this function has a maximum at $X = 210$.

3. $Y = 25 + 18.2X - .25X^2$
$y' = 18.2 - .5X = 0$
$-.5X = -18.2$
$X = 36.4$
$y'' = -.5 < 0$

Thus, this function has a maximum at $X = 36.4$.

Note that the y' and y'' notation is a little simpler to write and is just as good as the dY/dX and d^2Y/dX^2 forms.

In economics and business, maxima and minima are used to define marginal relationships. You will recall from your previous courses in economics that marginal revenue is the rate of change in total revenue. That means that marginal revenue is the slope of the total revenue function, or the first derivative of total revenue.

The graphs of total revenue and marginal revenue in Figure 3.6 should help refresh your memory of these relationships. Total revenue (TR) is a function of sales (Q).[6] For the function graphed in Figure 3.6, total revenue is

$TR = f(Q)$
$TR = 80Q - 2Q^2$

Marginal revenue, the rate of change in total revenue, is, then,

$MR = dTR/dQ = 80 - 4Q$

The first-order condition for total revenue to have a maximum is that the first derivative (marginal revenue) be equal to 0. Thus,

$MR = dTR/dQ = 80 - 4Q = 0$
$-4Q = -80$
$Q = 20$

To be sure that this critical value is for a maximum, you should check the second-order condition as follows:

$d^2TR/dQ^2 = -4 < 0$

Therefore, the total revenue function has a maximum at $Q = 20$, which is where the marginal revenue function is 0.

These results can be seen in Figure 3.6 as well. You can see that total revenue increases at a decreasing rate as quantity increases. That is, the

---

[6]We will see how this type of total revenue function is derived in Chapter 5, in which various demand and revenue concepts are discussed in detail.

slope of total revenue becomes less. This is shown by the declining marginal revenue curve, which is, after all, the slope of total revenue. When the slope of total revenue (i.e., marginal revenue) falls to 0 at $Q = 20$, you see that total revenue has reached its maximum value. That value can be found from the graph or from the total revenue function as follows:

$$TR_{max} = 80\,(20) - 2\,(20)^2 = 800$$

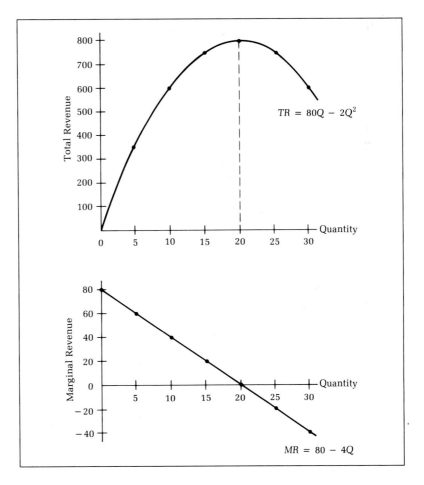

FIGURE 3.6   **Graphs of Total Revenue and Marginal Revenue** As quantity increases, total revenue rises at a decreasing rate until it reaches a maximum; then it declines. Marginal revenue is the slope (derivative) of total revenue. You can see that as the slope of total revenue decreases, marginal revenue does indeed decline. When marginal revenue is 0, the slope of total revenue is 0; this occurs at the maximum of total revenue.

3.7 ADDITIONAL CONCEPTS RELATED TO FINDING MAXIMA AND MINIMA

Two questions that may have come to your mind are (1) What if the second derivative is neither positive nor negative but is 0? and (2) Is there ever more than one critical value? To help in answering these questions, let us look at two slightly more complex examples. Consider the following functions, graphed in Figure 3.7:

Left quadrant: $Y = X^3$
Right quadrant: $Y = X^3 - 4X^2 + X + 2$

Let us first evaluate the function $Y = X^3$ for possible maxima or minima. The first-order condition is

$$y' = 3X^2 = 0$$
$$X = 0$$

The second-order condition gives us

$$y'' = 6X$$

which we must evaluate at the critical point, $X = 0$. At this point, you see that the second derivative is neither positive nor negative. It is 0:

$$y'' = 6(0) = 0$$

When this happens, the test for a maximum or minimum is said to fail. But there is a fairly easy solution to the problem this presents. You continue to find higher-order derivatives until you get one that is not 0 at the critical value. If this is an odd-numbered derivative, there is neither a maximum nor a minimum but, rather, a point of inflection (i.e., the curve changes shape from being convex to concave or vice versa). If the first nonzero derivative is even and has a positive value, the function has a minimum at that critical point. If it is even and has a negative value, the function has a maximum at the critical point.

In our present example, you find that the first nonzero derivative is the third derivative. That is,

$$y''' = 6$$

Since this is an odd-numbered derivative, the function $Y = X^3$ has a point of inflection at the critical value obtained from the first derivative. You can see this by looking at the left-hand graph in Figure 3.7.

Look now at the right-hand graph in Figure 3.7. The function graphed there at first rises, then falls, and then rises again. At point A, the function has what is called a local maximum. It is the maximum in a particular local area, but there are other values at which the function rises higher. Likewise, point B is a local minimum. As you will see, a critical value is associated with each of these points.

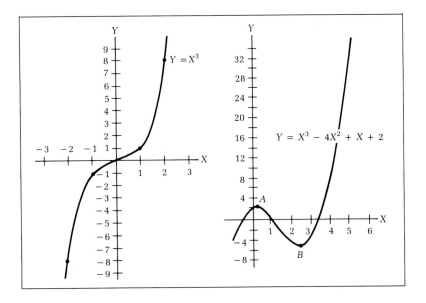

FIGURE 3.7   **Graphs of a Function with No Maximum or Minimum and One with Both a Maximum and a Minimum**   The left-hand function has a point of inflection at $X = 0$ but has no maximum or minimum. The right-hand function has a maximum at $X = .13$ and a minimum at $X = 2.53$.

Let us evaluate the function $Y = X^3 - 4X^2 + X + 2$ for possible maxima or minima. The first-order condition is

$$y' = 3X^2 - 8X + 1 = 0$$

To solve this for the values of X that will make the expression equal 0, you have to use the quadratic equation. In case you have forgotten, this little tool is given below:

For the general quadratic equation $aX^2 + bX + c = 0$, the two possible roots (values of X) are

$$X_1, X_2 = \frac{-b \pm \sqrt{b^2 - 4ac}}{2a}$$

This expression is called the quadratic equation.

For our present example $a = 3, b = -8$, and $c = 1$. So, the two values of X that make the first derivative equal 0 can be found as follows:

$$X_1, X_2 = \frac{-(-8) \pm \sqrt{(-8)^2 - 4(3)(1)}}{2(3)}$$

$$X_1, X_2 = \frac{8 \pm \sqrt{64 - 12}}{6}$$

$$X_1, X_2 = \frac{8 \pm \sqrt{52}}{6}$$

$$X_1, X_2 = \frac{8 \pm 7.2}{6}$$

$$X_1 = \frac{8 + 7.2}{6} = \frac{15.2}{6} = 2.53$$

$$X_2 = \frac{8 - 7.2}{6} = \frac{.8}{6} = .13$$

These are the critical values for the function being evaluated. You must now evaluate the second-order condition for each of these values. The second derivative is

$$y'' = 6X - 8$$

At

$$X = 2.53, y'' = 6(2.53) - 8 = 7.18$$

Since

$$y'' = 7.18 > 0$$

there is a minimum at this critical value. At

$$X = .13, y'' = 6(.13) - 8 = -7.22$$

Since

$$y'' = -7.22 < 0$$

there is a maximum at this critical value. These results are consistent with what you see on the right-hand graph in Figure 3.7.

3.8 PARTIAL DERIVATIVES

So far, our discussion has focused on functions with one independent variable, represented by the letter X. As you will see in later chapters, the techniques you have learned for such simple cases will be very valuable. But you are quite aware that in many business and economic situations, the dependent variable of interest is a function of more than one independent variable. The following two examples are representative:

1.   Sales may be a function of income, price, and advertising.

2.   Output may be a function of the usage of several inputs, such as labor, capital, and land.

In such cases, you may want to know how small changes in just one of the independent variables would influence the dependent variable if all other independent variables were constant. Partial derivatives are used for this purpose. As you will see, the basic concepts you have already learned are generally applicable to finding partial derivatives as well.

Suppose Y is a function of n independent variables. This could be written as

$$Y = f(X_1, X_2, X_3, \ldots, X_n)$$

where each X_i is a different independent variable. A partial derivative of Y with respect to any one of the n independent variables measures the change in Y that is caused by a very small change in just that one independent variable, with all the other independent variables constant.

The symbols used to represent partial derivatives are similar to those used for simple derivatives. The notations we will use in this text are as follows:

1. $\partial Y/\partial X_i$, which is similar to the dY/dX notation, is used in cases involving just one independent variable. The symbol $\partial Y/\partial X_i$ is read "the partial derivative of Y with respect to X_i," and is interpreted as the rate of change in Y as the variable X_i changes with all other independent variables remaining constant.

2. f_i, which is analogous to the $f'(X)$ notation you have seen before, may also be used to denote the partial derivative of the function $f(X_1, X_2, X_3, \ldots, X_n)$ with respect to X_i. The subscript i in f_i specifies the particular independent variable being changed (i.e., X_i). The partial derivative is interpreted the same way as above.

It is common practice to refer to $\partial Y/\partial X_i$ or f_i as the "partial of Y with respect to X_i," leaving out the term *derivative*. For example, for $Y = f(X_1, X_2)$, the function f_2 might be referred to as "the partial of Y with respect to X_2," and would represent the rate of change in Y as X_2 changes with X_1 constant.

There will be as many first-order partial derivatives as there are independent variables in the function. For $Y = f(X_1, X_2, X_3)$, there would be three partials: f_1, f_2, and f_3. For $Y = f(X_1, X_2, X_3, \ldots, X_n)$, there would be n partials: $f_1, f_2, f_3, \ldots, f_n$. In many cases, letters other than Y_i and X_i are used in functions. This does not affect the process of finding partial derivatives but changes how we denote them. For example, suppose output (Q) is a function of two inputs: labor (L) and capital (K). The function might be $Q = f(L, K)$, and its partials would be designated f_L and f_K. The partial f_L

would represent the rate of change in Q as L changes with K constant, while f_K would represent the rate of change in Q as K changes with L constant.

The process of determining partial derivatives is similar to differentiation of functions with a single independent variable. In partial differentiation, we allow only one of the n independent variables to change, while the other $n - 1$ independent variables are fixed and therefore can be *treated as constants*. As a result, in determining $\partial Y/\partial X_1$ (or f_1), X_1 is treated as the sole variable of the function, while the other $n - 1$ independent variables are considered constants. Thus, the problem becomes similar to those discussed for only one independent variable.

For example, if $Y = f(X_1, X_2) = X_1^2 + X_1 X_2 + 2X_2^2$, then f_1 is derived by applying the basic rules of differentiation. In deriving this partial derivative, X_1 is treated as the independent variable and X_2 is treated as a constant. Therefore,

$$f_1 = 2X_1^{2-1} + 1X_1^{1-1}X_2 + 0$$
$$f_1 = 2X_1 + X_1^0 X_2$$
$$f_1 = 2X_1 + X_2$$

To calculate the partial with respect to X_2, we consider X_1 a constant, and thus we find

$$f_2 = 0 + X_1 X_2^{1-1} + (2)2X_2^{2-1}$$
$$f_2 = X_1 X_2^0 + 4X_2$$
$$f_2 = X_1 + 4X_2$$

Suppose $Y = 20X^2 + 5X^2W^3 + 3W^4 + XW$ and we want to find the rate of change in Y as X or W changes with the other held constant:

$$f_X = 40X + 10XW^3 + 0 + W$$
$$f_W = 0 + 15X^2W^2 + 12W^3 + X$$

(Note the 0's that indicate where a particular term was just a constant in the original function in each case. Usually the 0's would not be written.)

A type of function that is very common in economic and business applications is a multiplicative function of the form

$$Y = f(W, X, Z) = KW^a X^b Z^c$$

This function would have three first-order partials (all of the partials we have discussed thus far are called first-order partials because they correspond to first derivatives). The three first-order partials for the function above would be

$$f_W = aKW^{a-1}X^b Z^c$$
$$f_X = bKW^a X^{b-1} Z^c$$
$$f_Z = cKW^a X^b Z^{c-1}$$

Let us consider two specific examples of such a function. Given $Y = 10X_1^3X_2^5$, the partials would be

$$f_1 = 30X_1^2X_2^5$$
$$f_2 = 5X_1^3X_2^{-.5}$$

For $Y = 10X^2W^3$, find the partials are

$$f_X = (2)(10)X^{2-1}W^3 = 20XW^3$$
$$f_W = (3)(10)X^2W^{3-1} = 30X^2W^2$$

You will see this general type of function used many times in the chapters that follow.

Just as we found second derivatives for functions with one independent variable, we can find second partials. For the function $Y = f(X_1, X_2)$, the first-order partials are f_1 and f_2. Each of these first-order partials may be differentiated with respect to X_1 or X_2, so there are four possible second-order partials. The partial of f_1 with respect to X_1 is denoted f_{11}, and the partial of f_1 with respect to X_2 is f_{12}. The partial of f_2 with respect to X_2 is written f_{21}. The second-order partials f_{12} and f_{21} are referred to as cross partials and are equal (i.e., $f_{12} = f_{21}$).

Let us return to the first of the functions used above as an example of calculating first-order partials and determine the four second-order partials for that function. Given the function $Y = f(X_1, X_2) = X_1^2 + X_1X_2 + 2X_2^2$, the partials are

$$f_1 = 2X_1 + X_2$$
$$f_2 = X_1 + 4X_2$$
$$f_{11} = 2$$
$$f_{12} = 1$$
$$f_{22} = 4$$
$$f_{21} = 1$$

It may be helpful to look at one more example of the determination of partial derivatives before going on to consider their usefulness. If $Y = f(X_1, X_2) = X_1^3 - 2X_1X_2^2 + X_2^4$, then the two first-order partials and four second-order partials are

$$f_1 = 3X_1^2 - 2X_2^2$$
$$f_2 = -4X_1X_2 + 4X_2^3$$
$$f_{11} = 6X_1$$
$$f_{12} = -4X_2$$
$$f_{22} = -4X_1 + 12X_2^2$$
$$f_{21} = -4X_2$$

Once more we see that the cross partials are equal (i.e., $f_{12} = f_{21} = -4X_2$).

3.9   MAXIMA AND MINIMA FOR MULTIVARIATE FUNCTIONS

You now have the concepts necessary to evaluate a function such as $Y = f(X, W)$ for possible maximum or minimum points.[7] Just as with bivariate functions, such as $Y = f(X)$, there are both first- and second-order conditions to consider. The first-order condition is that the first-order partials must all be *simultaneously equal to 0*. For $Y = f(X, W)$ this means that the first-order condition is

$$f_X = 0 \text{ and } f_Y = 0$$

Solving these two equations simultaneously will yield the critical values.

Suppose you want to evaluate the function $Y = 2X^2 + 5W^2 + 2XW - 10W + 50$ for values of X and W that would maximize or minimize Y. You would find the first-order condition as follows:

$$f_X = 4X + 2W = 0$$
$$f_W = 10W + 2X - 10 = 0$$

Solving the first of these (f_X) for X as a function of W, you would get

$$4X + 2W = 0$$
$$4X = -2W$$
$$X = -.5W$$

Solving the second (f_W) for W as a function of X, you obtain

$$10W + 2X - 10 = 0$$
$$10W = -2X + 10$$
$$W = -.2X + 1$$

By substituting $X = -.5W$ into this last equation, you can solve for W as follows:

$$W = -.2X + 1$$
$$W = -.2(-.5W) + 1$$
$$W = +.1W + 1$$
$$W - .1W = 1$$
$$.9W = 1$$
$$W = 1/.9$$
$$W = 1.11$$

And you know from setting $f_X = 0$ that

$$X = -.5W$$

---

[7] Only functions with three variables, one dependent and two independent, are discussed in this section and used in the rest of the text. Readers interested in the more general case of n independent variables should refer to the Weber or Chiang texts cited in the suggested readings at the end of the chapter.

Using the value of W found above, you can solve for the value of X:

$$X = -.5W$$
$$X = -.5(1.11)$$
$$X = -.56 \text{ (rounding to two places)}$$

Thus, there *may* be a maximum or minimum for the original function at the critical point $X = -.56$, $W = 1.11$.

To know for certain if there is a maximum or minimum, you have to check a set of second-order conditions that can be summarized as follows:[8]

A: $(f_{XX})(f_{WW}) - (f_{XW})^2 > 0$

If condition A is satisfied, that is, if the product of f_{XX} and f_{WW} minus the cross partial squared, $(f_{XW})^2$, is a positive value (at the critical point), there will be either a maximum or a minimum at that point. If condition A is not satisfied, this test for an extreme point fails, and more sophisticated tests must be evaluated. For problems in this course, condition A will normally be satisfied.

Given that condition A is satisfied, we can determine whether there is a maximum or a minimum from the following:

B1:   a *maximum* if both f_{XX} and f_{WW} are *negative*
B2:   a *minimum* if both f_{XX} and f_{WW} are *positive*

Evaluating the function in our example, you find

$$Y = f(X, W) = 2X^2 + 5W^2 + 2XW - 10W + 50$$
$$f_X = 4X + 2W = 0 \qquad \left.\begin{array}{l} \\ \\ \end{array}\right\} \begin{array}{l} \text{First-order} \\ \text{condition} \end{array}$$
$$f_W = 10W + 2X - 10 = 0$$

Solving for the values of X and W that make both equations equal to 0, you find

$$W = 1.11$$
$$X = -.56$$

The second-order partial derivatives are

$$f_{XX} = 4$$
$$f_{XW} = 2$$
$$f_{WW} = 10$$
$$f_{WX} = 2$$

Part A of the second-order condition is

$$(f_{XX})(f_{WW}) - (f_{XW})^2 > 0$$
$$(4)(10) - (2)^2 = 36 > 0$$

---

[8]The remainder of this section can be omitted without loss of continuity. It is often possible to know if a critical point represents a maximum or a minimum from the context of a problem, so some professors may choose not to cover the second-order conditions that follow.

Since this condition is satisfied, there is either a maximum or a minimum for Y at $X = -.56$, $W = 1.11$. Since

$$f_{XX} = 4 > 0 \text{ and } f_{WW} - 10 > 0$$

there is a minimum at $X = .56$, $W = 1.11$.

A Profit Maximization Example

Let us consider a function that represents a firm's profit function. We will let $Y = $ profit, $X = $ one of the firm's two products, and $W = $ the other product. Thus, profit is a function of the production and sale of X and W. The firm's revenue is given by $TR = 36X - 3X^2 + 40W - 5W^2$. The cost function is $TC = X^2 + 2XW + 3W^2$. Profit (Y) is defined as total revenue minus total cost. Thus, we find

$$Y = f(X, W)$$
$$Y = 36X - 3X^2 + 40W - 5W^2 - (X^2 + 2XW + 3W^2)$$
$$Y = 36X - 4X^2 + 40W - 8W^2 - 2XW$$
$$\left. \begin{array}{l} f_X = 36 - 8X - 2W = 0 \\ f_W = 40 - 16W - 2X = 0 \end{array} \right\} \quad \begin{array}{l} \text{First-order} \\ \text{condition} \end{array}$$

From f_X, we can solve for W:

$$-2W = 8X - 36$$
$$W = -4X + 18$$

From f_W, we can solve for X:

$$-2X = 16W - 40$$
$$X = -8W + 20$$

Combining these results, we have

$$W = -4X + 18$$
$$W = -4(-8W + 20) + 18$$
$$W = 32W - 80 + 18$$
$$W - 32W = -80 + 18$$
$$-31W = -62$$
$$W = -62/-31 = 2$$

We can then use this value to find the corresponding value for X as follows:

$$X = -8W + 20$$
$$X = -8(2) + 20$$
$$X = -16 + 20$$
$$X = 4$$

Thus, we find the critical point to be $X = 4$, $W = 2$.

Now consider the second-order condition. Evaluating part A of the second-order condition, we have

Is $(f_{XX}(f_{WW}) - (f_{XW})^2 > 0$?

$$f_{XX} = -8$$
$$f_{WW} = -16$$
$$f_{XW} = -2$$
$$f_{WX} = -2$$

thus,

$$(-8)(-16) - (-2)^2 = 124 > 0$$

Therefore, there is either a maximum or a minimum at $X = 4$, $W = 2$. And since both f_{XX} and f_{WW} are negative, there is a maximum at this point.

Let us summarize the conditions for a maximum or minimum when the function has two independent variables:

For $Y = f(X_1, X_2)$,

1.   *First-Order Condition*

$$f_1 = 0 \text{ and } f_2 = 0$$

2.   *Second-Order Conditions*

For a maximum:

$$(f_{11})(f_{12}) - (f_{12})^2 > 0$$
$$\text{and } f_{11} < 0 \text{ and } f_{22} < 0$$

For a minimum:

$$(f_{11})(f_{22}) - (f_{12})^2 > 0$$
$$\text{and } f_{11} > 0 \text{ and } f_{22} > 0$$

3.10   CONSTRAINED OPTIMIZATION

For many economic problems, the objective of maximizing or minimizing a function is constrained, in the sense that there are some limits on the values of the independent variables. For example, in the theory of consumer demand, the economist specifies a utility function of the general form $U = f(X_1, X_2, \ldots, X_n)$, where U represents the total satisfaction the individual receives from consuming some bundle of commodities, $X_1, X_2, \ldots, X_n$. In addition, the consumer is faced with a budget constraint that places limits on the amounts of $X_1, X_2, \ldots, X_n$ that the consumer can purchase. In general, the budget constraint is of the form $M = P_1X_1 + P_2X_2 + \cdots + P_nX_n$, where M is money income and P_i is the price of the ith commodity. Given this, we need a technique that will enable us to determine the critical values of $X_1, X_2, \ldots, X_n$, which will maximize the consumer's utility without exceeding the constraint.[9]

As another example of constrained optimization, businesses are often interested in the least-cost combination of inputs needed to produce a given level of output, say Q_0. If K and L are the two inputs, with prices P_K and P_L, and the output (Q) is given by the production function $Q = f(K, L)$, then this constrained cost-minimization problem can be formulated as follows: minimize $P_KK + P_LL$ subject to the constraint that $Q_0 = f(K, L)$. This situation is discussed further in Chapter 7, along with the problem of maximizing Q for a given expenditure on inputs (K and L).

The Lagrangian Multiplier Technique

The method normally used by economists to solve constrained optimization problems is the *Lagrangian multiplier* method. This technique involves setting up an augmented *function* (L) that consists of the function to be maximized or minimized, often called the objective function, plus a Lagrangian multiplier times the constraint that is to be satisfied. In mathematical notation,

$$L = f(X_1, X_2) + g(X_1, X_2)$$

where $f(X_1, X_2)$ is the objective function to be maximized or minimized and $g(X_1, X_2) = 0$ is the constraint. The Greek letter lambda (λ) is the symbol for the Lagrangian multiplier. It should be noted that the *constraint is always expressed in implicit form, that is, as some function set equal to 0.*

The critical values for a maximum or a minimum are derived from the first-order condition for constrained optimization, which consists of taking the partial derivative of L with respect to each independent variable and the Lagrangian multiplier (λ), then setting them equal to 0 and solving them simultaneously.[10] The first-order condition is

$$\partial L / \partial X_1 = f_1 + \lambda g_1 = 0$$
$$\partial L / \partial X_2 = f_2 + \lambda g_2 = 0$$
$$\partial 1 / \partial \lambda = g(X_1, X_2) = 0$$

---

[9]Some instructors may want to wait to cover this section until they get to the appendix of Chapter 5 or to Chapters 7 and 9, where constrained optimization is used in the discussions of demand, production, and cost, respectively.

[10]For second-order conditions, interested readers are again referred to the Weber or Chiang texts cited in the list of suggested readings at the end of the chapter. In economic problems, whether the result yields a maximum or minimum is usually clear from the context of the problem.

where, as before, f_1 and f_2 are the first-order partials of the function $f(X_1, X_2)$ with respect to X_1 and X_2 respectively. Likewise, g_1 and g_2 are partials of $g(X_1, X_2)$ with respect to X_1 and X_2 respectively.

The result of the first-order condition in this case is a set of equations with three unknowns $(X_1, X_2,$ and $\lambda)$. Since this set of equations is solved simultaneously, the critical values of $X_1, X_2,$ and λ will satisfy all three equations (the last equation guarantees that the values of X_1 and X_2 satisfy the constraint).[11]

Some Applications of the Lagrangian Method

In later chapters, you will use the Lagrangian technique in a number of different applications. But let us look at three such cases here to help demonstrate the mechanics of applying this useful tool. First, suppose we want to optimize $Y = X_1^2 + X_2^2$ subject to the constraint that $X_1 + 3X_2 = 4$. Writing the constraint in its implicit form yields

$$X_1 + 3X_2 - 4 = 0$$

Then the critical values for a constrained optimum of Y are found as follows:

$$L = X_1^2 + X_2^2 + \lambda(X_1 + 3X_2 - 4)$$

The first-order condition is

$$\partial L / \partial X_1 = 2X_1 + \lambda = 0$$
$$\partial L / \partial X_2 = 2X_2 + 3\lambda = 0$$
$$\partial L / \partial \lambda = X_1 + 3X_2 - 4 = 0$$

From the first two partials you can solve for λ:

$$\lambda = -2X_1$$

and

$$\lambda = -(2/3)X_2$$

Since λ must equal λ, you have

$$-2X_1 = -(2/3)X_2$$
$$X_1 = X_2/3$$

Substituting this result in the third partial, you get the following:

$$X_1 + 3X_2 - 4 = 0$$
$$(X_2/3) + 3X_2 = 4$$
$$X_2 + 9X_2 = 12$$
$$10X_2 = 12$$
$$X_2 = 1.2$$

---

[11]The value found for λ represents the marginal value of a one-unit change in the constraining factor. For example, in the constrained utility maximization problem introduced above, the constraining factor is money income. Thus, λ would measure the marginal utility of money.

Since $X_1 = X_2/3$, you can find X_1 as:

$$X_1 = X_2/3$$
$$X_1 = 1.2/3$$
$$X_1 = .4$$

You can find λ from either of the two expressions for λ that you found above:

$$\lambda = -2X_1 = -2(.4) = -.8$$
$$\lambda = -(2/3)X_2 = -(2/3)(1.2) = -.8$$

To apply these concepts in a specific economic setting, suppose that a firm has a cost function that depends on the levels of output of commodities X and W as follows:

$$C = 4X^2 + 10W^2$$

The production manager wants to determine the quantities of each commodity that should be produced to minimize cost if total output of X and W must equal 800 units. Thus, you want to minimize C, subject to the constraint that $X + W = 800$. The constraint can be written in its implicit form as

$$X + W - 800 = 0$$

Therefore, setting up the Lagrangian function, including the objective function along with the constraint, you have:

$$L = 4X^2 + 10W^2 + \lambda (X + W - 800)$$

The first-order condition is

$$\partial L/\partial X = 8X + \lambda = 0$$

Thus,

$$\lambda = -8X$$
$$\partial L/\partial W = 20W + \lambda = 0$$

Thus,

$$\lambda = -20W$$
$$\partial L/\partial \lambda = X + W - 800 = 0$$

From the first two partials, you can find

$$20W = 8X$$
$$W = .4X$$

Substituting this result into the third partial, you obtain the following:

$$X + W = 800$$
$$X + .4X = 800$$
$$1.4X = 800$$
$$X = 571.43$$

Therefore,

$$W = 800 - 571.43 = 228.57$$

And

$$\lambda = -8X = -8(571.43) = -4571.44$$

The cost can then be calculated from the original cost function as follows:

$$C = 4X^2 + 10W^2$$
$$C = 4(571.43)^2 + 10(228.57)^2$$
$$C = \$1,828,571.43$$

The interpretation of λ is that if we relax the constraint by one unit (i.e., to 799 units), the objective function (cost) would be reduced by \$4,571.44.

As a final comprehensive example of constrained optimization, let us compare the maximum profit a firm can get from selling two products $(X_1$ and $X_2)$ without and with a constraint. Suppose the profit function (P) is given as

$$P = 104 - 5X_1^2 + 40X_1 - 4X_2^2 + 16X_2 + 8X_1X_2$$

To maximize profit without any constraint, the first-order condition is

$$\partial P/\partial X_1 = -10X_1 + 40 + 8X_2 = 0$$
$$\partial P/\partial X_2 = -8X_2 + 16 + 8X_1 = 0$$

Solving the second partial for X_1 gives

$$X_1 = X_2 - 2$$

Substituting this in the first partial yields

$$-10(X_2 - 2) + 40 + 8X_2 = 0$$
$$-10X_2 + 20 + 40 + 8X_2 = 0$$
$$-2X_2 = -60$$
$$X_2 = 30$$

Then X_1 can be found as follows:

$$X_1 = X_2 - 2$$
$$X_1 = 30 - 2$$
$$X_1 = 28$$

To check the second-order conditions, you must first find the second-order partials. They are

$$f_{11} = -10$$
$$f_{22} = -8$$
$$f_{12} = 8$$
$$f_{21} = 8$$

You then need to check to see if $(f_{11})(f_{22}) - (f_{12})^2 > 0$. In this case, you find that

$$(f_{11})(f_{22}) - (f_{12})^2 = (-10)(-8) - (8)^2 = 16 > 0$$

so there is either a maximum or a minimum. Since both f_{11} and f_{22} are negative, you have found values of X_1 and X_2 that will give you a maximum profit. The actual amount of profit will be

$$P = 104 - 5(28)^2 + 40(28) - 4(30)^2 + 16(30) + 8(28)(30)$$
$$P = 904$$

Now suppose that these products are produced in a joint production process such that two units of X_1 are produced with every unit of X_2 (due to the nature of the production process). Assume that the production process cannot be changed to alter these proportions and that it is very costly to dispose of any excess of either product, so the firm must produce and sell exactly two of X_1 for each unit of X_2.

The constraint can be stated in algebraic form as $X_1 = 2X_2$, or written in implicit form, $0 = 2X_2 - X_1$. The Lagrangian function is thus

$$L = 104 - 5X_1^2 + 40X_1 - 4X_2^2 + 16X_2 + 8X_1X_2 + \lambda(2X_2 - X_1)$$

The first-order condition for a maximum is

$$\partial L/\partial X_1 = -10X_1 + 40 + 8X_2 - \lambda = 0$$
$$\partial L/\partial X_2 = -8X_2 + 16 + 8X_1 + 2\lambda = 0$$
$$\partial L/\partial \lambda = 2X_2 - X_1 = 0$$

Solving these simultaneously, we find that $X_1 = 12$ and $X_2 = 6$. Thus, with the production constraint, profit is reduced to

$$P = 104 - 5(12)^2 + 40(12) - 4(6)^2 + 16(6) + 8(12)(6)$$
$$P = 392$$

This is 512 less than the unconstrained maximum profit of 904 found above.

SUMMARY

In this chapter, you have worked through an overview of the calculus that is most useful in business and economic analysis. The following points of summary may constitute a useful reference as you work with these concepts in this and other courses:

1. A function shows how one or more independent variables can be transformed into, or associated with, a dependent variable. Functions can be expressed at various levels of generality as follows:

$Y = f(X)$	very general
$Y = a + bX$	more specific
$Y = 10 + 2X$	very specific

2. Slope refers to the rate of change in the dependent variable (Y) as an independent variable (X) changes. The average rate of change between the two points (X_1, Y_1) and (X_2, Y_2) can be expressed as

$$\text{Slope} = (Y_2 - Y_1)/(X_2 - X_1) = \Delta Y/\Delta X$$

A linear function has a constant slope: it is the same throughout the function. For nonlinear functions, the slope varies from point to point along the function.

3. A derivative is an instantaneous rate of change. That is, a derivative is the slope of a function at a point (as X becomes very small, approaching 0). Derivatives of bivariate functions such as $Y = f(X)$ can be written in any of the following forms:

$$dY/dX \text{ or } y' \text{ or } f'(X)$$

A derivative is defined as follows:

$$dY/dX = \lim_{\Delta X \to 0} \Delta Y/\Delta X$$

You should always think of a derivative as a rate of change in one variable as another changes over a very small interval.

4. Some basic rules will help you find derivatives for most functions you are likely to use in business and economic analysis:

- Constant rule: if $Y = C$ is a constant, $dY/dX = 0$.

- Power function rule: if $Y = aX^n$, $dY/dX = naX^{n-1}$.

- Sum or difference rule: if $Y = f(X) \pm g(X)$ where both $f(X)$ and $g(X)$ are functions of X, $dY/dX = f'(X) \pm g'(X)$.

- Rules for higher order derivatives: a second derivative is the derivative of the first derivative, a third derivative is the derivative of the second derivative, and so on. For $Y = f(X)$,

$$\begin{aligned} \text{First derivative} \quad & y' = dY/dX \\ \text{Second derivative} \quad & y'' = dy'/dX \end{aligned}$$

5. Partial derivatives reflect rates of change in the dependent variable (Y) of a multivariate function as one of the independent variables (X_1) changes and the others remain constant. For $Y = f(X_1, X_2, X_3, \ldots, X_n)$, partial derivatives are commonly written as

$$\partial Y/\partial X_1, \partial Y/\partial X_2, \partial Y/\partial X_3, \ldots \partial Y/\partial X_n$$

or

$$f_1, f_2, f_3, \ldots, f_n$$

6.   A very important application of calculus is in finding maxima or minima. First- and second-order conditions must be satisfied to determine the critical values for a function.

   a.   For $Y = f(X)$, the first-order condition for a maximum or minimum is that the first derivative (the slope of the function) be equal to 0. That is,

   $$f'(X) = 0$$

   The second-order condition is

   For a maximum, $f''(X) < 0$
   For a minimum, $f''(X) > 0$

   b.   For $Y = f(X_1, X_2)$, the first-order condition for a maximum or minimum is that both first-order partials equal 0. That is,

   $$f_1 = 0 \text{ and } f_2 = 0$$

   The second-order condition has two parts. The first is

   $$f_{11}f_{22} - (f_{12})^2 > 0$$

   If this is true, then

   For a maximum, $f_{11} < 0$ and $f_{22} < 0$
   For a minimum, $f_{11} > 0$ and $f_{22} > 0$

7.   In many cases, attempts to maximize or minimize something are restricted by some form of constraint. The Lagrangian multiplier technique provides a way of solving such constrained optimization problems. A Lagrangian function (L) is set up, composed of the function to be optimized $[f(X_1, X_2)]$ plus λ times the constraint function in its implicit form $[g(X_1, X_2) = 0]$. That is,

   $$L = f(X_1, X_2) + \lambda g(X_1, X_2)$$

   The optimum is found by solving the following set of equations:

   $$\partial L / \partial X_1 = f_1 + \lambda g_1 = 0$$
   $$\partial L / \partial X_2 = f_2 + \lambda g_2 = 0$$
   $$\partial L / \partial \lambda = g(X_1, X_2) = 0$$

SUGGESTED READINGS

Allen, R.G.D. *Mathematical Economics.* New York: Macmillan, 1966.

Archibald, G.C., and Lipsey, Richard G. *An Introduction to Mathematical Economics: Methods and Applications.* New York: Harper & Row, 1976.

Beer, Gerald Ann. *Applied Calculus for Business and Economics.* Winthrop, MA: 1978.

Chiang, Alpha C. *Fundamental Methods of Mathematical Economics,* 2d ed. New York: McGraw-Hill, 1974.

Dowling, Edward T. *Mathematics for Economists.* New York: McGraw-Hill Book Company, 1979.

Freilich, Gerald, and Greenleaf, Frederick P. *Calculus: A Short Course with Applications to Business, Economics, and the Social Sciences.* San Francisco: W.H. Freeman, 1976.

Weber, Jean E. *Mathematical Analysis: Business and Economic Applications*, 3d ed. New York: Harper & Row, 1976.

PROBLEMS

1. Find the values of X and Y that satisfy each of the following pairs of equations and graph each pair of equations:

    a. $2Y - 4X = 20$
        $Y + 2X = 10$
    b. $3Y + 6X = 12$
        $Y = 2 + 2X$
    c. $Y = 4 + .1X^2$
        $Y = 10 - X$
    d. $Y = 50 - .05X$
        $Y = .25X$
    e. $Y = 10 + 3X$
        $Y = 58$

2. Find the first derivatives for the following functions:

    a. $Y = 10X^2 + 6X - 100$
    b. $Y = 300X - .5X^2$
    c. $Y = 6X^4 + 3X^{-1} + 10X$
    d. $Y = (6X^3)(12X^4)$
    e. $Y = (6X^2 + X)(X^3 - 24X)$
    f. $Y = (X)/(X + 2)$
    g. $Y = X^{-1}(X^2 + 1)$

3. Find the first and second derivatives for the following functions:

    a. $Y = 500X - 2X^2$
    b. $Y = 90 + 20X^2 - X^3$
    c. $Y = X^2 + 10^{-1} + 50$
    d. $Y = 100 - 2X + .1X^2$

    Remember that a derivative is a slope, or rate of change, at a point. Keep this in mind as you work through problems 4, 5, and 6.

4. A retailer sells a product (X) at a price of \$4 per unit. She can sell as many units at this price as she can stock. Her revenue (R) from the sales of this product equals the price per unit times the number of units sold. That is,

   $R = 4X$

   Plot this line with revenue (R) on the vertical axis and sales (X) on the horizontal axis (use values of X from 0 to 10, and values of R from 0 to 40).

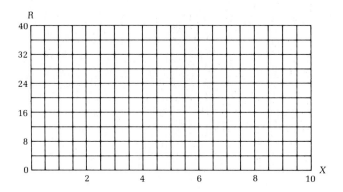

   What is the slope of this revenue function? _____ Is what you see about its slope in the graph consistent with what you get if you find the derivative of revenue (R) with respect to sales (X)? Explain why or why not.

5. Bob Batson runs a hobby shop at a local shopping mall. He has experimented with the pricing of one of his products (X) and finds that the revenue generated by the sale of X changes depending on the price of X but not in a linear manner. However, the relationship between the price of X and the amount of X sold is described quite well by the following equation: $P = 10 - .5X$. Since revenue is equal to price times the number of units sold at each price, Bob has been able to derive a revenue function as follows:

   $R = (P)(X)$

   and

   $P = 10 - .5X$
   $R = (10 - .5X)X$
   $R = 10X - .5X^2$

Plot this line with revenue (R) on the vertical axis and sales (X) on the horizontal axis (using the following values for X: 0, 2, 4, 6, 8, 10, and 14).

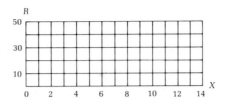

Connect this series of points with a smooth line. Just by looking at your line, what can you say about the slope of the revenue function at the point where $X = 3$? Is it positive, negative, or 0? How does the slope of the revenue function at $X = 7$ compare to the slope at $X = 3$? How does the slope at $X = 13$ compare to the slope at $X = 7$?

Find the first derivative of R with respect to X:

dR/dX = _____

Remember that this derivative is the slope of the function. Based on this information, complete the following statements:

At $X = 3$, the slope of R is _____ .

At $X = 7$, the slope of R is _____ .

At $X = 9$, the slope of R is _____ .

At $X = 11$, the slope of R is _____ .

At $X = 13$, the slope of R is _____ .

Look at the graph of the revenue function R. Are the values you found above for its slope at various points consistent with the graph? Why?

   If the slope of R is positive at $X = 9$ and negative at $X = 11$, does it make sense that somewhere between $X = 9$ and $X = 11$ the slope must be 0? You know that $dR/dX = 10 - X$. Find the value of X that would make this derivative (equation for slope) equal to 0 (X must = _____ for $10 - X$ to be 0).

   In your graph, it appears that R is at its highest point at $X = 10$. And you have found that the slope of R is 0 at $X = 10$. So you have demonstrated that this revenue function reaches its maximum value when sales are equal to 10 units.

6.   Shirley Lopez always liked to work with wood. To help pay her way through college, she started making small cribs for newborn children.

Over a period of nearly 40 months, she has kept careful track of her costs and with the help of a graduate student in business economics has estimated the following average cost function *(AC)* for making the cribs *(X)*:

$$AC = 40 - 2X + .1X^2$$

Plot this average cost function in the space provided, using the following values for X: 0, 2, 4, 6, 8, 10, 12, and 14.

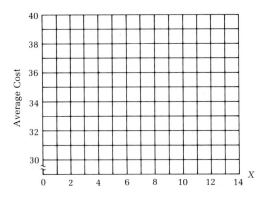

Connect these points to form a relatively smooth cost curve. By looking at the graph, what can you say about the rate of change in average cost as Shirley's output changes from three to four units? Does average cost stay the same, increase, or decrease? How is this related to the slope of the average cost function?

Would you say that the average cost function has a positive, negative, or 0 slope at $X = 11$? How does this compare to the slope at $X = 13$?

You know that the slope of a function can be described by the derivative of the function. What is the derivative of average cost as X changes?

$$dAC/dX = \text{_____}$$

Based on this equation for the slope of the cost function for cribs, complete the following statements:

At $X = 3$, the slope of *AC* is _____ .

At $X = 5$, the slope of *AC* is _____ .

At $X = 7$, the slope of *AC* is _____ .

At $X = 9$, the slope of *AC* is _____ .

At $X = 11$, the slope of AC is _____ .

At $X = 13$, the slope of AC is _____ .

What happens to the slope of average cost as X increases through this range of values? Where is the slope equal to 0? To be sure, solve the following equation for the value of X that makes the derivative of average cost 0:

$$dAC/dX = -2 + .2X = 0$$

Is your answer consistent with what the graph shows?

At what level of production (X) does average cost reach its lowest value? Show this on the graph and find the value of X mathematically.

7. Use your knowledge of calculus to find where the following functions have a maximum or minimum value. Use both first- and second-order conditions.

   a. $Y = 100X - .25X^2$
   b. $Y = 90X^2 - .02X^3$
   c. $Y = 80X - .002X^2$
   d. $Y = 100 - 2X + .02X^2$
   e. $Y = 100 - 4X + .06X^2$
   f. $Y = 8X + 2X^{-1}$
   g. $Y = X^3 + 3X^2 - 10$
   h. $Y = 10X - .5X^2$
   i. $Y = 40 - 2X + .1X^2$

8. The Dextro Corporation produces and markets two sugar substitutes $(S_1$ and $S_2)$ throughout the United States. The two products have been found to contribute to profits (P) according to the following functions:

   $$P = 120S_1 - 10S_1^2 + 80S_2 - 2S_2^2$$

   Both S_1 and S_2 are measured in millions of pounds per year, and profit is in hundreds of thousands of dollars. Use your knowledge of calculus to find the amounts of S_1 and S_2 to market in order to maximize the profit contributed to Dextro by these two products. Show both first- and second-order conditions.

9. Glacier Homes, Inc., produces kits for making two models of recreational log cabins $(H_1$ and $H_2)$. Glacier does not have data that allow them to isolate costs sufficiently to estimate individual cost functions for each model. However, studies have determined an average joint cost function (AC) that shows how unit costs vary as the level of production of the two types of kits varies. This joint average cost function is

   $$AC = 250,000 + 20H_1^2 + 25H_2^2 - 40H_1H_2 - 1920H_1$$

Based on this function, find the level of yearly production of the two models $(H_1$ and $H_2)$ that will minimize the average cost of production. Use second-order conditions to demonstrate that your solution yields a minimum. What is the corresponding value of AC?

10. CompuTech is a small firm that makes a 64K personal computer marketed primarily to educational institutions. One of CompuTech's principle marketing tools is a guarantee that assures schools that they will have no out-of-pocket repair costs for two years. CompuTech's engineers have estimated that the cost to the firm for repairs resulting from providing the guarantee is related to the average number of inspections per hour that the quality control department makes at two points in the assembly process. The yearly cost of repairs in thousands of dollars is

$$C = 2X^2 + 5Y^2 - 2XY - 90Y + 458$$

where X and Y represent the average number of inspections per hour at each of the two inspection points. Find the average number of inspections at each point that will minimize the yearly cost of repairs. What is that cost?

11. CompuTech, the computer firm referred to in problem 10, has decided to submit a bid to provide computers to some school districts in a state that requires that all bidders have a minimum of 20 production inspections per eight-hour shift. Such inspections can be made at any point in the production process, so both the X and Y inspections currently used by CompuTech can be used. CompuTech wants to minimize the cost function given in problem 10 subject to the following constraint:

$$X + Y = 20$$

What is the cost-minimizing combination of inspections given this constraint? What repair cost will result?

12. As the director of advertising for a corporation, you have been able to ascertain through sales studies, using regression analysis, that sales as a function of the amount spent on two types of media advertising is the following:

$$S = 500 + 60(1000X - X^2) + 20(500Y - Y^2)$$

Management has stated that the advertising budget for the year is $500.
   a.   If net profit $= .3S - X - Y$, find the values for X and Y that will maximize profit.
   b.   Assume that there is no advertising budget constraint and proceed to find the optimal solution.

4

Regression Analysis and
Model Building

Chapter 4 provides a concise overview of regression analysis and some of the applications of this tool in business and economics. Students with little or no background in statistics should be able to follow the pragmatic approach taken in this chapter. Students with more advanced training will find that this chapter provides a good review and may extend their horizons in some directions.

4.1 AN INTRODUCTION TO REGRESSION ANALYSIS AND MODEL BUILDING

Regression analysis is a statistical tool that allows us to describe the way in which one variable is related to another. This description may be a simple one involving just two variables in a single equation, or it may be very complex, having many variables and many equations, perhaps hundreds of each. From the most simple relationships to the most complex, regression analysis is useful in specifying the way in which one variable is affected by one or more other variables of interest.

The Consumption Function

A relatively simple model that can be specified using regression analysis is the consumption function, usually introduced to students in a basic macroeconomics course. In that model, the level of personal consumption expenditures in the economy is said to be a function of the level of aggregate income. That is, consumption is hypothesized to be dependent on the level of income.

When you construct such a hypothesis, you take the first step in building a model. You must define the variables used in the model carefully so that it can be tested and evaluated in a formal manner. Personal consumption expenditures represent a clearly defined statistical series that is published regularly, so there is little problem in defining that variable. The main question in this regard is whether you intend to build a model to explain variations in current dollar consumption or real consumption. We will come back to this issue of whether to use real or current dollar measures in business and economic models. For now, we will just note that when possible, *it is usually better to use real values,* so that the influence of inflation does not blur the structural relationship you are trying to identify.

In building this model, we also need some measure of aggregate income in the economy (the second variable). There are several measures that could be used, but for simplicity, let us look at gross national product (GNP) as our measure. To rid ourselves of some of the problems of using dollar values, we will use GNP and personal consumption expenditures in constant 1972 dollars (i.e., in real dollars).

To keep the data set small and easy to work with, suppose we look just at the 10 years of data from 1971 to 1980. As shown in Table 4.1, this gives us 10 values for each variable. Each value represents one observation of the respective variable. Thus, our data table has 10 rows: one for each observation of the two variables. The variables are listed by column.

TABLE 4.1   ***GNP* and Personal Consumption Expenditures in Billions of Constant 1972 Dollars: 1971–1981**

Observation	Year	GNP	Consumption
1	1971	1122.4	696.8
2	1972	1185.9	737.1
3	1973	1255.0	768.5
4	1974	1248.0	763.6
5	1975	1233.9	780.2
6	1976	1300.4	823.7
7	1977	1371.7	863.9
8	1978	1436.9	904.8
9	1979	1483.0	930.9
10	1980	1480.7	935.1

SOURCE: Economic Report of the President.

The data shown in Table 4.1 are called *time series data* because they represent numbers taken over a period of time for each of the variables involved in the model. In our example, we have one value for GNP and one value for consumption each year for 10 years. Thus, our data are *annual* time series data. If we had a value for each variable for each quarter during those 10 years, we would have a *quarterly* time series of data containing 40 observations. We might even have had values for each month, in which case our data would be a *monthly* time series with 120 observations for the 10 years.

In the consumption function model, we will hypothesize that consumption is primarily a function of income. Suppose that you want to state this proposed model mathematically. You might write

$$C = f(GNP)$$

where C represents personal consumption expenditures and GNP represents gross national product, both measured in billions of constant 1972 dollars. The econonmic assumption you have made is that changes in GNP *cause* changes in consumption. For this reason, C is referred to as the dependent variable, while GNP is the independent, or explanatory, variable.

A graphic representation of the data is often useful in helping us see if the model we are proposing is a good one. Such a graph can also help us in deciding some things about the specific form the model might take. The information given in Table 4.1 is shown graphically in Figure 4.1. In the

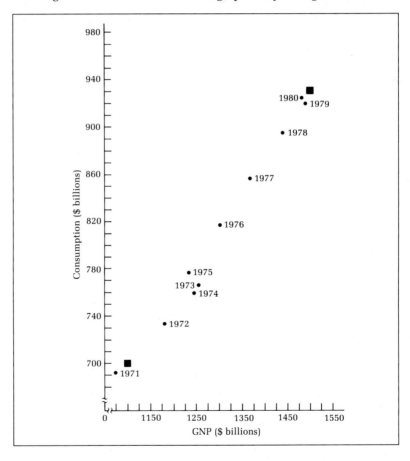

FIGURE 4.1   **Personal Consumption Expenditures as a Function of *GNP* Data for 1971–1980 in Billions of Constant 1972 Dollars**

graph, higher levels of consumption appear to be associated with higher levels of income. Also, the points representing the 10 observations appear to fall pretty much in a straight line. (Two additional points, represented by small squares, have been added to the graph. We will talk more about these shortly.)

If, on the basis of this observation, you believe that a linear equation might fit these data well, you might be more specific in writing the mathematical model as

$$C = f(GNP)$$
$$C = a + b(GNP)$$

In this second form, you not only are hypothesizing that there is some functional relationship between consumption and GNP but are also stating that you expect the relationship to be linear, with an intercept equal to a and a slope equal to b.

The obvious question to answer next in developing the model is: What are the appropriate values of a and b? Once you know these values, you will have made the model very specific. One way to get a quick estimate of these values is to draw through the data points the line that you think best fits the data. Take a minute now to draw in Figure 4.1 the straight line you think best fits these data points. Now, from that line, you can estimate values for the intercept and slope terms of the consumption function.

The method is pretty straightforward. Pick any two points on your line and write down the values of GNP and consumption that correspond to those two points. You might have something like this:

Point	GNP	Consumption
1	GNP_1	C_1
2	GNP_2	C_2

Now substitute each of these pairs of points into the general linear form of your equation for the consumption function. You would have

General form: $C = a + b(GNP)$
Point 1: $C_1 = a + b(GNP_1)$
Point 2: $C_2 = a + b(GNP_2)$

Subtract the equation for the second point from the first. That gives you

$$(C_1 - C_2) = (a - a) + b(GNP_1) - b(GNP_2)$$
$$C_1 - C_2 = b(GNP_1 - GNP_2)$$
$$\frac{C_1 - C_2}{GNP_1 - GNP_2} = b$$

This gives you an estimate of b, the slope of the consumption function. Once you know b you can find a from either the equation for point 1 or that for point 2. Do this for the line you have drawn.

Now find the two points in Figure 4.1 that are enclosed by small squares. Connect those points with a straight line. This is the line the authors picked to represent the data. Do not be surprised if it is a little different from your line. Any 10 reasonable people might have drawn 10 different but similar lines. For our points, we have

Point	GNP	Consumption
1	1100	700
2	1500	940

And so we find a and b as follows:

General form: $C = a + bY$
Point 1: $700 = a + b(1100)$
Point 2: $940 = a + b(1500)$

Subtracting the equation for point 2 from that for point 1 and solving for b, we get

$$-240 = b(-400)$$
$$-240/-400 = b$$
$$b = .6$$

Using point 1, we find a:

$$700 = a + .6(1100)$$
$$700 = a + 660$$
$$700 - 660 = a$$
$$a = 40$$

Our first approximation for the consumption function is, then,

$$C = 40 + .6GNP$$

Your equation will be different from this one if you have drawn your free-hand line through the data differently, but the results are likely to be very similar. If different people get different results, which is the correct or best model? We will address this issue in Section 4.2 and see that there is indeed a best regression line.

Retail Auto Sales as a Function of Population

The data used in the consumption function example are time series data: the values of the variables were collected at a different point in time for each observation. In our second example, we will use *cross-sectional* data. Such data are collected for one time period but for different entities, with each entity representing an observation.

The example involves retail auto sales and population for 10 cities in the northwestern United States. The hypothesis is that car sales are a function of population. The data all represent one point in time: the 1981 year. Each of the 10 observations represents one city. The data are shown in Table 4.2. As in Table 4.1, the data matrix contains 10 rows (one for each observation), and the variables are arranged in columns.

You might state the hypothesized model in mathematical notation as follows:

$$RAS = f(Pop)$$

where *RAS* represents retail auto sales in millions of dollars and *Pop* represents population in thousands. You might again further hypothesize the relationship to be linear and so may write the model as

$$RAS = a + b(Pop)$$

By hypothesizing a linear relationship, we are assuming that each one unit change in *Pop* causes *RAS* to change by an amount equal to the value of *b*. That value, *b*, is the rate of change in *RAS* per unit change in *Pop* regardless of the levels of *Pop* and *RAS*.

We can proceed, as above, to estimate values for *a* and *b*. Figure 4.2 will be helpful in this regard. Each point in the graph represents one of the 10 observations. Draw in the line that you think best fits the data, and calculate your own values for the intercept and slope terms.

TABLE 4.2   **Retail Auto Sales and Population for Ten Northwestern United States Cities: 1981**

Observation	City	Auto Sales ($ millions)	Population (thousands)
1	Seattle	1397	1644.3
2	Portland	1022	1277.3
3	Tacoma	367	503.4
4	Spokane	268	352.7
5	Boise	212	185.0
6	Yakima	138	178.7
7	Olympia	80	133.8
8	Billings	149	112.8
9	Bellingham	91	111.5
10	Great Falls	99	80.5

SOURCE: "1981 Survey of Buying Power," *Sales and Marketing Management*, July 27, 1981, pp.B1–B44 and C1–C228.

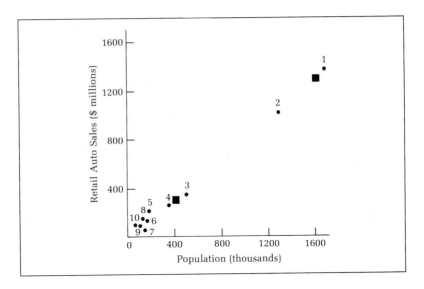

FIGURE 4.2   **Retail Auto Sales (*RAS*) as a Function of Population (*Pop*) in Ten Northwestern Cities for 1981.**   The numbers next to the points correspond to the cities numbered 1 through 10 in Table 4.2. The two squares do not represent any particular cities.

The authors' freehand line through these points can be found by connecting the two small squares. The equation for that line can be calculated as before:

Point	RAS	Pop
1	300	400
2	1300	1600

General form: $RAS = a + b(Pop)$
Point 1: $300 = a + b(400)$
Point 2: $1300 = a + b(1600)$

Subtracting two from one, we get

$$-1000 = b(-1200)$$
$$b = -1000/-1200$$
$$b = .833$$

Using point 2, we find a:

$$1300 = a + .833(1600)$$
$$1300 = a + 1332.8$$
$$a = -32.8$$

So our first approximation for the retail auto sales function for northwestern United States cities is

$$RAS = -32.8 + .833(Pop)$$

Once again, you probably got an equation that is a little different from this one. if you compare your equation with other students', you will be likely to find many different, yet similar, functions. Whose equation is the best? To know that, we must establish some basis for determining what is best. In the following section, we will do that, and then we will determine the best possible regression equation to represent the two models we have discussed in this section.

Before going on, let us summarize three important points:

1. Regression analysis is a statistical tool that helps us quantify functional relationships when we are building and working with economic models.

2. In building economic models, you, the analyst, must select and define relevant variables and then collect data that measure those variables. Business and economic logic led us to hypothesize that aggregate consumption would be a function of aggregate income. This type of reasoning also led us to expect that the level of car sales in cities would be a function of city size as measured by population.

3. Looking at data in a graphic form as well as in a tabular form is useful in helping us to see whether the data are well described by a linear equation. (Later in this chapter, we will consider some nonlinear cases.)

4.2 THE ORDINARY LEAST SQUARES REGRESSION MODEL

The simplest forms of regression analysis involve just one independent variable. The dependent variable is usually designated Y, and the independent variable is represented with an X. The simple linear regression model is often expressed as

$$Y = a + bX$$

This is called a *bivariate linear regression (BLR) model* because there are just two variables: Y and X.

In this expression, a represents the *intercept* or *constant* term for the regression equation. The intercept is where the regression line crosses the vertical, or Y, axis. It is the value that the dependent variable (Y) would have if the dependent variable (X) had a value of 0. We will have more to say about the interpretation of the value of a later.

The value of b tells us the slope of the regression line. The slope is the rate of change in the dependent variable for each unit change in the independent variable. From your understanding of calculus, you can see that

$$b = dY/dX$$

Understanding that the slope term (b) is the derivative of Y with respect to X, or the rate of change in Y as X changes, will be helpful to you in interpreting regression results. If b has a positive value, Y increases when X increases and decreases when X decreases. On the other hand, if b is negative, Y changes in the opposite direction of changes in X.

The freehand regression models developed earlier, for the consumption function and for retail auto sales, were based largely on judgment in estimating values for the intercept (a) and the slope (b). Let us now turn our attention to a better alternative. The most commonly used criterion is that the sum of the squared vertical differences between the observed values and the regression line be as small as possible. To illustrate this concept, Figure 4.3 shows 10 observations of the relationship between students' scores on the Graduate Management Admissions Test ($GMAT$) and their undergraduate grade point averages (GPA). You can see from the scattering of points

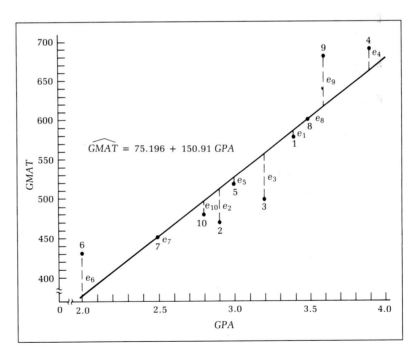

FIGURE 4.3   Ordinary Least Squares Regression Line for _GMAT_ Score as a Function of _GPA_.   Residuals, or deviations, between each point and the regression line are labeled e_i.

that no straight line would go through all of the points. We would like to find the one line that comes the closest to the points, based on the criterion of minimizing the sum of the squared vertical deviations of the observed values from the regression line.

The vertical distance between each point and the regression line is called a deviation. We will represent these deviations with e_i (where the subscript i refers to the number of the observation). A regression line is drawn through the points in Figure 4.3, and the deviations between the points and the estimates you would make from the regression line are identified as e_1, e_2, e_3, and so on. Note that some of the deviations are positive (e_4, e_6, and e_9), while the others are negative. Some errors are fairly large (e.g., e_3), while others are small (e.g., e_7). By our criterion, the best regression line is that which minimizes the sum of the squares of these deviations.

Using the method of least squares, we square each of the deviations and add them up. We square the deviations so that both positive and negative deviations are taken into account; if we do not square the deviations, the negative and positive deviations will cancel each other out as we find their sum. *The single line that gives us the smallest sum of the squared deviations from the line is the best line according to the method of least squares.*

The method of finding the values of a and b (i.e., the regression line) that minimizes the sum of these squared errors is called *ordinary least squares regression* (OLS). The OLS regression equation, as represented by the line in Figure 4.3, is

$$\widehat{GMAT} = 75.196 + 150.91 GPA$$

Using this equation, you can estimate the value of GMAT for each of the original 10 observations. The estimated variable is usually identified with a caret (^). Thus, the estimated values of this dependent variable are $\widehat{GMAT}$. The original data, estimated values, deviations from the estimated line, squared deviations, and the sum of the squared deviations are shown in Table 4.3. The deviations from the regression line are also frequently called

TABLE 4.3   **Regression Data and Residuals**

Observation	GPA	GMAT	$\widehat{GMAT}$	Residuals	Squared Residuals
1	3.4	580	588.290	−8.290	68.724
2	2.9	470	512.835	−42.835	1834.837
3	3.2	500	558.108	−58.180	3376.540
4	3.9	690	663.745	26.255	689.325
5	3.0	520	527.926	−7.926	62.821
6	2.0	430	377.016	52.984	2807.304
7	2.5	450	452.471	−2.471	6.106
8	3.5	600	603.381	−3.381	11.431
9	3.6	680	618.472	61.528	3785.695
10	2.8	480	479.744	−17.744	314.850
Sum of squared residuals					12957.633

residuals. You are likely to see the term *residuals* used in printouts from computer programs that perform regression analysis.

Interpreting the Intercept and the Slope

Let us consider how we should interpret the regression equation above. In particular, what do the estimated values of intercept (a) and slope (b) mean. The value of 75.196 for a indicates that if we were to extend the regression line to its intersection with the vertical axis, the value of the dependent variable would be 75.196. That is, if GPA were 0, GMAT would be estimated to have the value 75.196. However, we must be cautious in making such interpretations. The extrapolated value is far outside the range of data we have observed. Our data cover the GPA interval from 2.0 to 3.9. The further we go outside that range, the less reliable are the results. We really do not know what the graph of the function looks like below a GPA of 2.0. In many cases, it is erroneous to interpret the value of a as the expected value of the dependent variable when the independent variable is 0 because often our data do not include 0. In most cases the size of a is best interpreted as a positioning parameter. If we estimate the same regression in two time periods (or for two different cross-sectional populations), shifts in the function, up or down, will be seen by changes in a.

Recall that b represents the slope of the regression function. In this case the slope is positive and has a value of 150.91. This means that for each unit increase in GPA you would expect a rise in the GMAT score of nearly 151 points. In this situation, it is probably more useful to think in terms of the effect of a 0.1 change in GPA. Each tenth of a point change in GPA would be associated with an expected 15.1 change in GMAT score.

The Assumptions of the Ordinary Least Squares Model

Several assumptions underlie the ordinary least squares regression model. A general understanding of these assumptions is necessary to appreciate both the power and limitations of OLS regression.

First, for each value of X, there is a conditional probability distribution Y. Figure 4.4 shows the conditional probability distributions of Y for two of the possible values of X (X_1 and X_2). Y is specified as the dependent variable and X as the independent variable. The mean of the conditional probability distributions is assumed to lie on a straight line, according to the following equation:

$$Y = a + bX$$

In other words, the mean value of the dependent variable is assumed to be a linear function of the dependent variable (note that the regression line in Figure 4.4 is directly under the peaks of the conditional probability distributions for Y).

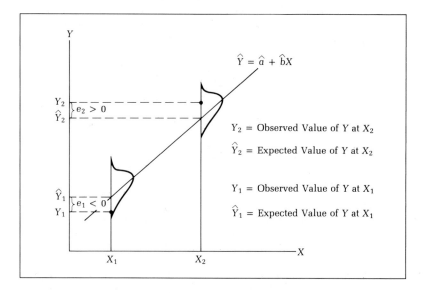

FIGURE 4.4   **Distribution of Y Values around the Ordinary Least Squares Regression Line.**   For any X, the possible values of Y are assumed to be distributed normally around the regression line. Further, the residuals (e_i) are assumed to be normally distributed with a mean of 0 and a constant standard deviation.

Second, OLS assumes that the standard deviation of each of the conditional probability distributions is the same for all values of the independent variable (such as X_1 and X_2). In Figure 4.4 the "spread" of both of the conditional probability distributions shown is the same (this characteristic of equal standard deviations is called *homoscedasticity*).

Third, the values of the dependent variable (Y) are assumed to be independent of one another; so if one observation of Y lies below the mean of its conditional probability distribution, this does not imply that the next observation will also be below the mean (or anywhere else in particular).

Fourth, all of the conditional probability distributions of the deviations or residuals are assumed to be normal. That is, the differences between the actual values of Y and the expected values (from the regression line) are normally distributed random variables with a mean of 0 and a constant standard deviation.

These four assumptions may be viewed as the ideal to which we aspire in calculating a regression line; while these underlying assumptions of regression are sometimes violated in practice, they are followed closely enough to ensure that estimated regressions represent true relationships between variables. For the practitioner, it is extremely important to note that if these four assumptions are not at least closely approximated, the resulting OLS regression analysis may be flawed. Summary statistics to be used with regression analysis allow us to check compliance with these assumptions. These statistics are described later in this chapter, as are the likely outcomes of violating these assumptions.

The Mathematics of the Ordinary Least Squares Model

In mathematical notation, a simple linear regression is expressed as

$$Y = a + bX$$

where

Y = dependent variable
X = independent variable
a = intercept of the regression line on the vertical, or Y, axis, often referred to as the constant term in the regression function
b = slope of the regression lines

Normally, the data do not follow an exactly linear relationship. In the scattergrams shown so far (see Figures 4.1, 4.2, and 4.3), it is impossible to draw one straight line in any of them that will go through all the points. Therefore, we have presented the method of ordinary least squares as a way of determining an equation for a straight line that best (according to the least squares criterion) represents the relationship inherent in the data points of the scatter diagram. The general form of this linear function may be stated as

$$\hat{Y}_i = \hat{a} + \hat{b}X_i$$

where $\hat{a}$ and $\hat{b}$ are the calculated values of the Y intercept and the slope of the line, respectively. $\hat{Y}_i$ is the calculated value for the dependent variable that is associated with the independent variable X_i.

Since the $(\hat{Y}_i)$ values are all located on our "calculated" straight line, the actual Y_1 values will, in most cases, differ from our calculated $(\hat{Y}_i)$ values by a residual amount, which we denote as e_i. These residuals may also be referred to as *deviation terms*.

Mathematically, this can be expressed as

$$Y_i - \hat{Y}_i = e_i$$

And thus,

$$Y_i = \hat{Y}_i + e_i$$

Further, since we have defined $\hat{Y}_i = \hat{a} + \hat{b}X_i$, the expression above may be written as

$$Y_i = \hat{a} + \hat{b}X_i + e_i$$

Figure 4.4 shows the relationships among Y_i, $\hat{Y}_i$, and e_i graphically.

There are at least two reasons for the existence of the residual (e_i): (1) it is impossible to know and have data for all the factors that influence the behavior of the dependent variable, and (2) there are errors in observation and measurement of economic data. Thus, it is normally impossible for one straight line to pass through all the points on the scatter diagram, and it becomes necessary to specify a condition or conditions that the line must satisfy to make the line in some sense better than any of the other lines that could be drawn through the scatter diagram. We have stated the ordinary least squares condition as follows:

> The line must minimize the sum of the squared vertical distances between each point on the scatter diagram and the line. In terms of Figures 4.3 and 4.4, the line must minimize the sum of the squared residuals, that is, minimize Σe_i^2.

The linear relationship, or line, that satisfies this condition is called an ordinary least squares regression line. The expression for the sum of the squared vertical distances is

$$\Sigma e_i^2 = \Sigma(Y_i - \hat{Y}_i)^2$$
$$= \Sigma(Y_i - \hat{a} - \hat{b}X_i)^2$$

where each expression is summed over the n observations of the data, that is, for $i = 1$ to $i = n$. In this expression the $\hat{a}$ and the $\hat{b}$ are the unknowns, or variables.

Given this equation, the objective is to obtain expressions, or *normal equations*, as they are called by statisticians, for $\hat{a}$ and $\hat{b}$ that will result in the minimization of Σe^2. The normal equations are derived by taking the partial derivatives of the above equation with respect to both $\hat{a}$ and $\hat{b}$ and setting them equal to 0 (this is the first-order condition for finding a minimum). Then, by solving the first-order partials for $\hat{a}$ and $\hat{b}$ we obtain the following results:

$$\hat{b} = (\Sigma Y_i X_i - n\overline{Y}\,\overline{X})/(\Sigma X_i - n\overline{X}^2)$$
$$\hat{a} = \overline{Y} - \hat{b}\overline{X}$$

These two equations can now be used to estimate the slope and intercept of the OLS regression function respectively.

In this text, we will not use these normal equations directly in estimating the intercept and slope terms for regression problems. In our modern business society, a computer and the appropriate software are available to anyone seriously interested in performing regression analyses. Mainframe computers usually support such statistical software as *TSP*, *SAS*, *BMD*, and/or *SPSS*, all of which provide good regression procedures. Further, many fine regression packages are available for personal computers and microcomputers. Micro *TSP*, *RATS*, *STATPAK*, *ESP*, and *SPSS/PC* are examples of such software available for microcomputers.

4.3   STATISTICAL EVALUATION OF ORDINARY LEAST SQUARES REGRESSION

There are a number of ways to evaluate the significance of an OLS regression function. In this section, we will first look at t-tests of hypotheses about the value of the slope term (b) of the regression. We will then consider the standard error of the estimate and the construction of confidence intervals. Finally, we will look at a measure of the percent of the variation in the dependent variable that is explained by the regression model.

Hypothesis Tests Related to the Slope of the Regression Line

Even if the numbers for X and Y that you entered into a regression program were random numbers, the program would yield some values for a and b. But would the regression equation have any useful meaning? Would you expect to find a real functional relationship between Y and X? You no doubt answered no to both of these questions. That is, if the values for X and Y are both selected from a random number table, you would not expect to find a functional relationship between them.

If Y is not a function of X, the best estimate of Y is the mean of Y, regardless of the value of X, since Y does not depend on X. If this is the case, the regression line would have a slope equal to 0 $(b = 0)$. The scattergram in Figure 4.5 illustrates such a case. The OLS regression equation for this set of points is

$$\hat{Y} = 14.66 - .012X$$

The mean value of Y is 14.5. Note that the a value in the regression equation is very close to the mean value of Y. In fact, if you draw the regression equation on Figure 4.5, you will find that it is very close to the horizontal line already drawn at the mean of Y.

We need to have some method of evaluating regression equations to see if there is a meaningful functional relationship between Y and X. This can be done by using a t-test to see if the estimated slope $(\hat{b})$ is statistically significantly different from 0. If it is, there is sufficient evidence in the data to support the existence of a functional relationship between Y and X. However, if the value of $\hat{b}$ is not significantly different from 0, we would conclude that Y is not a linear function of X.

A t-test is used to test the null hypothesis that the slope of the true relationship between Y and X is equal to 0. You could write this null hypothesis as

$$H_0: b = 0$$

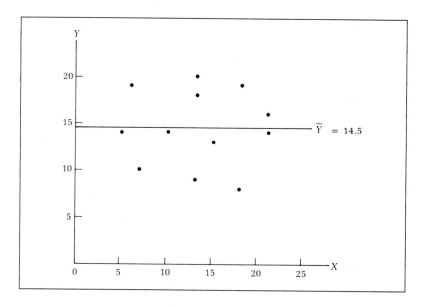

FIGURE 4.5   **Scattergram When Y Is Not a Function of X.**   Based on these 12 observations, there does not appear to be a functional relationship between X and Y. When no such relationship exists, the best estimate of Y for any observed X is the mean of Y.

The t-statistic used for this t-test is calculated as follows:[1]

$$t_c = \frac{\hat{b} - 0}{SE \text{ of } \hat{b}}$$

Where SE of $\hat{b}$ is the standard error of $\hat{b}$ (i.e., the standard deviation of the probability distribution of the estimator). This value is a standard part of the output of virtually all regression programs. The value of t_c indicates how many standard errors our estimate of b is from 0. The larger the absolute value of the t_c ratio, the more confident you can be that the true value of b is not 0. Most regression programs also give the calculated t-statistic (t_c) as a standard part of the regression output.

The alternative hypothesis could take any of the following three forms:

---

[1]In some situations, you might want to test to see if $\hat{b}$ is significantly different from some particular nonzero value. For example, perhaps you want to see if $\hat{b} = k$. Then the null hypothesis is $H_0: b = k$ and the t-statistic is

$$t + \frac{\hat{b} - k}{SE \text{ of } \hat{b}}$$

Case 1. H_1: $b \neq 0$

This form is appropriate when you are just testing for the existence of any linear functional relationship between Y and X. In this case, you have no reason to think that b will be either positive or negative.

Case 2. H_1: $b > 0$

This form is appropriate if you think that the relationship between Y and X is a direct one. That is, you would use this form when you expect an increase (decrease) in X to cause an increase (decrease) in Y.

Case 3. H_1: $b < 0$

This form is appropriate if you think that the relationship between Y and X is an inverse one. That is, you would use this form when you expect an increase (decrease) in X to cause a decrease (increase) in Y.

Situations such as described in case 1 imply the use of a two-tailed test. This means that if we want to be 95-percent confident that 0 is not in the confidence interval, we would have 2.5 percent of the total area under the t-distribution in the outer part of each tail of the t-distribution, as illustrated below:

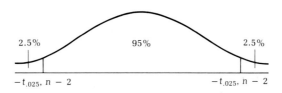

A 95-percent confidence interval is the same as a 5-percent significance level. The symbol α (alpha) is usually used to represent a significance level. Thus, in this example, $\alpha = .05$, and since we have a two-tailed test, $\alpha/2$ is the area under each tail of the t-distribution.

In performing a t-test, we not only have to decide on a significance level, but we also have to correctly identify the numbers of degrees of freedom to use. In bivariate linear regressions, the appropriate number of degrees of freedom can be found as follows:

$$df = n - 2$$

where n equals the number of observations used in determining the values of a and b and 2 is the number of parameters estimated. A t-table such as the one in Table 4.4 is then used to find the critical value of t for a t-test. We can reject the null hypothesis if the absolute value of t_c is greater than the table value (t).

As an example of using a two-tailed t-test, consider the data shown in the scattergram of Figure 4.5. In that case, you would have no reason to expect b to be either positive or negative. You would just be testing to see if the estimated value was indeed statistically significantly different from 0. Recall that the regression equation for that data is

$$\hat{Y} = 14.66 - .012X$$

Our null hypothesis is that the slope is equal to 0; that is, $H_0: b = 0$. The alternative hypothesis is that the slope is not equal to 0; that is, $H_1: b \neq 0$.

The computer output showed that the standard error of b for this data is .231, so we find

$$t_c = \frac{-.012 - 0}{.231} = -.052$$

There were 12 observations, so the number of degrees of freedom is

$$df = 12 - 2 = 10$$

Looking at Table 4.4 in the row for 10 degrees of freedom and under the .025 column, we find the critical value for t to be 2.228. We see that

$$|-.052| \not> +2.228$$

That is, the absolute value of t_c is not greater than the critical value, so we do not have enough evidence to reject the null hypothesis. Therefore, we conclude that there is no statistically significant linear relationship between Y and X at a 5-percent significance level.

Situations such as those described in cases 2 and 3 call for the use of a one-tailed test. In these cases, if we want to be 95-percent confident, we would have the entire 5 percent in the outer part of either the upper or lower tail of the distribution. Since the t-distribution is symmetrical and since we only test the absolute value of t_c, it is necessary to look at only the upper-tail, as illustrated below:

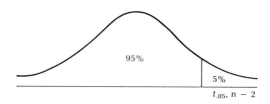

The number of degrees of freedom is still equal to $n - 2$.

As an example of the use of a one-tailed test, consider the data related to the relationship between retail auto sales (RAS) and population (Pop)

TABLE 4.4
Critical Values for the *t*-Distribution

df		Area under Clear Area of Curve		
	.10	.05	.025	.01
1	3.078	6.314	12.706	31.821
2	1.886	2.920	4.303	6.965
3	1.638	2.353	3.182	4.541
4	1.533	2.132	2.776	3.747
5	1.476	2.015	2.571	3.365
6	1.440	1.943	2.447	3.143
7	1.415	1.895	2.365	2.998
8	1.397	1.860	2.306	2.896
9	1.383	1.833	2.262	2.821
10	1.372	1.812	2.228	2.764
11	1.363	1.796	2.201	2.718
12	1.356	1.782	2.179	2.681
13	1.350	1.771	2.160	2.650
14	1.345	1.761	2.145	2.624
15	1.341	1.753	2.131	2.602
16	1.337	1.746	2.120	2.583
17	1.333	1.740	2.110	2.567
18	1.330	1.734	2.101	2.552
19	1.328	1.729	2.093	2.539
20	1.325	1.725	2.086	2.528
21	1.323	1.721	2.080	2.518
22	1.321	1.717	2.074	2.508
23	1.319	1.714	2.069	2.500
24	1.318	1.711	2.064	2.492
25	1.316	1.708	2.060	2.485
26	1.315	1.706	2.056	2.479
27	1.314	1.703	2.052	2.473
28	1.313	1.701	2.048	2.467
29	1.311	1.699	2.045	2.462
30	1.310	1.697	2.042	2.457
40	1.303	1.684	2.021	2.423
60	1.296	1.671	2.000	2.390
120	1.289	1.658	1.980	2.358
'	1.282	1.645	1.960	2.326

t-Distribution

For a 95-percent two-tailed test, .025 is under the clear area of this curve.

For a 95-percent one-tailed test, .05 is under the clear area of this curve.

SOURCE: Adapted with permission from *CRC Handbook of Tables for Probability and Statistics*, 1968. Copyright CRC Press, Inc., Boca Raton, Florida.

(see Table 4.2). You are likely to expect that the greater the population, the more cars will be sold. Our hypothesis could then be stated as

H_0: $b = 0$
H_1: $b > 0$

The data from Table 4.2 were analyzed with the OLS regression procedure on both Micro *TSP* and *SPSS/PC*. The results are shown in Table 4.5. From these results, we can write the estimated equation for retail auto sales as a function of population as

$$\widehat{RAS} = 6.5985 + .8203Pop$$

We want to see if the .8203 is significantly different from 0 and positive. The standard error of b in this case was calculated to be .0253. Thus,

$$t_c = \frac{.8203 - 0}{.0253} = 32.422$$

Note that our calculation of t_c is nearly .01 lower than the values in Table 4.5. This discrepancy is due solely to our rounding to four decimal places.

Since this data set contained 10 observations, the number of degrees of freedom is

$$df = 10 - 2 = 8$$

In Table 4.4 in the row for 8 degrees of freedom and under the .05 column, we find the critical value for t to be 1.860. We see that

$$|32.422| > 1.860$$

That is, the absolute value of t_c is greater than the critical value. Thus, we have enough evidence in this case to reject the null hypothesis and conclude that RAS is positively related to population size.

Try it yourself.[2] For the consumption and GNP data, the OLS equation is

$$C = -.55.5 + .6678GNP$$

The data for this regression are given in Table 4.1 and Figure 4.1. The standard error of b is .0247, and there are 10 observations. Set up the null and alternative hypotheses. Then perform the appropriate t-test using a 5-percent significance level.

A rule of thumb is often used in evaluating t-ratios when a t-table is not handy. The rule is that the slope term is likely to be significantly different from 0 if the absolute value of t_c is greater than 2. This is a valuable rule to remember.

---

[2]The null and alternative hypotheses are

$$H_0: b = 0, H_1: b > 0$$

This assumes that we expect consumption to be a positive function of income. The value of t_c is 27.04, and the critical value from Table 4.5 is 1.860. Thus the null hypothesis is rejected.

TABLE 4.5
Computer Results of OLS Regression Analysis of Retail Auto Sales *(RAS)* as a Function of Population *(Pop)*

TSP Results

SMPL   1   —   10
10 Observations
LS // Dependent variable is RAS

	COEFFICIENT	STANDARD ERROR	T-STATISTIC
C	6.5984767	17.576771	0.3754089
POP	0.8203090	0.0252943	32.430570

R squared	0.992451	Mean of dependent var	382.3000
Adjusted R squared	0.991507	SD of dependent var	453.5960
SE of regression	41.80136	Sum of squared resid	13978.83
Durbin-Watson stat	2.154237	F-statistic	1051.742
Log likelihood	-50.40296		

SPSS/PC Results

* * * * M U L T I P L E   R E G R E S S I O N * * * *

Equation Number 1   Dependent Variable..   RAS

Multiple R	.99622
R squared	.99245
Adjusted R squared	.99151
Standard error	41.80136

Analysis of Variance

	DF	Sum of Squares	Mean Square
Regression	1	1837765.26795	1837765.26795
Residual	8	13978.83205	1747.35401

F = 1051.74181   Signif F = .0000

——————————————— Variables in the Equation ———————————————

Variable	B	SE B	Beta	T	Sig T
POP	.82031	.02529	.99622	32.431	.0000
(Constant)	6.59847	17.57677		.375	.7171

End Block Number   1   All requested variables entered.

Point and Interval Estimates

Regression equations are often used to make estimates of the value of the dependent variable for a value of the independent variable that may or may not have been in the original data set. When such estimates are made, it is common to give both a point and an interval estimate.

The point estimate is generated directly from the regression equation. To illustrate, let us look again at the retail auto sales function introduced above. The equation is

$$\widehat{RAS} = 6.5985 + .8203Pop$$
$$(32.422)$$

Note that the t-ratio is written in parentheses under the slope term. This is a common practice that helps the reader make a quick judgment about the significance of the slope term. From this point on we will generally include the t-ratio in this form with each regression equation used in the text.

Suppose that you live in a city in the northwestern United States and want to use this regression equation to estimate auto sales in your area. If the population of the city you live in is 200,000, you would estimate sales as follows:

$$\widehat{RAS} = 6.5985 + .8203(200)$$
$$= 170.6585$$

Remember that the data used in estimating the function had population in thousands and auto sales in millions of dollars. Thus, the point estimate of sales for your city would be $170.6585 million, or $170,658,500.

While point estimates are useful, it is unlikely that they will be exactly correct. Thus, it is often preferable to make an interval estimate in such a way that we can say we are 95-percent (or some other percent) confident that the true value will be somewhere in the interval. A simple *approximation* for a 95-percent confidence interval for a general bivariate regression model can be given as

$$Y = \hat{Y} \pm 2(SEE)$$

where $\hat{Y}$ is the point estimate and SEE is the standard error of the estimate. The value for SEE is part of the output of nearly all regression programs. However, it can also be easily calculated as follows:

$$SEE = \sqrt{\Sigma(Y_i - \hat{Y}_i)^2/(n - 2)}$$

where n is the number of observations used in the estimation of the regression equation. The standard error of the estimate may also be represented by SER or SE (standard error of the regression or standard error, respectively).[3]

---

[3] See Robert S. Pindyck and Daniel L. Rubinfeld, *Econometric Models and Economic Forecasts* (New York: McGraw-Hill, 1981), p. 27.

Let us return to the retail auto sales example to illustrate the determination of an approximate 95-percent confidence interval. Our point estimate for RAS in a city with a population of 200,000 is $170,658,500 (or $170.6585 million). The computer output shows the SEE to be $41.8014 million. Thus, the approximate 95-percent confidence interval is

$$RAS = 170.6585 \pm 2(41.8014)$$
$$RAS = 170.6585 \pm 83.6028$$
$$RAS = 87.0557 \text{ to } 254.2613$$

Thus, we can say that we are 95-percent confident that the actual value of retail auto sales in a city of 200,000 people would be in the interval between $87,055,700 and $254,261,300.

Try making a point and an approximate interval estimate yourself.[4] The OLS regression equation for consumption as a function of GNP is

$$C = 55.5 + .6678\ GNP$$
$$(27.04)$$

with a standard error of the estimate of 9.325. Make point and 95-percent confidence interval estimates for consumption when income is $1200 billion (1972 terms).

While this approximation for a 95-percent confidence interval is often used because of its simplicity, a more precise interval estimation procedure is available:

$$Y = \hat{Y} \pm t(SEE) \sqrt{1 + (1/n) + (X_0 - \overline{X})^2 / \Sigma(X_i - \overline{X})^2}$$

where

$\hat{Y}_i$ = point estimate from the regression model

SEE = standard error of the estimate

t = t-value at an α significance level ($\alpha = .05$ for a 95-percent confidence interval) and $n - 2$ degrees of freedom

n = number of observations used in estimating the model

X_0 = value of the independent variable for which the estimate of Y is desired

$\overline{X}$ = mean value of the independent variable

$\Sigma(X_i - \overline{X})^2$ = sum of the squared deviations of the independent variable from its mean value for all n observations

---

[4]The point estimate is $745.86 billion, and the approximate 95-percent confidence interval is from $727.21 billion to $764.51 billion.

In this formulation for the confidence interval, you can see that the width of the interval depends on the value of the independent variable for which the estimation is made (i.e., on the value of X_0). Also, note that the confidence band becomes wider the farther X_0 is from $\overline{X}$.

Now let us apply this more precise method of determining the 95-percent confidence interval to the retail auto sales estimation that we considered earlier. In this case, $n = 10$, and, thus, from Table 4.4, we find that $t = 2.306$ (using 8 degrees of freedom and the .025 column such that 2.5 percent of the area is in each tail of the t-distribution). Given that the dependent variable, X, is population, the other values necessary for the calculation are

$$X_0 = 200 \text{ (representing the city of 200,000 population for which we want to estimate retail auto sales)}$$
$$\overline{X} = 458$$
$$\Sigma(X_i - \overline{X})^2 = 2{,}731{,}084$$
$$\hat{Y} = 170.6585 \text{ (as determined at the beginning of this section: } \hat{Y} = \widehat{RAS})$$
$$SEE = 41.8014 \text{ (see Table 4.5)}$$

Substituting these values into the confidence interval formulation, we have

$$Y = \hat{Y} + t(SEE) \sqrt{1 + (1/n) + (X_0 - \overline{X})^2/\Sigma(X_i - \overline{X})^2}$$
$$Y = 170.6585 \pm 2.306(41.8014) \sqrt{1 + (1/10) + (200 - 458)^2/2{,}731{,}084}$$
$$Y = 170.6585 \pm 96.394 \sqrt{1 + .1 + (66{,}564)/(2{,}731{,}084)}$$
$$Y = 170.6585 \pm 96.394 \sqrt{1.124}$$
$$Y = 170.6585 \pm 96.394(1.06)$$
$$Y = 170.6585 \pm 102.1777$$
$$Y = 68.4808 \text{ to } 272.8362$$

Thus, based on this more exact method, the range of our 95-percent confidence level for retail auto sales ($\widehat{RAS} = \hat{Y}$) in city of 200,000 people would be $68,480,800 to $272,836,200. Comparing this to the approximate range calculated earlier, we see that this procedure gives a wider confidence interval. If the city of interest had a population closer to the mean population for the sample (458,000) and/or if we had a larger sample, the two estimates of the 95-percent confidence interval would have been closer.

The Coefficient of Determination

There will always be some variation in the value of the dependent variable (Y) used in a regression analysis. It would be convenient to have a measure of how much of that variation is explained by the regression model. That is just what the coefficient of determination does for us.

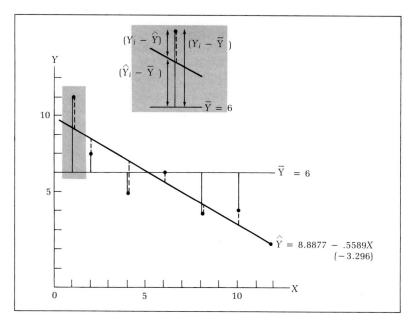

FIGURE 4.6   **Partitioning the Variation in Y.**   The total variation in the dependent variable (Y) can be separated into two components: variation that is explained by the regression model (see screened insert) and variation that is unexplained (residual variation): total variation $= \Sigma(Y_i - \overline{Y})^2$; explained variation $= \Sigma(\hat{Y}_i - \overline{Y})^2$; residual variation $= \Sigma(Y_i - \hat{Y}_i)^2$.

The total variation in Y is measured as the sum of the squared deviations of each Y_i value from the mean value of Y:

Total variation in $Y = \Sigma(Y_i - \overline{Y})^2$

Figure 4.6 will help you to see why this summary statistic is used to measure the variation in Y. The six large dots represent six observations on two variables, X and Y. (These data are also given in Table 4.6.)

In Figure 4.6, a horizontal line is drawn at the mean value for Y, that is, at $\overline{Y} = 6$. Only one of the six data points is on that line. All the other data points differ from the mean value of Y. The amount by which each observation differs from the mean of Y is shown by a solid vertical line from the data point to the horizontal line at $\overline{Y} = 6$. The length of these lines measures the variation of each observed Y_i from the mean of Y. If we added these distances to get the total variation in Y, we would get 0 because the negative values offset the positive ones [see the column headed $(Y_i - \overline{Y})$ in Table 4.6]. For this reason, we square these differences and then add the squared values to get a measure of the total variation in the Y data. As you see from Table 4.6, this sum is 26. So the total variation Y is 26.

TABLE 4.6
Calculation of the Coefficient of Determination (R^2)

X_i	Y_i	$(Y_i - \bar{Y})$	$(Y_i - \bar{Y})^2$	$\hat{Y}_i$	$(Y_i - \hat{Y}_i)$	$(Y_i - \hat{Y}_i)^2$	$(\hat{Y}_i - \bar{Y})$	$(\hat{Y}_i - \bar{Y})^2$
1	10	4	16	8.3288	1.6712	2.7929	2.3288	5.4233
2	7	1	1	7.7699	−.7699	.5927	1.7699	3.1325
4	5	−1	1	6.6521	−1.6521	2.7294	.6521	.4252
6	6	0	0	5.5343	.4657	.2169	−.4657	.2169
8	4	−2	4	4.4165	−.4165	.1735	−1.5835	2.5075
10	4	−2	4	3.2987	.7013	.4918	−2.7013	7.2970

$$\bar{X} = 5.1667 \qquad \Sigma(Y_i - \bar{Y})^2 = 26.0000 \qquad \Sigma(\hat{Y}_i - \bar{Y})^2 = 19$$
$$\bar{Y} = 6.0000 \qquad \Sigma(Y_i - \hat{Y}_i)^2 = 7$$

$$R^2 = \frac{\Sigma(\hat{Y}_i - \bar{Y})^2}{\Sigma(Y_i - \bar{Y})^2} = \frac{19}{26} = .7308$$

$\hat{Y}_i$ values are calculated from the OLS regression equation: $\hat{Y}_i = 8.8877 - .5589X_i$
$$(-3.296)$$

Part of that total variation in Y is explained by the regression model, but part is unexplained. Let us look at the latter. The difference between each observed value of Y (Y_i) and the value of Y determined by the regression equation ($\hat{Y}_i$) is a residual variation that has not been explained or accounted for (see the dashed vertical lines in Figure 4.6). We define the measure of residual variation as

$$\text{Residual variation in } Y = \Sigma(Y_i - \hat{Y}_i)^2$$

Look at Table 4.6 to see that the residual variation in this example is 7.

The part of the total variation in Y that is explained by the regression model is called the explained variation. For each observation, the explained variation can be represented by the distance between the value estimated by the regression line ($\hat{Y}_i$) and the mean of Y ($\bar{Y}$). These distances are shown in the inset in Figure 4.6. It follows that we define the measure of explained variation as

$$\text{Explained variation in } Y = \Sigma(\hat{Y}_i - \bar{Y})^2$$

From Table 4.6, you see that the explained variation in this example is 19.

We have shown that there is some total variation in Y and that some of that variation is explained by the regression model and some—the residual variation—is not explained. Does it not make sense that the sum of the explained plus the unexplained (residual) variations should equal the total variation? We can say that

$$\text{Total variation in } Y = \text{Residual variation in } Y + \text{Explained variation in } Y$$

Alternatively, we may write this partitioning of the total variation in Y as

$$\Sigma(Y_i - \bar{Y})^2 = \Sigma(Y_i - \hat{Y}_i)^2 + \Sigma(\hat{Y}_i - \bar{Y})^2$$

We now can measure the total variation in Y and how much of that variation is explained by the regression model.

This brings us back to the coefficient of variation (R^2). Recall that R^2 is the percentage of the total variation in Y that is explained by the regression equation. Thus, R^2 must be the ratio of the explained variation in Y to the total variation in Y:

$$R^2 = \frac{\text{Explained variation in } Y}{\text{Total variation in } Y}$$

$$R^2 = \frac{\Sigma(\hat{Y}_i - \overline{Y})^2}{\Sigma(Y_i - \overline{Y})^2}$$

For our present example, we can now find a value for R^2 using the data in Table 4.6:

$$R^2 = \frac{\Sigma(\hat{Y}_i - \overline{Y})^2}{\Sigma(Y_i - \overline{Y})^2}$$

$$R^2 = \frac{19}{26} = .7308$$

This means that 73.08 percent of the variation in the dependent variable (Y) is explained by the OLS regression model ($\hat{Y} = 8.8877 - .5589X$).

Since nearly all regression analyses are done using a computer, we rarely would have to calculate the coefficient of determination by hand. It will generally be given in the computer printout and is most often identified as "R squared" (see, for example, Table 4.5).

4.4 MULTIPLE LINEAR REGRESSION

In many applications, the dependent variable of interest is a function of more than one independent variable. In such cases, a form of OLS regression called multiple linear regression is appropriate. This technique is a straightforward extension of simple linear regression and is built on the same basic set of assumptions, with the following two additional assumptions: (1) the number of observations is greater than the number of variables, and (2) the independent variables are independent of one another.

The general form of the multiple linear regression model is

$$Y = f(X_1, X_2, \ldots, X_n)$$
$$Y = a + b_1X_1 + b_2X_2 + \cdots + b_nX_n$$

where Y represents the dependent variable, and the X_i terms represent different independent variables. The intercept, or constant, term in the regression is a, and the b_i terms represent slope terms, or rates of change, for the respective independent variables.

A Market Share Multiple Linear Regression Model

To understand the use and interpretation of multiple regression analysis, let us consider an example. The quarterly data in Table 4.7 contain the basic information used in this example and cover the three years from the first

TABLE 4.7 **Big Sky Foods' Market Share Multiple Regression Data**

Observation	Market Share	Price	Advertising	Interest Rate
1982.1	19	5.20	500	11
1982.2	17	5.32	550	11
1982.3	14	5.48	550	12
1982.4	15	5.60	550	12
1983.1	18	5.80	550	9
1983.2	16	6.03	660	10
1983.3	16	6.01	615	10
1983.4	19	5.92	650	10
1984.1	23	5.90	745	9
1984.2	27	5.85	920	10
1984.3	23	5.80	1053	11
1984.4	21	5.85	950	11

quarter of 1982 (1982.1) through the fourth quarter of 1984 (1984.4). Our objective is to develop a regression model that explains how Big Sky Foods' (BSF) price (P) and advertising (AD), as well as the interest rate (I), have influenced the firm's market share (MS). The regression results are summarized in Table 4.8.

From the results given in Table 4.8, you should be able to write the appropriate regression equation:

$$\widehat{MS} = 80.011 - 8.458P + .020AD - 2.541I$$
$$(-3.13) \quad (6.40) \quad (-3.92)$$

The interpretation of the slope for price, advertising, and interest is as follows:

1. *Price.* The coefficient -8.458 has a negative sign, which indicates that as price goes up, market share goes down. For every $1 increase in price, market share could be expected to fall by 8.458 percentage points; or for every 10-cent increase in price, market share would be expected to fall by .8458 percentage points. Price cuts would be expected to increase market share by like amounts.

2. *Advertising.* The coefficient .02 has a positive sign, which indicates that increasing advertising is expected to increase market share. Each $100 increase in advertising would increase market share by 2.0 percentage points. Decreases in advertising would lower market share in a like manner.

3. *Interest.* The negative sign of the interest rate variable's coefficient indicates that this firm's market share would fall when the interest rate rises. Every 1-percent rise in the interest rate is expected to lower market share by 2.541 percentage points. Decreases in the interest rate would be expected to increase market share in a like manner.

TABLE 4.8

Computer Results for Big Sky Foods' Market Share Regression

```
SMPL    1982.1 - 1984.4
12 Observations
LS // Dependent variable is MS
```

	COEFFICIENT	STANDARD ERROR	T-STATISTIC
C	80.010942	19.479236	4.1074990
P	-8.4575855	2.7044982	-3.1272291
AD	0.0204432	0.0031922	6.4040876
I	-2.5406584	0.6474311	-3.9242144

R squared	0.863030	Mean of dependent var	19.00000
Adjusted R squared	0.811666	SD of dependent var	3.861229
SE of regression	1.675675	Sum of squared resid	22.46309
Durbin-Watson stat	2.169941	F-statistic	16.80231
Log likelihood	-20.78906		

NOTE: Results were produced using Micro TSP regression software.

MS = market share AD = advertising

P = price I = interest rate

What can you say about the statistical significance of each of the independent variables? You can evaluate their significance using a t-test in the same way that we tested the significance of the slope term in simple linear regression. The only difference is that now the number of degrees of freedom must be defined more thoroughly. The number of degrees of freedom can be found as follows:

$$df = n - (K + 1)$$

where n is the number of observations and K represents the number of *independent* variables. In this example, there are 12 observations and three independent variables. Thus,

$$df = 12 - (3 + 1) = 8$$

The hypotheses you would want to evaluate are

For price $H_0: b_1 = 0, H_1: b_1 < 0$

For advertising $H_0: b_2 = 0, H_1: b_2 > 0$

For interest $H_0: b_3 = 0, H_1: b_3 < 0$

These all imply a one-tailed test. From Table 4.4, we find that the critical value of t at 8 degrees of freedom and a 95-percent confidence level for a one-tailed test is 1.860. Thus,

1. For price, we reject H_0, since $|-3.13| > 1.860$.
2. For advertising, we reject H_0, since $|6.40| > 1.860$.
3. For interest, we reject H_0, since $|-3.92| > 1.860$.

Suppose you wanted to know what market share would be expected if Big Sky Foods set the price at \$5.70 and spent \$700 on advertising, and if the interest rate was 10 percent. You could make a point estimate by substituting these values into the regression model as follows:

$$\widehat{MS} = 80.011 - 8.458(5.70) + .02(700) - 2.541(10)$$
$$\widehat{MS} = 20.39$$

How would you estimate an approximate 95-percent confidence interval for market share? From Table 4.8 you see that the standard error of the estimate is 1.676 (note that in Micro TSP, this is called the SE of regression). Thus, the approximate 95-percent interval is

$$MS = \widehat{MS} \pm 2\ SEE$$
$$MS = 20.39 \pm 2(1.676)$$
$$MS = 17.038 \text{ to } 23.742$$

This means that we would be 95-percent confident that BSF's market share would fall in the interval from 17.038 through 23.742 percent if the firm set a \$5.70 price and spent \$700 on advertising, and if the interest rate was 10 percent.

The Adjusted R^2

The adjusted coefficient of determination $(\overline{R}^2)$ is .812, which indicates that 81.2 percent of the variation in market share is explained by this regression model. This result is fairly good, but, of course, we would like to have this value be as close to 1.00 (or 100 percent) as possible. In the next section, we will consider another regression analysis of this market share problem, in which, by adding another variable, the adjusted R^2 is increased.

Since this is the first time we have looked at the adjusted coefficient of determination, let us define the nature of the adjustment. The adjusted coefficient of determination is usually designated $\overline{R}^2$. The relationship between $\overline{R}^2$ and R^2 is

$$\overline{R}^2 = 1 - (1 - R^2)\left(\frac{n-1}{n-K}\right)$$

where n represents the number of observations and K represents the number of independent variables. You can see that if n is large relative to K there will be little difference between $\overline{R}^2$ and R^2. It so happens that adding *any* additional independent variable will cause R^2 to go up but may or may not cause $\overline{R}^2$ to rise. Thus, in interpreting multiple linear regression results, it is preferable to look at the adjusted coefficient of determination if it is available.

The F-Test for Multiple Regression Models

One test of the overall significance of the multiple regression equation is related to the coefficient of determination. The test statistic is the F-statistic, which is defined as

$$F = \frac{\text{Explained variation}/K}{\text{Unexplained variation}/[n - (K + 1)]}$$

The explained and unexplained variations were introduced above in our discussion of the determination of R^2. The values n and K have been defined as the number of observations and independent variables, respectively.

As you have seen in Tables 4.5 and 4.8, the F-statistic is a standard part of most computer regression outputs. The F-distribution is shown in Table 4.9 for a 5-percent level of significance. For our present example, the appropriate numbers of degrees of freedom are

Numerator = $K = 3$
Denominator = $n - (K + 1) = 12 - (3 + 1) = 8$

The critical value of the F-statistic is then found at the intersection of the third column and eighth row of Table 4.9. It is 4.07.

The hypothesis being tested by the F-statistic is $H_0: b_1 = b_2 = b_3 = 0$. If this is true, there would be no relationship between this set of independent variables and our dependent variable (MS). Since the calculated F-statistic (16.80 from Table 4.8) is greater than the critical value (4.07), the null hypothesis (H_0) can be rejected. We can conclude that the regression function does show a statistically significant relationship between the dependent variable (MS) and the set of independent variables included in the regression function (P, AD, and I).

The graph in Figure 4.7 further illustrates how well this regression model explains variations in Big Sky Foods' market share. We see that the estimated market share follows the actual market share quite well, except during the second quarter of 1984.

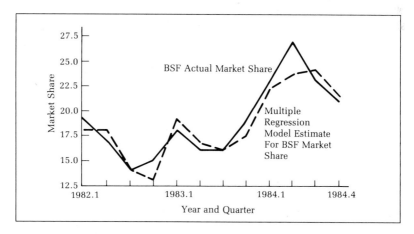

FIGURE 4.7   **Big Sky Foods' Market Share: Actual and First Estimate.**   The line representing the estimated market share for Big Sky Foods is derived from the following regression model (see Table 4.8): $\widehat{MS} = 80.011 - 8.458P + .020AD - 2.541I$.

TABLE 4.9
Critical Values of the *F*-Distribution at a 95-Percent Confidence Level

		Degrees of Freedom for the Numerator = K							
	1	2	3	4	5	6	7	8	9
1	161.4	199.5	215.7	224.6	230.2	234.0	236.8	238.9	240.5
2	18.51	19.00	19.16	19.25	19.30	19.33	19.35	19.37	19.38
3	10.13	9.55	9.28	9.12	9.01	8.94	8.89	8.85	8.81
4	7.71	6.94	6.59	6.39	6.26	6.16	6.09	6.04	6.00
5	6.61	5.79	5.41	5.19	5.05	4.95	4.88	4.82	4.77
6	5.99	5.14	4.76	4.53	4.39	4.28	4.21	4.15	4.10
7	5.59	4.74	4.35	4.12	3.97	3.87	3.79	3.73	3.68
8	5.32	4.46	4.07	3.84	3.69	3.58	3.50	3.44	3.39
9	5.12	4.26	3.86	3.63	3.48	3.37	3.29	3.23	3.18
10	4.96	4.10	3.71	3.48	3.33	3.22	3.14	3.07	3.02
11	4.84	3.98	3.59	3.36	3.20	3.09	3.01	2.95	2.90
12	4.75	3.89	3.49	3.26	3.11	3.00	2.91	2.85	2.80
13	4.67	3.81	3.41	3.18	3.03	2.92	2.83	2.77	2.71
14	4.60	3.74	3.34	3.11	2.96	2.85	2.76	2.70	2.65
15	4.54	3.68	3.29	3.06	2.90	2.79	2.71	2.64	2.59
16	4.49	3.63	3.24	3.01	2.85	2.74	2.66	2.59	2.54
17	4.45	3.59	3.20	2.96	2.81	2.70	2.61	2.55	2.49
18	4.41	3.55	3.16	2.93	2.77	2.66	2.58	2.51	2.46
19	4.38	3.52	3.13	2.90	2.74	2.63	2.54	2.48	2.42
20	4.35	3.49	3.10	2.87	2.71	2.60	2.51	2.45	2.39
21	4.32	3.47	3.07	2.84	2.68	2.57	2.49	2.42	2.37
22	4.30	3.44	3.05	2.82	2.66	2.55	2.46	2.40	2.34
23	4.28	3.42	3.03	2.80	2.64	2.53	2.44	2.37	2.32
24	4.26	3.40	3.01	2.78	2.62	2.51	2.42	2.36	2.30
25	4.24	3.39	2.99	2.76	2.60	2.49	2.40	2.34	2.28
26	4.23	3.37	2.98	2.74	2.59	2.47	2.39	2.32	2.27
27	4.21	3.35	2.96	2.73	2.57	2.46	2.37	2.31	2.25
28	4.20	3.34	2.95	2.71	2.56	2.45	2.36	2.29	2.24
29	4.18	3.33	2.93	2.70	2.55	2.43	2.35	2.28	2.22
30	4.17	3.32	2.92	2.69	2.53	2.42	2.33	2.27	2.21
40	4.08	3.23	2.84	2.61	2.45	2.34	2.25	2.18	2.12
60	4.00	3.15	2.76	2.53	2.37	2.25	2.17	2.10	2.04
120	3.92	3.07	2.68	2.45	2.29	2.17	2.09	2.02	1.96
∞	3.84	3.00	2.60	2.37	2.21	2.10	2.01	1.94	1.88

Degrees of Freedom for the Denominator $= n - (K + 1)$

Multicolinearity

Before leaving our discussion of the basic multiple linear regression model, we should discuss the problem referred to as *multicolinearity*. This problem can develop when the assumption of the independence of the independent variables is violated. If these variables are not independent, the regression results may not be reliable. In particular, the coefficients may be incorrectly estimated.

TABLE 4.9 (continued)
Critical Values of the *F*-Distribution at a 95-Percent Confidence Level

Degrees of Freedom for the Numerator = K									
10	12	15	20	24	30	40	60	120	∞
241.9	243.9	245.9	248.0	249.1	250.1	251.1	252.2	253.3	254.3
19.40	19.41	19.43	19.45	19.45	19.46	19.47	19.48	19.49	19.50
8.79	8.74	8.70	8.66	8.64	8.62	8.59	8.57	8.55	8.53
5.96	5.91	5.86	5.80	5.77	5.75	5.72	5.69	5.66	5.63
4.74	4.68	4.62	4.56	4.53	4.50	4.46	4.43	4.40	4.36
4.06	4.00	3.94	3.87	3.84	3.81	3.77	3.74	3.70	3.67
3.64	3.57	3.51	3.44	3.41	3.38	3.34	3.30	3.27	3.23
3.35	3.28	3.22	3.15	3.12	3.08	3.04	3.01	2.97	2.93
3.14	3.07	3.01	2.94	2.90	2.86	2.83	2.79	2.75	2.71
2.98	2.91	2.85	2.77	2.74	2.70	2.66	2.62	2.58	2.54
2.85	2.79	2.72	2.65	2.61	2.57	2.53	2.49	2.45	2.40
2.75	2.69	2.62	2.54	2.51	2.47	2.43	2.38	2.34	2.30
2.67	2.60	2.53	2.46	2.42	2.38	2.34	2.30	2.25	2.21
2.60	2.53	2.46	2.39	2.35	2.31	2.27	2.22	2.18	2.13
2.54	2.48	2.40	2.33	2.29	2.25	2.20	2.16	2.11	2.07
2.49	2.42	2.35	2.28	2.24	2.19	2.15	2.11	2.06	2.01
2.45	2.38	2.31	2.23	2.19	2.15	2.10	2.06	2.01	1.96
2.41	2.34	2.27	2.19	2.15	2.11	2.06	2.02	1.97	1.92
2.38	2.31	2.23	2.16	2.11	2.07	2.03	1.98	1.93	1.88
2.35	2.28	2.20	2.12	2.08	2.04	1.99	1.95	1.90	1.84
2.32	2.25	2.18	2.10	2.05	2.01	1.96	1.92	1.87	1.81
2.30	2.23	2.15	2.07	2.03	1.98	1.94	1.89	1.84	1.78
2.27	2.20	2.13	2.05	2.01	1.96	1.91	1.86	1.81	1.76
2.25	2.18	2.11	2.03	1.98	1.94	1.89	1.84	1.79	1.73
2.24	2.16	2.09	2.01	1.96	1.92	1.87	1.82	1.77	1.71
2.22	2.15	2.07	1.99	1.95	1.90	1.85	1.80	1.75	1.69
2.20	2.13	2.06	1.97	1.93	1.88	1.84	1.79	1.73	1.67
2.19	2.12	2.04	1.96	1.91	1.87	1.82	1.77	1.71	1.65
2.18	2.10	2.03	1.94	1.90	1.85	1.81	1.75	1.70	1.64
2.16	2.09	2.01	1.93	1.89	1.84	1.79	1.74	1.68	1.62
2.08	2.00	1.92	1.84	1.79	1.74	1.69	1.64	1.58	1.51
1.99	1.92	1.84	1.75	1.70	1.65	1.59	1.53	1.47	1.39
1.91	1.83	1.75	1.66	1.61	1.55	1.50	1.43	1.35	1.25
1.83	1.75	1.67	1.57	1.52	1.46	1.39	1.32	1.22	1.00

SOURCE: Reprinted with permission from *CRC Handbook of Tables for Probability and Statistics*, 1968. Copyright CRC Press, Inc., Boca Raton, Florida.

Two readily observable factors might indicate the existence of a multi-colinearity problem. First, if you observe that the standard errors of the coefficients are large, relative to the estimated coefficients, for variables you expect to be significant, there is some likelihood that multicolinearity exists. Second, if pairs of independent variables have high correlation coefficients, a multicolinearity problem may result. It is therefore important to examine the correlation coefficients for all pairs of the independent variables included in the regression.

For our market share regression, the correlation coefficients are

Variable Pair	Correlation Coefficients
AD, AD	1.000
AD, P	.468h
AD, I	−.092
P, P	1.000
P, I	−.590
I, I	1.000

Obviously, each variable is perfectly correlated with itself. Since none of the other correlation coefficients is particularly large, it is unlikely that there is a multicolinearity problem in this regression.

When multicolinearity exists, it does not necessarily mean that the regression function cannot be useful. The individual coefficients may not be reliable, but as a group they are likely to contain compensating errors. One may be too high, but another is likely to be too low. As a result, if your main interest is in using the regression for prediction, the entire function may perform satisfactorily.

Some things can be done to reduce multicolinearity problems. One is to use constant dollar terms when using money values. This removes the simultaneous effect of inflation from money-measured variables. You might also remove all but one of the highly intercorrelated variables from the regression.

4.5   USING DUMMY VARIABLES

Most of the variables you may want to use in developing a regression model are readily measurable with values that extend over a wide range. All of the examples we have used in this chapter have involved variables of this type. However, on occasion you may want to account for the effect of some event or attribute that has only two (or a few) possible cases. It either is or is not something. It either has or does not have some attribute. Some examples include the following: a month either is or is not June; a person either is or is not a woman; in a particular time period, there either was or was not a strike; a given quarter of the year either is or is not a second quarter; a teacher either has a doctorate or does not have one; a university either does or does not offer an MBA; and so forth.

A dummy variable (or several dummy variables) can be used to measure the effects of such seemingly qualitative attributes. A dummy variable is assigned a value of 1 or 0, depending on whether or not the particular observation has a given attribute. We will explain the use of dummy variables by looking at two examples.

Another Look at the Market Share Regression Model

The first example is an extension of the multiple linear regression we considered earlier dealing with a model of Big Sky Foods' market share. In that situation, we regressed the dependent variable market share (MS) on three independent variables: price (P), advertising (AD), and interest rate (I). The results of that regression are given in Table 4.8. It so happens that in the second quarter of 1984, another major firm had a fire that significantly reduced its production and sales. As an analyst, you might suspect that this event could have influenced the market share of all firms for that period. At the very least, it probably introduced some noise (error) into the data used for the regression and may have lowered the explanatory ability of the regression model.

   You can use a dummy variable to account for the influence of the fire on Big Sky Foods' market share and to measure its effect. To do so, simply create a new variable—call it D—that has a value of 0 for every observation except the second quarter of 1984 and a value of 1 for the second quarter of 1984. The data from Table 4.7 are reproduced in Table 4.10, along with the addition of this dummy variable.

   Using the data from Table 4.10 in a multiple regression analysis, we get the following equation for market share:

$$\widehat{MS} = 72.908 - 7.453P + .017AD - 2.245I + 4.132D$$
$$\quad\quad\quad (-3.84)\quad (7.05)\quad (-4.80)\quad (3.01)$$

The complete regression results are shown in the bottom of Table 4.10. The coefficient of the dummy variable representing the fire is 4.132. The fact that it is positive indicates that when there was a fire at a major competitor's facility, Big Sky Foods' market share increased. This certainly makes sense. In addition, we can say that that factor accounted for 4.132 percentage points of the 27-percent market share obtained during the second quarter of 1984.

   You should compare these regression results with those from Table 4.8. Note particularly the following:

1.   The adjusted R^2 increased from .812 to .906.

2.   The F-statistic increased from 16.80 to 27.54.

3.   The standard error of the estimate fell from 1.676 to 1.18.

TABLE 4.10
Big Sky Foods' Market Share Multiple Regression Data and Results

Observation	Market Share	Price	Advertising	Interest Rate	Dummy Variable
1982.1	19	5.20	500	11	0
1982.2	17	5.32	550	11	0
1982.3	14	5.48	550	12	0
1982.4	15	5.60	550	12	0
1983.1	18	5.80	550	9	0
1983.2	16	6.03	660	10	0
1983.3	16	6.01	615	10	0
1983.4	19	5.92	650	10	0
1984.1	23	5.90	745	9	0
1984.2	27	5.85	920	10	1
1984.3	23	5.80	1053	11	0
1984.4	21	5.85	950	11	0

Results

```
SMPL   1982.1 - 1984.4
12 Observations
LS // Dependent variable is MS
```

	COEFFICIENT	STANDARD ERROR	T-STATISTIC
C	72.908125	13.954634	5.2246532
P	-7.4530242	1.9385071	-3.8447238
AD	0.0173030	0.0024701	7.0454509
I	-2.2451057	0.4675622	-4.8017261
D	4.1323224	1.3738015	3.0079472

R squared	0.940254	Mean of dependent var	19.00000
Adjusted R squared	0.906113	SD of dependent var	3.861229
SE of regression	1.183117	Sum of squared resid	9.798362
Durbin-Watson stat	1.828370	F-statistic	27.54061
Log likelihood	-15.81111		

NOTE: MS = market share
       P = price
      AD = advertising
       I = interest rate
       D = dummy variable

It is clear that the regression with the dummy variable included is considerably better than the first model. This is further illustrated by the graph in Figure 4.8, which shows the actual market share and the market share as estimated with the multiple regression model above. Comparing Figure 4.8 with Figure 4.7 provides a good visual representation of how much the model is improved by adding the dummy variable to account for the abnormal influence in the second quarter of 1984.

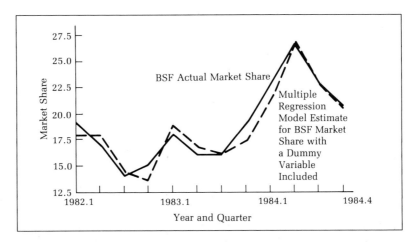

FIGURE 4.8   **Big Sky Foods' Market Share: Actual and Second Estimate.**   The line representing the estimated market share for Big Sky Foods is derived from the following regression model (see Table 4.10): $\widehat{MS} = 72.908 - 7.453P + .017AD - 2.245I + 4.132D$.

Accounting for Seasonality

As a second example of the use of dummy variables, let us look at how they can be used to account for seasonality. Table 4.11 contains data on a firm's quarterly sales over a 20-quarter period running from the first quarter of 1980 through the fourth quarter of 1984. This series of sales is also graphed in Figure 4.9. You see clearly in the graph that fourth-quarter sales are always high, while third quarters tend to have relatively low sales.

Three dummy variables can be used to identify and measure the seasonality in the firm's sales. (If you want to differentiate among M characteristics, $M - 1$ dummy variables will be used.) In Table 4.11, you see that for each second-quarter observation the dummy variable Q_2 has a value of 1, but Q_3 and Q_4 are 0. Note that for each first quarter none of the dummy variables has a value of 1. That is because first quarters are not second, third, or fourth quarters.

Let us first see what happens if we just estimate a simple time trend using sales as a function of time. The equation that results is

$$\widehat{Sales} = 12.605 + .352Time$$
$$(1.92)$$

This function is also plotted in the top graph of Figure 4.9. As you can see, it goes through the data without coming very close to any quarter's actual sales on a consistent basis. It is not surprising that the adjusted R^2 is only .123 for this model.

TABLE 4.11 **Seasonal Sales Data**

Observation	Time	Sales	Q_2	Q_3	Q_4
1980.1	1	12	0	0	0
1980.2	2	14	1	0	0
1980.3	3	10	0	1	0
1980.4	4	20	0	0	1
1981.1	5	13	0	0	0
1981.2	6	16	1	0	0
1981.3	7	12	0	1	0
1981.4	8	23	0	0	1
1982.1	9	13	0	0	0
1982.2	10	15	1	0	0
1982.3	11	11	0	1	0
1982.4	12	24	0	0	1
1983.1	13	14	0	0	0
1983.2	14	16	1	0	0
1983.3	15	13	0	1	0
1983.4	16	26	0	0	1
1984.1	17	15	0	0	0
1984.2	18	18	1	0	0
1984.3	19	14	0	1	0
1984.4	20	27	0	0	1

Now let us add the dummy variables to the regression model. The multiple regression model that results is

$$\widehat{Sales} = 11.094 + .256 Time + 2.144 Q_2 - 1.912 Q_3 + 9.831 Q_4$$
$$(7.26) \quad\quad (3.79) \quad\quad (-3.36) \quad\quad (17.10)$$

Complete regression results for both of these models are shown in Table 4.12. If we let Q_2, Q_3, and Q_4 equal 0, we get the first-quarter baseline, which is also graphed in the upper part of Figure 4.9. From the regression equation above, you can see that if all three dummy variables are set equal to 0, the first-quarter sales baseline is

First-quarter sales baseline $= 11.094 + .256 Time$

This is the function that would be used to make a point estimate for first-quarter sales.

The second-quarter dummy variable's coefficient (2.144) indicates that, on the average, second-quarter sales are 2.144 units *above* the first-quarter baseline. Similarly, third-quarter sales are, on the average, 1.912 units *below* the first-quarter baseline, while fourth-quarter sales are expected to be 9.831 units *above* that baseline.

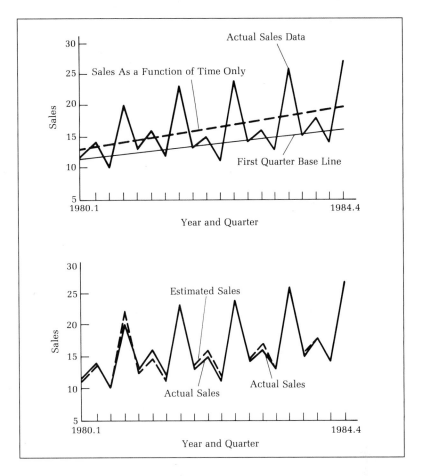

FIGURE 4.9   **Seasonal Sales Data.**   The top graph shows the sharp peaks and valleys of the pattern of the sales data along with the simple time trend line and the first-quarter baseline. The bottom graph shows estimated sales based on a trend model that includes quarterly dummy variables superimposed on the actual sales pattern. In many quarters, the estimated series performs so well that the two cannot be distinguished from one another.

Let us summarize some of the results of the two regression analyses of this firm's sales:

	Without Dummy Variables	With Dummy Variables
$\overline{R}^2$	.123	.969
F-statistic	3.67	148.50
Standard error or estimate	4.74	0.89

TABLE 4.12
Regression Results for Sales as a Function of Time and of Time and Dummy Variables (Q_2, Q_3, and Q_4) to Account for Seasonality

Sales as a Function of Time

```
SMPL  1980.1 - 1984.4
20 Observations
LS // Dependent variable is sales
```

	COEFFICIENT	STANDARD ERROR	T-STATISTIC
C	12.605263	2.2003632	5.7287193
Time	0.3518797	0.1836828	1.9156924

R squared	0.169354	Mean of dependent var	16.30000
Adjusted R squared	0.123207	SD of dependent var	5.058604
SE of regression	4.736737	Sum of squared resid	403.8602
Durbin-Watson stat	2.953488	F-statistic	3.669878
Log likelihood	-58.43213		

Sales as a Function of Time and Dummy Variables

```
SMPL  1980.1 - 1984.4
20 Observations
LS // Dependent variable is sales
```

	COEFFICIENT	STANDARD ERROR	T-STATISTIC
C	11.093750	0.5105935	21.727166
Time	0.2562500	0.0353185	7.2554062
Q2	2.1437500	0.5661985	3.7862164
Q3	-1.9125000	0.5694936	-3.3582469
Q4	9.8312500	0.5749434	17.099510

R squared	0.975370	Mean of dependent var	16.30000
Adjusted R squared	0.968802	SD of dependent var	5.058604
SE of regression	0.893495	Sum of squared resid	11.97500
Durbin-Watson stat	1.588518	F-statistic	148.5047
Log likelihood	-23.24966		

The model that includes the dummy variables to account for seasonality is clearly the superior model, and, as you have seen, the development of such a model is not difficult.

4.6   AUTOCORRELATION

Many times, business and economic applications of regression analysis rely on the use of time series data. In this chapter, we have seen examples of such applications in the estimation of a consumption function, the modeling of a firm's market share, and the development of a sales time trend (with and without seasonal dummy variables). In the use of such time series data, a problem known as autocorrelation can cause some difficulties.

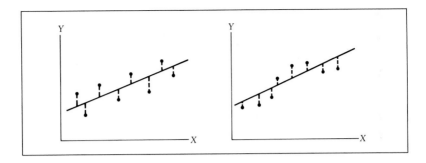

FIGURE 4.10 **Negative and Positive Autocorrelation Problems.** Negative auto-correlation is illustrated on the left, positive on the right. The residuals are indicated by dashed lines.

You will recall that one of the assumptions of the OLS regression model is that the error terms are normally distributed random variables with a mean of 0 and a constant variance. If this is true, we would not expect to find any regular pattern in the error terms. When a significant pattern is found in the error terms, autocorrelation is indicated.

Figure 4.10 illustrates the two possible cases of autocorrelation. In the left-hand graph, the case of negative autocorrelation is apparent. Negative autocorrelation exists when a negative error is followed by a positive error, then another negative error, and so on. The error terms alternate in sign. Positive autocorrelation is shown in the right-hand graph in Figure 4.10. In positive autocorrelation, positive errors tend to be followed by other positive errors, while negative errors are followed by other negative errors.

When autocorrelation exists, problems can develop in using and interpreting the OLS regression function. The existence of autocorrelation does not bias the coefficients that are estimated, but it does make the estimates of the standard errors smaller than the true standard errors. This means that the t-ratios calculated for each coefficient will be over-stated, which in turn may lead to the rejection of null hypotheses that should not have been rejected. That is, regression coefficients may be deemed statistically significant when indeed they are not. In addition, the existence of autocorrelation causes the $\overline{R}^2$ and F-statistics to be unreliable in evaluating the overall significance of the regression function.

There are a number of ways to test statistically for the existence of autocorrelation. The method most frequently used is the evaluation of the Durbin-Watson statistic (DW). This statistic is calculated as follows:

$$DW = \frac{\Sigma(e_t - e_{t-1})^2}{\Sigma e_t^{\,2}}$$

TABLE 4.13
Durbin-Watson Statistic (95-Percent Confidence Level)

n	K = 1		K = 2		K = 3		K = 4		K = 5	
	d_l	d_u	d_l	d_u	d_l	d_u	d_l	d_u	d_l	d_u
15	0.95	1.23	0.83	1.40	0.71	1.61	0.59	1.84	0.48	2.09
16	0.98	1.24	0.86	1.40	0.75	1.59	0.64	1.80	0.53	2.03
17	1.01	1.25	0.90	1.40	0.79	1.58	0.68	1.77	0.57	1.98
18	1.03	1.26	0.93	1.40	0.82	1.56	0.72	1.74	0.62	1.93
19	1.06	1.28	0.96	1.41	0.86	1.55	0.76	1.72	0.66	1.90
20	1.08	1.28	0.99	1.41	0.89	1.55	0.79	1.70	0.70	1.87
21	1.10	1.30	1.01	1.41	0.92	1.54	0.83	1.69	0.73	1.84
22	1.12	1.31	1.04	1.42	0.95	1.54	0.86	1.68	0.77	1.82
23	1.14	1.32	1.06	1.42	0.97	1.54	0.89	1.67	0.80	1.80
24	1.16	1.33	1.08	1.43	1.00	1.54	0.91	1.66	0.83	1.79
25	1.18	1.34	1.10	1.43	1.02	1.54	0.94	1.65	0.86	1.77
26	1.19	1.35	1.12	1.44	1.04	1.54	0.96	1.65	0.88	1.76
27	1.21	1.36	1.13	1.44	1.06	1.54	0.99	1.64	0.91	1.75
28	1.22	1.37	1.15	1.45	1.08	1.54	1.01	1.64	0.93	1.74
29	1.24	1.38	1.17	1.45	1.10	1.54	1.03	1.63	0.96	1.73
30	1.25	1.38	1.18	1.46	1.12	1.54	1.05	1.63	0.98	1.73
31	1.26	1.39	1.20	1.47	1.13	1.55	1.07	1.63	1.00	1.72
32	1.27	1.40	1.21	1.47	1.15	1.55	1.08	1.63	1.02	1.71
33	1.28	1.41	1.22	1.48	1.16	1.55	1.10	1.63	1.04	1.71
34	1.29	1.41	1.24	1.48	1.17	1.55	1.12	1.63	1.06	1.70
35	1.30	1.42	1.25	1.48	1.19	1.55	1.13	1.63	1.07	1.70
36	1.31	1.43	1.26	1.49	1.20	1.56	1.15	1.63	1.09	1.70
37	1.32	1.43	1.27	1.49	1.21	1.56	1.16	1.62	1.10	1.70
38	1.33	1.44	1.28	1.50	1.23	1.56	1.17	1.62	1.12	1.70
39	1.34	1.44	1.29	1.50	1.24	1.56	1.19	1.63	1.13	1.69
40	1.35	1.45	1.30	1.51	1.25	1.57	1.20	1.63	1.15	1.69
45	1.39	1.48	1.34	1.53	1.30	1.58	1.25	1.63	1.21	1.69
50	1.42	1.50	1.38	1.54	1.34	1.59	1.30	1.64	1.26	1.69
55	1.45	1.52	1.41	1.56	1.37	1.60	1.33	1.64	1.30	1.69
60	1.47	1.54	1.44	1.57	1.40	1.61	1.37	1.65	1.33	1.69
65	1.49	1.55	1.46	1.59	1.43	1.62	1.40	1.66	1.36	1.69
70	1.51	1.57	1.48	1.60	1.45	1.63	1.42	1.66	1.39	1.70
75	1.53	1.58	1.50	1.61	1.47	1.64	1.45	1.67	1.42	1.70
80	1.54	1.59	1.52	1.62	1.49	1.65	1.47	1.67	1.44	1.70
85	1.56	1.60	1.53	1.63	1.51	1.65	1.49	1.68	1.46	1.71
90	1.57	1.61	1.55	1.64	1.53	1.66	1.50	1.69	1.48	1.71
95	1.58	1.62	1.56	1.65	1.54	1.67	1.52	1.69	1.50	1.71
100	1.59	1.63	1.57	1.65	1.55	1.67	1.53	1.70	1.51	1.72

SOURCE: From J. Durbin and G.S. Watson, "Testing for Serial Correlation in Least Squares Regression," *Biometrika*, 38 (1951): 159–177. Reprinted with the permission of the authors and the trustees of *Biometrika*.

NOTE: K = number of independent variables
          n = number of observations

where e_t is the residual for time period t and e_{t-1} is the residual for the preceding time period $(t-1)$. Almost all computer printouts for regression analysis include the Durbin-Watson statistic, so you are not likely to ever have to calculate it directly.

The *DW* statistic will always be in the range of 0 to 4. As a rule of thumb, a value close to 2 indicates that there is no autocorrelation. As the value of the *DW* statistic approaches 4, the degree of negative autocorrelation increases. As the value of *DW* approaches 0, positive autocorrelation appears more severe.

To be more precise in evaluating the significance and meaning of the calculated *DW* statistic, we must refer to a Durbin-Watson table, such as Table 4.13. Note that for each number of independent variables (K), two columns of values labeled d_l and d_u are given. The values in these columns for the appropriate number of observations (n) are used in evaluating the calculated value of *DW*, as shown in Table 4.14.

TABLE 4.14   **Evaluating the Durbin-Watson Statistic**

Test	Value of the Calculated *DW*	Result
1	$(4 - d_l) < DW < 4$	Negative autocorrelation exists
2	$(4 - d_u) < DW < (4 - d_l)$	Result is indeterminate
3	$2 < DW < (4 - d_u)$	No autocorrelation exists
4	$d_u < DW < 2$	
5	$d_l < DW < d_u$	Result is indeterminate
6	$0 < DW < d_l$	Positive autocorrelation exists

Let us now evaluate for autocorrelation two of the applications of regression analysis used in this chapter. First, consider the market share model in which market share was estimated as a function of price, advertising, interest rate, and a dummy variable accounting for a fire in a competitor's facilities. Part of those regression results are reproduced below:

$$\widehat{MS} = 72.908 - 7.453P + .017AD = 2.245I + 4.132D$$
$$DW = 1.83$$

Using Table 4.13 for $K = 4$ independent variables and for $n = 15$ observations (we only had 12 observations, but since the table does not go that low, we will use 15 to illustrate), we find

$$d_l = 0.59$$
$$d_u = 1.84$$

We can use these values to evaluate each of the six tests shown in Table 4.14 for our *DW* of 1.83. In doing so, we find that only the conditions in test 5 are met.

Test 5: $d_l < DW < d_u$
         $.59 < 1.83 < 1.84$

Thus, we can only conclude that the Durbin-Watson test is indeterminate in this case.

Now let us look at the time trend analysis of sales with dummy variables to account for seasonality. The relevant part of those regression results are given below:

$$\widehat{Sales} = 11.094 + .256Time + 2.144Q2 - 1.1912Q3 + 9.831Q4$$
$$DW = 1.589$$

Using Table 4.13 for $K = 4$ independent variables and for $n = 20$ observations, we find

$$d_l = .79$$
$$d_u = 1.70$$

These values, along with our DW of 1.589, are then used to evaluate each of the six tests in Table 4.14. We find that only the conditions in test 5 are met:

Test 5: $.79 < 1.589 < 1.70$

Again, in this case, we have an indeterminate result. There is not enough evidence to say that positive autocorrelation exists but not enough to be sure that it is not a problem either.

Try using the Durbin-Watson test yourself.[5] In the simple time trend without dummy variables, we found that

$$Sales = 12.61 + .35Time$$

There were 20 observations, and DW was 2.953. Use the six tests in Table 4.10 to evaluate autocorrelation.

You might well ask: What causes autocorrelation and what can be done about it? A primary cause of autocorrelation is the existence of long-term cycles and trends in economic and business data. Such trends and cycles are particularly likely to produce positive autocorrelation. Autocorrelation can also be caused by a misspecification of the model. Either leaving out one or more important variables or failing to include a nonlinear term when one is called for can be a cause.

We can try several relatively simple things to reduce autocorrelation. One is to use first differences of the variables rather than the actual values when performing the regression analysis. That is, use the change in each variable from period to period in the regression. For example, in the market share regression, we might use the following function:

$$\Delta MS = f(\Delta P, \Delta AD, \Delta I, D)$$

---

[5]From Table 4.12, you should have found $d_l = 1.08$ and $d_u = 1.28$. In this case, only the conditions in test 3 are satisfied, so you would conclude that no autocorrelation exists.

where Δ represents the *change in*. (Note that it would not make sense to use ΔD, so that variable would be left in its original form.) Another possibility would be to add a linear trend, or time, variable if one has not already been included. For our market share problem, you might try

$$MS = f(PRICE, ADVERTISING, INTEREST\ RATE, DUMMY, TIME)$$

where $T = 1$ for the first quarter of data and $T = 12$ for the last observation in that data set. Finally, you could try introducing nonlinear terms, such as the square of one or more of the independent variables or even the cross products of two independent variables.

4.7 NONLINEAR REGRESSION MODELS

All of the regression models we have looked at so far have been linear. Some have had one independent variable, while others have had several independent variables, but all have been linear. Linear functions appear to work very well in many situations. However, cases do arise in which nonlinear models are called for.

In some situations, the economic theory underlying a relationship may lead us to expect a nonlinear relationship. Examples of such cases include the U-shaped average cost functions and S-shaped production functions, both of which are caused by the existence of the law of variable proportions or diminishing marginal returns. Profit and revenue functions often increase at a decreasing rate and then decline, shaped somewhat like an inverted U.

Earlier in this chapter, we suggested plotting data in a scattergram before doing a regression analysis. Among other things, this may help us decide on the appropriate form for the model. Perhaps some nonlinear form would appear more consistent with the data than would a linear function.

Quadratic Functions

Look now at the two graphs in Figure 4.11. The data for the scattergrams depicted in each graph are listed to the right of the graphs. In the upper graph, the 10 observations appear to form a U-shaped function such as one might expect of an average variable cost curve. The lower scattergram suggests a function that increases at a decreasing rate and then eventually declines. Clearly, a linear function would not fit either set of data very well.

These scattergrams are indicative of quadratic functions, that is, functions in which X^2 appears as an independent variable. But most regression programs are designed for linear problems. How can we use such programs to estimate this type of function? The answer is surprisingly simple. We

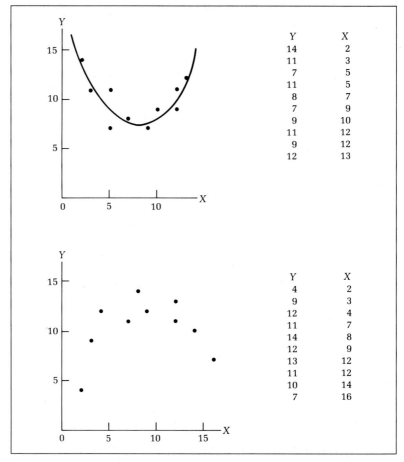

FIGURE 4.11   **Quadratic Functions.**   The OLS model for the upper graph is $\hat{Y} = 18.26 - 2.7X + .17X^2$. The data in the lower graph yield the following OLS model: $\hat{Y} = 1.73 + 2.49X - .14X^2$.

need only define a new variable to be the square of X. Let us use Z. Then $Z = X^2$. We can now estimate a multiple linear regression model of $Y = f(X, Z)$, which may be expressed as

$$Y = a + b_1X + b_2Z$$

This is a function that is linear in the variables X and Z.

Estimating a function such as this for the data in the upper graph of Figure 4.11, we get

$$\hat{Y} = 18.26 - 2.71X + .17Z$$
$$(-4.49) \quad (4.37)$$
$$\overline{R}^2 = .669$$

(Values for t-ratios are in parentheses.) But remember that $Z = X^2$. Rewriting the function in terms of Y, X, and X^2, we have

$$\hat{Y} = 18.26 - 2.71X + .17X^2$$

This is a quadratic function in X and has the U-shape we would expect to fit the scattergram. To get a visual image of how well this functions fits, we can estimate values for Y using this equation for X values ranging from 1 to 15. We get the following pairs of numbers:

X	$\hat{Y}$
1	15.7
2	13.5
3	11.7
4	10.1
5	9.0
6	8.1
7	7.6
8	7.5
9	7.6
10	8.1
11	9.0
12	10.2
13	11.8
14	13.6
15	15.9

The line formed by these 15 points is plotted on the lower graph in Figure 4.11. You will agree that it fits the data points quite well.

The data in the lower graph in Figure 4.11 also appear to be quadratic, but this time the function at first goes up and then down (rather than vice versa, as in the previous case). Let us again let $Z = X^2$ and proceed to estimate:

$$Y = a + b_1X + b_2Z$$

This time we expect the sign of b_1 to be positive and the sign of b_2 to be negative. (The opposite was true in the previous case.) The regression results are

$$\hat{Y} = 1.73 + 2.49X - .14Z$$
$$\quad\quad\quad (4.81) \quad (-4.70)$$
$$\overline{R}^2 = .701$$

(Values for t-ratios are in parentheses.) Substituting X^2 for Z, we have

$$\hat{Y} = 1.73 + 2.49X - .14X^2$$

This function would have the inverted U shape the data would suggest. Complete the following table based on the above equation, and on the lower graph in Figure 4.11 plot each pair of X, Y values. Then connect those points with a smooth line.

X	$\hat{Y}$
1	
2	
3	
4	
5	
6	
7	
8	
9	
10	
11	
12	
13	
14	
15	

Cubic Functions

Now take a look at the scattergrams and data shown in Figure 4.12. The data in the upper graph might represent a cost function, while that in the lower graph may be a production function. Both are polynomials, but they are cubic functions, rather than quadratic functions.

To estimate these cubic functions using a multiple linear regression program, let $Z = X^2$ and $W = X^3$. The linear function is then

$$Y = a + b_1X + b_2Z + b_3W$$

For the data in the upper graph in Figure 4.12, we get

$$\hat{Y} = 1.02 + 1.63X - .31Z + .021W$$
$$(1.15) \quad (-1.26) \quad (1.80)$$
$$\bar{R}^2 = .925$$

(Values for t-ratios are in parentheses.) Substituting X^2 for Z and X^3 for W, we get

$$\hat{Y} = 1.02 + 1.63X - .31X^2 + .21X^3$$

Construct a table of 15 X values from 1 through 15 and use this equation to calculate the corresponding values for $\hat{Y}$. Then plot the 15 points and connect them with a smooth line to see how well this equation fits the data.

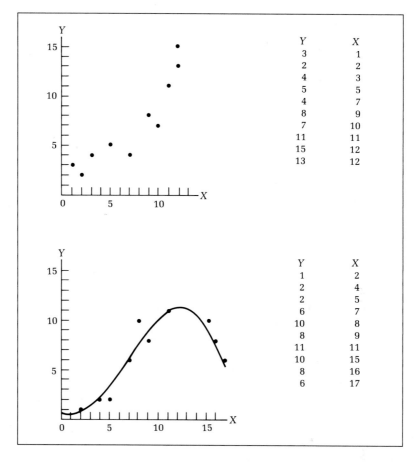

FIGURE 4.12   **Cubic Functions.**   The OLS model for the upper graph is $\hat{Y} = 1.02 +$ $1.63X - .31X^2 + .021X^3$. The data in the lower graph yield the following OLS model: $\hat{Y} = 1.03 - .80X + .33X^2 - .016X^3$.

You might be puzzled about why the t-ratios are fairly low even though the function fits the data pretty well. The main reason is related to the small number of data points relative to the number of variables. You would rarely do a regression analysis with just ten observations, especially when using three independent variables.

The lower scattergram in Figure 4.12 appears to have two turning points: one near $X = 6$ and the other in the vicinity of $X = 11$. This indicates that a cubic function might again be appropriate. We again let $Z = X^2$ and $W = X^3$, and estimate the function:

$$Y = a + b_1X + b_2Z + b_3W$$

The results are

$$\hat{Y} = 1.03 - .80X + .33Z - .016W$$
$$\quad\quad\quad\quad (-.65)\ \ (2.16)\ (-2.89)$$
$$\overline{R}^2 = .891$$

(Values for t-ratios are in parentheses.) Substituting X^2 for Z and X^3 for W, we have

$$\hat{Y} = 1.03 - .80X + .33X^2 - .016X^3$$

This time we have used 15 X values between 1 and 15 to solve for the corresponding values of $\hat{Y}$. These $\hat{Y}$ values have been plotted and connected with a smooth line to show how well the function represents the data in the scattergram.

Reciprocal Functions

Now let us focus our attention on the scattergrams and data in Figure 4.13. In the upper graph, we see that the Y values fall rapidly as X increases at first, but then as X continues to increase, the Y value seems to level off. The lower graph is similar except that, as X increases, at first Y increases rapidly but seems to reach a plateau. With either kind of pattern, consider using a *reciprocal transformation*; that is, use $1/X$ rather than X as the dependent variable.

We will let $U = 1/X$ and proceed to estimate the function:

$$Y = a + bU$$

For the upper graph the results are

$$\hat{Y} = 5.91 + 16.52U$$
$$\quad\quad\quad\quad (4.54)$$
$$R^2 = .720$$

(The value for the t-ratio is in parentheses.) Substituting $1/X$ for U, we have

$$\hat{Y} = 5.91 + 16.52(1/X)$$

This function is plotted on the upper graph in Figure 4.13. As X increases, the function approaches the value of the constant term of the regression ($a = 5.91$) from above. With the same method for the lower graph in Figure 4.13, the regression results yield

$$\hat{Y} = 12.38 - 11.53(1/X)$$
$$\quad\quad\quad\quad (-7.65)$$
$$R^2 = .880$$

Try plotting this function on the lower graph in Figure 4.13. As X increases, this function also approaches the value of the constant term of the regression ($a = 12.38$), but from below rather than above.

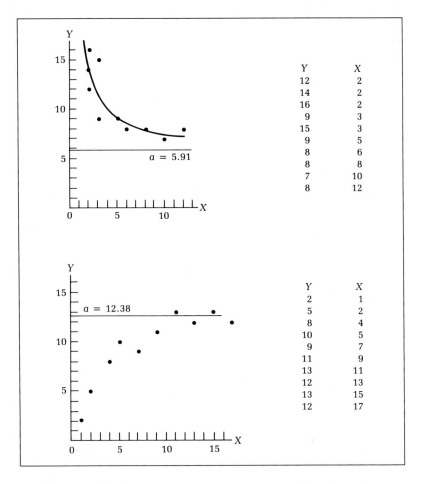

FIGURE 4.13 **Reciprocal Functions.** The OLS model for the upper graph on the left is $\hat{Y} = 5.91 + 16.52(1/X)$. The data in the lower graph yield the following OLS model: $\hat{Y} = 12.38 - 11.53(1/X)$.

Multiplicative Functions

The final type of nonlinear function we will consider involves a double-log transformation. This allows us to use a multiple linear regression program to estimate the following function form:

$$Y = AX_1^{b_1}X_2^{b_2}$$

Functions of this type are called power functions or multiplicative functions. The most common of these functions is the Cobb-Douglas production function. The general form for such a function is

$$Q = AL^{b_1}K^{b_2}$$

where Q is output, L is labor input, and K is capital.

These functions are clearly nonlinear, so we must use some transformation to get them into a linear form. If we take the logarithms of both sides of the equation, we get

$$Y = AX_1^{b_1}X_2^{b_2}$$
$$\ln Y = \ln A + b_1 \ln X_1 + b_2 \ln X_2$$

where ln represents the natural logarithm. Now, let $W = \ln Y$, $U = \ln X_1$, $V = \ln X_2$, and $a = \ln A$. The function is now linear in W, U, and V, as shown:

$$W = a + b_1 U + b_2 V$$

This function can be estimated using a standard multiple regression program.

For example, consider the data in Table 4.15. Y is the dependent variable, X_1 and X_2 are independent variables, and we would like to estimate the following function:

$$Y = AX_1^{b_1}X_2^{b_2}$$

We find the natural logarithms of all three variables ($W = \ln Y$, $U = \ln X_1$, and $V = \ln X_2$). These values are also shown in Table 4.15. Most computer regression programs have this type of transformation function, so you normally never even see the logarithms of your data.

TABLE 4.15 **Data for a Power Function**

Y	X_1	X_2	$W = \ln Y$	$U = \ln X_1$	$V = \ln X_2$
39.73	1	15	3.682	0.000	2.708
55.37	8	5	4.014	2.079	1.609
41.59	2	9	3.728	0.693	2.197
69.75	6	10	4.245	1.792	2.303
52.25	4	8	3.956	1.386	2.079
87.31	10	11	4.469	2.303	2.398
52.37	5	7	3.958	1.609	1.946
96.60	12	12	4.571	2.485	2.485
66.60	7	8	4.199	1.946	2.079
92.83	9	13	4.531	2.197	2.565

Using the natural logarithms as the variables, we estimate the following multiple linear regression:

$$\hat{W} = 2.401 + .408U + .475V$$
$$\phantom{\hat{W} = 2.401 + } (53.02) \quad (25.86)$$
$$\overline{R}^2 = .997$$

(Values for t-ratios are in parentheses.) Making the appropriate substitutions for W, U, and V, we have

$$\ln Y = 2.401 + .408 \ln X_1 + .475 \ln X_2$$

Taking the antilogarithm of the equation, we obtain

$$Y = (e^{2.401})X_1^{.408}X_2^{.475}$$

where e represents the Naperian number (2.7183), which is the base for natural logarithms. Thus,

$$Y = (2.7183)^{2.401}X_1^{.408}X_2^{.475}$$
$$Y = 11.03X_1^{.408}X_2^{.475}$$

This fairly complex-looking function can be estimated with relative ease using the power of multiple regression and the logarithmic transformation.

Power or multiplicative functions such as this are not only commonly found as production functions but are also sometimes used for utility functions and for demand functions. You will have the opportunity to estimate such functions in several later chapters.

SUMMARY

Regression analysis is a statistical tool that is useful in estimating the functional relationship between a dependent variable and one or more independent variables. It is up to the analyst to pick the variables that are used in the model being constructed and to select an appropriate measurement for each variable.

Simple linear regression, or bivariate linear regression, is based on the following assumptions:

1. The value of the dependent variable (Y) is assumed to be dependent on the value of the independent variable (X). Furthermore, Y is assumed to be a random variable, while X may or may not be a random variable.

2. The relationship between Y and X is assumed to be linear.

3. For each X value, there is a probability distribution for the Y values.

4. The error terms from the regression estimates are assumed to be a normally distributed random variable with a mean of 0 and a constant variance.

In addition, multiple regression analysis incorporates the following assumptions:

5. The number of observations is greater than the number of variables.

6. The independent variables are assumed to be statistically independent of one another.

Regression models can be evaluated using statistical tests (called summary statistics) to determine their adequacy. The regression coefficients are evaluated using t-tests, and the significance of the overall model is tested using an F-test. The coefficient of determination tells us the percentage of variation in the dependent variable that is explained by the regression model. The standard error of the estimate (also called the standard error of the regression) and the sum of the squared errors (or residuals) are also useful in evaluating regression models. The Durbin-Watson statistic helps in determining if autocorrelation is a problem in time series models. All of these evaluative statistics are a standard part of the output from most computer regression programs.

Even though the basic regression model is designed to estimate linear relationships, nonlinear models can be estimated by using various transformations of the variables. Polynomial functions can be estimated by using second, third, and/or higher powers of one or more of the independent variables. Logarithmic and reciprocal transformations are also commonly used.

SUGGESTED READINGS

Draper, N.R., and Smith, H. *Applied Regression Analysis*. New York: John Wiley & Sons, 1966.

Faub, Leon. "Econometrics Made Easy." *The Conference Board Record*, May 1972, pp. 60–64.

Frank, Charles R., Jr. *Statistics and Econometrics*. New York: Holt, Rinehart, & Winston, 1971.

Kimenta, Jan. *Elements of Econometrics*. New York: Macmillan, 1971.

McLagan, Donald L. "A Noneconometrician's Guide to Econometrics." *Business Economics*, May 1973, pp. 38–45.

Pindyck, Robert S., and Rubinfeld, Daniel L. *Econometric Models and Economic Forecasts*. New York: McGraw-Hill, 1981.

PROBLEMS

1. A slide rule manufacturer has the following sales data for 1971–1981 (sales are in thousands of units):

Year	Sales
1971	950
1972	880
1973	750
1974	680
1975	540
1976	420
1977	300
1978	290
1979	280
1980	200
1981	170

a. Plot these sales on the grid provided:

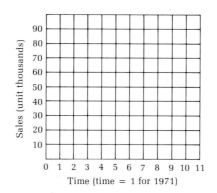

Time (time = 1 for 1971)

b. Estimate a simple linear time trend for the sales data (*Time* = 1 for
    1971, 2 for 1972, etc.):

$$Sales = f(Time)$$
$$Sales = a + b(Time)$$

Write the function you estimate below:

    Sales = _____

c. What does the value of the slope term b tell you? Is it statistically
    significant at a 95-percent confidence level?
d. How good a fit does this simple linear time trend give? Base your
    response on the coefficient of determination.
e. Evaluate autocorrelation for this model.

2. Use the following data to estimate a simple linear regression function
    of sales as a function of income:

Observation	Sales	Income	Observation	Sales	Income
1	1000	$4000	6	800	$2900
2	800	3000	7	1000	4600
3	900	3700	8	700	2700
4	1100	4400	9	1200	5000
5	1500	5900	10	600	2400

a. Write the regression equation using S to represent sales and I to
    represent income:

    Sales = $f(I)$ = _____

b. Interpret the value of the constant, or intercept, term and of the
    slope term in the equation.

c. Is the coefficient for the income variable significantly different from 0 at a 95-percent confidence level?

d. What level of sales in units would you predict if income was $4200? What if income was $6800? Are there any problems with making the latter estimate?

e. What 95-percent confidence interval would you estimate for sales at an income level of 4200?

3. Graph the 12 data points given below in the space provided:

Y	X	Y	X
0	0	80	6
2	1	91	7
7	2	90	8
19	3	79	9
41	4	68	10
65	5	37	11

a. Since, these data appear to have the general shape of a cubic function, try fitting the following form:

$$Y = f(X, X^2, X^3) = a + b_1X + b_2X^2 + b_3X^3$$

Write your equation below:

Y = _____

b. Graph the equation you found in part a using integer values of X from 1 to 11 on the grid provided. Does it appear to fit the data well?

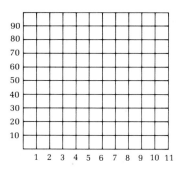

c. What does the adjusted R^2 tell you about how well your model fits the data?

d. Do the coefficients have the signs you would expect? Explain why or why not.

e. Are the coefficients statistically significant at a 95-percent confidence level? Explain.

4. Janis Brown is the new director of parks for the state. She has been concerned about the amount of money being budgeted for promoting usage of the park system. Her total budget has been cut, and she wants to revise the promotional budget downward but is fearful that usage may drop so much that the park system will no longer be fulfilling the governor's objective of having at least 18 million people per year use the state's parks. Before her arrival as director of parks, the department had developed the following linear relationship showing how use (*U*) was related to promotional expenditures (*PE*):

$$U = 10.1 + .0038PE$$

This function was estimated based on the following set of 14 observations, where usage (*U*) is in millions of park visitors and promotional expenditures (*PE*) are in thousands of dollars:

Year	Usage	Promotional Expenditures	Year	Usage	Promotional Expenditures
1971	6	320	1978	16	1320
1972	14	400	1979	17	1410
1973	12	500	1980	17	1700
1974	10	590	1981	19	2010
1975	14	700	1982	17	2190
1976	14	900	1983	18	2400
1977	17	1100	1984	19	2720

a. Using the function given above, estimate the number of park visitors Janis could expect if she cut the budget to $1,500,000?

Number of visitors = usage = _____

Will this satisfy the governor's objective?

b. Plot the usage and promotional expenditures data on the grid below:

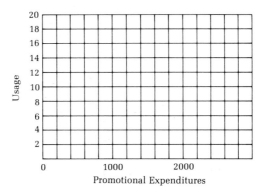

c. Having plotted the data, you see that a nonlinear function may fit it better than a linear function. Use a regression program to estimate the following function:

$$U = a + b(1/PE) = \underline{\hspace{4cm}}$$

Is the coefficient of the reciprocal of *PE* positive or negative? Does that make sense? Statistically, is it significantly different than 0 at the 95-percent confidence level? How can you tell?

d. What is the value of the coefficient of determination for the function you estimated in part c? What does this value tell you?

e. Use your equation to estimate the number of visitors to the parks Janis Brown would expect if she cuts the promotional budget to $1,500,000:

$$\text{Number of visitors} = \text{usage} = \underline{\hspace{4cm}}$$

Would this number satisfy the governor's objective?

f. In which estimate (the one from part a or the one from part e) would you have the most confidence? Explain why.

g. Plot both of these functions on the grid used in part b. Use the following values for *PE*: 200, 400, 600, 800, 1000, 1200, 1400, 1600, 1800, 2000, 2200, 2400, 2600, and 2800. Which function appears to fit the data best?

5. Sure-Skate Enterprises began making roller skates in 1973 and has been keeping track of the percentage of buyers from whom they have had complaints over the years. Donald Clark is the quality control manager of Sure-Skate. Anna Marsh, the director of public relations, has asked Donald to give her an estimate of the percentage of buyers who will be likely to write in with a complaint during each of the next two years. It is Anna's department that responds to each complaint, and she wants to forecast her personnel needs for the coming years. Donald has the following data available on which to base his estimate:

Year	Percent Complaints	Year	Percent Complaints
1973	19.2	1979	6.1
1974	22.1	1980	5.0
1975	12.0	1981	4.9
1976	10.8	1982	5.2
1977	7.2	1983	5.1
1978	8.1	1984	4.8

a. Letting *Time* = 1 for 1973 and 12 for 1984 and *PC* = percent complaints, estimate the following regression equations:

$$PC = a + bTime = \underline{\hspace{5cm}}$$

$$PC = a + b(1/Time) = \underline{\hspace{4cm}}$$

b. Which of the above equations represents a linear function and which represents a nonlinear function?

c. Which equation does the better job of modeling how the percent complaints has varied over the years? Explain the basis for your answer.

d. Use both equations to forecast the percent complaints for 1985, 1986, and 1987. Which set of projections seems the most reasonable? Why?

6. The following regression results were obtained in a study of faculty salaries at a small college:

Variable	Coefficient	Standard Error	T-Ratio
Constant	12,900	5160	2.50
YRS	800	160	_____
DEGR	3500	_____	3.50
PUB	400	160	_____
SEX	−1200	_____	−4.00

NOTE: Adjusted R^2 = .782
$n = 42$
SE of the regression = 1850
F-ratio = 88.4

where YRS is years of teaching experience; DEGR is 1 if the faculty member has a doctorate and 0 otherwise; PUB is the number of publications the faculty member has had in the past five years; and SEX is 1 if the faculty member is a female and 0 otherwise.

a. Fill in the four blanks in the table of regression results.

b. Write the regression equation below:

Salary = \underline{\hspace{6cm}}

c. Are all the variables statistically significant at a 95-percent confidence level? Why or why not?

d. What does the adjusted R^2 tell you?

e. Use this equation to estimate the faculty salary for a woman with 12 years' teaching experience, four publications, and a doctorate in Russian literature.

Salary = \underline{\hspace{6cm}}

    f.   Interpret each of the coefficients. That is, write out an explanation of what each one tells you.

    g.   On the basis of this information, does there appear to be sex discrimination in salaries? If so, does it favor men or women? Explain your answers.

7. Suppose that you observe the following 11 data points for two variables, Y and X:

Y	X	Y	X
0	0	72	6
30	1	52	7
51	2	50	8
42	3	29	9
60	4	21	10
71	5		

    a.   Find the simple bivariate linear regression for

$$Y = f(X) = a + bX$$

Evaluate the statistical significance of this function.

    b.   Now plot the 11 points on the grid below:

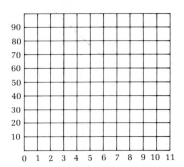

Based on this graph, does the relationship between Y and X appear linear? Draw the regression line estimated in part a on the graph.

    c.   Since the points appear to form a parabola, try fitting the following function:

$$Y = f(X, X^2) = a + b_1 X + b_2 X^2$$

Write your equation below:

$$Y = \underline{\hspace{6cm}}$$

Evaluate the statistical significance of this function. Does it provide a better fit than the linear function? Do the coefficients for X and X^2 have the signs you would expect? Explain.

d. Use integer values of X from 1 to 10 to plot the function estimated in part c on the graph in part b.

8. For 12 metropolitan areas in Michigan, retail auto sales (AS) in thousands of dollars, the number of people 25 years old and older (NPOP25) in thousands of people, and the median household effective buying income in thousands of dollars (MHEBI) are given below (data are for 1980):

Metropolitan Area	AS	MHEBI	NPOP25
1. Ann Arbor	185,792	23,409	133.17
2. Battle Creek	85,643	19,215	110.86
3. Bay City	97,101	20,374	68.04
4. Benton Harbor	100,249	16,107	99.59
5. Detroit	3,775,952	24,464	2,524.44
6. Flint	527,817	23,432	289.52
7. Grand Rapids	403,916	19,426	339.98
8. Jackson	78,283	18,742	89.53
9. Kalamazoo	188,756	18,553	155.78
10. Lansing	329,531	21,953	248.95
11. Muskegon	91,944	16,358	102.13
12. Saginaw	130,056	23,175	128.07

SOURCE: "1981 Survey of Buying Power," *Sales and Marketing Management*, July 27, 1981, pp. B1–B44 and C1–C228.

a. Use these data to estimate the multiple linear regression for auto sales as a function of median household effective buying income and the population age 25 and older. That is, for

$$AS = a + b_1 MHEBI + b_2 NPOP25$$

Find the values for a, b_1, and b_2.

b. What is the coefficient of determination for your regression model? Interpret its meaning.

c. Do each of the coefficients you have estimated have the expected sign? Are they statistically significant at a 95-percent confidence level? How can you tell?

9. For the 12 metropolitan areas identified in problem 8, food sales (FS) in thousands of dollars and population (POP) in thousands are given along with MHEBI in the table below (data are for 1980):

Area	MHEBI	FS	POP
1	23,409	153,186	267.4
2	19,215	121,058	187.9
3	20,374	108,604	120.0
4	16,107	173,921	171.7
5	24,464	4,411,732	4,345.0
6	23,432	469,726	522.6
7	19,426	349,649	607.1
8	18,742	82,357	152.0
9	18,553	199,942	281.2
10	21,953	354,617	472.4
11	16,358	121,155	179.8
12	23,175	215,614	228.7

SOURCE: "1981 Survey of Buying Power," *Sales and Marketing Management*, July 27, 1981, pp. B1–B44 and C1–C228.

a. Based on these data, estimate a multiple linear regression model of food sales as a function of median household effective buying income and population. Write your equation below:

FS = _____

b. Are the signs for the independent variables as you would expect? Explain why or why not. Are the independent variables both statistically significant at a 95-percent confidence level?

c. How good is this model in explaining variations in retail food sales for these Michigan metropolitan areas?

10. Once more, let us look at the 12 Michigan metropolitan areas identified in problem 8. Based on the following 1980 data, total retail sales (TRS) in thousands of dollars can be estimated as a function of median household effective buying income (MHEBI) and the number of households (HSHLDS) in thousands:

Area	TRS	MHEBI	HSHLDS
1	1,197,114	23,409	95.1
2	626,549	19,215	67.5
3	512,697	20,374	41.9
4	726,312	16,107	61.1
5	20,790,000	24,464	1,523.2
6	2,506,953	23,432	180.6
7	2,652,297	19,426	210.5
8	569,953	18,742	51.7
9	1,195,336	18,553	100.6
10	1,954,720	21,953	162.5
11	630,251	16,358	62.8
12	1,025,516	23,175	77.3

SOURCE: "1981 Survey of Buying Power," *Sales and Marketing Management*, July 27, 1981, pp. B1–B44 and C1–C228.

a. Use these data to estimate a multiple linear regression model of total retail sales as a function of MHEBI and HSHLDS. Write the equation you estimate below:

TRS = _____

b. Write an explanation of what each part of the above equation for TRS means.

c. Do the coefficients for MHEBI and HSHLDS have the signs you would expect? Explain.

d. Are the coefficients you estimated statistically significant at a 95-percent confidence level? Explain how you made this determination.

e. What is the value of the adjusted R^2 for this model? Write a brief explanation of what this statistic means.

11. There has been considerable interest in the demand for gasoline in the United States in recent years. Look up data on monthly domestic gasoline demand (Q), the retail price of gasoline (P), and personal income (M) for the most recent three-year period available.[6] Use these data to answer the following questions:

a. Estimate a multiple linear regression equation for gasoline demand, that is, for

$$Q = f(P, M)$$
$$Q = a + b_1 P + b_2 M$$

Estimate the values of a, b_1, and b_2. Are these coefficients significant at a 95-percent confidence level? What is the value of the adjusted coefficient of determination? Interpret its meaning. Write the regression equation below:

$Q =$ _____

b. Estimate a multiplicative demand model for gasoline in the following form:

$$Q = KP^{b_1} M^{b_2}$$

Remember that such a function is linear in logarithms such that

$$\ln Q = \ln K + b_1 \ln P + b_2 \ln M$$

where $\ln K$ is the intercept, or constant, term in the multiple linear regression equation. You need simply to use the natural logarithms of the three variables as inputs to your regression program.

---

[6]Use recent issues of *Survey of Current Business* to find data on these series.

Write the linear regression equation using the logaritms of the variables below:

$$\ln Q = \underline{\hspace{6cm}}$$

Now convert to the nonlinear form by finding the antilog of both sides (recall that $K = e^{\ln K}$):

$$Q = \underline{\hspace{6cm}}$$

Interpret the statistical significance of the exponents. Do they have the signs you would have expected?

12. Paul Tobel is the production manager of a small manufacturer of children's wooden puzzles. He is interested in knowing how variable costs (VC) are related to the level of production (Q) measured in thousands of puzzles. He has collected the following 12 observations from company records:

VC	Q	VC	Q
0	0	52	6
17	1	53	7
35	2	55	8
41	3	62	9
44	4	73	10
48	5	92	11

a. Estimate VC as a cubic function of output Q:

$$VC = f(Q, Q^2, Q^3) = a + b_1 Q + b_2 Q^2 + b_3 Q^3$$

Write your regression results below:

$$VC = \underline{\hspace{6cm}}$$

$$R^2 = \underline{\hspace{3cm}} \qquad F\text{-ratio} = \underline{\hspace{2cm}}$$

t-ratios: for Q _____ ,   for Q^2 _____ ,   for Q^3 _____

b. Write a brief interpretation of the regression equation and $\overline{R}^2$.
c. Are the signs of the coefficients in the regression equation as you would expect? Explain why or why not. Are the coefficients statistically significant at a 95-percent confidence level? How can you tell?

d. Plot the original data and the regression equation on the grid provided below:

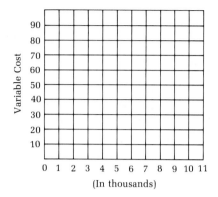

13. The following regression results were obtained in a study of how a
firm's sales (S) varied as the amount of newspaper (N) and radio (R)
advertising varied:

Variable	Coefficient	Standard Error	t-Ratio
Constant	2.30	1.10	2.09
LN	.52	.22	2.36
LR	1.51	.41	3.68

NOTE: Adjusted R^2 = .875
    n = 17
SE of the estimate = 1.24
    F-ratio = 62.4

where LN and LR represent the natural logarithms of newspaper and
radio advertising, respectively. The dependent variable is LS, the natural log of sales.

a. Write the multiple linear regression equation below:

$LS = F(LS, LR) = $ _____

b. Write the corresponding equation for sales as a function of newspaper and radio advertising below:

$Sales = f(N, R) = $ _____

c. If the firm uses 40 radio ads and 20 newspaper ads, what level of
sales would you predict based on this funciton?

$Sales = $ _____

d. Do you think this function does a good job of explaining the relationship between sales and these two forms of advertising? Explain.

14. In 1981, Ellen Blackwell was in charge of inventory control for Pinacle Industries, a major manufacturer of private-brand kitchen appliances. At a sales meeting, Ellen commented that she believed that sales of durable goods were heavily dependent on two factors: disposable personal income and the unemployment rate. Tom Noital, that national sales manager, told Ellen that she might be right that the disposable personal income is an important determinant but that the unemployment rate is not an important variable. He told the people at the meeting that he had personally looked at the correlation between manufacturers' sales of durable goods and the unemployment rate and found that it was $-.089$. Tom suggested that Ellen was not very edgeable about factors that influence sales and that perhaps she had better stick to strictly inventory-related problems. Keeping her good disposition, Ellen said that perhaps Tom was correct and that she would look into the relationship further and report her findings at the next month's sales meeting.

After the meeting, Ellen collected the following data for the most recent 13 months:

Year	Month	Sales	DPI	UR
1980	March	75925	1775.1	6.3
	April	72207	1775.6	6.9
	May	69443	1783.8	7.6
	June	69056	1793.0	7.5
	July	72544	1824.9	7.6
	August	72057	1837.7	7.6
	September	76571	1859.2	7.4
	October	79497	1880.2	7.6
	November	79741	1897.7	7.5
	December	80027	1913.1	7.4
1981	January	80259	1931.4	7.4
	February	81078	1946.1	7.3
	March	82397	1963.1	7.3

SOURCE: *Survey of Current Business,* Washington, D.C.: United States Department of Commerce/Bureau of Economic Analysis, pp. S1–S9.

where sales refers to millions of dollars of manufacturers' durable goods sales; *DPI* is billions of dollars of disposable personal income at a seasonally adjusted annual rate; and *UR* is the unemployment rate.

Ellen's analysis of correlation coefficients confirmed Tom's comments. The correlation between sales and *DPI* was .886, and between sales and *UR* − .069. From her business classes, Ellen remembered that it was possible that a regression analysis would tell her more about the relationships involved than would just looking at correlation coefficients.

a. Use a computer to estimate the following regression models:

$$\text{Sales} = a + b_1 DPI$$

Sales = _____

$$\text{Sales} = a + b_1 DPI + b_2 UR$$

Sales = _____

Which model does the best job of explaining variations in sales? Explain your answer.

b. Do the signs of the coefficients you have estimated make sense? Explain why or why not. Are they statistically significant at a 95-percent level?

c. Based on your analysis, write an outline of the points Ellen should make at the next sales meeting to support her original statement about sales being influenced by both *DPI* and *UR*.

d. Is autocorrelation a problem in this regression model? How can you tell?

15. The dean of your college thinks that the women students in the college show greater improvement in their grade point averages between the first term of their freshman year and the last term of their senior year than do men students. To control for influences other than gender, the dean has considered entrance exam scores and age at time of first enrolling. A dummy variable (*D*) was set equal to 1 for women and 0 for men. A regression analysis of the change in grade point averages (*ΔGPA*) as a function of entrance exam scores (*EES*) and age (*AGE*) was done on a random sample of 200 students. The following regression equation resulted:

$$\Delta GPA = -.0821 + .0007(EES) + .0073(AGE) + .1812(D)$$

a. Use this equation to estimate the most likely change in a male student's *GPA* if he scored 550 on the entrance exam and was 19 when he enrolled.

b. Use this equation to estimate the most likely change in *GPA* for a woman who starts school at age 25 and has an entrance exam score of 520.

c. Are the signs of the coefficients of *EES* and *AGE* reasonable? Explain.

d. Does the sign of the coefficient of the dummy variable support the dean's original hypothesis? Explain. What would it mean if this coefficient had a negative sign?

e. The adjusted coefficient of determination $(\overline{R}^2)$ for this equation was .8942. Explain what this means.

f. The t-ratios for each of the independent variables are given below:

Variable	t-Ratio
EES	12.25
AGE	1.54
D	1.79

Explain how each of these might influence your interpretation of the regression equation. Set up the null and alternative hypotheses you think are appropriate for each variable and do the related t-tests. Which variables are statistically significant at a 95-percent confidence level and which are not?

16. The student health service has been giving flu shots to students and has kept track of the cost of providing this service. The average cost (AC) per shot is shown below, along with the number of students treated (S), in thousands:

AC	S	AC	S
$.80	1	$.12	6
.61	2	.21	7
.49	3	.30	8
.20	4	.52	9
.15	5	.60	10

a. Plot these data points on the grid provided below:

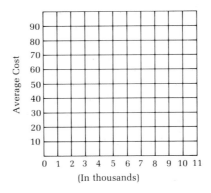

b. Based on these data, it appears that the average cost is a nonlinear function of the number of students treated. Estimate the following function:

$$AC = a + b_1S + b_2S^2$$

Write your model below:

$$AC = \underline{\hspace{6cm}}$$

c. What is the value of the adjusted R^2 for this model? Explain what this means.
d. Are the coefficients in this model significant at a 95-percent confidence level? Explain.
e. Graph your equation on the grid used in part a. Does the regression line appear to fit the data well?

17. A group of graduate students in outdoor recreation have been conducting a health and physical fitness program for students, faculty, and staff. One of the indexes they use to measure progress is the heart rate of participants after completing a one-mile run in nine minutes. The following data represent some of their results.

Observation	Heart Rate	Age	Weight	Miles Run per Week	Male or Female
1	136	30	170	10	M
2	133	22	165	3	M
3	167	45	184	3	M
4	132	19	190	4	M
5	122	23	105	8	F
6	123	22	176	2	M
7	153	41	142	4	F
8	149	37	131	7	F
9	104	28	110	22	F
10	118	25	165	15	M
11	150	32	204	8	M
12	139	31	150	12	M
13	181	55	118	6	F
14	113	24	118	11	F
15	117	22	167	9	M

a. Use a computer regression package to estimate coefficients and the constant term for the following multiple linear regression function:

$$HR = a + b_1A + b_2W + b_3MR + b_4D$$

where

$$HR = \text{heart rate after running one mile in nine minutes}$$
$$A = \text{age}$$
$$W = \text{weight}$$
$$MR = \text{miles run per week}$$
$$D = \text{dummy variable, which equals 1 for women and 0 for men}$$

b. What are the t-ratios for the four independent variables? Explain what these ratios tell you. Explain what you might do on the basis of this information.
c. What is the adjusted R^2 for your equation? Explain what this means.
d. What heart rate would you predict for a 118-pound, 32-year-old woman who normally runs 9 miles a week?
e. What heart rate would you predict for a 163-pound man who is 27 years old and who usually runs 2 miles a week? What 95-percent confidence interval would you have around this point estimate?

18. Consider the following regression results, in which the dependent variable is miles per gallon (*MPG*):

Variable	Coefficient	Standard Error	t-Ratio
Constant	6.507	1.280	
CID	0.031	0.012	
D	9.456	2.671	
M4	14.641	2.092	
M5	14.845	2.418	
US	4.643	2.481	

SOURCE: Based on a sample of data in *1982 Gas Mileage Guide*, Environmental Protection Agency and U.S. Department of Transportation, 1982.

NOTE: Adjusted R^2 = 0.569
Observations = 120
SE of regression = 8.208
F-statistic = 32.546

where

$$MPG = \text{miles per gallon}$$
$$CID = \text{cubic inch displacement (engine size)}$$
$$D = \text{1 for diesel cars and 0 otherwise}$$
$$M4 = \text{1 for a car with a four-speed manual transmission and 0 otherwise}$$
$$M5 = \text{1 for a car with a five-speed manual transmission and 0 otherwise}$$
$$US = \text{1 for cars made in the United States and 0 otherwise}$$

a. Evaluate the statistical significance of each of the independet variables. Use a 95-percent confidence level. (You will need to calculate each of the t-ratios to do this.)

b. Based on this model, how much of an increase in gas mileage would you say that a diesel engine provides?

c. Explain how an automatic transmission compares with four-speed and a five-speed manual transmission in terms of MPG. How much advantage does a five-speed have compared to a four-speed?

d. Is there any evidence in these regression results that cars made in the United States are less fuel efficient than imports? Explain.

e. Estimate MPG for the following two cars: (1) Ford LTD, automatic transmission, 255 CID gasoline engine; and (2) Isuzu Mark 1, manual five-speed, 111 CID diesel engine.

5

Demand

Demand and supply are at the very heart of business activity. You might even consider demand to be the lifeblood of any business. Without a demand for a firm's goods or services, the firm has no prospect of survival. A firm may have an ultraefficient managerial staff and use the most cost effective means of production, but without a demand for the goods or services produced, the firm is doomed to failure. Having a demand is not a sufficient condition for business success, but it is certainly a necessary condition. In this chapter, we focus on the demand side of the market, but starting with Chapter 7, we will investigate the supply side as well.

We will begin by first reviewing the basic elements of the economic concept of demand, including demand functions and demand curves for entire markets as well as for individual firms. In the process, we will look at actual regression estimates for both types of demand curves. We will then turn our attention to the interesting and useful concept of elasticity as a tool for measuring the responsiveness of sales to changes in various factors that affect demand. You will see that these elasticity concepts are very useful to managers of business activities as well as to public officials. Finally, we will look at some demand functions for the automobile industry in the United States that have been developed by a major econometric consulting firm for use by managers in both the private and public sectors of the economy.

5.1 AN INTRODUCTION TO CONSUMER DEMAND

The term *demand* refers to the quantities of a good or service that consumers in some market are willing and able to purchase at various prices in a given period of time. Note the words "willing and able." Both characteristics are necessary to have an effective demand. You may have a willingness to buy a condominium on one of the Caribbean islands to use over spring breaks and another near Jackson Hole, Wyoming, so you have a place to stay when you go for weekend ski trips; and, of course, you may be willing to buy a Lear jet to get you to and from these places. But if you are a typical student, you lack the ability to make such expensive purchases. Thus, you do not have an effective demand for them. There are just as many things that you have the ability but no willingness to buy. Each of us would have a different list of such things. One person's list might include bubble gum, cigarettes, kidney stew, crayons, stuffed animals, and so on. The person may be able to buy lots of these things but have no willingness to do so and thus not have an effective demand for them. For consumers to have an effective demand, they must be both willing and able to buy the particular goods and services in question.

The Law of Demand

Basic economics courses usually introduce a principle known as the law of demand. This law states that consumers are willing and able to purchase more units of a good or service at lower prices than at higher prices, other things being equal. The law of demand is illustrated by the negatively sloped demand function shown in Figure 5.1. That demand curve shows the different quantities demanded at various prices. The same information can also be given in a table, or schedule, such as Table 5.1 or by an equation for the demand function such as the following:

$$P = 100 - 0.25Q$$

where P is price and Q is quantity. We will work primarily with demand information in the form of equations in this chapter because (1) the equations are easier to work with, and (2) modern managers in both the private and public sector are relying on such functions (which have been estimated using regression analyses) with increasing frequency. When appropriate, we will also use graphs and tables to help clarify and illustrate the information contained in demand functions.

TABLE 5.1   **Simple Demand Schedule**

Price ($)	Quantity (units)
90	40
70	120
50	200
30	280
10	360

Note that the simple demand function used to illustrate the law of demand is a linear function. Not all demand functions are linear, but in many cases linear functions work well in explaining the relationship

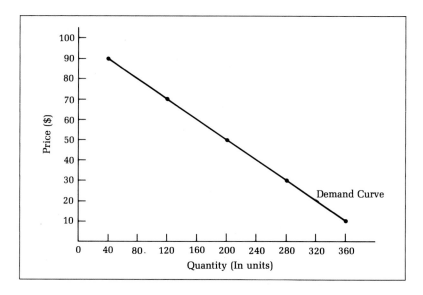

FIGURE 5.1   **Simple Demand Curve.**   Consumers are willing and able to purchase more units at a lower price than at a higher price.

between price and the quantity demanded. We will consider a number of useful linear demand functions later in this chapter.

It seems logical to most people that demand functions would slope downward to the right, that is, that the law of demand would be true for most products. If this were not true, we would expect to observe strange behavior in the business world. For example, during the 1970s, the Chrysler Corporation was on the brink of bankruptcy. Under the capable leadership of Lee Iacocca and with the help of the government, the company survived. Think how much easier it would have been to get Chrysler back on a good financial foundation if the demand function for Chrysler cars were positively rather than negatively sloped. The solution would have been simple: raise price and as a result sell more cars. It is doubtful that Lee Iacocca would have paid very much for such advice. He knew the demand function for Chrysler's cars was negatively sloped and that raising price would have the effect of lowering sales, other things being equal.

Have you ever thought about why the law of demand is true for nearly all goods and services? Two influences, known as the income effect and the substitution effect, are particularly important in explaining the negative slope of demand functions.[1] The *income effect* is the influence of a change in a product's price on real income, or purchasing power. If the price of

---

[1]For a more complete discussion of income and substitution effects, see J. Holton Wilson, *Microeconomics: Concepts and Applications* (New York: Harper & Row, 1981), pp. 99–103.

something that we buy goes down, our income will go farther and we can purchase more goods and services (including the good for which price has fallen) with a given level of money income. The *substitution effect* is the influence of a reduction in a product's price on quantity demanded such that consumers are likely to substitute that good for others that have thus become relatively more expensive.

5.2 THE DETERMINANTS OF DEMAND

Many forces influence our decisions regarding the bundle of goods and services we choose to purchase. It is important for managers to understand these forces as fully as possible in order to make and implement decisions that enhance their firms' long-term health. It is probably impossible to know about all such forces, let alone be able to identify and measure them sufficiently to incorporate them into a manager's decision framework. However, a small subset of these forces is particularly important and nearly universally applicable.

The Product's Price As a Determinant of Demand

It has already been noted that we normally expect consumers to be willing and able to purchase more of a product at lower prices than at higher prices. In evaluating a demand or sales function for a firm or an entire industry, one of the first things a thoughtful analyst or manager will consider is the price of a product.

If inventories have built up, a firm may consider lowering price to stimulate demand. In the 1970s, rebates became a popular way of doing this. Rebate programs of one type or another appeared for cars, home appliances, toys, lawn and garden equipment, farm implements, and even food products. Such rebates constitute a way of lowering the effective purchase price and thereby increasing the quantity consumers demand without the negative repercussions of raising price once the excess inventory is eliminated. Instead of raising the price back to its normal level, the firm simply allows the rebate program to quietly come to an end.

A firm's management may not be the only source of decisions that influence the effective selling price to consumers. Federal, state, and local government officials may also make decisions that influence the effective purchase price of a product. As these officials consider policies in the area of sales and excise taxes, they make decisions that alter the prices we pay for goods and services. As a marketing manager for a tire manufacturer, you would probably not be pleased to see the federal excise tax (FET) on tires increased. On the other hand, if that excise tax were reduced, you could anticipate some favorable impact on tire sales.

Income as a Determinant of Demand

Nearly all goods and services are what economists refer to as *normal goods*. These are goods for which consumption goes up as the incomes of consumers rise and vice versa. In fact, it is rare to find a demand function that does not include some measure of income as an important independent variable.

This relationship between product demand and income is one of the reasons that so much national attention is given to the level of GNP and changes in the rate of growth of GNP. The GNP is the broadest measure of the income generated in the economy. In demand analysis, we often use other, more narrowly defined measures, such as personal income or disposable personal income, but these measures are highly correlated with GNP. So watching what is happening to the GNP is helpful in understanding what may happen to the demand for a product you are concerned with.

The importance of income as a determinant of consumer demand has been underscored by public policy at the federal level. In order to decrease unemployment and increase economic growth, public officials have used the fiscal policy tool of implementing tax cuts. Tax cuts have the effect of increasing the amount of income people have available to spend on goods and services. This in turn increases demand, which prompts firms to hire more production, sales, and other workers.

This relationship among government policy, disposable income, and demand is an important reason why people in the business community are concerned about the government's fiscal policy actions. At the state and local level, such government actions can affect buying power in those subnational markets. Nearly all states have an income tax, as do some cities and counties. The income tax rates at the state and local levels are lower than at the federal level but may still significantly affect local purchasing power and are thus of particular concern to owners and managers of small businesses.

In addition to analyzing national income accounts data on disposable income, managers also use a measure called *effective buying income*, which is published each year in *Sales and Marketing Management's* "Survey of Buying Power." Effective buying income is often a useful measure of the income variable in analyzing demand relationships.

Tastes and Preferences as Determinants of Demand

We all like certain things and dislike others. A pair of identical twins brought up in the same environment may have different preferences in what they buy. Exactly how these preferences are formed and what influences them is not easy to know. Psychologists, sociologists, and social-psychologists have a lot to offer in helping economists and other business analysts understand how preferences are formed and altered.

Even if we do not have a thorough understanding of preference structures, one thing is clear: preferences and changes in preferences affect demand for goods and services. We have all observed how such changes in tastes and preferences have influenced various markets. For example, consider the automotive market. In the United States, people appeared to have a preference for big, powerful cars throughout the 1950s and 1960s. During the 1970s, the preference structure started to change in favor of smaller, less powerful, but more fuel efficient cars. Part of this change was probably related to changing prices of gasoline, a relationship we will look at more fully in the next section. In part, the change in our preference structure for cars may also have been related to psychographic (life-style) factors, such as being sportier and more concerned with resource conservation. Convenience factors, such as ease of driving and parking, may also have been important. Demographic changes, especially a trend toward smaller families, may have had some effect as well. Clearly, many factors have affected our preference structure for cars. And so it is with many other goods and services as well.

As much as we may like to think that we know our own minds and make our own purchase decisions without the influence of others, we are very likely influenced quite strongly by various peer groups, including the people with whom we work, classmates, roommates, the people with whom we socialize, our church groups, neighbors, and so on. Our decisions about clothes, entertainment, college courses, food, and many other things are influenced by these peer groups.

From the business perspective, advertising is a key factor in the formation and alteration of consumers' tastes and preferences.[2] We can think of advertising as being either primarily informational or primarily transformational. Informational ads are designed to increase demand for a particular product by providing information about a product: how it is used, how much it costs, where you can buy it, what attributes it has (size, weight, etc.). Newspaper ads often have the strongest informational component. They are designed to elicit direct purchase action on the part of consumers.

Transformational advertisements are designed to influence our image of a product or service. They attempt to enhance the satisfaction we get from a product by evoking positive images of how we will feel if we buy it. Think about television commercials for a beer or soft drink. How much usable information do they give you? Usually not much. They tell you the name of the product; associate its consumption with some reference group of happy, healthy-looking people (often famous people as well); and generally try to create a positive image in an attempt to alter your preference structure in favor of that beer or soft drink. A single exposure to such an ad is not usually

---

[2]We will consider other aspects of advertising in a later section of this chapter and in Chapter 8, in which the media selection process is analyzed using linear programming.

very effective, but repeated exposure to that ad and similar ones has been shown to influence consumer preferences.

In terms of measurement, this determinant of demand—tastes and preferences — is the most difficult for an analyst to handle. It is hard to identify all the things that influence tastes and preferences and often just as hard to measure those that are identified. Measures of advertising effort are sometimes used to help account for this determinant of demand.

Other Prices as Determinants of Demand

How much consumers buy of one product may be affected by the prices charged for other goods or services as well. Earlier we noted that the rise in the price of gasoline during the 1970s had some effect on the demand for large versus small cars in the United States. Gasoline and cars are complementary goods: they are used together and complement one another. When the price of gasoline rose, there were at least two effects on the automobile market. First, the higher price of gas increased the cost of driving and thus reduced the total number of miles individuals tended to drive. This situation, in turn, had the long-term effect of making cars last longer and thus reduced scrappage and replacement car demand. Second, smaller, more fuel-efficient cars became more attractive relative to big cars.

Let us state this relationship in more general terms. Suppose we observe two goods, A and B, and B is complementary to A. If the price of B goes up, we can expect the demand for A to be reduced. The reverse is also true: if the price of B falls, the demand for A will rise. It should be clear why business analysts are concerned not only about the effect that their product's price has on sales but also with the effect of the prices of complementary products.

What effect would you expect an increase in the price of movie tickets to have on the demand for home video disks and tapes? These are substitute goods. In this case, as the price of movie tickets goes up, we would expect the demand for video disks and tapes to rise as well. In general, if we have two products, C and D, which are substitutes, we can expect that a rise in the price of C (or D) will cause the demand for D (or C) to go up.

Economists and other business analysts are, therefore, concerned with all other prices that may affect the products they are analyzing. The prices of both complementary and substitute products can be expected to influence demand. Later in this chapter, we will see how a measure called the cross-price elasticity of demand can be helpful in determining whether two goods are complements, substitutes, or neither.

Other Determinants of Demand

It would be a monumental task to identify everything that might have some influence on the demand for any product. So far, we have identified the four most important influences: a product's price, income, tastes and preferences, and the price of complementary or substitute products. Three others are population, legal restrictions, and public policy.

Population growth obviously causes the potential demand for nearly all products to rise. In many cases, economists involved in analyzing the demand for particular products look at individual components of the population as determinants of demand. The changing age distribution, for example, may have differential effects on different markets. The growing proportion of people over 65 in our population has important ramifications for demand for such things as retirement villages and certain kinds of health care products. Changes in other demographic characteristics and in the geographical distribution of the population may also be important.

Legal restrictions imposed on the primarily free market also affect demand. For example, suppose that a state that currently sets the legal drinking age at 18 years raises that age to 21 years. This change could have the effect of decreasing the demand for alcoholic beverages. Similarly, if the driving age was raised (or lowered), insurance companies would have a decrease (or an increase) in the demand for car insurance.

Public policy can have a number of effects on demand. We have already cited the effects of sales, excise, or income taxes. Now let us consider the public policy concerning whether tuition payments for private kindergarten through twelfth-grade education should be tax deductible. If the tuition is tax deductible, the effective price of private schools is lower to the users. Demand theory suggests that a greater quantity of private education would be purchased.

A Change in Demand versus a Change in the Quantity Demanded

The terms *change in demand* and *change in quantity demanded* refer to different kinds of effects. To see the distinction, look at Figure 5.2. The left-hand graph shows a change in quantity demanded (ΔQ_D). If price falls from P_A to P_B, the quantity demanded increases from Q_A to Q_B. But note that demand does not change. The demand curve is still the same line through points A and B. The only thing that will change the quantity demanded is a change in the price of the product or service. The notation ΔQ_D refers to movement along a given demand curve.

Now look at the right-hand graph in Figure 5.2. Here, the demand curve has shifted from D_1 to D_2. There has been a change in demand (ΔD). At each price, such as P_A or P_B, the amount purchased would be greater along D_2 than along D_1. So a change in demand means a shift in the entire demand curve. What do you think would cause demand to change? The determinants of demand discussed above are the most important: income, consumers' tastes and preferences, the price of substitute or complementary goods, the size of a relevant segment of the population, legal restrictions, and public policy.

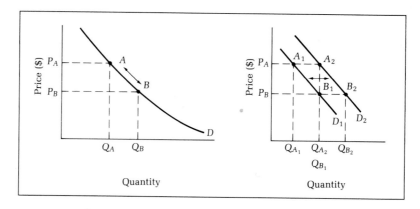

FIGURE 5.2   **Change in Quantity Demanded and Change in Demand.**   A change in quantity demanded is represented by movement along a given demand curve, such as from A to B in the graph on the left. A change in demand is a shift in the entire demand function, as shown in the graph on the right.

5.3   MARKET DEMAND FUNCTIONS

The market demand function is the total of the quantities demanded by all individual consumers at each price. Business logic and economic theory both support the proposition that individual consumers will purchase more of a good at lower prices than at higher prices. If this is true of individual consumers, then it is also true of all consumers combined. This relationship is demonstrated by the example in Figure 5.3, which shows three individual demand curves and the market demand found by adding those three curves together.

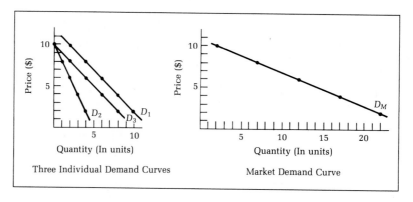

FIGURE 5.3   **Derivation of a Market Demand Curve**

The demand data supporting the curves in Figure 5.3 are also shown in Table 5.2. The three equations below represent the three consumers' demand functions:

Consumer 1: $P = 12 - Q_1$
Consumer 2: $P = 10 - 2Q_2$
Consumer 3: $P = 10 - Q_3$

You should substitute some value of Q (such as $Q = 4$) in each of these equations to verify that they are consistent with the data in Table 5.2 and the curves in the left portion of Figure 5.3.

TABLE 5.2   **Derivation of a Market Demand Schedule**

	Individual Demand Schedules			
Price	Q_1	Q_2	Q_3	Market Demand Schedule Q_M
10	2	0	0	2
8	4	1	2	7
6	6	2	4	12
4	8	3	6	17
2	10	4	8	22

Let us now add these three demand functions together to get an equation for the market demand curve. Be careful in doing this. There is sometimes a temptation to just add equations without thinking about what we want to accumulate. In both Table 5.2 and Figure 5.3, it is easy to see that the quantities sold to each consumer at each price have been added. For example, at a price of $6, consumer number 1 would buy six units ($Q_1 = 6$), consumer number 2 would buy two units ($Q_2 = 2$), and consumer number 3 would buy four units ($Q_3 = 4$). Thus, the total market demand at a price of $6 is 12 units ($6 + 2 + 4 = 12$). The important point is to remember that in nearly all cases we want to add the quantities, *not* the prices.

To add the three demand equations given above, we must first solve each for Q, since we want to add the quantities (i.e., we want to add the functions horizontally, so we must solve them for the variable represented on the horizontal axis). Solving the individual demand functions for Q as a function of P,

$Q_1 = 12 - P$
$Q_2 = 5 - 0.5P$
$Q_3 = 10 - P$

Adding these, we get

$Q_1 + Q_2 + Q_3 = 27 - 2.5P$

And letting $Q_M = Q + Q_2 + Q_3$, where Q_M is market demand,

$$Q_M = 27 - 2.5P$$

This is the algebraic expression for the market demand function. You could solve this expression for P:

$$P = 10.8 - 0.4Q_M$$

Now check to see that this form of expressing the market demand is consistent with the data shown in Table 5.2 and Figure 5.3.

Empirical Estimation of a Market Demand Function

Now let us look at some data representing the total sales of a consumer good in a particular subnational market. Market sales are hypothesized to be primarily a function of the average price of the four firms selling the product in that market and the total disposable income in the market. These data are shown in Table 5.3 for the period from the fourth quarter of 1981 through the first quarter of 1985 (a total of 14 observations).

The OLS multiple regression results based on this information are:

$$MD = 119.539 - 23.198AP + .029INC$$
$$(-4.17) \qquad (10.30)$$

$$\overline{R}^2 = .931$$
$$\text{SE of the estimate} = 3.964$$
$$F\text{-statistic} = 88.21$$
$$DW = 1.751$$

where

MD = market demand in thousands of units
AP = average price
INC = income in millions of dollars

Values in parentheses are t-ratios.

As you would expect, the coefficient of the average price has a negative sign and is statistically significant at a 95-percent confidence level. This is consistent with the law of demand. Note from Table 5.3 that both average price and sales increase over the 14-quarter period covered by these data. In fact, the simple correlation between sales and average price is .61. A naive observer might suggest that increases in sales are caused by increases in the average price (i.e., the demand function is positively sloped). But this is not consistent with business logic or economic theory. Looking at just the relationship between sales and average price does not adequately identify the market demand model. The $\overline{R}^2$ for a simple regression on these two data series would be only .37, and a positive relationship between price and

TABLE 5.3   **Data for Market Demand Function**

Observation	Market Sales (thousands of units)	Average Price	Income ($ millions)
1981.4	80	5.00	2620
1982.1	86	4.87	2733
1982.2	93	4.86	2898
1982.3	99	4.79	3056
1982.4	106	4.79	3271
1983.1	107	4.87	3479
1983.2	109	5.01	3736
1983.3	110	5.31	3868
1983.4	111	5.55	4016
1984.1	113	5.72	4152
1984.2	110	5.74	4336
1984.3	112	5.59	4477
1984.4	131	5.50	4619
1985.1	136	5.48	4764

sales violates any logical expectation. This would indicate that one or more other independent variables of importance had been omitted from the model.

We have specified the model more fully by including the income variable in addition to a price variable. The coefficient of income has the expected positive sign, which is consistent with such data for a normal good. The coefficient of determination ($\overline{R}^2$) for this model is quite good, at .931. This tells us that 93.1 percent of the variation in sales is explained by this model.

Can this demand function be represented graphically? The answer is yes, *if* we specify some level of income and hold that constant. Remember that demand is defined as the quantities consumers are willing and able to purchase at various prices, *other things being equal*. Suppose that we let income be its average value for the period, which is 3716. The demand function is then

$$MD = 119.539 - 23.198AP + .029(3716)$$
$$MD = 119.539 - 23.198AP + 107.764$$

$$MD = 227.303 - 23.198AP$$

This function is graphed in Figure 5.4 for the four prices $P = 4.80$, $P = 5.10$, $= 5.40$, and $P = 5.70$. The corresponding values of the quantity sold are MD 116, $MD = 109$, $MD = 102$, and $MD = 95$, respectively. The demand func- has the expected negative slope.

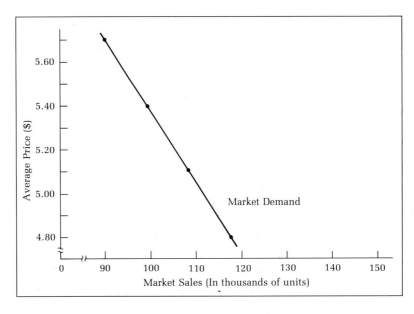

FIGURE 5.4   **Market Demand Curve.**   This market demand (MD) is based on the regression function $MD = 119.539 - 23.198AP + .029INC$, with income held constant at $INC = 3716$.

Suppose you want to know what the demand curve would look like for some other level of income. Let us pick the most recent level of income from Table 5.3 (i.e., 4764). Find the levels of sales that correspond to the following prices:

$P = 4.80$ $MD =$ _____

$P = 5.10$ $MD =$ _____

$P = 5.40$ $MD =$ _____

$P = 5.70$ $MD =$ _____

Now plot these four points on Figure 5.4 and connect them with a straight line. You see that an increase in the level of income causes the demand curve to shift to the right.

Market Demand for Sweet Potatoes

Before considering the demand curves for the output of individual firms, let us briefly review two studies of market demand. The first comes from the agricultural sector of the economy, in which considerable applied economic analysis is performed. The study concerned the demand for sweet potatoes.[3] The dependent variable in the analysis was the total quantity of sweet potatoes sold in 1000 hundredweight (cwt.), denoted Q_s. The following five independent variables were included:

P_s = real farm prices in dollars per cwt. received for sweet potatoes
N = two-year moving average of total United States population in millions as of July 1
Y = real per capita personal disposable income in thousands of dollars
P_w = real farm price in dollars per cwt. received for white potatoes
T = a time trend (T = 1 for 1949, 2 for 1950, etc.)

Data included the 1949–1972 crop years. The estimated regression equation representing the commercial market demand for sweet potatoes is

$$Q_s = 7609 - 1606P_s + 59N + 947Y + 479P_w - 271T$$

Let us consider the coefficient of each of these independent variables. The negative coefficient of the variable representing the price of sweet potatoes (P_s) is consistent with the law of demand. An increase in price would cause Q_s to decline (i.e., there would be a decrease in the quantity demanded). The positive relationship between population (N) and market demand is also reasonable. In addition, we see that as real income increases, the market demand for sweet potatoes also increases, since Y has a positive coefficient. The other price included in this demand study was the price of white potatoes (P_w). Simple logic would lead us to expect a positive relationship between Q_s and P_w. White potatoes and sweet potatoes may be considered substitutes for one another. Thus, when the price of white potatoes increases, fewer white potatoes are purchased, and many consumers substitute sweet potatoes for white potatoes, causing the demand for sweet potatoes to increase. The negative coefficient of the time trend may reflect a number of factors, one of which may be a general decline in the taste and preference of consumers for sweet potatoes.

Market Demand for Crude Oil

Now let us look at a study of the demand for crude oil in the United States using data from 1929 through 1973, excluding the period between 1942 and

---

[3]Ronald A. Schrimper and Gene E. Mathia, "Reservation and Market Demands for Sweet Potatoes at the Farm Level," *American Journal of Agricultural Economics*, February 1975, pp. 119–121. We include only that portion of the analysis related to market demand. The authors also estimated the on-farm or on-reservation demand for sweet potatoes and relationships between the two.

1947, for which World War II caused abnormalities in the data. The study employed several regression analyses and various data transformations.[4]

The authors note that "the demand for crude oil is influenced by numerous phenomena, including its own price, the income of consumers, the stock of automobiles/trucks/buses/airplanes, and the availability and cost of substitutes such as coal and natural gas. It also depends on habits of individuals such as their desired thermostat setting, driving and vacation patterns, and upon phenomena not subject to human choice such as the severity of weather."[5] The independent variables used in their analyses include

P = real own crude oil price per barrel at the well
I = income, measured as real per capita GNP
A = number of motor vehicles per captia
C = coal consumption per capita

The dependent variable was crude oil consumption per capita designated as O.

The regression results reported here are for a logarithmic transformation of the data in terms of yearly changes for only the later time period (1948–1973). The demand equation estimated is

$$\Delta \ln O = .78 - .26 \Delta \ln P + .10 \Delta \ln I + .79 \Delta \ln A + .10 \Delta \ln C$$

As in the sweet potato study, the signs of the coefficients are reasonably consistent with our expectations. The coefficient of determination (R^2) was .586, meaning that 58.6 percent of the variation in the dependent variable $\Delta \ln O$ is explained by variations in this set of independent variables. Since the regression was done on logarithms, the coefficients represent the *percentage* change in the dependent variable for each 1-percent change in its respective independent variable. For example, a 1-percent increase in the price of gasoline (P) would decrease consumption (O) by .26 percent. This responsiveness is measured using the concept of elasticity, which we will discuss in detail shortly.

5.4   THE FIRM'S DEMAND

There is some demand for the output of each firm in an industry that represents some fraction of the total market demand. That fraction can be a very small part of the total (such as the sales of a single wheat farmer compared to total wheat sales), or it may be a substantial fraction of the total (such as

---

[4]Albert L. Danielson and Charles D. DeLorme, Jr., "Elasticities of Demand for Crude Oil in the United States, 1929–1941 and 1948–1973," *Review of Business and Economic Research*, Winter 1975–1976, pp. 19–29. Only a portion of the analysis is reported here.

[5]Danielson and DeLorme, p. 20.

General Motors' share of United States auto sales). In the limiting case of a monopoly, the firm's demand and the market demand are identical. In this section, we will consider only the vast middle ground between the extremes of monopoly and perfect competition.

The majority of firms in the economy face demand curves that have a negative slope. That is, most firms can sell more at lower prices than at higher prices. The market represented by the data in Table 5.3 has four dominant firms that account for nearly all of the market sales. Let us consider one of those firms, Big Sky Foods, and estimate its demand function (this is the same firm we looked at in estimating market share in Chapter 4). Big Sky Foods' sales and price data are given in Table 5.4, along with the income data from Table 5.3 and data on the price charged by the largest firm in the market.

TABLE 5.4   **Data Used to Estimate Big Sky Foods' Demand Function**

Observation	Sales (thousands of units)	Price	Income ($ millions)	Competitor's Price
1981.4	20	5.00	2620	5.00
1982.1	16	5.20	2733	4.80
1982.2	16	5.32	2898	4.80
1982.3	14	5.48	3056	4.50
1982.4	16	5.60	3271	4.44
1983.1	19	5.80	3479	4.55
1983.2	17	6.03	3736	4.60
1983.3	18	6.01	3868	4.85
1983.4	21	5.92	4016	5.10
1984.1	26	5.90	4152	5.40
1984.2	30	5.85	4336	5.00
1984.3	26	5.80	4477	4.95
1984.4	27	5.85	4619	5.00
1985.1	29	5.80	4764	5.00

The regression results are as follows:

$$Q = 15.939 - 9.057P + .009INC + 5.092PC$$
$$(-2.90) \qquad (5.55) \qquad (1.97)$$

$$\overline{R}^2 = .867$$
$$F\text{-statistic} = 29.22$$
$$SE \text{ of the estimate} = 1.99$$
$$DW = 1.81$$

where

Q = sales in thousands of units
P = price
INC = income in millions of dollars
PC = the competitor's price

Values in parentheses are t-ratios.

The negative coefficient of Big Sky Foods' price indicates that the firm has a downward sloping demand curve (i.e., more can be sold at lower prices than at higher prices). Each 10-cent decrease in price would be expected to cause sales to increase by .905 units. Since sales are in thousands, this means sales would go up by 905. The positive coefficient of income shows that this firm's product is seen as a normal good by consumers. Both of these coefficients are statistically significant at a 95-percent confidence level (see the corresponding t-ratios).

The positive coefficient of the variable representing the major competitor's price indicates that when the competition raises price, Big Sky Foods' sales go up (i.e., the products are substitutes). Note that this variable (PC) is not statistically significant at the 95-percent confidence level. It is, however, significant at a 90-percent confidence level (you may want to check the t-ratio given against the t-table in Chapter 4).

The .867 value for $\overline{R}^2$ tells us that this model accounts for 86.7 percent of the variation in Big Sky Foods' sales. While this is not as high as the R^2 for the market demand equation, it is still quite high. We should note that this comparison between the firm and market demand curves is typical. It is usual to get a higher R^2 when estimating the demand function for an entire industry than for any one firm in that industry.

Let us now graph this demand function for the average values of income and competitor's price, which are $INC = 3716$ and $PC = 4.86$, respectively. The demand equation is

$$Q = 15.939 - 9.057P + .009(3716) + 5.092(4.86)$$
$$Q = 15.939 - 9.057P + 33.444 + 24.747$$

$$Q = 74.130 - 9.057P$$

Using the same four prices we used to plot the market demand, we find

If $P = 4.80$, then $Q = 30.7$
If $P = 5.10$, then $Q = 27.9$
If $P = 5.40$, then $Q = 25.2$
If $P = 5.70$, then $Q = 22.5$

These points are plotted in Figure 5.5 and connected with a straight line to show the demand curve.

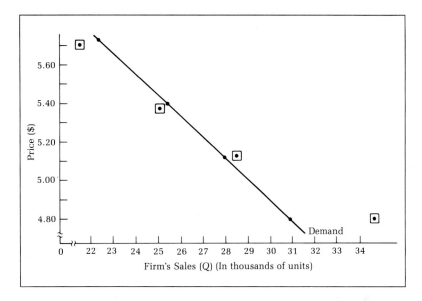

FIGURE 5.5   **Big Sky Foods' Demand Curve.**   This demand curve is based on the demand function $Q = 15.939 - 9.057P + .009INC + 5.092PC$, with income ($INC$) and the price of the largest competitor (PC) held constant at their mean values (3716 and 4.86, respectively).

Complete the following exercises:[6]

1. Let $I = 3716$ (no change), but let the competitor's price rise to $PC = \$5.40$. Complete the following table:

$P = 4.80$ $Q =$ _____

$P = 5.10$ $Q =$ _____

$P = 5.40$ $Q =$ _____

$P = 5.70$ $Q =$ _____

Graph these points on Figure 5.5 and connect them to form the new demand curve. Is it as you would expect?

---

[6]For exercise 1, the demand curve should shift to the right, since the firm sells more when the price of the substitute product rises. For exercise 2 (see next page), the demand curve should shift to the left due to the fall in income, since the product is a normal good.

2. Let $I = 3500$ (a decline) and let $PC = \$4.86$ (as in our original example). Complete the following table:

$P = 4.80$ $Q =$ _____

$P = 5.10$ $Q =$ _____

$P = 5.40$ $Q =$ _____

$P = 5.70$ $Q =$ _____

Graph these points on Figure 5.5 and connect them to form another new demand curve. Is this one as you would expect?

Let us compare the slope of this linear equation for the firm's demand function with the linear equation for the corresponding market demand function. The two functions are

Industry demand: $MD = 119.539 - 23.198AP + .029INC$

Firm's demand: $Q = 15.939 - 9.057P + .009INC + 5.092PC$

The slopes are found by taking the partial derivatives of the respective functions with respect to the relevant price variables:

$\partial MD/\partial AP = -23.198$
$\partial Q/\partial P = -9.057$

We see that the firm's demand curve is flatter than the market demand curve. This is nearly always true (note that in Figures 5.4 and 5.5 the slopes do not appear very different because the horizontal axes are scaled differently).

Now let us investigate what the equation for the firm's demand function would look like in a multiplicative form. The form we want to fit is

$$Q = A(P)^{b_1}(INC)^{b_2}(PC)^{b_3}$$

which is linear in logarithms as follows:

$$\ln Q = \ln A + b_1\ln P + b_2\ln INC + b_3\ln PC$$

Using the natural logarithms of the four variables as inputs to a multiple linear regression equation, we estimate the following equation:

$$\ln Q = -6.756 - 2.755\ln P + 1.512\ln INC + 1.364\ln PC$$
$$(-2.988) \qquad (5.174) \qquad (2.316)$$

where

$$\overline{R}^2 = .869$$
$$F\text{-statistic} = 29.85$$
$$SE \text{ of the estimate} = .092$$
$$DW = 1.70$$

Values in parentheses are t-ratios. Finding the antilogarithm of this regression equation yields

$$Q = .0012P^{-2.755}INC^{1.512}PC^{1.364}$$

For $INC = 3716$ and $PC = 4.86$ (the average values of these variables), we obtain

$$Q = .0012P^{-2.755}(3716)^{1.512}(4.86)^{1.364}$$

$$Q = .0012P^{-2.755}(250,008.323)(8.641)$$

$$Q = 2592.433P^{-2.755}$$

Using this function to estimate values of Q for the four prices used earlier, we get the four points enclosed by small squares in Figure 5.5. Try connecting all four of those points with one straight line — it does not work. You should, however, be able to connect those points with a smooth nonlinear curve that bows slightly toward the origin.

5.5   ELASTICITY: A METHOD OF MEASURING THE SENSITIVITY OF SALES

Economists and other business analysts are frequently concerned with the responsiveness of one variable to changes in some other variable. It may be useful to know, for example, what effect a given percentage change in price would have on sales. The measure of responsiveness most widely adopted is elasticity. *Elasticity* may be defined as the percentage change in some dependent variable given a 1-percent change in an independent variable, *ceteris paribus*. If we let Y represent the dependent variable, X the independent variable, and E the elasticity, then

$$E = \%\Delta Y / \%\Delta X$$

There are two forms of elasticity: arc elasticity and point elasticity. The former reflects the average responsiveness of the dependent variable to changes in the independent variable over some interval. The numeric value of an arc elasticity can be found as follows:

$$E = \left(\frac{Y_1 - Y_2}{Y_1 + Y_2}\right)\bigg/\left(\frac{X_1 - X_2}{X_1 + X_2}\right)$$

where the subscripts refer to the two data points observed, or the extremities of the interval for which the elasticity is calculated.

Point elasticities indicate the responsiveness of the dependent variable to the independent variable at one particular point on the demand curve. Point elasticities will be denoted with a lowercase e and are calculated as follows:

$$e = \frac{dY}{dX} \cdot \frac{X}{Y}$$

This form works well when the function is bivariate: $Y = f(X)$. However, when there are more independent variables, partial derivatives must be used. For example, suppose $Y = f(W, X, Z)$ and we want to find the elasticities for each of the independent variables. We would have

$$e_W = W\text{-elasticity} = \frac{\partial Y}{\partial W} \cdot \frac{W}{Y}$$

$$e_X = X\text{-elasticity} = \frac{\partial Y}{\partial X} \cdot \frac{X}{Y}$$

$$e_Z = Z\text{-elasticity} = \frac{\partial Y}{\partial Z} \cdot \frac{Z}{Y}$$

For power functions, the point elasticity results are particularly interesting. Consider the following function:

$$Y = aW^b X^c Z^d$$

The elasticity with respect to W is

$$e_W = \frac{\partial Y}{\partial W} \cdot \frac{W}{Y}$$
$$e_W = b(aW^{b-1} X^c Z^d)(W/Y)$$

Substituting $Y = aW^b X^c Z^d$ in for Y, we have

$$e_W = b(aW^{b-1} X^c Z^d)(W/aW^b X^c Z^d)$$

Multiplying the last two terms, we obtain

$$e_W = b(aW^b X^c Z^d) / (aW^b X^c Z^d)$$

Dividing by the denominator, we find

$$e_W = b$$

We see that the elasticity of the function Y with respect to W is equal to b, the exponent of W in the original function.

This convenient result can be generalized as follows: *for all power functions, the elasticity for each independent variable is equal to that variable's exponent in the demand function.* Thus, for the general function $Y = aW^b X^c Z^d$, the point elasticities are

$$e_W = b$$
$$e_X = c$$
$$e_Z = d$$

We will apply this principle to specific functions as you progress in sections 5.6 – 5.9.

While a great variety of elasticities are used by economists, three deserve particular attention because of their wide application in the business world: price elasticity, income elasticity, and cross-price elasticity.

5.6   PRICE ELASTICITY OF DEMAND

Price elasticity of demand measures the responsiveness of the quantity sold to changes in the product's price, *ceteris paribus*. It is the percentage change in sales divided by a percentage change in price. We shall use the notation E_p for the arc price elasticity of demand and e_p for the point price elasticity of demand. If the absolute value of E_p (or e_p) is greater than 1, a given percentage decrease (increase) in price will result in an even greater percentage increase (decrease) in sales. In such a case, the demand for the product is considered *elastic*; that is, sales are relatively responsive to price changes. When the absolute value of the price elasticity of demand is less than 1, the percentage change in sales is less than a given percentage change in price. Demand is then said to be *inelastic* with respect to price. *Unitary price elasticity* results when a given percentage change in price results in an equal percentage change in sales. The absolute value of the coefficient of price elasticity is equal to 1 in such cases. These relationships are summarized below:

> If $|e_p|$ or $|E_p| > 1$, demand is elastic
> If $|e_p|$ or $|E_p| < 1$, demand is inelastic
> If $|e_p|$ or $|E_p| = 1$, demand is unitarily elastic

Arc Price Elasticity

Let us consider the hypothetical prices of some product and the corresponding sales as given in Table 5.5. We could calculate the arc price elasticity between the two lowest prices as follows:

$$E_p = \left(\frac{360 - 280}{360 + 280} \right) \bigg/ \left(\frac{10 - 30}{10 + 30} \right) = -.25$$

Thus, demand is inelastic in that range. This value of $E_p = -.25$ means that a 1-percent change in price results in a .25-percent change in the quantity demanded (in the opposite direction of the price change) over this region of the demand function.

TABLE 5.5   **Demand Schedule to Demonstrate Price Elasticities**

Price ($) (P)	Quantity (units) (Q)	Arc Elasticity	Point Elasticity
90	40		−9.00
70	120	−4.00	−2.33
50	200	−1.50	−1.00
30	280	−0.67	−0.43
10	360	−0.25	−0.11

If we calculate the arc price elasticity between the prices of 50 and 70, we have

$$E_P = \left(\frac{200 - 120}{200 + 120} \right) \bigg/ \left(\frac{50 - 70}{50 + 70} \right) = -1.5$$

We would say that demand is price elastic in this range because the percentage change in sales is greater than the percentage change in price.

Point Price Elasticity

The algebraic equation for the demand schedule given in Table 5.5 is

$$P = 100 - .25Q$$

or

$$Q = 400 - 4P$$

We can use this demand function to illustrate the determination of point price elasticities. Let us select the point at which $P = 10$ and $Q = 360$:

$$e_P = \frac{dQ}{dP} \cdot \frac{P}{Q}$$
$$e_P = (-4)(10/360)$$
$$e_P = -.11$$

Since $|e_P| < 1$, we would say that demand is inelastic at a price of \$10. Now consider a price of \$70:

$$e_P = \frac{dQ}{dP} \cdot \frac{P}{Q}$$
$$e_P = (-4)(70/120)$$
$$e_P = -2.33$$

Here $|e_P| > 1$, and demand is price elastic.

We have seen in the above example that the price elasticity of demand may (and usually does) vary along any demand function depending on the portion of the function for which the elasticity is calculated. It follows that we usually cannot make such statements as "the demand for product X is elastic," because it is likely to be elastic for one range of prices and inelastic for another.

Demand Functions with a Constant Price Elasticity

Some nonlinear demand functions do have a constant price elasticity. Suppose that empirical studies show a demand function to be of the form

$$Q = aP^b \qquad b < 0$$

Then the point price elasticity would be

$$e_P = \frac{dQ}{dP} \cdot \frac{P}{Q}$$

$$e_P = (baP^{b-1})\,(P/Q)$$

$$e_p = (baP^{b-1})\,(P/aP^b)$$

$$e_P = b$$

If $|b| > 1$, the demand would be price elastic throughout; if $|b| < 1$, it would be inelastic throughout; and if $|b| = 1$, the demand function would be unitarily elastic at all points.

To illustrate the constant elasticity concepts, let us look back at the firm's demand function we estimated earlier in a multiplicative form. Recall that sales (Q) were found to be a function of price (P), income (INC), and a competitor's price (PC). The demand function was

$$Q = .0012P^{-2.755}INC^{1.512}PC^{1.364}$$

The price elasticity in point form is

$$e_P = \frac{\partial Q}{\partial P} \cdot \frac{P}{Q}$$

$$e_P = (-2.755)(.0012P^{-2.755-1}INC^{1.512}PC^{1.364}) \cdot$$

$$\left(\frac{P}{.0012P^{-2.755}INC^{1.512}PC^{1.364}} \right)$$

$$e_P = (-2.755) \cdot \left(\frac{.0012P^{-2.755}INC^{1.512}PC^{1.364}}{.0012P^{-2.755}INC^{1.512}PC^{1.364}} \right)$$

$$e_P = -2.755$$

Since $|e_P = -2.755| > 1$, this demand function is classified as elastic with respect to price.

What would you expect to find if you calculated arc price elasticities for this function? Since a multiplicative power function such as this has been demonstrated to have a constant price elasticity equal to the price exponent, all arc price elasticities should equal that same value. Let us look at two examples from the data points enclosed by small squares in Figure 5.5. The points are

1. $P = 4.80$ $\qquad$ $Q = 34.43$
2. $P = 5.10$ $\qquad$ $Q = 29.13$
3. $P = 5.40$ $\qquad$ $Q = 24.89$
4. $P = 5.70$ $\qquad$ $Q = 21.44$

Arc elasticity between points 1 and 2 is

$$E_P = \left(\frac{34.43 - 29.13}{34.43 + 29.13} \right) \Bigg/ \left(\frac{4.8 - 5.1}{4.8 + 5.1} \right) = -2.752$$

Arc elasticity between points 3 and 4 is

$$E_p = \left(\frac{24.89 - 21.44}{24.89 + 21.44} \right) \Big/ \left(\frac{5.4 - 5.7}{5.4 + 5.7} \right) = -2.755$$

You see that both arc price elasticities equal the point price elasticity (except for a minor rounding difference). Calculate the arc price elasticity between points 2 and 3 to further verify this relationship.

Determinants and Use of Price Elasticity

A knowledge and understanding of the concept of price elasticity of demand is very useful in many economic decisions. For example, consider a problem of the manager or directors of a metropolitan mass transit authority. Suppose the bus transportation system is running a deficit because most buses are used only at a fraction of capacity, but the transit authority has a legal commitment to maintain present service (i.e., to keep the same routing and frequency of service). Should fares be raised in order to eliminate the deficit? The answer depends on the relative price elasticity of demand. If demand is relatively elastic — that is, if ridership is very sensitive to price changes — an increase in fares would actually result in reduced revenue. When demand is inelastic, price and revenue change in the same direction.[7] Thus, if demand is price elastic, the transit authority can reduce the deficit (increase revenue) by reducing fares. The opposite would, of course, be true if demand was estimated to be price inelastic. For example, a study of fare elasticity for urban bus transit in Hartford, New Haven, and Stamford, Connecticut, showed that "the fare elasticity of demand does appear to be elastic" with values ranging from 1.82 to 3.45.[8] Thus, revenues could be expected to rise if the fare was lowered.

Several general factors have been found to influence the degree of price elasticity of any good or service. The most important is the number of substitutes available. If there are many good substitutes for a product, demand will be fairly elastic. For example, demand for a particular brand of gasoline is fairly elastic because other brands provide nearly perfect substitutes, whereas the industry demand for gasoline is not very elastic, since there is no really good substitute for this fuel at present. This relationship between the elasticity of a brand and the entire product class holds for most goods (i.e., soft drinks, soap, beer, televisions, etc.). To verify this, let us look at the market and firm demand functions estimated above. To be consistent,

---

[7]The relationship between sales revenue and price elasticity is examined in more detail in the section on "Price Elasticity and Revenue."

[8]R.W. Schmenner, "The Demands for Urban Bus Transit: A Route by Route Analysis," *Journal of Transport Economics and Policy,* January 1976, pp. 68–86.

we will use the linear form of the firm's demand and the same price for both sets of calculations. Further, all other variables are set equal to their respective mean values, so the simple bivariate demand functions are

For market demand: $MD = 227.303 - 23.198AP$
For the firm's demand: $Q = 74.130 - 9.057P$

You will recognize these equations from our earlier discussion. The point elasticities at $P = \$5.20$ are

For market demand: $e_P = \dfrac{dMD}{dAP} \cdot \dfrac{AP}{MD}$

$e_P = -23.198\,(5.20/106.7) = -1.131$

For the firm's demand: $e_P = \dfrac{dQ}{dP} \cdot \dfrac{P}{Q}$

$e_P = -9.057\,(5.20/27.0) = -1.744$

You see that the firm's demand is more elastic than the market demand at the price of $5.20.

If expenditures for a particular product represent a relatively small fraction of a consumer's total budget, such as expenditures for salt, we can expect demand to be less elastic than for products that represent a larger fraction of the budget. The relative necessity of a good also influences elasticity. For example, the demand for insulin is probably pretty inelastic, since it is necessary for those diabetics who rely on this drug.

The time period being considered also affects elasticity. The long-run elasticity is generally greater than the short-run elasticity because over a longer period more product substitution is possible. For example, a sharp increase in the price of natural gas would not reduce consumption by nearly as much in the short run as over a longer period, during which consumers could switch to heating systems that use alternative fuels.

Price Elasticity and Revenue

We have defined demand to be elastic when the absolute value of the price elasticity is greater than 1. For that to be true, the percentage change in quantity must be greater than the percentage change in price (i.e., $\%\Delta Q > \%\Delta P$). If this is true, what would you expect to happen to a firm's receipts if the price was lowered? Recall from your principles of economics course that total revenue (TR) is equal to price (P) times quantity (Q):

$TR = P \cdot Q$

Consider an extreme case. Suppose a 5-percent cut in price stimulates a 50-percent increase in sales (the price elasticity would be 10). You would expect revenues to rise. The relatively small drop in price would be more than compensated for by a large increase in sales.

To see exactly the relationship between total revenue and price elasticity, let us return to the demand function given by the equation

$$Q = 400 - 4P$$

which was used as the basis for Table 5.5. That table shows how the price elasticity of demand varies along the demand curve.

Table 5.6 is based on the same demand function. In this table, total revenue and marginal revenue are included, as well as the point price elasticities. Marginal revenue (MR) is defined as the rate of change in total revenue, or

$$MR = dTR/dQ$$

In this example, the demand function can be solved for P in terms of Q as follows:

$$Q = 400 - 4P$$
$$4P = 400 - Q$$
$$P = 100 - .25Q$$

Total revenue and marginal revenue are then

$$TR = P \cdot Q$$
$$TR = (100 - .25Q) \cdot Q$$
$$TR = 100Q - .25Q^2$$
$$MR = dTR/dQ$$
$$MR = 100 - .5Q$$

TABLE 5.6   **Demand, Price Elasticity, and Revenue**

Price (P)	Quantity (Q)	Total Revenue (TR = P·Q)	Marginal Revenue $\left(MR = \dfrac{dTR}{dQ}\right)$	Point Price Elasticity $\left(e_P = \dfrac{dQ}{dP} \cdot \dfrac{P}{Q}\right)$
100	0	0	100	
90	40	3,600	80	−9.00
80	80	6,400	60	_____
70	120	8,400	40	−2.33
60	160	9,600	20	_____
50	200	10,000	0	−1.00
40	240	9,600	−20	_____
30	280	8,400	−40	−0.43
20	320	6,400	−60	_____
10	360	3,600	−80	−0.11

NOTE: Use this table to practice calculating point price elasticity by filling in the four blank spaces in the last column. As a check, make certain each of your answers is between the elasticities immediately above and below your estimate. Note that no point elasticity can be calculated when $Q = 0$, since division by 0 is not defined.

These revenue functions, along with the demand curve, are graphed in Figure 5.6.

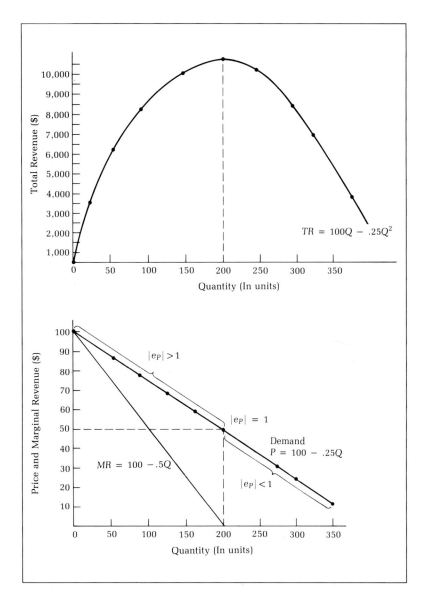

FIGURE 5.6   **Demand, Total Revenue, Marginal Revenue, and Price Elasticity and Demand.**   Note that demand is elastic above the $50 price and inelastic below it. When price is decreased and demand is elastic, total revenue rises. However, if price is decreased and demand is inelastic, total revenue also decreases.

You see in Figure 5.6 that demand is price elastic over the range of quantities for which marginal revenue is positive. Since marginal revenue is the slope of total revenue (remember that $MR = dTR/dQ$), you can tell that increasing sales by lowering price will cause total revenue to rise over this interval. However, lowering price when demand is inelastic (beyond $Q = 200$) will result in reduced revenues.

From an examination of Figure 5.6 and Table 5.6, we can reach some important conclusions about the relationship between elasticity and total revenue. These can be summarized as follows:

Elastic Demand

1. Decrease price .... Increase total revenue

2. Increase price .... Decrease total revenue

Price and total revenue move in opposite directions.

Inelastic Demand

1. Decrease price .... Decrease total revenue

2. Increase price .... Increase total revenue

Price and total revenue move in the same direction.

If demand is unitarily elastic between two points, both will yield the same total revenue. If a demand function of the constant elasticity type (such as the power functions we looked at above) has a unitary elasticity, then the same level of revenue will be generated regardless of price.

You see that for a linear demand function, as price falls, demand becomes less elastic until at some point it becomes inelastic. You have also seen that when demand is elastic, price cuts are associated with increases in total revenue. But if price continues to be lowered in the range in which demand is inelastic, total revenue will fall. Thus, total revenue will be maximized at the price (and related quantity) at which demand is unitarily elastic. You can see from Figure 5.6 that this point is also where $MR = 0$. This observation makes sense, since marginal revenue is the slope of total revenue. Recall that any function may have a maximum where its slope is 0. For total revenue, we have

$$TR = P \cdot Q = (100 - .25Q)Q$$
$$TR = 100Q - .25Q^2$$
$$dTR/dQ = 100 - .5Q$$

Setting the first derivative equal to 0 and solving for Q, we find

$$dTR/dQ = 100 - .5Q = Q$$
$$-.50Q = -100$$
$$Q = 200$$

Checking the second-order condition, we see that

$$dTR^2/dQ^2 = -.5 < 0$$

Since the second derivative is negative, we know that total revenue is a maximum at $Q = 200$. The price at which 200 units will sell is $50, so that is the revenue-maximizing price.

5.7   INCOME ELASTICITY OF DEMAND

The income elasticity of demand measures the responsiveness of sales to changes in income, *ceteris paribus*. It is defined as the percentage change in sales divided by the corresponding percentage change in income. The methods used to calculate arc income elasticity (E_I) and point income elasticity (e_I) are

$$E_I = \left(\frac{Q_1 - Q_2}{Q_1 + Q_2} \right) \bigg/ \left(\frac{I_1 - I_2}{I_1 + I_2} \right)$$

$$e_I = \frac{dQ}{dI} \cdot \frac{I}{Q}$$

Given information on sales and income relationships similar to the sales price data used above, the calculation of income elasticities is strictly analogous to the calculation of price elasticities.

If the income elasticity of demand for a product is greater than 1, the product is said to be income elastic; if it is equal to 1, the product has unitary income elasticity; and if the income elasticity is less than 1, the product is income inelastic. For normal goods, the income elasticity is greater than 0, since with rising incomes, consumers will purchase a greater quantity of such goods, *ceteris paribus*. If the income elasticity for a commodity is negative, the good is an inferior good; that is, people will choose to purchase less of the product when their income increases. Potatoes or hamburger may represent examples of inferior goods for some households, as would purchases from the Goodwill store or Salvation Army store. These relationships can be summarized as follows:

Normal goods are indicated by e_I or $E_I > 0$.

If e_I or $E_I > 1$, the good is income elastic
If e_I or $E_I < 1$, the good is income inelastic
If e_I or $E_I = 1$, the good is unitarily income elastic

Inferior goods are indicated by e_I or $E_I < 0$.

To illustrate just one way in which income elasticity may be useful, consider the following situation. A firm has obtained a fairly reliable estimate of the projected percentage increase in income for their market area for the next year, let us say 4.5 percent. They know that sales are currently running at an annual rate of 200,000 units, and the marketing or economic analysis group has estimated the arc income elasticity of demand for the product at 1.2. If other factors are expected to remain relatively constant, we can use this information as one input into projecting sales for the next year, as follows:

$$E_I = \frac{\%\Delta Q}{\%\Delta I}$$

and subsequently,

$$\%\Delta Q = (E_I)(\%\Delta I)$$
$$\%\Delta Q = (1.2)(4.5)$$
$$\%\Delta Q = 5.4$$

Thus, next year's sales would be projected to be 5.4 percent above the current level, or 1.054 times this year's sales:

$$(1.054)\,(200{,}000) = 210{,}800 \text{ units}$$

Let us now look once more at the Big Sky Foods demand functions that we estimated in section 5.4. We estimated the following linear and nonlinear forms. The linear demand function is

$$Q = 15.939 - 9.057P + .009INC + 5.092PC$$

The nonlinear demand function is

$$Q = .0012P^{-2.755}INC^{1.512}PC^{1.364}$$

Using the linear form, let us calculate the arc income elasticity over the income interval of $3500 to $4000, with Big Sky Foods' price and the competitor's price at their mean values of $5.88 and $4.86, respectively. The calculation of Q for a $3500 income level is

$$Q = 15.939 - 9.057(5.88) + .009(3500) + 5.092(4.86)$$
$$Q = 18.93$$

The calculation of Q for a $4000 income level is

$$Q = 15.939 - 9.957(5.88) + .009(4000) + 5.092(4.86)$$
$$Q = 23.43$$

The arc income elasticity is calculated as

$$E_I = \left(\frac{Q_1 - Q_2}{Q_1 + Q_2}\right)\Big/\left(\frac{I_1 - I_2}{I_1 + I_2}\right)$$
$$E_I = \left(\frac{18.93 - 23.43}{18.93 + 23.42}\right)\Big/\left(\frac{3500 - 4000}{3500 + 4000}\right)$$
$$E_I = 1.593$$

On this basis, we would judge this product to be a normal good ($E_I > 0$) and elastic with respect to income ($E_I > 1$).

The point income elasticity at each of the end points of the above interval ($3500 to $4000) is as follows:

$$\text{At } I = 3500: \quad e_I = \frac{\partial Q}{\partial INC} \cdot \frac{INC}{Q} = (.009)(3500/19.83)$$

$$e_I = 1.664$$

$$\text{At } I = 4000: \quad e_I = \frac{\partial Q}{\partial INC} \cdot \frac{INC}{Q} = (.009)(4000/23.43)$$

$$e_I = 1.536$$

This demonstrates that income elasticities, like price elasticities, will vary within a linear demand function as the level of income varies.

For the multiplicative power function (nonlinear) form of the demand function, we can find the point income elasticity as follows:

$$e_I = \frac{\partial Q}{\partial INC} \cdot \frac{INC}{Q}$$

$$e_I = (1.512)(.0012 P^{-2.755} INC^{.512} PC^{1.364})(INC/.0012 P^{-2.755} INC^{1.512} PC^{1.362})$$

$$e_I = (1.512) \left(\frac{.0012 P^{-2.755} INC^{1.512} PC^{1.364}}{.0012 P^{-2.755} INC^{1.512} PC^{1.364}} \right)$$

$$e_I = 1.512$$

Since none of the variables is included in the final expression for the point income elasticity, we can conclude that for this function, the income elasticity of demand is constant. That is, $e_I = 1.512$ for all values of the variables. Once more we see that for this type of function, the elasticity is equal to the value of the relevant variable's exponent in the demand function.

5.8   CROSS-PRICE ELASTICITY

The sales volume of one product may be influenced by the price of either substitute or complementary products. Cross-price elasticity of demand provides a means to quantify that type of influence. It is defined as the ratio of the percentage change in sales of one product to the percentage change in price of another product. The relevant arc (E_C) and point (e_C) cross-price elasticities are determined as follows:

$$E_C = \left(\frac{Q_{A_1} - Q_{A_2}}{Q_{A_1} + Q_{A_2}} \right) \bigg/ \left(\frac{P_{B_1} - P_{B_2}}{P_{B_1} + P_{B_2}} \right)$$

$$e_C = \frac{\partial Q_A}{\partial P_B} \cdot \frac{P_B}{Q_A}$$

where the alphabetic subscripts differentiate between the two products involved.

A negative coefficient of cross-price elasticity implies that a decrease in the price of product B results in an increase in sales of product A or vice versa. We know that a decrease in the price of product B will normally result in increased sales of product B, and if that is accompanied by increased sales of product A (*ceteris paribus*), we can conclude that the products are complementary to one another (such as cassette tape recorders and cassette tapes). Thus, when the coefficient of cross-price elasticity for two products is negative, we classify the products as complements.

A similar line of reasoning leads to the conclusion that if the cross-price elasticity is positive, the products are substitutes. For example, an increase in the price of sugar would cause less sugar to be purchased but would increase the sale of sugar substitutes. When we calculate the cross-price elasticity for this case, both the numerator and the denominator ($\%\Delta Q$ of sugar substitutes and $\%\Delta P$ of sugar, respectively) would have the same sign, and the coefficient would be positive.

If two goods are unrelated, a change in the price of one will not affect the sales of the other. The numerator of the cross-price elasticity ratio would be 0, and thus the coefficient of cross-price elasticity would be 0. In this case, the two commodities would be defined as independent. For example, consider the expected effect that a 10-percent increase in the price of eggs would have on the quantity of electronic calculator sales. These relationships can be summarized as follows:

If e_C or $E_C > 0$, goods are substitutes
If e_C or $E_C < 0$, goods are complementary
If e_C or $E_C = 0$, goods are independent

Let us return once more to Big Sky Foods' demand functions as estimated earlier. The linear demand function is

$$Q = 15.939 - 9.057P + .009INC + 5.092PC$$

The nonlinear demand function is

$$Q = .0012P^{-2.755}INC^{1.512}PC^{1.364}$$

For the nonlinear form, the point cross-price elasticity of demand is calculated as

$$e_C = \frac{\partial Q}{\partial PC} \cdot \frac{PC}{Q}$$

You know that for the nonlinear function, this reduces to the value of the exponent on the variable representing the competitor's price. Thus, in this example, the estimate of the cross-price elasticity would be

$$e_C = 1.364$$

Since this is a positive value, you would conclude that the two firms' products are substitutes in the eyes of consumers.

The arc cross-price elasticity of demand is calculated in a manner similar to the calculation of other arc elasticities. Using the linear demand function given above, with $P = 5.68$, $INC = 3716$, $PC_1 = 4.50$, and $PC_2 = 5.00$, we find Q_1 and Q_2 as follows:

$$Q_1 = 15.939 - 9.057(5.68) + .009(3716) + 5.092(4.50)$$
$$Q_1 = 20.85$$
$$Q_2 = 15.939 - 9.057(5.68) + .009(3716) + 5.092(5.00)$$
$$Q_2 = 23.40$$

The arc cross-price elasticity is

$$E_C = \left(\frac{20.85 - 23.40}{20.85 + 23.40} \right) \bigg/ \left(\frac{4.50 - 5.00}{4.50 + 5.00} \right)$$
$$E_C = 1.095$$

Calculate the arc cross-price elasticity for another pair of values for PC. Let $PC_1 = 4.20$ and $PC_2 = 4.60$. Fill in the remaining values given that $P = 5.68$ and $INC = 3716$:[9]

$$Q_1 = \underline{\hspace{5cm}}$$

$$Q_2 = \underline{\hspace{5cm}}$$

$$E_C = \left(\frac{-}{+} \right) \bigg/ \left(\frac{4.20 - 4.60}{4.20 + 4.60} \right)$$

$$E_C = \underline{\hspace{4cm}}$$

---

[9] $Q_1 = 19.33$, $Q_2 = 21.36$, $E_C = 1.098$.

5.9 MORE EXAMPLES OF ELASTICITIES IN THE PRIVATE AND PUBLIC SECTORS

Earlier we cited market demand functions for sweet potatoes and for crude oil. We will now consider various elasticities for these studies. In the report on the demand for sweet potatoes, the authors estimate a coefficient of price elasticity of .65, reflecting an inelastic demand. They also report that their results are generally consistent with a 0 income elasticity of demand. While the authors did not report a cross-price elasticity, it would clearly be positive, given the sign of the white potato price variable, indicating the "substitution effect between the two types of potatoes."[10]

---

[10] Schrimper and Mathia, p. 120.

In the study of crude oil demand, elasticities were calculated for each subset of the data (i.e., 1929–1941 and 1948–1973) and may be summarized as follows:[11]

Type of Elasticity	1929–1941	1948–1973
Gasoline price	.06	−.26
Income	.20	.10
Auto stock	.43	.79

The statistical significance of these estimates varies, but one important conclusion of policy concern is clear: the coefficient of price elasticity is quite low (inelastic). This implies that public policy measures that might attempt to conserve oil consumption by increasing price would not be very effective unless the price increases were quite substantial. Demand is simply not very responsive to changes in price, as evidenced during the gasoline crisis of the early 1970s, when price rose sharply but consumption decreased very little.

An interesting example of the application of demand analysis and elasticity estimation in the public sector is found in a study of outdoor recreation in Arizona.[12] Using a sample of nearly 3000 households, the authors estimate price elasticities for various recreational activities using variable cost per household trip as the measure of price. The results are summarized in Table 5.7.

TABLE 5.7   **Price Elasticities for Various Recreational Activites**

Region of State	Hunting		Small Game	Fishing		General Rural Outdoor Recreation
	Deer	Other Big Game		Cold Water	Warm Water	
1	.43	.33	1.06	.40	.48	.12
2	.30	.39	.52	.38	.65	.15
3	.44	—	.74	.41	.31	.35
4	.21	—	.68	—	.33	.56
5	.87	.23	.54	.74	.44	.30
6	.27	.40	.36	.59	.83	.14
7	.27	.62	.52	.97	.85	.36

SOURCE: Russell L. Gum and William E. Martin, "Problems and Solutions in Estimating the Demand for Value of Rural Outdoor Recreation," *American Journal of Agricultural Economics*, November 1975, pp. 558–566.

---

[11]Danielson and DeLorme, p. 27.

[12]Russell L. Gum and William E. Martin, "Problems and Solutions in Estimating the Demand for and Value of Rural Outdoor Recreation," *American Journal of Agricultural Economics*, November 1975, pp. 558–566.

One conclusion that could be derived from these elasticity estimates is that the variable costs involved in obtaining the benefits of outdoor recreation could generally be increased substantially with little loss of activity. This may imply, for example, that greater revenue could be generated from hunting and fishing licenses and from fees for the use of parks and campgrounds.

In another public sector application, the direct (own) price elasticity and a cross-price elasticity were estimated for a school lunch program in Pittsburgh. The study concerned the effect of an increase in hot lunch prices during the 1972–1973 school year on participation by fully paying students and on participation in free hot lunch programs by students qualifying for the free lunch.[13]

The important results of this study are summarized by the graphs in Figure 5.7. The left-hand graph shows the simple demand relationship between price and quantity, along with four elasticities calculated by the authors based on their empirical findings. The equation for this demand curve is

$$Q = 16{,}415.21 - 262.743P$$

The demand function exhibits the expected relationship between price and quantity. Furthermore, it should be noted that the coefficient of price elasticity of demand is lower (less elastic, or more inelastic) as the demand function moves from left to right. Students may wish to verify the elasticities presented in this graph. Because estimates of price and quantity made from the graph may not be precise, calculated values may differ slightly from those shown. In discussing their research findings, the authors give more precise data. For example, at the original price of 20 cents in January 1973, 11,160 paid meals were served. Using these data, we can calculate the point price elasticity at point C as follows:

$$e_P = \frac{dQ}{dP} \cdot \frac{P}{Q}$$

$$Q = 16{,}415.21 - 262.743P$$

$$dQ/dP = -262.743$$

$$e_P = (-262.743)\,(20/11{,}160)$$

$$e_P = -.471$$

---

[13]George A. Braley and Paul E. Nelson, Jr., "Effect of a Controlled Price Increase on School Lunch Participation: Pittsburgh 1973," *American Journal of Agricultural Economics*, February 1975, pp. 90–96; and "Pricing the School Lunch: A Consumer Problem," *The Journal of Consumer Affairs*, vol. 9, no. 2, 1975, pp. 139–147. When this research was conducted, Braley was a food program specialist with the Food and Nutrition Service, and Nelson was an economist with the Economic Research Service of the United States Department of Agriculture, illustrating the kind of opportunities available in the public sector for people with good managerial economics skills.

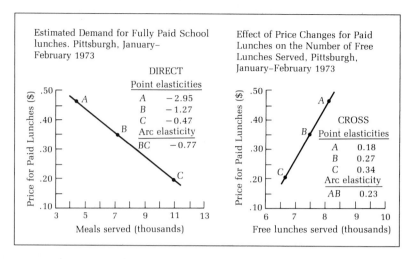

FIGURE 5.7   **Effect of Paid Lunch Price Changes on Paid and Free Lunches Served.**   The point price elasticities in the left-hand graph indicate that demand becomes less elastic (more inelastic) as price decreases. (Adapted from George A. Braley and Paul E. Nelson, Jr., "Effect of a Controlled Price Increase on School Lunch Participation: Pittsburgh, 1973," *American Journal of Agricultural Economics*, February 1975, pp. 92–94.)

The right-hand graph in Figure 5.7 illustrates the effect of the price increase for paid lunches on the number of free lunches served. We should expect this relationship to be positive and therefore the cross-price elasticity to be positive. Free lunches are clearly a substitute for paid lunches. In fact, if it were not for qualification requirements, we would expect everyone to make the substitution. The empirical results support the reasoning that a higher price for paid lunches would encourage more students to attempt to qualify for the free lunch program. Thus, the results from the Pittsburgh study are consistent with deductive economic reasoning. The relatively low cross-price elasticities, however, suggest that relatively few students who quit purchasing a lunch at higher prices become participants in the free lunch program.

5.10   THE EFFECT OF ADVERTISING ON DEMAND

Advertising influences our attitudes toward the product or service being promoted. In most cases, the intent of a firm's advertising is to stimulate sales of a particular product or product line. When the Chrysler Corporation decides to sponsor a television show or to place an advertisement in a national magazine, it is hoped that doing so will increase the sales of Chrysler products. Such product promotions have their impact on consumers through the tastes and preferences determinant of demand discussed earlier in this chapter.

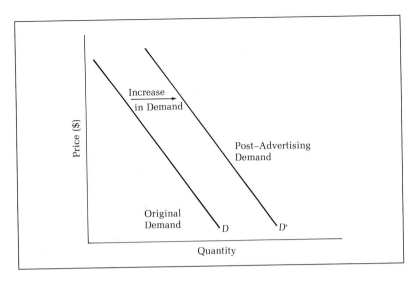

Price ($)

Increase in Demand

Post–Advertising Demand

Original Demand

D

D′

Quantity

FIGURE 5.8   **Effect of Advertising on Demand.**   We usually expect advertising to cause the demand curve to shift to the right. Such an increase in demand is shown by the shift from D to D′. At any given price, consumers will purchase more along D′ than along D.

As shown in Figure 5.8, advertising is expected to shift the firm's demand function to the right. As a result, more will be purchased at each price after the advertising campaign than before it. Why? Part of the answer lies in the information component of the advertising message. From advertising, consumers are able to learn about new products and to gain additional information about how existing products may satisfy perceived needs. We certainly will not buy a product that we do not know exists, and the more we know about how a product can bring us satisfaction, the more likely we are to purchase the product.

In addition to shifting the demand function to the right, advertising may have the effect of making it somewhat more steep. The reason for this is that advertisements can create stronger consumer brand preferences, thus making consumers less sensitive to price changes for that product. This means that one effect of advertising can be to make the demand for a firm's product more price inelastic. To the extent that this is true, management has an increased ability to raise price without losing as many sales as would have been lost otherwise. We have seen that raising the product's price will increase total revenue for the firm if demand is inelastic.

While this relationship between sales and advertising is generally true, advertising may also be used to decrease sales. The term *demarketing* is sometimes used to describe this process. Consider, for example, the effort to convince consumers to use less energy resources during the late 1970s and early 1980s. People were urged to lower thermostat settings, add insulation to their homes, and make their homes more energy efficient through other weatherization measures, such as reducing air infiltration. Advertising messages sponsored by electric and natural gas utilities were directed at getting us to reduce consumption.

5.11   DERIVED DEMAND

Thus far our discussion has related primarily to the demand for consumers' goods and services. Now let us briefly consider the demand for inputs to the production process. The general characteristic of a negatively sloped demand function (the law of demand) holds for the demand for factors of production, raw materials, and manufactured inputs as well as for consumer goods.

The demand curve for inputs to the production process slopes downward because of the principle of diminishing marginal productivity of factors.[14] Since additional units of a factor of production typically yield less incremental output than did the previous unit, it is reasonable to expect greater quantities of any one factor to be used at lower prices, *ceteris paribus*.

The demand for a factor input is called a derived demand because the level of the demand is determined by, or derived from, the demand for the final products for which it is an input. For example, the level of demand for inputs into the production of a cotton crop is determined by the demand for clothing, drapes, book bindings, canvas, adhesive tape, glycerin, paints, and other products composed in part or in whole of cotton fibers or cottonseed. In this example, there are two levels of derived demand. The demand for the inputs to cotton production is derived from the demand for cotton, which in turn is derived from the demand for cotton products.

5.12   DEMAND FOR PUBLIC GOODS

Public goods are jointly consumed by all members of society and are characterized by nonrival consumption and nonexclusion. *Nonrival consumption* means that one person's consumption of the goods does not limit consumption by others. *Nonexclusion* refers to the fact that it would be impossible, or prohibitively expensive, to exclude any one person from consuming the good. The best example is probably national defense, although such things as police and fire protection, highways, public libraries, and flood control projects are also illustrative.

---

[14]This principle is developed in detail in Chapter 7.

You almost surely have some demand for these and other public goods. But you do not buy them through the same kind of markets you use to obtain a bike, a haircut, a magazine, or other private goods. The public goods are provided through public sector decisions that we influence with our political votes rather than our dollar votes. We do, of course, pay for public goods, albeit indirectly, through taxes.

Even though we do not express our demand for public goods through direct private sector purchases, we do get some benefit from public goods. That is, public goods yield satisfaction, or utility, just as do private goods. Consider, for example, police protection. If asked to think about it, most people would say that they would rather have police protection than live without it and suffer the greater risk of being a crime victim. Thus, we can conclude that people get some benefit from police protection. It also seems reasonable to assume that there are diminishing marginal benefits from such public goods as police protection.

The marginal benefit received from having a particular unit of a public good available for "consumption" is taken as a measure of its worth to the consumer. That means that *if there were a way* to charge a consumer for each unit of the public good available, the appropriate price would be equal to the marginal benefit of the last unit made available. Thus, the diminishing marginal benefit function is considered to be the individual's demand curve for a public good. This is illustrated in Figure 5.9, in which price is considered to measure the value, or marginal benefit, of successive units of the public good.

Now let us consider how we might hypothetically get the total demand for a public good. You will recall that for private goods, we added all of the individual consumers' demand functions *horizontally* to get a market demand function. That is, we added the quantities consumers

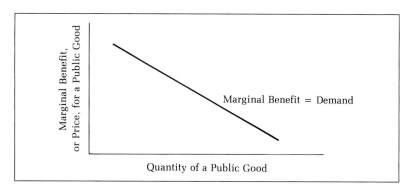

FIGURE 5.9   **Individual Demand Curve for a Public Good.**   Individual demand for public goods is usually related to the marginal benefit the individual gets from the good. Since marginal benefits generally decline as quantity increases, the demand for public goods is negatively sloped.

would purchase at various prices. This would not work for public goods because once a decision is made about how much police protection, national defense, or any other public good is to be made available, that amount is available for all of us to consume and receive its benefits. Our intent for public goods is to find the total value society places on each possible level of provision of the public good in question. This implies a *vertical* summation of the demand curves for all individual consumers.

To illustrate this process and to facilitate comparison with a private good, let us use the same three individual demand functions used in Figure

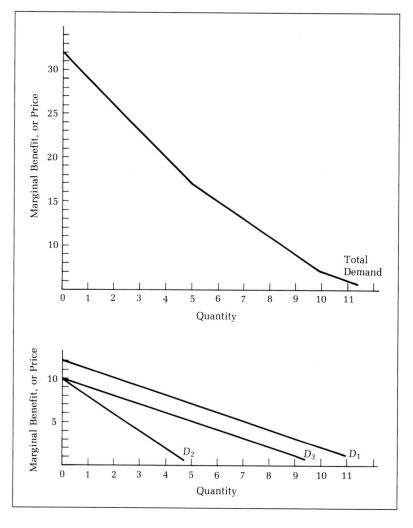

FIGURE 5.10   **Determining Demand for a Public Good**

5.3. The only difference is that now we will assume that these functions represent the individuals' demand functions for a public good rather than a private good. The demand functions are

Consumer 1: $P = 12 - Q$
Consumer 2: $P = 10 - 2Q$
Consumer 3: $P = 10 - Q$

For a public good, these functions are added vertically, as shown in Figure 5.10. Compare this figure to Figure 5.3, which illustrates the horizontal addition for a private good. The total demand curve can be thought of as a function that shows the marginal benefit for all of society for various levels of the public good. In determining the total demand for a public good in this way, we are weighing each consumer's marginal benefit equally.

5.13   DEMAND FOR CARS IN THE UNITED STATES

According to a study of the period from 1945 to 1975, the number of cars in use in the United States rose at an annual rate of 4.5 percent, from 25.2 million to 95.2 million units.[15] This was more than three times the growth rate of the population, so other forces must also have been instrumental in causing a rise in the demand for cars. Chief among these were rising incomes and more active life-styles. However, from 1975 to 1980, the annual growth rate in the number of cars dropped to 1.5 percent. Not only has the growth rate dropped, but there has also been a change in tastes and preferences in favor of smaller, more fuel-efficient cars.

The study divides the total demand for cars into two components: a demand for replacement vehicles and a demand for additions to the stock of cars. (Since light-duty trucks are frequently used in place of cars, both types of vehicles are considered part of the fundamental automobile demand.) Let us look at these two components of automobile demand in detail, beginning with the largest component: replacement demand.

Replacement demand is defined as "consisting of vehicles needed to replace those being retired from the fleet."[16] Since this is difficult to measure directly, scrappage data are used as a proxy variable for actual replacement demand. Total units scrapped is the dependent variable for the replacement demand (*RD*) component of the total demand. The independent variables include

---

[15]Robert Gough and Scott Mayfield, "Is Automobile Demand Slowing," *Data Resources U.S. Review*, October 1981, pp. 1.9–1.16.

[16]Gough and Mayfield, p. 1.11.

1. T = a time trend with 1947.1 = 1

2. RU = rate of unemployment

3. ΔCPI = year-over-year percent change in the consumer price index

4. ΔINC = year-over-year percent change in real disposable personal income

5. ΔGP = year-over-year percent change in the implicit price deflator for consumption of gasoline

6. ΔP = percent change in the implicit price deflator for consumption of motor vehicles and parts minus the percent change in the implicit price deflator for consumption of durable goods

The time period included in estimating this regression model covered the period from the first quarter of 1967 (1967.1) to the fourth quarter of 1980 (1980.4). The regression results that the authors report are

$$RD = .233 + \underset{(9.27)}{.032T} - \underset{(4.01)}{.111RU} - \underset{(4.51)}{.085\Delta CPI} +$$

$$\underset{(2.13)}{.031\Delta INC} + \underset{(2.02)}{.006\Delta GP} - \underset{(2.05)}{.017\Delta P}$$

$$\overline{R}^2 = .8277$$
SE of the estimate = .1363
$$DW = 1.9609$$
Absolute values of t-ratios are in parentheses.

All the signs of the independent variables are reasonable, and all variables are significant at the 95-percent confidence level. The negative signs on the unemployment (RU) and inflation (ΔCPI) variables indicate that as consumers' economic circumstances worsen, they are likely to postpone replacing their vehicles. The positive sign for the income variable shows that people are more likely to change to a new car when incomes are rising. What about the positive sign on the energy variable (ΔGP)? Remember that the dependent variable is replacement demand. It makes sense that as fuel costs rise, people will be more inclined to discard an older, less fuel-efficient car for a new, smaller, more fuel-efficient one. You see that the variable used to measure automotive prices has the expected negative sign. The positive sign of the time variable indicates an increase over time in the rate of scrappage, again consistent with a change in tastes and preferences toward a different type of car: a smaller, more fuel-efficient model.

The second component of the total demand for cars is the demand for additions to the stock of cars, which the study refers to as the trend demand (TD). This dependent variable is the change in the total stock of vehicles (light trucks and automobiles). The independent variables in the regression model for TD are

1. ΔN = yearly change in the number of people in the population aged 16 years and older

2. ΔDI = yearly change in real permanent disposable personal income (1972 dollars)

3. ΔFR = yearly change in the finance rate for consumer installment credit for automobile loans

4. D = dummy variable to account for the effect of the energy price shock starting with the fourth quarter of 1974: $D = 0$ for 1974.3 and before; $D = 1$ for 1974.4 and after

5. ΔGP = year-over-year percent change in the implicit price deflator for consumption of gasoline

6. S = variable that measures the share of personal consumption expenditure spent for energy-related purchases

The time period used in estimating this regression model covered the period from 1967.2 through 1980.4. The results are as follows:

$$TD = 1.112\Delta N + .034\Delta DI - .050\Delta FR$$
$$(4.43)\qquad (1.90)\qquad (2.03)$$
$$-.004\Delta GP - .118(D)(S)(\Delta GP)$$
$$(.097)\qquad\qquad (2.46)$$

$$\overline{R}^2 = .7367$$
$$\text{SE of the estimate} = .1162$$
$$DW = 1.7821$$

Absolute values of t-ratios are in parentheses.

The coefficient of the population variable (ΔN) indicates that there is nearly a one-to-one relationship between the increase in the driving-age population and the increase in the stock of vehicles. The positive sign of the income variable is expected, indicating that a rise in the stock of vehicles is associated with increasing incomes. The negative sign of the variable representing the interest rate (ΔFR) supports the proposition that people may buy cars when finance rates drop and delay buying when rates rise. This proposition provides a rationale for the use of special financing arrangements as a promotional inducement to increase auto sales. Notice that the gas price variable has the expected sign (increasing gas prices reducing the long-term growth in the automotive stock) but that its level of statistical significance is quite low.

Finally, look at the last term in the model and its sign. The term is the product of the dummy variable, the share variable, and the gas price variable. The product of the last two terms ($S \cdot \Delta GP$) provides a weighted measure of the effect of changing gas prices. Multiplying this measure by the dummy variable makes it operative only for the period from 1974.4 and after (recall that $D = 0$ before 1974.4 and $D = 1$ starting with 1974.4). The coefficient of the last term (–.118) has the expected sign (i.e., this energy variable has had the effect of decreasing the trend demand for cars).

Total demand is found by adding the trend demand (TD) to the replacement demand (RD) for each period estimated.

SUMMARY

In this chapter, you learned that demand is the force that drives all business. Without a demand for its goods or services, a firm is doomed to failure. Several determinants of demand have been identified. The most important of these are the product's price, the level of income, consumer's tastes and preferences, and the prices of complementary or substitute goods.

The effect of the determinants of demand on sales is often measured using an elasticity. Elasticities measure the relative responsiveness of sales to changes in the determinants of demand. The three most important elasticities are

$$\text{Price elasticity} = \%\Delta Q / \%\Delta P$$
$$\text{Income elasticity} = \%\Delta Q / \%\Delta I$$
$$\text{Cross-price elasticity} = \%\Delta Q_A / \%\Delta P_B$$

These elasticities can be calculated for market demand functions as well as for the demand functions of individual firms.

You have seen that demand functions can be estimated statistically using regression analysis. This is true for some public sector activities, such as providing school lunches, and for private sector demand functions, such as automotive demand.

SUGGESTED READINGS

Braley, George A., and Nelson, Paul E., Jr. "Pricing the School Lunch: A Consumer Problem." *The Journal of Consumer Affairs*, vol. 9, no. 2, 1975, pp. 139–147.

Hogarty, Thomas F., and Elzinga, Kenneth G. "The Demand for Beer." *The Review of Economics and Statistics,* May 1972, pp. 195–198.

Hughes, David. *Demand Analysis for Marketing Decision.* Homewood, IL: Richard D. Irwin, 1973.

Morgan, W. Douglas, and Belknap, Andrew. "The Determinants of Mobile Home Shipments: Time Series Evidence." *Business Economics,* May 1982, pp. 30–37.

Reekie, W.D. "The Price Elasticity of Demand for Evening Newspapers." *Applied Economics,* March 1976, pp. 69–79.

Suits, D.B. "The Elasticity of Demand for Gambling." *Quarterly Journal of Economics,* February 1979, pp. 155–162.

Working, E.J. "What Do Statistical Demand Curves Show?" *Quarterly Journal of Economics,* February 1927, pp. 212–235.

PROBLEMS

1. Given that an individual consumer's demand curve is $P = 200 - 4Q$:
   a. Find the quantity this consumer would purchase at a price of $20.
   b. Suppose that the price increased to $60. How much would the consumer now purchase? Would this represent a change in demand or a change in quantity demanded? Why?
   c. What is the arc price price elasticity of demand between these observations? What does this imply about how the price increase would affect the total amount of money the consumer would spend on this product? Explain. Verify your answer by calculating total expenditures at both prices.

2. Calculate all of the meaningful arc elasticities of demand (price, income, and cross price) based on the following observations. Consider only contiguous points in evaluating potential elasticities.

Observation	Quantity	Price	Income	Other Price
A	10	100	3000	14
B	20	90	3000	14
C	30	80	4000	12
D	40	80	5000	12
E	50	70	6000	10
F	60	70	6000	8
G	70	60	7000	6
H	80	50	7000	6

For each of the elasticities you calculate, explain in one or two sentences what your result means.

3. Answer the following questions based on the following demand curve:

$$P = 400 - 5Q$$

a. Complete the following table:

P	Q	Total Revenue	Marginal Revenue
180			
160			
140			
120			
100			
80			
60			
40			
20			

b. What are the algebraic equations that represent total revenue (TR) and marginal revenue (MR)?

     $TR = $ _____

     $MR = $ _____

c. What is the arc price elasticity between the prices of 180 and 160?

     $E_p = $ _____

What is the arc price elasticity between the prices of 120 and 100?

     $E_p = $ _____

What is the arc price elasticity between the prices of 60 and 40?

     $E_p = $ _____

Are these results consistent for the values of TR and MR calculated above?

d. What is the point price elasticity at a price of 100?

     $e_p = $ _____

4. Use the data given in problem 2 to estimate a multiple linear regression model of demand. Use quantity (Q) as the dependent variable and price (P), income (M), and other price (PC) as the independent variables.
   a. Write your model below:

$Q =$ _____

Variable	t-Ratio
Price	————
Income	————
Other price	————

$\overline{R}^2 =$ _____

   Interpret the statistical significance of each variable and of the entire regression model.
   b. Use your regression model to estimate sales for each of the eight observations and write the estimated value as well as the amount of error in the table below.

Observation	Actual Quantity	Estimated Quantity	Error
A	10		
B	20		
C	30		
D	40		
E	50		
F	60		
G	70		
H	80		

   c. Calculate the point price elasticities of demand for observations A, E, and H. Are these results consistent with the arc price elasticities calculated in problem 2? Explain.

5. Table 5.4 presents data related to the demand function for Big Sky Foods. A multiple linear regression model of sales (Q) as a function of price (P), income (INC), and the competition's price (P) was estimated to be

$$Q = 15.939 - 9.05P + .009INC + 5.092PC$$
$$\qquad\qquad (-2.90)\quad (5.55)\qquad (1.97)$$

$$\overline{R}^2 = .867$$
$$DW = 1.81$$
$$\text{SE of the estimate} = 1.99$$

a. A fire at the major competitor's facilities during the second quarter of 1984 (period 1984.2) had some impact on all firms in the industry. To evaluate that fire's effect on Big Sky Foods' sales, assign a dummy variable (D) to equal 0 for every quarter except 1984.2 and let $D = 1$ for that period. Run a multiple linear regression using P, INC, PC, and D as independent variables and Q as the dependent variable. Write your results below:

$Q = $ _____

Variable		t-Ratio
P		_____
INC		_____
PC		_____
D		_____

$$\overline{R}^2 = \text{_____}$$
$$DW = \text{_____}$$
$$\text{SE of the estimate} = \text{_____}$$

b. How do these results compare with those given above? Which model do you think is best? Explain why. Does the sign of the coefficient of the dummy variable make sense to you? Explain.

6. The demand for ATA Systems' new long-life, felt-tipped pen has been estimated as a function of the price ATA charges (P), the average

monthly income of professional workers (M), the price charged by ATA's major competitor (P_o), and the level of ATA's annual advertising budget in thousands of dollars (A). The resulting equation follows:

$$Q = 10.3P^{-1.2}M^{1.2}P_o{}^{.7}A^{.4}$$

a. If ATA sets the price for the new pen at $10 while income is at $1890, the competitors' price is $5.70, and ATA's advertising budget is $500,000, what level of sales can be expected?

b. What is the point price elasticity of demand? Is demand elastic or inelastic? What does this mean in terms of the effect that a change in price would have on total revenue?

c. What is the cross-price elasticity of demand? Does this indicate that the two products are substitutes? Explain.

d. Is the demand for the new long-life pens income elastic or inelastic? Explain your answer.

e. If income is projected to go up by 4 percent next year, what percentage change in sales can be expected? Explain.

f. How responsive are sales to advertising expenditures? Explain the basis for your answer.

g. If income increases to $2020 while the other independent variables remain constant, what level of sales will result? Find the arc income elasticity based on the change between part a and part g. Could you have predicted this result?

7. MonDak Foods sells premade sandwiches through convenience stores and gas stations. They have been experimenting with different prices in 10 isolated test markets to determine how sales and price are related. The following results have been obtained:

Market	Price ($)	Sales (units/1000 people/month)
1	3.50	80
2	3.40	85
3	3.30	90
4	3.20	95
5	3.10	100
6	3.00	105
7	2.90	110
8	2.80	115
9	2.70	120
10	2.60	125

a. Does this relationship follow the law of demand? Explain.

b. Calculate the value of the arc price elasticity for a change in price from $3.40 to $3.30. Is demand elastic or inelastic in this region?

c. Plot these 10 observations on the grid below and connect them to form a demand curve.

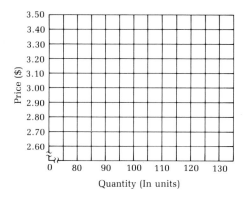

d. Based on this graph, how many units would you expect MonDak to sell at a price of $2.95?

8. The algebraic equation for MonDak's demand function based on the data from problem 7 is

$$P = 5.10 - .02Q$$

a. If MonDak has a target sales level of 118 units, what price should be used?

b. Find the algebraic expression for MonDak's total revenue (TR) as a function of sales (Q).

$$TR = f(Q) = \text{_____}$$

c. What is the algebraic equation for marginal revenue (MR)?

$$MR = dTR/dQ = \text{_____}$$

d. Based on these algebraic functions, find the price and the corresponding level of sales that would maximize total revenue for MonDak.

e. Rewrite MonDak's demand function with Q as a function of P rather than P as a function of Q, as given above.

$$Q = \text{_____}$$

f. What is the point price elasticity of demand at a price of $3.15? Is demand elastic or inelastic at this point?

9. Complete the following table based on the demand schedule for MonDak Foods given above (problem 8):

Price ($)	Sales (units)	Total Revenue ($)	Marginal Revenue* ($)	Arc Price Elasticity*
3.50	80	280		
3.40	85	289	1.8	−.209
3.30				
3.20				
3.10				
3.00				
2.90				
2.80				
2.70				
2.60				

*Place the values you calculate for these columns at the end of the relevant intervals, as shown for the first case.

a. In problem 8 you found the demand function, with sales as a function of price, to be

$$Q = 255 - 50P$$

Use this information to calculate the point price elasticity of demand for a price of $2.85.

$$e_p = \underline{\hspace{6cm}}$$

b. Is your answer to part a consistent with the arc price elasticities you calculated for the interval between $P = \$2.90$ and $P = \$2.80$? Explain.

c. What price-quantity combination would result in a point price elasticity of -1.0 for MonDak? What relationship does this answer have to your answer to problem 8, part d? Explain.

10. EVAS Enterprises manufactures a desk designed as a microcomputer work station. Bill Enith, the son of the company's founder, started working for EVAS last summer after completing his MBA program at Ohio State University. Bill was anxious to apply some of the tools he had learned and so estimated a demand function for the desks. His results were

$$Q = -180 - 8.5P + .25INC + .019A$$
$$\quad\quad\quad (-2.68) \quad (4.21) \quad\quad (8.71)$$

where

$$Q = \text{sales}$$
$$P = \text{price}$$
$$INC = \text{average household income}$$
$$A = \text{annual advertising budget}$$

Values in parentheses are t-ratios. The coefficient of determination (adjusted) is .876.

a. Based on this regression model for EVAS Enterprises' demand, what level of sales would you expect if the price was set at $400, average household income was $16,500, and EVAS spent $200,000 on advertising?

$$Q = \underline{\hspace{6cm}}$$

b. If the sales manager had a target of reaching 10 percent of the total market (estimated to be 48,000 units), what price should be established?

$$P = \underline{\hspace{6cm}}$$

c. What is the arc price elasticity of demand between the $400 price used in part a and the price you found in part b?

$$E_p = \underline{\hspace{6cm}}$$

d. What would be the difference in EVAS Enterprises' total revenue resulting from these two different price-quantity combinations? Is this difference consistent with the elasticity you calculated above? Explain.

11. The following regression results were obtained in a study of demand for a local bakery:

Variable	Coefficient	Standard Error	t-Ratio
Constant	12.42	2.43	5.11
Price	−0.83	0.27	−3.07
Income	0.04	0.02	2.00
Advertising	1.91	0.86	2.22

$$\text{Adjusted } \overline{R}^2 = .875$$
$$\text{SE of the estimate} = 4.89$$
$$F\text{-ratio} = 8.42$$
$$n = 34$$

a. The dependent variable is sales (S) in thousands of units per week. Write the regression equation:

$$S = \underline{\hspace{6cm}}$$

b. Given that advertising is in hundreds of dollars per week and income is in average weekly earnings, write a paragraph in which you interpret these results as though you were explaining them to the owner of the bakery, who has no background in economics.

c. What level of sales would result if the firm set the price at $7.50 while income was $580 and advertising was $1200?

$$S = \underline{\hspace{6cm}}$$

d. For the conditions given in part c, what is the point price elasticity of demand?

$$e_P = \underline{\hspace{6cm}}$$

What is the point income elasticity of demand?

$$e_I = \underline{\hspace{6cm}}$$

What is the point advertising elasticity of demand?

$$e_A = \underline{\hspace{6cm}}$$

e. If income is constant at $580 and advertising stays at $1200, what is the equation for the relationship between sales and price?

$$Q = f(P) = \underline{\hspace{6cm}}$$

f. Graph this demand on the grid below.

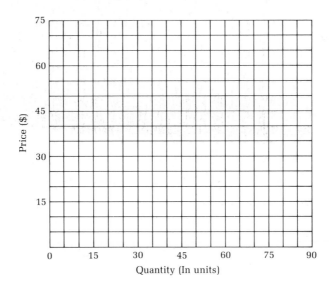

g. Find the algebraic expressions for total revenue (TR) and marginal revenue (MR) as functions of sales (Q):

$$TR = f(Q) = \text{\underline{\hspace{6cm}}}$$

$$MR = f(Q) = \text{\underline{\hspace{6cm}}}$$

Plot the marginal revenue function, along with the demand function, on the graph above.

h. What level of sales will maximize the bakery's total revenue? At what price would that level of sales result?

12. A local restaurant, Franklin's, has found that the number of lunch specials served each week is primarily a function of the level and composition of its advertising expenditures. Franklin advertises on the radio and in the local newspaper. Each radio spot (R) costs $80, and each newspaper ad (N) costs $40. The sales ($S$) response function has been estimated as

$$S = 11.2R^{.5}N^{1.5}$$

a. Assuming that the total advertising budget is $500 per week, use the Lagrangian multiplier method to find the sales-maximizing combination of radio and newspaper advertising.

b. What percentage increase in sales would result from a 1-percent increase in radio advertising? (Apply the general concept of elasticity.)

13. Harden Electronics sells a switching device to the automotive industry. Bruce Harden, the founder and president of the company, hired a consulting firm to do some demand analysis. In part, the results showed that the demand for the switching devices could be represented by the following function:

$$P = 100 - 4Q$$

a. Find the algebraic expression for Harden's total revenue:

$$TR = \text{\underline{\hspace{7cm}}}$$

b. Find the albegraic expression for Harden's average and marginal revenue functions:

$$AR = \text{\underline{\hspace{6cm}}}$$

$$MR = \text{\underline{\hspace{6cm}}}$$

c. What price should Harden set if the objective is to sell 15 switching devices?

$$P = \text{\underline{\hspace{6cm}}}$$

d. What price and quantity would maximize total sales revenue for Harden?

P = _____

Q = _____

14. TV Shack, a television store near campus, sells a line of 32K private-brand computers that use a TV screen as a monitor. The computer comes with almost no software, and other hardware, such as a disk drive, a cassette tape storage system, and a printer are available only at an extra cost. TV Shack's owner, Alice O'Hagan, has experimented using different prices for the basic computer and has collected the following data:

Price	Sales	Price	Sales
110	30	103	60
105	40	104	40
101	100	102	80
107	30	108	20
101	140	101	120

a. Plot these observations on the grid provided below.

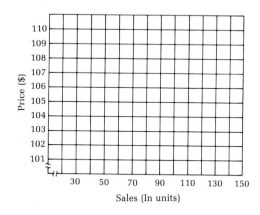

b. The data do not appear to form a linear demand function. Use OLS regression to see which of the following models fits these data the best:

Linear: $P = a + bQ$
Nonlinear: $P = a + b/Q$

(For the nonlinear form, use the reciprocal of Q as the independent variable.) Write your two equations and the respective values for R^2 below:

Linear form: $P =$ _____ $R^2 =$ _____

Nonlinear form: $P =$ _____ $R^2 =$ _____

c. For the nonlinear model, find the equations for total revenue and marginal revenue.

d. Based on the nonlinear demand function, calculate the point price elasticity of demand for the following points:

$P = 108$ $Q =$ _____ $e_p =$ _____

$P = 105$ $Q =$ _____ $e_p =$ _____

$P = 102$ $Q =$ _____ $e_p =$ _____

15. Alice O'Hagan, the owner of the TV Shack store, has a son, Warren, who is a business major at Allegheny University. Warren was looking at the regression results for sales of the 32K computer and suggested that there might be some other factor influencing sales in addition to price changes. In discussing the problem with Alice, he learned that advertising expenditures had also been changed. So Warren suggested incorporating that variable into a demand model as well. Warren fit several types of models to the data but found that the following model seemed to work the best:

$$\ln Q = 88.02 - 18.85(\ln P) + .78(\ln A)$$
$$(-7.27) \qquad (2.04)$$
$$R^2 = .874$$

where

$\ln Q =$ natural logarithm of sales (Q)
$\ln P =$ natural logarithm of price (P)
$\ln A =$ natural logarithm of advertising (A)

a. Write the multiplicative form of this function below, [i.e., $Q = f(P, A) = KP^a A^b$]:

$Q =$ _____

b. What sales level could be expected if price was 105 and advertising expenditures were 100?

c. What is the point price elasticity of demand? Is demand elastic or inelastic? Is this consistent with the results you found in problem 14 related to TV Shack's sales of the computer? Explain.

d. You might try verifying these regression results yourself using the following data:

Sales	Price	Advertising
30	110	100
20	108	80
30	107	110
40	105	85
40	104	95
60	103	70
80	102	85
100	101	85
140	101	140
120	101	120

16. Suppose that you were given the following data representing 14 observations of a firm's sales, the price charged for the product, and a measure of income:

Price	Sales	Income
5.00	20	2620
5.20	16	2733
5.30	16	2898
5.48	14	3056
5.60	16	3271
5.80	19	3479
6.03	17	3736
6.01	18	3868
5.92	21	4016
5.90	26	4152
5.85	30	4336
5.80	26	4477
5.85	27	4619
5.80	29	4764

a. Estimate the linear equation for the demand curve using just price
   (P) and sales (Q), with $Q = f(P)$:

$$Q = \underline{\hspace{5cm}}$$

$$\overline{R}^2 = \underline{\hspace{5cm}}$$

$$t\text{-ratio for } P = \underline{\hspace{5cm}}$$

b. Interpret this regression equation, including a statement of what the
   t-ratio and $\overline{R}^2$ tell you. Does the relationship you have estimated
   between P and Q make sense, given what you know about the law
   of demand? Explain.

c. Now estimate sales (Q) as a function of both price (P) and income
   (M) in a multiple linear regression:

$$Q = \underline{\hspace{5cm}}$$

Variable	Coefficient	Standard Error	t-Ratio
P	_____	_____	_____
M	_____	_____	_____
$\overline{R}^2 =$			

Which model is better, this one or the one estimated in part a? Explain why.

17. A firm has the following demand curve:

$$P = 1000Q^{-.2}$$

a. What is the equation for total revenue?

TR = _____

b. What is the equation for marginal revenue?

MR = _____

c. What is the equation for average revenue?

AR = _____

d. What is point price elasticity of demand at a price of $1000? Is demand inelastic, elastic, or unitarily elastic at $P = 1000$?

$e_p =$ _____

Demand: _____

18. The following results were obtained from an OLS regression analysis of sales (Y) as a linear function of price (P), income (M), and a dummy variable (D), which equaled 1 if a television advertising campaign was used in a given city and 0 otherwise. Sales are in units per 1000 people, price is in real 1967 dollars, and income is in real (1967 dollars) disposable personal income per capita.

Variable	Coefficient	Standard Error	t-Ratio
Intercept	10.20	2.60	3.92
P	−2.40	1.10	−2.18
M	0.02	0.009	2.22
D	18.50	5.70	3.25

$$\overline{R}^2 = .887$$
$$F = 12.45$$
Number of observations = 24

a. Write the algebraic equation for this regression model:

$$Y = \underline{\hspace{10cm}}$$

b. Interpret the value of $\bar{R}^2$.

c. If price was \$10.00 and the income variable was \$8,800 for a city where the advertising campaign was used, what would be the best point estimate for sales?

d. What is the point income elasticity, given your answer in part c?

APPENDIX   A Formal Model of Consumer Demand

Consumers are faced with a wide variety of goods and services from which they select items for consumption while omitting others from their market basket of purchases. How much of any commodity is consumed is determined by many factors. The most important of these are the individual's tastes and preferences, the prices of various commodities, and the consumer's income.

The tastes and preferences of a consumer are influenced by many factors, including the media he or she is exposed to, education, life experiences, advertising, and social norms, to name a few. These variables will determine the satisfaction to be obtained from consuming various bundles of goods. This satisfaction can be expressed in terms of a utility function: $U = f(X_1, X_2, \ldots, X_n)$. It appears that, for most people, the function U increases as consumption increases (i.e., $\partial U/\partial X_i > 0$ for all i). In general, we can say that more is preferred to less with respect to consumption. The number of commodities available (n) is so large and diverse that few people can honestly claim that there is nothing more they would like to have. It is reasonable to assume that people conduct themselves in the economic world in such a manner as to attempt to maximize their expected satisfaction, that is, to maximize U.

Unfortunately, we are not free to consume whatever we may like. We are constrained by our income and by the reality that the goods and services we consume have positive money prices. We are faced, therefore, with the problem of allocating our scarce money resources among alternative bundles of commodities in such a way as to yield the greatest possible satisfaction. Thus, the limitation imposed on increasing the value of the function U is referred to as a budget constraint and can be stated as $M = \Sigma P_i X_i$, where M is money income, P_i is the price of the ith commodity, and X_i is the number of units of the ith commodity purchased.

The consumer's problem can be stated in mathematical terms as follows:

Maximize: $U = f(X_1, X_2, \ldots, X_n)$
Subject to: $M = P_1 X_1 + P_2 X_2 + \ldots + P_n X_n$

Such a problem can be solved using the Lagragian multiplier technique. If we set up the Lagrangian function L, with the Lagrangian multiplier λ, we can maximize U subject to the budget constraint by maximizing L:

$$L = f(X_1, X_2, \ldots, X_n) + \lambda(M - P_1X_1 - P_2X_2 - \ldots - P_nX_n)$$

Then, finding partial derivatives, we get

$$\partial L/\partial X_1 = f_1 - \lambda P_1 = 0$$
$$\partial L/\partial X_2 = f_2 - \lambda P_2 = 0$$
$$\cdots\cdots\cdots\cdots$$
$$\cdots\cdots\cdots\cdots$$
$$\cdots\cdots\cdots\cdots$$
$$\partial L/\partial X_n = f_n - P_n = 0$$
$$\partial L/\partial \lambda = M - P_1X_1 - P_2X_2 - \ldots - P_nX_n = 0$$

From the preceding equation, it follows that in order for the consumer to maximize the constrained utility function the following must hold:

$$\frac{f_1}{P_1} = \frac{f_2}{P_2} = \ldots = \frac{f_n}{P_n}$$

Since f_i represents the marginal utility of the ith commodity, we arrive at the important conclusion regarding consumer behavior that satisfaction will be maximized when the budget is so allocated that marginal utility per dollar spent is equal for all goods. From the last partial derivative above, it also follows that all of the consumer's budget will be spent.

Let us now consider a specific utility function for a consumer along with a budget constraint to illustrate the concept of consumer equilibrium, that is, the determination of the actual bundle of commodities that will maximize satisfaction. We shall use a simplified two-commodity case for two reasons: (1) the computations are reduced (but remain applicable to the n-dimensional case presented in general form above), and (2) the concept can be adequately illustrated graphically by using just two goods. Assume that

$$U = XY$$
$$M = P_XX + P_YY$$
$$M = 100, P_X = 10, P_Y = 5$$

where X and Y represent the number of units of the two commodities consumed. Thus, the Lagrangian function is

$$L = XY + \lambda(100 - 10X - 5Y)$$
$$\partial L/\partial X = Y - 10\lambda = 0$$
$$\partial L/\partial Y = X - 5\lambda = 0$$
$$\partial L/\partial \lambda = 100 - 10X - 5Y = 0$$

Solving the first two partials, we find

$$Y/10 = X/5$$
$$Y = 2X$$

Substituting this result in the third partial and rearranging terms,

$$100 = 10X + 5(2X)$$
$$100 = 20X$$

Therefore, $X = 5$ and $Y = 10$. The equilibrium for the consumer is to purchase 5 units of X and 10 units of Y. This exhausts the budget of $100. Utility equals 50 ($U = XY = 5 \cdot 10$).

From the first two partials, we can solve $\lambda = Y/10$ and $\lambda = X/5$, respectively. From the equilibrium values of X and Y determined above, we find that $\lambda = 10/10 = 5/5 = 1$. But does this value have any economic meaning? The answer is a definite yes. The value of λ can be interpreted in a manner analogous to the interpretation of shadow prices in linear programming. That is, the value of λ indicates the amount of change in the objective function that would result if the consumer had $1 more of income (utility could be increased by 1). Thus, in the example of utility maximization subject to a budget constraint, λ measures the marginal utility of income (money).

This result can be verified by solving the constrained maximization problem above with a budget constraint of $101 rather than $100:

$$L = XY + \lambda(101 - 10X - 5Y)$$
$$\partial L / \partial X = Y - 10\lambda = 0$$
$$\partial L / \partial Y = X - 5\lambda = 0$$
$$\partial L / \partial \lambda = 101 - 10X - 5Y = 0$$

From the first two partials, we still find $Y = 2X$. Substituting this in the third partial, we determine that $X = 5.05$ and thus $Y = 10.1$. Utility is then $U = (5.05)(10.1) = 51.0$, or one unit greater than when income was 100 rather than 101. Thus, the marginal utility of money is 1 at this point.

The original situation is illustrated graphically in Figure 5A.1. The line AB represents the consumer's budget constraint. The budget constraint is $10X + 5Y = 100$. When this is solved for $Y (Y = 20 - 2X)$, we see that the slope is -2. The curve labeled U_{50} represents the various combinations of X and Y for which the utility function has a value of 50. Such a curve is referred to as an *indifference curve* because the consumer receives the same degree of satisfaction (i.e., utility is constant at 50) at any point along such a curve. The point C represents the point of tangency between U_{50} and AB. The slope of U_{50} (or any indifference curve) is the negative of the ratio of the marginal utility of X to the marginal utility of Y ($-MU_X/MU_Y$), and the slope of the budget constraint is $-P_X/P_Y$, the negative of the ratio of the price of X to the price of Y. Since at a point of tangency two curves have equal slopes, it follows that at a point of tangency between an indifference curve and a budget constraint

$$MU_X/MU_Y = P_X/P_Y$$

or, by rearranging terms,

$$MU_X/P_X = MU_Y/P_Y$$

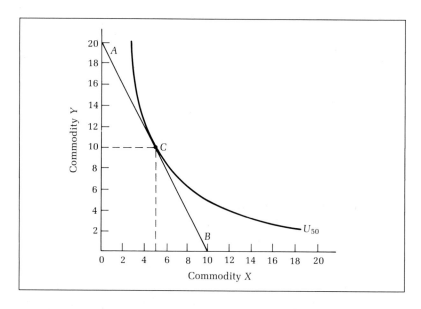

FIGURE 5A.1   Consumer Equilibrium at the Tangency of an Indifference Curve and a Budget Constraint

This is, of course, the same condition for consumer equilibrium given above because $MU_X = f_X$ and $MU_Y = f_Y$ (here we have denoted the goods as X and Y instead of X_1 and X_2).

If the ratios of marginal utility to price are not equal, the consumer could increase satisfaction by spending less on the good with the lower ratio and more on the good with the higher ratio. To illustrate, suppose that we have the following ratios: $MU_X/P_X = 10$ and $MU_Y/P_Y = 4$. At the level of consumption for which these ratios are calculated, the consumer would increase utility by 10 units if an additional dollar were spent on X but would lose only 4 units of utility if that dollar came from decreasing the expenditure for Y. Total utility would be increased by 6 units due to the reallocation of the consumer's budget (money income). If X, Y, or both are subject to diminishing marginal utility, such reallocations will not increase utility indefinitely. The marginal utility of X will decrease, or the marginal utility of Y will increase (or both will happen) as more of X is consumed and the consumption of Y declines. Assuming that prices to the consumer remain constant, the ratios MU_X/P_X and MU_Y/P_Y will eventually become equal, and no further change in the bundle of X and Y purchased will increase the consumer's total utility.

Now let us use this model of consumer behavior to derive a demand function for an individual consumer. This can be done either mathematically or graphically. We will start with the latter method. In the left-hand graph in Figure 5A.2, three budget constraints are drawn for a given level of income ($M = 1000$), a constant price of Y ($P_Y = 10$), and three different prices of the good $X (P_{X_1} = 50, P_{X_2} = 33,$ and $P_{X_3} = 25$). The respective X intercepts for these budget constraints are 20 (M/P_{X_1}), 30.3 (M/P_{X_2}), and 40 (M/P_{X_3}). These intercepts represent the maximum amount of the good X that a consumer could purchase with the given money income if no Y was purchased for each price of X. We see that as the price of X declines, a given income allows a greater maximum consumption of X.

The points of consumer equilibrium are circled and are, of course, at the points of tangency between the budget constraints and the indifference curves (U_1, U_2, and U_3). The quantity of X purchased at each price is found on the horizontal axis by dropping a perpendicular line from each point of equilibrium to that axis.

The horizontal axes in both parts of Figure 5A.2 are exactly the same. Thus, we can see that when the price of X is 50, 10 units are consumed; when the price drops to 33 and 25, 18 and 25 units are demanded, respectively. This relationship between price and quantity purchased is plotted on the right-hand graph in Figure 5A.2 and is defined as the demand curve for X. Since there is an inverse relationship between price and the quantity demanded at each price, the relationship graphed in Figure 5A.2 follows the law of demand. This law is a generalization that for most goods, a greater quantity will be purchased at a lower price than at a higher price, *ceteris paribus*.

To derive a demand curve from the mathematical model of consumer behavior, we will consider just two cases (X and Y will represent the two goods) with income (M) held constant. Since we will derive the demand for X, we will also hold the price of Y constant. Suppose the consumer has the following simple utility function:

$$U = XY$$

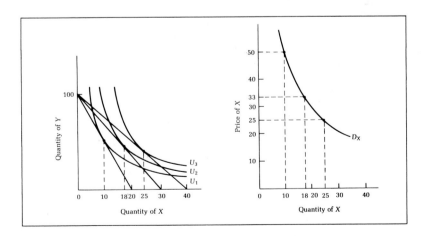

FIGURE 5A.2   Graphic Derivation of a Demand Curve

The consumer would want to maximize utility for each possible price of X. Thus, our problem may be stated as follows:

Maximize: $U = XY$
Subject to: $M = P_X X + P_Y Y$

The Lagrangian function is

$$L = XY + \lambda(M - P_X X - P_Y Y)$$
$$\partial L/\partial X = Y - \lambda P_X = 0$$
$$\partial L/\partial Y = X - \lambda P_Y = 0$$
$$\partial L/\partial \lambda = M - P_X X - P_Y X = 0$$

Solving the first two partial derivatives

$$Y/P_X = X/P_Y$$

and rearranging terms, we see that

$$Y = (P_X/P_Y)\, X$$

If we substitute this result in the third partial derivative, we have

$$M = P_X X - P_Y\,[(P_X/P_Y)X] = 0$$

and solving this for M, we find

$$M = P_X X + P_X X = 2P_X X$$

or, solving for X,

$$X = (M/2)P_X{}^{-1}$$

We now have a single equation derived from the constrained utility maximization model, which represents the demand curve for the commodity X. Since we have followed the convention of graphing a demand curve with price on the vertical axis, let us solve the above expression for P_X and assume that income is given as 100 (i.e., $M = 100$). We find that the equation for the demand curve is

$$P_X = M/2X$$
$$P_X = (M/2)X^{-1}$$
$$P_X = 50X^{-1}$$

Note that this demand curve follows the law of demand, since there is an inverse relationship between price and quantity. You can see that the demand function is downward sloping by finding its slope as follows:

$$dP_X/dX = -50X^{-2}$$

which is negative for all values of X. This same demand function is shown graphically in Figure 5A.3.

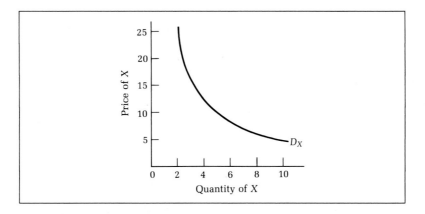

FIGURE 5A.3   Demand Curve Described by $P_X = 50X^{-1}$

6
FORECASTING

Forecasting involves making the best possible judgment about the future value of some variable based upon a thoughtful analysis of factors that have influenced that variable in the past and those that are expected to influence it in the future. Judgments are important to the forecasting effort in every case. Mere acceptance of the results of some purely mechanical statistical-mathematical technique does not constitute forecasting. However, this is not to say that analytical methods of analysis are not important in forecasting. They are, and their importance is becoming more pronounced as the methods become more refined, as computers and the appropriate software become more widely available, and as more people who understand and appreciate the techniques reach middle and upper management positions.

Forecasting involves both art and science. Managers who make intuitive forecasts based just on their "gut feelings" do disservice to their firms by not taking into account the input of the best scientific analysis available. A blending of the manager's experience and insight with the analyst's ability to develop sophisticated quantitative models can be expected to yield the most reliable forecasts.

In this chapter, our primary focus is on sales forecasting because of its importance to the management of most businesses. The methods suggested and techniques covered are also applicable to a wide variety of other activities. For example, you might use the material presented here to forecast such things as

School enrollment	*Automobile registrations*
Employment	*Law school graduates*
Population	*Welfare recipients*
Tax revenues	*New housing starts*
Business failures	*Open heart surgeries*
Cattle prices	*National income*
Unemployment rate	*Number of child abuse cases*

From this list, you see that forecasting can be useful in both private and public sector activities.

6.1 THE ROLE OF FORECASTING

Forecasts provide information that helps managers to make better decisions. Business decisions are made under conditions of risk or uncertainty, and forecasts about the future economic environment can help to reduce that risk or uncertainty or at least identify reasonable boundaries around the relevant variables. The importance of forecasting is difficult to measure, but the following observations, reported in *The Journal of Business Forecasting*, indicate significant activity in the forecasting area:[1]

1. During 1980, 1981, and 1982, at least 155 English-language articles related to just business forecasting appeared in 91 different journals.

2. In a survey of large United States business firms, the mean amount of resources committed annually to develop sales forecasts was $265,000. One firm reported a $2-million forecasting budget.

This certainly suggests that business firms in the United States find forecasts useful and valuable inputs to the managerial decision process.

The information provided by forecasts is important to the short-term and long-term planning process of almost every department, division, and functional area within a firm. Every responsibility center that must prepare an annual budget has to have some forecast of what the coming year's needs will be. Let us consider just four areas within a typical firm:

1. *Marketing.* The marketing manager needs to have reasonable sales forecasts in order to budget for sales staff functions and personnel, to plan an appropriate distribution program, and to establish the overall promotional budget, among other marketing-related functions.

2. *Production.* The production manager needs a sales forecast to plan for material needs, equipment needs, the number of production workers to be employed, warehousing requirements for both raw materials and finished goods, inventories, maintenance schedules, and other production activities.

---

[1]David C. Carlson, Robin T. Peterson, and David J. Lill, "State of the Art Advances but Its Use Is Still Sparse," *Journal of Business Forecasting*, Summer 1983, pp. 14–15.

3. *Personnel.* The personnel manager needs to know the forecasted level of activity for the firm to make appropriate plans to hire or release personnel throughout the company, including production workers, clerks, secretaries, supervisors, maintenance workers, quality-control analysts, and so on.

4. *Finance.* The manager in charge of financial functions relies on the sales forecast in part to determine what the firm's cash flow will be, when the firm may need to obtain outside funds, and how much money will be needed, as well as to prepare the firm's projected profit and loss statement and balance sheet for the year ahead. In addition to relying on the annual sales forecast for these functions, a long-term forecast is used in capital budgeting decisions.

To further illustrate how forecasts are used by business firms, let us look specifically at three major United States companies: Armstrong World Industries, the B. F. Goodrich Company, and the Union Carbide Company.

Forecasting at Armstrong World Industries

Armstrong World Industries is one of the leading firms in the production of interior furnishings with four principal markets: (1) home improvement and refurbishing (about 50 percent of sales), (2) new residential building (about 20 percent of sales), (3) commercial and institutional building (about 20 percent of sales), and (4) industrial specialty products for the automotive, textile, and building industries (about 10 percent of sales). Annual sales in 1982 were $1,285,590,000, and the firm employed 20,824 people.[2]

Armstrong World Industries has an economic research department that makes broad-based economic forecasts of

- Year-to-year gain in real output

- Gross national product price deflator

- Short- and long-term interest rates, monetary policy, and fiscal policy

- Likelihood of price and wage controls, and federally administered capital allocation programs

- Capital spending by business and its effect on productive capacity

---

[2]This discussion is adapted from George F. Johnston, "Putting Forecasts to Work in the Corporate Planning Function," *Business Economics*, January 1976, pp. 35–40. Sales employment data for 1982 are from "The Fortune 500," *Fortune*, May 2, 1983, pp. 238–239.

- Aggregate disposable personal income, as well as real disposable income, along with employment and productivity trends

- Raw material price and availability expectations

- Energy price and availability expectations

In addition to these broad economic forecasts, estimates are also developed for specific markets, along with a rationale behind them and how they may affect Armstrong World Industries. Examples of these market forecasts include

- Consumer spending for furniture and home furnishings

- Home improvement and refurbishing expenditures

- Nonresidential building contract awards

- Mobile home production

- Industrial markets production

These forecasts and their analysis of such things as seasonal and cyclical patterns are used throughout Armstrong World Industries' four-phase planning process. In the area of corporate planning, George F. Johnston (vice president and chief planning officer) has said: "One of the valuable tools we have is forecasting, and day by day we are learning how to use it better" (p. 40).

Forecasting at B. F. Goodrich

At B. F. Goodrich, a firm with 1982 annual sales of $3,005,300,000 and 30,042 employees, forecasts are also used extensively throughout the firm.[3] The business research department provides forecast information critical to the planning process. Through the entire planning cycle, forecasts of market size and market share provide essential information for determining such things as capacity requirements, size of sales staff, methods of distribution, and operating budgets. In the tire business, forecasts are segmented in several ways: "by wheel size — 13, 14 or 15; by channel — OE and replacement with replacement further divided into dealer, oil company, company store and department store" (p. 43; OE refers to original equipment tire sales to automobile manufacturers).

---

[3]This discussion is based on T. W. Blazey, "Putting Forecasts to Work in the Firm," *Business Economics*, January 1976, pp. 41–44. Sales and employment data for 1982 are from "The Fortune 500," *Fortune*, May 2, 1983, pp. 232–233.

B. F. Goodrich is also a major user of cotton, for sale as converted yarn, and of crude rubber. The business research department is expected to forecast supplies and prices for both of these commodities for use in decisions about whether to lengthen or shorten inventory coverage. These forecasts are also segmented by various grades of rubber and by staple length of cotton.

T. W. Blazey (vice president and controller) has said: "Forecasting plays an integral part in the operations of our company" (p. 44). Once more, you see a testimonial to the importance of forecasting by someone in a top management position of a major corporation.

Forecasting at Union Carbide

Union Carbide is the largest of the three firms used as examples here.[4] In 1982, Union Carbide had sales of $9,061,500,000 and employed 103,229 people. As a very large firm, Union Carbide has the resources to have memberships in a number of economic services, including Chase Econometrics, Inc.; Data Resources, Inc.; the Research Seminar on Quantitative Economics of the University of Michigan; and Wharton Econometric Forecasting Associates, Inc. These memberships give Union Carbide access to some of the best macroeconomic data and forecasts available in the United States. (Additional nationally recognized sources of such forecasts are identified under "Macroeconomic Forecasts," below.)

The macroeconomic forecasts used by Union Carbide provide "estimates of the future levels and rates of change of a large number of variables, all of which relate to the entire U.S. economy. No company-specific variables are produced in this forecasting process. Rather, the corporate economic forecast serves as one of the many possible sources of information to those who develop financial projections, the outlook for raw material prices, the cost of future plant and equipment expenditures or specific business plans" (p. 27).

Relying primarily on the Wharton model, Union Carbide prepares a best case and a worst case scenario to provide a band of probable error around the base forecast. The same type of procedure is used with long-term forecasts, for which case as many as five alternative scenarios may be produced. James F. Smith (chief economist for Union Carbide) notes: "The purpose of all of these forecasts is to provide business planners, marketing and operating executives, purchasing agents, and financial planners a background and a range to consider when preparing their own budgets, forecasts and plans."

---

[4]This discussion is based on James F. Smith, "How Union Carbide Uses Macroeconomic Forecasts," *Journal of Business Forecasting*, Fall 1982, pp. 27–28. Sales and employment data for 1982 are from "The Fortune 500," *Fortune*, May 2, 1983, pp. 228–229.

These three examples are not unique. Forecasting is an important function in helping to improve decisions in both the private and public sectors of the economy. It has been said that "all decisions — decisions to do nothing as well as those to do something — are contingent upon a prior assessment of the probable consequences of the status quo. The only thing worse than a bad forecast is no forecast."[5] Students who are interested in seeing how over 20 other companies use forecasting and the methods that are used should look in their library for *Sales Forecasting*, a research report published by The Conference Board.[6]

6.2   TYPES OF FORECASTS

Forecasts can be classified by a number of dimensions. It is not our purpose here to specify all of these. Rather, it is simply to give you further insight into the breadth of the forecasting function and of the ways management uses forecasts.

First, we can distinguish between macro and micro forecasts. Macro forecasts involve such aggregate measures as gross national product, the overall unemployment rate, the rate of inflation, changes in the money supply, and other variables that are macroeconomic in nature. Forecasted values for these variables are often used in preparing micro forecasts.

Micro forecasts have several subsets. An industry forecast is usually the largest of the micro forecasts. For example, you might want to forecast the total national demand for new single-family housing. At a more micro level, you might want to forecast the demand for new modular single-family housing throughout the United States. Or you might want to forecast the demand for new modular single-family housing in the mountain states. Further geographic breakdowns to the state, county, or city level may be needed in some situations.

Another subset of micro forecasts involves individual market segments rather than entire industries. Continuing our housing example, you may want to forecast the demand for new ultra–energy-efficient modular single-family housing. You may go even further to forecast a firm's individual product line demand (i.e., expected sales for different models of ultra–energy-efficient houses).

Forecasts can also be categorized by the time horizon covered. Short-term forecasts are generally considered to be for less than two years, and most often, for one year or less, into the future. Long-term forecasts are those

---

[5]Stephen K. McNees, "The Recent Record of Thirteen Forecasters," *New England Economic Review*, September-October 1981, pp. 5–21, as quoted in James F. Smith, p. 28.

[6]David K. Hurwood, Elliott S. Grossman, and Earl L. Bailey, *Sales Forecasting* (The Conference Board, 1978).

that extend more than two years out, with five years being a typical outer limit for reasonably reliable forecasts. Projections are sometimes made 10 and 20 years ahead, but it is usually recognized that such forecasts are very tentative ballpark figures and are quite likely to change. Nonetheless, such very long-term forecasts are useful for strategic planning.

6.3   MACROECONOMIC FORECASTS

Macroeconomic forecasts focus on the big picture of what is going on in the total national economy. Generally, it is not cost effective for a firm to prepare such forecasts internally, since they are available on a subscription basis from a number of vendors. Some of the most prominent vendors are

- Data Resources
- Chase Econometrics
- Kent Economic and Development Institute
- Wharton Econometric Forecasting Associates
- UCLA Business Forecasting Project
- Merrill Lynch Economics
- Georgia State University Economics Forecasting Group
- Evans Economics

In addition, part of the information available on a subscription basis from vendors is available at little or no cost, *but with a time lag,* in such publications as

- *Business Forecasts* (published annually by the Federal Reserve Bank of Richmond)
- *Highlights of NABE Economic Outlook Survey* (National Association of Business Economists)
- *Quarterly Survey of Economic Forecasts* (American Statistical Association)
- *Statistical Bulletin* (The Conference Board)
- *The Journal of Business Forecasting*
- *The Wall Street Journal* (limited detail)

Macroeconomic forecasts rely primarily on large econometric models of the economy. An econometric model is a statistical and mathematical model made up of a set of equations that explain certain elements of the behavior of a given economic system. Regression analysis is the most important statistical tool upon which econometric models are built. Two types of equations are used in building econometric models: (1) *identities*, which are mathematical statements of relationship between variables that are true by virtue of the way the variables are defined; and (2) *behavioral equations*, which are mathematical expressions that show how one variable behaves in relationship to one or more other variables, and are typically estimated using regression analysis. The variables included in identities and behavioral equations are classified as either endogenous or exogenous. Endogenous variables are determined within the model being used, while exogenous variables are determined by forces outside it.

A Small Macroeconomic Model

Let us consider a very simple econometric macroeconomic model as a way of illustrating these concepts and the process of building such a model. First, let us define GNP to be composed of personal consumption expenditures (C), investment spending (I), and government spending (G). We can write this relationship in mathematical form as

$$GNP \equiv C + I + G$$

This is an identity. The variables are defined to have this relationship. A three-tiered equals sign is used to represent something that is equal by definition.

Now let us hypothesize that personal consumption expenditures are primarily a function of GNP and that we expect that functional relationship to be linear. In mathematical form, we have

$$C = f(GNP)$$
$$C = a + b(GNP)$$

This is a behavioral equation that can be estimated using regression analysis. You may recall that this equation was estimated in Chapter 4 as an example of the use of the regression technique. The resulting values of a and b were

$$C = -55.5 + .668GNP$$

Both C and GNP are considered endogenous variables because they will be determined within our macroeconomic model.

The other two variables, investment and government spending, will be considered exogenous. That is, we will assume that their values are given as

$$I = I_0$$
$$G = G_0$$

where I_0 and G_0 represent the exogenously determined values of I and G. We will assume these values to be

$$I_0 = 400$$
$$G_0 = 500$$

This macroeconomic model can be summarized as

$$GNP = C + I + G$$
$$C = a + b(GNP)$$
$$I = I_0$$
$$G = G_0$$

Substituting the last three equations into the first, we have

$$GNP = a + b(GNP) + I_0 + G_0$$

and solving for GNP, we find

$$GNP = \left(\frac{1}{1-b}\right)(a + I_0 + G_0)$$

This is called a reduced form equation for our model because the endogenous variable (GNP) is expressed in terms of the exogenous variables (I_0 and G_0) and the parameters a and b.

You can now substitute the regression estimates for a and b into the model, along with the exogenous values for investment and government spending, to obtain

$$GNP = \left(\frac{1}{1-.668}\right)(-55.5 + 400 + 500)$$
$$GNP = (3.012)(844.5)$$
$$GNP = 2,543.634$$

Now suppose that you expect government spending in the next year to increase to 550 and investment to rise to 450. Your forecast of GNP would be

$$GNP = (3.012)(-55.5 + 450 + 550)$$
$$GNP = 2,844.834$$

Consult the most recent issue of the *Economic Report of the President* or another publication that would have the latest values for investment and government spending in the United States economy, and use this model to estimate GNP:

$$GNP = \left(\frac{1}{1-b}\right)(a + I_0 + G_0)$$

$$GNP = \left(\frac{1}{1-.668}\right)(-55.5 + \underline{\hspace{1.5cm}} + \underline{\hspace{1.5cm}})$$

$$GNP = (3.012)(\underline{\hspace{1.5cm}})$$

$$GNP = \underline{\hspace{1.5cm}}$$

How does your estimate of GNP compare with the actual value for that year? Why is there a difference between your predicted value and the actual value?

Large Macroeconomic Models

The large macroeconomic models of the United States economy are developed in a manner similar to that in which we developed this very simple model. The difference is that the large models have many more equations and, instead of just two variables, they forecast the values of a great many economic variables. The Kent Economic and Development Institute model, for example, forecasts over 40,000 variables. The data in Table 6.1 illustrate the type of information provided to subscribers of the Kent model (or other similar services). You may want to compare the predictions for 1985 and 1986 with the actual values, given the most recent data available as you read this chapter.

The projections of macroeconomic variables made by the large econometric models are useful to individual firms in preparing specific forecasts of sales and other variables of direct concern to the firm. You will see applications of such use in later sections of this chapter.

A natural question is: How precise are these macroeconomic forecasts? The data in Table 6.2 provide at least a partial answer to that question. You see that average errors for the median forecasts are fairly low.[7] If you want to forecast macroeconomic variables, looking at median values for a number of forecasts or some other form of consensus forecast is a very good approach to take.

6.4 SALES FORECASTING: AN OVERVIEW

Most firms are very much concerned with forecasting sales. You have seen that the sales forecast is an important driving force in the planning and budgeting process throughout a business (and in public sector activities as well). Appropriately, firms allocate a substantial amount of resources, both monetary and personnel, to the forecasting function.

There are many approaches to forecasting sales, and they vary from being naive to very sophisticated, and from qualitative to highly quantitative.[8] We cannot say that any single approach is the best. It is desirable to

---

[7]A median is the middle value in an array of numbers that are ordered from low to high. Thus, the median forecast is the middle forecast from some set of forecasts. About 40 forecasts used in the compilation of the Federal Reserve Bank of Richmond provide the basis for Table 6.2.

[8]Case examples of firms that use each of the techniques described in this and subsequent sections of this chapter can be found in David K. Hurwood, Elliott S. Grossman, and Earl L. Bailey, *Sales Forecasting* (The Conference Board, 1978).

TABLE 6.1
KEDI Forecast of Selected Indicators as of December 15, 1984

Variable	Unit	1984.2	1985.2	1985.3	1985.4	1986.1	1985	1986
Gross national product	Billions of $	3644.7	3875.6	3943.3	4028.3	4096.3	3913.9	4218.3
Personal income	Billions of $	2984.6	3222.2	3286.4	3326.4	3404.8	3242.4	3508.5
Personal consumption expenditures	Billions of $	2332.9	2499.0	2546.3	2611.8	2669.0	2524.1	2744.7
Unemployment rate	%	7.5	7.4	7.5	7.6	7.7	7.5	7.4
Personal disposable income	Billions of $	2554.3	2755.6	2811.0	2842.1	2910.1	2771.6	3000.4
Personal savings	Billions of $	146.8	160.9	162.3	161.8	160.9	161.6	165.7
Consumer instalment credit*	Billions of $	427.6	461.3	464.6	475.2	477.5	475.2	487.2
Auto sales (domestic and foreign)	Millions of units	10.6	10.2	10.0	9.8	9.5	10.1	9.8
Commercial and industrial loans	Billions of $	240.5	258.4	260.7	263.2	264.4	259.6	266.1
GNP price deflator	1972 = 100	222.4	230.8	233.8	237.0	239.8	232.4	244.3
Consumer price index	1967 = 100	309.7	322.5	328.6	332.7	336.4	325.7	343.0
Producer price index**	1967 = 100	291.4	297.5	301.1	306.0	311.7	299.8	319.6
Industrial capacity utilization	%	81.6	81.9	81.4	81.1	81.1	81.6	81.1
Index of industrial productivity	1967 = 100	163.1	168.1	168.5	169.1	169.0	168.0	172.2
Nonresidential fixed investments	Billions of $	422.1	463.2	468.7	474.3	473.2	466.2	475.7
Treasury bills yield (3-month)	%	9.81	8.45	9.10	10.14	10.81	9.00	9.66
Federal funds rate	%	10.87	8.89	9.83	10.82	11.48	9.54	10.38
Aaa corporate bonds rate	%	12.97	11.06	11.32	11.55	12.24	11.37	11.87
Money supply M1	Billions of $	540.8	570.1	573.6	576.4	584.2	570.8	599.5
Private housing starts	Millions of units	1.906	1.661	1.751	1.495	1.466	1.617	1.544
Gross national product	Billions of 1972$	1638.8	1679.2	1686.6	1699.7	1708.2	1683.9	1726.3

SOURCE: *Journal of Business Forecasting*, Winter 1984–1985, p. 43. Reprinted by permission.
*End of the period data. **Finished goods.
NOTE: Data for consumer price index, producer price index, consumer installment credit, commercial and industrial loans, treasury bills yield, federal funds rate, and Aaa corporate bonds rate are not seasonally adjusted. All other quarterly data are seasonally adjusted at annual rates.

TABLE 6.2
The Record of Median Forecasts

	Real GNP (Percent Change)			Inflation Rate (GNP Deflator)			Treasury Bill Rate		
	Actual	Predicted	Error	Actual	Predicted	Error	Actual	Predicted	Error
1971	4.7	3.8	0.9	4.7	3.6	1.1			
1972	7.0	5.6	1.4	4.3	3.2	1.1			
1983	4.3	6.0	6.0	7.0	33	3.7			
1974	−2.7	1.2	3.9	10.1	5.5	4.6	7.3	6.0	1.3
1975	2.2	−0.6	2.8	7.7	7.1	0.6	5.7	7.1	1.4
1976	4.4	6.0	1.6	4.7	5.4	0.7	4.7	7.1	2.4
1977	5.8	5.0	0.8	6.1	5.7	0.4	6.1	5.8	0.3
1988	5.3	4.2	1.1	8.5	5.9	2.6	8.7	6.5	2.2
1979	1.7	1.5	0.2	8.1	7.1	1.0	11.8	8.1	3.7
1980	−0.3	−0.8	0.5	9.8	8.2	1.6	13.7	8.6	5.1
1981	0.9	2.4	1.5	8.9	9.1	0.2	11.8	10.8	1.0
1982 (preliminary)	1.2	2.8	4.0	4.5	7.1	2.6	8.0	11.2	3.2
Average error			1.7			1.7			2.3

Source: *Business Forecasts 1983*, Federal Reserve Bank of Richmond, p. 7.

Note: Predictions are from *Business Forecasts*, pubished annually by the Federal Reserve Bank of Richmond. The error is the absolute value of the difference between predicted and actual values. Real growth and inflation are from the fourth quarter of the previous year to the fourth quarter of the stated year. The Treasury bill rate is the average value in the fourth quarter.

employ *at least* two different methods and then use managerial judgment to reconcile the results.

Let us look briefly at some of the most widely used sales forecasting techniques, beginning with the more qualitative ones. First, consider what is usually called the *jury of executive opinion*. Forecasts of sales are developed by combining the subjective opinions of key managers and executives who are most likely to have the best insights about the firm's business. This may be done on an individual basis, with results collected by the person ultimately responsible for the sales forecast, or it may be done in group discussions that allow for an interplay of ideas among the participants. The latter has the advantage of stimulating deeper insights, but a very real disadvantage is that one or two dominant individuals and various peer pressures may make one or a few opinions disproportionately important in the consensus that is reached.

To eliminate the undesirable effects of group interactions, a procedure called the *Delphi method* can be used in conjunction with the jury of executive opinion technique of sales forecasting. The Delphi method can be summarized by the following steps:

1. Participants are selected.

2. Questionnaires asking about the variables in question (e.g., expected sales) are distributed to each participant.

3. Results are collected anonymously, tabulated, and summarized.

4. Summary results are distributed to participants, who are asked to revise their previous responses in light of this new information.

5. Steps 2–4 are repeated until no significant changes result.

The group forecast is not necessarily a consensus but is a statistical average of the participants' final round responses. Using written questionnaires can make the data collection, distribution of results, and revised response sequence time-consuming. Computer networks and electronic mail hold out the promise of making the Delphi method more efficient, especially when geographically dispersed personnel are involved.[9]

The *sales force composite* method of developing a sales forecast is another qualitative and judgmental approach. It is particularly useful among firms that sell industrial goods. Members of the sales force are asked to estimate sales, usually by product. These estimates are then combined by the sales manager for a given product line (or geographic area), and ultimately by the person who has the responsibility for preparing final sales forecasts, to arrive at the firm's total forecast. This method has the advantage of incorporating grass roots information that comes from the people who know customers the best. However, there is a major disadvantage in that sales are likely to be underestimated by the sales force. This is particularly true when the people involved have sales quotas that are assigned on the basis of their forecasts and receive bonuses that depend on their performance relative to those quotas.

Firms may also find *surveys of user's expectations* helpful in preparing a sales forecast. This method is particularly applicable when users form a well-defined population that is easily sampled. For example, a natural gas utility can use a survey of customers to identify their expectations for their consumption patterns over the coming year. Are any major changes from natural gas to other energy sources (or vice versa) anticipated? Answers to this type of question can provide valuable insight into the preparation of the firm's sales forecast.

An *evaluation of time trends* and projection of those trends is also a useful and not technically difficult method of forecasting sales. The analysis of trends can go well beyond simple trend projections to include such methods as *time series decomposition* and *exponential smoothing.* (These quantitative techniques are considered in more detail later in this chapter.)

Multiple regression models and *input-output models* are also useful in preparing sales forecasts. These techniques are considerably more sophisticated and require well-trained personnel to prepare and use them. These models are discussed in section 6.7 and the appendix to this chapter.

---

[9]See, for example, Bernard S. Husbands, "Electronic Mail System Enhances Delphi Method," *Journal of Business Forecasting,* Summer 1982, pp. 24–27.

6.5   TIME SERIES DECOMPOSITION

Some economic and business data have a long-term trend that may be estimated using a simple bivariate linear regression model. However, for many data series, this long-term trend is clouded by seasonal, cyclical, and irregular movements around the trend. Time series decomposition is a method of isolating each of these components.

The method of decomposition we will demonstrate in this section assumes a multiplicative relationship between the components of the time series, as follows:

$$Q = T \cdot S \cdot C \cdot I$$

where

Q = quantity of sales (or other variable to be forecast)
T = long-term trend component
S = seasonal component
C = cyclical component
I = irregular component

The long-term trend is most often estimated, using OLS regression, as a linear function of the sales data after the seasonality in the data has been removed. However, nonlinear trends may be estimated using transformations such as the reciprocal, logarithmic, or power (squared, cubic, etc.) ones discussed in Chapter 4.

The seasonal component reflects regular movements in the data that are repeated within the duration of a year and are similar year after year. Typically, these are either quarterly or monthly movements in sales data, although other regular periods may be identified for particular series (semi-annual, weekly, etc.). Many sales data have fairly strong seasonal patterns related to weather changes, holidays, the school year, sports seasons, and so on.

The cyclical component represents longer-term movements above and below the overall trend in the data. It is usually more difficult to identify why the cycle is moving up or down than it is to explain the ups and downs of the seasonal pattern.

The irregular component is caused by random events that are not repeated (or at least not with any regularity) over time. Wars, strikes, abnormally severe weather, and a fire at a firm's warehouse are all examples of irregular forces. These events are impossible to model in a formal way, due to their random nature.

Table 6.3 contains 20 quarters of sales data, in thousands of units, which we will use to illustrate this forecasting technique. The column headed *MA* contains *moving averages* of the sales data. These are *four-period moving averages* because each is calculated as the mean of a set of four consecutive quarters. The moving average located in the third line of the table is found as follows:

$$MA_3 = (Q_1 + Q_2 + Q_3 + Q_4)/4$$

The next moving average (MA_4) is found in the same manner, except that the four quarters used are moved ahead by one quarter. The first quarter is dropped, and the fifth quarter is added. Thus,

$$MA_4 = (Q_2 + Q_3 + Q_4 + Q_5)/4$$

In general, we can calculate the four-period moving average for any period as

$$MA_t = (Q_{t-2} + Q_{t-1} + Q_t + Q_{t+1})/4$$

Note that Table 6.3 shows no moving averages for periods 1, 2, or 20. This is because we do not have enough data before periods 1 or 2 or after period 20 to make those calculations.

Look at Table 6.3 and compare the variability in the sales data with the variability in the moving averages. There is a great deal less fluctuation in the latter. The reason is that the seasonality in the original sales data is removed by calculating the moving averages. Each moving average contains one first-quarter value, one second-quarter value, one third-quarter value, and one fourth-quarter value. Thus, each moving average represents the typical level of sales for a given one-year period (which may or may not correspond to a calendar year).

From the definition above and the data in Table 6.3, you see that

$$MA_3 = (7 + 6 + 4 + 6)/4 = 5.75$$

This value represents the typical (average) level of sales for the year represented by the time periods 1, 2, 3, and 4. We find MA_4 similarly:

$$MA_4 = (6 + 4 + 6 + 8)/4 = 6.00$$

which represents the typical level of sales for the year covered by quarters 2, 3, 4, and 5.

Ideally each of these moving averages should be centered at the midpoint of the year it represents. To do this, we calculate a centered moving average (CMA):

$$CMA_3 = (MA_3 + MA_4)/2$$

or, in more general terms,

$$CMA_t = (MA_t + MA_{t+1})/2$$

Note that ideally we should have placed MA_3 at time period 2.5 and MA_4 at time period 3.5 to center them at the midpoints of their respective years. By averaging the values appropriate to period 2.5 and period 3.5, we get the number that best represents the typical level of sales of the year centered around period 3. That value is denoted CMA_3 and in this example is

TABLE 6.3
Time Series Decomposition Analysis of Sales to Determine Trend, Seasonal, and Cyclical Components of Sales Data

Observation	Time Index	Sales (Q)	MA	CMA	CMAT	SF	CF	SI	Estimated Sales
1980.1	1	7			5.073			1.237	
1980.2	2	6			5.446			1.009	
1980.3	3	4	5.75	5.875	5.819	.681	1.010	.759	4.46
1980.4	4	6	6.00	6.125	6.192	.980	.989	.995	6.09
1981.1	5	8	6.25	6.500	6.565	1.231	.990	1.237	8.04
1981.2	6	7	6.75	6.875	6.938	1.018	.991	1.009	6.94
1981.3	7	6	7.00	7.250	7.311	.828	.992	.759	5.50
1981.4	8	7	7.50	7.750	7.684	.903	1.009	.995	7.71
1982.1	9	10	8.00	8.00	8.057	1.250	.993	1.237	9.90
1982.2	10	9	8.00	8.250	8.430	1.091	.979	1.009	8.33
1982.3	11	6	8.50	8.750	8.803	.686	.994	.759	6.64
1982.4	12	9	9.00	9.125	9.176	.986	.994	.995	9.08
1983.1	13	12	9.25	9.625	9.549	1.247	1.008	1.237	11.91
1983.2	14	10	10.00	10.375	9.922	.964	1.046	1.009	10.47
1983.3	15	9	10.75	10.875	10.295	.826	1.056	.759	8.25
1983.4	16	12	11.00	11.000	10.668	1.091	1.031	.995	10.96
1984.1	17	13	11.00	10.875	11.041	1.195	.985	1.237	13.45
1984.2	18	10	10.75	10.625	11.414	.941	.931	1.009	10.72
1984.3	19	8	10.50		11.787		.97 e	.759	8.68
1984.4	20	11			12.160		.98 e	.995	11.86
1985.1	21	?			12.533		1.01 e	1.237	15.66 f
1985.2	22	?			12.906		1.04 e	1.009	13.54 f
1985.3	23	?			13.279		1.06 e	.759	10.68 f
1985.4	24	?			13.652		1.04 e	.995	14.13 f

NOTE: Sales data are in thousands of units.

MA = four-quarter moving average
CMA = centered four-quarter moving average
$CMAT$ = long-term trend (T) through centered moving averages: $CMAT = 4.701 + .373(\text{Time})$
SF = seasonal factor: $SF = Q/CMA$
CF = cycle factor (C): $CF = CMA/CMAT$; (e indicates estimates from Figure 6.2)
SI = seasonal index (S): SI = standardized mean of seasonal factors
Estimated sales = $T{\cdot}S{\cdot}C$ (f represents values forecasted ahead)
? = sales for 1985 were not known
f = denotes forecasted values for sales during the next year (1985)

$$CMA_3 = (MA_3 + MA_4)/2$$
$$CMA_3 = (5.75 + 6.00)/2 = 5.875$$

Identifying the Long-Term Trend

This series of centered moving averages best represents the typical level of sales for each quarter, after the seasonality has been taken out. Since these data are void of seasonality, we use them to estimate the long-term trend of the sales data. That is,

$$\text{Trend} = CMAT = f(\text{Time})$$

where $CMAT$ is centered moving average trend. Using OLS regression to estimate this function in linear form, we get

$$CMAT = 4.701 + .373 \, (\text{Time})$$
$$(21.96)$$

The value in parentheses is the t-ratio. Substituting successive values of the time index ($T = 1$ for first quarter 1980) in this equation yields the set of values shown in the $CMAT$ column of Table 6.3. Remember that this set of values represents the trend component of our time series decomposition model:

Trend component $= T = CMAT$

A Method of Measuring Seasonality

Now take a minute to compare the actual sales in each quarter with the corresponding centered moving average. Keep in mind that the centered moving averages are "deseasonalized" (i.e., the seasonality in the data has been removed through the process of calculating the CMA). Looking at 1980.3, you see that the actual sales of four units are not as high as the typical average quarterly sales for the year, which centers on 1980.3. That means that this third quarter is below the deseasonalized third-quarter value.

Multiplying the deseasonalized value for 1980.3 (i.e., $CMA_3 = 5.875$) by four gives us a better approximation of total sales in either the year 1980.1–1980.4 or the year 1980.2–1981.1 than does multiplying the actual 1980.3 value (i.e., 4.0) by four. This is illustrated below:

Year	Actual Sales	$(4)(Q_3)$	$(4)(CMA_3)$
1980.1–1980.4	23	16	23.5
1980.2–1981.1	24	16	23.5

This demonstrates the fact that the actual value in quarter 3 is not typical of either of these years.

Looking through the rest of the third-quarter sales data, you will see that the third quarter of each year is always a low quarter. To get a measure of this seasonality, a seasonal factor (SF) is calculated:

$$SF_t = Q_t/CMA_t$$

For the third quarter of 1980, we find

$$SF_3 = 4/5.875 = .681$$

Glancing down the SF column of Table 6.3, you see that, while there is a definite pattern to the seasonal factors, they do not repeat themselves exactly in a four-quarter sequence. Not all of the third-quarter seasonal factors equal .681. Which, then, should be used as the seasonal component of the time series decomposition model? The answer is none of these SF values. Rather, the normalized values of the average seasonal factor for each quarter are used in the model. These are called seasonal indexes.

The seasonal indexes (SI) are calculated as shown in Table 6.4. These indexes represent the seasonal component of the time series decomposition model. That is,

$$\text{Seasonal component} = S = SI$$

TABLE 6.4
Determination of Seasonal Indexes from Seasonal Factors

	Seasonal Factors				
Year	Quarter 1	Quarter 2	Quarter 3	Quarter 4	
1980			.681	.980	
1981	1.231	1.018	.828	.903	
1982	1.250	1.091	.686	.986	
1983	1.247	.964	.826	1.091	
1984	1.195	.941			
Totals	4.923	4.014	3.021	3.960	
Means	1.231	1.004	.755	.990	Sum of means = 3.980
Normalized Means	1.237	1.009	.759	.995	

where

Normalization factor = (N)/(sum of means)

N = number of seasons per year (4 in this example)

Normalized means = (mean)(normalization factor) = seasonal index

The calculation of each seasonal index is shown below:

Quarter 1: $SI_1 = (1.231)(4/3.980) = 1.237$
Quarter 2: $SI_2 = (1.004)(4/3.980) = 1.009$
Quarter 3: $SI_3 = (.755)(4/3.980)\ = .759$

Calculate the last one to verify your understanding:

Quarter 4: $SI_4 = ($ $)($ $) = $ _____

The Cyclical Component

Finally, we need to find a way of accounting for the cyclical component of the model. Looking at Figure 6.1 will help you to see how this might be done. Compare the line representing the centered moving averages (CMA)

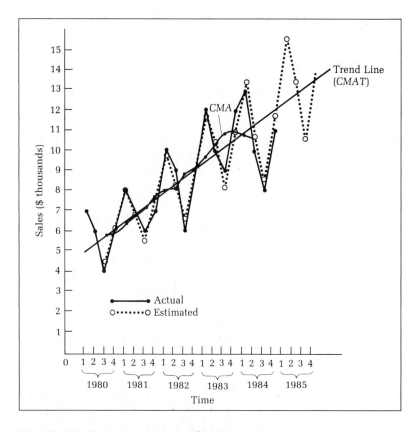

FIGURE 6.1   **Time Series Decomposition of Sales Data.**   The trend line component of the time series, based on the centered moving averages (*CMA*),
passes through the middle of the data but would not be a consistently
good predictor for any quarter. However, the complete model represented by the dotted line follows the path of the actual data quite
closely.

and the long-term trend line (*T* = *CMAT*). The *CMA* line follows a
smooth, wavelike pattern above and below the *CMAT*. These long-term
movements above and below the trend are called the cyclical movements in
the data.

The cyclical component of the model is calculated based on this relationship between the *CMA* and the *CMAT*, specifically,

$$CF_t = CMA_t/CMAT_t$$

where CF_t refers to the cycle factor for period t. So we now have a method of
measuring the cyclical component (*C*) of the time series decomposition
model:

$$\text{Cyclical component} = C = CF$$

These values are shown in the *CF* column of Table 6.3. Calculate several of these yourself and compare your results to the values in Table 6.3 to verify your understanding.

Using the Time Series Decomposition Model

The column headed "Estimated Sales" in Table 6.3 is calculated as the product of the trend component, the seasonal component, and the cycle component. That is,

Estimated sales = *(T)(S)(C)*
Estimated sales = *(CMAT)(SI)(CF)*

Compare the values in this column with the actual sales data. The estimated values are relatively close to the actual values. This can also be seen in Figure 6.1, where the estimated sales pattern is shown by the dotted line and the actual sales pattern is represented by the solid line.[10]

So the model does a nice job of "backcasting" the data. How can it be used to forecast sales? In essentially the same way as we used it to backcast. We simply find the product of the three components of the model. The long-term trend *(T)* can be projected as far into the future as we wish, using the linear trend line:

CMAT = 4.701 + .373(Time)

The seasonal component *(S = SI)* is repetitive year after year, and so it too can be projected as far as we wish.

Our real problem comes in projecting the cycle component. It is helpful to prepare a graph such as the one in Figure 6.2, which shows the cycle factors plotted over time. Note that they move above or below the 1.00 baseline in the same manner that the *CMA* moves above or below the trend line *(CMAT)* in Figure 6.1.

The first approach the analyst may take is to look for a clear pattern in the graph of *CF* and then try to extrapolate that pattern into the future on the graph. Estimates of each future quarter's cycle factor can then be read from the graph. In addition to looking at the pattern, an analyst also draws on experience in the industry, the opinions of other experts, and other judgments to make such estimates.

For our example, the cycle is projected to turn back up and continue up for five quarters, as it did in the last upturn, before turning down again.

---

[10]The arithmetic involved in developing this model is fairly easy to do by computer. If you have a microcomputer with one of the electronic spread sheets (such as VISICALC, SuperCalc, or 1-2-3), you can set up a time series decomposition fairly easily.

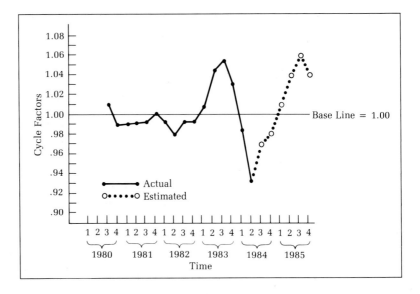

FIGURE 6.2   **Cycle Factors and Projections.** The cycle factor (CF) shows long-term movements above and below the overall trend in the data as represented by the baseline in this figure.

The corresponding *CF* values are estimated from the graph and are used in Table 6.3 to forecast estimated sales through 1985.

A more sophisticated approach to explaining and estimating the cycle component involves developing a regression model with *CF* as the dependent variable and one or more business cycle indicators as the independent variables. Nearly 300 series, 150 of which are classified as business cycle indicators, are published monthly by the United States Department of Commerce, Bureau of Economic Analysis, in *Business Conditions Digest* (*BCD*). This is an invaluable resource for business and economic forecasters. A brief description of business cycle indicators is found in Exhibit 6.1.[11] The *BCD* list of leading economic indicators, roughly coincident indicators, and lagging indicators is as follows:

Leading Indicators
- Average workweek (production workers in manufacturing)
- Average weekly initial claims, state unemployment insurance
- New orders for consumer goods and materials in 1972 dollars
- Stock prices, 500 common stocks

[11]Elizabeth W. Angle, *Keys for Business Forecasting*, 5th ed., Federal Reserve Bank of Richmond, April 1980, pp. 26–27. Reprinted by permission.

- Contracts and orders for plant and equipment in 1972 dollars
- New building permits, private housing units
- Vendor performance, companies receiving slower deliveries
- Change in inventories on hand and on order in 1972 dollars
- Change in sensitive crude materials prices
- Change in total liquid assets
- Money supply in 1972 dollars

Roughly Coincident Indicators
- Employees on nonagricultural payrolls
- Industrial production, total
- Personal income less transfers in 1972 dollars
- Manufacturing and trade sales in 1972 dollars

Lagging Indicators
- Labor cost per unit of unemployment
- Manufacturing and trade inventories, total in 1972 dollars
- Commercial and industrial loans outstanding
- Average duration of unemployment
- Ratio of consumer installment credit to personal income
- Average prime rate charged by banks

EXHIBIT 6.1   Business Cycle Indicators

In recent years, the indicator approach to business cycle analysis, developed by the National Bureau of Economic Research (NBER), has been cited more and more in private and government publications. The businessman is confronted with such economic expressions as reference dates, peaks, troughs, turning points, composite indexes, and leading, coincident, and lagging indicators. The purpose of this [exhibit] is to define briefly these terms as used in business forecasting and analysis of current economic conditions.

The Business Cycle Defined
A business cycle as defined by the NBER "consists of expansions occurring at about the same time in many economic activities, followed by similarly general recessions, contractions, and revivals which merge into the expansion phase of the next cycle." Thus business cycles are alternating and recurring movements. They relate to aggregate economic activity, as distinguished from the cycle of an individual statistical series. There are two essential ingredients in the NBER definition: first, many economic activities cumulate into a composite

picture of the U. S. economy; and second, forces working contrary to the general course of the economy gain sufficient strength to cause a directional change in the economy's path.

Reference Dates

The "turning points," or "peaks" and "troughs," of the business cycle have been dated for the period from 1854 to 1975 by the NBER. These dates, termed "business cycle reference dates," mark off 28 U. S. business cycles for the period. The cycles range in duration from 28 months (from the trough of March 1919 to that of July 1921) to 117 months (February 1961 to November 1970). At the time of this writing, the March 1975 trough is the latest to be dated.

The expansion phase — the rise in business activity from the trough to the peak — is usually of longer duration than the contraction phase — the decline from the peak to the trough. For the 28 complete cycles, the average expansion lasted 33 months and the average contraction ran 19 months. For six post–World War II cycles, the disparity in length between the two cycle phases is more evident; expansions averaged 48 months in contrast to an average contraction of 11 months. The expansion from February 1961 to December 1969 lasted 106 months, the longest to be recorded.

Coincident Series

The reference dates provide a framework for classifying individual economic series into three groups according to whether their turning points tend to lead, lag, or coincide with the turning points in general business. Individual series whose peaks and troughs roughly parallel those in general business are termed the "roughly coincident series." Three of the four most commonly used "coincident indicators" . . . are personal income less transfers in 1972 dollars; industrial production (charted on the next page); and nonagricultural employment. The fourth major coincident indicator is manufacturing and trade sales in 1972 dollars. The turning points of these individual series do not always coincide with the NBER reference dates. Individual analysts sometimes prefer to designate peaks and troughs in general business on the basis of the behavior of a single indicator, particularly gross national product.

Leading and Lagging Series

Turning points in some series typically precede the reference dates marking the peaks and troughs of general business. These series are accordingly termed "leading indicators." The 12 major series in this category include such measures as building permits for new private housing, the average workweek in manufacturing, change in sensitive

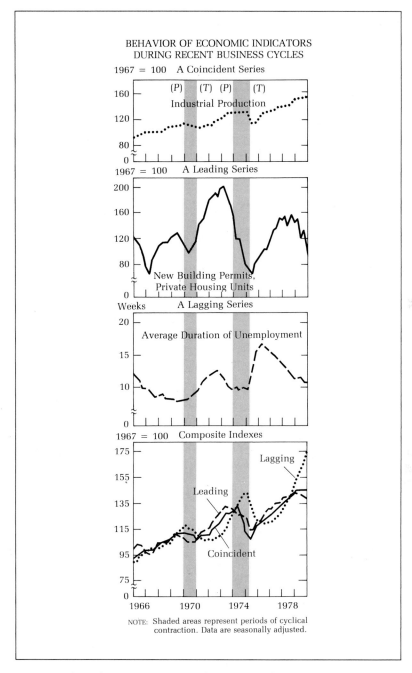

BEHAVIOR OF ECONOMIC INDICATORS
DURING RECENT BUSINESS CYCLES

1967 = 100   A Coincident Series

Industrial Production

1967 = 100   A Leading Series

New Building Permits,
Private Housing Units

Weeks   A Lagging Series

Average Duration of Unemployment

1967 = 100   Composite Indexes

Lagging

Leading

Coincident

1966   1970   1974   1978

NOTE: Shaded areas represent periods of cyclical
contraction. Data are seasonally adjusted.

prices, index of 500 common stock prices, and money supply (M₂) in
1972 dollars.

On the other hand, peaks and troughs in some important economic
series typically follow the turning points in general business. These

series termed "lagging indicators" reflect chiefly business investment costs. Included in the group of six major series are business loans outstanding, prime rate charged by banks, and average duration of unemployment.

Composite Indexes

The number of months an individual series precedes or follows the turning points in general business varies from cycle to cycle. Moreover, the average length of leads and the average length of lags at peaks differ from those at troughs. Thus a summary measure can be more useful to the business cycle analyst than tracking an individual series. This need is met by the composite indexes prepared by the Bureau of Economic Analysis, Department of Commerce.

There is one composite index for leading indicators, another for the coincident indicators, and a third for the lagging indicators. Consistency of timing at both business cycle peaks and troughs was a major factor in determining which individual indicators were included in the composite indexes. Other criteria used to assess the individual series were economic significance, statistical adequacy, conformity to business expansions and contractions, smoothness, and prompt availability. The major series included in each composite index are those discussed above. Each series included is consistent in timing at both peaks and troughs.

Some Warnings

There is no surefire, short-cut method of calling the turns in the business cycle. The discriminating forecaster must make a careful, detailed analysis of the statistical evidence on hand and weigh his evaluation against an understanding of the nature and causes of fluctuations in aggregate economic activity. He realizes that complete reliance on past performance of an individual statistical series or a group of series is foolhardy. The one fact accepted by all economists is the inconstancy of the business cycle. No period of expansion or contraction is identical with earlier business cycles movements in duration, in intensity, or in causation.

6.6 EXPONENTIAL SMOOTHING

If you are attempting to forecast a time series of sales or other data that are fairly stable (i.e., exhibit little upward or downward trend) but have considerable erratic movement, a simple exponential smoothing model may work well.[12] This technique calculates a forecast based on a weighted average of the actual and forecasted values in all previous periods. The weights assigned to previous periods become successively smaller in an exponential manner, hence the name *exponential smoothing*.

Fortunately, the model can be simplified readily to a form that, while implicitly taking into account all previous periods, needs only the actual value of current sales (A_t) and the previously forecast value for sales in the current period (F_t) along with a weighting factor (w) to forecast sales in the next period (F_{t+1}). The model may be written as

$$F_{t+1} = F_t + w(A_t - F_t)$$

Multiplying through the parentheses, we find

$$F_{t+1} = F_t + wA_t - wF_t$$
$$F_{t+1} = wA_t + F_t - wF_t$$
$$F_{t+1} = wA_t + (1 - w)F_t$$

In this form, we can best see how much weight is given to the current level of sales and the current forecast of sales in determining the forecasted value for the next period.

To illustrate the application of this exponential smoothing model, let us use it to forecast market share for Big Sky Foods (BSF). The data for BSF's market share were first used in Chapter 4 when we developed a regression model to explain market share. These share data are given again in Table 6.5 and Figure 6.3.

Besides the actual data for Big Sky Foods' market share in each period, Table 6.5 also shows forecasted values using five different weighting factors. Note that the forecasted value for 1982.1 is the same in all five cases. This is because we cannot forecast the first period with the exponential smoothing model, since no previous data are available. Thus, regardless of the weighting factor, the first forecast value $(F_{1982.1})$ must be assigned some initial value, such as the mean value of the actual market share for the entire period (19.0). A forecast for 1985.1 is given for each value of the weighting factor (w).

Which of these five models does the best job of forecasting BSF's market share? Forecasters use a number of criteria to help answer this kind of question. One evaluative statistic that can be used is called the root mean squared error $(RMSE)$. It is calculated as

$$RMSE = \sqrt{\Sigma (A_t - F_t)^2/n}$$

---

[12]If a positive or negative trend does exist, a related method, double exponential smoothing, may be used. See, for example, Charles W. Gross and Robin T. Peterson, *Business Forecasting*, 2d ed. (Boston: Houghton-Mifflin, 1983), Chapter 3.

TABLE 6.5 **Big Sky Foods' Market Share Forecast Using Exponential Smoothing**

Period	Actual Market Share	Forecasted Market Share at Different Weightings				
		$w = .1$	$w = .3$	$w = .5$	$w = .7$	$w = .9$
1982.1	19	19.0	19.0	19.0	19.0	19.0
1982.2	17	19.0	19.0	19.0	19.0	19.0
1982.3	14	18.8	18.4	18.0	17.6	17.2
1982.4	15	18.3	17.1	16.0	15.1	14.3
1983.1	18	18.0	16.5	15.5	15.0	14.9
1983.2	16	18.0	16.9	16.8	17.1	17.7
1983.3	16	17.8	16.6	16.4	16.3	16.2
1983.4	19	17.6	16.5	16.2	16.1	16.0
1984.1	23	17.8	17.2	17.6	18.1	18.7
1984.2	27	18.3	19.0	20.3	21.5	22.6
1984.3	23	19.1	21.4	23.6	25.4	26.6
1984.4	21	19.5	21.9	23.3	23.7	23.4
1985.1	?	19.7	21.6	22.2	21.8	21.2
RMSE		3.74	3.41	3.11	2.92	2.77

NOTE: RMSE = root mean squared error; w = weighting factor

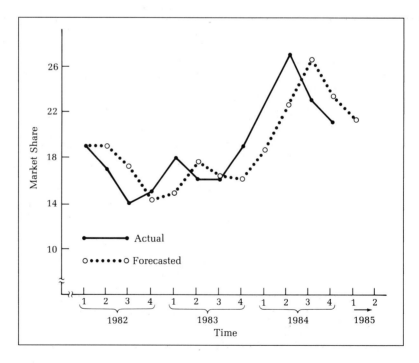

FIGURE 6.3 **Exponential Smoothing Forecast of Big Sky Foods' Market Share.**
Forecasts shown here are based on a weighting factor of .9 for the previous period's actual sales and of .1 for the previous period's forecasted sales.

where

A_t = actual value in period t
F_t = forecasted value in period t
n = number of periods used

A lower *RMSE* is preferred to a larger one in evaluating different forecasting models, since the *RMSE* is a measure of the average error in the forecasts. The *RMSE* for each model is given at the bottom of Table 6.5. On the basis of this criterion, a weighting factor of $w = .9$ appears to provide the best forecast. The forecasts based on this weighting factor are shown in Figure 6.3, along with the actual market shares for Big Sky Foods over the 1982.1–1984.4 period.

6.7   REGRESSION MODELS IN FORECASTING

You have already seen some ways in which regression analysis is used in the forecasting process. It is the primary statistical tool used in developing major macroeconometric models and is useful in the estimation of long-term trends. This section describes several applications of multiple regression analysis to the forecasting process.

Let us begin by looking at a model that has been used to help hospital administrators forecast the number of patients to be served at various care levels.[13] This could be particularly helpful in setting up daily and weekly schedules for personnel:

$$CL1 = 1.03 + .49\,(3N) + .67(3T) + 1.75(4T) + .84(5T) + .27(PEDS)$$
$$+ 5.12(OB) + 5.72(NSY) - .45(April) - .30(June)$$
$$- .35(August) - .36(Sunday) - .33(Monday) - .31(Tuesday)$$
$$- .18(Friday) - .34(Saturday) - 1.31(Night\ shift)$$
$$- .00097(Time)$$

where

$CL1$ = number of patients at care level 1
$3N$ = medical cases and surgical and orthopedic overflow
$3T$ = medical cases
$4T$ = surgical cases
$5T$ = orthopedic cases

---

[13]F. Theodore Helmer, Edward B. Opperman, and James D. Suver, "Forecasting Nursing Staffing Requirements by Intensity-of-Care Level," *Interfaces*, June 1980, pp. 50–55.

$$PEDS = \text{pediatrics}$$
$$OB = \text{obstetrics and maternity-gynecology cases}$$
$$NSY = \text{nursery}$$
$$Time = \text{day of the year, numbered 1 through 365}$$

Day of the week and monthly variables are self-defined. All variables except the dependent variable ($CL1$) and Time are dummy variables equal to 1 if a case fits a particular class and 0 otherwise. All variables are significant at the 95-percent level, and $R^2 = .61$. The adjusted R^2 is not given, but since nearly 10,000 observations were used, the adjustment would be slight.

The model was used to predict the number of patients requiring level 1 of care in Ward 4T (surgical cases) on Monday, July 17, 1978, during the day shift. In this example, $4T = 1$, Monday $= 1$, Time $= 195$, and all other variables are 0. The estimated number of patients in care level 1 is

$$CL1 = 1.03 + 1.75(1) - .33(1) - .00097(195)$$
$$CL1 = 2.26 \text{ patients}$$

The authors report that the actual number of patients was 2.

Next, let us consider a public sector application. Brooke Saladin has developed a regression model to predict the call-for-service work load (W) of the police force in a metropolitan area of 650,000 as follows:[14]

$$W = 5.6587 + 1.8432P + 1.69874AR - .92643AF + .61478V + .128723D$$

where

$$P = \text{population factor}$$
$$AR = \text{arrest factor}$$
$$AF = \text{affluence factor}$$
$$V = \text{vacancy factor}$$
$$D = \text{density factor}$$

Using the projected values of the independent variables, we could estimate the call-for-service work load (demand) for the police force using the multiple regression model given above. The projected changes in the independent variables could be obtained using a simple trend, a moving average trend, or through exponential smoothing.

Now let us return to the demand for Big Sky Foods as estimated in Chapter 5. The demand function we estimated was

$$Q = 15.939 - 9.057P + .009INC + 5.092PC$$

---

[14]Brooke A. Saladin, "A Police Story with Business Implications and Applications," *Journal of Business Forecasting*, Winter 1982–1983, pp. 3–5.

where

$$Q = \text{sales}$$
$$P = \text{BSF's price}$$
$$INC = \text{income}$$
$$PC = \text{price charged by BSF's major competitor}$$

Big Sky Foods has access to forecasts from one of the macroeconometric service firms that provide a good estimate of the income variable by quarter for one year ahead. In addition, BSF has had reasonable success using a simple exponential smoothing model (with $w = .8$) to predict the competitor's price one quarter in advance. And, of course, BSF controls its own price. Thus, the above model can be used to forecast sales one quarter at a time. Assume that BSF plans to price at $P = 5.85$ next quarter, that the competitor's price is forecast to be $PC = 4.99$, and that income is forecast at $INC = 4800$. Sales for BSF is forecast as

$$Q = 15.939 - 9.057(5.85) + .009(4800) + 5.092(4.99)$$
$$Q = 31.565$$

Notice that, in making this forecast, BSF starts with a macro forecast that provides a projection for income and an exponential smoothing model that provides a projected value for the competitor's price. These are then combined with the multiple regression model of demand and BSF's own pricing plan to arrive at a forecast for sales. BSF can then use this procedure to experiment with the effect of different prices.

> Try this yourself.[15] Suppose forecasts for income and the competitor's price are the same as those in our example and that you want to evaluate the effect of setting BSF's price at $5.75 rather than $5.85. What estimate for sales (Q) would you obtain?
>
> $$Q = 15.939 - 9.057(\underline{\hspace{1cm}}) + .009(\underline{\hspace{1cm}}) + 5.092(\underline{\hspace{1cm}})$$
>
> $$Q = \underline{\hspace{1cm}}$$
>
> What can you say about price elasticity based on this result?

Before leaving the discussion of applications of multiple regression analysis to forecasting, let us demonstrate how the data forecast with time series decomposition (see Table 6.3) could also be forecast using a multiple regression model. You will see that the multiple regression model can also

---

[15]You should find $Q = 32.419$ for $P = 5.75$, $INC = 4800$, and $PC = 4.98$. Since total revenue (PQ) goes from 184.357 to 186.409 when price is lowered, demand must be elastic.

account for the seasonality in the data. (You may recall that this concept was introduced in Chapter 4 but was not applied to developing a forecast.)

Suppose we assign dummy variables for quarters 2, 3, and 4 as follows:

Q_2 = 1 for quarter 2 observations and 0 otherwise
Q_3 = 1 for quarter 3 observations and 0 otherwise
Q_4 = 1 for quarter 4 observations and 0 otherwise

We would then have the following regression model:

$$Sales = a + b_1(Time) + b_2Q_2 + b_3Q_3 + b_4Q_4$$

The data used to estimate this function are shown in Table 6.6, and the regression results are

$$Sales = 7.019 + .331(Time) - 1.931Q_2 - 4.062Q_3 - 1.994Q_4$$
$$(10.17) \qquad (3.70) \qquad (7.74) \qquad (3.76)$$

R^2 = .884, the absolute value of t-ratios are in parentheses, and the Durbin-Watson statistic is 1.18.

TABLE 6.6   **Sales Data and Quarterly Dummy Variables**

Period	Time Index	Sales	Quarterly Dummy Variables		
			Q_2	Q_3	Q_4
1980.1	1	7	0	0	0
1980.2	2	6	1	0	0
1980.3	3	4	0	1	0
1980.4	4	6	0	0	1
1981.1	5	8	0	0	0
1981.2	6	7	1	0	0
1981.3	7	6	0	1	0
1981.4	8	7	0	0	1
1982.1	9	10	0	0	0
1982.2	10	9	1	0	0
1982.3	11	6	0	1	0
1982.4	12	9	0	0	1
1983.1	13	12	0	0	0
1983.2	14	10	1	0	0
1983.3	15	9	0	1	0
1983.4	16	12	0	0	1
1984.1	17	13	0	0	0
1984.2	18	10	1	0	0
1984.3	19	8	0	1	0
1984.4	20	11	0	0	1

We can use this model to forecast sales for 1985 as follows:

1985.1:
$$Sales = 7.019 + .331(21) - 1.931(0) - 4.062(0) - 1.994(0)$$
$$Sales = 13.97$$

1985.2:
   Sales = 7.019 + .331(22) − 1.931(1) − 4.062(0) − 1.994(0)
   Sales = 12.37
1985.3 (you do this one):[16]
   Sales = 7.019 + .331(__) − 1.931(__) − 4.062(__) − 1.994(__)
   Sales = _____
1985.4:
   Sales = 7.019 + .331(24) − 1.931(0) − 4.062(0) − 1.994(1)
   Sales = 12.97

Compare these results with those obtained from the decomposition model (see Table 6.3). They are quite consistent. In both models, you see that the third quarter has the lowest and the first quarter the highest sales. As mentioned earlier in this chapter, it is a good idea to use more than one method in preparing any forecast. Managerial judgment should also be used to establish a high, a low, and a most likely forecast.

An excellent example of how a company might actually construct a forecast from the bottom up is provided in Exhibit 6.2. This article appeared originally in *Business Economics*, published by the National Association of Business Economists.[17]

EXHIBIT 6.2   A Comprehensive Forecasting Example

The sales of any product line are determined by many factors in combination. In general these factors can be separated into four categories — the economic environment, those factors controlled internally by management, the actions of competitors, and random events.

Relevant economic factors may include the general state of the economy, the level of interest rates, the level of production or sales in the markets to which the product line is sold, and so forth. But, too much economic data presented in an inappropriate format can be as useless for product line forecasting as too little awareness of the effect of the economic environment. An economic information system *structures* data so that the relevant data are identified and their effects on the product line are shown.

Modern statistical packages enable users to model econometrically the historical relationships between the relevant economic factors and the performance of the product line. Then this information

---

[16]You should find sales = 10.57.

[17]Stephen J. Browne and Dennis O'Brien, "Product Line Forecasting and Planning," *Business Economics*, September 1974, pp. 63–71. Reprinted with permission of the National Association of Business Economists.

can be used in conjunction with an econometric macro-economic forecasting model to forecast product line performance. The following example illustrates how an economic information system is helping one company structure the effect of national economic and market conditions on the performance of one of its product lines. The company's data have been disguised to insure confidentiality and yet not to influence the results. Each step is spelled out so that the general applicability of this approach can be seen.

Examining Historic Data

The dotted line in Figure 1 is a graph of the units of widgets sold, per quarter, from 1961:1 to 1972:1. Information was provided on units of widgets sold (not seasonally adjusted), relative price, and promotional outlays, in current dollars.

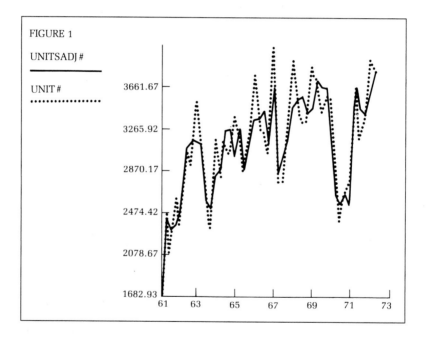

FIGURE 1

UNITSADJ #

UNIT #

Seasonal Adjustment

The initial step taken in building the Widget Model is to seasonally adjust the raw data. There are two reasons for doing so. First, quarterly time series have much of their fluctuations caused by such factors as customs, shifts in regional distribution patterns, and new car introduction cycles. It is important to isolate the contributions of these events in order to evaluate clearly the more important movements of the series. Second, the economic time series that we will be using as explanatory variables have been adjusted for seasonal variations. If an unadjusted product line series were related to an adjusted economic series, spurious relationships might be generated and real correlations could be disguised. For example, a downturn in the fourth quarter of an adjusted economic series might seem to explain a downturn in the fourth quarter of the unadjusted product line series, whereas in actuality this latter downturn may have been caused by the fact that there were fewer trading days due to holidays, or that the product was a fair weather good, etc. It is preferable to relate seasonally adjusted series to other adjusted series, rather than to use all unadjusted series, as the seasonal patterns in the several variables could be different.

In this model the Census X11 method with multiplicative seasonal adjustment is used. One of the features of X11 is its ability to calculate a trend in the seasonal pattern. In the Widget Model, the seasonal factors have a pronounced trend.

In 1961 the first quarter's seasonal factor was 95.6, a subnormal quarter. By 1972 it had grown at the expense of other quarters to 99.6, a normal quarter. Conversely, the second quarter in 1961 had a normal seasonal of 100.3; by 1972 this had deteriorated to 92.2. Table 1 is a printout of the historic seasonal factors for the four quarters and the forecast made by the X11 package of these factors one year ahead.

Once the factors have been determined, the seasonally adjusted series is created by simple division:

Unadjusted Data/Seasonal Factors = Adjusted Data

TABLE 1
Final Seasonal Factors, 3 × 5 Moving Average

Year	1st Quar	2nd Quar	3rd Quar	4th Quar
1961	95.571	100.305	91.916	112.077
1962	95.947	99.760	92.264	112.003
1963	96.420	98.802	92.739	112.102
1964	97.115	97.214	93.440	112.660
1965	97.142	95.947	94.415	112.698
1966	97.457	94.514	95.612	112.728
1967	97.274	93.751	96.720	112.155
1968	97.641	93.023	97.541	111.568
1969	97.986	92.763	98.124	110.531
1970	98.854	92.409	98.497	109.832
1971	99.415	92.217	98.695	109.548
1972	99.609	********	********	********

Series Units
Seasonal Factors One Year Ahead

Year	1st Quar	2nd Quar	3rd Quar	4th Quar
1972	*************	92.121	98.793	109.407
1973	99.707	********	********	********

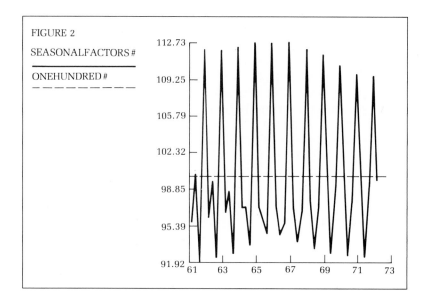

FIGURE 2

SEASONALFACTORS #
————————

ONEHUNDRED #
— — — — — — — —

Later, when the adjusted series has been forecast and it is desirable to put it back into its adjusted form, simply reverse the procedure:

$$\text{Adjusted Data Forecast} * \text{Seasonal Factor Forecast} = \\ \text{Unadjusted Data Forecast}$$

Figure 1 shows seasonally adjusted unit sales (UNITSADJ#) versus unadjusted sales to demonstrate the results of the seasonal adjustment procedure; Figure 2 is a graph of the seasonal factors (100 = normal).

Economy-Wide Variables

Correlation with Economic Variables. Widgets are sold chiefly to the transportation industry and the construction industry and are also an important item in inventories. Starting with this knowledge of the markets for widgets, the following simple correlation matrix between widget output and three variables representing these markets may be calculated.

The variable JFRB37Q is the Federal Reserve Board Production Index for the transportation industry. HUSTLAG is the number of housing starts (millions), both single and multiple family, lagged one quarter; the lag is used since widgets are not required in the initial phase of construction. JINVEAF58 is the change in non-agricultural inventories in 1958 dollars; constant (1958) dollars are used so that this variable does not include the effect of inflation, as the variable we are explaining is the number of widgets sold, not the dollar value of sales.

Correlation Matrix				
	UNITSA DJ	QFRB37 Q	HUSTSL AG	JINVEA F58
UNITSADJ	1.0000			
JFRB37Q	0.7890	1.000		
HUSTLAG	0.4844	0.0825	1.000	
JINVEAF58	0.3295	0.3954	− 0.3599	1.000

The correlation matrix displays the *correlation coefficients* between pairs of variables. The coefficient measures the strength of the correlation between the members of a pair. It is an important tool, but does not take the place of regressions. Regressions allow one not only to measure the strength of the relationship between variables, (e.g., R-bar squared) but also to calculate what that numerical relationship is (e.g., the regression coefficients). More importantly, regressions allow one to use more than one variable to explain the dependent variable (e.g., widgets sold); such multiple regressions measure the combined impact of the several explanatory variables, as well as their particular numerical relationships to the dependent variable. It should be noted that the relatively low correlation coefficients of widgets sold to (lagged) housing starts and change in inventories do not adequately reflect their true importance as explanatory variables within a multiple regression, as will be seen shortly.

Regression with Economic Variables.   A multiple regression is performed, relating widget sales to three economic variables. (See Regression 1.) At this point the equation is:

Regression 1			

Ordinary Least Squares

Frequency Quarterly
Interval
Left-hand Variable: UNITSADJ

Right-hand Variable	Estimated Coefficient	Standard Error	T-Statistic
Constant	− 94.3493	270.331	− 0.349013
JFRB37Q	1700.51	239.630	7.09640
HUSTLAG	1005.01	147.836	6.79812
JINVEAF58	34.8039	10.1635	3.42440

R-Bar Squared: 0.7718
Durbin-Watson Stat.:   1.0399
Standard Error of the Regression: 219.260

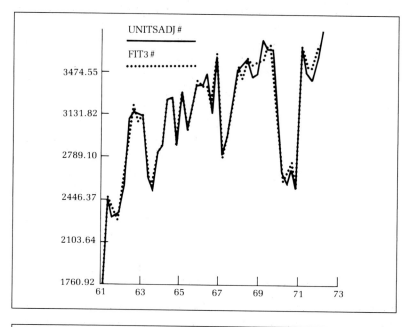

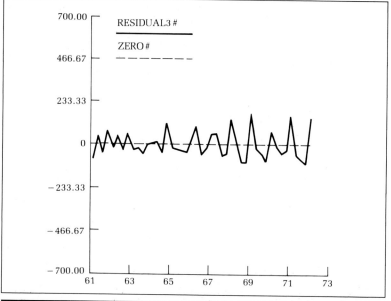

$$\text{UNITSADJ} = -94.35 + 1700.5 * \text{JFRB37Q} +$$
$$1005.01 * \text{HUSTSLAG} + 34.80 *] \text{INVEAF58}$$

The estimated coefficient of the transportation industry index is positive and can be interpreted to mean that for an increase of 0.1 in the index, widgets sold will increase by 170. The lagged housing starts variable has a positive coefficient, as expected, implying that additional housing starts in one quarter will lead to increased widget production in the next quarter. Change in inventories also has a positive coefficient.

R-bar squared, a measure of the overall fit of the equation, is .77, indicating that 77% of the variation in widget sales around their mean value is explained by movements in the three economic variables. All three variables have statistically significant coefficients, as indicated by the t-statistics printed out in Regression 1. The standard error of ther regression is 219, meaning that 67% of the time the sales of widgets estimated by the equation were within ± 219 of actual widget output.

The plot of actual versus fitted values shows that the equation tracks the major movements, but could still use improvement. The plot of the residuals makes the pattern of errors clearer. The residual is defined as the actual value of widgets sold minus the estimated value; it is the amount by which the equation is in error for each quarter.

Management Decision Variables

At this point, factors over which management has control can be used to explain the pattern of the residual. One might be tempted to add more economy-wide variables, but there may be pitfalls in doing so. For example, the transportation industry has motor vehicles and airplanes as two of its component industries. However, the FRB production indices for these two industries are highly correlated. Including both of them causes what is known as the *multicollinearity* problem, making it difficult to tell what the true coefficient is for each of these two variables. The total transportation industry index, JFRB37Q, serves as a proxy for the two separate indices.

From 1962:2 to 1963:1 the model underestimates, what the actual sales of widgets were. In the period of 1969:4 to 1970:4 the model overestimates the sales of widgets. Perhaps the difference between actual widget company sales and the model's estimate is accounted for by variations in the widget company's market share. Thus, when the model underestimates widget company sales, market share may have increased; when the model overestimates, actual widget company sales may be depressed due to a loss in customary market share.

In this light variables such as price and promotional expenditures are introduced to the model. Called Management Decision Variables, they are used to explain fluctuations in the company's market share.

Effects of Pricing.   The first step is to try to relate relative price (defined as 100 * [company price of widgets/industry price]) to the residual variance left unexplained by the markets for widgets. The relative price of widgets is always less than one; that is, the company price is always below the industry price. Since this product always sold below the market price, one might expect to observe a continuous gain in market share. As this did not occur, it appears that this product is to some extent inferior in terms of quality or service than the products against which it competes, or the reported industry price is characteristically inflated. Hence, the apparent relative price advantage may be merely a discount to make up for the quality or service differential or to offset traditional discounts in the industry.

Regression 2

Ordinary Least Squares

Frequency Quarterly
Interval 61:1 to 72:1
Left-hand Variable: UNITSADJ

Right-hand Variable	Estimated Coefficient	Standard Error	T-Statistic
Constant	2384.77	817.285	2.91791
JFRB37Q	1630.90	217.868	7.48571
HUSTLAG	1046.15	134.355	7.78647
JINVEAF58	41.0572	9.40178	4.36696
RELPRICELAG	−31.4263	9.88563	−3.17899

R-Bar Squared: 0.8133
Durbin-Watson Stat.:   1.1558
Standard Error of the Regression: 198.338

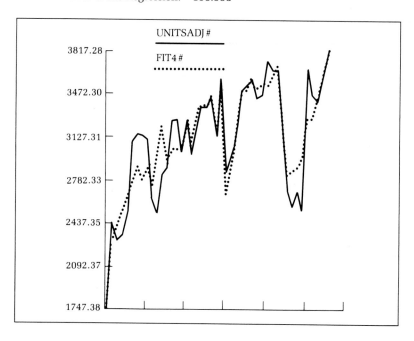

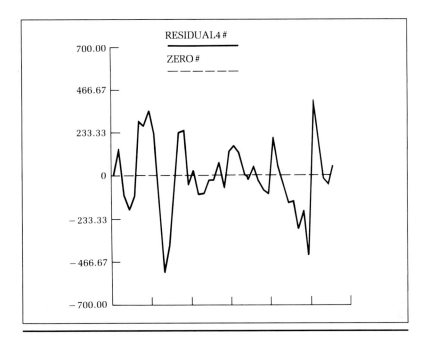

Still, fluctuations in relative price will probably affect market shares. The best results are found when relative price is lagged one quarter. The lagged relative price is included in our widgets model, and a multiple regression is performed. (See Regression 2.) The price variable has a negative and significant coefficient. The coefficient indicates that if the company increases the relative price of widgets from 80 (per cent) to 81 (per cent), they would lose 31.4 units of sales. Company management is in agreement with the lag and the estimated magnitude of the price effect.

Effects of Promotion.   The plot of the residual still shows significant variation not accounted for by the markets or the relative price factor. At this point the effects of promotional activities are investigated by postulating a theory concerning the effects of promotional expenditures. Since promotional activity here includes advertising as well as discounts, we believe that there would be more of a distributed lag effect rather than just a simple one-period effect. It is also postulated that it is only extraordinary activity in this area which has any effect. Normal discounts or advertising are simply met by the competition. Only expenditures above or below normal cause gains or losses of market share. But the questions remain: What is normal, and what is the structure of the lag?

As a first step in answering these questions, promotional expenditures are deflated. Since we are trying to explain the forecast units rather than sales dollars we want to remove the effects of inflation from promotional expenditures. Lacking a good measure of inflation in advertising, the promotion-advertising series is deflated by the GNP deflator:

$$ADV/PGNP = ADV\$$$

The data are plotted along with the trended mean bracketed by plus and minus 1/2 standard deviation. Only expenditures either above 1/2 standard deviation above the trended mean or below 1/2 standard deviation below the trended mean are included (blacked-in area in Figure 3).

The residual (the error that remains after the effects of market fluctuations and relative price are accounted for) is regressed against the extreme values of promotional expenditures, lagged 0, 1, and 2 quarters, to establish distributed lag weights.

The effect of the advertising variable in the current period is less than its effect lagged one period, while its effect further diminishes two periods out. From this analysis the following weights are assigned to the extreme promotional expenditures variable:

.3 at time t
.5 at time t − 1
.2 at time t − 2

A new variable is created using these lags and weights:

$$\text{Advertising} = [.3*X + .5*X_{-1} + .2*X_{-2}]$$

where

$$X = (Y \text{ when } Y > 0) \text{ and } (Z \text{ when } Z < 0)$$

and

$$Y = ADV\$ - (1/2 \, \sigma \text{ above the trended mean})$$
$$Z = ADV\$ - (1/2 \, \sigma \text{ below the trended mean})$$

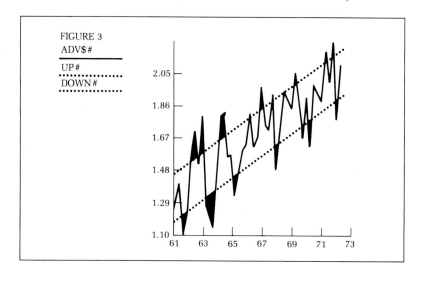

FIGURE 3
ADV$ #

UP #
....

DOWN #
....

This variable is included in the model and we perform a multiple regression (not shown). The advertising variable has a positive and statistically significant sign, indicating that promotion expenditures well above normal result in increased widget sales, even with no change in the levels of the economy-wide variables. Similarly, well-below normal expenditures will reduce the widget company's market shares. (More rigorously, the extreme expenditures variable could have been incorporated in the regression using the technique of polynomial distributed lags to determine the lag weighting structure.)

Effects of Strikes.   The model fits quite well, with the exception of the fourth quarter of 1970 through the second quarter of 1971. As it is known that widgets are sold to the automotive industry, the model's overestimate for the fourth quarter of 1970 would appear to come from the auto strike in that quarter. A strike dummy is created to estimate the effect of the strike on widgets sales. The dummy has a value of zero except for those quarters when a strike effect presumably occurs. For the fourth quarters of 1964 and 1970, the dummy is assigned negative values, −0.6 in 1964 and −1.0 in 1970, their sizes reflecting the relative strength of the two strikes. Not only are widget sales depressed during a strike compared with what they otherwise would have been, but also in the following quarters widget sales are boosted by postponed auto production by the struck auto company. Hence, positive values are assigned to the dummy in the two quarters following a strike (+ 0.3 in 1965, + 0.5 in 1971; 1st and 2nd quarters). A multiple regression is performed including this strike dummy. (See Regression 3.)

Regression 3

Ordinary Least Squares

Frequency Quarterly
Interval 61:1 to 72:1
Left-hand Variable: UNITSADJ

Right-hand Variable	Estimated Coefficient	Standard Error	T-Statistic
Constant	3568.07	304.969	11.6998
JFRB37Q	1555.40	78.7228	19.7561
HUSTLAG	1041.40	47.9157	21.7340
JINVEAF58	45.7966	3.36520	13.6089
RELPRICELAG	− 45.5687	3.65880	− 12.4545
ADVERTISING	2975.12	196.177	15.1655
STRIKEDUMMY	410.225	51.9248	7.90035

R-Bar Squared: 0.9764
Durbin-Watson Stat.:   2.3489
Standard Error of the Regression: 70.5684

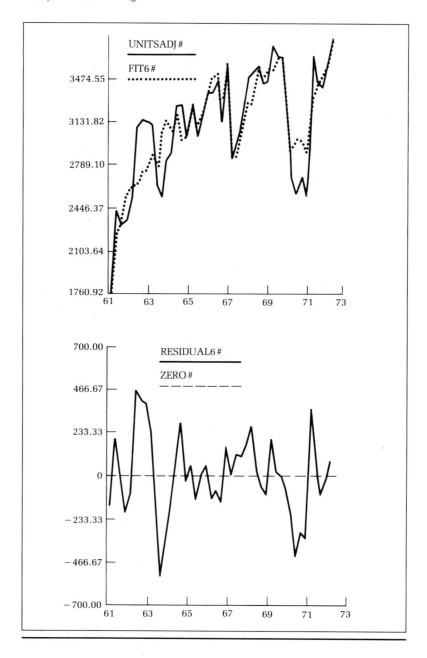

The strike dummy is significant and has a positive coefficient of 410. This can be interpreted to mean that the 1970 4th quarter sales of widgets would have been 410 units higher if there had been no strike.

The R-bar squared in this final version of the model is .9764, meaning that 97.6% of the variance of widgets sales from their mean value can be accounted for by this model. The standard error of the regression is 70.6, meaning that there is a probability of 67% that the estimated value will be within ± 70.6 of the true value of widgets sales. All the independent (right-hand side) variables have significant t-statistics. The plot of the error of residual can be compared with the previous residual plots, as all are on the same scale. The residual error has been reduced markedly, and exhibits only random fluctuations.

In Figure 4, labeled "Final Model Fit," the actual seasonally-unadjusted widget data versus the estimated unadjusted values are graphed. The latter come from multiplying the seasonal factors discussed earlier by the estimated seasonally-adjusted values from the model.

Note that the values of the several coefficients may change somewhat as more variables are added. For example, the coefficient of JFRB37Q changes from 1700 before the internal decision variables are included to 1555 in the final model regression. Including these variables not only provides a better overall fit of actual sales, but also provides estimates closer to the true coefficients of the several righthand-side variables. With these more accurate coefficients, the effect on widget sales of changes in any one of these variables can be determined more accurately.

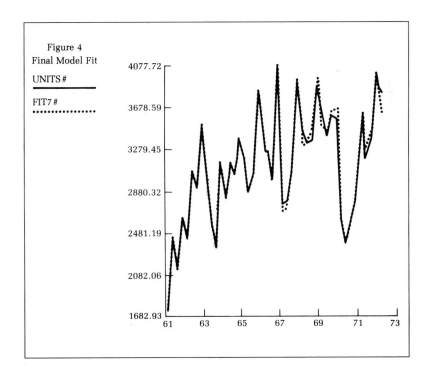

Figure 4
Final Model Fit

UNITS #

FIT7 #

Forecasting

How can this model be used to forecast widget sales? Computer packages linked with macro-economic models provide simulation capabilities for product line models and produce forecasts for products under a variety of assumptions about the future. The procedure is to generate forecasts of the economic variables included in the model, and to plug into the model these values along with appropriate values for the internal decision variables in order to calculate projected product line sales.

Using a Macro-Economic Forecast.   An econometric model's short-term forecast of the economy is used to produce values for the economy-wide variables included in the widget model — that is, to forecast the level of housing starts, change in inventories, and the transportation industry production index. Values for the internal decision variables are entered (relative price, promotional expenses) as is the strike dummy, and the model is solved. The results are displayed in Report 1.

Widget Report 1 Control							
General Economic Variables							
	72: 4	73: 1	73: 2	73: 3	73: 4	74: 1	74: 2
GNP — Current $	1193.	1225.	1249.	1273.	1298.	1324.	1346.
GNP — 1958 $	808.8	820.9	829.4	838.0	849.2	857.7	866.5
Independent Variables							
FRB Prod. Index — Transportation	1.014	1.035	1.029	1.029	1.034	1.031	1.037
Housing Starts — Lagged 1 Qtr.	2.224	2.218	2.184	2.087	2.095	2.098	1.921
Change in Inventories — Non-Agric — 1958 $	8.9	10.1	10.8	10.5	12.4	11.3	10.7
Assumptions — Decision Variables							
Relative Price — Lagged 1 Qtr.	80.00	80.00	80.00	80.00	80.00	80.00	80.00
Promotional Expenses — 1958 $	2.000	2.000	2.000	2.000	2.000	2.200	2.200
Effect of Promotional Expenses	0.0000	0.0000	0.0000	0.0000	−.1200J	−.2000J	−.0800J
Strikedummy — Automobiles	0.0000	0.0000	0.0000	0.0000	0.0000	0.0000	0.0000
Widgets Forecast							
Widgets — Units	4223.	4305.	4292.	4176.	4279.	4222.	4024.
Widgets — Not Seasonally Adjusted	4620.	4292.	3954.	4125.	4682.	4210.	3707.
Seasonal Adjustment Factors	109.4	99.71	92.12	98.79	109.4	99.71	92.12

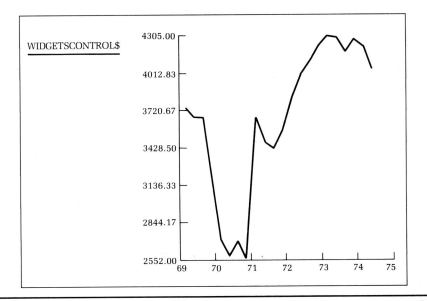

Risk of Economic Change. Changes in the economy affect production by the firm. If the economy were to take a downturn at the close of 1973, this would have definite implications for widget sales, as the regression analysis shows that the company was not isolated from the economy in past years. Such an alternative forecast for the economy can be generated with an econometric model of the economy, and this can be used as the basis for alternative forecasts of widget production. Report 2 and the associated graph show the effect of such a forecast on widget output. In this example, note that the pessimistic forecast shows that not only will GNP be lower than in the *most likely* forecast, but also housing starts, change in inventories, and transportation industry production will be off.

Simulating Management Reactions to Economic Change. These forecasts can be used not only to learn what level of production will be needed and what the future will look like, but also to provide a guide to management's reaction to that future. The model demonstrated that price and promotional expense policies have affected widget sales. Thus, management can test various strategies designed to change the future of widget sales.

For example, management could try to offset the effect of the declining economy in the pessimistic forecast above by lowering widget's relative price. Report 3 and the following plot show how a price policy change could yield the same widget output with the pessimistic economy forecast as with the more optimistic economic forecast. Alternatively, heavier promotional outlays can achieve the same goal,

Widget Report 2
PESSIM

General Economic Variables

	72: 4	73: 1	73: 2	73: 3	73: 4	74: 1	74: 2
GNP — Current $	1167.	1215.	1237.	1260.	1286.	1315.	1342.
GNP — 1958 $	802.6	809.8	814.4	821.1	831.3	840.4	850.1

Independent Variables

	72: 4	73: 1	73: 2	73: 3	73: 4	74: 1	74: 2
FRB Prod. Index — Transportation	0.9608	0.9582	0.9401	0.9392	0.9486	0.9559	0.9725
Housing Starts — Lagged 1 Qtr.	2.066	2.070	1.951	1.875	1.916	1.960	.921
Change in Inventory — Non-Agric — 1958 $	8.6	8.2	8.2	7.5	9.5	8.6	8.5

Assumptions — Decision Variables

	72: 4	73: 1	73: 2	73: 3	73: 4	74: 1	74: 2
Relative Price — Lagged 1 Qtr.	80.00	80.00	80.00	80.00	80.00	80.00	80.00
Promotional Expenses — 1958 $	2.000	2.000	2.000	2.000	2.000	2.200	2.200
Effect of Promotional Expenses	0.0000	0.0000	0.0000	0.0000	− .1200J	− .2000J	− .0800J
Strikedummy — Automobiles	0.0000	0.0000	0.0000	0.0000	0.0000	0.0000	0.0000

Widgets Forecast

	72: 4	73: 1	73: 2	73: 3	73: 4	74: 1	74: 2
Widgets — Units	3964.	3945.	3794.	3681.	3825.	3840.	3821.
Widgets — Not Seasonally Adjusted	4337.	3934.	3495.	3636.	4185.	3829.	3520.
Seasonal Adjustment Factors	109.4	99.71	92.12	98.79	109.4	99.71	92.12

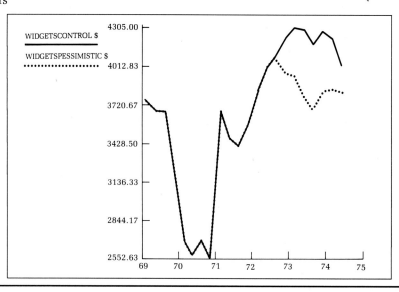

	72: 4	73: 1	73: 2	73: 3	73: 4	74: 1	74: 2
Widget Report 3 Price							
General Economic Variables							
GNP — Current $	1167.	1215.	1237.	1260.	1286.	1315.	1342.
GNP — 1958 $	802.6	809.5	814.4	821.1	831.3	840.4	850.1
Independent Variables							
FRB Prod. Index — Transportation	0.9608	0.9582	0.9401	0.9392	0.9486	0.9559	0.9725
Housing Starts — Lagged 1 Qtr.	2.066	2.070	1.951	1.875	1.916	1.960	1.921
Change in Inventory — Non-Agric — 1958 $	8.6	8.2	8.2	7.5	9.5	8.6	8.5
Assumptions — Decision Variables							
Relative Price — Lagged 1 Qtr.	74.00	72.00	70.00	70.00	70.00	72.00	76.00
Promotional Expenses — 1958 $	2.000	2.000	2.000	2.000	2.000	2.200	2.200
Effect of Promotional Expenses	0.0000	0.0000	0.0000	0.0000	−.1200J	−.2000J	−.0800J
Strikedummy — Automobiles	0.0000	0.0000	0.0000	0.0000	0.0000	0.0000	0.0000
Widgets Forecast							
Widgets — Units	4236.	4310.	4249.	4136.	4281.	4204.	4004.
Widgets — Not Seasonally Adjusted	4636.	4297.	3915.	4086.	4683.	4192.	3688.
Seasonal Adjustment Factors	109.4	99.71	92.12	98.79	109.4	99.71	92.12

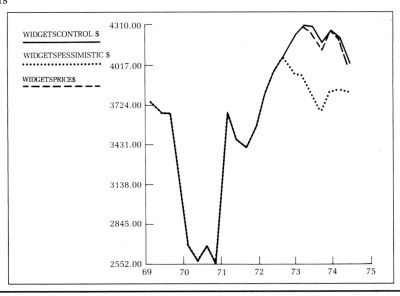

offsetting the economic lull and generating widget production nearly the same as with the stronger economy.

These alternative strategies can be filtered through an economic information system to test their effects on the income statement of the firm. That is, cash flow, income statement, and balance sheet models can be developed which will measure the effect of management strategies on earnings per share and so forth. In this manner, the two strategies above can be tested to see which is the more profitable way of meeting the sluggish economy, and indeed, whether either policy is better than no reaction at all. Similarly, the optimum pricing and advertising strategies under a variety of economic assumptions can be determined.

Anticipating Strike Effects.   Lastly, it was shown that auto strikes affected widget sales. With this model, we can see what the effect of an auto strike would be on widget output in the future. For example, suppose we want to test the effect of a strike about one half the size of 1970's occurring in the fourth quarter of 1973. A new forecast of the economy can be simulated using the macro-economic model, a forecast which captures the repercussions of the strike throughout the economy. This, along with the appropriate values for the strike dummy for widgets, will provide the best estimate of widget sales in the presence of an auto strike. The same model simulation procedure can be used to develop alternative economic forecasts under a variety of assumptions, if desired, with these forecasts then used to drive the widgets model to provide widgets forecasts given these economic scenarios.

SUMMARY

In this chapter, you have learned that firms spend a great deal of money on the forecasting function and that forecasts are used extensively in a firm's planning process. Most sales forecasts begin with a macroeconomic forecast of key variables. Firms usually obtain macroeconomic forecasts by subscribing to one of the macroeconometric forecasting services or through one of several published reports.

The sales forecast can be developed using qualitative methods, such as the sales force composite method, or quantitative models, such as exponential smoothing, time series decomposition, and multiple regression analysis. It is advisable to obtain more than one sales forecast, preferably through different kinds of techniques, and then use the good judgment of management to reconcile the results.

SUGGESTED READINGS

Angle, Elizabeth W. *Keys for Business Forecasting*, 5th ed. Richmond, VA: Federal Reserve Bank of Richmond, 1980.

Armstrong, J. Scott. *Long-Range Forecasting: From Crystal Ball to Computer*. New York: John Wiley & Sons, 1978.

Cleary, James P., and Levenbach, Hans. *The Professional Forecaster*. Belmont, CA: Lifetime Learning Publications, 1982.

Granger, C.W.J. *Forecasting in Business and Economics*. New York: Academic Press, 1980.

Gross, Charles W., and Peterson, Robin T. *Business Forecasting*, 2d ed. Boston: Houston-Mifflin, 1983.

Hanke, John E., and Reitsch, Arthur G. *Business Forecasting*. Boston: Allyn & Bacon, 1981.

Hurwood, David K., Grossman, Elliott S., and Bailey, Earl L. *Sales Forecasting*. The Conference Board, 1978.

Levenbach, Hans, and Cleary, James P. *The Beginning Forecaster*. Belmont, CA: Lifetime Learning Publications, 1981.

Pindyck, Robert S., and Rubinfeld, Daniel L. *Econometric Models and Economic Forecasts*. New York: McGraw-Hill, 1981.

Trubac, Edward R. "Fluctuations in Non-electrical Machinery Unfinished Goods Inventories During Recent Recessions." *Business Economics*, May 1983, pp. 13–21.

PROBLEMS

1. In Chapter 5, data relating to a market demand function were given in Table 5.3. Use that data, except that for 1985.1, to estimate the equation for the market demand function with market demand (MD), a function of average price (AP), and income (INC) (1985.1 is withheld since you will use the model to forecast that quarter's sales). Is your model for demand the same as the one given in Chapter 5? Why not?

    a. Prepare a forecast of income (INC) for 1985.1 using a simple time trend (use data for 1981.4–1984.4 only):

    $$INC = f(T)$$
    $$INC = a + bT$$

    where T is a time index ($T = 1$ for 1981.4).

    $$INC = \underline{\hspace{2cm}} + \underline{\hspace{2cm}} T$$

    $$(\underline{\hspace{2cm}}) \, t\text{-ratio}$$

    $$\overline{R}^2 = \underline{\hspace{2cm}} \quad DW = \underline{\hspace{2cm}}$$

    1985.1 forecast value for income = \underline{\hspace{2cm}}

b. Prepare a forecast of average price (AP) for 1985.1 using either an exponential smoothing model or a simple time trend (again, use only the 1981.4–1984.4 data):

1985.1 forecast value for average price = _____

c. Prepare a forecast of market demand (MD) using a simple time trend by first estimating the basic linear trend with the 1981.4–1984.4 data and then projecting that trend through 1985.1:

$$MD = f(T)$$
$$MD = a + bT$$

$$MD = \underline{\hspace{2cm}} + \underline{\hspace{2cm}} T$$

$$(\underline{\hspace{2cm}})\ t\text{-ratio}$$

First 1985.1 forecast value for market demand = _____

d. Now add dummy variables Q_2, Q_3, and Q_4 to the data set to see if there is any seasonality to the data. Estimate the following regression function:

$$MD = a + b_1T + b_2Q_2 + b_3Q_3 + b_4Q_4$$

Based on these results, what can you say about the amount and significance of seasonality in this set of market sales data?

e. The model you should have estimated for market demand (MD) in the opening part of this question is

$$MD = 114.64 - 21.04AP + .027INC$$
$$ (-3.68) \quad\ \ (8.72)\ \ t\text{-ratios}$$
$$\overline{R}^2 = .913 DW = 1.99$$

Use the model above to prepare a forecast of market demand for the first quarter of 1985 (1985.1) using your forecasted values of income and average price from parts a and b, respectively:

Second 1985.1 forecast value for market demand = _____

f. In which of your two forecasts of 1985.1 market demand do you have the most confidence? Explain why.

2. Look at Table 5.4 in Chapter 5. That table contains a set of data related to Big Sky Foods' sales and price, consumer income, and the price charged by their major competitor. The data cover the period 1981.4–1985.1. As in the previous problem, you should ignore the actual values given for the first quarter of 1985 and see how well you can forecast them using the tools covered in this chapter.

a. Start by estimating a new demand function using just the first 13 observations, with sales (S) a function of price (P), income (INC), and the competitor's price (CP). Write your function and related statistical results below:

$$S = a + b_1P + b_2INC + b_3PC$$

$$S = \underline{\hspace{1cm}} - \underline{\hspace{1cm}} P + \underline{\hspace{1cm}} INC + \underline{\hspace{1cm}} PC$$
$$(\quad) \qquad (\quad) \qquad (\quad)$$

Put t-ratios in the parentheses above.

$$\overline{R}^2 = \underline{\hspace{1cm}} \quad DW = \underline{\hspace{1cm}}$$

b. Now estimate a simple linear time trend for income based on data for 1981.4–1984.4:

$$INC = a + bT$$

$$INC = \underline{\hspace{1cm}} + \underline{\hspace{1cm}} T$$
$$(\quad) \; t\text{-ratio}$$

$$\overline{R}^2 = \underline{\hspace{1cm}} \quad DW = \underline{\hspace{1cm}}$$

Project the trend ahead one quarter to forecast an income for the first quarter of 1985:

Income forcast for 1985.1 = \underline{\hspace{2cm}}

c. Use an exponential smoothing model to make a forecast of the competitor's price (CP) for the first quarter of 1985:

Competitor's price forecast for 1985.1 = \underline{\hspace{2cm}}

d. Assuming that Big Sky Foods does intend to set its price at $5.80 during the first quarter of 1985, use the information in parts a through c to make a sales forecast for 1985.1:

First 1985.1 sales forecast = \underline{\hspace{2cm}}

e. Now prepare another sales forecast based on just a simple linear time trend of the sales data:

Second 1985.1 sales forecast = \underline{\hspace{2cm}}

f. Knowing that the actual level of sales in the first quarter of 1985 was 29, which model gave the best forecast? Without knowing actual sales, how might you have judged the two models used, and in which one do you think you would have had the most confidence? Why?

3.   In 1984, as part of her job responsibilities, Sally Cerny was concerned with forecasting sales from Goodwill Stores in the Rocky Mountain region. Reliable sales records were available only back to the fourth quarter of 1979. Sally had several questions concerning sales at one of the stores for which she needed to make a forecast: (1) Was the store manager who was there from the second quarter of 1980 through the first quarter of 1984 effective in promoting sales? (2) Did the introduction and sale of some forms of new clothes (mainly undergarments) at the store in the second quarter of 1980 influence total sales (most of the sales would still be expected to be in the used goods class)? and (3) Was there any significant seasonality for sales in that store (Sally thought fourth-quarter sales should always be high because of the Christmas season)? The data available to Sally are given below:

Quarter	Time	Total Sales	New Clothes Sales
1979.4	1	20933	0
1980.1	2	19125	0
1980.2	3	26064	192
1980.3	4	30691	263
1980.4	5	36613	160
1981.1	6	26726	375
1981.2	7	29611	583
1981.3	8	32686	1350
1981.4	9	38408	3466
1982.1	10	23059	1546
1982.2	11	31572	2164
1982.3	12	27741	1596
1982.4	13	43194	2662
1983.1	14	40394	1982
1983.2	15	40083	3972
1983.3	16	47672	7049
1983.4	17	48880	4490
1984.1	18	47160	5053
1984.2	19	37342	2700

a.   Based on these data, develop a simple linear trend equation for total sales (S) as a function of time (T), and use your results to fill in the blanks below:

$$S = a + bT$$

$$S = \underline{\hspace{2cm}} + \underline{\hspace{2cm}} T$$

$$\overline{R}^2 = \underline{\hspace{2cm}} \qquad DW = \underline{\hspace{2cm}}$$

t-ratio for the slope term = \underline{\hspace{2cm}}

b. Assign a dummy variable (D) equal to 1 for quarters 1980.2–1984.1 to measure the effect of the store manager who resigned in April 1984. Then estimate the following multiple linear regression function:

$$S = a + b_1 T + b_2 NG$$

$$S = \underline{\hspace{2cm}} + \underline{\hspace{2cm}} T + \underline{\hspace{2cm}} D$$

$$(\underline{\hspace{1cm}}) \quad (\underline{\hspace{1cm}})$$

$$\overline{R}^2 = \underline{\hspace{2cm}} \qquad DW = \underline{\hspace{2cm}}$$

Fill in the blanks above based on your results, placing the t-ratios in the parentheses beneath the corresponding coefficients. Would you say that the manager helped to promote sales or not based on this evidence? Why or why not?

c. Now test to see if Christmas seasons have had a significant effect on total sales. Do this by assigning a dummy variable (Q_4) equal to 1 for each fourth quarter and equal to 0 otherwise. Estimate the following model, filling in the blank spaces based on your results:

$$S = a + b_1 T + b_2 Q_4$$

$$S = \underline{\hspace{2cm}} + \underline{\hspace{2cm}} T + \underline{\hspace{2cm}} Q_4$$

$$(\underline{\hspace{1cm}}) \quad (\underline{\hspace{1cm}})$$

$$\overline{R}^2 = \underline{\hspace{2cm}} \qquad DW = \underline{\hspace{2cm}}$$

Based on these results, what can you conclude about Sally's hypothesis that total sales are higher during the Christmas season? Explain.

d. To evaluate whether or not the introduction of new goods (NG) has influenced total sales (S), estimate the following regression:

$$S = a + b_1 T + b_2 NG$$

$$S = \underline{\hspace{2cm}} + \underline{\hspace{2cm}} T + \underline{\hspace{2cm}} NG$$

$$(\underline{\hspace{1cm}}) \quad (\underline{\hspace{1cm}})$$

$$\overline{R}^2 = \underline{\hspace{2cm}} \qquad DW = \underline{\hspace{2cm}}$$

How would you interpret these results?

e. Now estimate a more comprehensive model in which total sales are a function of a time trend (T), the effect of the interim manager (D), the Christmas season (Q_4), and the sales of new goods (NG). Complete the following table:

Variable	Coefficient	t-ratio
Intercept	――――――	――――――
T	――――――	――――――
D	――――――	――――――
Q_4	――――――	――――――
NG	――――――	――――――
$\overline{R}^2 =$ ――――――	$DW =$ ――――――	

Write a paragraph interpreting these results for a nonstatistical user.

f. To use the model developed in part e as an aid in forecasting, you would first need some means of forecasting new goods sales (NG). Estimate a linear time trend equation for $NG = f(T)$, and use that function to estimate new goods sales for 1984.3 and 1984.4:

1984.3 forecast $NG =$ ―――――――――

1984.4 forecast $NG =$ ―――――――――

g. Now use the model developed in part e, along with your projections for new goods sales, to make a forecast of total sales for this Goodwill Store for the last two quarters of 1984:

1984.3 Goodwill total sales $=$ ―――――――――

1984.4 Goodwill total sales $=$ ―――――――――

4. During the summer of 1980, graduate students Joan and Bill Casper decided to build a canoe in the north country of Wisconsin. Not only did they enjoy the experience, but the canoe also worked marvelously. Further, many people commented about how much they liked the birch canoe. Later that year, Joan and Bill consented to make 2 more canoes for friends but to do so had to give up part-time jobs. To make up for this opportunity cost, they agreed to sell each canoe to their friends for $400 over their material costs. After the Christmas holiday, 5 other people who had seen these canoes inquired about having ones made, under the same pricing agreement, for use during the summer of 1981. Joan and Bill once more consented. During the spring of 1981, 9 more people asked about having birch canoes custom-made, and the Caspers filled their requests. Other people inquired during the summer and fall of 1981, but not as many (3 and 4, respectively). However, during the first quarter of 1982, 9 more requests came in, and then in the second quarter of that year, Joan and Bill were surprised when 17 people asked them to make canoes. The Caspers had been putting their initials on each canoe, along with the date it was completed, so they decided to formalize their backyard business as J & B Enterprises. Word of mouth alone continued to bring in orders. A sales history through the third quarter of 1984 follows:

Period	Actual Sales	Time Index	MA	CMA	SF	CMAT	CF
1980.4	2	1	—	—	—	—	—
1981.1	5	2	—	—	—	—	—
1981.2	9	3					
1981.3	3	4					
1981.4	4	5					
1982.1	9	6					
1982.2	17	7					
1982.3	6	8					
1982.4	7	9					
1983.1	13	10					
1983.2	24	11					
1983.3	6	12					
1983.4	8	13					
1984.1	15	14					
1984.2	26	15					
1984.3	6	16	—	—	—		e
1984.4	—	17	—	—	—		e
1985.1	—	18	—	—	—		e
1985.2	—	19	—	—	—		e
1985.3	—	20	—	—	—		e
1985.4	—	21	—	—	—		e

a. Calculate the four-period moving average and the centered moving average for J & B's sales, placing the calculated values in the table as appropriate. Write a sentence or two explaining what the CMA values represent.

b. Using the actual sales data, along with the CMA, calculate the seasonal factors (SF). Explain the meaning of these factors. Record them to three decimal places in the appropriate column of the table.

c. Use the following grid to determine the seasonal indexes (SI) for J & B's canoe sales:

Seasonal Factors by Quarter

Year	1	2	3	4	
1981	—				
1982					
1983					
1984		—	—	—	Sum of
Totals					Means
Means					
SI					

where, for each quarter, SI = (mean)(4/sum of means).

d. Estimate the centered moving average trend (CMAT) by using OLS regression, with CMA as the dependent variable and the time index (T) as the independent variable. Write the equation below:

$$CMAT = a + bT$$

CMAT = _____ + _____ T

Use this equation to find CMAT for each row of the table above, from 1980.4–1985.4.

e. Now calculate the cycle factors (CF) by dividing the CMA for each quarter by the corresponding CMAT. Plot these CF values on the graph below and make projections, or estimates, through 1985.

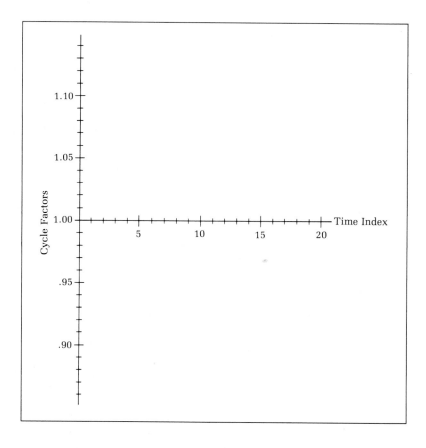

f. Use the CMAT, SI, and CF developed above to forecast sales for J & B Enterprises through the end of 1985:

Period	CMAT	SI	CF	Forecast
1984.4				
1985.1				
1985.2				
1985.3				
1985.4				

    g. The actual sales for this period turned out to be 9, 20, 35, 8, and 10, respectively. Calculate the root mean squared error (*RMSE*) for these five quarters.

    h. Write a paragraph explaining your forecasts for Joan and Bill Casper.

5. Joan Casper's cousin, Larry Taylor, an MBA student who had just purchased a microcomputer, came to visit in November 1984. He suggested that sales for J & B Enterprises might be better forecast by using regression techniques for which he had appropriate computer software.

    a. Put yourself in Larry's place and estimate the simple linear time trend for sales, based on the data given in the previous problem. The model you are to fit, for data from 1980.4–1984.3, is

$$S = a + bT$$

where S represents sales, and T is the time index ($T = 1$ for 1980.4). Fill in the blanks in the equation below:

$$S = \underline{\hspace{2cm}} + \underline{\hspace{2cm}} T$$
$$(\quad\quad)$$
$$\overline{R}^2 = \underline{\hspace{1.5cm}} \quad\quad DW = \underline{\hspace{1.5cm}}$$

Put the *t*-ratio in the parentheses below the slope term.

    b. Write a paragraph explaining this model to Joan and Bill Casper.

    c. Use the model developed in part a to forecast sales for 1984.4–1985.4. The actual sales data for these quarters are given in the following table. Add your forecast values, complete the rest of the table, and calculate the root mean squared error (*RMSE*) for your model.

Period	Actual Sales	Forecast Sales	Error	Squared Error
1984.4	9			
1985.1	20			
1985.2	35			
1985.3	8			
1985.4	10			

Sum of the squared errors = _____

RMSE = _____

Based on this RMSE and on your results in part g of problem 4, which model appears to work better, the time series decomposition model or the simple linear trend model?

d. In looking at your results, Joan and Bill remark that the model does not take into account the seasonal nature of their sales. See if you can improve on the regression model by incorporating dummy variables to account for the seasonality. Letting Q_2, Q_3, and Q_4 represent dummy variables for the second, third, and fourth quarters, respectively, estimate the following model using a multiple regression program:

$$S = a + b_1T + b_2Q_2 + b_3Q_3 + b_4Q_4$$

Write your related statistical results in the table below:

Coefficient	Value	t-ratio
a		
b_1		
b_2		
b_3		
b_4		
$\overline{R}^2$ = _____	DW = _____	

e. Use this multiple regression model to develop another forecast of sales for 1984.4–1985.4, and complete the following table:

Period	Actual Sales	Forecast Sales	Error	Squared Error
1984.4	9			
1985.1	20			
1985.2	35			
1985.3	8			
1985.4	10			
Sum of the squared errors =				_____
RMSE = _____				

Now compare all three models. Which one provides the best forecasts based on the RMSE criterion?

6. Greg Masters is the assistant administrator of the Green River Community College (GRCC) and has been asked to prepare a method for forecasting enrollment so that the school can better plan its facilties and personnel needs. The city of Green River (population 55,000) is also the home of a small private college, River Falls College (RFC). Greg believes that RFC and GRCC compete for some of the same students, since the former runs several two-year certificate programs. In addition, he has observed what he thinks is significant seasonality in enrollments at GRCC.

Greg gathered data on enrollment at GRCC and the average tuition charged at RFC for every quarter between the first quarter of 1970 (1970.1) and the fourth quarter of 1983 (1983.4). Using his data (which are given below), along with dummy variables for the second (Q_2), third (Q_3), and fourth (Q_4) quarters, estimate the following regression models for use in forecasting enrollments:

Model 1: Enrollment as a function of time (let $T = 1$ for 1970.1)
Model 2: Enrollment as a function of time and seasonal dummy variables
Model 3: Enrollment as a function of time, seasonal dummy variables, and RFC tuition

Write a short paragraph interpreting and explaining each of these three models.

Knowing that RFC has made a pledge to hold tuition at $100 per credit hour through the 1984 calendar year, prepare a forecast of GRCC enrollment for each quarter of 1984 based on these models. Below are two tables. The first contains data for use in developing the forecast model. Enter your values in the second table and calculate the root mean squared error for each forecast:

Period	GRCC Enrollment	RFC Tuition	Period	GRCC Enrollment	RFC Tuition
1970.1	73	36	1977.1	169	55
1970.2	282	36	1977.2	288	55
1970.3	291	36	1977.3	302	55
1970.4	308	36	1977.4	328	55
1971.1	124	36	1978.1	202	60
1971.2	319	36	1978.2	303	60
1971.3	297	36	1978.3	301	60
1971.4	330	36	1978.4	298	60
1972.1	133	36	1979.1	204	75
1972.2	311	36	1979.2	286	75
1972.3	308	36	1979.3	303	75
1972.4	330	36	1979.4	323	75
1973.1	181	45	1980.1	229	85
1973.2	356	45	1980.2	636	85
1973.3	356	45	1980.3	287	85
1973.4	290	45	1980.4	299	85
1974.1	181	45	1981.1	299	85
1974.2	356	45	1981.2	473	85
1974.3	295	45	1981.3	410	85
1974.4	276	45	1981.4	437	95
1975.1	154	45	1982.1	265	95
1975.2	268	45	1982.2	518	95
1975.3	319	45	1982.3	480	95
1975.4	306	45	1982.4	528	95
1976.1	188	55	1983.1	231	100
1976.2	308	55	1983.2	563	100
1976.3	279	55	1983.3	480	100
1976.4	284	55	1983.4	522	100

Period	Actual Enrollment	Model 1 Forecast Enrollment	Model 2 Forecast Enrollment	Model 3 Forecast Enrollment
1984.1	256			
1984.2	563			
1984.3	480			
1984.4	531			
RMSE		_____	_____	_____

7. In problem 6, you may have noticed a larger than usual jump in enrollment at Green River Community College during the second quarter of 1980 (1980.2 in the data set). Near the end of the previous quarter,

there was a strike of maintenance workers at River Falls College that threatened to shut the school down. It is likely that this could have caused some students to switch to GRCC for the 1980.2 quarter.

Given the additional information, reestimate the models in problem 6 using a dummy variable (D) to represent this influence on the data. Let $D = 1$ for 1980.2 and $D = 0$ for all other quarters. Does the use of the dummy variable seem to improve the models based on their adjusted R-squared values? How are the forecasts effected? Are the *RMSE*s for the forecasts better?

8. Black Bear Lodge (BBL) is a family restaurant located on the edge of Black Bear Lake in the north central part of the state. Pat McKittrick bought BBL in 1980 and has kept careful track of the number of customers served each day since she took over the facility. In 1984, the total number of customers served was about 2.6 times the number served in 1981, and Pat found that her facilities were being used to capacity. She decided that she would like to consider an expansion and so had plans drawn up and went to a local bank for financing. Bob Bell, the loan officer, told her that he thought the bank could help her, but that they would need a forecast of sales for each of the next four quarters. The table below shows the data that Pat has for the number of customers served for the 17 quarters since she took over (data are in hundreds of people):

Quarter	Year				
	1980	1981	1982	1983	1984
1		19	40	49	68
2		30	59	72	92
3		51	81	82	111
4	22	31	50	61	70
Yearly totals	?	131	230	264	341

a. Plot these customer counts on a quarterly basis, allowing room on the graph to extend through the four quarters of 1985.

b. Use a simple linear regression program on your calculator or on a computer to estimate the time trend in the BBL data. Let CS represent customers served and T represent time, where $T = 1$ for the fourth quarter of 1980. Then complete the following equation:

$$CS = a + bT$$

$$CS = \underline{\hspace{1cm}} + \underline{\hspace{1cm}} T$$

What is the coefficient of determination for this model? What does that number mean?

c. The raw data and the graph you prepared in part a both lead you to think that there is some seasonality in the data. To account for the seasonality, try using the dummy variable technique with the following dummy variables: Q_2, Q_3, and Q_4.

Quarter 1: $Q_2 = 0$, $Q_3 = 0$, $Q_4 = 0$
Quarter 2: $Q_2 = 1$, $Q_3 = 0$, $Q_4 = 0$
Quarter 3: $Q_2 = 0$, $Q_3 = 1$, $Q_4 = 0$
Quarter 4: $Q_2 = 0$, $Q_3 = 0$, $Q_4 = 1$

Using CS as a function of T, Q_2, Q_3, and Q_4, estimate the following multiple linear regression:

$$CS = a + b_1 T + b_2 Q_2 + b_3 Q_3 + b_4 Q_4$$

Complete the following:

Coefficient	Value	t-ratio
a		
b_1		
b_2		
b_3		
b_4		
$\overline{R}^2 = $ _____	$DW = $ _____	

Write the algebraic equation below:

$CS = $ _____

d. Does each of the seasons have dummy variables with the signs you expected based on your eyeball view of the data in either table or graphic form? Explain why or why not. Is there significant seasonality in all quarters? Explain.

e. How would you interpret this equation for Pat McKittrick? (Include an interpretation of each coefficient and the adjusted R^2 in your discussion.)

f. Now use this model to make a forecast of the number of customers served for each of the quarters in 1985. Complete the following table:

Period	Forecast of Customers Served
1985.1	
1985.2	
1985.3	
1985.4	

g. To show Pat McKittrick how well your model fits past data, complete the following table:

Period	Actual Customers	Estimated Customers	Error
1980.4			
1981.1			
1981.2			
1981.3			
1981.4			
1982.1			
1982.2			
1982.3			
1982.4			
1983.1			
1983.2			
1983.3			
1983.4			

Graph the estimated values on the graph prepared in part a of this problem.

9. Suppose Pat McKittrick, the owner of Black Bear Lodge (see problem 8), asks you for help in preparing an alternative forecast of the number of customers she should expect for the coming year because she feels uncomfortable with having just one forecast. Pat recently read an arti-

cle in a business magazine about time series decomposition and asks you to prepare an alternative forecast based on this methodology.

a. Prepare a table like Table 6.3 for the sales data for Black Bear Lodge, filling in the columns for the time index, sales (BBL customers, in this case), the moving average (*MA*), and the centered moving average (*CMA*). Use the time frame of 1980.4–1985.4. Did you get 84.125 for the *CMA* in 1984.2?

b. Using an OLS regression program on a computer or on your calculator, find the equation that represents the overall trend in customers served by quarter, based on the deseasonalized *CMA* series. Write the trend equation below:

$$CMAT = a + bT$$

$$CMAT = \underline{\hspace{2cm}} + \underline{\hspace{2cm}} T$$

Now fill in the *CMAT* column of your table based on this function, extending the time trend through the four quarters of 1985. Did you get 91.51 for the 1984.4 *CMAT*?

c. Calculate the seasonal factors (*SF*) for 1981.2–1984.2, and write them in the *SF* column of your table. *SF* for 1984.2 should be 1.094.

d. Using the format shown in Table 6.4, calculate the seasonal indexes (*SI*). Do you get .814 for the first quarter seasonal index? Write the seasonal indexes in the *SI* column of the table. Write a brief explanation of what these indexes mean and how they could be useful to Pat McKittrick. Are these seasonal indexes consistent with the results of the multiple regression model developed above? Explain.

e. Calculate the cycle factors (*CF*) for the quarters from 1981.2–1984.2, and write them in the *CF* column of your table. Graph these cycle factors on a piece of graph paper, using a range of .90–1.10 for *CF*, plotted on the verticle axis. Based on the pattern you see, make your best judgement about what the cycle factor would be for the quarters 1984.3–1985.5. Write these estimates in your table followed by an *e* to show that they are estimated values.

f. To see how well the model you have developed worked for the period during which actual customer counts were known, fill in the "Estimated Sales" column for 1981.2–1984.4. Plot these values on the graph of BBL customers that you used in the previous questions. How does backcasting with this model compare to backcasting with the multiple regression model?

g. Now prepare your forecast for each quarter of 1985 using this time series decomposition model. How do these results compare with those from the multiple regression model? Which results do you think provide the better forecast? Why?

10. J. R. Ashby, a wealthy businessman from Houston, has a cabin on the west shore of Black Bear Lake and eats at the Black Bear Lodge frequently during his summer vacations at the lake. In talking with Pat McKittrick one day, J. R. became interested in investing in her business. He told Pat that if she thought her 1985 sales would be 25 percent or more above the 1984 level, he would lend her the money she needed for expansion at 2 percent less than the bank would charge.

a.   Based on the results you obtained in problems 8 and 9, what estimates of total customers served would you make for 1985?

Model	1985 Forecast
Multiple regression	
Time series decomposition	

b.   J. R. Ashby has always been cautious in his investment decisions, so he wants you to prepare a third estimate of 1985 sales (customers served) using an exponential smoothing model with weighting factors of $w = .2$, $w = .5$, and $w = .8$. Complete the following table for Mr. Ashby, including the root mean squared error ($RMSE$) for each of the three forecasts:

Year	Actual Customers Served	Forecast Customers Served at Three Weighting Factors		
		$w = .2$	$w = .5$	$w = .8$
1981	131			
1982	230			
1983	264			
1984	341			
1985	?			
$RMSE =$		___	___	___

c.   Compare the best of these three forecasting models with the multiple regression model and with the time series decomposition model. Are the results comparable? Which model would you say is the best for forecasting the number of customers served at BBL on an annual basis?

d.   Given these results, and with knowledge of J. R.'s 25-percent criterion for a sales increase, would you recommend that he finance Pat McKittrick's expansion? Explain.

11. Clare Wharton manages a health and fitness center in a small mid-western town. She has been in business at her present location for four years and, due to growth, has started to press the capacity of her facilities. During her four years of experience, she has found that the first quarter of the year seems to be her best in terms of customers served, while the third quarter is her low season. Clare reasons that people have fewer options for exercise during the winter months and that during the summer people are more likely to get their exercise through a variety of outdoor activities. Before making any plans for expansion, she would like to have a forecast of her next year's level of business. Her sales history is given in the following table (data are in hundreds of customers served):

| | | Year | | |
Quarter	1981	1982	1983	1984
1	7	8	10	12
2	6	7	9	10
3	4	6	6	9
4	6	7	9	12
Yearly totals	23	28	34	43

a. Use a simple exponential smoothing model to estimate total sales for 1985. Are there any problems in using such a model in this case? Explain.

   1985 forecast = _____

b. Now use a simple linear time trend on just the yearly totals to make a forecast for 1985. Your model is

   $$YS = a + bT$$

   where YS represents yearly sales and T is the time index, with $T = 1$ for 1981, $T = 2$ for 1982, $T = 3$ for 1983, and $T = 4$ for 1984.

c. Which model do you think works best? Explain why.

12. In problem 11, you were given data for sales at a health and fitness center by quarter for a four-year period. Clare Wharton, the manager of the center, has indicated that she believes there is some seasonality to her sales, and she would like you to develop a model of her sales that would help her measure the seasonality and also provide the basis for a forecast of 1985 sales on a quarterly basis.

a. Use a multiple linear regression model of the following form to model Ms. Wharton's sales:

   $$S = a + b_1T + b_2Q_2 + b_3Q_3 + b_4Q_4$$

where S represents sales, T represents a time index that increases by 1 each quarter ($T = 1$ for 1981.1), and Q_2, Q_3, and Q_4 represent dummy variables for quarters 2, 3, and 4, respectively. From your computer results, complete the following table:

Coefficient	Value	t-ratio
a		
b_1		
b_2		
b_3		
b_4		
$\overline{R}^2 =$ _____	$DW =$ _____	

Does it make sense for all three dummy variables to have negative coefficients? Explain.

b. Write a paragraph explaining these results to Clare Wharton, assuming that, while she is an excellent manager, she does not know much about statistics.

c. Use this model to forecast sales for each quarter of 1985, writing your results below:

Period	Sales Forecast
1985.1	
1985.2	
1985.3	
1985.4	
Yearly total	

d. The actual sales for each quarter of 1985 were 13, 10, 8, and 11 for the first, second, third, and fourth quarters, respectively. Calculate the root mean squared error ($RMSE$) for this forecasting model based on these four quarters:

$RMSE =$ _____

e. Prepare a graph on which you plot the actual sales series for 1981.1–1985.4, along with your forecasted values for the four quarters of 1985.

13. In problems 11 and 12, you worked with data for a health and fitness center in a small midwestern town. In this problem, you are to prepare a quarterly forecast of sales using a time series decomposition model. You will then be asked to compare the results of all three of these problems.

a. Calculate the moving average (MA) and centered moving average (CMA) series for these data and write them in the table below (use only data for 1981–1984):

Year	Time Index	Actual Sales	MA	CMA	SF	CMAT	CF
1981.1	1	7	—	—	—		—
1981.2	2	6	—	—	—		
1981.3	3	4					
1981.4	4	6					
1982.1	5	8					
1982.2	6	7					
1982.3	7	6					
1982.4	8	7					
1983.1	9	10					
1983.2	10	9					
1983.3	11	6					
1983.4	12	9					
1984.1	13	12					
1984.2	14	10					
1984.3	15	9	—	—	—		—
1984.4	16	12	—	—	—		—
1985.1	17		—	—	—	—	e
1985.2	18		—	—	—	—	e
1985.3	19		—	—	—	—	e
1985.4	20		—	—	—	—	e

b. Calculate the seasonal factors (SF) by dividing each sales (S) value by the corresponding centered moving average (CMA) (i.e., SF = S/CMA). Enter these in the table above and also in the table below. Use the format provided below to determine the four seasonal indexes (SI):

Seasonal Factors by Quarter

Year	1	2	3	4	
1981					
1982					
1983					
1984					Sum of Means
Totals					
Means					

$$\text{First-quarter } SI = \text{(first-quarter mean)(4/sum of means)}$$

$$= \underline{\hspace{6cm}}$$

$$\text{Second-quarter } SI = \text{(second-quarter mean)(4/sum of means)}$$

$$= \underline{\hspace{6cm}}$$

$$\text{Third-quarter } SI = \text{(third-quarter mean)(4/sum of means)}$$

$$= \underline{\hspace{6cm}}$$

$$\text{Fourth-quarter } SI = \text{(fourth-quarter mean)(4/sum of mean)}$$

$$= \underline{\hspace{6cm}}$$

Write a paragraph explaining to Clare Wharton the meaning of these seasonal indexes.

c. Use your calculator's regression program or a computer program to find the trend component of this time series using the CMA as the dependent variable and the time index as the independent variable. The model for the trend component is

$$CMAT = a + bT$$

$$CMAT = \underline{\hspace{2.5cm}} + \underline{\hspace{2.5cm}} T$$

(Use the values you estimate to fill in the blanks above.) Based on this regression equation, calculate the values of CMAT from 1981.1–1985.4 and enter these values in the table provided in part a of this problem.

d. Calculate the cycle factors (CF) by dividing the centered moving average (CMA) by the centered moving average trend (CMAT) for each quarter (i.e., CF = CMA/CMAT). Enter these values in the table provided above, and graph them in the space below:

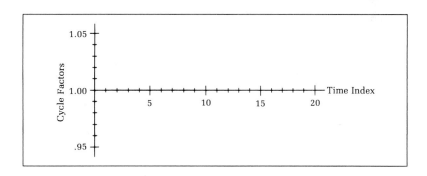

e. Project the cycle factor ahead through 1985 (through time index 20) on the graph above using your best judgment. From the graph, read estimates of the cycle factors for time periods 17–20 and enter these values in the table provided in part a of this problem.

f.   Use the table below to summarize the information necessary in making the 1985 forecast, and complete the forecast column by calculating forecast values as follows:

$$\text{Forecast value} = (CMAT)(SI)(CF)$$

Period	Time Index	CMAT	SI	CF	Forecast
1985.1	17				
1985.2	18				
1985.3	19				
1985.4	20				
Forecast of yearly total sales =					_____

g.   Calculate the root mean squared error for this forecasting method, using the data for 1985.1–1985.4, given that actual sales for that year were 13, 10, 8, and 11 for the first, second, third, and fourth quarters, respectively:

$$RMSE = \underline{\hspace{5cm}}$$

h.   In part e of problem 12, you graphed the actual sales data for 1981.1–1985.4 along with the forecast values from your regression model. Add the forecast values from part f of this problem to that graph.

14.   In problems 11–13, you developed several different forecasts of 1985 sales for Clare Wharton's health and fitness center. You know now that total sales for 1985 were 42 (actually 4200, since the data were given in hundreds).

a.   Summarize your yearly sales forecasts below:

Exponential smoothing forecast = \underline{\hspace{4cm}}

Simple time trend forecast = \underline{\hspace{4cm}}

Multiple regression forecast = \underline{\hspace{4cm}}

Decomposition forecast = \underline{\hspace{4cm}}

Calculate the percentage error for each of the forecasting methods. Would you have made a better forecast if you had taken the average of these individual forecasts rather than relying on any one method? Explain.

b. You have also developed quarterly sales forecasts based on two methods. Compare these, using *RMSE* as the criterion. Which model appears to work the best in this case?

15. The 1979 *Commodity Yearbook* has the following data for per capita turkey consumption (in pounds) in the United States:

Period	Turkey Consumption	Period	Turkey Consumption
1970.1	.9	1972.1	1.1
1970.2	.9	1972.2	1.3
1970.3	2.1	1972.3	2.2
1970.4	4.1	1972.4	4.4
1971.1	1.0	1973.1	1.2
1971.2	1.2	1973.2	1.3
1971.3	2.1	1973.3	2.1
1971.4	4.1	1973.4	3.9

Use this information as the basis for a time series decomposition analysis of turkey consumption and to make a forecast of 1974 turkey consumption by quarter. Following the method described in the text, use the tables below for your calculations:

Period	Time Index	Turkey Consumption	MA	CMA	SF	CMAT	CF
1970.1	1						
1970.2	2						
1970.3	3						
1970.4	4						
1971.1	5						
1971.2	6						
1971.3	7						
1971.4	8						
1972.1	9						
1972.2	10						
1972.3	11						
1972.4	12						
1973.1	13						
1973.2	14						
1973.3	15						
1973.4	16						

Graph the cycle factor and make a projection of it through 1974. Use the format provided below to calculate the four seasonal indexes (*SI*):

Seasonal Factors by Quarter

Year	1	2	3	4	
1970					
1971					
1972					
1973					Sum of
Totals					Means
Means					

First-quarter *SI* = (first-quarter mean)(4/sum of means)

= _____

Second-quarter *SI* = (second-quarter mean)(4/sum of means)

= _____

Third-quarter *SI* = (third-quarter mean)(4/sum of means)

= _____

Fourth-quarter *SI* = (fourth-quarter mean)(4/sum of means)

= _____

Use the table below to calculate your 1974 forecasts:

Period	CMAT	SI	CF	Forecast
1974.1				
1974.2				
1974.3				
1974.4				

The actual values for per capita turkey consumption in 1974 were quarter 1 = 1.2, quarter 2 = 1.6, quarter 3 = 2.0, and quarter 4 = 4.1. On the basis of this information, calculate the root mean squared error for your forecast.

16. In problem 15, a data set for per capita turkey consumption in the United States was given.

a. Using that data, develop quarterly forecasts of consumption for 1974 based on a multiple regression model with dummy variables to account for seasonality. Begin by using a first-quarter base period and Q_2, Q_3, and Q_4 dummy variables for the second, third, and fourth quarters. The model is

$$C = a + b_1T + b_2Q_2 + b_3Q_3 + b_4Q_4$$

where C represents per capita consumption and T is the time index, with $T = 1$ for the first quarter of 1970. From your computer output, complete the following table:

Variable	Coefficient	t-ratio
Intercept		
T		
Q_2		
Q_3		
Q_4		
$\overline{R}^2 =$ _____	$DW =$ _____	

b. Use this model to make the 1974 forecast by quarter, and then calculate the root mean squared error, as indicated below:

Period	Forecast	Actual	Error	Squared Error
1974.1		1.2		
1974.2		1.6		
1974.3		2.0		
1974.4		4.1		
Sum of squared errors =				_____
$RMSE =$ _____				

c. Which model appears to provide the best forecast for per capita turkey consumption: the time series decomposition model of the previous problem, or the multiple regression model used in this problem? Explain your answer.

17. Problems 15 and 16 used data on per capita turkey consumption in the United States. From those data, yearly consumption can be found for 1970 through 1973 as follows:

Year	Per Capita Turkey Consumption
1970	8.0
1971	8.4
1972	9.0
1973	8.5

a. Use exponential smoothing with weights of .2, .5, and .8 to forecast sales for 1974. Use the following table to show your results, including the RMSE for each forecast. (The average for the four years, 8.48, is used as the first forecast.)

Year	Actual Consumption	Forecast Turkey Consumption $w = .2$	$w = .5$	$w = .8$
1970	8.0			
1971	8.4			
1972	9.0			
1973	8.5			
1974	?			
RMSE =		____	____	____

b. If you also did problems 14 and 15, you have two other forecasts for 1974. Compare those two forecasts with the one developed in this problem for 1974. Given that total turkey consumption per capita in 1974 was 8.9 pounds, which model gave the most accurate forecast? Is the average of the three forecasts any better than any one of them alone?

c. What factors do you think could cause variations in turkey consumption from year to year? Explain.

18. Suppose that you worked for the passport office in 1983 and needed to develop a quarterly budget and a personnel schedule by quarter for 1984. You were able to put together the following data on the number of passports issued for each quarter of 1978 through 1983:

Year	Quarter			
	1	2	3	4
1978	835	1102	794	502
1979	793	1089	777	511
1980	804	987	725	487
1981	808	1015	820	487
1982	739	1262	923	739
1983	1156	1336	944	696

SOURCE: *Survey of Current Business,* various issues between February 1979 and February 1984.

a. Prepare a simple linear time trend based on these data, with passports issued (P) as a function of time (T), where $T = 1$ for the first quarter of 1978:

$$P = a + bT$$

$$P = \underline{\hspace{2cm}} + \underline{\hspace{2cm}} T$$
$$\qquad\qquad\qquad (\qquad\qquad)\ t\text{-ratio}$$

$$\overline{R}^2 = \underline{\hspace{2cm}} \qquad DW = \underline{\hspace{2cm}}$$

How well do you think this time trend would work in forecasting the number of passports issued for each quarter of 1984?

b. Plot the data in the table above to see if there appears to be any seasonality to the number of passports issued.

c. Use a multiple linear regression with dummy variables Q_2, Q_3, and Q_4 in addition to time (T) as independent variables to see if there is significant seasonality in the data. Write your model below:

$$P = a + b_1 T + b_2 Q_2 + b_3 Q_3 + b_4 Q_4$$

$$P = \underline{\hspace{1cm}} + \underline{\hspace{1cm}} T + \underline{\hspace{1cm}} Q_2 - \underline{\hspace{1cm}} Q_3 - \underline{\hspace{1cm}} Q_4$$
$$\qquad\qquad (\quad) \qquad (\quad) \qquad (\quad) \qquad (\quad)$$

Write t-ratios in parentheses.

$$\overline{R}^2 = \underline{\hspace{2cm}} \qquad DW = \underline{\hspace{2cm}}$$

d. Use both of the models developed in parts a and c to make forecasts for each quarter of 1984:

Period	Simple Time Trend	Trend with Seasonality Included
1984.1		
1984.2		
1984.3		
1984.4		
Total for 1984		

e. Use an exponential smoothing model to make a third forecast of the total number of passports issued in 1984. Does this forecast seem consistent with the results found above?

f. Go to the library and look up the actual number of passports issued in 1984. How does the actual result compare to your forecasts?

APPENDIX Input-output Forecasting

Input-output forecasts are generated through the use of a device developed by Wassily Leontief, the *input-output table*. An input-output table is a matrix with each row showing how the output or sales of a particular sector of the economy are distributed among all the sectors of the economy, including final demand. In the same manner, each column indicates all the inputs used by a particular sector of the economy. All figures are in dollars. As a very simple illustration, if we have an economy that is composed of three industries, A, B, and C, an input-output table for this economy might look like Table 6A.1.

TABLE 6A.1 Input-Output Total Transactions Table

Selling Industries	Purchasing Industries			Final Demand	Total
	A	B	C		
A	10	50	20	100	180
B	5	10	60	30	105
C	70	5	0	45	120
Value added	95	40	40		
Total	180	105	120	175	

In this example, note that the output of any sector of the economy can be purchased by the same sector, purchased by other producing sectors, or consumed as a final good by individuals, government, or businesses. When the output of a supplying sector is consumed as a final good (i.e., it is not an input for further processing), the transaction is listed under "Final Demand" in the input-output table. It should be obvious that the input-output table records all transactions, including both interindustry and intraindustry activity in the economy (whereas, in order to avoid double counting, the national income and product accounts deal only with transactions of final goods and services). Therefore, the input-output table affords the forecaster an opportunity to discern the markets in which the outputs of the industry involved are being purchased.

The "Value added" row shows the resource cost of the labor and capital used and the profit earned by the sector listed in the column heading. As you can see, the row total for each sector equals the column total for the respective sector. The reason for this equality is that the rows and columns of an input-output table are accounting identities; that is, the sum of revenues for an industry equals the sum of costs incurred plus the profits earned.

Although several input-output studies have been developed (many econometric forecasting services provide industry forecasts generated by input-output analysis) at various levels of disaggregation for commercial and academic use, the most widely used are the input-output tables produced by the United States Department of Commerce. Three different tables are available, with the most detailed tables containing four-digit SIC data:[1] the transaction table, the direct requirements table, and the total requirements table.

The transaction table, which most economists refer to as an input-output table (as shown in Table 6A.1), indicates in each row how the output of goods and services of a given industry is distributed to all industries and final users in the economy. According to our example, industry A produces $180 of total output, of which $80 are intermediate goods sold to other industries (including industry A) for use in producing products, while the remaining $100 of output are finished goods that are sold to final consumers. Each column, in turn, shows the consumption of goods and services from all industries and the value added for a given industry.

The direct requirements table, which is derived from the input-output table, presents in each column the dollar amount of input each industry listed down the left side of the table must supply for the industry named in the column heading to produce $1 of output. Table 6A.2 is the direct requirements table generated from our simple transaction table. The shortcoming of the direct requirements table is that, as its name suggests, only direct requirements are shown. In other words, looking at Table 6A.2, you see that, in order for industry C to produce $1 of output, $.50 of input from industry B would be required, along with $.167 of output from industry A. But for industry B to produce $.50 of output, it would in turn require inputs from industries A and C and also from its own industry and so on ad infini-

TABLE 6A.2   Direct Requirements Table for Input-Output Analysis

Selling Industries	Purchasing Industries		
	A	B	C
A	.056	.476	.167
B	.028	.095	.500
C	.389	.048	

[1]SIC refers to Standard Industrial Classifications, according to which business activities are arranged by type of product or service produced. See *Standard Industrial Classification Manual* (Washington, DC: Statistical Policy Division, Office of Management and Budget, U.S. Government Printing Office, 1972).

tum. The direct requirements table does not take into account these "second round" effects of an increase in output for one industry.

The total requirements table, often called the Leontief inverse matrix, which is generated from data contained in the direct requirements table, shows in each column the amount of total input, both direct and indirect, that each industry listed down the left side of the table must supply for the industry named in the column heading to produce $1 of output for final demand. For our example, these data are given in Table 6A.3.[2] Such a table can be used in conjunction with the econometric models in deriving industry forecasts.

TABLE 6A.3   **Total Requirements Table for Input-Output Analysis**

Selling Industries	Purchasing Industries		
	A	B	C
A	1.312	.726	.584
B	.335	1.319	.716
C	.530	.345	1.262

The following relationship is fundamental to the input-output model. The $(I - A)^{-1}$ matrix (the total requirements matrix) can be multiplied by the final demand vector (which is an $[n \times 1]$ matrix) to determine the total output for each industry. In the present example,

$$
\begin{array}{ccc}
\text{Total} & \text{Final} & \text{Total} \\
\text{requirements} & \text{demand} & \text{demand} \\
\text{matrix} & \text{vector} & \text{vector}
\end{array}
$$

$$
\begin{pmatrix} 1.321 & .726 & .584 \\ .335 & 1.319 & .716 \\ .530 & .345 & 1.262 \end{pmatrix}
\begin{pmatrix} 100 \\ 30 \\ 45 \end{pmatrix}
=
\begin{pmatrix} 180 \\ 105 \\ 120 \end{pmatrix}
$$

Note that this product corresponds to the total demand or total output for industries A, B, and C, respectively. While this result is trivial, consider its ramifications: (1) we can now find the total demand vector for any composite of industry final demand; and (2) given the total demand for each industry's production, we can further calculate the new transaction matrix, that is, how much industry B will have to purchase from industries A and C, and how much industry B will use of its output. The latter is determined by multiplying each element in any column of the direct requirements matrix by the total demand for the corresponding industry. Recall that the direct

---

[2] The calculation of the values in the total requirements matrix is performed by solving for the elements of the $(I - A)^{-1}$ matrix, where I is an identity matrix and A is the $(n \times n)$ matrix of direct requirements. In our example, $n = 3$, since we have three interrelated industry sectors.

requirements table shows in each column the amount of input each industry listed down the left side of the table must supply to enable the industry named in the column heading to produce $1 of output. For example, multiplying each element of column B in the direct requirements matrix by 105 gives us 50, 10, and 5, the elements of the transaction matrix in column B ($105 \times .476 = 50$; $105 \times .095 = 10$; and $105 \times .048 = 5$). This means, of course, that in order for industry B to produce $105 of total output, industry B requires $50 of output from industry A, $10 of its own output, and $5 of output from industry C.

Econometric models are used to generate final demand, with the large econometric models providing very detailed consumption forecasts. These forecasts of final demand are then "driven" through the total requirements table to arrive at total industry forecasts. One of the greatest benefits of working with the input-output table is that the forecasts thus derived are internally consistent. This type of analysis also quickly points out bottlenecks and supply problems in the economy.

For example, suppose we have a reliable econometric forecast of the final demand for industry C. If the final demand for industry C is expected to increase to 60, what will be the total outputs of industries A, B, and C? The answer is found by multiplying the total requirements matrix by the new final demand vector:

$$\begin{pmatrix} 1.321 & .726 & .584 \\ .335 & 1.319 & .716 \\ .530 & .345 & 1.262 \end{pmatrix} \begin{pmatrix} 100 \\ 30 \\ 60 \end{pmatrix} = \begin{pmatrix} 189 \\ 116 \\ 139 \end{pmatrix}$$

Therefore, the new total outputs for industries A, B, and C are 189, 116, and 139, respectively. These new output levels give the new total demand for each industry, including all "second round" effects. We can use these values, as indicated above, to construct a new transactions table showing how much each industry will demand from each of the industries. The revised transactions matrix is given in Table 6A.4.

TABLE 6A.4   **Input-Output Total Transactions Table for Revised Final Demand for Industry C**

Selling Industries	Purchasing Industries			Final Demand	Total
	A	B	C		
A	11	55	23	100	189
B	5	11	70	30	116
C	73	6	0	60	139

Another benefit of input-output analysis and forecasts is that the forecaster is able to specify and analyze changes in technology by changing the direct requirement coefficients, a_{ij}. These are the values given in the body of

Table 6A.2. The a_{ij} values show the dollar amount of product from the industry in row i that is used by the industry in column j to produce a dollar worth of industry j's output. Estimating these direct requirement coefficients can be accomplished by using engineering studies and/or from historical data.

In summary, input-output analysis is a valuable tool for the forecaster because it gives a total picture of the markets for any group of commodities.[3] In addition, forecasts generated by input-output analysis are internally consistent, making it possible for the forecaster to determine what effect changes in demand will have on various industries. Since input-output tables give a total picture of the markets for a commodity, they also often indicate independent variables that may possibly be used in regression analysis.

---

[3]For an interesting application of input-output modeling for sales forecasts for the Montreal Expos, see N. Carroll Mohn, et al., "Input/Output Modeling: New Sales Forecasting Tool," *University of Michigan Business Review*, July 1976, pp. 7–15.

7 PRODUCTION

In this chapter, the focus moves from the consumer side of the market to the production, or supply, side. All firms engage in the production of some good or service. Some firms produce physical products, such as calculators, cars, shirts, jewelry, tape recorders, corn flakes, laundry detergent, wheat, and so forth. Other firms provide (produce) services, such as those provided by a travel agent, a barber, a cab driver, an entertainer, a house cleaner, a marketing consultant, a teacher, or a surgeon. The production concepts discussed in this chapter are appropriate to the analysis of all forms of production, whether the output is a good or a service and whether it is produced in the private or the public sector.

In the production process, various inputs are transformed into some form of output. Inputs are broadly classified as land, labor, capital, and entrepreneurship (which embodies the managerial functions of risk taking, organizing, planning, controlling, and directing resources). Each of these can be broken down into subsets. For example, we might want to analyze how different types of labor contribute to higher education. In such a case, the following classifications might be useful:

Administrators	Library staff
Maintenance workers	Work-study students
Secretaries	Computer center staff
Faculty	Food service workers

How you might choose to divide the factors of production into subsets depends on the production system you wish to analyze.

7.1 WHY STUDY PRODUCTION?

The discussion in this chapter covers decision rules for determining the quantity of various inputs to use in producing a firm's output under different circumstances. It also develops a basis upon which an understanding of a firm's costs can be constructed. After all, the reason a firm incurs costs is because it must pay for the productive factors used in the production process. Thus, an understanding of production helps provide a foundation for the study of cost. Knowledge about the behavior of costs can then be combined with the revenue concepts derived from consumer demand to establish criteria for determining the product price and the optimal level of output.

Business firms produce a good or service as a means to an end. That end, or objective, may be to maximize profits (as usually assumed in economic analysis), to "satisfice" (i.e., to obtain a "satisfactory" rate of profit but not necessarily the maximum profit), to gain or maintain market share, to achieve a target return on investment, or to obtain any number of other end results. In the case of public goods, the objective may be to provide a particular level of service (such as education) within the bounds of a budget constraint. Regardless of the firm's objectives, it seeks to operate as efficiently as possible, given those objectives. That is, a firm attempts to combine various inputs in such a way that the product is produced with as few resources as possible (assuming that the firm must pay for all resources used). To accomplish this, persons in decision-making positions should have a basic understanding of the process of production.

7.2 PRODUCTION FUNCTIONS: AN INTRODUCTION

The production process involves collecting various inputs at the production site and combining them in such a way as to yield the desired finished product. For example, a farmer growing tomatoes combines, soil, fertilizers, pesticides, water, seeds, labor (of several types perhaps), and capital (farm equipment, storage sheds, etc.) to yield a crop of tomatoes. Some of these inputs may be relatively fixed in supply: the land or soil available, and the existing amount of capital. The other inputs may be varied and, as different quantities of each are used, the level of output may be expected to vary.

The relationship between the amount of various inputs used in the production process and the level of output is called a production function. Production functions describe only efficient levels of output; that is, the output associated with each combination of inputs is the maximum output possible with that set of inputs, given the existing level of technology. Production functions change as the technology used in the production process changes.

A Production Function with One Variable Input

Production functions may be presented in tabular, graphic, or algebraic form and may consist of one, two, or more variable inputs. Let us begin with the tabular and graphic forms of a function that represents the production of custom belt buckles in a small stamping plant. We will represent the number of buckles produced by the letter Q and the number of laborers per eight-hour shift by the letter L. Table 7.1 shows the output that results for different levels of use of the labor input.

TABLE 7.1 **A Production Function for Custom Belt Buckles [$Q = f(L)$]**

Labor (L)	Output (Q)	Labor (L)	Output (Q)
1	7	8	224
2	26	9	243
3	54	10	250
4	88	11	242
5	125	12	216
6	162	13	169
7	196	14	98

We assume in this example that the labor input combines with other input factors of fixed supply and that there is a constant technology. The relationship given in Table 7.1 between the labor input and the quantity of output is shown in graphic form in Figure 7.1. The production function goes through the origin, indicating that without labor, no output is produced. No matter what advances are made in robotic production, it is likely that, for the foreseeable future, some labor will be necessary to obtain the first units of output.

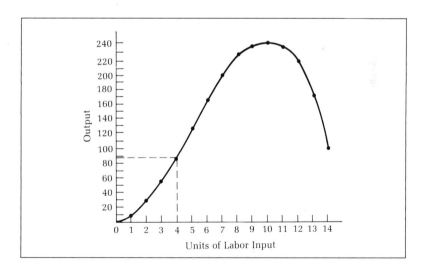

FIGURE 7.1   **Graphic Depiction of the Belt Buckle Production Function.**   This function shows how the number of buckles produced varies as the number of units of labor employed changes.

The same information contained in the production schedule in Table 7.1 and in the graphic production function in Figure 7.1 can also be represented by an algebraic function:

$$Q = f(L)$$
$$Q = 7.5L^2 - 0.5L^3$$

In this form, we see most clearly that if the number of laborers is 0, the level of output is also 0. For positive values of labor input, the corresponding level of output can be determined from the production function. For example, if four laborers are hired for a given eight-hour shift, Table 7.1 indicates that 88 buckles can be produced. Similarly, from Figure 7.1 we see that if four units of labor are hired, the graphic production function is 88 units above (in the vertical direction) the horizontal (labor) axis. Algebraically, we have

$$Q = 7.5(4)^2 - 0.5(4)^3 = 88$$

What if we wanted to know how many buckles could be produced if four workers were hired for the full eight-hour shift but one worker was hired for just one-half shift? That is, what output level should be expected from $L = 4.5$? The tabular form of the production function is not helpful in this case, since $L = 4.5$ is not specified. We could estimate the level of output as the midpoint between $L = 4$ and $L = 5$ ($Q = 106.5$), but this assumes that the production function is linear between four and five units of labor, when in fact it is not. As it turns out, in this case, the production function is very nearly linear in this range, and the estimate of 106.5 units of output for 4.5 units of labor input is not too far off. Similarly, using the graph in Figure 7.1 to estimate the rate of output for 4.5 units of labor also involves considerable individual judgment. One person might make an estimate of 107 units, while others might pick different values.

The most accurate method of determining the output of 4.5 units of labor is to use the algebraic form of the production function:

$$Q = 7.5(4.5)^2 - 0.5(4.5)^3 = 106.3$$

Every person would get exactly the same result from this calculation. You will see that the use of algebraic production functions becomes even more desirable as additional variable factors of production are used.

A Production Function with Two Variable Inputs

Bivariate production functions such as the one we have been using are quite useful in some applications. However, in many cases, it is necessary to model output as a function of two or more variable inputs. Using just two inputs, we can still use tables and graphs to represent production functions, although their use becomes cumbersome. Table 7.2 and Figure 7.2 illustrate a production function for baked goods using two variable inputs.

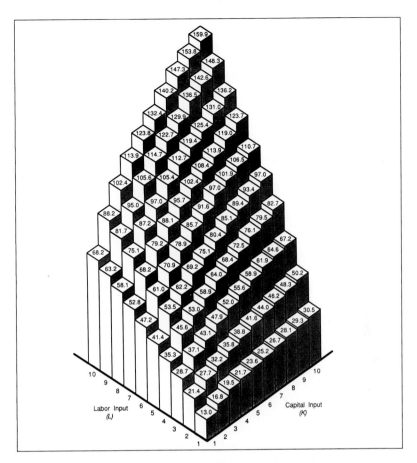

Labor Input (L)

Capital Input (K)

FIGURE 7.2   **Graphic Depiction of the Output of Baked Goods as a Function of Both Labor and Capital Inputs.**   We see that the output surface rises as either or both of the inputs are increased.

TABLE 7.2   **Output of Baked Goods as a Function of Both Labor and Capital Inputs**

Labor Input (L)										
10	68.2	88.2	102.4	113.9	123.8	132.4	140.2	147.3	153.8	159.9
9	63.2	81.7	95.0	105.6	114.7	122.7	129.9	136.5	142.6	148.3
8	58.1	75.1	87.2	97.0	105.4	112.7	119.4	125.4	131.0	136.2
7	52.8	68.2	79.2	88.1	95.7	102.4	108.4	113.9	119.0	123.7
6	47.2	61.0	70.9	78.9	85.7	91.6	97.0	101.9	106.5	110.7
5	41.4	53.5	62.2	69.2	75.1	80.4	85.1	89.4	93.4	97.0
4	35.3	45.6	53.0	58.9	64.0	68.4	72.5	76.1	79.5	82.7
3	28.7	37.1	43.1	47.9	52.0	55.6	58.9	61.9	64.6	67.2
2	21.4	27.7	32.2	35.8	38.8	41.6	44.0	46.2	48.3	50.2
1	13	16.8	19.5	21.7	23.6	25.2	26.7	28.1	29.3	30.5
	1	2	3	4	5	6	7	8	9	10

Capital Input (K)

In this production function, we see that if the amount of the labor (L) input is increased, for any given stock of capital (K), output (Q) increases as well. However, the rate at which output rises, diminishes as more labor is used. This is due to diminishing marginal productivity, a principle that will be discussed in some detail in the following section. Similarly if labor is fixed at some level and the amount of capital used is increased, output increases, but at a diminishing rate.

When output is being analyzed as a function of two or more input variables, algebraic production functions provide the best tools for analysis. One of the most widely used forms of production function is the Cobb-Douglas type, which may be written as

$$Q = AK^aL^b$$

where A is a positive constant called a scale factor and the values a and b are positive fractions that represent elasticities. For example, a 1-percent increase in labor will increase output by b percent. A more general form of the Cobb-Douglas type of function, allowing for n variable factors of production, is

$$Q = AX_1^{a_1}X_2^{a_2}X_3^{a_3}, \cdots, X_n^{a_n}$$

where each X_i is a factor input and each a_i is a positive constant $(0 < a_i < 1)$ representing the elasticity of output for that input. Cobb-Douglas production functions have several interesting mathematical properties. Constant output elasticity is one such property: each a_i represents the precentage increase in output for a 1-percent increase in the X_i input, holding the quantities of other inputs constant.

For the production function, $Q = AK^aL^b$, the percent increase in Q for a 1-percent increase in L is equal to $\%\Delta Q \div \%\Delta L$, or $(\Delta Q/Q) \div (\Delta L/L)$. This can be written as $(\Delta Q/\Delta L) \cdot (L/Q)$. In terms of partial derivatives, we have

$$\begin{aligned}
\frac{\partial Q}{\partial L} \cdot \frac{L}{Q} &= (bAK^aL^{b-1})(L/Q) \\
&= (bAK^aL^{b-1})(L/AK^aL^b) \\
&= bAK^aL^b/AK^aL^b \\
&= b
\end{aligned}$$

Thus, if $b = .4$, we know that a 1-percent increase in the amount of labor used (holding capital constant) will increase output by .4 percent.

Table 7.3 illustrates representative values for the exponents in Cobb-Douglas production functions for major industries in Western industrial economies. As above, a represents the exponent for the capital input, and b the exponent for the labor input. We see, for example, that in the gas industry, a 1-percent increase in the labor input would increase output by .83 percent with no change in the amount of capital. Similarly, we see that 1-percent increase in capital for the automobile industry would increase output by .41 percent without any change in labor input.

TABLE 7.3   **Estimates of the Exponents for Representative Cobb-Douglas Production Functions**

Industry	Capital Exponent (a)	Labor Exponent (b)	$a + b$
Gas	.10	.83	.93
Foods	.35	.72	1.07
Coal	.29	.79	1.08
Metals and machinery	.26	.71	.97
Montana livestock	.94	.08	1.02
Automobiles	.41	.96	1.37

SOURCE: A. A. Walters, "Production and Cost Functions: An Econometric Survey," *Econometrica*, January-April 1973, pp. 26–33.

The production function given in Table 7.2 and Figure 7.2 can also be expressed in the algebraic form of a Cobb-Douglas function. The equation relating output (Q) to the amount of labor (L) and capital (K) used is

$$Q = 13K^{.37}L^{.72}$$

This equation is found from the 100 observations in Table 7.2 by regressing the natural logarithm of output on the natural logarithm of the two inputs, capital and labor. That is,

$$\ln Q = C + a\ln K + b\ln L$$

The result of this regression is

$$\ln Q = 2.57 + .37\ln K + .72\ln L$$
$$Q = e^{2.57}K^{.37}L^{.72}$$
$$Q = 2.718^{2.57}K^{.37}L^{.72}$$
$$Q = 13K^{.37}L^{.72}$$

7.3   THREE IMPORTANT MEASURES OF PRODUCTION

In the production functions we have been discussing, the measure of output represented by Q has been the total product that results from each level of input use. For example, we see from Table 7.1 that a total of 88 belt buckles would be produced if we employed four units of the labor input. You will often see total product represented by TP as well as by Q. In addition to this measure of total output, two other measures of production are important to understand: marginal product and average product.

Marginal Product

From a decision-making perspective, it is often particularly important to know how production will change as a variable input is changed. For example, we may want to know if it would be profitable to hire an additional unit of labor for some productive activity. Thus, we need to have a measure of the rate of change in output as the use of any one of the variable inputs is changed. We call this rate of change the marginal product of the variable input. To find the effect that changing one input has on output, it is necessary to hold all other inputs constant. If more than one input is changed at a time, we could not tell how much of the change in output should be attributed to each of the input variables that have been changed.

The marginal product (*MP*) of a variable factor of production is the rate of change in total product (*TP* or *Q*) per unit change in the amount of the variable input while other factors are held constant. More explicitly, if

$$TP = Q = f(X_1, X_2, \ldots, X_n)$$
$$MP_i = \frac{\partial TP}{\partial X_i}$$

where the X_i's are inputs to the production process. Of course, if the production function is stated solely in terms of a single variable factor of production [e.g., $Q = f(L)$],

$$MP_L = \frac{dTP}{dL}$$

Would you expect output to increase at a constant rate as more of any one input is added to the production process? To help your thinking about this question, let us assume that you have a small garden plot, say 10 feet by 20 feet. You want to grow beans, tomatoes, zucchini squash, and onions. In preparing the soil for planting, you may decide that some fertilizer would help improve your yield. So you call a garden supply store for advice about how much to use. Suppose the gardening expert suggests that, as a rule of thumb, gardeners in your area should apply 1 ounce (by weight) of fertilizer per square foot of garden twice each year. For your 200 square feet of garden, that would amount to 12.5 pounds. You spread that amount over your garden, and then someone suggests that if one application of fertilizer is good, two applications would be better. If two are better, perhaps three or four would be better yet. Do you think that each successive application of fertilizer would do as much to increase your yield as the first? Probably not. What would you expect to happen if you bought enough fertilizer to spread 6 inches deep over the entire garden? Nothing would grow at all. You could use so much of this variable input that output would be driven down to 0.

It is safe to say that most production functions react in the same general way as more of a variable input is added to other fixed factors (such as the fixed land area in the example above). *Output does not increase at a constant rate.* Note that the production function graphed in Figure 7.1 at first increases at an increasing rate (for *L* less than 5), then increases at a decreasing rate (for *L* between 5 and 10), and finally begins to decline (for *L* greater than 10). Look also at Table 7.2 to see what happens to the rate of increase in output as more labor is used and the amount of capital is held fixed (i.e., reading across any row of the table). You see that as more labor is used, the rate at which output increases becomes less.

The *principle of diminishing marginal productivity* states that as additional units of a variable input are added to other inputs that are fixed in supply, the increments to output eventually decline (for a constant technology). This principle of diminishing marginal productivity has been observed in a great many productive environments and has been well documented by empirical research. Business managers can safely assume that it will operate in nearly all situations if the use of a variable input is continually increased while other inputs are kept constant. As we shall see shortly, the marginal productivity of an input plays an important part in determining how much of that input will be employed.

Average Product

At times, we want to know the productivity per worker, per pound of fertilizer, per machine, and so on. This calls for the use of another measure of productivity: average product. The average product (AP) of a variable factor of production is defined as total output divided by the number of units of the variable factor used in producing that output:

$$AP_i = TP/X_i$$

This represents the mean (average) output per unit of land, labor, or other factor input. AP_i and X_i refer to the average product of the ith factor and the number of units of the ith factor employed, respectively.

The concept of average product is widely used. When people make comparisons of labor productivity between industries or between countries, they almost always are referring to the average product of labor (i.e., the average amount of output produced per labor hour). In recent years, various political, social, and economic issues, such as inflation and balance of payments problems, have focused considerable attention on the average productivity of workers in the United States. It is often argued that employee wage increases should be tied to increases in productivity (meaning *average* productivity) and that one reason for our diminished competitiveness in world markets is that domestic labor has not increased in productivity as fast as has labor in some other countries. The advent of the use of quality circles and other forms of employee participation in management are, in part, attempts to increase the average productivity of the work force.

Marginal, Average, and Total Product Compared

The production function presented in Table 7.1 is reproduced in Table 7.4 along with the average and marginal products of the variable factor labor. Remember that the amount of other inputs and the state of technology are

TABLE 7.4   **Total, Average, and Marginal Product ($TP = 7.5L^2 - 0.5L^3$)**

Labor Input (L)	Total Product (TP)	Average Product (AP = TP/L)	Marginal Product (MP = dTP/dL)
0	0		7
1	7	7	19
2	26	13	28
3	54	18	34
4	88	22	37
5	125	25	37
6	162	27	34
7	196	28	28
8	224	28	19
9	243	27	7
10	250	25	−8
11	242	22	−26
12	216	18	−47
13	169	13	−71
14	98	7	

NOTE: Other inputs and the level of technology are held constant.

assumed fixed in this example. The values for marginal product are written between each increment of labor input because those values represent the marginal productivity over the respective intervals. In the table, marginal product has been calculated as $MP = \Delta TP / \Delta L$. The data in Table 7.4 are also graphed in Figure 7.3.

In both the table and the graphic representation, we see that both average and marginal productivity at first increase, eventually reach a maximum, and then decline. Note that $MP = AP$ at the maximum of the average product function. This is necessarily the case. If $MP > AP$, the average will be pulled up by the incremental unit, and if $MP < AP$, the average will be pulled down. It follows that the average product function will reach its peak where $MP = AP$.

We know that the quantity of output (Q or TP) can also be expressed as an algebraic function of the labor input for this production relationship. Working with the algebraic production function, we can determine the amount of labor to employ if we want to maximize the production of the belt buckles. Recall that

$$TP = 7.5L^2 - 0.5L^3$$

It follows that marginal product is

$$MP = \frac{dTP}{dL}$$
$$MP = 15L - 1.5L^2$$

Setting marginal product equal to 0, we find that $MP = 0$ when $L = 0$ and $L = 10$, as follows:

$$MP = 15L - 1.5L^2 = 0$$
$$L(15 - 1.5L) = 0$$

which has two solutions: $L = 0$ and $L = 10$. These points correspond to where marginal product crosses the labor axis in the graph of marginal prod-

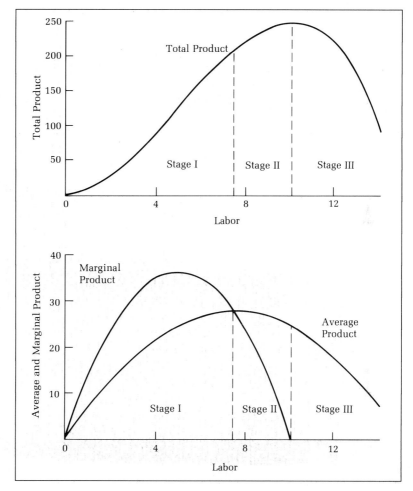

FIGURE 7.3   **Total, Average, and Marginal Product Functions for the Production of Custom Belt Buckles.**   Early in stage I, where marginal product is increasing, total product increases at an increasing rate. When marginal product starts to decline, total product begins to increase at a decreasing rate. Once marginal product becomes negative, total product starts to decline. As long as marginal product is above average product, the latter rises; but when marginal product is less than average product, it pulls average product down. Thus, $MP = AP$ at the peak of AP.

uct (Figure 7.2). Since setting $MP = 0$ is the same as setting $dTP/dL = 0$, we should expect total product to have a maximum at one of these points and a minimum at the other. Checking the second-order conditions, we find

$$\frac{d^2TP}{dL^2} = \frac{dMP}{dL} = 15 - 3L$$

1.   At $L = 0$, $15 - 3L = 15 > 0$, so total product has a minimum at $L = 0$.

2.   At $L = 10$, $15 - 3L = -15 < 0$, so total product has a maximum at $L = 10$.

These results are consistent with Figure 7.3 and Table 7.4, which show this production function.

In Figure 7.3, we see that for this production function, both marginal product and average product at first rise, then reach a maximum, and then fall. We can find the point at which marginal product reaches a maximum as follows:

$$MP = 15L - 1.5L^2$$
$$\frac{dMP}{dL} = 15 - 3L = 0$$
$$L = 5$$

For amounts of labor input beyond 5, the marginal product has a negative slope (i.e., $dMP/dL < 0$ for $L > 5$).

Let us now look at the average product function. We know that average product equals total product divided by the number of units of the relevant factor of production. Thus, in this case,

$$AP = \frac{TP}{L} = 7.5L - 0.5L^2$$

Finding the first derivative of the average product function, setting it equal to 0, and solving for L, we obtain

$$\frac{dAP}{dL} = 7.5 - L = 0$$
$$L = 7.5$$

Thus, the average product function reaches its peak at $L = 7.5$. We have said that $MP = AP$ at the maximum of average product, and this can be shown in two ways. First, we could find the value of average product and marginal product at $L = 7.5$ and see that they are equal. For marginal product, we have $MP = 15(7.5) - 1.5(7.5)^2 = 28.13$, and for average product, $AP = 7.5(7.5) - .5(7.5)^2 = 28.13$. Alternatively, we could set the equation for marginal product equal to the equation representing average product and solve for the value of L for which the equality holds. Then, we would have

$$MP = AP$$
$$15L - 1.5L^2 = 7.5L - 0.5L^2$$
$$15 - 1.5L = 7.5 - 0.5L$$
$$-1.0L = -7.5$$
$$L = 7.5$$

Note also that for $L > 7.5$, $dAP/dL < 0$, and $dMP/dL < 0$. Thus, beyond 7.5 units of labor, both marginal and average product are subject to diminishing returns.

7.4 THREE STAGES OF PRODUCTION

In Figure 7.3, we have divided the graph into three parts, labeled stage I, stage II, and stage III. The first stage includes the region from the origin to the level of labor input at which the average product of labor reaches its maximum. We have shown that this is at $L = 7.5$. So throughout stage I, average product is rising, even though marginal product has begun to fall as we near the end of stage I.

Stage II includes the region between the maximum point on the average product function and the point at which marginal product falls to 0. In the example in Figure 7.3, this is the region between $L = 7.5$ and $L = 10$. Throughout stage II, both marginal and average product are falling, but both are still positive.

Stage III is the entire region for which the marginal product of labor is negative (i.e., to the right of $L = 10$). In this stage, the amount of the fixed resource available *per unit of labor* has become too small for efficient production to take place. While we will not prove this here, the same type of problem occurs in stage I. In stage I, the amount of labor is too small for the existing amount of the fixed resource, which results in a negative marginal product for that resource. This means that of the three stages of production, only stage II has a positive marginal product for all inputs (we will demonstrate this point more thoroughly later in the chapter).

The important business consequence of this relationship is that *the relevant range of production is restricted to stage II*. No manager would knowingly employ any resources for which the marginal product is negative.

7.5 HOW MUCH LABOR SHOULD BE EMPLOYED?

Suppose that you are the owner-manager of the small casting shop that makes the custom belt buckles in our example. How much labor would you hire? That is a question you would have to answer, and it is one with which the tools of managerial economics can help. We already know that the only range of production to consider is stage II, or between $L = 7.5$ and $L = 10$. Let us address this problem by first asking ourselves: Under what conditions would we want to hire any additional workers?

Would you hire a worker if the cost of doing so, including wages and all benefits, was more than the revenue you could get by selling the added output attributable to that worker? Probably not. But you would hire another unit of labor if you could sell the added output for more than the added cost of employing that unit of labor. This is the basis upon which the decision to employ more of any resource should be made. Before formalizing this criterion, let us first define some terms.

Marginal revenue product (MRP) is the additional revenue the firm receives when the output from one additional worker is sold. It is, then, a dollar measure of the additional output attributable to the efforts of an added worker. It is calculated as

$$MRP = (MR)(MP)$$

where *MR* is marginal revenue, and *MP* is the marginal product of labor. *MRP* is a negatively sloped function because *MP* diminishes, and *MR* is either constant or diminishing.

Marginal resource cost (MRC) is the additional cost to the firm of employing one more unit of labor. *MRC* is made up of the wage rate plus other costs to the firm of employing that additional worker (e.g., insurance, social security, and retirement). We will assume that the number of workers hired by this firm is small relative to the entire labor market, and so the *MRC* is independent of the number of workers hired. That is, we will consider *MRC* to be equal to some constant dollar amount per additional worker employed.

Now suppose that you can sell each belt buckle for $4 and that the *MRC* for the labor you hire is $6.75 per hour ($5.25 as the wage rate per hour plus $1.50 per hour in benefits). Further, let us assume that you can hire workers for less than a full day but that you have an agreement to employ people only in two-hour blocks of time. For example, 7.75 labor units would be seven people working an eight-hour shift plus one person working six hours. Based on this information, Table 7.5 can be completed. As long as $MRP > MRC$, it pays to continue employing more labor. This is true for up to 9.00 units of labor, as we can see in Table 7.5 and in Figure 7.4. This result can be generalized as follows:

> The optimum number of units of any variable resource to employ is determined by the condition that
>
> $$MRP = MRC$$

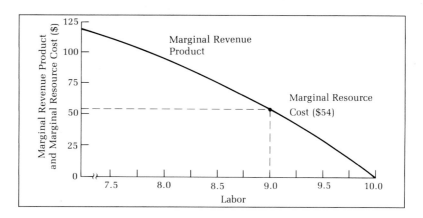

FIGURE 7.4   **Determination of the Amount of Labor to Employ.**   As long as *MRP* > *MRC*, the firm benefits by hiring additional labor and increasing production. If it was found that at the current level of production *MRP* < *MRC*, production should be cut back and fewer units of labor employed. In this example, the optimum level of employment is at 9.0 units of labor.

TABLE 7.5   **Marginal Revenue Product and Marginal Resource Cost for Stage II of Production**

L	MP	MR	MRP	MRC
7.50	28.125	$4	$112.50	$54
7.75	26.156	4	104.62	54
8.00	24.000	4	96.00	54
8.25	19.125	4	86.62	54
8.50	19.125	4	76.50	54
8.75	16.406	4	65.62	54
9.00	13.500	4	54.00	54
9.25	10.406	4	41.62	54
9.50	7.125	4	28.50	54
9.75	3.656	4	14.62	54
10.00	0	4	0	54

NOTE: $MP = dTP/dL = 15L - 1.5L^2$
$MR = \$4$
$MRP = (MP)(MR)$
$MRC = \$6.75$ per hour, or $54.00 per labor unit (eight-hour day)

7.6   EVALUATING COBB-DOUGLAS PRODUCTION FUNCTIONS FOR DIMINISHING MARGINAL PRODUCTIVITY

Are Cobb-Douglas production functions characterized by diminishing marginal productivity? We can answer this question by investigating the nature of the marginal and average product functions for this type of production function. We have

$$TP = AK^aL^b$$
$$MP_L = \frac{\partial TP}{\partial L}$$
$$MP_L = bAK^aL^{b-1}$$

The slope of marginal product is the rate of change in MP as the labor input is changed:

$$\text{Slope of } MP_L = \frac{\partial MP_L}{\partial L} = (b-1)(b)AK^aL^{b-2}$$

Since $0 < b < 1$, this partial must be negative, and so the slope of marginal product is always negative for Cobb-Douglas production functions. Thus, they are subject to diminishing marginal productivity throughout the entire range of production. Similar analysis shows that

$$MP_K = aAK^{a-1}L^b \text{ and } \partial MP_K/\partial K < 0$$

Thus, Cobb-Douglas production functions also have diminishing marginal productivity for capital. This can be generalized for all inputs in such production functions.

In the case of a Cobb-Douglas production function, average product also diminishes throughout and is always greater than marginal product. In fact,

$$MP_L = bAP_L \text{ and } MP_K = aAP_K$$

Recall that

$$AP_L = \frac{TP}{L}$$
$$AP_L = \frac{AK^aL^b}{L}$$
$$AP_L = AK^aL^{b-1}$$
$$MP_L = bAK^aL^{b-1}$$
$$MP_L = bAP_L$$

and since $0 < b < 1$, $MP_L < AP_L$. The relationship that $MP_K = aAP_K$ can be shown in a strictly analogous manner.

Let us look at marginal product and average product for the Cobb-Douglas production function given in Table 7.2 and in Figure 7.2. Recall that the algebraic equation for this production function is

$$Q = 13K^{.37}L^{.72}$$

The marginal productivity of labor (MP_L) can be found as

$$\frac{\partial Q}{\partial L} = (.72)(13K^{.37}L^{-.28})$$
$$MP_L = 9.36K^{.37}L^{-.28}$$

To determine whether the marginal productivity of labor is decreasing, we need to find its slope (that is, we need to find the rate of change in MP_L as labor changes, or the partial derivative of MP_L with respect to L):

$$\frac{\partial MP}{\partial L} = -2.62K^{.37}L^{-1.28}$$

This is the slope of MP_L, and as you can see by the negative sign, it has a negative value for all positive values of K and L. Thus, we can conclude that the marginal productivity of labor does diminish.

What about the average productivity of labor? Does it also diminish? If so, over what range? We can find the average product of labor as follows:

$$AP_L = \frac{Q}{L} = \frac{13K^{.37}L^{.72}}{L}$$
$$AP_L = 13K^{.37}L^{-.28}$$

The slope of labor's average product is found as

$$\frac{\partial AP_L}{\partial L} = (-.28)(13K^{.37}L^{-1.28})$$

$$\frac{\partial AP_L}{\partial L} = -3.64K^{.37}L^{-1.28}$$

Once more, we see from the negative sign that the average product of labor has a negative slope and therefore diminishes throughout. The marginal and average products for this Cobb-Douglas production function are shown in Table 7.6 for both 5 and 10 units of capital.

There are several things you should be certain to see in the data of Table 7.6. First, note that for any level of capital and labor you select, the ratio of the marginal product of labor to the average product of labor is always .72. Thus, we see that marginal product is always less than average

TABLE 7.6   **Marginal Product and Average Product of Labor for the Cobb-Douglas Production Function ($Q = 13K^{.37}L^{.72}$)**

	For $K = 5$		For $K = 10$	
L	MP	AP	MP	AP
1	16.98	23.58	21.94	30.47
2	13.98	19.42	18.07	25.10
3	12.48	17.34	16.13	22.41
4	11.52	16.00	14.88	20.67
5	10.82	15.03	13.98	19.42
6	10.28	14.28	13.29	18.45
7	9.85	13.68	12.72	17.67
8	9.48	13.17	12.26	17.02
9	9.18	12.75	11.86	16.47
10	8.91	12.38	11.52	15.99

NOTE: The ratio MP/AP always equals .72.

product. Second, we see that both marginal and average product diminish throughout.

Finally, you should compare the productivity of labor at the two different levels of capital. When $K = 10$, the marginal product of labor is higher than when $K = 5$. The same is true for average product. Thus, if we provide the labor resource with more capital, we can expect that labor productivity will be improved.

> Test yourself on these concepts.[1] Find the equations for the marginal and average products of capital for the same production function used in our example. What is the MP_K at $K = 4$ if $L = 10$? What is the AP_K at this same point?

7.7   RETURNS TO SCALE

The previous section focused on how output changed as one input was changed and all others were held constant. Now we will look at what happens if we change all inputs simultaneously. This removes the restriction that at least one input is fixed and moves us from a short-run analysis of production to long-run decisions in which all inputs can be varied.

By observing what happens to the level of output as all input variables are increased proportionately, we can evaluate the concept known as *returns to scale*. As the name implies, this concept is related to the change in output as the entire scale of the production process changes. Returns to scale are categorized as follows:

1. *Increasing Returns to Scale.* If all inputs are increased by some proportion, output will increase by a greater proportion.

2. *Constant Returns to Scale.* If all inputs are increased by some proportion, output will increase by the same production.

3. *Decreasing Returns to Scale.* If all inputs are increased by some proportion, output will increase by a lesser proportion.

For homogeneous production functions,[2] returns to scale can be evaluated with relative ease. Assume that output (Q) is a function of n inputs:

---

[1] You should find $MP_K = 4.18K^{-.63}L^{.72}$ and $AP_K = 13K^{-.63}L^{.72}$. At $K = 4$ and $L = 10$, $MP_K = 10.54$, and $AP_K = 28.49$. Note that $MP_K = .37 AP_K$.

[2] A production function is said to be homogeneous of degree r if, when each of its independent variables is multiplied by the factor P, the value of the function changes by the factor P^r for all levels of production.

$$Q = f(X_1 X_2, \ldots, X_n)$$

If all inputs are increased by a factor P, the new level of output Q^* may be written as

$$Q^* = P^r Q = f(PX_1, PX_2, \ldots, PX_n)$$

If $r > 1$, there are increasing returns to scale; if $r = 1$, there are constant returns to scale; and if $r < 1$, there are decreasing returns to scale.

Let us look specifically at Cobb-Douglas functions; that is, $Q = AK^a L^b$. If we multiply each input by the factor P, we have

$$Q^* = A(PK)^a (PL)^b$$
$$Q^* = AP^a K^a P^b L^b$$
$$Q^* = AK^a L^b P^{a+b}$$
$$Q^* = (P^{a+b})Q$$

In this case, $r = a + b$. For the more general form of the Cobb-Douglas production function with n inputs, r equals the sum of the exponents in all n input variables.

Applying this to the industries in Table 7.3, we find that the gas and the metals and machinery industries are characterized by decreasing returns to scale: $r = .93$ and $r = .97$, respectively. The Montana livestock industry has very nearly constant (or slightly increasing) returns to scale, according to the parameters reported. The coal ($r = 1.08$), food ($r = 1.07$), and automobile ($r = 1.37$) industries demonstrate increasing returns to scale. If, for example, the amount of both labor and capital used in the automobile industry was increased by 20 percent (i.e., $P = 1.2$), output would be expected to increase by a factor of 1.284 ($1.284 = 1.2^{1.37}$), or 28.4 percent.

What about the Cobb-Douglas production function represented in Table 7.2 and Figure 7.2? Do there appear to be increasing, constant, or decreasing returns to scale? Refer to Table 7.2. At $K = 2$ and $L = 3$, we see that $Q = 37$. If K and L are doubled (i.e., $K = 4$ and $L = 6$), we see from the table that output rises to $Q = 79$. Output has increased by a factor of 2.14 (where $2.14 = 79/37$). Thus, in this region, we see that this production function has increasing returns to scale, since doubling the inputs more than doubles the level of output.

This can be demonstrated more generally by the algebraic form of the production function:

$$Q = 13K^{.37} L^{.72}$$

Let Q^* equal the output that would be obtained using $2K$ and $2L$, rather than K and L, amounts of the inputs:

$$Q^* = 13(2K)^{.37}(2L)^{.72}$$
$$Q^* = 13(2)^{.37}(K)^{.37}(2)^{.72}(L)^{.72}$$
$$Q^* = 13(2)^{1.09} K^{.37} L^{.72}$$
$$Q^* = (2)^{1.09} 13K^{.37} L^{.72}$$
$$Q^* = (2)^{1.09} Q$$
$$Q^* = 2.13Q$$

Thus, when the inputs are doubled, output increases by 2.13 times. Why did we get 2.14 above and 2.13 here? Tables are inherently bulky, and the values in the table are rounded to integers. Thus, the values obtained for particular points in the table may vary a bit from the true value determined from the algebraic form of the production function.

For nonhomogeneous production functions, we must test each case individually to tell if there are increasing, decreasing, or constant returns to scale. Consider, for example, the following production function:

$$Q = f(K,L)$$
$$Q = 10K + 8L - 0.2KL$$

For $K = 10$ and $L = 20$, we find Q as follows:

$$Q = 10(10) + 8(20) - 0.2(10)(20)$$
$$Q = 220$$

If we double the amount of the inputs to $K = 20$ and $L = 40$, we then find Q^* as follows:

$$Q^* = 10(20) + 8(40) - 0.2(20)(40)$$
$$Q^* = 360$$

Since the ratio Q^*/Q equals 1.64, output increases by only 64% when the amount of both inputs used is doubled. Thus, this function exhibits decreasing returns to scale over this range of values.

7.8   PRODUCTION THEORY IN PRACTICE: A POLICE PRODUCTION FUNCTION

Before continuing with the discussion of production theory, let us pause briefly to consider a specific example of how the concepts developed thus far may be applied. Beyond just showing a specific application, the example selected illustrates that these concepts are useful in the public sector as well as in the private sector of the economy. The situation reviewed here involves the estimation and evaluation of a police production function.[3]

The measure of output for a police production function is not as easily specified as for a firm producing physical units of some product. To some extent, the output is an intangible protective service, but the output of a police department has quantifiable attributes. One of these is the felony

---

[3]The discussion in this section is based on the work of Jeffrey I. Chapman, Werner Z. Hirsch, and Sidney Sonenblum, as reported in "Crime Prevention, the Police Production Function, and Budgeting," *Public Finance*, 30, 2 (1975), pp. 197–215. Only part of their analysis is presented here; for example, they estimate five different production functions, and we discuss only the one with the highest coefficient of determination (R^2). Their analysis is based on data for the city of Los Angeles.

arrest rate, which is measured as the number of arrests divided by the number of crimes committed. The higher this ratio, the greater the productivity of the police department. Productive factors include

MT = log of the number of motorcycle teams
FO = log of the number of field officers
NFO = log of the number of nonfield officers
CE = log of the number of civilian employees
XC = log of the number of newly released criminals in the community

While police service is highly labor intensive, this list of people-related productive factors does not imply that capital is not important as well. Rather, since each class of labor is generally related to a particular class of capital (e.g., motorcycle officers and motorcycles), "resource inputs are defined as the joint labor and capital input by occupational class, and this input is approximated by the number of employees in each class. Capital inputs are therefore assumed to enter into the production process through the combined productivity of the labor and capital package as represented by the input coefficients."[4] The last of the input variables listed above, XC, is a proxy for police knowledge about the potential criminal population in the jurisdiction. As this knowledge increases, we would expect it to be easier to make arrests and prevent crimes. Thus, all the input variables would be expected to have a positive relationship to output.[5] All inputs are specified in per capita terms to eliminate the effect of population change.

A multiplicative production function can be estimated using multiple regression analysis. Letting Q represent output, we have the production function:

$$Q = 17.20 MT^{.01} FO^{.718} NFO^{1.02} CE^{.74} SC^{.078}$$

The coefficient of determination for this police production function is $R^2 = .9013$. The input variables FO, NFO, and CE have t-ratios of 1.66, 2.29, and 2.16, respectively, and are the only significant variables at the 90-percent level. From a public policy perspective, the conclusion is that "the production function analysis indicates that increasing police resources significantly affects police output . . . [and that] . . . there appears to be some indication of increasing returns [to scale] to the police agency as a whole."[6]

---

[4]Chapman, Werner, and Sonenblum, p. 204.

[5]One additional variable was used in the estimated production functions that are not discussed here. That variable was a dummy variable to account for possible structural crime changes during the period covered by the data. Its value was 0 until 1965 (the year of the Watts riots) and 1 thereafter.

[6]Chapman, Werner, and Sonenblum, p. 207.

7.9 ISOQUANT CURVES

Now that we have some common basis of understanding related to production and production functions, we can take a big step toward the goal of applying these concepts in a decision framework. Two particularly important types of decisions involving an analysis of production functions can be summarized by the following questions:

1. What combination of inputs will be most efficient for the production of some target level of output?

2. For a given expenditure of money, what combination of inputs will provide the maximum level of production?

In answering both these questions, it is helpful to use an analytical device known as a mapping of isoquant curves.

For a production function, $Q = f(L,K)$, an isoquant curve shows all the possible combinations of labor (L) and capital (K) that can be used to produce a given amount of output. There is a separate isoquant curve for each level of production. To help you see what the isoquant curves are likely to

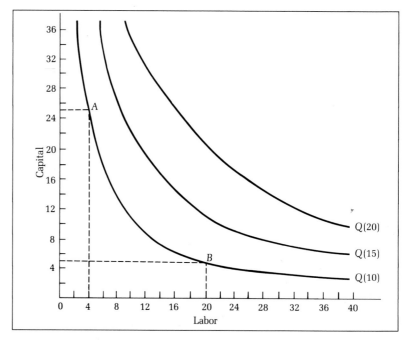

FIGURE 7.5   **Isoquant Mapping of the Production Function $Q = K^{.5}L^{.5}$.** Three representative isoquant curves representing 10, 15, and 20 units of output are graphed. Note that they are all negatively sloped, continuous, and convex to origin, and do not intersect one another.

look like, three typical isoquants are drawn in Figure 7.5 for the production function

$$Q = K^{.5}L^{.5}$$

These isoquants are for 10, 15, and 20 units of output.[7] All of the combinations of labor and capital along isoquant $Q(10)$ will provide 10 units of output. For example, if $L = 4$ and $K = 25$, such as at point A, we have

$$Q = (4^{.5})(25^{.5}) = (2)(5)$$
$$Q = 10$$

or if $L = 20$ and $K = 5$, such as at point B, we have

$$Q = 20^{.5} + 5^{.5} = (4.47)(2.24)$$
$$Q = 10$$

Properties of Isoquant Curves

Isoquants have several important properties. First, they are negatively sloped in the relevant range,[8] which indicates that if the amount of one input is decreased, additional units of the other input must be used if the level of output is to remain constant (i.e., if we are to stay on the same isoquant curve). For example, given the production function $Q = K^{.5}L^{.5}$, we have seen that if we want to maintain output at $Q = 10$ and if we reduce the capital input from 25 to 5, the amount of labor used must increase from 4 to 20. The change in capital required per unit change in labor, keeping output constant, is called the marginal rate of technical substitution ($MRTS$).

The $MRTS$ is measured as the negative of the slope of an isoquant and is equal to the ratio of the MP_L to the MP_K. Using some calculus, this can be shown as follows. Let

$$Q = f(K,L)$$

The total differential of Q is

$$dQ = f_L\, dL + f_K\, dK$$

---

[7]The equation for each of these isoquants can be found as follows. Let Q_o be a given level of output. Then,

$$Q_o = K^{.5}L^{.5}$$
$$K = Q_o^2/L$$

Letting $Q = 10$, 15, and 20, we can derive the equations, for $Q(10)$, $Q(15)$, and $Q(20)$, respectively:

$$K = 100/L$$
$$K = 225/L$$
$$K = 400/L$$

[8]The relevant range is defined as the range of production in which the marginal products of all inputs are positive. This corresponds to stage II of production and is explained in more detail in the following section.

where f_L and f_K denote the partial derivatives of the production function with respect to labor and capital, respectively, and dQ, dL, and dK represent changes in output, labor, and capital, respectively. If Q is constant along an isoquant curve $dQ = 0$, then

$$f_L \, dL = -f_K \, dK$$

or, by rearranging terms,

$$-dK/dL = f_L/f_K$$

The left-hand term is the negative of the slope of an isoquant curve, while on the right side, the numerator is the MP_L and the denominator is the MP_K. For the isoquants graphed in Figure 7.5 (and derived from the production function $Q = K^{.5}L^{.5}$), the MRTS is

$$MRTS = f_L/f_K$$
$$MRTS = (.5K^{.5}L^{-.5})/(.5K^{-.5}L^{.5})$$
$$MRTS = K/L$$

Look at the point A in Figure 7.5. At that point, 25 units of capital and 4 units of labor are used to produce 10 units of output. Since the isoquant appears quite steep at that point, we should expect the MRTS to be relatively high. It is

$$MRTS = K/L$$
$$= 25/4$$
$$= 6.25$$

Remember that this is the negative of the slope of the isoquant at point A (i.e., the slope is –6.25). This means that in the vicinity of point A, a 1-unit change in the amount of labor used must be compensated for by a 6.25-unit change (in the opposite direction) in the amount of capital to keep production at $Q = 10$ units.

We can also calculate the MRTS for any of the industries listed in Table 7.3. For example, consider the gas industry. From the values of a and b given in the table, you know that $Q = AK^{.1}L^{.83}$. It follows that $MP_K = .1AK^{-.9}L^{.83}$ and $MP_L = .83AK^{.1}L^{-.17}$. Thus, $MRTS = MP_L/MP_K = 8.3K/L$.

A second characteristic of isoquants is that they are generally convex to the origin. This indicates that the MRTS declines as we move from left to right along any given isoquant. Thus, as successively fewer units of capital (labor) are used in production, the additional increments of labor (capital) necessary to maintain the same output become greater. As we move from left to right along an isoquant, the marginal productivity of capital increases, while the marginal productivity of labor decreases (thus, the MRTS decreases). Therefore, greater increments of labor must be used to compensate for the loss of output due to decreases in the amount of capital as we move to the right along any isoquant curve. This is illustrated by the isoquant for 10 units of output in Figure 7.5. At point B, where 5 units of capital and 20 units of labor are used, the marginal rate of technical substitution is

$$MRTS = K/L$$
$$= 5/20$$
$$= .25$$

Thus, as we move from point A to point B, the marginal rate of technical substitution falls from 6.25 to .25 (and the isoquant becomes less steep). At point B, it is more difficult to substitute labor for capital while maintaining output at 10 units.

Another characteristic of isoquants is that they do not intersect one another. If they did intersect, there would be a logical inconsistency. By definition, each isoquant represents a given constant level of output. If two isoquants were to intersect, this condition would be violated, since at the intersection, a single point would represent two different values. Finally, we should note that, due to the assumed continuity of the production function, the isoquant map is dense; that is, there is an isoquant for each possible level of output. Normally, only a small subset of these isoquants is graphed.

The Three Stages of Production: Another View

In our earlier discussion of the three stages of production, we indicated that stage III was not a meaningful region to consider because, in that stage, the marginal productivity of labor was negative. This can also be seen in the isoquant mapping of Figure 7.6. Let us focus our attention on isoquant Q_1 over the interval from point A to point E. We now know that as we substitute labor for capital and move from A toward E, the marginal productivity of labor diminishes. But look what happens if we move beyond E, continuing to use more labor. The isoquant Q_1 turns upward, indicating that if we use more labor and still want to produce Q_1 units, we must now also use *more* capital. Why? Because beyond E, the marginal product of labor has become negative, and so to compensate for using more labor, we must add to the amount of capital used as well.

If we follow Q_2, Q_3, or Q_4 from left to right, we see that a similar result occurs. Beyond points F, G, and H in Figure 7.6, the isoquant curves turn up. That is, the slopes of the isoquants become positive due to the negative marginal productivity of labor. The line (R') connecting all points, such as E, F, G, and H, is called a ridge line; it marks off the boundary between stage II and stage III of production. No one would want to produce in stage III, since the same level of production could be obtained with fewer of both inputs by moving to the left along the appropriate isoquant until stage II was reached.

We can now apply this same line of reasoning to rule out stage I. Again let us concentrate attention on isoquant Q_1. This time, suppose we move up and to the left toward point A. As we do so, substituting capital for labor, the marginal productivity of capital diminishes and becomes negative if we go

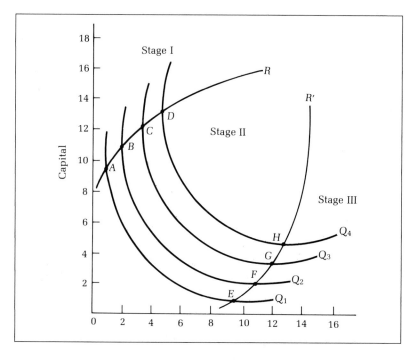

FIGURE 7.6   **The Three Stages of Production.**   To the right of the ridge line R', labor has negative marginal productivity and to the left of ridge line R, capital has negative marginal productivity. Only between the ridge lines is the marginal product of both inputs positive. Thus, stage II is the only logical region in which production should take place.

beyond A. Thus, if we add more capital above A while maintaining output at the Q_1 level, we must use *more* labor. This does not make much sense from a managerial perspective. Points B, C, and D are analogous to point A for their respective isoquants. Beyond these points, the marginal productivity of capital is negative, and so we would not wish to operate in that region, which we refer to as stage I.

The ridge line R marks the boundary between stage I and stage II just as R' marks the boundary between stages II and III. We see that neither stage I nor stage III is desirable for production, since the marginal productivity of at least one input is negative in those stages. We can then conclude that *the only relevant region for production is stage II*, which is bounded by the two ridge lines, R and R'.

7.10   ISOQUANTS FOR SPECIFIC TYPES OF PRODUCTION

As we have seen, production functions may be estimated using regression analysis. They can also be determined from the physical relationships defined by engineering studies of the production process. The first example in this section is based on an engineering production function for the transport of crude petroleum through a pipeline.[9] The output (Q) is the throughput of crude petroleum, measured in barrels per day (b/d) through a pipeline of 1000 miles.

Given the viscosity of the oil, its flow through a pipeline is determined by two forces: the driving pressure of pumps and the frictional resistance of the walls of the pipe. The first is measured as the horsepower supplied by the pumps and is denoted H. We expect that the greater the value of H, the greater the throughput. The second variable (friction) is related to the size of the inside diameter of the pipe (D). The larger the diameter of a cylindrical container, the greater the ratio of volume to inside surface area (excluding ends). Thus, a large pipe has less friction per barrel of oil than does a pipe with a smaller inside diameter. Therefore, we would expect both H and D to be positively related to output.

As reported by Pearl and Enos, the relevant physical laws can be combined in a fairly simple production function:

$$Q = 24.95 H^{.36} D^{1.72}$$

By plotting the inside pipe diameter on the vertical axis and horsepower on the horizontal axis, we may derive a mapping of isoquants. Figure 7.7 illustrates 17 such isoquants for the transport of crude oil via pipeline.

Let us look at the upper left point along the isoquant for 200,000 barrels per day. Reading from the horizontal axis, we see that this point corresponds to roughly 5000 horsepower. From the vertical axis, we can interpolate to estimate the pipe diameter at 31.3 inches. If these input values are substituted into the production function, we have

$$Q = 24.95(5000)^{0.36}(31.3)^{1.72}$$
$$Q = 24.95(22.46)(373.54)$$
$$Q = 200,000$$

We could verify the location of each isoquant by letting Q equal a given value and solving for alternative values of H and D that will yield that throughput, given the parameters of the production function.[10] The marginal rate of technical substitution of horsepower for pipe diameter can be calculated at various points by measuring the slope of the isoquants. For example, along $Q = 100,000$ b/d, at point A, the MRTS is approximately

---

[9] D.J. Pearl and J.L. Enos, "Engineering Production Functions and Technological Progress," *Journal of Industrial Economics*, September 1975, pp. 55–72.

[10] For example, try letting $Q = 600,000$, and solve for values of D that would correspond to $H = 10,000$, $H = 50,000$, $H = 100,000$, and $H = 500,000$. Then plot the four points corresponding to these values for the inputs H and D on Figure 7.7. The line connecting these points should be between the isoquant for 500,000 barrels per day and the one for 650,000 barrels per day.

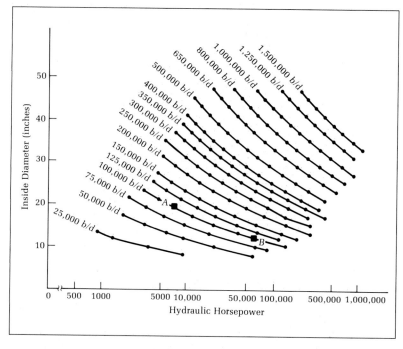

FIGURE 7.7   **Isoquants for Oil Transport via a Pipeline.**   These isoquants have all the properties suggested by economic theory. They are derived from the production function $Q = 24.95H^{.36}D^{1.72}$, where Q = throughput of oil, H = horsepower of pumps, and D = inside diameter of the pipe. (*Source:* Adapted from D.J. Pearl and J.L. Enos, "Engineering Production Functions and Technological Progress," *Journal of Industrial Economics* (Sept. 1975), p. 56. Reprinted with permission of Basil Blackwell & Mott.)

0.00045; at B, it is roughly 0.000033. As our theory suggests, the *MRTS* diminishes.

Before leaving this discussion of isoquants, let us look at one further example of an industry production function and the corresponding isoquants. H. D. Vinod has developed a production function for the Bell System in which output (measured as real net value added) is a function of the net capital stock employed (C) and the labor input in person-hours (L).[11] The production function used is a nonhomogeneous modification of the Cobb-Douglas formulation. Letting Q represent output, we get

$$\ln Q = 69.9 - 6.4(\ln C) - 10.6(\ln L) + 1.1(\ln C)(\ln L)$$

[11]H.D. Vinod was with the applied statistics department of Bell Telephone Laboratories at the time of this research, which is reported in "Nonhomogeneous Production Functions and Applications to Telecommunications," *Bell Journal of Economics and Management Science*, Autumn 1972, pp. 531–543.

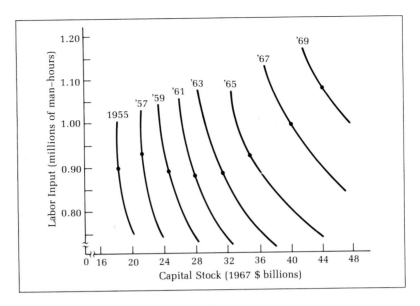

FIGURE 7.8   **Value-Added Isoquants for the Bell System.**   These isoquants have the expected properties. Each represents a different level of output as measured by real net value added. Dots represent the actual labor and capital used for eight selected years. (*Source:* H.D. Vinod, "Nonhomogeneous Production Functions and Applications," *The Bell Journal of Economics and Management Science*, Autumn 1972, p. 540. Reprinted with permission from The Rand Corporation.)

This production function provides the basis for the eight isoquants depicted in Figure 7.8.

Yet another example of the use of isoquants in a fully developed decision context is presented later in this chapter. This concept will be used in an optimization framework to help in determining the optimum mix of feeds to use in order to obtain a given amount of weight gain in hog production. But first, let us develop the optimization process in more general terms.

7.11   OPTIMIZATION IN PRODUCTION: A GRAPHIC APPROACH

You can now put your production background to work in a decision model. Suppose that a firm wants to produce Q^* units of output at the lowest possible resource cost. The decision involves selecting from many possible combinations of inputs the one combination that will produce the desired output at the lowest cost.

To explore this problem, we shall use the simple two-input Cobb-Douglas production function specified by $Q = K^{.5}L^{.5}$. The firm's cost is a function of the inputs used and, if the per-unit input costs are constant to the firm, the cost function (C) may be written as

$$C = P_K K + P_L L$$

where P_L represents the cost per unit of labor and P_K is the cost per unit of capital. Thus, $P_K K$ equals the total expenditure on capital, and $P_L L$ is the total expenditure on labor. Solving for K, we have

$$K = \frac{C}{P_K} - \frac{P_L}{P_K}(L)$$

which is linear, with intercepts at $L = 0, K = C/P_K$ and $K = 0, L = C/P_L$. The slope is equal to the ratio of the per-unit labor cost (P_L) to the per-unit capital cost (P_K) and is negative.

Since P_L and P_K are given, the slope is constant and the intercepts vary only as total production cost (expenditure on inputs) varies. Note that as C increases, the capital and labor intercepts $(C/P_K$ and C/P_L, respectively) shift outward, yet the slope (P_L/P_K) does not change; thus, changing C causes parallel shifts in the cost line, resulting in a parallel family of cost functions, each representing a specific level of cost. Each of these is called an *isocost curve*. Figure 7.9 illustrates three isocost curves and the same isoquants as in Figure 7.5. Since we shall assume for now that $P_L = P_K$, the slope of each isocost curve is -1 in this case.

Now let us suppose that each unit of capital costs $50 and that each unit of labor also costs $50. The three isocost functions shown in Figure 7.9, C_1, C_2, and C_3, then represent expenditures of $1000, $1500, and $1800, respectively. Let us further assume that the firm wants to produce 15 units of output (i.e., $Q^* = 15$). We know that any combination of labor and capital that satisfies

$$Q^* = K^{.5}L^{.5}$$
$$15 = K^{.5}L^{.5}$$

will enable the firm to produce the desired output. Three such combinations are points A, B, and D in Figure 7.9.

Point A represents approximately 28 units of capital and 8 units of labor, costing a total of $1800. At this point, the marginal productivity of each of the inputs is

$$MP_K = \partial Q/\partial K = .5K^{-.5}L^{.5}$$
$$MP_K = .5(28)^{-.5}(8)^{.5} = .27$$
$$MP_L = \partial Q/\partial L = .5K^{.5}L^{-.5}$$
$$MP_L = .5(28)^{.5}(8)^{-.5} = .94$$

If we were to reduce the capital input by $1 worth of capital, we would sacrifice .0054 units of output ($MP_K/P_K = .27/50 = .0054$). If we used that $1 to hire additional labor, output would increase by .0188 units ($MP_L/P_L = .94/50 = .0188$) and *total output would increase at the same cost!* It follows

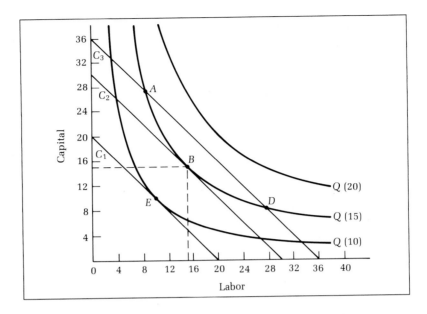

FIGURE 7.9   **Optimization in Production with Isoquant and Isocost Curves.**
Isoquant curves representing $Q = 10$, 15, and 20 units of output are graphed along with isocost curves representing expenditures of $1000, $1500, and $1800 on labor and capital. The lowest cost of producing 15 units is $1500 by using the combination of inputs represented by point B (i.e., $L = 15$ and $K = 15$).

that we could keep output constant by spending $1 less on capital while spending approximately an additional $.29 on labor (a cost savings of about $.71).[12] As long as the marginal productivity per dollar for labor is greater than the marginal productivity per dollar for capital, costs can be reduced for a given level of output by using more labor and less capital.

Similar analysis of point D (total expenditure again is $1800) leads us to the realization that at that point

$$MP_L/P_L < MP_K/P_K$$

and the Q^* units could be produced less expensively by moving along isoquant $Q(15)$ in a leftward direction, that is, by substituting capital for labor. As long as the marginal productivity per dollar for capital is greater than the marginal productivity per dollar for labor, costs can be reduced for a given level of output by using more capital and less labor.

It follows that costs will be minimized for a given level of output when the marginal productivities per dollar for the inputs are equal:

$$MP_L/P_L = MP_K/P_K$$

---

[12]The $.29 is found by the ratio $(MP_K/P_K)/(MP_L/P_L) = .0054/.0188 = .2872$.

We can show that this is true at point B, where the marginal productivities of capital and labor are

$$MP_K = .5(15)^{-.5}(15)^{.5} = .5$$
$$MP_L = .5(15)^{.5}(15)^{-.5} = .5$$

and since $P_L = P_K = 50$, we have

$$MP_L/P_L = MP_L/P_K$$
$$.5/50 = .5/50$$
$$.01 = .01$$

No further reallocation of inputs will allow the production of Q^* at a cost lower than the \$1500 represented by isocost curve C_2. There is no point along C_1 (or any isocost below C_2) that would provide sufficient inputs to produce the desired output $(Q^* = 15)$.

7.12 OPTIMIZATION IN PRODUCTION: AN ALGEBRAIC APPROACH

If we had more than two input variables, we would not be able to use a graphic form of analysis. However, the constrained optimization technique of the Lagrangian multiplier provides a method that is applicable to any number of input factors. We shall use this technique for the same problem as was evaluated above using the graphic method. The cost function to be minimized is

$$C = 50K + 50L$$

subject to the constraint that output must equal 15:

$$15 = K^{.5}L^{.5}$$
$$15 - K^{.5}L^{.5} = 0$$

The Lagrangian function (Z) is

$$Z = 50K + 50L + \lambda(15 - K^{.5}L^{.5})$$

Taking the partial derivatives, setting them equal to 0, and solving for L and K, we have

$$\partial Z/\partial K = 50 - .5K^{-.5}L^{.5}\lambda = 0$$
$$\partial Z/\partial L = 50 - .5K^{.5}L^{-.5}\lambda = 0$$
$$\partial Z/\partial \lambda = 15 - K^{.5}L^{.5}$$

From the first two of these partials, we find

$$K^{-.5}L^{.5} = 100/\lambda$$

and

$$K^{.5}L^{-.5} = 100/\lambda$$

Thus,

$$K^{-.5}L^{.5} = K^{.5}L^{-.5}$$
$$K = L$$

Substituting this result in the third partial, we get

$$15 - K^{.5}K^{.5} = 0$$
$$K = 15$$

and so

$$L = 15$$

and

$$C = 50(15) + 50(15) = \$1500$$

This solution corresponds to point B in Figure 7.9. Solving for λ, we find that $\lambda = 100$. The value of λ can be interpreted as the additional cost of increasing output by one unit using the most efficient (cost-minimizing) combination of inputs. This can be verified by resolving the problem, substituting 16 for 15 in the constraint function. Then, we find that C increases to $1600. You may recognize λ as being equal to the marginal cost of producing an additional unit of output.

Let us now examine the first two partials a bit more closely. Solving each for $1/\lambda$, we have, respectively,

$$1/\lambda = \frac{.5K^{-.5}L^{.5}}{50}$$

$$1/\lambda = \frac{.5K^{.5}L^{-.5}}{50}$$

Thus, we find that

$$\frac{.5K^{-.5}L^{.5}}{50} = \frac{.5K^{.5}L^{-.5}}{50}$$

Since the numerators are marginal products and the denominators are input prices, we have

$$MP_K/P_K = MP_L/P_L = 1/\lambda$$

Thus, we see that the marginal product per dollar is equal to the reciprocal of the marginal cost.

The importance of these results is far reaching. The condition that the marginal products per dollar are equal for all inputs can be shown to apply to output maximization problems for a given constraint on cost, as well as to cost minimization for a given output. Consider the following general form of that problem:

Maximize: $Q = f(K, L)$
Subject to: $C_o = P_K K + P_L L$

where C_o is a given level of expenditure. The Lagrangian function is

$$Z = f(K, L) + \lambda(C_o - P_K K - P_L L)$$

Finding the partials, we have

$$\partial Z/\partial K = f_K - P_K \lambda = 0$$
$$\partial Z/\partial L = f_L - P_L \lambda = 0$$
$$\partial Z/\partial \lambda = C_o - P_K K - P_L L = 0$$

where f_L is the marginal product of labor, and f_K is the marginal product of capital. From the first two partials, we find

$$\lambda = f_K/P_K$$
$$\lambda = f_L/P_L$$

Setting $\lambda = \lambda$, we get the same condition as above:

$$f_K/P_K = f_L/P_L$$
$$MP_K/P_K = MP_L/P_L$$

That is, the marginal products per dollar are equal for labor and capital.

Let us find the maximum output we can obtain from the function $Q = K^{.5}L^{.5}$ for an expenditure of $1000 (corresponding to C_1 in Figure 7.9). We have

$$Z = K^{.5}L^{.5} + \lambda(1000 - 50K - 50L)$$

finding the three partial derivatives, we get

$$\partial Z/\partial K = .5K^{-.5}L^{.5} - 50\lambda = 0$$
$$\partial Z/\partial L = .5K^{.5}L^{-.5} - 50\lambda = 0$$
$$\partial Z/\partial \lambda = 1000 - 50K - 50L = 0$$

Solving the first two partials, we find $L = K$, and substituting this result in the third partial, we obtain $L = 10$ and $K = 10$ as the combination of labor and capital that will maximize output $(Q = 10)$ for an expenditure of $1000 on the two inputs. Note that this corresponds to point E in Figure 7.9, where C_1 is tangent to $Q(10)$. We also find that $\lambda = .01$. The value of λ means that output could be increased by .01 units if $1 more was used to purchase inputs (in efficient combinations). Thus, in this context, λ represents the marginal productivity of money. This can be verified by solving the problem with $1001 rather than $1000. (You will find that $Q = 10.01$.)

In the two problem situations just analyzed, we have found optimal solutions at points B and E in Figure 7.9, where the isocost curves C_2 and C_1 are tangent to the isoquants $Q(15)$ and $Q(10)$, respectively. At any point of tangency, the curves that are tangent have the same slope. The slope of an isocost curve is the negative of P_L/P_K, and the slope of an isoquant is the negative of the $MRTS = MP_L/MP_K$. Thus, to minimize cost for a given output or to maximize output for a given cost,

$$P_L/P_K = MP_L/MP_K$$

Rearranging terms, we obtain the familiar condition that

$$MP_L/P_L = MP_K/P_K$$

While we have used the mathematical technique of the Lagrangian multiplier for a two-input, one-constraint case, it can easily be extended to any number of inputs and constraints (as long as the number of equality constraints is less than the number of inputs). We have used this simple problem as an example so that you can see the relationship between the geometric and mathematical relationships and thereby gain a better understanding and appreciation of the latter.

7.13   DETERMINATION OF THE OPTIMAL DIET MIX

To illustrate the optimization concept in a specific case, let us look at the work of Sonka, Heady, and Dahm involving hog production.[13] The total quantities of corn and a protein supplement needed to achieve three levels of weight gain were determined using a sample of 648 hogs that were fed various rations. These levels were (1) a gain of 40 pounds (from 60–100); (2) a gain of 50 pounds (from 100–150); and (3) a gain of 65 pounds (from 150–215).

Equations for the three isoquants, one for each weight-gain interval, were estimated as follows:[14]

1. $\ln C_1 = 6.163 - 0.5898 \ln PS_1$
   (32.99)   (9.33)
   $R^2 = 0.740$

2. $\ln C_2 = 6.2292 - 0.4405 \ln PS_2$
   (63.26)   (13.14)
   $R^2 = 0.691$

3. $\ln C_3 = 6.4378 - 0.3526 \ln PS_3$
   (81.61)   (14.16)
   $R^2 = 0.769$

where C_i represents the number of pounds of corn consumed in the ith interval and PS_i the number of pounds of protein supplement consumed in the ith interval. The values in parentheses are t-ratios, which along with the

---

[13] This section is based on Steven T. Sonka, Earl O. Heady, and P. Fred Dahm, "Estimation of Gain Isoquants and a Decision Model Application for Swine Production," *American Journal of Agricultural Economics*, August 1976, pp. 466–474.

[14] Sonka, Heady, and Dahm, p. 469.

values for R^2, indicate a good statistical fit in each case. The isoquant equations can be written in arithmetic, rather than logarithmic, form as follows:

$$C_1 = 474.85PS_1^{-.5898}$$
$$C_2 = 507.35PS_2^{-.4405}$$
$$C_3 = 625.03PS_3^{-.3526}$$

by finding the antilogarithm of each side of the respective equations (note that natural logarithms were used).[15]

We know that the marginal rate of technical substitution ($MRTS$) between two inputs is equal to the negative of the slope of the isoquant. For the interval-1 isoquant,

$$MRTS = -dC/dPS$$
$$dC/dPS = -.5898(474.85)PS^{-1.5898}$$
$$MRTS = 280.06PS^{-1.5898}$$

For $PS = 12$,

$$MRTS = 280.06(12)^{-1.5898}$$
$$MRTS = 5.39$$

Thus, in interval 1, one pound of protein supplement replaces 5.39 pounds of corn at $PS = 12$. At $PS = 20$, the $MRTS$ falls to 2.39, and at $PS = 36$, the $MRTS$ is just .94. We see that the marginal rate of technical substitution diminishes; that is, the slope of the isoquant becomes less steep as we move from left to right. This can be seen in Figure 7.10, which shows these same three isoquants graphically.

In Figure 7.10, the isoquants are labeled Q_1 for interval 1 (40-pound gain), Q_2 for interval 2 (50-pound gain), and Q_3 for interval three (65-pound gain). We see that for any interval there are alternative diets that would achieve the desired weight gain. But the equations and isoquants presented above describe only the dietary input factors in determining weight gain for swine. To determine the economically optimum ration, we must also consider the relative costs of corn and of the protein supplement. The least-cost ration "is attained when corn and protein supplement are mixed in a ratio that allows the marginal rate of (technical) substitution of protein for corn to just equal the protein supplement, corn-price ratio."[16] This is, of course, the same condition that we have already established as a general rule.

---

[15]To illustrate these calculations, let us look more closely at C_1:

$$\ln C_1 = 6.163 - .5898\ln PS$$

Taking the antilog of both sides of this expression, we have

$$C_1 = (e^{6.163})PS_1^{-.5898}$$
$$C_1 = (2.718^{6.163})PS_1^{-.5898}$$
$$C_1 = 474.85PS_1^{-.5898}$$

[16]Sonka, Heady, and Dahm, p. 471.

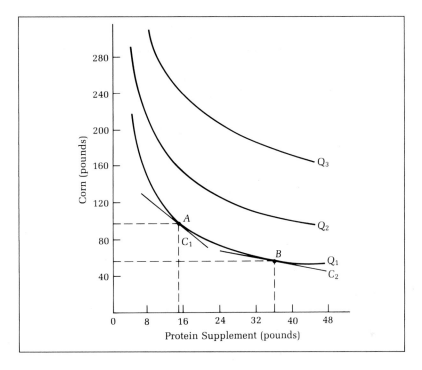

FIGURE 7.10   **Determination of an Optimum Diet Mix.**   The determination of the least-cost combination of protein supplement and corn to feed hogs in order to achieve a weight gain of 40 pounds (Q_1), given a .95 ratio of the price of protein supplement to the price of corn, is at point B, where the slope of Q_1 is $-.95$.

Sonka, Heady, and Dahm give data on the price ratio (price per pound of protein supplement to the price per pound of corn) for every November and April from November 1970 to April 1975.[17] For illustrative purposes, we shall look at the high- and low-price ratios during this period. In April 1975, the ratio was 0.95, and in April 1973, it was 3.62. Since the optimum diet mix is the one for which the *MRTS* equals the price ratio, we can solve for the least-cost diet mix as follows. For April 1973 and interval 1,

$$MRTS = 280.06PS^{-1.5898}$$
$$\text{Price ratio} = 3.62$$

Therefore,

$$280.06PS^{-1.5898} = 3.62$$
$$PS = 15.41$$

---

[17] Sonka, Heady, and Dahm, p. 472.

and from the equation for the isoquant, we find C as follows:

$$C = 474.85PS^{-.5898}$$
$$C = 474.86(15.41)^{-.5898}$$
$$C = 94.62$$

For April 1971 and interval 1,

$$MRTS = 280.06PS^{-1.5898}$$
$$\text{Price ratio} = 0.95$$

Therefore,

$$280.06PS^{-1.5898} = 0.95$$
$$PS = 35.76$$

Also from the equation for the isoquant, we find C as follows:

$$C = 474.85PS^{-.5898}$$
$$C = 474.85(35.76)^{-.5898}$$
$$C = 57.59$$

As expected, we see that when the price of the protein supplement is high relative to the price of corn (i.e., a higher price ratio), less of the protein supplement and more corn is used in the least-cost diet mix for a given weight gain.

These same results may be seen in graphic form in Figure 7.10. We know that an isocost curve has a slope equal to the ratio of the input prices: the ratio of the price of PS to the price of C in this example. The lowest isocost with a slope equal to 3.62 (absolute value) and tangent to Q_1 is drawn in Figure 7.10 and is labeled C_1. The tangency between this isocost and the isoquant Q_1 is at the same input combination derived above for April 1973, when the price ratio was 3.62. The isocost curve labeled C_2 has a price ratio, or slope, of 0.95 (absolute value) and is tangent at the same input combination as determined above for April 1971.

7.14 PRODUCTION THEORY AND THE QUALITY OF EDUCATION

For a final application of the production concepts we have been discussing, let us turn again to the public sector.[18] The problem we will consider involves the decision concerning how many teacher and nonteacher inputs a school district should hire to maximize the *quality* of education, given (1) some number of students (n), (2) a given dollar amount of resources (money

---

[18]This section is based on Daniel G. Gallagher and Edwin C. Hackleman, "Isoquants, Collective Bargaining, and Public School Resource Allocation," *Journal of Economics and Business*, Spring 1979, pp. 160–165.

available), (3) some set of costs per unit of teacher and nonteacher inputs, and (4) a set of quality isoquant curves.

Look first at an initial situation, as described in Figure 7.11, that has an equilibrium at point A. The monetary constraint imposed on the school district is represented by the isocost curve RL. You have learned that, given this constraint, the highest quality level attainable is found where RL is just tangent to one of the quality isoquant curves. From Figure 7.11, you see that this is at point A, with T_A teacher inputs being hired along with NT_A nonteacher inputs. The quality level is given by Q_3.

Now, suppose that teachers demand higher salaries and fringe benefits. This will raise the cost per unit for teacher inputs. If we assume that the cost of nonteacher inputs and the school district's budget remain the same, the isocost curve will become steeper, as does the one labeled RM. What is the new optimal combination of inputs? Economic reasoning indicates that using T_B and NT_B teacher and nonteacher inputs, respectively, will

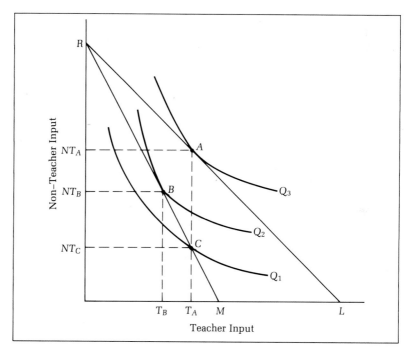

FIGURE 7.11   **Allocation of Inputs to Education.**   If teacher inputs become more expensive relative to nonteacher inputs, the isocost curve becomes steeper (it moves from RL to RM). This results in a lower level of output, as measured by educational quality, as the equilibrium moves from A to B. If the school system must maintain T_A teaching inputs, the educational quality level will drop still further, to Q (see point C).

maximize the quality of education for the n students. The new quality level (Q_2) is lower, however.

There may be legal and/or sociopolitical pressure to keep the student-to-teacher ratio constant. If this ratio must be maintained at the original level, with T_A teacher inputs, what will happen to the quality of education? If we are constrained to both operate under the budget represented by RM and to hire T_A teachers, the highest quality level that can be reached is Q_1, at point C.

SUMMARY

Production is the process of providing goods or services that have value to consumers. These goods or services can include such disparate things as cars, the transport of crude oil, police protection, hog weight gain, and education. The principle of diminishing marginal productivity affects nearly all types of production. Thus, adding additional units of any variable input to other inputs that are fixed results in successively smaller increments to output.

When all inputs can be varied simultaneously, production may be characterized by increasing, constant, or decreasing returns to scale, summarized as follows:

1. Increasing returns to scale: increasing all inputs by some proportion increases output by a greater proportion.

2. Constant returns to scale: Increasing all inputs by some proportion increases output by the same proportion.

3. Decreasing returns to scale: increasing all inputs by some proportion increases output by a lesser proportion.

The optimum mix of inputs to use in a production process is always the combination for which the marginal productivities per dollar are equal for all inputs. This can be demonstrated graphically using isoquant and isocost curves or mathematically using the Lagrangian constrained optimization model.

SUGGESTED READINGS

Baumol, William J. *Economic Theory and Operation Analysis*, 4th ed. Englewood Cliffs, NJ: Prentice-Hall, 1977, Chapter 11.
Gallagher, Daniel G., and Hackleman, Edwin C. "Isoquants, Collective Bargaining, and Public School Resource Allocation." *Journal of Economics and Business*, Spring 1979, pp. 160–165.

Griliches, Zvi. "R & D and the Productivity Slowdown." *American Economic Review*, May 1980, pp. 343–348.

Heady, Earl O., and Dillon, John. *Agricultural Production Functions*. Ames: Iowa State University Press, 1961.

Mansfield, Edwin. *The Economics of Technical Change*. New York: Norton, 1968.

Nadiri, M. Ishaq, and Schankerman, M.A. "Technical Change, Returns to Scale, and the Productivity Slowdown." *American Economic Review*, May 1981, pp. 314–319.

Walters, A.A. "Production and Cost Functions: An Econometric Survey." *Econometrica*, January-April 1963, pp. 1–66.

PROBLEMS

1. The production manager of a small manufacturing firm wishes to estimate the functional relationship betweeen the amount of labor input and output. For a given size of plant (and fixed amounts of other factors of production), the following data were obtained:

Output (Q)	15	13	10	10	12	15	11	14	16	9
Labor (L)	10	6	2	1	4	8	2	6	10	1

   where output is in thousands of units and labor is in hundreds of labor hours.

   a. You are asked to help the production manager by estimating a production function of the form $Q = a + bL$. Using regression analysis, derive estimates for a and b. Do these estimates have the expected signs? Is b significant at the 95-percent confidence level? What is the coefficient of determination (R^2)?

   b. Write a brief explanation of your production function and related statistics for the production manager, assuming that the manager knows little or nothing about the technique you used.

   c. If 550 labor hours were used, what amount of output would you expect? Could you use the function you estimated to predict the level of output that would be obtained using 1600 labor hours? Why or why not?

2. Suppose that the economic research staff of a company for which you work has estimated the following production function:

$$Q = 10L + 6L^2 - .02L^3$$

where Q is output in thousands, and L is hours of labor input in thousands. This production function is for a given plant and other fixed factors of production.

a.   Find the algebraic equations for average product (AP) and for marginal product (MP).

b.   Does this production function exhibit diminishing marginal productivity for labor? Explain your answer.

c.   Graph the production function, the MP function, and the AP function for $L = 20, 40, 60, \ldots, 200$ (i.e., you will have 10 observations to plot for each function).

d.   Show that for this production function, $MP = AP$ at the maximum of AP.

e.   Your firm is currently employing 150,000 hours of labor (i.e., $L = 150$). In a monthly staff meeting, the vice president for marketing reports that sales could easily be increased to 103,500 from the current level ($Q = 69,000$ at $L = 150$) if more units were available. Since this represents a 50-percent increase in sales and needed production, someone at the meeting suggests that you hire 50 percent more workers (i.e., $L = 225$) to increase output sufficiently to satisfy the potential demand. How would you respond to this proposition? How would you convince others to agree with your position relative to the suggestion to increase the labor input? Are there other potential alternatives?

3.   Qwik-Serve Stores (QSS) are providers of fast film processing in several midwestern communities. Data for August 1985 have been gathered on the number of labor hours employed (L) and the number of rolls of film processed (P) for 14 Qwik-Serve Stores. These data are given below:

Store	P	L
1	11,000	800
2	13,000	1,600
3	5,000	300
4	8,000	800
5	4,000	100
6	11,000	2,000
7	7,000	600
8	8,000	2,200
9	4,000	300
10	14,000	1,300
11	15,000	1,600
12	4,000	600
13	12,000	1,000
14	14,000	2,000

a. Plot these observations on the graph below:

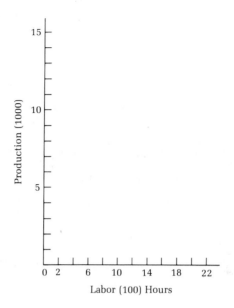

b. From your graph, does there appear to be diminishing marginal productivity for the labor input? Explain.

c. Use a regression program to estimate the production function in a linear form:

$$Q = \underline{\hspace{2cm}} + \underline{\hspace{2cm}} L$$

$$(\quad\quad) \, t\text{-ratio}$$

$$R^2 = \underline{\hspace{4cm}}$$

d. Now estimate a cubic function for the production data given above. Use the general form:

$$P = f(L, L^2, L^3)$$

$$P = \underline{\hspace{1.5cm}} - \underline{\hspace{1.5cm}} L + \underline{\hspace{1.5cm}} L^2 - \underline{\hspace{1.5cm}} L^3$$

$$(\quad\quad) \quad (\quad\quad) \quad (\quad\quad)$$

$$t\text{-ratios}$$

$$R^2 = \underline{\hspace{4cm}}$$

e. Which function do you think best describes the film processing production function? Based on your answer, does the principle of diminishing marginal productivity appear to apply to film processing? Explain.

4. From your cubic production function in problem 3, derive the marginal and average product functions:

$$AP_L = \text{_____}$$

$$MP_L = \text{_____}$$

a. Over what range of labor input is average product diminishing? Over what range of labor input is marginal product declining?
b. Find the value of the labor input at which $MP_L = AP_L$. How does this point relate to your answer to part a?
c. Find the labor input level that provides the maximum level of output. Does this seem consistent with the graph in problem 3?

5. Assume that you are an economic consultant to a firm that has the following Cobb-Douglas production function:

$$Q = 10L^{.5} K^{.5}$$

The current wage rate is $50 per labor unit, and the cost per unit of capital is $80.

a. If the firm wishes to produce 400 units of output, how much of each input would you tell the managers to use to minimize the cost of producing the 400 units? What would that cost be?
b. Suppose that instead of having a target amount of output, the firm's managers have told you that they spend $6000 on labor and capital and that they would like to maximize the amount of output produced. Now how many units of labor and capital would you recommend? How many units could they produce?
c. For parts a and b, show that the marginal productivity per dollar spent on each input is equal for the values of L and K that you suggest.
d. If the labor union demands wage increases and other benefits that push the cost per unit of labor up to $80, how would this influence your response in parts a and b? Rework each of these problems to show how the added labor costs would influence the employment of labor and the cost of production in part a and the level of output in part b.

6. An economic study of communications in Canada reported the following Cobb-Douglas production function was estimated for Bell Canada:[19]

$$V = .56L^{.705} K^{.405} D^{.01}$$

The t-ratios were 4.9, 6.8, and 9.5 for the variables L, K, and D, respectively. The coefficient of determination was .998, and the Durbin-

---

[19] A.R. Dobell et al., "Telephone Communications in Canada," *Bell Journal of Economics and Management Science*, Spring 1972, pp. 175–219.

Watson statistic was 1.78. V is the value added (in thousands of dollars), L is labor-hours (in millions,) K is net capital stock (in thousands of dollars), and D is a proxy for technological change (measured as the percentage of station-to-station toll calls dialed by the customer). All data are on a yearly basis, and values in parentheses under each variable are the t-ratios.

a. Is this production homogeneous and, if so, to what degree?

b. Does this production function exhibit increasing, constant, or decreasing returns to scale? Why?

c. Suppose that $K = 2500$, $L = 60$, and $D = 52$. What would be your estimate of value added for Bell Canada?

d. For the same values of K, L, and D used in part c, determine the marginal productivity of labor and capital.

e. Is this function characterized by diminishing marginal productivity for labor and for capital? Prove that you are correct.

f. Given the value calculated in part c and assuming a constant state of technology (i.e., D is fixed at 52), derive the equation for the isoquant. Using this equation, plot the isoquant with labor on the horizontal axis and capital on the vertical axis (use odd values of labor from 45–65). Does this isoquant have the expected shape? Explain.

g. Show what happens to that isoquant if technology improves such that $D = 60$. Plot the new isoquant along with the original. Is the relationship between the two as you expected? Explain.

7. EDM is a producer of casings used to house electronic products such as televisions, stereos, VCRs, and related products. EDM was founded by Jim Conant and Mary Lou Hamilton in 1968 and has now been successful and profitable for well over 15 years. Jim and Mary Lou have been talking with several microcomputer manufacturers about expanding into the production of shock-resistant cases for portable micros. Mary Lou wants to look at their production history in detail before considering this expansion. As a starting point, she has gathered a sample of 20 months' data on production and the corresponding labor input. These data are given below:

Labor Hours	Output	Labor Hours	Output
1000	7050	100	250
200	2500	2000	7600
1500	7350	1700	7450
500	6000	300	4050
1200	7230	1900	7580
1600	7390	700	6670
800	6980	1400	7280
600	6430	1800	7490
1100	7170	900	7100
400	5240	1300	7310

From Jim's engineering background, he suspects that the proper functional form for their production should be:

$$Q = f(1/L) = a + bL^{-1}$$

a. Estimate this function using regression analysis for EDM's production. What sign do you expect for b? (Remember that you are using the reciprocal of labor as the independent variable.)

$$Q = \underline{\hspace{2cm}} +/- \underline{\hspace{2cm}} L^{-1}$$

$$(\hspace{2cm}) t\text{-ratio}$$

$$R^2 = \underline{\hspace{2cm}}$$

b. Based on your result for part a, does labor appear to have diminishing marginal productivity? Why? Write the marginal product function below:

$$MP = \underline{\hspace{2cm}}$$

c. Find the algebraic function for average product:

$$AP = \underline{\hspace{2cm}}$$

Is the average product of labor increasing, decreasing, or constant? Explain your answer.

8. a. Based on the production function you found in problem 7, how many units of labor would EDM need to produce 3000 units of output? How much labor would be needed to produce 6000 units?

$$L_{3000} = \underline{\hspace{2cm}}$$

$$L_{6000} = \underline{\hspace{2cm}}$$

b. If each unit of labor costs $40, find the average labor cost (ALC) to produce both 3000 and 6000 units of output:

$$ALC_{3000} = \underline{\hspace{2cm}}$$

$$ALC_{6000} = \underline{\hspace{2cm}}$$

c. Are your results for part b consistent with your answer to problem 7c?

9. The following table gives data relating output (Q) to the number of units of labor (L) and capital (K) used in a production process:

Capital	\multicolumn{5}{c}{Labor}
	1	2	3	4	5
1	10	35	51	70	81
2	31	52	70	91	104
3	39	60	81	105	120
4	45	70	95	120	140
5	49	77	104	125	150

a. Using these data, estimate the production function in the linear form $Q = a + b_1 K + b_2 L$. Do the coefficients b_1 and b_2 have the expected signs? Are they significant at the 95-percent level? What is the coefficient of determination? Does this function exhibit constant, increasing, or decreasing returns to scale? Why?

b. Estimate the Cobb-Douglas form for the production function $Q = AK^b L^c$. (If the regression package on your computer does not have a logarithmic transformation, change the data to logarithms before entering it into the regression program.) Do these coefficients have the expected signs? Are they significant at the 95-percent level? What is the coefficient of determination? Does this function exhibit constant, decreasing, or increasing returns to scale? What is the marginal productivity of labor? Of capital?

c. Use the Cobb-Douglas form of the production function to estimate how much output would be expected if 3.5 units of labor and 4.2 units of capital were used.

10. GroMor, Inc., manufactures fertilizer products that are sold throughout the Midwest. In a controlled study of a new product, the firm has collected production data in bushels of grain per acre for applications of from 1 pound of fertilizer per acre to 20 pounds per acre. The results from this experiment are given below:

Pounds of Fertilizer (PF)	Bushels of Grain (B)	Pounds of Fertilizer (PF)	Bushels of Grain (B)
1	2.0	11	83.0
2	6.0	12	90.0
3	12.4	13	92.6
4	20.4	14	93.0
5	29.0	15	89.0
6	38.0	16	81.6
7	49.0	17	70.0
8	60.0	18	55.0
9	69.5	19	46.5
10	78.0	20	34.0

a. Use a regression program to estimate the fertilizer production function in cubic form based on these results:

$$B = f(PF, PF^2, PF^3)$$
$$B = a + b_1 PF + b_2 PF^2 + b_3 PF^3$$

From your results, complete the following table:

Term	Value	t-ratio
a		
b_1		
b_2		
b_3		
$R^2 =$ _____		

b. Write the algebraic expressions for total product, average product, and marginal product:

TP = _____

AP = _____

MP = _____

c. Is there diminishing marginal productivity in the use of this fertilizer? If so, over what range of fertilizer use?
d. At what level of fertilizer use is the average productivity highest?
e. At what level of fertilizer use is the total product maximized?

11. In the text, a study by Sonka, Heady, and Dahm concerning weight gain isoquants was discussed. The two inputs to weight gain were pounds of corn consumed (C) and pounds of protein supplement consumed (PS). The gain intervals and corresponding equations for the isoquants are given below:

Gain Interval	Isoquant
60–100 pounds	$C = 474.85PS^{-.5898}$
100–150 pounds	$C = 507.35PS^{-.4405}$
150–215 pounds	$C = 625.03PS^{-.3526}$

a. Assume that the ratio of the price of protein supplement to the price of corn is 3.0. What would be the optimum mix of PS and C to increase hog weight from 150 to 215 pounds?
b. Now assume that the PS to C price ratio increases to 5.0. What is the best mix of the two feeds to increase weight from 150 to 215 pounds?
c. Write a paragraph in which you explain the relationship between the two answers found above.

12. ADCO is a small and relatively new advertising agency that Mary Hallom started after finishing her MBA. She has an office in one room of

her house and so far has done all of the work herself. For her first 10 months of operation, she has collected the following data related to her services (she is measuring output as the dollars of net revenue generated):

Month	Output	Labor Hours
1	400	10
2	410	30
3	500	30
4	400	60
5	700	60
6	1200	100
7	1400	120
8	1300	170
9	1600	160
10	1400	180

a. Based on these data, estimate the production functions $Q = f(L)$ and $Q = f(L, L^2)$:

$$Q = \underline{\hspace{2cm}} + \underline{\hspace{2cm}} L$$

$$(\underline{\hspace{2cm}}) t\text{-ratio}$$

$$R^2 = \underline{\hspace{3cm}}$$

$$Q = \underline{\hspace{2cm}} + \underline{\hspace{2cm}} L - \underline{\hspace{2cm}} L^2$$

$$(\underline{\hspace{2cm}}) \quad (\underline{\hspace{2cm}})$$
$$t\text{-ratios}$$

$$\overline{R}^2 = \underline{\hspace{3cm}}$$

Which of the above do you think best describes Mary's production function? Why?

b. Do you think that the principle of diminishing marginal productivity applies to ADCO? Explain.

13. Eagle Manufacturing, Inc., produces plastic ballpoint pens that are sold to schools and other institutions in bulk form. The production functions for the pens has been estimated as

$$Q = 100K^{.2} L^{.9}$$

Eagle currently pays $20 per unit of the labor input and $10 per unit of the capital input. Based on this information answer the following questions:

a. Find the algebraic expressions for the marginal product of labor (MP_L) and for the marginal product of capital (MP_K).

$$MP_L = \underline{\hspace{2cm}}$$

$$MP_K = \underline{\hspace{2cm}}$$

b. Determine whether there is diminishing marginal productivity for labor and capital.

c. Find the maximum output that Eagle can produce if $2000 is available to spend on labor and capital inputs. How many units of each input should be used?

d. In part c, what value would the Lagrangian multiplier have? Interpret its meaning. How could this information be useful to management?

e. For the level of production determined in part c, what is the average cost per unit of output?

14. Refer to the production function for Eagle Manufacturing given in problem 13. Suppose that the marketing division has projected sales for the coming period to be 16,000:

a. What combination of labor and capital should be used to minimize the cost of producing the 16,000 pens?

b. Interpret the value of the Lagrangian multiplier, explaining how this information could be useful to management.

c. What is the average cost of producing these 16,000 pens? How does this compare to the average cost of production that you found in problem 13e? What can you say about returns to scale based on what has happened to average cost?

15. Suppose that a technological change causes the production function for Eagle Manufacturing (see problems 13 and 14) to become

$$Q = 100K^{.5}L^{.7}$$

a. Did the technological change influence the existence and/or degree of economies of scale?

b. Did the change affect the rate to which L and K are subject to diminishing marginal productivity?

c. Now what is the maximum output that can be obtained for a $2000 expenditure on L and K (assume P_L and P_K are $20 and $10, respectively)? How much L and K should be used?

d. Given the new technology, what is the minimum cost to produce 16,000 units, and how much L and K would be used?

Linear Programming

Linear programming is a technique used to solve allocation problems when constraints, such as limited budgets, time limits, legal restrictions, technological constraints, and the like, are imposed on the decision maker. The technique most used for solving such allocation problems in business is linear programming; it is a powerful, yet relatively simple technique. Any situation in which scarce resources must be allocated to achieve an organization's goals represents a possibility for solution through linear programming.

The linear programming technique is actually a model, that is, a simplified or idealized representation of the real world. This chapter describes the model — that is, the set of simplifying assumptions — on which linear programming is based. This chapter also reviews a variety of applications. The conditions that must be fulfilled before a given problem can be analyzed using linear programming are presented in the form of the assumptions underlying this type of analysis. If these conditions are met, the firm's problem may then be translated into a linear objective function and a set of linear constraints that can be stated in precise algebraic form. This phase of applying linear programming is called formulating the LP problem. Once the problem is formulated, it may be solved using any one of a number of different techniques.

The word linear, as used in linear programming, means that we are dealing with proportional relationships between variables. For example, in a linear relationship between hours of work and output, a doubling of hours of work would cause a doubling in output. The term programming means that we use mathematical algorithms, or steps, to arrive at an optimal solution.

8.1 REPRESENTATIVE APPLICATIONS OF LINEAR PROGRAMMING

Economic and business decisions often involve the allocation of limited resources (raw materials, time, space, money, people, etc.) among competing projects with the objective of maximizing some performance objective (output, sales, return on investment, market share, etc.) or minimizing some cost objective (dollar cost, waste, pollution, etc.). In many cases, decisions such as these can be analyzed using linear programming.

The variety of problem situations to which linear programming applies is vast. The following eight situations in which linear programming has been used are examples of the versatility of this technique:

1. *Product Mix Problems.* The problem of deciding on the optimal mix of products to be produced with a company's limited supply of personnel, materials, and plant capacity can be analyzed using linear programming. We shall use this relatively common application in explaining linear programming throughout this chapter. Consider, for example, a food processing firm that specializes in tomato products. Tomatoes may be used to produce chili sauce, tomato paste, stewed tomatoes, ketchup, tomato soup, tomato juice, and canned whole tomatoes. A given tomato processing plant can normally produce any or all of these products. The firm is usually limited by the available crop of tomatoes, time (since the crop is perishable), available labor, and availability of other material inputs, such as sugar and starch. Each of the products is likely to have a different profit contribution, and thus management is faced with a complex decision regarding how much of each product should be produced. Furthermore, management may want to know how much the company can afford to pay for additional units of the factors constraining production. These questions and others can be answered with information provided by the linear programming technique.

2. *Diet Problems.* In the production of animal feeds, specific nutritional levels must be met. Feeds are prepared from a number of ingredients each of which contains a different content of various nutritional components (protein, vitamins, minerals, etc.) and each of which is likely to have a different cost. A firm's management wants to produce feeds that meet the nutritional requirements of buyers or the government, and to do so at the lowest cost. Management may also be interested in evaluating how much cost will increase when the nutritional level of the feed is increased. Linear programming is helpful in determining the best solution to these problems. This type of problem also arises in the chemical, pharmaceutical, fertilizer, lawn seed, and pet food industries.

3. *Process Selection.* A problem in some respects similar to the diet case involves the production of a product that can be made using any one or more of several processes. A firm's management wants to produce the product using the process or processes that will combine inputs in such a manner so as to minimize production costs.

4. *Allocation of an Advertising Budget.* Given a fixed budget for advertising, a firm's management wants to get the maximum possible benefit from spending these dollars. The money spent on advertising must be allocated among various media, such as television, radio, billboards, newspapers, and magazines. In addition, the money spent on a given medium may have to be allocated within subsets of that medium. For example, television advertising could be split between daytime and evening shows, depending on the audience management hopes to reach.

5. *Distribution Problems.* Many firms have multiple plants producing a given product, and several have many warehouses in which the product is stored before being distributed to retail outlets. The distribution cost varies depending on the route the product takes between the point of production and the point of sale. The firm's management must determine how many units should go from each plant to each warehouse and from each warehouse to each sales outlet. Determining the mix of shipments that will minimize shipping cost is a complex problem for which suboptimal solutions are likely without the aid of linear programming.[1]

6. *Personnel Assignment Problems.* Some characteristics of the assignment of personnel to various activities are similar in many respects to the distribution problem discussed above. For example, an accounting firm or division may wish to find the best method of assigning audit staff personnel to various audit activities while conforming to the limitations of the audit office and at the same time meeting the unique professional and economic objectives of the office.[2]

7. *The Petroleum Industry.* Any large petroleum firm has crude oil from several sources that must be transported to one of several refineries where it is made into a variety of products, each of which must be distributed for sale. The products are jointly produced in a cracking process that can be manipulated, within limits, to vary the mix of outputs. Linear programming can be used to determine the optimum mix of products and the best method of allocating crude oil from various sources to the several refineries and of distributing the final products for sale. Thus, the petroleum industry represents a case in which linear programming can be used at virtually every stage of the production process.

8. *Long-Range Capacity Planning.* As energy-related problems become increasingly severe, there is even greater need for good long-range

---

[1]See, for example, Dan Arramovich, Thomas Cook, Gary Langston, Frank Sutherland, "A Decision Support System for Fleet Management: A Linear Programming Approach," *Interfaces,* June 1982, pp. 1–9.

[2]See, for example, Edward L. Summers, "The Audit Staff Assignment Problem: A Linear Programming Analysis," *The Accounting Review,* July 1972, pp. 443–449.

planning models. Such models must be capable of incorporating demand projections for future years with information on operating and investment costs. John R. McNamara has developed a linear programming capacity planning model for electric utilities to minimize the costs of satisfying projected demands. Some of the advantages of the model being used at the time this study was reported were stated as follows: "The model is user oriented and compatible with the form of the data commonly used by planning departments of the electric utilities. It should be stressed that the model is very easy to use and solutions are obtained very quickly."[3]

These eight examples illustrate the broad range of problems for which linear programming models may be useful.[4] In many applications, more complex variations of the basic model presented in this chapter are necessary. However, the more complex models are built on the foundation of the linear programming technique presented below.

8.2 REQUIREMENTS OF A LINEAR PROGRAMMING PROBLEM

While a great variety of problem situations can be analyzed using linear programming, certain requirements or assumptions must be fulfilled. First, an explicit *objective* that a firm's management wants to maximize or minimize must be involved. Multiple objectives can be incorporated in the analysis,[5] but it is necessary that all objectives be stated in a concrete operational form.

Second, alternatives must be available to the firm. If there are no alternatives, there is no decision: the firm is faced with a single course of action. For example, if only one advertising medium is available, the firm need not allocate funds among media; if a product can be produced by only one process, no decision must be made regarding which process to use; and so on.

Third, optimization of the objective function must be subject to some type of *restriction*. Such restrictions may be related to limited supply of resources (materials, time, money, etc.), capacity of a firm's plant, legal

---

[3]John R. McNamara, "A Linear Programming Model for Long-Range Capacity Planning in an Electric Utility," *Journal of Economics and Business*, Spring/Summer 1976, pp. 227–235 (quote from pp. 233–234).

[4]Readers may find it interesting to consult *Business Periodicals Index* under the linear programming heading to find reference to current applications of this technique. For a bibliography of linear programming applications, see P. G. Moore, S. D. Hodges, eds., *Programming for Optimal Decisions* (Baltimore: Penguin Books, 1970).

[5]In solving a linear programming problem, we must use a single objective function. Multiple objectives can often be combined to form a single, comprehensive objective function. Alternatively, all but one of the objectives may be stated as a constraint. For example, the objective that an advertising campaign reaches 20 percent of the male population could be set up as a constraint on the objective to minimize advertising cost.

considerations, contractual agreements, marketing quotas, or anything else that may impinge on the firm's attempt to optimize its objective. In linear programming, these restrictions are called *constraints*.

Fourth, the firm's objective and the firm's constraints must be able to be represented by linear mathematical equations or inequalities. Fortunately, many business and economic relationships are linear or close to linear in the relevant range of activity.

The use of inequalities is less familiar to most students than the use of equations, and it is the use of inequalities that distinguishes linear programming from the type of calculus optimization (minimizing and maximizing) demonstrated in Chapter 3. How do inequalities differ from equations? Equations are specific statements in which the left-hand expression is mathematically identical to the right-hand expression. For example,

$$12 = 8 + 4$$

or

$$12 = 8 + X$$

Inequalities, on the other hand, are not so specific and provide only the information that one expression is either larger or smaller than another. Many business situations require the use of inequalities. For example, a company's management desires to spend *not more than* $120. Thus,

$$\text{Costs} \leq \$120$$

The sign $\leq$ means "is equal to or less than." Costs in this case must either be equal to or less than $120. While most resource limitations in linear programming are expressed as inequalities, some are represented by equations.

8.3 FORMULATING THE LINEAR PROGRAMMING PROBLEM

Let us consider a production problem and evaluate how each of the requirements is related to that problem. The Lumin Company is a small manufacturer of specialty lamps. Its product line consists of two lamps, both made out of a bronze sculpture. The standard lamp is less intricate than the deluxe model but is polished to a high gloss. The sculpture for the deluxe model is more complex, with many more folds and undulations in the metal. Only the high points are polished on the deluxe lamps.

The casting is done on two machines, each of which provides 8 hours of usable time each day. The polishing is done by hand, and 12 hours of labor are available each day for this purpose. Each standard lamp takes 1 hour to cast and 2 hours to polish, while each deluxe lamp requires twice as much casting time but only two-thirds as much polishing time. The profit contribution is $20 per unit for standard lamps and $30 per unit for deluxe lamps. The profit contribution is equal to price minus average variable cost.

For this problem, the *objective function* may be explicitly stated as follows: *Lumin Company management wants to maximize profit from the sale of standard and/or deluxe lamps.* As long as the $20 and $30 contribution margins do not change with the number of lamps produced, this objective is linear. Each additional standard lamp contributes $20 to profit, and each additional deluxe lamp contributes $30 to profit. Clearly, management has alternatives: it can seek to make a profit by producing only standard lamps, only deluxe lamps, or some of each. Given the objective stated above, Lumin Company management should select the alternative that yields the greatest profit.

In this problem, the firm is restricted, or constrained, in its quest for maximum profits by the limited time available for casting and polishing the lamps. The constraints are linear because the time necessary to cast or polish a given lamp is unchanged no matter how many lamps are produced.

The process of formulating the linear programming problem involves transforming the descriptive information about the situation into mathematical statements. This phase of the analysis is often the most difficult. It is not always easy to take a given problem situation and to express the relationships involved in the form of mathematical functions.

One usually begins by constructing the objective function. For the Lumin Company, this is a relatively simple task. If we let X_1 represent the number of standard lamps produced and X_2 represent the number of deluxe lamps produced, then the total profit contribution equals $20X_1 + 30X_2$. Letting Z represent the total profit contribution, we get the objective function:

Maximize: $Z = 20X_1 + 30X_2$ (objective function)

where 20 and 30 are the contribution margins for standard and deluxe lamps, respectively.

The next step in formulating the linear programming problem is to specify the constraints. This is most easily accomplished by first summarizing what is known about the relationships involved in the problem. This can be done by answering the following questions: (1) Which activities or phenomena limit the objective function? and (2) How are the variables in the objective function related to these restrictions? Let us see how these questions are answered for the Lumin company.

In answer to the first question, the objective function is limited by two factors: 12 hours of polishing time and 16 hours of casting time are available each day. The second question can be answered by recalling that each standard lamp (X_1) requires 1 hour of casting time and 2 hours of polishing time. Furthermore, from the general presentation of the Lumin case given above, we know that each deluxe lamp (X_2) requires 2 hours of casting time and 40 minutes (two-thirds of an hour) of polishing time.

It is often helpful to summarize such information in a table such as Table 8.1. This table is relatively simple because the Lumin Company problem is not complex. Other problems may involve more complicated data tables than those used in this chapter, but the purpose here is to explain the method of linear programming without getting involved in vast amounts of computational detail.

TABLE 8.1 **Time Requirements for the Production of Standard and Deluxe Lamps**

Type of Lamp	Hours Required per Lamp for: Polishing	Casting
Standard (X_1)	2	1
Deluxe (X_2)	$\frac{2}{3}$	2
Total hours available	12	16

From Table 8.1, the constraint functions can be readily constructed. We see that 1 hour times the number of standard lamps produced plus 2 hours times the number of deluxe lamps produced must not exceed the 16 total casting hours available. That is,

$$X_1 + 2X_2 \leqslant 16$$

Furthermore, 2 hours times the number of standard lamps plus two-thirds hour times the number of deluxe lamps must not be greater than the 12 total polishing hours available. That is,

$$2X_1 + \tfrac{2}{3}X_2 \leqslant 12$$

The complete linear programming problem can then be stated as follows:

Maximize: $Z = 20X_1 + 30X_2$ (objective function)
Subject to: $X_1 + 2X_2 \leqslant 16$ (casting constraint on output)
                    $2X_1 + \tfrac{2}{3}X_2 \leqslant 12$ (polishing constraint on output)
                            $X_1, X_2 \geqslant 0$ (nonnegativity constraint)

The final constraint $(X_1, X_2 \geqslant 0)$ is called a nonnegativity constraint. In most economic situations, it would make little sense to talk about producing a negative standard lamp (X_1) or a negative deluxe lamp (X_2).

In this form, the problem is ready to be solved. If there are only two variables, as in this case, the problem can be solved by a simple graphic procedure. However, most problems have more variables and must be analyzed using another method.

8.4 THE ECONOMIC ASSUMPTIONS

It is important to note at this point the economic assumptions embodied in linear programming problems. For example, we have assumed that the

Lumin Company may be represented by a series of linear relationships involving decision variables: standard lamps and deluxe lamps. With regard to resource inputs, such as casting and polishing, this amounts to assuming that the prices of these resources to the firm are constant over some relevant range of production. This implies that management may purchase as much of these resources as it likes and that the per unit cost will remain unchanged. This assumption rules out quantity discounts.

A second assumption embedded in the Lumin Company model, and in every linear programming model, is that of constant returns to scale in production. Thus, if the Lumin Company were to double its use of casting and polishing (the resources), we would expect a doubling of the quantity of output.

The final economic assumption embedded in the model is that of constant profit contributions for each of the two final products, standard and deluxe lamps. This assumption is found in the objective function when we specify that Lumin Company earns a $20 profit contribution for each standard lamp (the coefficient of X_1 in the objective function) and earns a $30 profit contribution for each deluxe lamp (the coefficient of X_2 in the objective function). If any of these assumptions is not true, the linear programming model presented for the Lumin Company will result in solutions that are not necessarily optimal.

8.5   GRAPHIC SOLUTIONS: MAXIMIZATION

This section evaluates the production problem discussed above using the graphic method of solving linear programming problems. This approach is limited to problems that have two variables and therefore is rarely useful in practical applications. However, this solution does provide an excellent foundation for understanding more complex linear programming problems.

Graphing the Constraints

Having already formulated our product mix problem, we have all the necessary information represented in the form of an objective function and a set of constraints. There are two decision variables in these functions: standard lamps (X_1) and deluxe lamps (X_2). These variables are measured along the vertical and horizontal axes of Figure 8.1. The constraints are represented graphically as follows: (1) by graphing the line that represents the linear equality form of each constraint, and (2) by indicating the direction of the inequality with arrows.

For our production problem, the constraints are

Casting: $X_1 + 2X_2 \leq 16$ (inequality form)
$X_1 + 2X_2 = 16$ (equality form)
Polishing: $2X_1 + \frac{2}{3}X_2 \leq 12$ (inequality form)
$2X_1 + \frac{2}{3}X_2 = 12$ (equality form)

These constraints are illustrated in Figure 8.1. The entire triangle *OBD* (perimeter and interior) specifies possible combinations of standard and deluxe lamps that can be produced without violating the constraint imposed only by the amount of casting time available. The entire triangle *OAE* (perimeter and interior) specifies combinations that satisfy only the polishing constraint.

The area common to both these two triangles (*OBD* and *OAE*) forms a set of points that satisfies both of the restrictions imposed on the Lumin Company. In Figure 8.1, the area common to both triangles is represented by the shaded polyhedron *OACD*. That is, any combination of standard and deluxe lamps that lies either inside *OACD* or on the perimeter of *OACD* satisfies both the casting and polishing constraints. Any other point (e.g., *B*, *E*, or *F*) violates one or both of the constraints and thus does not represent a possible level of production. For this reason, the points in and on the perimeter of *OACD* are called *feasible solutions* to the linear programming

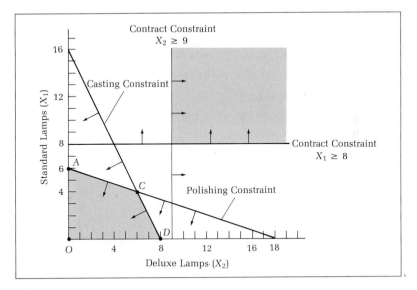

FIGURE 8.1 **Graphic Representation of Constraints.** The casting constraint is represented by the triangle *OBD*, while the polishing constraint is represented by the triangle *OAE*. The set of feasible solutions is the area common to both constraints, or *OACD*, including interior and perimeter points.

problem. While defining the set of feasible solutions greatly reduces the number of solution points, it does not solve the problem.

Given that the goal is to maximize or minimize some objective function, the viable alternatives can be even more significantly reduced. The *fundamental theorem of linear programming* states that the objective function is optimized at an extreme point of the convex set of feasible solutions. This means that only the corner points of the polyhedron *OACD* need be evaluated to determine the maximum profit for the Lumin Company. That is, the objective function is maximized at either *O*, *A*, *C*, or *D*.[6] The reason why the optimal solution must occur at a corner will become apparent shortly, when we discuss Figure 8.2.

Point *C* is called the *optimal basic feasible solution*, since it is the basic feasible solution for which the objective function is optimized (try substituting in the objective function the values of X_1 and X_2 at each corner; corner *C* yields the highest profit contribution). We must conclude that if the Lumin Company management wishes to maximize the profit from the sale of standard and deluxe lamps, they should allocate the casting and polishing time so that four standard lamps and six deluxe lamps are produced.

Graphing the Objective Function

Figure 8.2 is identical to Figure 8.1 except that three isoprofit lines have been added.[7] An isoprofit line is a graphic representation of all possible combinations of the two products that yield the same level of profit contribution. These combinations are represented by dotted lines in Figure 8.2. The general form of each isoprofit line is

$$Z = 20X_1 + 30X_2$$

This, of course, is the objective function specified earlier for the Lumin Company.

All combinations of X_1 and X_2 along the isoprofit line *I* yield a total profit contribution of $60. For example, if $X_1 = 3$ and $X_2 = 0$, the total profit contribution is 60, and if $X_1 = 0$ and $X_2 = 2$, it is also 60. Along I_2, the total profit contribution equals $260 ($Z = 260$), and I_3 identifies combinations of output that yield a total profit contribution of $340 ($Z = 340$).

---

[6]The values of X_1 and X_2 for points *O*, *A*, and *D* can be determined easily by inspection of the graph in Figure 8.1. For point *C* the values of X_1 and X_2 may be read from the respective axes of that graph, or they may be found by simultaneously solving the two constraint equations, which intersect at *C* ($X_1 + 2X_2 = 16$ and $2X_1 + 2/3X_2 = 12$), for the values of X_1 and X_2 that satisfy both constraints in their equality form.

[7]These lines are called isoprofit lines because the objective function is to maximize profit. If the objective was to maximize advertising exposure, isoexposure functions would be graphed. If the objective was to maximize sales, isosales functions would be appropriate, and so on.

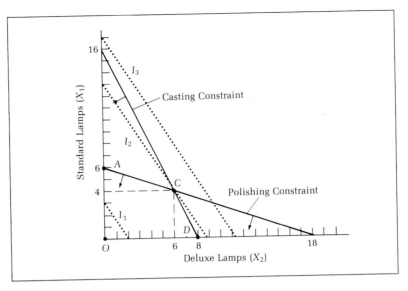

FIGURE 8.2   **Isoprofit Lines.**   The total profit contribution objective function can be represented by the equation

$$Z = 20X_1 + 30X_2$$

For $Z = 60$, $Z = 260$, and $Z = 340$, the isoprofit lines are I_1, I_2, and I_3, respectively. Note that all isoprofit lines have the same slope.

From Figure 8.2, we can observe three important characteristics of the isoprofit functions: (1) they all have the same slope, that is, they are parallel;[8] (2) the farther an isoprofit function is from the origin, the greater the profit; and (3) an infinite number of isoprofit functions could be drawn, one for each level of profit (of course, many are not meaningful, since they lie outside the set of feasible solutions). To determine the optimal basic feasible solution to the linear programming problem, we can draw one isoprofit function, such as I_1, and then "slide" the line outward parallel to I_1 until the isoprofit function is found, which is as far from the origin as possible, while still having at least one point in common with the set of feasible solutions. That point is the optimal basic feasible solution to the linear programming problem.

Determining the Maximum from the Graph

In the present example, we see that I_2 is the isoprofit function that is farthest from the origin while still having one point in common with the set of

---

[8]The slope is determined by solving the objective function Z for the variable measures along the vertical axis. In this case, $Z = 20X_1 + 30X_2$, thus $X_1 = Z/20 - (30/20)X_2$. The slope of isoprofit functions is therefore equal to $(-30/20)$, or -1.5.

feasible solutions. The point C in Figure 8.2 (corresponding to $X_1 = 4$, $X_2 = 6$) is the common point between I_2 and the feasible solutions. Therefore, the optimal basic feasible solution to this product mix problem is to produce four standard lamps and six deluxe lamps, yielding a profit contribution of $260.

Note that an optimal basic feasible solution always occurs at a corner if this procedure is followed.[9] The observation that the optimal basic feasible solution is always found at a corner provides a clue as to how a computer finds an optimal solution. Using a routine called the *simplex method*, the computer examines the corners of the feasible region to locate the optimal point (this simplex method is explained in detail in the appendix to this chapter). Because of the computer's ability to perform the "corner examination" so rapidly, the solution of linear programming problems with a computer software package has become routine. The actual setup or formulation of the problem, however, still requires the knowledge of what economic assumptions are being made and whether those assumptions apply in a particular case, and an ability to interpret the output from a software package.

An alternative method of obtaining the optimal basic feasible solution by hand is to check for a maximum at each of the corners of the feasible space. We can evaluate each of the four basic feasible solutions to determine the one that generates the greatest profit as follows:

1. Point O: $X_1 = 0$, and $X_2 = 0$
   therefore,
   $$Z = (20 \times 0) + (30 \times 0) = 0$$

2. Point A: $X_1 = 6$, and $X_2 = 0$
   $$Z = (20 \times 6) + (30 \times 0) = 120$$

3. Point C: $X_1 = 4$, and $X_2 = 6$
   $$Z = (20 \times 4) + (30 \times 6) = 260$$

4. Point D: $X_1 = 0$, and $X_2 = 8$
   $$Z = (20 \times 0) + (30 \times 8) = 240$$

Again, we see that the optimal solution is to produce four standard lamps and six deluxe lamps, yielding a total profit contribution of $260.

8.6   GRAPHIC SOLUTIONS: MINIMIZATION

Let us assume that a problem has been formulated and that we have the following objective function and constraints:

---

[9] It is possible that two extreme points would give the same optimum value for an objective function. In such a case, either of the extreme points or any point on a straight line connecting the points will optimize the objective function at precisely the same value of Z. In actual practice, this is a rare situation.

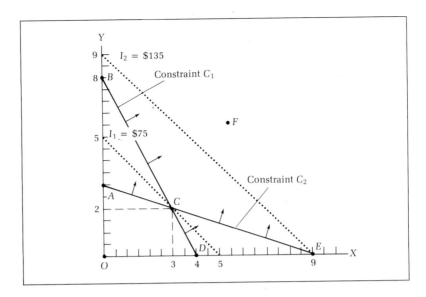

FIGURE 8.3   **Isocost Lines for a Minimization Problem.** Isocost line I_1 ($75) and isocost line I_2 ($135) are defined by the variable cost function $VC = 15X = 15Y$. The constraints in this problem are greater than or equal to constraints as indicated by the arrows pointing upward from the two constraints. The feasible solution space is the area above or on the line BCE, the vertical axis beyond B, and the horizontal axis beyond E. I_1 is the lowest (minimum) isocost line that has a point in common with the feasible solution space.

Minimize: $VC = 15X + 15Y$
Subject to: C_1: $2X + Y \geqslant 8$ (state-imposed production constraint)
 C_2: $X + 3Y \geqslant 9$ (federally imposed production constraint)
 $X, Y \geqslant 0$

The constraints C_1 and C_2 are graphed in Figure 8.3, along with two isocost functions (we will assume that the objective function, VC, represents the variable cost of producing X and Y). The constraints represent the legal limitations imposed by two different government agencies, one state and one federal, on the combinations of products that must be made available. The isocost line I_1 illustrates combinations of X and Y that result in a variable cost of $75, while I_2 represents a variable cost of $135.[10]

---

[10]There are an infinite number of possible isocost lines, each representing combinations of X and Y that have a given (constant) variable cost — thus the term *isocost* meaning the same cost. The two dotted lines in Figure 8.3 represent two such lines.

Feasible solutions to this problem are found in the region bounded by the line BCE, the vertical axis beyond B, and the horizontal axis beyond E. Thus, in this case, F is a feasible solution, while A and D are not. The basic feasible solutions are again found at the corner points, B, C, and E. The variable costs (VC) at these points are \$120, \$75, and \$135, respectively. Point C (\$75 variable cost) is therefore the optimal basic feasible solution to this minimization problem. We can see in Figure 8.3 that I_1 is the lowest isocost function that has only one point in common with the set of feasible solutions. This common point is, of course, C, and the optimal basic feasible solution is to let $X = 3$ and $Y = 2$, with a minimum cost of \$75.

As with maximization problems, most practical linear programming problems involving minimization are usually solved by the nongraphic approach known as the simplex method and run on a computer.

8.7 SPECIAL CONSIDERATIONS IN LINEAR PROGRAMMING

Is it possible for a linear programming problem to fail to have an optimal basic feasible solution? Yes, this possibility may occur in one of two ways.

The first possibility in which there is no solution is called *infeasibility*. Infeasibility is the situation in which there is no area of feasible solutions that satisfies all the constraints. Figure 8.4 depicts the Lumin Company example with the addition of two constraints: (1) contracts entered into by the Lumin Company require the delivery of at least eight standard lamps (i.e., $X_1 \geq 8$), and (2) contracts also require the delivery of at least nine deluxe lamps (i.e., $X_2 \geq 9$). We can see from Figure 8.4 that no possible combination of standard and deluxe lamps satisfies all four constraints. The old feasible space of $OACD$ and the new contract-imposed feasible space in the upper right-hand corner are mutually exclusive. They have no point in common. In this case, then, there is no feasible solution to the problem. Unless additional casting and polishing time becomes available, the contract-imposed constraints cannot be met and a solution is infeasible.

A second possibility in which there is no solution is called *unboundedness*. In cases of unboundedness, we may assume that a mistake has been made in the formulation of the problem. Unboundedness refers to a situation in which the solution can be made infinitely large without violating any one of the constraints in the problem. In such a case, we would know that the problem setup was incorrect, since no situation could permit a truly infinitely large profit. Figure 8.5 shows the Lumin Company with only the contract-imposed constraints. With the problem stated in this manner, the area of feasible solutions is infinite. Isoprofit line I_4 can be shifted upward and to the right without bound, increasing profit at each shift. Profit may be as high as we want it. Isoprofit line I_4 may be followed by any number of higher isoprofit lines, such as I_5 and others representing yet higher profits.

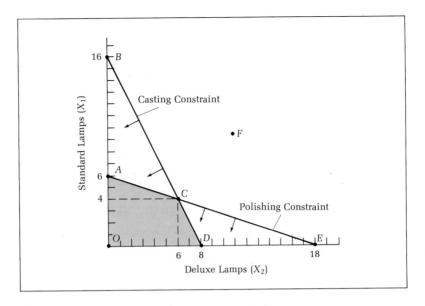

FIGURE 8.4   **Example of Infeasibility in Linear Programming.**   The two capacity constraints limit feasible solutions to the shaded area bounded by *OACD* and its perimeter. The two contract constraints limit feasible solutions to the shaded area in the upper right and its lower boundary lines ($X_1 = 8$ and $X_2 = 9$). Because the two shaded areas have no point in common, there is no feasible solution. No combination of X_1 and X_2 can simultaneously satisfy all four constraints.

Besides unfeasibility and unboundedness, a situation called *redundancy* sometimes occurs in linear programming. Any constraint that does not affect the size or shape of the feasible space is called a redundant constraint. Consider the contract constraint added to the original Lumin Company situation in Figure 8.6. The contract constraint specifies that Lumin Company may not produce more than 17 standard lamps (i.e., $X_1 \leq 17$). Such a contract may exist because of a patent licensing arrangement entered into by the Lumin Company.

In the original specification of the Lumin Company case, the greatest number of standard lamps that could be produced was 6. Since this number is already less than the limit of 17 in the new constraint, the contract constraint is redundant. The contract constraint may be removed from the problem, and the optimal solution would remain the same; removing the redundant constraint can save considerable computation time.

One final special consideration has already been mentioned but bears repeating. Consider Figure 8.2 again; in this figure, the isoprofit lines are lines I_1 through I_3. Each of these isoprofit lines has a slope identical to that of every other isoprofit line (i.e., they are all parallel to one another). But the isoprofit lines in this example are not parallel to either of the constraints

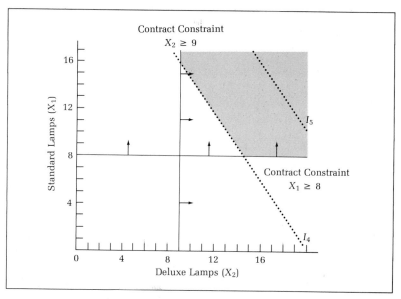

FIGURE 8.5   **An Unbounded Linear Programming Problem.**   In this graph, iso-profit lines I_4 and I_5 are both in the feasible space, so I_5 would be selected. But other isoprofit lines above I_5 would also exist in this limitless feasible space, bounded only at the lower end by the two constraints.

(i.e., the isoprofit lines do not have the same slope as either constraint). Let us see what the solution would be if the isoprofit lines were exactly parallel to the casting constraint. In this rare case, an optimal solution would still occur at a corner of the feasible space; in fact, either corner point C (6, 4) or corner point D (8, 0) would be optimal solutions. In addition to these specific points, any point on the casting constraint between C and D would be an optimal solution as well. Every one of these points would result in an identical value of the objective function. Thus, more than one optimal solution is possible, but not common, in practice.

8.8   DUAL AND SHADOW PRICES

The solution to every linear programming problem presents us with additional valuable information. Often, we would like to know the value of relaxing one of the constraints. How much extra profit would be generated if one of the constraints was relaxed by one unit? We could rewrite that single constraint and resolve the problem, but more often we resort to solving the *dual*.

The dual is a linear programming problem associated with the original problem. The original problem, by convention, is called the *primal*. The

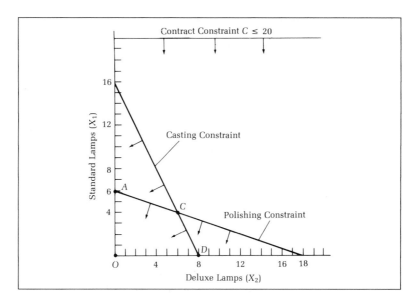

FIGURE 8.6   **Illustration of a Redundant Constraint.**   Given that the casting and polishing constraints combine to limit the feasible space to the area bounded by $OACD$, adding the constraint that the number of standard lamps produced must be no more than 17 (i.e., $X_1 \leq 17$) does not affect the solution. It is a redundant constraint.

concept of duality is essentially mathematical, but it has some important economic interpretations as well.

We can think of every linear programming maximizing problem as having a doppelgänger, or corresponding, dual that is a minimizing problem; likewise, every linear programming minimization problem has a dual that is a maximization problem. Consider the Lumin Company problem solved earlier in the chapter; it was a maximization problem, or a primal:

Maximize:	$Z = 20X_1 + 30X_2$	(objective function)
Subject to:	$X_1 + 2X_2 \leq 16$	(casting constraint)
	$2X_1 + \frac{2}{3}X_2 \leq 12$	(polishing constraint)
	$X_1, X_2 \geq 0$	(nonnegativity constraint)

Assume for a moment that you are working late and have just completed the formulation of the problem above. You decide to take a break before solving the problem, which is written on a sheet of paper lying in the middle of your desk. You leave the room to get a snack. At just that moment, your roommate enters the room and notices the problem lying on the desk. You roommate knows little about linear programming and decides to play a joke on you. He or she proceeds to "turn around" everything in the problem, writing the altered problem on a new sheet of paper and leaving it for you to solve. The hope is that you will return, notice nothing, solve the altered problem, hand it in the next day, and make a fool of yourself by having nothing at all correct in the problem.

You return, notice nothing, solve the altered problem, turn it in the next day, and, much to the dismay of your roommate, get a perfect grade for having the correct value of the objective function! How could such a thing be possible? Well, if your roommate had succeeded in turning the primal linear programming maximization problem into the dual linear programming minimization problem, the answer (optimal value of the objective function) would be identical.

Consider the *altered* Lumin Company problem, or the dual:

Minimize: $Q = 16A + 12B$ (objective function)
Subject to: $1A + 2B \geqslant 20$ (first constraint)
$2A + \frac{2}{3}B \geqslant 30$ (second constraint)
$A, B \geqslant 0$ (nonnegativity constraint)

This dual is actually the mathematical equivalent of the primal; we are just writing the problem in two different formats in order to gain some economic insight into the problem. Note how the problem changed. It is now a minimization problem; the values on the right-hand side of the primal constraints are the coefficients of the dual objective function; the coefficients of the primal objective function are the values on the right-hand side of the dual constraints; the coefficients of the first primal constraint are now the first column of the dual constraint coefficient matrix; and the coefficients of the second primal constraint are now the second column of dual constraint coefficient matrix. The diagram below may help you see this relationship between the constraint coefficients of the primal and the dual (the numbers used refer to the Lumin problem described above):

Primal constraint coefficients:

1	2

2	$\frac{2}{3}$

Dual constraint coefficients:

1
2

2
$\frac{2}{3}$

The constraints of the dual are *greater than or equal tos* and those of the primal are *less than or equal tos*. Only the nonnegativity constraint remains unchanged (recall that, in economics, a negative value of most variables is nonsense).

8.9   SHADOW PRICES

You may have noted in the previous section that the names of variables change in the dual. The variables are called A and B, rather than X_1 and X_2, as in the primal. The names given to A and B by economists are *shadow prices*. The values of these variables in the optimal solution of the dual have an interesting economic meaning. They are the *imputed values* of the scarce resources they represent; more precisely, they are the value to the firm, in dollars, of one extra unit of that input.

Were you to solve the dual problem, the value of the objective function would be 260, the same answer we arrived at for the optimal value of the primal objective function.

The interpretation of the dual variables depends on the statement of the original problem, but in the Lumin Company case the value of A would be the shadow price of casting. The value of A would then be the dollar value of one more unit of casting time to the Lumin Company. The value of B in the dual of the Lumin Company problem would be the dollar value to the firm of one additional unit of polishing time. The actual solution to the dual yields

$$Q = 260$$
$$A = 14$$
$$B = 3$$

Thus, the value of one extra unit of casting time is $14, while the value of one extra unit of polishing time is $3. In order to verify that these shadow prices are correct, solve the original Lumin Company problem with one small variation: add one more unit of casting time:

Maximize: $Z = 20X_1 + 30X_2$ (objective function)
$X_1 + 2X_2 \leqslant 17$ (casting constraint)
$2X_1 + \frac{2}{3}X_2 \leqslant 12$ (polishing constraint)
$X_1, X_2 \geqslant 0$ (nonnegativity constraint)

The optimal Z value is $274, or $14 more than the value when only 16 units of casting time were available (X_1 is 3.8, and X_2 is 6.6).

Now add one more unit of polishing time to the original problem, leaving the casting time constrained to 16:

Maximize: $Z = 20X_1 + 30X_2$ (objective function)
$X_1 + 2X_2 \leqslant 16$ (casting constraint)
$2X_1 + \frac{2}{3}X_2 \leqslant 13$ (polishing constraint)
$X_1, X_2 \geqslant 0$ (nonnegativity constraint)

The optimal value of Z is now $263, or $3 more than the value when only 12 units of polishing time were available (X_1 is 4.6, and X_2 is 5.7).

The shadow price, then, tells us what it would be worth to the firm to relax a particular constraint by one unit. If the shadow price equals $0 for some resource, this means the input is not being fully used up (i.e., some of that resource is left over). In such a case, it would make little sense for the firm to buy more of the resource, since it already has too much. Buying extra units of a resource with a $0 shadow price adds nothing to profit.

The shadow price should be compared to the market price of the resource when the firm makes decisions. If the market price of an extra unit of casting time is $10, Lumin Company would be wise to purchase at least one unit at $10, which would increase its profit by $14, which is the shadow price. How many units of casting should the company purchase at $10? A shadow price of $14 does not mean that management can purchase as many extra casting units as they desire and that each extra unit will increase profit by $14. There is a finite limit to the usefulness of a shadow price. A shadow price is valid only until another binding constraint comes into play; that is, the shadow price is the marginal value to the firm of a particular resource, assuming the availability of other resources with which to combine it as stated in the problem formulation. As a given resource is actually combined with other resources, sooner or later one of the other resources becomes depleted, thus lowering the shadow price of the given resource. Shadow prices, then, are constant, not for *any* amount of a given resource, but only over some finite range.

8.10 APPLICATIONS: ALLOCATING ADVERTISING EXPENDITURES

Before leaving our general discussion of linear programming, let us look at some representative applications.[11] We will start with the use of linear programming to allocate advertising expenditures. The first situation involves the allocation of $25,000 in advertising for the Pennsylvania Transformer Division of McGraw-Edison.

The company's transformers were sold in past years primarily to plants and large institutions, where an engineer usually made the purchase decision. The objective was to reach as many of these engineers as possible through 10 available magazines (other types of communications media could be included as the situation required). Let P_i represent the number of engineers reached by medium i per dollar spent on that medium and X_i represent the number of dollars allocated to medium i. The objective function is, then,

$$\text{Maximize:} \quad E = P_1 X_1 + P_2 X_2 + \cdots + P_{10} X_{10}$$

The following table represents the determination of each P_i for the 10 available media:

[11]This section is based on James F. Engel and Martin R. Warshaw, "Allocating Advertising Dollars by Linear Programming," *Journal of Advertising Research*, September 1964, pp. 42–48.

Magazine	Engineers Reached ÷ Cost per Ad (C_i)	Engineers Reached per Dollar (P_i)
1. *Consulting Engineer*	0/475	$P_1 = 0$
2. *Electrical Construction*	12,000/792	$P_2 = 15.15$
3. *Electrical World*	24,000/730	$P_3 = 32.87$
4. *Power*	44,000/890	$P_4 = 49.44$
5. *Plant Engineering*	52,000/918	$P_5 = 56.65$
6. *Electrical West*	8,000/456	$P_6 = 17.54$
7. *Electrified Industry*	44,000/756	$P_7 = 58.20$
8. *Public Power*	0/700	$P_8 = 0$
9. *Electric Light & Power*	16,000/680	$P_9 = 23.53$
10. *Transmission & Distribution*	23,000/575	$P_{10} = 40.00$

These values for $P_1, P_2, \ldots, P_{10}$ can be inserted in the objective function for the solution using a computerized linear programming algorithm.

The constraints in this case were that the total expenditures (ΣX_i) could not exceed \$25,000 and that no more could be spent on any one medium than would permit advertising in that medium in each of 12 issues throuogut the year (i.e., $X_i \le 12C_i$). These constraints may be summarized as

$$X_1 + X_2 + \cdots + X_{10} \le 25,000$$

$X_1 \le 5700$	$X_6 \le 5472$
$X_2 \le 9504$	$X_7 \le 9072$
$X_3 \le 8760$	$X_8 \le 8400$
$X_4 \le 10,680$	$X_9 \le 8160$
$X_5 \le 11,016$	$X_{10} \le 6900$

The simplex solution gave the following optimal solution:

$$X_4 = \$4912 \quad \text{(Power)}$$
$$X_5 = \$11,016 \quad \text{(Plant Engineering)}$$
$$X_7 = \$9072 \quad \text{(Electrified Industries)}$$

In this simple case, we would likely have at least selected the correct media just by looking at the P_i values and with some manipulation could well have found the optimal solution. However, this problem does not contain some refinements that would provide a more thorough analysis.

Consider that all media are not equally effective in achieving the desired objective. For example, we might place a greater degree of confidence in an advertisement for business calculators appearing in *Business Week* than for the same ad appearing in a movie magazine. Engel and Warshaw suggest using an "effectiveness rating" to adjust for such differences. Furthermore, the mix of buyers seeing each medium may differ, and, if so, an "audience profile match" may be developed to adjust for such differentials.

A more complex problem including such adjustments may be illustrated by a case involving the expenditure of \$1 million on advertising women's electric razors in the following consumer magazines:

Magazine	Amount to Spend on Ads for each Magazine
1. Cosmopolitan	X_1
2. Mademoiselle	X_2
3. Family Circle	X_3
4. Good Housekeeping	X_4
5. McCall's	X_5
6. Modern Romances	X_6
7. Modern Screen	X_7
8. Motion Picture	X_8
9. True Confessions	X_9
10. Woman's Day	X_{10}
11. Seventeen	X_{11}
12. Ladies' Home Journal	X_{12}

In developing a weighting scheme based on effectiveness and matching of audiences with media, it was first determined that the primary market was composed of white women aged 18 to 44 years, living in metropolitan areas, and having incomes of $7000 or more (remember that this and other dollar measures are more than 10 years old and represent much greater purchasing power than the same dollar amounts would command today). A rating scale of 0 to 1.0 was developed indicating which of these characteristics was most important and the weight to be attached to it. Then each medium was evaluated on each of these four dimensions and on the proportion of its readers who purchased an electric razor in the previous 12 months. Using this information and the rating scale, an overall effectiveness rating was developed for each medium.

Multiplying the total audience reached by each magazine by this rating factor gave the "effective audience" for each. This figure divided by the cost per ad yielded the "effective readings per dollar spent," which are the coefficients of the objective function (comparable to the P_i values of the simpler case). The objective function so developed was

$$\text{Maximize: } E = 158X_1 + 263X_2 + 106X_3 + 108X_4 + 65X_5 + 176X_6 + 285X_7 + 86X_8 + 120X_9 + 51X_{10} + 190X_{11} + 101X_{12}$$

In addition to the budget constraint ($\Sigma X_i \leq \$1$ million) there is the same type of maximum insertion constraint for each magazine as in the simple example, except that management set an insertion limit of 7 on *Mademoiselle* and a limit of 2 on *Ladies' Home Journal*. These constraints are then expressed as

$$X_1 \leq 58{,}080 \qquad X_7 \leq 52{,}380$$
$$X_2 \leq 30{,}075 \ (7) \qquad X_8 \leq 53{,}580$$

$$X_3 \leqslant 349,000 \qquad X_9 \leqslant 57,960$$

$$X_4 \leqslant 288,000 \qquad X_{10} \leqslant 333,000$$

$$X_5 \leqslant 407,400 \qquad X_{11} \leqslant 72,360$$

$$X_6 \leqslant 52,380 \qquad X_{12} \leqslant 81,200 \; (2)$$

In addition, management set minimum levels of expenditures on the following magazines, and these constraints must be added:

Mademoiselle	$X_2 \geqslant 13,275$
Family Circle	$X_3 \geqslant 58,166$
McCall's	$X_5 \geqslant 33,950$
Woman's Day	$X_{10} \geqslant 27,750$

Also, management decided that no more than \$280,000 should be allocated to *Family Circle* (X_3), *True Confessions* (X_9), *Woman's Day* (X_{10}), and *Ladies' Home Journal* (X_{12}) combined and that a total of exactly \$85,870 should be spent on *Cosmpolitan* (X_1) and *Motion Picture* (X_8) combined. Thus, we have two additional constraints:

$$X_3 + X_9 + X_{10} + X_{12} \leqslant 280,000$$
$$X_1 + X_8 = 85,870$$

This case is clearly more complex than the McGraw-Edison problem, and it is unlikely that an individual (or staff) would correctly identify the optimal solution in any reasonable period of time. The computer solution was

Cosmopolitan	X_1 =	\$ 58,080
Mademoiselle	X_2 =	30,075
Family Circle	X_3 =	194,290
Good Housekeeping	X_4 =	288,000
McCall's	X_5 =	180,484
Modern Romances	X_6 =	52,380
Modern Screen	X_7 =	52,380
Motion Picture	X_8 =	27,790
True Confessions	X_9 =	57,960
Woman's Day	X_{10} =	27,750
Seventeen	X_{11} =	72,360
Ladies' Home Journal	X_{12} =	0

The alert reader will notice that this totals $1,041,549, which exceeds the budget constraint. This is because the magazines offer volume discounts and, based on the initial solution, those discounts amounted to $41,549. That money was allocated to *McCall's* based on the sensitivity analysis accompanying the simplex solution (see the appendix to this chapter) and is included in the $180,484 given above for X_5.

8.11   LINEAR PROGRAMMING APPLICATIONS IN PRODUCTION ANALYSIS

In the discussion of production in Chapter 7, we assumed that inputs could be substituted for one another in a continuous manner. This gave rise to nice, smooth isoquant curves. While this is fine for some types of productive activity, it may not be adequate for other situations, in which the technology limits production to certain combinations of inputs. As a consequence of such limitations, isoquants are not smooth functions, and the production functions are not continuous. The Lagrangian method of optimization is no longer appropriate. But linear programming can be applied to many such cases.

Let us consider a simple case. Suppose that a product is produced in such a way that each unit of output requires 0.3 unit of labor input (L) and 0.3 unit of capital input (K). Isoquants representing 10, 20, and 30 units of output are graphed in Figure 8.7. At point A, 10 units of output are produced using 3 units of labor and 3 units of capital. Point B represents 20 units of output (using $6L$ and $6K$), and point C represents 30 units of output (from $9L$ and $9K$). Note that with 3 units of labor input, the isoquant, $Q(10)$, is vertical above point A, because additional capital will not increase output unless labor is increased as well. In this case, labor and capital cannot be substituted for one another in production, and the isoquants are rectangular. Production requires that the inputs be combined in fixed proportions: $0.3L$ and $0.3K$ per unit of output.

The ray connecting A, B, and C illustrates this production *process*. The idea of a process is basic to many production situations and to the application of linear programming to such problems. A process is a method or technique of combining inputs to produce a product. The process defines the rate of use of each input necessary to produce a unit of output by that technique. Each process can be described by a set of technical coefficients $(a_1, a_2, \ldots, a_m)$ that represent the amount of each of the m inputs necessary to produce one unit of output by that process.

In many situations, firms have more than one available process (although, at least in the short run, the number of processes is finite). Each process can be represented by a ray through the input space, and a variable, X_i, can represent the number of units of output produced by each process. Suppose that, in addition to the process depicted in Figure 8.7, our output

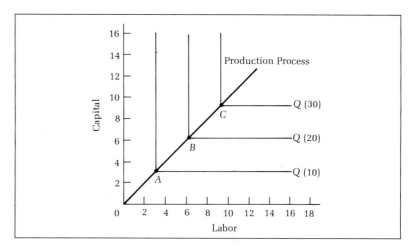

FIGURE 8.7 **A Single Production Process.** These isoquants represent 10, 20, and 30 units of output that must be produced using a process that requires 0.3 unit of labor and 0.3 unit of capital per unit of product. The ray connecting A, B, and C represents the production process.

could be produced by two additional processes: in one, 0.2 unit of labor and 0.4 unit of capital are necessary to produce each unit of output; in the other, 0.6 unit of labor and 0.2 unit of capital are necessary per unit of output. The technical coefficients for each of these processes are summarized in Table 8.2. These three processes are graphed in Figure 8.8. (Process 2 corresponds to the process depicted in Figure 8.7.)

TABLE 8.2 **Technical Coefficients of Three Production Processes**

	Process 1	Process 2	Process 3
Labor required per unit of output	0.2	0.3	0.6
Capital required per unit of output	0.4	0.3	0.2

We shall define the number of units of output produced with process 1 as X_1, the number of units produced with process 2 as X_2, and the number of units produced with process 3 as X_3. If we want to produce $Q = 10$ units of output with process 1 ($X_1 = 10$), we have to use $2L$ and $4K$. This is point A in Figure 8.8. Using process 2 to produce 10 units ($X_2 = 10$), we use $3L$ and $3K$ at point A'. The same output could be produced at A'', using process 3 ($X_3 = 10$). The points labeled B, B', and B'' represent $X_1 = 20$, $X_2 = 20$, and $X_3 = 20$, respectively, while C, C', and C'' indicate $X_1 = 30$, $X_2 = 30$, and $X_3 = 30$, respectively.

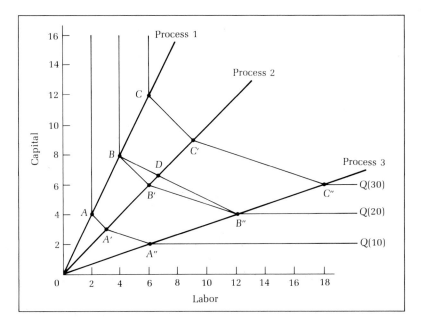

FIGURE 8.8 **Three Production Processes.** These isoquants represent 10, 20, and 30 units of a product that can be produced using three alternative processes. In process 1, 0.2 unit of labor and 0.4 unit of capital combine to produce 1 unit of output. In process 3, 0.6 unit of labor and 0.2 unit of capital combine to produce 1 unit of output. Process 2 is the same as the process in Figure 8.7, combining 0.3 unit of both labor and capital per unit of product.

The 20 units of output could be produced at B, B', or B'', as well as by using combinations of processes 1, 2, and 3 and the corresponding amounts of labor and capital represented by the points along the three line segments connecting these points. However, the combinations of inputs along the line BB'' are inefficient. This line represents combinations of processes 1 and 3 and the required labor and capital to yield 20 units of output. At point D on that line segment, if the same amounts of the two inputs are used in process 2 (rather than split between 1 and 3), output will be greater than 20 (D lies farther from the origin along the ray for process 2 than does B'). We can conclude that for this example the only relevant combinations of processes lie along the lines connecting two adjacent processes at some given output level.

All points along the line segments running through points A, A', and A'' represent combinations of labor and capital that can be used to produce 10 units of output. Some combinations employ just one process ($L = 2$, $K = 4$; $L = 3$, $K = 3$; and $L = 6$, $K = 2$), and other combinations use a mix of two processes. That set of line segments thus corresponds to our earlier definition of an isoquant, and therefore we have labeled it $Q(10)$. Other isoquants, labeled $Q(20)$ and $Q(30)$, are also illustrated in Figure 8.8. We could identify an isoquant for each level of output in a similar manner. Note that these isoquants have a negative slope and are convex, as are those depicted in earlier sections of this chapter. The only difference is that the isoquants derived from a finite set of production processes are a series of linear segments rather than being smooth, continuous curves. As more different processes are available, the isoquants become more like the smooth ones developed earlier.

Output Maximization with Input Constraints

Having developed this method of specifying isoquants, we can use them — along with a knowledge of linear programming — to answer a number of interesting questions involving different decisions a firm's management must make. We shall look at two types of questions that can be answered by using these isoquants and the linear programming optimization model.[12]

First, let us assume that the quantities of labor and capital available are limited to 15 and 7 units, respectively. What is the maximum output that can be produced, and how much of that output should be produced with each process? Output (Q) can be units produced with process 1 (X_1), process $2(X_2)$, process 3 (X_3), or some combination of the three processes. That is,

$$Q = X_1 + X_2 + X_3$$

We want to maximize Q subject to the limitation that $L \leqslant 15$ and $K \leqslant 7$.

From the technical coefficients given in Table 8.2., we can determine the following algebraic statement of the constraints in terms of the process variables X_1, X_2, and X_3:

$$0.2X_1 + 0.3X_2 + 0.6X_3 \leqslant 15$$
$$0.4X_1 + 0.3X_2 + 0.2X_3 \leqslant 7$$

Since our problem has just two inputs, we can solve this problem graphically. The production processes and isoquants shown in Figure 8.8 are reproduced in Figure 8.9, along with the constraints on labor and capital. The space bounded by the rectangle $OABC$ represents the set of feasible solutions. The highest isoquant within the set of feasible solutions is at point B, on $Q(30)$. This gives us only the maximum number of units of output possible. We still must determine how much should be produced with

---

[12]For excellent extensions of the discussion presented here, see D.C. Vandermeulen, *Linear Economic Theory* (Englewood Cliffs, NJ: Prentice-Hall, 1971), Chapters. 8, 9, 10, and 11; and W.J. Baumol, *Economic Theory and Operations Analysis,* 3d ed. (Englewood Cliffs, NJ: Prentice-Hall, 1972), Ch. 12.

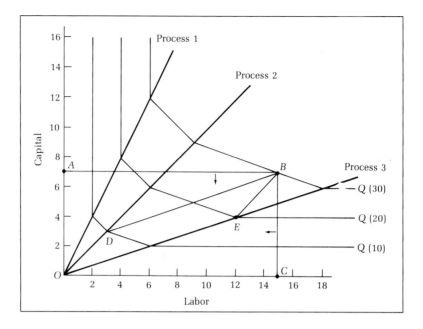

FIGURE 8.9 **Output Maximization with Input Constraints.** These isoquants represent 10, 20, and 30 units of output that can be produced using any of three processes with the constraints that no more than 15 units of labor and 7 units of capital are available. The objective is to maximize Q subject to those constraints. The rectangle $OABC$ is the set of feasible solutions, and the points O, A, B, and C are basic feasible solutions. At B, production is maximized, but B is not one of the possible processes. Thus, 30 units ($Q = 30$ at B) would be produced at points D and E on processes 2 and 3, respectively. Ten units of output would be made using process 2, and 20 units using process 3. We see that, between the two processes, all 15 units of labor and all 7 units of capital are used.

each process. Since B lies between process 2 and process 3, we know that the 30 units of output will be produced using those two processes.

The method of solution is not difficult. To determine the number of units to be produced by process 2, we draw a line parallel to process 3 connecting point B with process 2: line BD in Figure 8.9. At point D, three units of both labor and capital are used in process 2. Since one unit of output can be produced with $0.3L$ and $0.3K$ using process 2, ten times as many units of each input will produce 10 units of output; that is, $X_2 = 10$.

To find the number of units produced with process 3, we draw a line parallel to process 2 connecting point B with process 3: line BE in Figure 8.9. We see that at E, $12L$, and $4K$ are used in process 3. This is 20 times the requirement for each unit of production in process 3; thus, $X_3 = 20$. Since $Q = X_1 + X_2 + X_3$ and $X_1 = 0$, $X_2 = 10$, and $X_3 = 20$, total output Q must be 30, which checks with our original conclusion that the maximum Q is at point B along $Q(30)$.

Cost Minimization with an Output Constraint

Let us now consider a second type of production problem that can be investigated using this methodology. Suppose that the firm's management wants to produce 20 units of output at the lowest possible cost. If we assume that the firm pays $90 per unit of capital and $60 per unit of labor, the cost function may be expressed as

$$C = 90K + 60L$$

or, in terms of output,[13]

$$C = 48X_1 + 45X_2 + 54X_3$$

Our objective is to minimize C, subject to $Q = 20$. From the above, it is clear that the least expensive way to produce $Q = 20$ is by process 2, using $6K$ and $6L$. Thus, using either expression for cost, we have

$$C = 90(6) + 60(6) = 900$$

and

$$C = 48(0) + 45(20) + 54(0) = 900$$

We can reach the same conclusion by graphic analysis, but in such a simple case, that is not necessary. However, let us look at a more interesting case.

Suppose we want to minimize the cost of producing $Q = 20$ but are further constrained by resource limitations of $L \leqslant 12$ and $K \leqslant 5$. The above solution, $L = 6$ and $K = 6$, is no longer feasible. Our problem may now be stated as follows:

Minimize: $C = 48X_1 + 45X_2 + 54X_3$
Subject to: $X_1 + X_2 + X_3 = 20$
       $0.2X_1 + 0.3X_2 + 0.6X_3 \leqslant 12$
       $0.4X_1 + 0.3X_2 + 0.2X_3 \leqslant 5$

where these constraints represent the output, labor, and capital constraints, respectively.

The problem is solved graphically in Figure 8.10. The rectangle $OABC$ represents the set of feasible solutions as defined by just the input constraints. When we take into account the constraint that $Q = 20$, the feasible

---

[13]The cost per unit of X_1 equals $0.4(90) + 0.2(60)$, where 0.4 is the number of units of capital per unit of output, and 0.2 is the number of units of labor per unit of output using process 1. In a similar manner, the cost per unit of X_2 equals $0.3(90) + 0.3(60)$, and the cost per unit of X_3 is equal to $0.2(90) + 0.6(60)$.

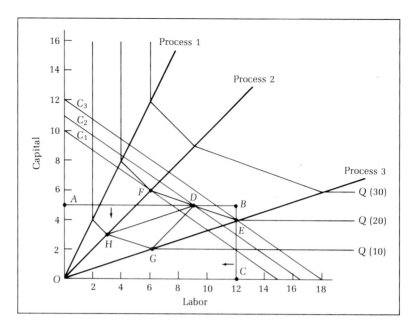

FIGURE 8.10 **Cost Minimization with Input Constraints and a Target Output.**
This is the graphic solution to the problem of minimizing the cost of producing 20 units of output when 12 units of labor and 5 units of capital
are available. If it were not for the input constraints, 20 units could be
produced at point F, which is on isocost C_1. With the input constraints,
only points along the line segment DE satisfy all constraints. The cost at
E (C_3) is greater than that at D (C_2), so D is the optimal basic feasible solution. Since D is not on any process, the 20 units would be produced
using processes 2 and 3 (at points H and G, respectively) with 10 units
produced by each process. All 12 units of labor and all 5 units of capital
will be used.

solution set is reduced to points along the line segment DE in the space
$OABC$. The question is: Which of those points represents the lowest cost?
We can incorporate isocost functions in Figure 8.10. We know that there is
a whole family of parallel isocost functions, each with a slope of minus the
ratio of unit labor cost to unit capital cost, that is, 60/90, or $-2/3$.

Three of these cost functions, $C_1 = 900$, $C_2 = 990$, and $C_3 = 1080$, are
drawn on Figure 8.10. We see that C_1 represents the least-cost solution to the
simple problem posed above (i.e., minimize cost, subject to $Q = 20$) with
the optimum at point F, using just process 2. But given the added constraints, there is no point along C_1 that satisfies all three conditions: $L \leq 12$,
$K \leq 5$, and $Q = 20$. We note that the lowest isocost curve that will satisfy
these conditions is $C_2 = 990$, at point D. The question yet to be answered is:
How much should be produced with each process?

Clearly, since D lies between process 2 and process 3, $X_1 = 0$, and we can solve for X_2 and X_3 in the same manner as in Figure 8.9. Drawing the relevant parallelogram (see line segments DH and DG), we find that at point H along process 2, $L = 3$ and $K = 3$, so X_2 must be 10. Also at point G along process 3, $L = 6$ and $K = 2$, so X_3 must also equal 10. Thus,

$$Q = 0 + 10 + 10 = 20$$
$$L = 3 + 6 = 9 \leqslant 12$$
$$K = 3 + 2 = 5 \leqslant 5$$

and from either expression for cost, we find that

$$C = 90K + 60L = 90(5) + 60(9) = 990$$

or

$$C = 48X_1 + 45X_2 + 54X_3 = 48(0) + 45(10) + 54(10) = 990$$

It should be evident in this example that, since all 12 available units of labor were not used, there is excess labor, and thus capital represents the binding constraint.

SUMMARY

Linear programming is quite useful for solving the class of maximization and minimization problems characterized by constraints that are equalities or inequalities and in which the functional relationships are linear. The values of the objective function are assumed to be related to the values of one or more decision variables. The relationship assumed is one of certainty, meaning that each set of values of the decision variable invariably leads to a known specific value of the function.

Linear programming has the advantage over classical calculus techniques for optimization because it can be applied to problems with inequality constraints that are common in business practice. Even the necessity that the objective function and constraints must be expressed as linear functions leaves a wide variety of problems to be formulated and solved in the linear programming framework. The assumption of linearity, while often untrue in the real world, is often close enough to being true over the relevant range of decision variables to make linear programming a valuable technique.

One of the most important parts of the solution to a linear programming problem is the value of the dual variables, or shadow prices. Shadow prices are useful in making marginal resource allocation decisions.

SUGGESTED READINGS

Baumol, William J. "Activity Analysis in One Lesson." *American Economic Review*, December 1958, pp. 837–873.

Daellenbach, Hans G., and Bell, Earl J. *User's Guide to Linear Programming.* Englewood Cliffs, NJ: Prentice-Hall, 1970.

Dorfman, Robert. "Mathematical or 'Linear' Programming: A Nonmathematical Exposition." *American Economic Review*, December 1953, pp. 797–825.

Loomba, N.P., and Turban, E. *Applied Programming for Management.* New York: Holt, Rinehart and Winston, 1974.

McNamara, John R. "A Linear Programming Model for Long-Range Capacity Planning in an Electric Utility." *Journal of Economics and Business*, Spring-Summer 1976, pp. 227–235.

Stimson, David H., and Ronald P. Thompson. "Linear Programming, Busing, and Educational Administration." *Socio-Economic Planning Sciences*, August 1974, pp. 195–206.

Summers, Edward L. "The Audit Staff Assignment Problem: A Linear Programming Analysis." *The Accounting Review*, July 1972, pp. 443–449.

Thompson, Gerald E. "Linear Programming and Microeconomic Analysis." *Nebraska Journal of Economics and Business*, Autumn 1972, pp. 25–36.

Vandermeulen, Daniel. *Linear Economic Theory.* Englewood Cliffs, NJ: Prentice-Hall, 1971.

PROBLEMS

1. Which of the following are *unacceptable* as linear programming constraints? (Assume a standard linear programming format.)
   a. $101A + 96B = 252$
   b. $12X_1 + 14X_2 + \emptyset X_3 \leq 74$
   c. $13X_1 X_2 + 23X_3 \leq 61$
   d. $12A + 9B \leq 16/A$
   e. $14X_1 + 8X_2 \geq 35$

2. Which of the following are *acceptable* as linear programming constraints?
   a. $3A + 4B \geq 16$
   b. $1A^2 + 3B \geq 23$
   c. $12AB + 14C \geq 44$
   d. $12X_1 + 2X_2 = 14$
   e. $12A + 14 A/B \geq 21$

3. In the poultry industry, it is common to try to ensure the health of the poultry by fulfilling certain minimum daily requirements (MDRs) for several kinds of nutrients. Assume that the chickens of Fisher Chickens require only three kinds of nutrients and that their feed is a combination of only two types of grains, A and B. The table below lists the minimum daily requirements for each nutrient:

	MDR in Units
Nutrient 1	20
Nutrient 2	20
Nutrient 3	12

Each grain provides the following nutrients per pound of grain:

	Grain A	Grain B
Nutrient 1	10 units	4 units
Nutrient 2	5 units	5 units
Nutrient 3	2 units	6 units

Grain A sells for $.60 per pound and grain B sells for $1.00 per pound. Given this information, the manager of Fisher Chickens wishes to mix the two grains in such a way as to meet the minimum daily requirement of nutrients in the least expensive manner.

a. Set up the problem in the standard format shown in the chapter (including an objective function, a number of constraints, and a nonnegativity constraint).

b. On a graph whose axes are labeled Grain A and Grain B, plot the constraints related to the three nutrient requirements (there are three constraints, one for each nutrient).

c. Show which area of your completed graph is the "feasible space" and explain why this is true.

d. Plot any objective function on this graph and proceed to "slide" it up or down to find the optimal solution. What is that optimal solution? (Hint: The optimal solution involves only whole pounds of each grain.)

e. Try any combination of grains in the "feasible space" other than the optimal solution and explain why it is *not* the optimal solution.

f. Assume that the price of the grains changes to $1.20 per pound for grain A and $2.00 per pound for grain B. Draw a new objective function and proceed to the optimal solution as in part d. What is the new optimal solution?

g. Assume now that the price of the grains changes to $1.00 per pound for grain A and $1.00 per pound for grain B. Draw the new objective function again and try to find the optimal solution, as you did in part d. What is the new optimal solution? Is there any other solution that is optimal? Is an optimal solution still found at a corner of the feasible space?

4. The management of Moreau Manufacturing wish to use linear programming as an aid in determining their optimal product mix (i.e., the "correct" number of each of its products to produce). Moreau produces only two products: 80-column printers and 100-column letter-quality printers. The manufacture of the two products is limited in several ways: final assembly time available for 80-column printers, final assembly time available for 100-column printers, casings for each printer, motors for each printer, and internal components for each printer. Moreau is limited to 100 units per day in final assembly of 80-column printers. Final assembly time is limited to 120 units per day for 100-column printers. The casing department can supply 150 80-column casings, 150 100-column casings, or any combination. The motor department can supply 180 motors for 80-column printers, 180 motors for 100-column printers, or any combination. The internal components department can supply components for 120 80-column printers, components for 240 100-column printers, or any combination. The profit margin on 80-column printers is $20 per unit, while the profit margin on letter-quality printers is $30 per unit.
   a. Set up the problem in standard linear programming format with an objective function, constraints, and a nonnegativity condition.
   b. On a set of axes with 80-column printers on one axis and 100-column printers on another axis, plot each of the constraints. Indicate where the feasible space is located.
   c. Plot an objective function on the axes above and "slide" it to determine the optimal solution. (Note: no fractional printers will be produced at this optimum point.)
   d. Choose any other corner of the feasible space and demonstrate that it is not the optimal solution.
   e. If Moreau was to add a third printer to its line (say, a color printer), would you be able to graphically solve for the optimal solution? Explain.

5. Flanner Industries produces two different types of tires: conventional tires and radial tires. Each tire requires the use of two resources: labor and capital. A radial tire uses one unit of labor and four units of capital, and a conventional tire uses one unit of labor and two units of capital. Flanner has only three thousand units of labor and eight thousand units of capital available. The profit margin on the two products is

$3.50 for the radial and $2.50 for the conventional tire. Flanner's management must decide how many radial tires and how many conventional tires should be produced in order to maximize profit.

a. Formulate the problem in standard linear programming format (i.e., objective function, constraints, and a nonnegativity constraint).

b. Graph the constraints, indicate the feasible space, and solve the problem by graphing an objective function and "sliding" it to the optimal solution.

c. Formulate the dual for Flanner Industries in standard linear programming format.

d. Graph the dual problem and indicate the feasible space. Solve the problem for the optimal solution graphically.

e. The optimal values of the dual variables calculated in part d are the shadow prices of Flanner's two inputs. Give an economic interpretation of these values.

f. Would Flanner be willing to buy more units of labor at a market price of $1.25 per unit?

g. At a market price of $.25, Flanner would be willing to purchase more units of capital according to the shadow price calculated for capital in part e. Would Flanner purchase "many" extra units of capital? Explain.

6. The management of Nieuland Manufacturing wish to determine the best method of cutting metal circles from standard rolled metal. Nieuland produces four-, six- and eight-inch circles for use in the manufacture of lids for scientific storage jars. Nieuland currently needs 48,000 four-inch tops, 50,000 six-inch tops, and 36,000 eight-inch tops to fulfill a contract. A standard rolled metal sheet may be cut using either of two patterns. Pattern number one produces 12 eight-inch tops, 10 six-inch tops, and 6 four-inch tops but wastes three inches of rolled metal per sheet. Pattern number two produces 6 eight-inch tops, 10 six-inch tops, 16 four-inch tops, and only two inches of waste per sheet. The company is able to cut some sheets according to one pattern and some sheets according to the other pattern.

a. If Nieuland's management wishes to minimize waste (measured in inches of waste per sheet cut), set up the linear programming problem in standard format.

b. Graph the constraints, indicate the feasible space, and solve for the optimal solution by graphing at least one objective function and "sliding" it. Note that the answer to this problem will be in cuts per pattern rather than in dollars, hours, or units.

7. A chemical company with a personal products division mixes three ingredients to make two different shampoos. Aida is a shampoo for

oily hair, and Celeste is a shampoo for dry hair. Each of the shampoos is some combination of three ingredients labeled I_1, I_2, and I_3. Aida now contributes $.09 per bottle, and Celeste contributes $.06 per bottle to profit. The mixing requirements for the products are:

	I_1	I_2	I_3
Aida	.2 units	.3 units	.5 units
Celeste	.1 units	.1 units	.8 units

Currently available stocks of ingredients are 48 units of I_1, 30 units of I_2, and 60 units of I_3. What combination of Aida and Celeste will maximize profits? What are the marginal values of each of the ingredients?

8. Surgicare, Inc., is a freestanding clinic specializing in outpatient care at prices below those charged for similar services performed in hospitals. The four most common procedure categories are plastic surgery, dermatology, orthopedic procedures, and laboratory tests. The average profit contribution in each of these areas is plastic surgery, $200; dermatology, $150; orthopedic procedures, $150; and laboratory tests, $250. The administrator of the clinic believes that patients are not being processed in an optimal manner. The following information on time limitations and requirements is available to the administrator. Data are given in hours required per patient:

Output	Laboratory	X-Ray	Therapy	Outpatient Surgery	Physician
Plastic surgery	5	2	1	4	10
Dermatology	5	8	10	8	14
Orthopedic procedures	2	1	0	16	8
Laboratory tests	4	5	8	10	12
Total hours available with current staff and facilities	200	140	110	240	320

a. Plastic surgery and orthopedic procedures, in addition, are limited to a combined 120 hours per week of physician time. From the administrator's point of view, what is the optimal weekly patient mix?

b. What areas of the clinic appear to be bottlenecks that, if expanded, could significantly increase profits?

9. Many institutional food preparers (universities, hospitals, nursing homes, etc.) run operations in which the institution chooses the complete menu. Menu planning is most commonly done in conjunction with a dietician to ensure that satisfactory menus are developed at minimum cost. Suppose that a university food service is planning menus for the coming school year. The university must have entrees for each of 200 days. The poultry entrees (usually chicken) cost $2.25 each, the fish entrees cost $2.00 each, and the beef entrees cost $2.50 each. The entree costs include salad and vegetable costs. Each of the three types of entrees has been arranged to meet protein requirements. Student surveys in the past have rated the entrees on a scale of 1 to 10; poultry is rated 7, fish is rated 4, and beef is rated a 9. The university administrators wish to attain at least a total of 1400 taste points per year. Vitamins required total 2100 units for the year, with fish providing 8 units, poultry providing 8.5 units, and beef providing 12 units. What number of each entree will the university be wise to choose?

10. Hurley Electronics manufactures two types of radio control equipment for model airplanes and cars. Each piece of equipment requires a certain amount of skilled assembly time, of which there is a limited supply (80 hours per week). Each piece of equipment also requires a certain amount of technician time, which is also limited (60 hours per week). To produce radio control equipment for an airplane requires .2 hours of skilled assembly time and .3 hours of technician time. To complete radio control equipment for a model automobile requires .4 hours of skilled assembly and .1 hours of technician time. Radio control equipment for airplanes contributes $100 to profit, while the model automobile equipment contributes $80. What weekly mix of production would exactly maximize profit contribution? Formulate the corresponding dual problem. Calculate the shadow prices and explain their meaning.

11. The Hayes-Healy Brokerage Firm has been named trustee of a $250,000 estate. The trust fund is to be invested by Hayes-Healy, subject to a number of restrictions in the trust agreement: (1) at least 40 percent of the funds are to be invested in the common stock of high-technology firms in such industries as aerospace, microelectronics, computers, and genetic engineering; (2) tax-free municipal bonds must constitute at least 20 percent of the portfolio; and (3) not more than 50 percent of the amount invested in the municipal bond share of the portfolio should be invested in utilities. Within the trust agreement guidelines, which investment would you choose if the only approved investments were as follows:

Investment	Forecasted Rate of Return (%)
Northeast Municipal Bonds	11.8
Southwest Municipal Bonds	5.3
Hi-Tech Microelectronics	6.8
Genetic Engineers, Inc.	4.9
Corby Computers	8.4
Dillon Aerospace	7.6
Midland Telephone	8.6

Would Hayes-Healy change its investment portfolio if the trust agreement was rewritten to allow less than 40 percent of the portfolio in high-technology firms?

12. Farley Forms, Inc., produces and markets paper and business forms (e.g., invoices, billing slips, and labels). The firm's computer paper inventory is warehoused in either San Francisco, Chicago, or New York. Farley expects to sell 100,000 cases in New York, 80,000 cases in Chicago, and 150,000 cases in San Francisco. Farley produces the forms either in Des Moines, Iowa, or Biloxi, Mississippi. The Des Moines plant is capable of producing up to 150,000 cases per year, while the Biloxi plant can produce up to 200,000 cases per year. The cost of shipping a single case from each factory to each warehouse is presented below:

From	To		
	New York	Chicago	San Francisco
Biloxi	$.20	$.30	$.50
Des Moines	.30	.10	.40

Farley's management wishes to set a shipping schedule that will minimize its total annual transportation charges. What will that schedule be?

13. The South Bend, Indiana, superintendent of schools must assign all students in South Bend to one of the city's three high schools. The superintendent has arbitrarily divided the city into five sections, or geographic neighborhoods. The district administrators would like to minimize the number of student miles traveled by bus. The superintendent has indicated that no student living in a geographic area and assigned to a school in that same area should be bused. The three high schools are located in areas 2, 3, and 5. The following table outlines the number of students and distances involved:

Geographic Neighborhoods	Distance to School			Number of Students
	School in 2	School in 3	School in 5	
1	5	8	6	700
2	0	4	12	500
3	4	0	7	100
4	7	2	5	800
5	12	7	0	400

Each high school is the same size and can accept up to 900 students. What allocation of students will minimize student miles traveled?

14. The management of Martins Supermarkets decide to allocate $1000 on advertising for their local chain of grocery stores during a given period. Since Martins is running a special promotion to draw children into the store (who will, of course, bring their parents), the goal of the advertising campaign is to reach the maximum audience while reaching at least 6000 children. Martins may use any combination of radio, television, and newspaper advertising. The costs of each medium and the latest audience estimates are shown below:

	Radio	Television	Newspaper
Cost per unit of advertising	$ 150	$ 400	$ 200
Total audience	14,000	36,000	20,000
Children	1,000	3,000	1,000

What is the optimal advertising mix for Martins? Could there be more than one optimal solution to this problem? What would be the increase in audience reach achieved by spending one extra dollar?

15. Greenlawn, Inc., has a lawn care business in each of three Indiana cities: South Bend, Ft. Wayne, and Indianapolis. Greenlawn's major product is a liquid fertilizer applied to lawns up to four times per year. Greenlawn purchases the liquid fertilizer from local wholesale suppliers in each of the three cities. Managers are currently trying to decide how much liquid fertilizer to purchase from each of three suppliers. They need the following amounts of liquid fertilizer in each city: 600,000 gallons in South Bend, 500,000 gallons in Ft. Wayne, and 300,000 gallons in Indianapolis. The three suppliers have indicated that they can provide the following total amounts of liquid fertilizer: company A, 300,000 gallons; company B, 400,000 gallons; company C, 700,000 gallons. The cost per gallon of fertilizer varies from supplier to supplier and city to city. The following table gives the per

gallon prices for each supplier delivering products in each of the three cities:

	Company A	Company B	Company C
South Bend	$.25	$.30	$.28
Ft. Wayne	.26	.28	.29
Indianapolis	.30	.29	.29

What would be the optimal purchase pattern for Greenlawn to follow (assume Greenlawn has no opportunity itself to transport the liquid fertilizer from city to city)?

16. Pangborn Industries, Inc., is a small, new firm that manufactures tents for backpacking. They currently produce two styles, one called the Ranger (R) and the other called Forester (F). The Forester is less complex to produce, easier to set up, but less stable than the Ranger, which is a freestanding tent (it needs no stakes). Pangborn has a very strong quality reputation and has been able to sell all the tents that their employees can produce each quarter in 12,000 work hours (allowing for single-shift operation, lunchtime, breaks, and cleanup). Each Forester tent uses 140 square feet of nylon that takes two hours to cut and sew and 10 sections of tubing, each of which is 2.5 feet long. The tubing must be cut and tapered at one end, which takes on the average 3 minutes per section. The profit on each Forester is $6.90. The freestanding Ranger uses less nylon (120 square feet per tent) but more sections of tubing (15 per tent), each of which is 2 feet long. The cutting and sewing of the nylon for each Ranger tent takes 1.8 hours, and each section of tubing averages 2 minutes to cut and taper. Because the Ranger is freestanding, it requires two tubular braces to hold the five poles (made from the 15 two-foot sections of tubing) together. These two braces each use .5 feet of tubing and are made on the same equipment used to cut and taper the tubing (they are made from the same size tubing). Each brace takes 7.5 minutes to make. Pangborn makes a profit of $7.50 on each Ranger tent. The company is limited in production because they can use only 12,000 hours of labor per quarter; they can obtain only 300,000 square feet of nylon per quarter; and the amount of tubing is limited to 72,000 feet per quarter. Because of equipment constraints, no more than 3200 hours of time can be allocated to cutting and tapering tubing each month. Pangborn has contracted with a sporting goods chain to supply them with at least 1500 Foresters per quarter. How many of each type of tent should Pangborn produce to maximize profits and satisfy all of their production constraints as well as their commitment to the sporting goods chain?

17. A firm can produce its product using any of three processes. Process A uses 0.3 unit of labor and 0.6 unit of capital per unit of output. Process B uses 0.4 unit of each input per unit of output, and process C uses 0.8 unit of labor and 0.3 unit of capital per unit of output. Graph the three processes and the isoquants for 10, 20, and 30 units of output.

18. Suppose that in problem 17, the amount of labor is limited to 60 and capital is limited to 80. What is the maximum possible level of production, and how many units should be produced with each process?

19. Suppose that the firm in problem 17 pays $100 per unit of capital and $50 per unit of labor. What is the least-cost combination of processes that will enable the firm to produce 200 units of output, assuming there are no restrictions on the amount of labor and capital used? How would your answer change if only 80 units of capital could be used?

APPENDIX   The Simplex Method: An Introduction

The graphic solutions discussed in this chapter are useful for the insight they provide into the nature of linear programming problems. However, such procedures are limited to the simplest types of problems, for which optimal decisions can usually be made without formal analysis. Complex linear programming requires a more sophisticated solution technique. The most common method employed by computers in solving large-scale linear programming problems is the simplex method. This procedure involves an orderly evaluation of basic feasible solutions until an optimum is obtained. This appendix explains the use of a hand-calculated simplex method for solving a maximization problem, the Lumin Company case.

In our example, Lumin Company management wish to maximize the profit from the production and sale of standard and deluxe lamps, subject to constraints on the casting and polishing time available. In the chapter, we stated the problem in algebraic form as follows:

Maximize: $Z = 20X_1 + 30X_2$ (objective function)
Subject to: $X_1 + 2X_2 \leq 16$ (casting constraint)
$2X_1 + \frac{2}{3}X_2 \leq 12$ (polishing constraint)
$X_1, X_2 \geq 0$ (nonnegativity constraint)

In order to use the simplex method, all constraints must be represented as equalities, rather than inequalities such as these. The process for converting inequalities to equalities is simple. In the case of less-than-or-equal-to inequalities, we add a slack variable to the left-hand side of the constraint.

A slack variable represents the unused amount of the element that is the constraining factor for a given inequality. In our present example, we can convert the casting time constraint to an equality by adding a slack variable that represents unused casting time. Thus, the first constraint becomes

$$X_1 + 2X_2 + S_1 = 16$$

where S_1 is used to denote slack casting time. If Lumin does not produce any standard or deluxe lamps ($X_1 = 0$ and $X_2 = 0$), then they have 16 hours of slack (unused) casting time; that is, $S_1 = 16$.

By letting S_2 stand for the slack variable in the polishing time constraint, we can write that constraint in equality form as

$$2X_1 + \tfrac{2}{3}X_2 + S_2 = 12$$

If $X_1 = 0$ and $X_2 = 0$, there will be 12 hours of unused, or slack, polishing time; that is, $S_2 = 12$.

Of course, idle casting or polishing time makes no contribution to the firm's profit. Therefore, slack variables always have a coefficient of 0 in the firm's objective function. The Lumin Company problem can now be written as

$$\text{Maximize:} \quad Z = 20X_1 + 30X_2 + 0S_1 + 0S_2$$
$$\text{Subject to:} \quad X_1 + 2X_2 + S_1 = 16$$
$$2X_1 + \tfrac{2}{3}X_2 + S_2 = 12$$
$$X_1, X_2, S_1, S_2 \geqslant 0$$

The problem is now ready for solution using the simplex method.

The Initial Simplex Table

The simplex method is a repetitive (iterative) procedure in which each iteration represents a basic feasible solution. A series of *simple tables* is used to organize and manipulate the data. The initial simplex table for the Lumin Company problem is Table 8A.1. The first step in constructing the initial simplex table is to write down the heading row, which contains the following headings: sol mix, b_0, and the designation for each variable in the problem. In this case, the variables are X_1, X_2, S_1, and S_2:

TABLE 8A.1   **Initial Simplex Table: Lumin Company**

C_j	Sol mix	b_0	20 X_1	30 X_2	0 S_1	0 S_2	N
0	S_1	16	1	②	1	0	8 ← Key row
0	S_2	12	2	$\tfrac{2}{3}$	0	1	18
	Z_j	0	0	0	0	0	
	$C_j - Z_j$		20	30	0	0	

Key column

The column headed "Sol mix" (meaning "solution mix") contains the variables that make up the solution for any given iteration. The b_0 column represents the value assigned to the solution mix variables in each solution. For the initial simplex table, the constant terms in the constraint functions make up the b_0 column. In this problem, the constant terms are 16 and 12. To the right of the constant terms, the values in the initial simplex table are the coefficients that each of the variables heading a column have in their respective constraint functions.

Immediately above the heading row is the C_j row, which contains the contribution that each of the variables makes to the objective function. In the present example, each standard lamp (X_1) contributes \$20 to profit (Z), each deluxe lamp (X_2) contributes \$30 to Z, and the slack variables $(S_1$ and $S_2)$ contribute nothing to profit.

The next step is to determine which variables should make up the initial solution to the linear programming problem, that is, to determine the variables to be written in the solution mix column. The procedure is to read across each row until a column is found that has a 1 in that row and a 0 in every other row (under the heading row) and write the variable heading that column in the solution mix column for that row. For example, in our table, reading across the row that has 16 in the b_0 column, we find a 1 in the X_1 column, but that column does not contain a 0 in every other row, thus we read on. We find a 1 in the S_1 column, and every other number under that column heading is 0, so we write S_1 in the first row of the solution mix column. We do the same for all other rows of the initial simplex table. For the row that has a 12 in the b_0 column, we find that the S_2 column has a 1 in that row and a 0 in the other row. Thus, we enter S_2 in the second row of the solution mix column.

To the left of the solution mix column, we have written the contribution that each unit of the variables in that solution mix makes to the objective function. In this case, they are both 0. This is called the C_j column.

Let us recall that the values of the b_0 column represent the values assigned to each variable in a given solution mix. For this initial solution, we see that these are 16 of S_1 and 12 of S_2. Any variable that does not appear in the solution mix column for a given solution has a value of 0 for that solution. Thus, our initial solution corresponds to point O in Figure 8.1, at which $X_1 = 0$ and $X_2 = 0$. If no lamps are produced, we should expect there to be 16 hours of slack casting time (S_1) and 12 hours of slack polishing time (S_2).

Let us now consider the Z_j of the simplex table. The numbers in the Z_j row are found by multiplying the values in each column of the simplex table by the corresponding values in the C_j column and adding the resulting products. For the Z_j value under the b_0 column, we find $(0 \times 16) + (0 \times 12)$, or 0. We see that, since the C_j column is composed of all 0's, each element in the Z_j row will be 0 in this case. It is important to note that the number in the b_0 column of the Z_j row represents the value of the objective function for the present solution. In the Lumin Company problem, there is 0 profit if the solution mix column contains only slack variables (and thus, X_1, X_2 = 0). This determination of the value of the objective function is equivalent to putting the value of each variable as determined by the simplex solution into the objective function and calculating Z. For the present example, we have

$$Z = 20X_1 + 30X_2 + 0S_1 + 0S_2$$

or, for the initial solution,

$$Z = 20(0) + 30(0) + 0(16) + 0(12)$$
$$Z = 0$$

Next we must calculate values for the $C_j - Z_j$ row. This is called the index row of the simplex table because the values in this row provide an index to indicate the best variable to bring into the solution for the next iteration. These values are determined by subtracting each value in the Z_j row from the corresponding value in the C_j row above the heading row. Since there is no C_j value for the b_0 column, we can leave that spot blank. If any of the values in this index row is greater than 0, the objective function can be improved by changing the solution mix.

Changing the Solution Mix

The positive values in the index row represent the amount of change in the objective function for each unit of the variable heading that column that is added to the solution mix at that iteration. For example, at this point, each unit of X_1 that enters the solution would increase profit by $20, and each unit of X_2 would increase profit by $30. Since our objective is to maximize Z, we should select X_2 as the variable to enter the solution. The general rule is that the largest positive value of the index row identifies the variable that should be brought into the solution mix. The column headed by that variable is called the key column.

Because we had two constraints in this problem, there were just two values in the b_0 column and thus only two variables in the solution mix column. If we want to bring variable X_2 into the solution mix, one of the variables currently there must be removed. To determine which variable should be taken out of the solution, we calculate the values of N, which are written on the far right side of the simplex table. These values are found by dividing each element in the b_0 column by the corresponding element in the key column. For the present example, the first value in the N column is 16 ÷ 2 = 8, and the second value of N is 12 ÷ 2/3 = 18. These values represent the number of units of the incoming variable (X_2 in this case) that can be brought in at this point without violating the constraints. For example, we could bring in 8 units of X_2 without violating the polishing constraint. Since we must satisfy all the constraints, the maximum number of units of X_2 we can bring in is 8. The general rule is that the variable to be deleted from the solution mix is the variable with the smallest (but positive) value of X. This row is referred to as the key row.

The number that appears at the intersection of the key column and the key row plays a very important part in the development of the next simplex table. For this reason, it is called the key number and is circled in Table 8A.1.

The second and all succeeding simplex tables have the same format as the first, or initial, simplex table. The heading row and the C_j row are exactly the same. All simplex tables for a given problem have the same number of rows and columns. However, the values that constitute the body of the table and the variables represented in the solution mix vary from table to table.

Deriving the Second Simplex Table

For the present example, we have determined that variable X_2 (the variable heading the key column) should be brought into the solution mix and that variable S_1 (the variable in the solution mix column of the key row) should be removed from the solution mix. Thus, in constructing the second simplex table, X_2 replaces S_1 in the solution mix column. We refer to this new row (the X_2 row) as the incoming row, meaning that it is the row for the variable coming into solution at this iteration. The values in the incoming row are found by dividing each of the corresponding values in the key row by the key number. For Table 8A.2, these were found as follows:

incoming row value = key row value key number
b_0 column = 16/2 = 8
X_1 column = 1/2 = 1/2
X_2 column = 2/2 = 1
S_1 column = 1/2 = 1/2
S_2 column = 0/2 = 0

A different technique is necessary to determine the values for the remaining rows of the new simplex table. At first the procedure may seem a little confusing, but after several applications, the method becomes very easy. Let us begin by simply stating the process verbally. The values in each new row are found by subtracting from the corresponding value in the old row (in the previous simplex table) the product of the key row number in the same column and the ratio of the value in the key column of the old row to the key number. For any given row, this ratio is a constant, which we shall denote K. In general,

$$\begin{array}{c}\text{Value in column } j \\ \text{of the new row}\end{array} = \left(\begin{array}{c}\text{value in column } j \\ \text{of the old row}\end{array}\right) - \left(\begin{array}{c}\text{value in column } j \\ \text{of the key row}\end{array}\right)K$$

where K is the value in the key column of the old row divided by the key number. For our current example, the values for the new S_2 row (the S_2 row of the second simplex table) are determined as follows:

$$K = \frac{(2/3)}{2} = 1/3$$

New S_2 row, b_0 column $= 12 \;-\; 16(1/3) = 20/3$
New S_2 row, X_1 column $= 2 \;\;-\; 1(1/3) \;\;= 5/3$
New S_2 row, X_2 column $= 2/3 - 2(1/3) \;\;= 0$
New S_2 row, X_2 column $= 0 \;\;-\; 1(1/3) \;\;= -1/3$
New S_2 row, S_2 column $= 1 \;\;-\; 0(1/3) \;\;= 0$

These values have been placed in the second simplex table, Table 8A.2.

TABLE 8A.2   **Second Simplex Table: Lumin Company**

C_j →	Sol mix	b_0	20 X_1	30 X_2	0 S_1	0 S_2	N
30	X_2	8	$\frac{1}{2}$	1	$\frac{1}{2}$	0	16
0	S_2	$\frac{20}{3}$	$\frac{5}{3}$	0	$-\frac{1}{3}$	1	4 ← Key row
Z_j		240	15	30	15	0	
$C_j - Z_j$			5	0	−15	0	

Key column (points to X_1 column)

We can now determine the Z_j row for the second simplex table as follows:

Z_j row, b_0 column $=$ (30×8) $\;+\; (0 \times 20/3)$ $= 240$
Z_j row, X_1 column $=$ $(30 \times 1/2) + (0 \times 5/3)$ $\;\;= 15$
Z_j row, X_2 column $=$ (30×1) $\;\;+\; (0 \times 0)$ $\;\;= 30$
Z_j row, S_1 column $=$ $(30 \times 1/2) + (0 \times -1/3) = 15$
Z_j row, S_2 column $=$ (30×0) $\;\;+\; (0 \times -1)$ $\;\;= 0$

Recall that the Z_j value in the b_0 column represents the value of the objective function for the basic feasible solution represented by that iteration. Thus, for this solution ($X_1 = 0, X_2 = 8, S_1 = 0, S_2 = 20/3$), the Lumin Company's profit from producing lamps is $240. This corresponds to point D in Figure 8.1. Earlier we noted that the values in the index row of a given simplex table represent the amount of change in the objective function for each unit of the variable heading the column that is added to the solution mix. Looking back at the first simplex table (Table 8A.1), we see that the index row value X_2 was 30. By comparing the solutions of the first two simplex tables, we see that 8 units of X_2 were brought in to the solution and that profit increased by \$240, and \$30 per unit of X_2.

The index row values of the second simplex table are found as follows:

$$C_j - Z_j, X_1 \text{ column} = 20 - 15 = 5$$
$$C_j - Z_j, X_2 \text{ column} = 30 - 30 = 0$$
$$C_j - Z_j, S_1 \text{ column} = 0 - 15 = -15$$
$$C_j - Z_j, S_2 \text{ column} = 0 - 0 = 0$$

The only index row value that is greater than 0 is in the X_1 column; thus, that becomes the key column.

Subsequent Simplex Tables

Remember that the criterion for identifying the key column, and thus the next variable to enter the solution, is the largest positive value in the index row. This value (5) indicates that for each unit of X_1 that enters the solution in the coming iteration, the objective function will increase by \$5. The increase in Z per unit of X_1 is \$5, rather than the \$20 profit contribution, because as units of X_1 must be removed from the solution in order to satisfy the first constraint (casting time), some profit is lost as X_2 is reduced below 8 units.

To determine the variable that must leave the solution to make room for X_1, we calculate the value of N for each row:

$$N \text{ for the } X_2 \text{ row} = 8 \div 1/2 = 16$$
$$N \text{ for the } S_2 \text{ row} = 20/3 \div 5/3 = 4$$

Since 4 is the smallest positive value for N, we identify that row as the key row and replace the variable S_2 with X_1 in the next solution. The smallest N value represents the number of units of the incoming variable that can be brought into solution at that iteration, and thus we know that in the third simplex table, X_1 will equal 4. Having determined in the index row that each unit of X_1 will increase profit by \$5, we expect that, after completing the next simplex table, the level of profit will be \$240 + (\$5 × \$4) = \$260.

After identifying the key number in the second simplex table as 5/3 (at the intersection of the key column and the key row), we can set up the third simplex table. The C_j row and the heading row are the same as in the first two tables. The solution mix column now contains the variables X_2 and X_1 in the first and second rows, respectively.

The incoming row is the X_1 row, and the values in it are found by dividing the corresponding values in the key row of the second table by the key number:

incoming row value = key row value ÷ key number

$$b_0 \text{ column} = 20/3 \div 5/3 = 4$$
$$X_1 \text{ column} = 5/3 \div 5/3 = 1$$
$$X_2 \text{ column} = 0 \div 5/3 = 0$$
$$S_1 \text{ column} = -1/3 \div 5/3 = -.2$$
$$S_2 \text{ column} = 1 \div 5/3 = .6$$

These values are entered in the X_1 row of Table 8A.3, the third simplex table. We can now calculate each of the values for the new X_2 row as follows:

$$\begin{pmatrix} \text{Value in column } j \\ \text{of the new } X_2 \text{ row} \end{pmatrix} = \begin{pmatrix} \text{value in column } j \\ \text{of the old } X_2 \text{ row} \end{pmatrix} - \begin{pmatrix} \text{value in column } j \\ \text{of the key row} \end{pmatrix}(K)$$

where K is the value in the key column of the old X_2 row key number:

$$K = 1/2 \div 5/3 = .3$$

For the new X_2 row, we find

$$\begin{array}{llll} \text{New } X_2 \text{ row, } b_0 \text{ column} = 8 & - (20/3).3 & = 6 \\ \text{New } X_2 \text{ row, } X_1 \text{ column} = 1/2 & - (5/3).3 & = 0 \\ \text{New } X_2 \text{ row, } X_2 \text{ column} = 1 & - (0).3 & = 1 \\ \text{New } X_2 \text{ row, } S_1 \text{ column} = (1/2) & - (-1/3)(.3) & = .6 \\ \text{New } X_2 \text{ row, } S_2 \text{ column} = 0 & - (1)(.3) & = -.3 \end{array}$$

Having entered these values in the third simplex table, we can calculate the Z_j row:

$$\begin{array}{lll} Z_j, b_0 \text{ column} = (30 \times 6) & + (20 \times 4) & = 260 \\ Z_j, X_1 \text{ column} = (30 \times 0) & + (20 \times 1) & = 20 \\ Z_j, X_2 \text{ column} = (30 \times 1) & + (20 \times 0) & = 30 \\ Z_j, S_1 \text{ column} = (30 \times .6) & + (20 \times -.2) & = 14 \\ Z_j, S_2 \text{ column} = (30 \times -.3) & + (20 \times .6) & = 3 \end{array}$$

TABLE 8A.3   Third Simplex Table: Lumin Company

C_j			20	30	0	0
	Sol mix	b_0	X_1	X_2	S_1	S_2
30	X_2	6	0	1	.6	-.3
20	X_1	4	1	0	-.2	.6
	Z_j	260	20	30	14	3
	$C_j - Z_j$		0	0	-14	-3

We know that for any simplex table the value of the objective function can be determined by examining the value in the b_0 column of the Z_j row. For the present solution ($X_1 = 4, X_2 = 6, S_1 = 0, S_2 = 0$), we see that the objective function, or profit, is equal to $260. This is exactly what we predicted based on our earlier interpretation of the second simplex table. We must now determine whether 260 represents a maximum for our objective function. To do this, we need to calculate the index row values.

If all of the index row values are either negative or 0, we shall have obtained the optimal solution to the Lumin Company problem. These values are calculated as follows:

$$C_j - Z_j, X_1 \text{ column} = 20 - 20 = 0$$
$$C_j - Z_j, X_2 \text{ column} = 30 - 30 = 0$$
$$C_j - Z_j, S_1 \text{ column} = 0 - 14 = -14$$
$$C_j - Z_j, S_2 \text{ column} = 0 - 3 = -3$$

Thus, by producing six deluxe lamps (X_2) and four standard lamps (X_1), the Lumin Company will maximize profit subject to the constraints on the casting and polishing time available.

The index row values for the slack variables in the final simplex table have a very important economic interpretation. Their absolute value represents the amount of change in the optimal value of the objective function that would result from relaxing the corresponding constraint by one unit. This is the shadow price. Consider the index row value in the S_1 column of the third simplex table. The absolute value of -14 is 14. Therefore, we can say that if one more hour of casting time is available,[1] Lumin Company profits would increase by $14; that is, the shadow price for casting time is $14. The interested student can verify this by solving (using either the graphic or the simplex method) the following linear programming problem:

Maximize: $Z = 20X_1 + 30X_2$
Subject to: $X_1 + 2X_2 \le 17$
$$2X_1 + \tfrac{2}{3}X_2 \le 12$$
$$X_1, X_2 \ge 0$$

where the first constraint represents the new restriction on casting time.[2]

If the Lumin Company can increase profit by $14 for each additional unit of casting time (in this range), they should be willing to pay up to that amount for each unit. This is why the term *shadow price* is used for these values. The shadow price for polishing time is $3, which indicates that if the

---

[1] The constraint associated with S_1 is the casting constraint. To relax this constraint by one unit would mean increasing the number of hours of available casting time by one.

[2] Solving this new LP problem will give a maximum profit of $274, with $X_1 = 3.8$ and $X_2 = 6.6$. Note that this solution yields noninteger values of X_1 and X_2. While it may not be meaningful to consider producing 3.8 standard lamps, we might evaluate the result to be that three such lamps should be completed and one should be 80 percent completed in this production period. If it is necessary that solution variables be integer values, a related technique known as integer programming can be employed.

Lumin Company can obtain an additional unit of polishing time for less than \$3, it can increase profit.[3]

Additional Aspects of the Simplex Method

In the preceding simplex solution, all the constraints facing the Lumin Company were of the less-than-or-equal-to type. Many practical problems involve constraints that are in the form of equalities or are greater-than-or-equal-to inequalities. Having now mastered the basics of the simplex method, we can extend our discussion to include the use of these kinds of constraints. We can also show how the maximization method developed above can be used to solve problems for which the objective function is to be minimized.

The Use of Equality and Greater-Than-or-Equal-to Constraints

Let us recall that in order to use the simplex method to solve linear programming problems, all constraints must be stated in (or converted to) equality form. With less-than-or-equal-to inequalities, we have added a slack variable to form an equality. When the constraint is of the greater-than-or-equal-to type, we must therefore subtract a slack variable to form an equality constraint. Suppose, for example, that the Lumin Company had contracted with retail stores to provide the stores with 15 deluxe lamps (X_2) each week. Assuming that the firm operates on a five-day workweek, it would have to produce deluxe lamps at a rate of at least three per day. In algebraic form, this constraint is

$$X_2 \geq 3$$

which can be converted to an equality by subtracting a slack variable (S_3 is used to denote this slack variable, since S_1 and S_2 have been used for the first two constraints). In equality form, this additional constraint is

$$X_2 - S_3 = 3$$

If we were to try to set up the initial simplex table using the three constraints

$$X_1 + 2X_2 + S_1 = 16$$
$$2X_1 + X_2 + X_2 = 12$$
$$X_2 - S_3 = 3$$

we would have three rows under the heading row of the table and above the Z_j row (one row for each constraint). We would need to have three variables

---

[3]It is important to note that the shadow prices are only valid when one constraint is relaxed at a time and only over a relevant range of values. This range can be determined through sensitivity analysis that is beyond the scope of this text. However, such analysis is a standard part of most computer solutions, and thus the range of values over which the shadow prices are valid is generally known.

in the solution mix column, but by using the simplex method presented earlier, we find that only variables S_1 and S_2 would qualify. S_2 would not qualify because it has a coefficient of -1, not $+1$.

TABLE 8A.4   **Incomplete Initial Simplex Table — Lumin Company: Expanded (with Greater-Than-or-Equal-to Constraint)**

	Sol mix	b_0	X_1	X_2	S_1	S_2	S_3
$C_j \rightarrow$			20	30	0	0	0
0	S_1	16	1	2	1	0	0
0	S_2	12	2	$\frac{2}{3}$	0	1	0
		3	0	1	0	0	-1
Z_j							
$C_j - Z_j$							

This situation is illustrated in Table 8A.4, where we see that it is not possible to identify a set of variables that would provide a basic feasible solution. There is a relatively simple way to overcome this problem. In order to generate an initial basic feasible solution when $\geq$ constraints are involved, an "artificial variable" is added to each such constraint. Unlike slack variables, artificial variables have no economic meaning and are simply artificial constructs used to establish an initial basic feasible solution. Adding the artificial variable A_1 to the third constraint for the expanded Lumin Company problem, we have the following three constraint functions:

$$X_1 + 2X_2 + S_1 = 16$$
$$2X_1 + (2/3)X_2 + X_2 = 12$$
$$X_2 - S_3 + A_1 = 3$$

Since the artificial variable has no economic meaning, we want to be certain that it does not appear in the final solution mix; thus we shall assign it a large negative value in the objective function. We can then write the objective as

$$\text{Maximize: } Z = 20X_1 + 3X_2 + 0S_1 + 0S_2 - MA_1$$

where M is an arbitrarily large number.

The complete initial simplex table for this problem is presented in Table 8A.5. We see that in the index row of this table the large positive value appears in the X_2 column, which is therefore the key column and X_2 the incoming variable. We note also that the smallest positive value of N (3) is associated with the artificial variable, and thus X_2 will replace A_1 in the solution mix.

TABLE 8A.5
Complete Initial Simplex Table — Lumin Company:
Expanded (with Greater-Than-or-Equal-to Constraint)

C_j →	Sol mix	b_0	X_1	X_2	S_1	S_2	S_3	A_1	N
		20	30	0	0	0	$-M$	
0	S_1	16	1	2	1	0	0	0	8
0	S_2	12	2	$\frac{2}{3}$	0	1	0	0	18
$-M$	A_1	3	0	①	0	0	-1	1	3 ← Key row
	Z_j	$-3M$	0	$-M$	0	0	M	$-M$	
	$C_j - Z_j$		20	$(30 + M)$	0	0	$-M$	0	

Key column

It so happens that adding this third constraint will not alter the optimum solution mix for the Lumin Company. Students can verify this by returning to Figure 8.2 and drawing in this additional constraint as the area to the right of a vertical line at $X_2 = 3$. Alternatively, we may work through the simplex method starting with the initial solution given in Table 8A.5 until an optimal basic feasible solution is found (that is, until all index row values are ≤ 0).

Let us now consider constraints that are already expressed as equalities. For example, we shall assume that the Lumin Company has contracted with one chain of retail stores to provide their stores with exactly 15 deluxe lamps each week (three per day). Included in the contract is a guarantee that the Lumin Company will not sell deluxe lamps to any other buyer. Thus they must produce exactly three deluxe lamps each day. In algebraic form, the constraint is $X_2 = 3$.

Slack variables are not necessary for this constraint because it is already stated as an equality. However, if we were to try to set up the first simplex table, we would find that no initial basic feasible solution would exist; therefore, we must again add an artificial variable to obtain the initial solution. The linear programming problem for this expansion of the Lumin Company case is formulated as

$$\text{Maximize:} \quad Z = 20X_1 + 30X_2 + 0S_1 - MA_1$$
$$\text{Subject to:} \quad X_1 + 2X_2 + S_1 = 16$$
$$2X_1 + \tfrac{2}{3}X_2 + S_2 = 12$$
$$X_2 - A_1 = 3$$

The initial simplex table for this problem is presented in Table 8A.6.

TABLE 8A.6
Initial Simplex Table — Lumin Company: Expanded (with Equality Constraint)

C_j			20	30	0	0	$-M$		
	Sol mix	b_0	X_1	X_2	S_1	S_2	A_1		N
0	S_1	16	1	2	1	0	0		8
0	S_2	12	2	$\frac{2}{3}$	3	1	0		18
$-M$	A_1	3	0	①	0	0	1		3 ← Key row
	Z_j	$-3M$	0	$-M$	0	0	$-M$		
	$C_j - Z_j$		20	$(30 + M)$	0	0	0		

Key
column

We see that X_2 should be brought into the solution to replace the artificial variable A_1. This problem can again be solved graphically or by completing the simplex method. In either case, the optimal basic feasible solution is $X_1 = 5$, $X_2 = 3$, $S_1 = 0$, and $A_1 = 0$. That is, Lumin Company would produce five standard lamps and three deluxe lamps to be sold to the retail chain. By producing this product mix, they will use up all of the polishing time available but will have five hours of slack casting time. Profit would equal \$190 $[(5 \times 20) + (3 \times 30)]$.

Minimization Problems

The simplex method, as developed above, solves the linear programming problem for values that maximize the objective function. Many practical problems, however, require that the objective function be minimized. In this section we shall develop a procedure whereby the maximization technique described earlier can be used to minimize an objective function.

Suppose that we have a linear objective function, $Z = f(X, Y)$, which we would like to minimize, subject to a set of linear constraints. The values of X and Y that cause Z to be a minimum are exactly those values for which $-Z$ is a maximum; thus:

Minimum Z = maximum $(-Z)$

This relationship provides a mechanism through which we can use the maximizing simplex procedure to solve minimization problems.

We shall illustrate this technique by solving the minimization example. In that example we had a cost function:

$Z = 15X + 15Y$

which was to be minimized, subject to two greater-than-or-equal-to inequalities:

$$4X + 2Y \geqslant 16$$
$$X + 3 \geqslant 9$$

These constraints must be converted to the equality form by subtracting a slack variable from the left-hand side of each. Artificial variables must also be added to provide an initial basic feasible solution. The slack variables will have 0 coefficients in the objective function. Since we want to minimize Z, we must assign arbitrarily large coefficients (M) to the artificial variables in the objective function. The objective function can then be written as

Minimize: $Z = 15X + 15Y + 0S_1 + 0S_2 + MA_1 + MA_2$

However, since our simplex method is a maximization procedure, we shall write the problem in the form

Maximize: $-Z = -15X - 15Y - 0S_1 - 0S_2 - MA_1 - MA_2$
Subject to: $4X + 2Y - S_1 + A_1 = 16$
$X + 3Y - S_2 + A_2 = 9$

From this set of relationshps we can set up the initial simplex table as shown in Table 8A.7.

We see that there is a tie for the largest positive value in the index row $(C_1 - Z_1)$ of the initial simplex table. This indicates that each unit of the variables heading these tied columns will have the same effect on the objective function if it was to enter the solution. In our example we could bring either X or Y into solution and increase the value of the objective function by $(-15 + 5M)$.

TABLE 8A.8
Second Simplex Table: Minimization Example

C_j			-15	-15	0
	Sol mix	b_0	X	Y	S_1
-15	X	4	1	.5	$-.25$
$-M$	A_2	5	0	2.5	.25
	Z_j	$(-60 - 5M)$	(-15)	$(-7.5 - 2.5M)$	$(3.75 - .25M)$
	$C_j - Z_j$		0	$(-7.5 + 2.5M)$	$(-3.75 + .25M)$

Key column

TABLE 8A.7
Initial Simplex Table: Minimization Example

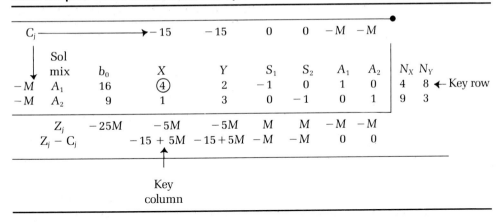

C_j			-15	-15	0	0	$-M$	$-M$		
	Sol mix	b_0	X	Y	S_1	S_2	A_1	A_2	N_X	N_Y
$-M$	A_1	16	④	2	-1	0	1	0	4	8 ← Key row
$-M$	A_2	9	1	3	0	-1	0	1	9	3
	Z_j	$-25M$	$-5M$	$-5M$	M	M	$-M$	$-M$		
	$Z_j - C_j$		$-15 + 5M$	$-15 + 5M$	$-M$	$-M$	0	0		

Key column

When this occurs, the determination of the tied variable to be brought into the solution mix is made by evaluating the calculated values of N of each of the tied variables. These are shown in Table 8A.7 as N_X and N_Y. We see that if X is to be the incoming variable, the smallest positive value of N_Y is 4. Thus 4 units of X could be brought into the solution. If Y were to enter, the N_Y column indicates that only 3 units could enter the solution. Since each unit of X or Y has the same impact on the objective function, our decision is to bring in the variable X because more units of that variable can enter the solution without violating any constraints.

The second and third simplex tables for this cost minimization problem are shown in Tables 8A.8 and 8A.9. In the second simplex table the largest positive value in the index row is associated with the variable Y and

TABLE 8A.8
Second Simplex Table: Minimization Example (continued)

0	$-M$	$-M$	
S_2	A_2	A_1	N
0	.25	0	8
-1.0	$-.25$	1.0	2 ← Key row
(M)	$(-3.75 + .25M)$	$(-M)$	
$(-M)$	$(3.75 - 1.25M)$	0	

TABLE 8A.9
Third Simplex Table: Minimization Example

C_j	Sol mix	b_0	-15 Z	-15 Y	0 S_1	0 S_2	$-M$ A_1	$-M$ A_2
-15	X	3	1	0	$-.3$	.2	.3	$-.2$
-15	Y	2	0	1	.1	$-.4$	$-.1$	.4
	Z_j	-75	-15	-15	3	3	-3	-3
	$C_j - Z_j$		0	0	-3	-3	$3 - M$	$3 - M$

the smallest value for N is associated with the artificial variable A_2. Thus Y replaces A_2 in the solution mix of the third simplex table. All index row values in the third simplex table are either 0 or negative, and therefore we have reached an optimal solution.

In the optimal solution, we see that $X = 3$ and $Y = 2$, while all other variables equal 0 (because they do not appear in the solution mix). The value of the objective function given in the table is $Z = -75$. Recall, however, that we have been maximizing $-Z$ in order to minimize Z. Therefore, the optimum value given in the simplex table must be multiplied by -1 to find the minimum for our original objective function. This can be verified by returning to that function:

$$Z = 15X + 15Y$$
$$Z = 15(3) + 15(2) = 75$$

This solution is, of course, the same as the result we found using the graphic method in Chapter 8 and illustrated in Figure 8.3.

Cost Theory and Analysis

⑨

Trade-offs, or sacrifices, are pervasive in human action. Everyone is confronted daily with situations in which one choice implies that some other alternative must be foregone. For example, the selection of a Pioneer tape deck for purchase may preclude the purchase of a Sony video player (after all, you're not "made of money"). We can think of an economic system as a means of rationing inadequate supplies, and in this sense, cost has a new meaning. The cost of any good is the cost of the raw materials used in making it; and their cost, in turn, is the cost of the foregone alternative, or the opportunity cost. For example, if you use the electrical components available to manufacture a tape deck, the real cost of the tape deck is the video player or phonograph that could have been produced with the same materials.

This is the view economists take of costs. It is actually the way the real world works and not just a whimsical way of looking at things. The more tape decks produced, the fewer video players and phonographs produced, all other things being equal. In an economy coordinated by prices, as in the United States, when the demand for tape decks increases, electrical components that might have found their way into video players and phonographs are often absorbed into the production of tape decks. The quantity of electrical components allocated for tape deck production depends on the respective values placed on tape decks, video recorders, and phonographs by consumers. Those values are subjective values: when people say they want a tape deck and are willing to pay for it, they mean they are willing to sacrifice other alternatives for the tape deck; a tape deck, then, has more value to them than do the alternatives considered.

The cost of any good can usually be given quite easily in physical terms. A given quantity of electrical components is needed for a tape deck, and at least some of those components could alternatively be used in video player or phonograph production. To make such a statement, however, says nothing about whether tape decks or video players or phonographs or some combination of all three will actually be produced in an economy. That depends on the subjective values placed on those respective goods by individuals. More about the actual allocation of resources in an economy

441

is discussed in the next three chapters, which deal with market structures and pricing.

The purpose of this chapter is to explore cost and its relevance to decision making. We begin by developing the important concepts of explicit and implicit costs and demonstrating how the identification of the various cost components of a decision-making situation can not only explain the behavior of business managers but can also aid in making correct decisions. We will then consider the concepts of short- and long-run costs and show that they, in conjunction with the concepts of production studied in Chapter 7, can give us a more complete understanding of the applications of cost theory to decision making.

9.1 EXPLICIT AND IMPLICIT COSTS

The opportunity cost (or cost of the foregone alternative) of an item is a definition of cost in its most basic form. While this particular definition of cost is the preferred baseline for economists in describing cost, not all costs in decision-making situations are completely obvious; one of the skills of a good manager is the ability to uncover hidden costs. The manner in which costs are classified or defined is largely dependent on the purpose for which the cost data are being used. For a long time, there was considerable disagreement between accountants and economists on how costs should be treated. The reason for the difference of opinion was that the two groups wanted to use the cost data for dissimilar purposes.

Traditionally, the accountant was primarily concerned with the collection of historical cost data for use in reporting a firm's financial behavior and position and in calculating its taxes. Business economists, on the other hand, were primarily concerned with using cost data in decision making. These purposes called for different types of cost data and classifications. A better understanding of the alternative uses of the data, along with a closer working relationship between cost accountants and managerial, or business, economists has reduced the intensity of the disagreement over cost classifications. Accountants, however, still correctly rely primarily on historical cost in determining the profit or loss of a firm during some past period of time or in establishing the tax liability of the firm at some point in time.

Economists prefer to use the opportunity cost baseline concept in evaluating economic decisions. The opportunity cost of a resource can be defined as the value of the resource in its next best use, that is, if it were not being used for the present purpose. The opportunity cost is the benefit of using a resource for the next most attractive alternative. For example, the opportunity cost of a student's college education could be the income that could have been earned had the student employed his or her labor resources at a job, rather than spending that time studying literature, accounting, economics, and so on.

As a further example, consider the costs of attending this course in managerial economics. The out-of-pocket costs (*explicit costs*) include the average tuition cost of this course (say, $300) and the cost of books and other supplies (perhaps another $50). We could view this as the cost of the course (a total of $350). Alternatively, we could use the opportunity cost concept and consider what you could have been doing instead of taking this course. To attend the course involves about 45 class meetings per semester, each about 60 minutes in length. In addition, time must be spent in coming and going, homework assignments, test preparation, and so on. The actual total number of hours spent on managerial economics may be closer to 135 hours per semester (three times the 45 60-minute class meetings). Now, what could you have done in lieu of taking this course? One alternative could be to work at, say, $4 per hour. Your time cost in money terms is then $540 ($4 per hour times 135 hours). The total cost of taking the course is then

Tuition and supplies (explicit):	$350
Time cost (implicit):	540
Total cost of course:	$890

The major portion of the total cost of the course turns out to be the *implicit* time cost. The implicit cost could have been 0 if you had no opportunity to work, or it could have been much higher than $540 if your skills were highly valued in the market. Relatively fewer older persons take managerial economics (or any other college courses), and this can be explained, at least in part, by the high implicit time cost to them of attending college.

Accountants typically use only those costs that are recorded in their various accounts as representing an actual transfer of money. These are explicit, or nominal, costs and often do not represent the full economic costs that should be considered in a given decision. *In addition to explicit costs, the business economist uses implicit, or imputed, cost in evaluating a problem.*

9.2   RELEVANT COSTS FOR A BUSINESS DECISION: AN EXAMPLE

To further illustrate the consequences of using the alternative views of cost, consider the following decision situation. Suppose that Mr. Ditton, owner of Ditton Heating and Air Conditioning Company of Muskogee, Oklahoma, has been contracted by the City Council concerning the installation of a climate control system in the Muskogee City Hall, which is being renovated. The City Council has given Ditton the first chance at the job because his company is the only local one with the necessary size and expertise to handle the contract. The climate control system must be completely installed during the 21 workdays in June. Mr. Ditton has been offered $65,000 to do the job.

After careful analysis of the type of system the City Council has requested, Mr. Ditton has been able to establish reasonably accurate estimates of the time and resource requirements necessary to complete the task in the given time period. The best estimate of the labor requirements indicates that 82 labor-days will be needed. Since June is one of the busiest months for Ditton, only three men who are trained and have experience in this type of work can be allocated to the job because of other commitments the company has for June. Thus, from his present work force, only 63 labor-days can be used for this job (21 days in June times 3 laborers). Fortunately, Mr. Ditton's son, Murray, will be home from college at the end of May and can perform much of the unskilled work. Mr. Ditton figures that, for his regular employees, each labor-day costs the company $106 (including wages, hospitalization insurance, social security payments, and other miscellaneous expenses). Thus, the labor cost for his three employees for 21 days will be $6678 (3 × 21 × 106).[1] Murray expects to be able to get his usual summer job back at $40 per day but would be willing to work for his father if asked.

The Ditton Company has all the necessary equipment for the job and has most of the materials available in inventory, except one major component. The materials in inventory cost $47,500, and the other component can be specially ordered in time for installation at a cost of $8500. Table 9.1 summarizes Mr. Ditton's first estimate of the cost of the project based on explicit and historical cost concepts. The decision is obvious: since costs are $2322 less than the revenue from the project, Mr. Ditton should accept the contract.

Upon seeing these estimates, Murray suggests to his father that this is not a true depiction of the relevant costs involved. First, Murray notes that his labor time has an opportunity cost of $40 per day; thus, if he works 19 days on this project, his labor should be included at $760 (40 × 19). Furthermore, since the costs of the heating and air-conditioning materials to be used from inventory have increased an average of 6 percent, their replacement cost is $50,350 ($47,500 × 1.06). This is, then, the best estimate of

TABLE 9.1   **Explicit Costs and Revenues of the City Hall Project**

Revenue		$65,000
Costs		
Labor	$ 6,678	
Materials (inventory cost)	47,500	
Special component	8,500	
Total costs		62,678
Profit		$ 2,322

[1]This assumes that Mr. Ditton may lay off employees when there is no work for them, which may be the case if the city hall project is not obtained.

TABLE 9.2   **Explicit and Implicit Costs of the City Hall Project**

Revenue		$65,000
Costs		
Labor (explicit)	$ 6,678	
Labor (implicit)	760	
Materials (replacement costs)	50,350	
Special component	8,500	
Total costs		66,288
Profit (Loss)		($ 1,288)

the cost to the Ditton Company of using those materials to install the new climate control system in the Muskogee City Hall. Mr. Ditton agrees with Murray's analysis and reevaluates the situation as shown in Table 9.2. Using the opportunity cost concept (including the imputed cost of Murray's labor), we see that if this project is undertaken, the company would incur a loss of $1288, rather than Mr. Ditton's initial estimate of $2322 in profit.[2]

We should emphasize several important points. First, there is not always a right and a wrong way to look at cost. The interpretation and determination of costs must be consistent with the use for which the information is generated. For example, the relevant cost data for determining a company's tax liability may be quite different from the relevant data for decision making. Second, the determination of costs is not always a purely objective matter; considerable judgment must be used, and there is often disagreement among analysts on the appropriate costs in a given situation. This is particularly true when imputed, or indirect, costs and the opportunity cost concept are involved. Finally, we must realize that most of the cost data available in a business have been collected and categorized by accountants. Therefore, it is imperative that, in using historical cost data as input into economic decision models, economists know how to interpret various accounts.

9.3   PRIVATE COSTS VERSUS SOCIAL COSTS

A further distinction that confounds many discussions of costs, particularly in the public sector, is that between private and social costs. *Private costs* are those that accrue directly to the individuals engaged in the relevant

---

[2]This example is fairly simple and does not include all variations of the possible implications of various cost concepts. For example, it may be that by taking this job, the Ditton Company would realize promotional benefits equal to $3000 worth of advertising. If so, the project may be profitable if the firm can save that $3000 (a negative cost). The net profit from the contract would then be $1712. On the other hand, Mr. Ditton may have been able to use these workers and other resources in some alternative way that would have produced a profit. If so, that profit should be included as an opportunity cost of the city hall project.

activity. External costs, on the other hand, are passed on to persons not involved in the activity in any direct way (i.e., they are passed on to society at large). Consider the classic case of a manufacturer located on the edge of a lake or river who dumps waste into the water rather than disposing of it in some other manner. The private cost to the firm of dumping is 0. If the waste was hauled away to a landfill or otherwise treated, some explicit private cost would be involved. Production costs thus appear lower than they really are. Third parties located downcurrent are adversely affected by the waste and incur higher costs in terms of treating the water for their use, having to travel to alternative recreation facilities and so on. If these external costs were included in the production costs of the producing firm, a truer picture of real, or *social costs*, of the output would be obtained. Ignoring external costs may lead to an inefficient and undesirable allocation of resources.

9.4   AN INTRODUCTION TO THE RELATIONSHIP BETWEEN PRODUCTION AND COSTS

The concept of cost is closely related to production theory. A *cost function* is the relationship between a firm's costs and the firm's output. While the production function specifies the technological maximum quantity of output that can be produced from various combinations of inputs, the cost function combines this information with input price data and gives information on various outputs and their prices. The cost function (any cost function) can thus be thought of as a combination of the following two pieces of information:

---

1. PRODUCTION FUNCTION

plus

2. INPUT PRICES

yields

FIRM'S COST FUNCTION

For example, consider the two following pieces of information. First, Firm A has a production function with constant returns to the variable inputs (i.e., its production function is a straight line). Second, the firm faces constant input prices (i.e., no matter what quantity of inputs is purchased, the per unit price remains the same to the firm; there are no quantity discounts).

Considering these two pieces of information, Firm A's resulting variable cost function would be drawn as pictured in the upper part of Figure 9.1. The production function ($Q = 10L$) is shown in the lower part of the graph. Only one variable input is used just to simplify the analysis. The results would hold for more variable inputs as long as the production function was linear in all inputs. Firm A's variable cost function is linear because as inputs are increased (say, doubled), output increases proportionately (doubles), and with constant input prices, variable cost increases along the straight line path exhibited in Figure 9.1 (i.e., $VC = 1.5Q$).

To be sure that the relationship between the production function and the variable cost function is clear, let us look at it carefully:

$$\text{Production function:} \quad Q = 10L$$
$$\text{Assumed price per unit of labor:} \quad P_L = 15$$

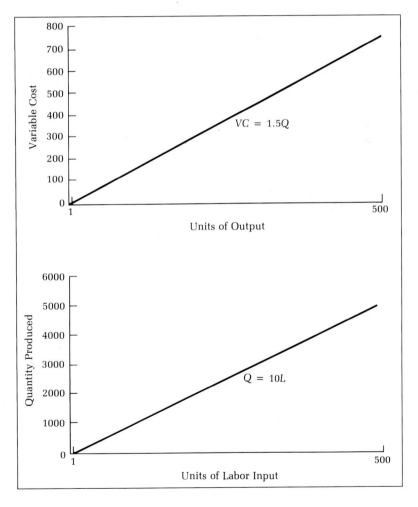

FIGURE 9.1   **Production and Cost Functions: Firm A.** This firm has constant returns to the variable input (labor), which results in a linear variable cost function.

The variable cost is equal to the price per unit of the variable input times the number of units of the input employed. Thus,

Variable cost: $VC = 15L$

But we usually consider cost a function of the level of output (Q). Since we know how output (Q) and input (L) are related, we can find VC as a function of Q as follows:

$$Q = 10L$$

Thus,

$$L = .1Q$$
$$VC = 15L$$
$$VC = 15(.1Q)$$
$$VC = 1.5Q$$

This variable cost function is the one graphed in the upper part of Figure 9.1.

If the assumption of either a linear production function or of a constant input price is changed, the shape of the resulting variable cost curve will also change. The important point to keep in mind is that the shape of the variable cost curve (all the cost curves, in fact) depends on these two bits of information.

Now consider Firm B. It is also faced with a constant input price (we shall assume only one variable input, labor, with a price of $15 per labor unit), but B's production function exhibits decreasing returns to the variable input. Its production function could be

$$Q = 10 \sqrt{L}$$

With decreasing returns, each successive unit of production costs (in input terms) a little more than the preceding unit. Thus, Figure 9.2, which depicts Firm B's variable cost function, shows that variable cost increases at an increasing rate as the quantity produced increases. The variable cost function is

$$VC = .15Q^2$$

This is found as follows:

$$Q = 10\sqrt{L}$$

Thus,

$$L = Q^2/100$$
$$VC = 15L$$
$$VC = 15(Q^2/100)$$
$$VC = .15Q^2$$

The change in the shape of the variable cost function of Firm A to that of Firm B was solely the result of a change in the nature of the production function (from constant to decreasing returns to the variable input).

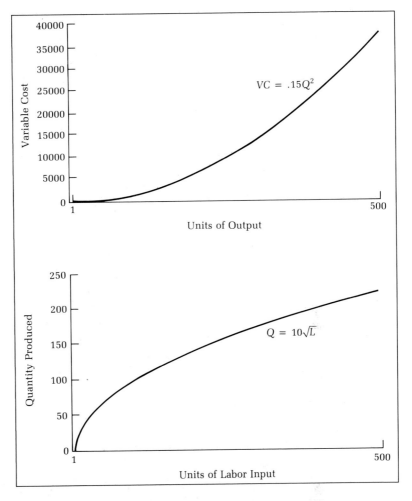

FIGURE 9.2   **Production and Cost Functions: Firm B.**   This firm has decreasing returns to the variable input (labor), which results in a variable cost function that increases at an increasing rate.

Next let us look at Firm C, with a constant input price (again, $15 per labor unit) but with a production function that has increasing returns to the variable input. Again, the shape of the variable cost curve is determined by the characteristics of the production function ($Q = 10L^2$) and by the supply conditions of the input (price of labor is constant at $15 per labor unit). Firm C's variable cost function is pictured in Figure 9.3; the cost curve increases at a decreasing rate throughout its entire range, in line with our two assumptions. In this case, $VC = 4.74Q^{.5}$, which is found as follows:

$$Q = 10L^2$$

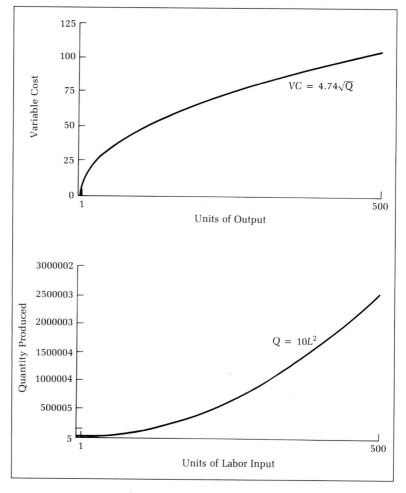

FIGURE 9.3   **Production and Cost Functions: Firm C.**   This firm has increasing returns to the variable input (labor), which results in a variable cost function that increases at a decreasing rate.

Thus,

$$L = \sqrt{Q/10}$$
$$VC = 15L$$
$$VC = 15\sqrt{Q/10}$$
$$VC = (15/\sqrt{10})\sqrt{Q}$$
$$VC = 4.74\sqrt{Q}$$

Note also that the cost curve could have just as easily changed its shape in response to a changed assumption about input prices. A common situation in the real world is the offering of quantity discounts: the more a firm purchases of a resource, the less its unit cost. If we had assumed a production

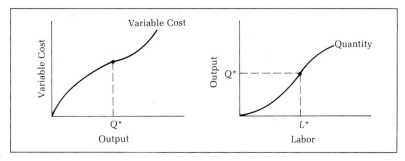

FIGURE 9.4   **Production and Cost Functions: Firm D.**   This firm has a production function that exhibits increasing returns to the variable factor input (labor) up to L^* and decreasing returns after L^*. The input level L^* corresponds to the output level Q^*. The variable cost function increases at a decreasing rate up to Q^* and at an increasing rate beyond Q^*.

function with constant returns to the variable inputs and decreasing input prices (quantity discounts), we would again have a variable cost curve like Firm C's in Figure 9.3.

It is also common for a production function to have different returns to variable inputs over different ranges. The firm represented in Figure 9.4, Firm D, first has increasing returns and then has decreasing returns to the variable input along with constant input prices. This combination of assumptions yields the variable cost function in Figure 9.4, which has a shape that is characteristic of many actual variable cost functions: *increasing at a decreasing rate and then increasing at an increasing rate.* This characteristic shape of many real world total cost functions is used later in the chapter.

9.5   THE SHORT RUN AND THE LONG RUN

The *short run* may be defined as a time period over which some factors of production are fixed and others are variable. In the *long run*, all factors of production are variable. Note that these periods are not defined by some specified length of time but, rather, are determined by the variability of factors of production. Thus, what one firm may consider the long run may correspond to the short run for another firm.

Consider Ann's Bakery and the Mobil Oil Company, for example. If the proprietors of Ann's should decide to expand the scope of their operations, they could hire more labor and/or add to their capital equipment (with a larger oven, perhaps) in a matter of a day, a week, or a month. These would be short-run changes because their building (a factor of production) remains fixed in size. However, given six or eight months, they could likely expand their present facility or move to a new, larger building. This would then represent the long run, since all productive factors could be varied.

For Mobil, the short run may extend over a very long time span. To expand all the factors involved in producing commercial oil products takes considerable time in planning and generating the funds for expansion and construction, not to mention such difficult decisions as the selection of a site for a new facility. A large company such as Mobil may find it impossible to change all factors of production in less than five years. Thus, the short run for such a firm will be far longer than for firms in some other types of productive activities. We should expect the time span covered by the concepts of long and short run to vary among industries and, to a lesser extent, among firms within a single industry.

9.6   DERIVATION OF SHORT-RUN COST FUNCTIONS

In the short run, a firm incurs some costs that are associated with variable factors and others that result from fixed factors. The former are referred to as *variable costs*, and the latter represent *fixed costs*. Variable costs (VC) change as the amount of output changes and can therefore be expressed as a function of output (Q), that is, $VC = f(Q)$. Variable costs typically include such things as raw materials, labor, and utilities. Fixed costs, on the other hand, are not a function of the level of output and are constant in the short run, that is, $FC = K$. Fixed costs may include such things as property taxes, the cost of leases on land, buildings and some types of equipment, interest on bonds sold to purchase capital equipment, and some kinds of insurance.

We have seen that, when a variable factor of production is added to some fixed factor or factors, the variable factor eventually becomes subject to diminishing marginal returns (see Chapter 7). That is, as more of the variable factor is employed, output eventually increases at a decreasing rate. With constant input prices, it follows that variable costs will increase at an increasing rate, since output is increasing at a decreasing rate (see Figure 9.4).

Consider a typical short-run production function with labor as the variable factor that combines with some fixed factors of production. For such a production function, output will first increase at an increasing and then at a decreasing rate when expressed as a function of the variable factor. As a general rule, we should then expect variable costs to increase first at a decreasing rate and subsequently at an increasing rate. To see this explicitly, let us consider a numerical example.

The data in Table 9.3 will help us translate information about production into the corresponding short-run cost functions. The first two columns of this table represent a production function in which daily output at first increases at an increasing rate and then at a decreasing rate as the amount of a variable input, labor, is increased from 0 to 10

TABLE 9.3   **Determination of Variable and Total Cost from a Production Schedule**

Units of Labor (L)	Quantity of Output (Q)	Price per Unit of Labor (P_L)	Variable Cost of Production (VC)*	Fixed Cost (FC)**	Total Cost (TC)†
0	0	$160	$ 0	$400	$ 400
1	8.4	160	160	400	560
2	31.2	160	320	400	720
3	64.8	160	480	400	880
4	105.6	160	640	400	1040
5	150.0	160	800	400	1200
6	194.4	160	960	400	1360
7	235.2	160	1120	400	1520
8	268.8	160	1280	400	1680
9	291.6	160	1440	400	1840
10	300.0	160	1600	400	2000

*$VC = P_L L = 160L$
**FC is given as 400
†$TC = FC + VC$

units. Some amount of fixed factors with a daily cost allocation of $400 is also used.

The production schedule from Table 9.3 is plotted on the right-hand side of the graph in Figure 9.5. It is drawn as a solid line only up to 10 units of the labor input, since beyond that point total product diminishes (marginal product is negative). Each of the 10 points used to plot the production function is labeled with a letter (A through J).

Now assume that each unit of labor costs $160 (i.e., a unit equals one eight-hour day at $20 per hour, including fringe benefits, social security, etc.). Then one labor unit, or 8.4 units of output (point A), would represent a variable cost of $160. Two labor units, or 31.2 units of output (point B), would have a variable cost of $320. Production of 150 units of output (point E) would involve five units of labor, or $800 of variable cost. Thus, each point on the production function has a corresponding variable cost. These points are graphed in the left-hand part of Figure 9.5 as points A' through J'. We usually think of variable cost as a function of the level of output. Therefore, to see the general shape of a variable-cost curve, the diagram should be turned clockwise 90 degrees so that the quantity ($TP = Q$) axis becomes the horizontal axis and the variable cost axis the vertical.

Doing this, we see that VC intersects at the origin because 0 output results when no labor is used, and if no labor is used, there is no labor cost (here labor is the only variable factor). We also see that variable cost first increases at a decreasing rate (the slope becomes less steep) and then increases at an increasing rate (the slope becomes steeper). Remember that we are considering the quantity axis the horizontal, so the slope is measured as dVC/dQ.

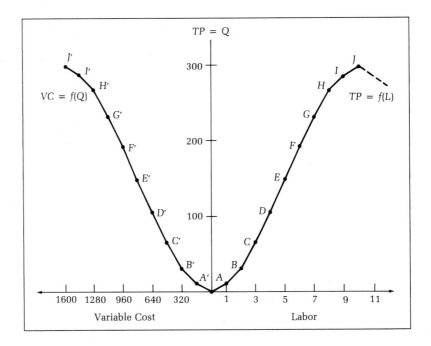

FIGURE 9.5   **Derivation of Variable Cost.**   This graph depicts the derivation of the variable cost curve from the production function given in Figure 9.3, with a labor cost of $160 per unit.

9.7 SHORT-RUN VARIABLE, FIXED, AND TOTAL COSTS: AN ALGEBRAIC EXAMPLE

Another variable cost function is shown in Table 9.4 and Figure 9.6. We see that variable cost increases at a decreasing rate up to $Q = 6$, and beyond that point, variable cost increases at an increasing rate. This variable cost function is represented by the equation

$$VC = 18Q - 2.7Q^2 + .15Q^3$$

We have seen that in the short run the total cost (TC) of production is composed of variable costs and fixed costs (FC). That is,

$$TC = FC + VC$$

If fixed costs in this case are equal to 30, we can express total cost as follows:

$$TC = 30 + 18Q - 2.7Q^2 + .15Q^3$$

The total cost function and the fixed cost function are illustrated in Figure 9.6

TABLE 9.4

Variable Cost (VC) as a Function of Output (Q):
$VC = 18Q - 2.7Q^2 + .15Q^3$

VC	Q
0.0	0
15.45	1
26.40	2
33.75	3
38.40	4
41.25	5
43.20	6
45.15	7
48.00	8
52.65	9
60.00	10
70.95	11
86.40	12
107.25	13
134.40	14
168.75	15

The total cost function has a positive intercept because the firm incurs certain fixed costs (30) in the short run even if output is 0. At nonzero levels of output, the total cost function increases at a decreasing rate up to some

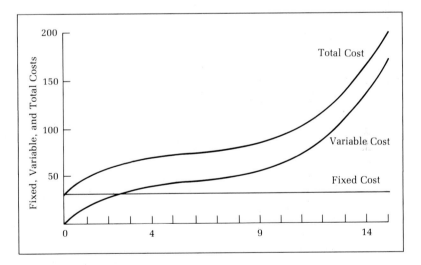

FIGURE 9.6

Typical Cost Functions. This graph illustrates the following cost functions:

$$FC = 30$$
$$VC = 18Q - 2.7Q^2 + .15Q^3$$
$$TC = 30 + 18Q - 2.7Q^2 + .15Q^3$$

Note that total cost (TC) and variable cost (VC) at first increase at a decreasing rate and then at an increasing rate.

point ($Q = 6$) and beyond that increases at an increasing rate. The total cost function always lies above the variable cost function by the amount of fixed costs (30). That is, the vertical distance between the total and variable cost functions is constant throughout and exactly equals fixed costs.

9.8 SHORT-RUN UNIT COSTS

Having developed an understanding of fixed, variable, and total cost, we can now proceed to evaluate per unit, or average, costs. Dividing each of these three costs (fixed cost, variable cost, and total cost) by the quantity of output yields average fixed cost, average variable cost, and average total cost, respectively. The term *average cost* is often used instead of *average total cost*. We shall follow the common convention of using the term *average cost* (AC) throughout the remainder of the text. Thus, when referring to the average cost of producing some product, we mean the total cost divided by the number of units of output. These per unit cost functions may be written as follows:

$$AFC = FC/Q$$
$$AVC = VC/Q$$
$$AC = TC/Q$$
$$AC = (FC + VC)/Q$$
$$AC = AFC + AVC$$

The most important cost concept in economic analysis is marginal cost (MC). Marginal cost represents the rate of change in total cost as output changes and can be represented as the first derivative of total cost with respect to quantity.[3] That is,

$$MC = dTC/dQ$$

If the cost data are given in tabular form, marginal cost is approximated as the change in total cost divided by the change in quantity in each interval (i.e., $MC = \Delta TC/\Delta Q$). This is frequently referred to as *incremental cost*, since it represents the change in cost over an interval rather than at a particular point, as is the case with marginal cost. Since marginal analysis lies at the core of the economic decision process, the concept of marginal cost is very important in our subsequent analysis.

Let us now look into the general nature of each per unit cost function. The average fixed cost, average variable cost, average cost, and marginal cost functions that correspond to the cost functions graphed in Figure 9.6 are illustrated in Figure 9.7 and are also shown in Table 9.5.

---

[3]Since fixed costs are constant, the only change in total cost must result from changes in variable cost; thus, we also define $MC = dVC/dQ$, since $dVC/dQ = dTC/dQ$.

TABLE 9.5
Cost as a Function of Output

Q	Fixed Cost (FC)	Total Variable Cost (VC)	Total Cost (TC)	Marginal Cost* (MC)	Average Fixed Cost (AFC)	Average Variable Cost (AVC)	Average Total Cost (AC)
0	30	0.0	30.00				
				15.45			
1	30	15.45	45.45		30.00	15.45	45.45
				10.95			
2	30	26.40	56.40		15.00	13.20	28.20
				7.35			
3	30	33.75	63.75		10.00	11.25	21.25
				4.65			
4	30	38.40	68.40		7.50	9.60	17.10
				2.85			
5	30	41.25	71.25		6.00	8.25	14.25
				1.95			
6	30	43.20	73.20		5.00	7.20	12.20
				1.95			
7	30	45.15	75.15		4.29	6.45	10.74
				2.85			
8	30	48.00	78.00		3.75	6.00	9.75
				4.65			
9	30	52.65	82.65		3.33	5.85	9.18
				7.35			
10	30	60.00	90.00		3.00	6.00	9.00
				10.95			
11	30	70.95	100.95		2.73	6.45	9.18
				15.45			
12	30	86.40	116.40		2.50	7.20	9.70
				20.85			
13	30	107.25	137.25		2.31	8.25	10.56
				27.15			
14	30	134.40	164.40		2.14	9.60	11.75
				34.35			
15	30	168.75	198.75		2.00	11.25	13.25

NOTE: $FC = \$30$ $AFC = FC/Q$
$VC = 18Q - 2.7Q^2 + .15Q^2$ $AVC = VC/Q$
$TC = FC + VC$ $AC = TC/Q$
$MC = TC/Q$

*Marginal cost shown in this table refers to an intraunit marginal cost and not the calculated (i.e., $MC = 18Q - 2.7Q^2 + .15Q^3$) value at individual values of Q.

Average Fixed Cost

We see that average fixed cost diminishes throughout as the fixed cost (30) is spread over ever-increasing levels of output. The average fixed cost function is

$$AFC = 30/Q$$

This function is a rectangular hyperbola approaching each axis asymptotically.

Marginal Cost

The marginal cost (MC), average variable cost (AVC), and average (AC) cost functions all decrease over some range of output, reach a minimum, and subsequently increase as the level of output expands. For this reason, these functions are referred to as *U-shaped cost functions*. Given the total cost function (presented above), we can derive the equation for MC, AVC, and AC and determine the range of output over which each decreases or

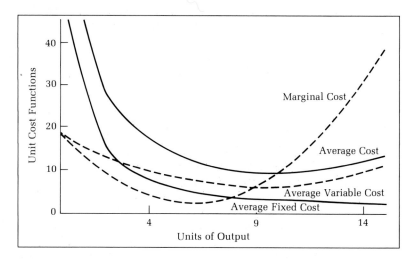

FIGURE 9.7   **Typical Unit Cost Curves.**   This figure illustrates the unit cost func-
tions corresponding to the total, variable, and fixed cost curves shown in
Figure 9.6. The data related to these curves are shown in Table 9.5.
These functions can also be represented by the following equations:

$$AFC = 30/Q$$
$$AVC = 18 - 2.7Q + .15Q^2$$
$$AC = (30/Q) + 18 - 2.7Q + .15Q^2$$
$$MC = 18 - 5.4Q + .45Q^2$$

increases. In this section, our focus is on just the marginal cost function. For
MC, we have

$$TC = 30 + 18Q - 2.7Q^2 + .15Q^3$$
$$MC = dTC/dQ = 18 - 5.4Q + .45Q^2$$
$$dMC/dQ = -5.4 + .9Q = 0$$
$$.9Q = 5.4$$
$$Q = 6$$

Therefore, there is a critical value for the marginal cost function at $Q = 6$.
Looking at the second-order condition, we see

$$d^2MC/dQ^2 = .9 > 0$$

Thus, marginal cost reaches a minimum at $Q = 6$, at which point $MC =$
1.80. MC is a decreasing function up to $Q = 6$ and an increasing function
beyond that level of output. This result should be compared with the MC
data given in Table 9.5 and the MC curve illustrated in Figure 9.7.

The Relationship between Marginal Cost and Marginal Product

Marginal cost reaches its minimum when marginal productivity is at a
maximum. Using difference notation (Δ = change in), we can show this as

follows. Let F be the variable factor of production, P_F be the price of that factor, and Q be output. Then,

$$MP = \Delta Q/\Delta F \qquad (1)$$
$$MC = \Delta TC/\Delta Q, \text{ and } \Delta TC = (P_F)(\Delta F)$$
$$MC = (P_F)(\Delta F)/\Delta Q \qquad (2)$$

Solving equation 1 for ΔQ yields

$$\Delta Q = (MP)(\Delta F)$$

Substituting this in equation 2, we get

$$MC = (P_F)(\Delta F)/(MP)(\Delta F)$$
$$MC = P_F/MP = P_F(1/MP)$$

Thus, marginal cost equals the price of the variable factor times the reciprocal of marginal product. If marginal product increases, marginal cost decreases and vice versa. Therefore, when MP reaches a maximum, MC is at its minimum.

Average Variable Cost

Since variable cost is that portion of total cost that changes as the level of output changes, it can be represented as

$$VC = 18Q - 2.7Q^2 + .15Q^3$$

The average variable cost can then be found as follows:

$$AVC = VC/Q$$
$$AVC = 18 - 2.7Q + .15Q^2$$

To find the minimum point on the average variable cost function, we must find where its first derivative is 0:

$$dAVC/dQ = -2.7 + .3Q = 0$$
$$.3Q = 2.7$$
$$Q = 9$$

Therefore, there is a critical value for the average variable cost function at $Q = 9$. Looking at the second-order condition, we find

$$d^2AVC/dQ^2 = .3 > 0$$

Thus, average variable cost reaches a minimum at $Q = 9$, at which point $AVC = 5.85$. AVC is a decreasing function for output less than 9 and increases beyond that point. This result should be compared with the AVC data given in Table 9.5 and with the AVC curve shown in Figure 9.7.

The Relationship between Average Variable Cost and Average Product

Because variable costs are derived from the variable factor of production, we expect average variable cost to reach a minimum when the average productivity of the variable factor is at a peak. Let F be the amount of a variable factor used in production, P_F be the constant price per unit of the variable factor, and Q be the qauntity of output produced. Then,

$$AP = Q/F \qquad (1)$$
$$AVC = VC/Q = (P_F)(F)/Q \qquad (2)$$

Solving equation 1 for Q yields

$$Q = (AP)(F)$$

Substituting this in equation 2, we get

$$AVC = (P_F)(F)/(AP)(F)$$
$$AVC = P_F/AP = P_F(1/AP)$$

Thus, average variable cost equals the price of the variable factor times the reciprocal of the average product. If average product increases, average variable cost must decrease and vice versa. It follows that when AP is at a maximum, AVC is at a minimum.

Average Cost

We have seen that the average cost of production is total cost divided by the number of units produced. Alternatively, we can think of average cost as the sum of average variable cost and average fixed cost. For our current example, we have

$$AC = TC/Q = AFC + AVC$$
$$AC = 30/Q + 18 - 2.7Q + .15Q^2$$
$$AC = 30Q^{-1} + 18 - 2.7Q + .15Q^2$$

To find where average cost has a minimum, we must evaluate its first derivative as follows:

$$dAC/dQ = -30Q^{-2} - 2.7 + .3Q = 0$$

The only economically meaningful root for this first-order condition is $Q = 10$, which is therefore our critical value. The second-order condition is

$$d^2AC/dQ^2 = 60Q^{-3} + .3 > 0$$

Thus, average cost reaches a minimum at $Q = 10$, at which point $AC = 9.00$. AC decreases up to 10 units of output and increases beyond that level. This result should be compared with the data for average cost in Table 9.5 and the average cost function graphed in Figure 9.7.

Some Further Points of Interest

Let us now investigate some further interrelationships between various cost concepts. Recall that both the total cost and variable cost functions were found to increase, first at a decreasing rate and then at an increasing rate. Recall, too, that marginal cost is the first derivative of either of these cost functions with respect to quantity. That is, marginal cost measures the rate of change in both total cost and variable cost. If marginal cost decreases (but is positive), the rate of increase in TC and VC must decrease. We see in Table 9.5 and Figure 9.6 that TC and VC increase at a decreasing rate up to $Q = 6$, that is, as long as marginal cost is declining. When marginal cost is increasing (for $Q > 6$), TC and VC increase at an increasing rate. Furthermore, note that for $Q < 6$, $dMC/dQ < 0$, while for $Q > 6$, $dMC/dQ > 0$. We can generalize as follows:

> 1.   If the slope of MC is negative ($dMC/dQ < 0$), total cost and variable cost increase at a decreasing rate.
>
> 2.   If the slope of MC is positive ($dMC/dQ > 0$), total cost and variable cost increase at an increasing rate.

When $dMC/dQ = 0$, the rate of increase in TC and VC is constant. This is true at only one point for the cost functions that we have been considering. However, in some situations, the TC and VC functions may be linear (or approximately linear) in the relevant range of output. In such cases, marginal cost is constant (equal to the slope of TC and VC, as always) and has a slope of 0, which is indicative of the constant rate of increase in TC and VC.

Figure 9.8 illustrates the marginal cost, average cost, and average variable cost curves for the data in Table 9.5 (Figures 9.7 and 9.8 are identical except that AFC is omitted from the latter). Two points on this graph are of particular interest. Point A is the intersection of marginal cost with average variable cost, and point B is the intersection of marginal cost with average cost. Note that at A and B, and AVC and AC have their respective minimum values. If these average cost functions (AC and AVC) have a minimum, the marginal cost function will intersect each at its minimum point.[4] For our functions, this can be shown as follows. We are given

---

[4]For average cost, this can be proved in general form as follows. We know that at the minimum of AC, $dAC/dQ = 0$. Furthermore, we have defined $AC = TC/Q$. Thus, at the minimum AC, $d(TC/Q)/dQ = 0$. Following the quotient rule, we have

$$\frac{d(TC/Q)}{dQ} = \frac{Q(dTC/dQ) - TC}{Q^2} = 0$$

$$Q(dTC/dQ) = TC$$
$$dTC/dQ = TC/Q$$
$$MC = AC$$

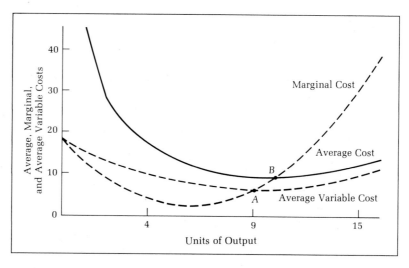

FIGURE 9.8   **Relationship among Marginal, Average, and Average Variable Costs.**   Note that the marginal cost curve (*MC*) intersects the average variable cost curve (*AVC*) at its minimum (point *A*) and the average cost curve (*AC*) at its minimum (point *B*).

$$MC = 18 - 5.4Q + .45Q^2$$
$$AC = 30/Q + 18 - 2.7Q + .15Q^2$$
$$AVC = 18 - 2.7Q + .15Q^2$$

And we know from above that *AC* is a minimum at $Q = 10$, while *AVC* is a minimum at $Q = 9$. At $Q = 10$, we have

$$MC = 18 - 5.4\,(10) + .45(10)^2 = 9$$
$$AC = 30/10 + 18 - 2.7(10) + .15(10)^2 = 9$$

And at $Q = 9$, we have

$$MC = 18 - 5.4(9) + .45(9)^2 = 5.85$$
$$AVC = 18 - 2.7(9) + .15(9)^2 = 5.85$$

The short-run cost functions and interrelationships that we have investigated are typical of a wide variety of business situations. An understanding of these concepts is essential for short-run economic decision making based on marginal analysis. For long-run decisions, we must consider how costs are affected when all factors of production are variable.

9.9   TOTAL COST IN THE LONG RUN

Most decisions involve short-run cost concepts because they are made in a context in which some fixed inputs exist. However, long-range plans and decisions are made based on the ability to change the level of use of all inputs. Thus, all short-run decisions are made within the framework of having certain fixed factors, the level of which was determined by an earlier long-run plan or decision. For this reason, long-run cost curves are often used to depict a firm's planning horizon.

Cost-Production Relationships in the Long Run

Long-run total-cost curves are derived from long-run production functions in which all inputs are variable. Such a production function is represented by the five isoquant curves in Figure 9.9. Although successive isoquants appear to be the same distance apart, the change in the level of output between successive isoquants is not constant. As we move from Q_1 to Q_2, output increases by 150 units (250 − 100); from Q_2 to Q_3, output increases by 250 units (500 − 250); from Q_3 to Q_4, output increases by 100 units (600 − 500); and from Q_4 to Q_5, output increases by 50 units (650 − 600).

The five isocost curves tangent to these isoquants at the points A, B, C, D, and E represent expenditures on resources (total costs) of $300, $400, $500, $600, and $700, respectively. Since the costs per unit of capital (r) and

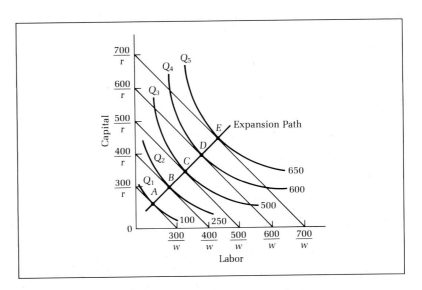

FIGURE 9.9   **Expansion Path and Returns to Scale**   These isoquant and isocost curves are for a production function that at first has increasing returns to scale $(A$ to $C)$, then constant returns to scale $(C$ to $D)$, and finally decreasing returns to scale $(D$ to $E)$. Points A, B, C, and E form the expansion path. The vertical and horizontal intercepts equal total cost divided by the cost per unit of capital (r) and the cost per unit of labor (w), respectively. Isoquants are labeled according to the number of units of output each represents.

labor (w) are assumed to be constant, these five isocost curves are parallel to one another, and the distance between them is constant along the expansion path traced out by A, B, C, D, and E.

Taking the values for total cost and output from the expansion path of Figure 9.9, we can construct the following table for total cost and output:

Output (Q)	Long-Run Total Cost (LRTC)
100	300
250	400
500	500
600	600
650	700

These points are graphed in Figure 9.10 as the long-run total-cost (LRTC) curve. The points A', B', C', D', and E' correspond to the equilibrium points in Figure 9.9 (A, B, C, D, and E, respectively). Note the LRTC curve at first increases at a decreasing rate, then at a constant rate, and finally at an increasing rate.

The graph of LRTC is extended from A' to the origin, since in the long run all costs are variable and if nothing is produced, no resources will be used (i.e., the firm will leave the industry entirely). Thus, the LRTC curve is analogous to the short-run VC curve. But the similarity is only superficial.

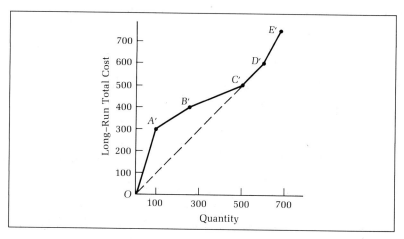

FIGURE 9.10 **Long-Run Total Cost Curve.** This is the long-run total cost curve (LRTC) derived from the expansion path of Figure 9.9. The LRTC curve increases at a decreasing rate (O through C'), then at a constant rate (C' to D'), and then at an increasing rate (beyond D'), representing the stages of increasing, constant, and decreasing returns to scale, respectively.

Although these two curves have the same general shape, the reasons for their shapes are quite different. The shape of VC is due to the fact that production is subject to the law of variable proportions in the short run. In the long run, however, it is the existence of increasing, constant, and decreasing returns to scale that accounts for the shape of $LRTC$.

Long-Run Cost and Economies of Scale

By comparing the relative change in resources to the relative change in output, we can determine whether there are economies of scale over any interval. Since r and w are constant, the percentage change in cost equals the percentage change in resources employed. The percentage changes are as follows:

Region	%Δ Total Cost		%Δ Output
AB	33	<	150
BC	25	<	100
CD	20	=	20
DE	17	>	8

Thus, this production function is characterized by increasing returns to scale over the range from A to C, constant returns to scale from C to D, and decreasing returns to scale from D to E.

9.10   UNIT COSTS IN THE LONG RUN

In the long run, costs are not dichotomized into fixed and variable components; all costs are variable. Thus, the only long-run unit-cost functions of interest are long-run average cost ($LRAC$) and long-run marginal cost ($LRMC$). These are defined as follows:

$$LRAC = LRTC/Q$$
$$LRMC = \Delta LRTC/\Delta Q$$

or

$$LRMC = d(LRTC)/dQ$$

For the long-run total cost given in Figure 9.10, these unit costs can be presented in tabular form as follows:

Output (Q)	Long-Run Total Cost (LRTC)	Long-Run Average Cost (LRAC)	Long-Run Marginal Cost (LRMC)
0	0		
100	300	3.00	3.00
250	400	1.60	.67
500	500	1.00	.67
600	600	1.00	1.00
650	700	1.08	2.00

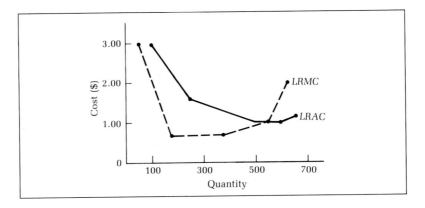

FIGURE 9.11   **Long-Run Unit-Cost Curves.** Graphed are the long-run marginal cost (LRMC) and the long-run average cost (LRAC) for the LRTC function graphed in Figure 9.10. LRMC equals LRAC at the minimum of LRAC.

These LRAC and LRMC values are graphed in Figure 9.11. We see, both in the table and in the graph, that LRAC and LRMC are U-shaped and that they are equal at the minimum of LRAC. The values of LRMC are graphed at the midpoints of the output intervals they represent.

The values for LRMC could be obtained from the table or from the LRTC function in Figure 9.10. LRAC can also be determined from Figure 9.10. For example, the LRAC of producing 100 units is the slope of OA' (300/100), and the LRAC of producing 500 units is the slope of the dashed line OC' (500/500 = 1).

Long-Run Average Cost as an Envelope Curve

The long-run average-cost curve is sometimes shown as the envelope curve of a series of all the possible short-run average cost curves, as shown in Figure 9.12. Five short-run average cost curves, each representing a different-sized plant (or set of fixed factors) are illustrated, although many more may exist. For any given rate of output, one plant size will accommodate that level of production at the lowest possible unit cost. Interestingly, the lowest cost of producing some rate of output is not generally at the minimum point of a short-run average-cost curve.

Consider, for example, the production of Q^* units in Figure 9.12. That level of output could be produced with the plant size represented by $SRAC_1$, $SRAC_2$, or $SRAC_3$. It represents the *optimum rate of output* for the size plant represented by $SRAC_1$ (i.e., it is at the minimum point of $SRAC_1$). However, if the firm expects to produce at that rate, the best size of plant is the one related to $SRAC_2$. Q^* units could be produced at a cost savings of FB per unit over $SRAC_1$. However, if the firm expanded too much, say, to the plant

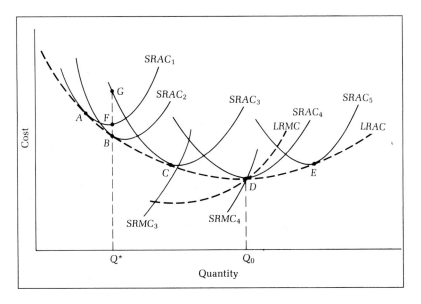

FIGURE 9.12   Long-Run Average Cost as an Envelope Curve.   The *LRAC* curve as the envelope curve of a series of *SRAC* curves, each representing a different size of plant. The minimum possible cost of producing each level of output (such as points *A, B, C, D,* and *E*) determine *LRAC*. Economies of scale exist up to Q_0, and diseconomies of scale are evident beyond that level. The *LRMC* is composed of a single point from each *SRMC* and intersects *LRAC* at its minimum (*D*).

with $SRAC_3$, the unit cost would be even higher (at point *G*) than with $SRAC_1$. The series of points such as *A, B, C, D,* and *E* that represent the lowest possible cost of producing each rate of output trace out the *LRAC* curve. Each of these points represents a tangency of a *SRAC* with the *LRAC* envelope curve.

The plant size associated with $SRAC_4$ is the *optimum size of plant* because its minimum point is the lowest of all possible unit costs.[5] Given the *LRAC* in Figure 9.12, we can say that there are increasing returns to scale (or economies of scale) up to Q_0 and decreasing returns to scale (or diseconomies of scale) beyond Q_0.[6]

---

[5]More than one scale may provide the lowest unit cost for certain levels of output. In such cases, management considers other factors in selecting the appropriate scale of production.

[6]We have used the terms *increasing returns to scale* and *economies of scale* (and *decreasing returns to scale* and *diseconomies of scale*) interchangeably. Strictly speaking, this is incorrect. Returns to scale are determined by production and technological factors. Economies (and diseconomies) of scale may also result from monetary effects alone, as when a larger firm is able to purchase large lots of inputs at reduced cost. However, in relationship to *LRAC*, it does little harm to think of these terms as representing the same concept.

The long-run marginal cost (*LRMC*) is composed of a single point from each *SRMC* curve, as shown in Figure 9.12. Only two representative short-run marginal-cost curves are illustrated ($SRMC_3$ and $SRMC_4$).

Some Reasons for the Shape of the *LRAC*

LRAC typically declines over some range of output for a number of reasons. The most important is that, as the scale of output is expanded, there is greater potential for *specialization* of productive factors. This is most notable with regard to labor but may apply to nonlabor factors as well. Specialization and the corresponding division of labor contribute to reduced unit costs in several ways. First, the laborer becomes more adept at his or her particular task, performs the function with greater skill and consistency, and, as a result, produces more output per unit of labor cost. There is also time saved when each worker does not have to move from one job to another at various stations throughout the production facility. Furthermore, specialized workers are more likely to see ways in which their functions can be performed more efficiently.

Other factors contributing to declining *LRAC* include ability to use more advanced technologies and more sophisticated capital equipment; opportunity to take advantage of lower costs for some inputs by purchasing large quantities; purely geometric factors, such as doubling the number of bricks used to build a warehouse, which can more than double the capacity; certain administrative costs that may not need to be increased at all for successive scales of output (over some range), for example, the employment of one purchasing agent for several plant sizes; and advances in the technology of management, including the use of computers to sort and organize vast quantities of data.

Not all economists agree that the *LRAC* will be U-shaped. This is in part because the evidence in support of the existence of diseconomies of scale is much less compelling than the evidence for economies of scale. As you will see shortly, many long-run average curves may be L-shaped. Such a shape results from a region of increasing returns to scale at low levels of production that is followed by an extended region of constant returns to scale.

9.11   ECONOMIES OF SCALE: SOME EVIDENCE

In this section, we will look at some industry studies that provide evidence concerning the existence of economies of scale. An entire text could be devoted to this topic, but the industries discussed here should give you a reasonably representative picture of the existence of scale economies.

The Soft Drink Industry

In the soft drink industry, it has been reported that a soft drink plant producing 1 to 2 percent of the total market is large enough to realize any possible economies of scale. This is true for several reasons.[7] First, the technology involved is relatively simple and generally well known, since it is not protected by patents. Also, the ingredients used are agricultural products easily obtained by all existing or potential producers. Furthermore, the capital costs of entering the industry are not very large relative to the costs of entering other industries, perhaps less than $10 million for a plant of minimum optimal size (capable of producing a volume of 1 to 2 percent of the total market). Thus, the long-run average cost probably declines slightly and then levels off.

Grain Production

Grain production, which also has a relatively simple technology, uses readily available inputs, and has low capital requirements, is another example of an industry exhibiting evidence of significant economies of scale. Using data on corn and soybean production in Illinois, Mueller and Hinton find that costs per bushel are relatively constant for farms over 500 acres.[8] Part of their data is reproduced in Table 9.6, which shows some fluctuation in per bushel grain costs for farms above 500 acres, but, clearly, any important scale economies are realized by that size interval.

TABLE 9.6   **Grain Production Cost per Bushel by Size of Farm**

Farm Size (acres)	Corn	Soybeans
180–259	$2.61	$6.43
260–339	2.27	5.93
340–499	2.20	5.73
500–649	2.11	5.43
650–799	2.09	5.42
800–949	2.17	5.55
950 +	2.04	5.41

SOURCE: A.G. Mueller and R.D. Hinton, "Farmer's Production Cost for Corn and Soybeans by Unit Size," *American Journal of Agricultural Economics,* December 1975, p. 937. Reprinted by permission.

---

[7]See James F. Mongoven, "Advertising as a Barrier to Entry: Structure and Performance in the Soft-Drink Industry," *Antitrust Law and Economics Review,* vol. 8, no. 1, 1976; pp. 93–101. More details from this article are reported in Chapter 13.

[8]See A.G. Mueller and R.A. Hinton, "Farmers' Production Cost for Corn and Soybeans by Unit Size," *American Journal of Agricultural Economics,* December 1975, pp. 934–939.

It is worth noting that cash, noncash, and implicit costs are all included in the determination of the average cost of producing corn and soybeans, as follows:

Cash Costs (explicit costs) per Acre	Noncash and Implicit Costs per Acre
Fertilizer	Labor, unpaid charges
Seed and crop expenses	Machinery depreciation
Labor costs	Building depreciation
Machinery repairs, fuel, and higher taxes	Land charges
	Interest on other capital
Building repairs	Machinery investment
Cash overhead expenses	Building investment
	Stored grain inventory
	Operating capital

Over 50 percent of the cost per bushel comes from categories in the right-hand column. This illustrates the importance of including implicit costs in the analysis of economic activities, as discussed earlier in this chapter.

The Electric Power Industry

In contrast to cases that illustrate only economies of scale in lower ranges of production and relatively constant costs thereafter, the electric power industry is an industry in which there are decreasing costs for most firm sizes in the industry. Perhaps the single most important difference between the soft drink and grain industries and the electric power generation industry is with regard to the amount of capital needed. For example, Commonwealth Edison had over $4 billion in plant and equipment (at original cost) as of December 1970.[9] This is clearly much larger than the necessary capital in the soft drink industry or in grain production. Of course, it should be noted that Commonwealth Edison is one of the larger electric utility companies in the United States, as indicated by its rank on the sample of 25 such companies listed in Table 9.7.

The data in this table are indicative of the decrease in average cost as the volume of output (in millions of kilowatt hours) increases.[10] The right-

---

[9]From the Commonwealth Edison Company 1970 Annual Report. The 1970 observation is used so that this measure of plant and equipment is consistent in time with the data on economics of scale in electric power generation given in this section.

[10]See L.R. Christensen and W.H. Greene, "Economies of Scale in U.S. Electric Power Generation," *Journal of Political Economy*, August 1976; pp. 655–676. See also footnote 5 in this chapter.

TABLE 9.7
Estimates of Scale Economies for Selected Firms (firms ordered by 1970 output)

Company	Output (million kwh) 1970	Average Cost ($1000 kwh) 1970	SCE
Newport Electric	50	10.75	.324
Community Public Service	183	7.03	.247
United Gas Improvement	467	8.44	.216
St. Joseph Light & Power	938	5.45	.181
Iowa Southern Utilities	1,328	6.07	.160
Missouri Public Service	1,886	5.47	.143
Rochester Gas & Elecric	2,020	8.89	.136
Iowa Electric Light & Power	2,445	5.37	.133
Central Louisiana Gas & Electric	2,689	5.54	.127
Wisconsin Public Service	3,571	6.02	.103
Atlantic City Electric	4,187	7.00	.094
Central Illinois Public Service	5,316	4.43	.097
Kansas Gas & Electric	5,785	3.36	.094
Northern Indiana Public Service	6,837	4.96	.079
Indianapolis Power & Light	7,484	3.94	.080
Oklahoma Gas & Electric	10,149	3.01	.066
Niagara Mohawk Power	11,667	6.40	.049
Potomac Electric Power	13,846	6.95	.037
Gulf States Utilities	17,875	3.27	.036
Virginia Electric Power	23,217	4.85	.015
Consolidated Edison	29,613	8.43	− .003
Detroit Edison	30,958	6.05	− .004
Duke Power	34,212	4.84	− .012
Commonwealth Edison	46,871	5.43	− .014
Southern	53,918	4.30	− .028

NOTE: kwh = kilowatt-hour
        SCE = scale economies where SCE = 1 − MC/AC

SOURCE: L.R. Christensen and W.H. Greene, "Economies of Scale of U.S. Electric Power Generation," *Journal of Political Economy*, August 1976, p. 672. Reprinted with permission of the University of Chicago Press.

hand column (*SCE*) provides a measure of economies of scale, which the authors define as follows:

$$SCE = 1 - MC/AC$$

where *MC* is marginal cost and *AC* is average cost. If $MC < AC$, average cost is declining and increasing returns to scale exist. In such instances, *SCE* is positive. If, however, $MC > AC$, average costs are rising, and that region is characterized by decreasing returns to scale. *SCE* is negative in this range. If $SCE = 0$, that region is characterized by constant returns to scale.

Christensen and Greene determined the range of output for which statistically significant scale economies or diseconomies exist using a 5-percent significance level. They found that statistically significant scale economies existed up to an output level of 19.8 billion kilowatt-hours. This meant that 97 of the 114 firms in their study fell within the range of output for which increasing returns to scale were evident. These firms accounted for about 48.7 percent of total output. Between 19.8 billion and 67.1 billion kilowatt-hours, no significant economies of scale were evident. Sixteen firms, accounting for 44.6 percent of all output, were in this range. Statistically significant diseconomies were found to exist above 67.1 billion kilowatt-hours. Only one firm was above this level, and it produced 6.7 percent of the total output.

The diagram in Figure 9.13 illustrates the average cost curve for electric power generation in the United States with arrows separating the regions of economies of scale, no significant economies or diseconomies of scale, and diseconomies of scale. Immediately below the graph is a bar indicating the number of firms in each interval. It is clear that, for this industry, significant economies of scale exist and that many firms have not reaped all the possible potential scale economies.

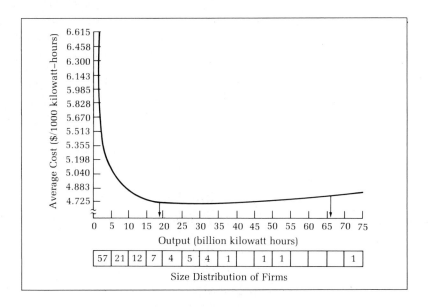

FIGURE 9.13   **Long-Run Average Cost for the Electric Power Industry.** The *LRAC* curve for United States electric power generation, shows an initial stage of substantial economies of scale. (*Source:* L.R. Christensen and W.H. Greene, "Economies of Scale of U.S. Electric Power Generation," *Journal of Political Economy*, August 1976, p. 674. Reprinted by permission of the University of Chicago Press.)

Other Empirical Evidence

To illustrate a wide range of industries studied under consistent methodology, let us look at Gupta's study of 29 Indian manufacturing industries.[11] His results are summarized in Table 9.8. We see that in 18 of the industries studied, the long-run average cost curve is L-shaped, in 5 it is U-shaped, and in 6 it is linear. The observation that so many are L-shaped does not necessarily refute the theory of U-shaped long-run average costs. It may well be that the scale of output at which costs would turn up had not been reached.

In another classic article, which includes a review of 18 cost studies, Walters concluded that "there is no large body of data which convincingly contradicts the hypothesis of a U-shaped long-run cost curve and the fruitful results which depend on it."[12]

9.12   TWO METHODS OF DETERMINING COST FUNCTIONS

Thus far, we have reviewed the fundamentals of the microeconomic theory of a firm's cost structure and examined some empirical evidence concerning costs. This section discusses the empirical determination of cost functions and some of the major problems that confront economists engaged in this process.

Using Regression Analysis to Estimate Cost Functions

The most widely adopted method of determining cost functions is the "statistical" estimation of the relationship between cost and output. The basic technique is that of regression analysis (see Chapter 4), and, as usual, the data may be time series or cross-sectional. At first glance, the application of regression techniques to the estimation of various cost functions seems deceptively simple: just regress cost on output. However, the job is fraught with difficulties.

Johnston and Walters have suggested some particularly important and often vexing problems in statistical cost analysis.[13] First, in collecting the cost and output data, we must be certain that they are properly paired, that is, that the cost data are, in fact, applicable to the corresponding data on

---

[11]See Vinod K. Gupta, "Cost Functions, Concentration, and Barriers to Entry in Twenty-nine Manufacturing Industries of India," *Journal of Industrial Economics*, November 1968, pp. 57–72.

[12]A.A. Walters, "Production and Cost Functions: An Econometric Survey," *Econometrica*, January-April 1963, pp. 1–66.

[13]See J. Johnston, *Statistical Cost Analysis* (New York: McGraw-Hill, 1960), pp. 26–30; and A.A. Walters, "Production and Cost Functions: An Econometric Survey," *Econometrica*, January-April 1963, pp. 42–43.

TABLE 9.8
Long-Run Average Cost Functions for 29 Manufacturing Industries in India

Industry	Average Cost Function	Shape
Sewing machines	$AC = 76.6 + 139/Q + .0003Q$	L +
Starch	$AC = 76.0 + 413/Q + .02Q$	U
Electric lamps	$AC = 80.4 + 224/Q - .005Q$	L −
Electric fans	$AC = 81.9 + 302/Q$	L
Soap	$AC = 92.2 + 130/Q - .014Q$	L −
Iron and steel	$AC = 92.6 - .003Q$	S −
Woolen textiles	$AC = 89.5 + 140/Q - .003Q$	L −
Bicycles	$AC = 82.5 + 65/Q - .003Q$	L −
Matches	$AC = 71.4 + 876/Q + .004Q$	U −
Paints and varnishes	$AC = 82.0 - .011Q$	S −
Paper and paperboard	$AC = 73.6 + 963/Q$	L
Fruit and vegetable processing	$AC = 82.0 + 46/Q + .004Q$	L +
Cement	$AC = 65.6 + 5622/Q + .005Q$	U −
Ceramics	$AC = 78.4 + 348/Q$	L
Biscuit making	$AC = 89.2 + 143/Q - .031Q$	L −
Plywood and tea chests	$AC = 86.1 + 151/Q - .026Q$	L −
Vegetable oil (edible)	$AC = 93.0 + 207/Q - .009Q$	L −
Vegetable oils (not edible)	$AC = 100 - .013Q$	S −
Aluminum, copper, and brass	$AC = 88.6 - .001Q$	S
Distilleries and breweries	$AC = 67.8 + 349/Q + .909Q$	U −
Chemicals	$AC = 73.9 - .0002Q$	S
Glass and glassware	$AC = 89.2 + 130/Q$	L
Tanning	$AC = 95.7 + 83/Q - .009Q$	L −
Wheat flour	$AC = 91.9 + 54/Q - .003Q$	L −
Cotton textiles	$AC = 89.7 + 273/Q$	L
Jute textiles	$AC = 94.4 - .0003Q$	S
General and electrical engineering	$AC = 84.4 + 49/Q + .002Q$	L −
Sugar	$AC = 85.0 + 124Q + .001Q$	L +
Rice milling	$AC = 86.4 + 151/Q + .038Q$	U

NOTE: AC = average cost
    Q = output
    U = U-shaped
    U − = U-shaped with flatter rising arm
    L + = L-shaped with slightly rising leg
    L = L-shaped with virtually horizontal leg
    L − = L-shaped with slightly falling leg
    S − = slightly falling straight line
    S = virtually horizontal straight line

SOURCE: Adapted from Vinod K. Gupta, "Cost Functions, Concentration, and Barriers to Entry in Twenty-nine Manufacturing Industries of India," *Journal of Industrial Economics*, November 1968, pp. 59–60.

output. For example, if wages paid in a given week are based on the number of hours worked for a previous week, the pairing of accounting data for wages and output for a particular week, say, the *n* th week, would lead to an incorrect assignment of labor cost to output. A related problem may arise, particularly for short-run cost functions, when the period for which accounting data is available may differ from what might be the most meaningful economic period.

We must also try to obtain data on costs and output during a time period when the output has been produced at a relatively even rate. If, for example, a month is chosen as the relevant time period over which the variables are measured, it would not be desirable to have wide weekly fluctuations in the rate of output. The monthly data would in such a case represent an average output rate that could disguise the true cost-output relationship. Not only should the rate of output be uniform, but it also should be a rate to which the firm is fully adjusted. Furthermore, it should not be contaminated by such external factors as power failures, delays in receiving necessary supplies, and variations in the prices paid for raw materials, labor, and other inputs. These difficulties are exacerbated by the fact that, to generate the data necessary for a meaningful statistical analysis, the observations must include a wide range of rates of output. To observe 24 months of cost-output data when the rate of output was the same each month would provide little information concerning the appropriate cost function.

Still other problems are created by the fact that cost data are normally collected and recorded by accountants for their own purposes and in a manner that makes the information less than perfect from the perspective of economic analysis. Three problems of this nature are particularly widespread. First and most obvious, perhaps, is the use of historic cost for valuation of both assets and inventories. We saw an example of the impact of this problem in the Ditton case, discussed earlier in this chapter. The second difficulty in this respect is related to depreciation. The distribution of depreciation over the life of an asset is determined, not by what might be reasonable according to economic function, but, rather, by various tax laws. The use of straight line depreciation, for example, introduces a linearity bias into the estimated cost function. Other depreciation methods may create a related bias, since they do not necessarily reflect a true relationship between the asset's productivity and the cost assigned.

Finally, for situations in which more than one product is being produced with given productive factors, it may not be possible to separate costs according to output in a meaningful way. We learn in cost accounting courses that the various ways of allocating costs among products is usually based on the relative proportion each product represents of the total output. These methods are helpful, but in some cases costs may interact such that the methods may not accurately reflect the cost appropriate to each product.

Using Engineering Relationships to Determine Cost Functions

A second, and quite different, approach to determining cost functions does not use regression analysis. This approach relies on engineering studies, or data, on the relationship of inputs to output and uses the price of inputs to determine costs. This method of estimating real world cost functions rests clearly on the knowledge that the shape of any cost function is dependent on (1) the production function and (2) the price of inputs.

Let us say, for example, that we know the technology of production is such that output (Q) can be expressed as a function of two inputs (X_1 and X_2) as follows:[14]

$$Q = AX_1^a X_2^b$$

where A is a constant. The variable cost (assuming constant factor prices) is then

$$VC = P_1 X_1 + P_2 X_2$$

where P_1 and P_2 are the factor prices for X_1 and X_2, respectively. Assuming that the firm's management attempts to minimize cost for a given level of output (or to maximize output for a given cost, which would yield the same result), we can determine the variable cost function from our knowledge of factor prices (P_1 and P_2) and the production parameters (A, a, and b).

The relevant Lagrangian function can be written as

$$L = P_1 X_1 + P_2 X_2 + \lambda(AX_1^a X_2^b - Q)$$

Note that we must use a Lagrangian function here because we are minimizing costs *subject to* some given level of output. The following first-order condition emerges:

Minimize: $L = P_1 X_1 + P_2 X_2 + \lambda(AX_1^a X_2^b - Q)$

To minimize, take the partial derivatives and set each of them equal to 0.	$\dfrac{\partial L}{\partial X_1} = P_1 + a\lambda\, AX_2^b X_1^{a-1} = 0$ $\dfrac{\partial L}{\partial X_2} = P_2 + b\lambda\, AX_1^a X_2^{b-1} = 0$ $\dfrac{\partial L}{\partial \lambda} = AX_1^a X_2^b - Q = 0$

Now divide the first partial derivative by the second partial derivative.	$\dfrac{P_1}{P_2} = \dfrac{a\lambda AX_2^b X_1^{a-1}}{b\lambda AX_1^a X_2^{b-1}}$ $\dfrac{P_1}{P_2} = \dfrac{aX_2}{bX_1}$

---

[14]The number of inputs need not be restricted to two. We have done so to keep the algebra simple.

Rearranging terms, we can solve for X_1.	$\dfrac{P_1}{P_2} \cdot \dfrac{b}{a} = \dfrac{X_2}{X_1}$ $\dfrac{P_1}{P_2} \cdot \dfrac{b}{a} \cdot \dfrac{1}{X_2} = \dfrac{1}{X_1}$ $\dfrac{P_2}{P_1} \cdot \dfrac{a}{b} \cdot X_2 = X_1$
Substitute the above value for X_1 into the third partial derivative.	$Q = A \left(\dfrac{P_2}{P_1} \cdot \dfrac{a}{b} \cdot X_2 \right)^a X_2^b$ $Q = A \left(\dfrac{P_2}{P_1} \cdot \dfrac{a}{b} \right)^a X_2^{a+b}$

Now define a new variable called C (note that this variable is not cost and has no clearcut economic meaning but allows us to arrive at a mathematical solution with some meaning):

$$C = [A\,((a/b)\cdot(P_2/P_1))^a]^{-1/(a+b)}$$

Using our new variable, C, in the previous equation allows us to solve for X_2 as follows:

$$X_2 = CQ^{1/(a+b)}$$

Now substitute the value of X_1 computed above in the variable cost (VC) function:

$$VC = P_1 \left(\dfrac{a}{b} \cdot \dfrac{P_2}{P_1} \right) X_2 + P_2 X_2$$

$$VC = \left[P_1 \left(\dfrac{a}{b} \cdot \dfrac{P_2}{P_1} \right) + P_2 \right] X_2$$

Next, define a second new variable called D (note again that this new variable has no clear economic meaning but serves to allow a clear mathematical solution to our problem; note also that C and D contain only values of our factor prices, P_1 and P_2, and production function parameters, A, a, and b:

$$D = \left[P_1 \left(\dfrac{a}{b} \cdot \dfrac{P_2}{P_1} \right) + P_2 \right]$$

Finally, define one last variable, K, which is simply equal to C times D:

$$K = CD$$

Now the variable cost equation may be rewritten:

$$VC = KQ^{1/(a + b)}$$

where K is simply a constant made up of the factor prices and the parameters of the production function.

The variable cost can thus be determined by knowing the factor prices and production parameters. Once the variable cost function is known, the other cost functions can easily be developed. We see that if $a + b = 1$, the variable cost function is linear (average and marginal cost are both equal to K). If $a + b > 1$, both average and marginal cost are declining (variable cost increases at a decreasing rate), and if $a + b < 1$, average and marginal cost are increasing (variable cost increases at an increasing rate). Remember that in the long run all inputs are variable, so variable cost is the same as total cost.

Let us consider three examples of how the variable cost function can be derived from Cobb-Douglas production functions and input prices, where the only difference is in the degree of homogeneity of the production functions. Using the general form

$$Q = AX_1^a X_2^b$$

we shall keep A constant at 10 and vary a and b. Furthermore, we shall assume that the price per unit for input X_1 is constant at $P_1 = 20$ and that the price per unit for input X_2 is constant at $P_2 = 40$ for all three cases. From the above, we know that variable cost is

$$VC = KQ^{1/(a + b)}$$

or, substituting $K = CD$ and the appropriate terms for C and D, we have

$$VC = \left[A\left(\frac{a}{b} \cdot \frac{P_2}{P_1}\right)^a\right]^{-1/(a + b)} \left[P_1\left(\frac{a}{b} \cdot \frac{P_2}{P_1}\right) + P_2\right] Q^{1/(a + b)}$$

For the first case, assume that $a = b = .5$ such that the production function is homogeneous of degree 1 and, according to our analysis in Chapter 7, exhibits constant returns to scale. Given these parameters and the values of A, P_1, and P_2 above, we can calculate variable cost as

$$VC = \left[10\left(\frac{.5}{.5} \cdot \frac{40}{20}\right)^{.5}\right]^{-1/(.5 + .5)} 20\left[\left(\frac{.5}{.5} \cdot \frac{40}{20}\right) + 40\right] Q^{1/(.5 + .5)}$$

$$VC = 5.66Q$$

We see that the variable cost function is linear and thus depicts constant returns to scale.

Now suppose that $a = .4$ and $b = .3$, while A, P_1, and P_2 retain the values given above. Since $a + b = .7$, the production function is homogeneous of degree .7 and has decreasing returns to scale. Solving for variable cost, we find

$$VC = \left[10\left(\frac{.4}{.3}\cdot\frac{40}{20}\right)^{.4}\right]^{-1/(.4 + .3)}\left[20\left(\frac{.4}{.3}\cdot\frac{40}{20}\right) + 40\right]Q^{1/(.4 + .3)}$$
$$VC = 1.99Q^{1.43}$$

This variable cost function is nonlinear and increases at an increasing rate. It thus represents a case of decreasing returns to scale.

Finally, let $a = .6$ and $b = .7$, keeping the same values for A, P_1, and P_2. Because $a + b = 1.3$, the production function is homogeneous of degree 1.3 and illustrates a case of increasing returns to scale. The variable cost function is

$$VC = \left[10\left(\frac{.6}{.7}\cdot\frac{40}{20}\right)^{.6}\right]^{-1/(.6 + .7)}\left[20\left(\frac{.6}{.7}\cdot\frac{40}{20}\right) + 40\right]Q^{1/(.6 + .7)}$$
$$VC = 9.85Q^{.77}$$

This variable cost function increases at a decreasing rate and thus represents an example of increasing returns to scale.

A shortcoming of this approach to determining the cost function for a firm is that it relies on a sophisticated knowledge of the production process that is sometimes not available. However, there are situations in which such knowledge exists. In the petroleum industry, for example, various production processes are well defined and linear. Griffin has shown that such an analysis can be used to generate cost functions for the petroleum industry that substantiate the microeconomic theory concerning U-shaped average costs.[15]

9.13   BREAK-EVEN ANALYSIS

One of the simplest, yet most useful, techniques of all economic analyses is break-even analysis. This section presents only the fundamental model and a sample of variations that may be developed. The break-even graph is the most frequent mode of using this form of the analysis. Such a graph is presented in Figure 9.14. It is common to use linear revenue and cost functions in using break-even analysis. For many practical applications, this is often satisfactory because these functions are either linear or very nearly linear in the relevant range of output. Nonlinear functions can be used if it is determined that the use of linear approximations is accompanied by unacceptable errors.

Several facts should be readily apparent from Figure 9.14. First, the vertical distance between the total-cost line and the horizontal fixed-cost line represents the variable cost of alternative levels of output. Second,

[15]See James M. Griffin, "The Process Analysis Alternative to Statistical Cost Functions: An Application to Petroleum Refining," *American Economic Review*, March 1972, pp. 46–50.

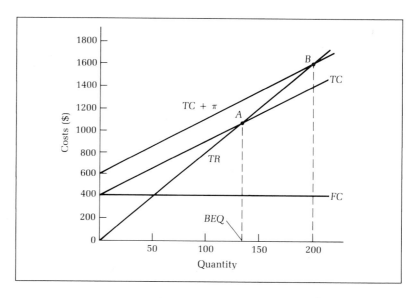

FIGURE 9.14   **Break-Even Analysis.**   This is the graphic determination of the break-even level of output (*BEQ*), given fixed costs of $400, an average variable cost of $5 per unit, and a price of $8 per unit. The break-even point is *A*, where *BEQ* = 133. For a target profit of $200, the necessary level of output is determined at *B*, or 200 units.

since total revenue (*TR*) is linear, price (*P*) must be constant over the relevant range of output. Furthermore, average variable costs (*AVC*) must also be constant over this range in order for total cost (*TC*) to be linear. Finally, note that the break-even level of output (*BEQ*) is at the point on the horizontal axis directly below the intersection of *TR* and *TC* (this intersection is the break-even point).

This graphic model may be expressed in algebraic forms as well. By definition, profit (π) equals total revenue minus total cost:

$$\pi = TR - TC$$

and

$$TR = P \cdot Q$$
$$TC = FC + VC$$
$$TC = FC + AVC \cdot Q$$

Furthermore, by definition, profit is 0 if the firm breaks even. Thus, for the break-even quantity, we have

$$0 = P \cdot Q - FC - AVC \cdot Q$$
$$FC = (P - AVC)Q$$
$$Q = \frac{FC}{P - AVC} = BEQ$$

In this form, the denominator $(P - AVC)$ is often referred to as the contribution margin per unit because that value represents the portion of selling price that contributes to paying the fixed costs (and to profit, as we shall see).

If the only use of break-even analysis were to determine the level of sales at which the firm would break even, given price and costs, the technique would not be so widely adopted. A single break-even graph also shows how much profit (for $Q > BEQ$) or loss (for $Q < BEQ$) the firm will make at each level of output. Suppose that the firm has a target profit of X dollars. By adding that to fixed costs, we can use break-even analysis to determine how great a sales volume will be necessary to achieve that rate of profit. In addition, suppose that the firm has econometric or marketing studies that indicate expected sales at each of three different prices. By plotting the total revenue line representing each price, the firm can quickly determine which price and corresponding level of sales will be most profitable. These are just examples of the types of situations in which break-even analysis can be used.

Let us illustrate these concepts with a numerical example. First, suppose that a firm has fixed costs of $400 and average variable costs of $5, and sells its product for $8. The break-even level of sales is calculated as

$$BEQ = \frac{400}{8 - 5}$$
$$BEQ = \frac{400}{3}$$
$$BEQ = 133$$

This result can also be seen by examining Figure 9.14 for the intersection of total revenue (TR) and total cost (TC) at point A. Now if the firm decided that they would set a target rate of profit of $200, how many units must be sold to achieve that objective? If the contribution margin is $3 per unit, then we should expect them to have to sell 67 more units to get the desired profit. This can be seen by adding the target rate of profit, 200, to fixed costs in either graphic or algebraic forms. For the latter, we simply calculate

$$Q = \frac{FC + \text{target profit}}{P - AVC}$$
$$Q = \frac{400 + 200}{8 - 5} = 200$$

This result is determined at point B in Figure 9.14.

Let us complicate the problem a little further. Suppose that the firm has a fixed cost of $200 and an average variable cost of $10 per unit but that management is uncertain about the price to set for this product. Their marketing and economic research personnel have found that the demand for the product is negatively sloped (as would be expected). They have collected data that indicate that expected sales at three alternative prices are

P	Q
$20.00	25
15.00	60
12.50	110

Each of these prices would give rise to a different total revenue function, as shown in Figure 9.15 (TR_1 for $P = 20$, TR_2 for $P = 15$, and TR_3 for $P = 12.5$).

We see that as price is reduced, the break-even level of sales increases from 20 (at A, for $P = 20$) to 40 (at B, for $P = 15$) and finally to 80 (at C, for $P = 12.5$). More important, we see that as price is reduced and sales increase, profit increases from $\pi_1 = 50$ to $\pi_2 = 100$ and then decreases to $\pi_3 = 75$ for the prices $20, $15, and $12.50, respectively. Thus, management should select a price of $15 if their objective is to maximize profits.

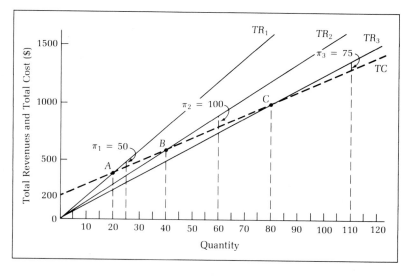

FIGURE 9.15 **Break-Even Levels and Potential Profit for Three Total Revenue Functions.** With a fixed cost of $200 and an average variable cost of $10 per unit, we find the following break-even levels for the three possible prices along with the profit based on expected sales at those prices:

Price	BEQ	Expected Sales	Expected Profit
$20	20	25	$ 50
15	40	60	100
12	80	110	75

If profit maximization is the objective, a price of $15 is best. However, if the objective is related to sales volume or market share, the $12 price may be preferred.

Other objectives might lead to different decisions. For example, if their objective is to increase market share subject to making at least $50 profit per time period, then a price of $12.50 would be appropriate.

There are many more extensions and modifications of the basic break-even analysis model, which we cannot cover in a managerial economics text. You may want to try some variations on your own; for example, determine how much sales would have to be increased to make a lump sum advertising expenditure of a given amount worthwhile.

SUMMARY

At first it may appear to be a fairly simple matter to determine the cost involved in a particular economic activity. However, in practice, several factors complicate the process. Accounting practices are such that the data that are generally collected and reported on costs do not necessarily coincide with the concept of cost as used by economists. For example, the use of historical cost or the failure to match cost with output in the same period create some problems for economic analysis. Accounting data also generally do not include implicit costs such as the cost of a farmer's own labor in planting and harvesting a crop. Economists prefer to use an opportunity cost concept as a baseline in evaluating economic decisions. The opportunity cost is the value of what must be given up when resources are allocated to a particular activity.

In the short run (the period in which there is at least one factor of production that is fixed and at least one that is variable), the total cost of an economic activity is composed of a fixed and a variable component. Variable cost, and thus total cost, typically increases first at a decreasing rate and then at an increasing rate. The reason for this type of behavior of variable and total cost is related to the principle of diminishing marginal productivity. If marginal product increases at first, marginal cost at first declines (that is, the rate of increase in variable and total cost declines). However, once marginal product begins to decline, marginal cost increases (the rate of increase in variable and total cost increases). It follows that in the short run, marginal cost (MC), average variable cost (AVC), and average total cost (AC) curves are generally U-shaped.

The long run is defined as the period for which all factors of production are variable. Thus, in the long run, total costs are identical to variable costs. The long-run total cost curve may also at first increase at a decreasing rate and then increase at an increasing rate. If this is true, the long-run average cost (LRAC) will also have a U shape. The long-run cost functions may be derived from the series of most efficient short-run cost curves or from an expansion path.

In the region in which LRAC is declining, there are increasing returns to scale in the economic activity. If LRAC is horizontal, there are constant *returns to scale, and if LRAC is rising, there are decreasing returns to scale. Empirical evidence reported in this chapter suggests that most industries are characterized by some initial range of output in which there are increasing returns to scale. However, in some cases, the economies of scale are exhausted at a relatively low level of production (see, for example, the discussion of the soft drink and grain industries).*

Break-even analysis is frequently used in economic analysis, applying the short-run cost concepts presented in this chapter. If the revenue per unit of output is constant (i.e., price is constant for the firm), then we can determine the level of sales necessary for the firm to break even by dividing fixed cost by the difference between price and average variable cost (called the contribution margin). This simple break-even format can be extended to determine the sales volume necessary to obtain any specified level of profit or to determine which of several price-quantity combinations will yield the maximum profit for a given cost structure.

The cost analysis presented in this chapter has been framed in the context of traditional business activity. However, the concepts developed are equally applicable to the analysis of not-for-profit activities and of economic activities in the public sector. For example, an important consideration for administrators in most colleges and universities is the determination of the break-even level of enrollment for summer sessions.

SUGGESTED READINGS

Anthony, Robert N. "What Should 'Cost' Mean?" *Harvard Business Review*, June 1970, pp. 121–131.

Baumol, William J. *Economic Theory and Operations Analysis*, 3d ed. Englewood Cliffs, NJ: Prentice-Hall, 1972, Chapter 11.

Benston, George J. "Multiple Regression Analysis of Cost Behavior." *Accounting Review*, October 1966, pp. 657–672.

Dean, Joel. "Statistical Cost Curves." *Journal of American Statistical Association*, March 1937, pp. 83–89.

Johnston, J. *Statistical Cost Analysis*. New York: McGraw-Hill, 1960.

Keating, Barry P. "Cost Shifting: An Empirical Examination of Hospital Bureaucracy," *Applied Economics*, April 1984, pp. 279–289.

Longbrake, William A. "Statistical Cost Analysis." *Financial Management*, Spring 1973, pp. 49–55.

Rakowski, James P. "Economies of Scale in U.S. Trucking." *Journal of Economics and Business*, Spring-Summer 1978, pp. 166–176.

Roth, Timothy P. "Empirical Cost Curves and the Production-Theoretic Short Run: A Reconciliation." *Quarterly Review of Economics and Business*, Autumn 1979, pp. 35–47.

Walters, A.A. "Production and Cost Functions: An Econometric Survey." *Econometrica*, January-April 1963, pp. 1–66.

PROBLEMS

1. Given the total cost function

   $$TC = 12 + 3Q + .6Q^2$$

   where Q = units of output (note that this is not a cubic total cost function but only a quadratic one),
   a. Determine the equations for fixed cost and variable cost. Graph the total cost, fixed cost, and variable cost, and show graphically their relationships to one another. How would you describe the behavior of variable cost as output increases?
   b. Determine the equations for average fixed cost, average variable cost, average total cost, and marginal cost. Graph each of these functions and show graphically their relationships to one another.
   c. What is the nature of the underlying production function? What will its shape be?

2. Given the total cost function

   $$TC = 100 + 15Q - 6.5Q^2 + Q^3$$

   where Q is units of output,
   a. Determine the equations for fixed costs and variable costs. Graph the total cost, fixed cost, and variable cost functions and show graphically their relationships to one another. How would you describe the behavior of variable cost as output increases?
   b. Determine the equations for average fixed cost, average variable cost, and marginal cost. Graph each of these functions and show graphically their relationships to one another.
   c. How would you describe the nature of the production function from which these cost curves are derived? What will its shape be?

3. Pasquerilla Fashions, Inc., manufactures designer jeans for the export market. A statistical analysis of the firm's short-run total cost function gave the following results:

   $$TC = 10 + 18Q - 6Q^2 + Q^3$$

   where Q is output in thousands of units and TC is in thousands of dollars.
   a. What is total cost at an output rate of 500 units? 1000 units?
   b. What is the average fixed cost at an output rate of 500 units? 1000 units?
   c. At approximately what output rate is the point of diminishing marginal returns to variable input encountered?
   d. At approximately what output rate does stage 2 begin?

4. Fill in the following table using your knowledge of the relationships among the cost functions:

MC	TC	Q	FC	VC	AFC	AVC	ATC
—	428.5	1			—	—	—
67.5		2	340				181.83
		3				68.5	
		4		240			
22.5		5					
	616	6				40.5	
	623.5	7					
		8					78.5
		9		292.5			70.28
	640	10		300		30	

5. The cardiac care unit (CCU) of a nonprofit hospital (over 90 percent of all hospitals are nonprofit) is estimated to have the following total cost function:

$$TC = 5Q - .03Q^2 + .0005Q^3$$

where Q is the average number of patients using the facility and TC is the total cost per year of the CCU.

   a. Does this cost function have the characteristic shape mentioned in the chapter, that is, first increasing at a decreasing rate and then increasing at an increasing rate? What average number of patients ensures the lowest cost per patient?

   b. Could the hospital perhaps change the size (i.e., scale) of the CCU and thus change the cost curve above?

   c. If the CCU is currently averaging 40 patients, what is the estimated increase in costs per year of increasing that average by one?

6. Sorin Engineering is currently producing a product selling for $10 per unit. Sorin will decide shortly on which of two production processes to use in order to produce these units. Sorin has collected the following data on each process, and management believes that 150,000 units will be sold:

	Production Process 1	Production Process 2
Sales	$1,500,000	$1,500,000
Variable costs	800,000	950,000
Fixed costs	400,000	250,000
Profit	$ 300,000	$ 300,000

   a. Calculate the break-even point for both processes.

    b.   Which process would be preferred if management felt there was a high probability of exceeding sales of 150,000 units? Why?

    c.   Which process would be preferred if management felt there was a high probability of selling considerably less than 150,000 units? Why?

7.   Moreau Industries produces a single product, which sells for $25 per unit. Its variable operating costs are $10, and its fixed operating costs are $2 million.

    a.   Calculate Moreau's profit for 100,000 units and 200,000 units.

    b.   Calculate the break-even volume.

    c.   Draw the break-even chart for Moreau Industries.

8.   Moreau Industries' management is considering changing its operations. Calculate both the profit level and the break-even point under the following conditions:

    a.   10-percent increase in selling price

    b.   10-percent increase in selling price coupled with a 10-percent increase in variable costs

    c.   10-percent increase in selling price coupled with a 10-percent increase in fixed costs

    d.   10-percent increase in variable costs coupled with a 10-percent decrease in fixed costs

    e.   10-percent decrease in variable costs coupled with a 10-percent increase in fixed costs

9.   Moreau is trying to classify the following costs as either fixed or variable. To which category would you assign each cost?

    a.   Office supplies for executive offices

    b.   Property taxes on the plant property

    c.   Transportaton costs for delivery of raw material

    d.   Raw material cost

    e.   Insurance on the plant and equipment

    f.   Insurance on production employees

    g.   Costs associated with the customer billing department

    h.   Plant heating and cooling costs

    i.   Executive office building heating and cooling costs

    j.   Executive salaries

    k.   Maintenance personnel wages

10.   Morrissey Aviation runs charter flights for individuals and corporations. This week, it allowed its Boeing 737 aircraft to sit idle in the hangar; were any costs incurred in this decision? If a group of vacationers had requested the use of the plane for a fee and Morrissey had no other requests for the craft at the same time, what costs would be

relevant in deciding whether to accept the fee offered by the vacationers? Morrissey pays a licensing fee of $75,000 per year on the 737.
Should this fee be taken into account in considering the vacationers'
request?

11. Using the average cost functions in Table 9.8, determine the algebraic
     equations for total cost and long-run marginal cost for the following
     industries:
     a. Sewing machines
     b. Soap
     c. Chemicals
     d. Rice milling

12. Given the following total cost function for ABE Industries,

$$TC = 100 + 200Q - 3Q^2 + .02Q^3$$

     a. What is the firm's fixed cost?
     b. What is the algebraic equation for variable cost?
     c. Plot FC, VC, and TC on a sheet of graph paper.
     d. Find the equations for marginal cost, average variable cost, and
         average cost.
     e. Plot each of these unit cost curves on another sheet of graph paper.
         Does marginal cost intersect the average variable cost and average
         cost functions at their minimum points?

13. Suppose that you work for a firm whose management has estimated
     the following production function for one of its products:

$$Q = 25L^{.8}K^{.4}$$

     The current cost per unit of labor (L) is $120, and the cost per unit
     of capital (K) is $90. Your boss tells you that labor negotiations
     are likely to result in an increase in labor costs to $140 per unit
     and asks you to find the cost function for output under each of the
     two sets of factor prices (the cost per unit of capital will remain con-
     stant). After deriving both cost functions, determine the cost of pro-
     ducing 1000 units before and after such an increase in labor cost. If you
     were asked to explain to labor the consequence of this $20 increase
     in terms of employment assuming the firm maintains output at 1000,
     how would you do it? Exactly how many fewer labor units would
     be hired?

14. In higher education, many costs and revenues are nearly linear
     with relation to the level of activity, as measured by enrollment. It has

been suggested that break-even analysis may thus be a useful management tool for the combined analysis of costs and revenue in higher education.[16] Suppose that fixed cost of top-level administrative salaries, maintenance, building and grounds expenses, and so on for South Central State University (SCSU) totaled $1.2 million per year. Also, let us assume that revenue per student is composed of a tuition charge of $25 per credit hour for in-state students and $65 per credit hour for out-of-state students, plus a state appropriation of $50 per in-state student credit hour and $10 for each credit hour for out-of-state students. In addition, SCSU has some revenue from sources not related directly to student credit hours, such as federal grants and private research grants, which amounts to about $300,000 per year.

SCSU is divided into two colleges: the College of Arts and Sciences and the College of Agricultural Studies. Each college has four departments. The college and department budgets for variable costs, such as faculty salaries and supplies, are given in the table below, along with the number of credit hours taught by each department:

	Faculty Salaries	Other Variable Costs	Total Variable Costs	Credit Hours Taught	Allocated Fixed Cost
College of Arts and Sciences	$1,900,000	$320,000	$2,220,000	39,690	
Department 1	600,000	100,000	700,000	14,000	
Department 2	450,000	70,000	520,000	9,450	
Department 3	500,000	90,000	590,000	9,440	
Department 4	350,000	60,000	410,000	6,800	
College of Agricultural Studies	1,800,000	310,000	2,110,000	34,400	
Department 5	400,000	80,000	480,000	8,400	
Department 6	700,000	110,000	810,000	10,200	
Department 7	200,000	50,000	250,000	4,000	
Department 8	500,000	70,000	570,000	11,800	

Assuming that the fixed costs should be allocated on the basis of each unit's share of total credit hours, complete the final column of the above table.

a. Determine the break-even level of enrollment for each college and each department (for now, ignore the $300,000 of revenue that is not related directly to enrollment).

---

[16]See for example, L. Keith Larimore, "Break-Even Analysis in Higher Education," *Management Accounting*, September 1974, on which part of this question is based.

    b.   Rank the departments according to profitability. How many departments operate at a net loss? Does each college "pay its own way?"

    c.   Suppose that the $300,000 of grant revenue is obtained by departments as follows: department 1, 10 percent; department 2, 12 per-cent; department 3, 28 percent; department 4, 0 percent; department 5, 10 percent; department 6, 15 percent; department 7, 10 percent; and department 8, 15 percent. Which departments break even?

    d.   The faculty in department 6 have been concerned because the board of regents has been under pressure to cut costly programs. The faculty argue that their work and their graduates are vital to the agricultural base of the state's economy and that, because of the positive externalities they create for the rest of the state, their state appropriation per credit hour should be increased by $5. If this was done, would department 6 still have a deficit, would they have a net surplus, or would they break even? If they would not break even, how much revenue per credit hour would be necessary for them to break even with the current enrollment?

    e.   Is it reasonable to expect each department to "pay its own way?" What about each college?

15.   a.   Given the following cost data, use regression analysis to estimate the corresponding cubic total cost function:

Quantity	10	20	30	40	50	60	70	80	90	100
Total cost	485	705	790	825	850	935	1100	1500	2200	3100

    b.   Given the total cost function estimated above, derive algebraic equations for average cost, marginal cost, and average variable cost.

    c.   Plot the data given above along with the curve for the total cost function you estimated. Does your cost equation provide a good fit to the data? What is the R^2 value for your cost function?

    d.   Show average cost and marginal cost in tabular form and plot the data points. Also plot the equations for average cost and marginal cost derived in part b. Do these equations correspond reasonably well to the scatter diagram of data points for marginal and average cost?

16.   Given the production data in Table 7.2 (see Chapter 7, "Production"), estimate the cost function for output, assuming that both labor and capital are variable and that the cost per unit of labor is $50 and the cost per unit of capital is $100. That is, estimate the OLS regression function:

$$TC = aQ^b$$

by using the logarithmic transformation:

$$\ln TC = \ln a + b \ln Q$$

Find the total cost for each of the 100 levels of production from:

$$TC = 50L + 100K$$

10

Market Structure and Pricing: Perfect Competition and Monopoly

This and the next two chapters put the demand and production sides of the market together in a context that will help you understand how firms make optimal pricing and output decisions. You will see that how an industry is organized in terms of its market structure has a significant effect on the pricing and output decisions managers make. You may recall from an introductory economics course that there are four major forms of market structure, or organization: perfect competition, monopolistic competition, oligopoly, and monopoly.

If we were to array market structures according to the degree of control the individual firm has over its own price, assuming no government interference, it would look like this:

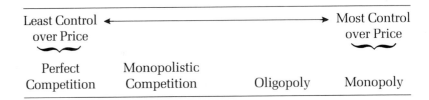

Least Control over Price			Most Control over Price
Perfect Competition	Monopolistic Competition	Oligopoly	Monopoly

This chapter focuses on the two extreme cases: perfect competition and monopoly. The intermediate cases and some special topics related to pricing are discussed in Chapters 11 and 12.

Throughout the three chapters that deal with pricing and output decisions faced by managers, you will see the importance of using marginal analysis. You will see many applications of the profit maximizing rule that marginal revenue should equal marginal cost and, in addition, how the way of thinking inherent in marginal analysis can help a manager make more profitable and/or efficient decisions.

The "marginal revenue equals marginal cost" rule is so widely applicable that it may be useful to quickly see how this rule is derived. We define profit (π) as the difference between total revenue (TR) and total cost (TC):

$$\pi = TR - TC$$

Both total revenue and total cost are functions of the quantity (Q) produced and sold; thus, profit is also a function of quantity. Further, we know that any function can be evaluated for a possible maximum by finding where its slope is equal to 0 (i.e., by finding its first derivative and setting that equal to 0). For profit, we have

$$\pi = TR - TC$$
$$d\pi/dQ = (dTR/dQ) - (dTC/dQ) = 0$$

Thus,

$$(dTR/dQ) = (dTC/dQ)$$

The left-hand term in this equality is the rate of change in total revenue as quantity changes, or marginal revenue. The right-hand term is the rate of change in total cost as quantity changes, or marginal cost. Thus, the first-order condition for a maximum profit is

$$(dTR/dQ) = (dTC/dQ)$$
$$MR = MC$$

Note that there is nothing in this rule, or in its development, that is directly related to the form of market structure within which the firm operates. The profit maximizing rule is independent of the market structure involved. You will see this principle applied for each market structure in the following chapters on market structure and pricing.

10.1   THE COMPETITIVE MARKET AND THE INVISIBLE HAND

The study of markets dates back at least to 1776 and the publication by Adam Smith of *The Wealth of Nations*.[1] An often quoted passage from that book summarizes Smith's thinking about competitive markets: "It is not from the benevolence of the butcher, the brewer, or the baker, that we expect our dinner, but from their regard to their own interest. We address ourselves, not to their humanity but to their self-love, and never talk to them of our own necessities but of their advantages."

Smith's point was simply that you cannot rely on the charity of others to support you in all the things you want; charity has limits. Instead, you

---

[1] The title is *An Inquiry into the Nature and Causes of the Wealth of Nations*. See the current edition by the University of Chicago Press, 1976.

must stand ready to do something that others value. Adam Smith viewed a market as an institution that facilitated cooperation between people who might rarely, if ever, meet. It was Smith who first used the term *invisible hand* to suggest that individuals pursuing their self-interest in a market would ultimately benefit society.

When Smith published his book in England in 1776, his views were in direct opposition to the prevailing opinion. Common opinion had it that only one party stood to gain in any exchange. Smith pointed out that, on the contrary, both parties stood to gain in a voluntary exchange. The system of voluntary exchanges taking place in competitive markets has come to be called *capitalism*.

It is interesting to note that the term *capitalism* was applied to the competitive market system, not by a proponent of the system, but by someone very opposed to it: Karl Marx. There is no reason, however, to reject the term *capitalism* as an appropriate description. It does describe very clearly the source of the great economic improvements brought about by a competitive market system. Those improvements are the result of capital accumulated through the division of labor and based on the observation that people do not consume everything they produce. They save part of what is produced, and part of the savings is invested in tools of production. That savings, which allows one generation to pass along to the next the additional tools needed to sustain an increase in the standard of living, is the true source of capitalism's ability to encourage economic improvement.

10.2   WHAT IS A MARKET?

In order to discuss markets, we must shift our emphasis from individual behavior—the emphasis up to this point in the text—to market phenomenon. Likewise, we must move from an emphasis on *optimization* to a *description of equilibrium*. We will, however, return to individual behavior, decision making, and optimization within the context of each type of market.

When economists talk about markets, they are not referring to a grocery store or an open-air market. Indeed, the term *market* does not even refer to a place; it refers, rather, to a process. Any market is a process by which buyers and sellers interact in order to exchange information about what the participants are willing to buy and sell. Some markets, like the market for corporate stock, are located primarily in a small geographic area. The New York Stock Exchange (the "Big Board") is located on Wall Street in New York City and handles the major portion of stock bought and sold in the United States. However, even the concentrated corporate stock market is not located in just one place. The American Stock Exchange, or Amex, located a few blocks from Wall Street, also deals in stocks. In addition, there are a number of smaller exchanges in various cities across the United States (e.g., Philadelphia). No one location can bill itself as *the* market for stocks.

You see, it is not the location of the stock markets that is important in defining them as part of a market. Each of the locations noted is just a place where the *process of exchange* can occur. The market is a *process* where the terms of trade—price, quantity, quality, and so on—are agreed upon by the participants. On any of the stock exchanges, which are part of the larger stock market, buyers and sellers can interact with one another to exchange shares of corporate stock.

10.3   PERFECTLY COMPETITIVE MARKETS

Since the time of Adam Smith, the perfectly competitive market has been the ideal type of market for economists. In a perfectly competitive market, buyers try to outdo other buyers by offering sellers the most attractive terms, and sellers try to outdo other sellers by offering lower prices. A perfectly competitive market exists when the following criteria are met:

1.   *Many buyers and sellers in the market.* The market has so many participants that each can have only a negligible affect on price, and the participants act independently of one another.

2.   *Free entry and exit.* Any firm that believes it can earn higher profits by moving from one industry to another is free to do so. That is, there is complete mobility of productive resources.

3.   *A homogeneous or standardized product.* Each firm's product is neither superior nor inferior to the products made by other firms. The products are identical.

4.   *Perfect knowledge.* All firms have access to the same types of technology, and prospective buyers are familiar with prevailing prices.

Actual examples of the economist's ideal perfectly competitive market are a bit difficult to come by; in fact, there may be no situations that *exactly* match the four conditions outlined. However, markets for some agricultural products, say, wheat, tend to be very close to perfectly competitive. Many wheat producers exist in the market and they sell to many buyers. The product is more or less standardized and any buyer or seller can stop buying or producing at any time. Don't be misled, though, into believing that all agricultural markets are perfectly competitive in every way. Various government programs reduce the degree to which many of these markets fit the perfectly competitive model (see Chapter 13, "Regulation").

The perfectly competitive market has some characteristics that make it very attractive. Because there are many sellers of the product in a competitive market, buyers may easily switch purchases from one seller to another.

This ease of transfer encourages sellers to compete with one another by attempting to change the terms of trade—to offer lower prices, offer better service, give better quality, and the like. If any one seller refuses to compete with fellow sellers, the buyers may transfer their sales to a competitor. Because the products of each seller are perfect substitutes for the products of every other seller, a single firm must offer to sell its entire production at the market price. Thus, any one seller in a competitive market is said to be a *price taker* because that seller cannot refuse to compete with other sellers offering lower prices: the consequence of doing so would be to lose all one's customers to other sellers. One result of this situation is that an individual firm's demand curve will be perfectly elastic at the market price, as shown in Figure 10.1. From a buyer's point of view, this is an ideal situation, since the buyer is assured that the market will result in the lowest price being offered, i.e., the lowest price that is consistent with firms' not losing money in the long run.

Another attractive characteristic of a perfectly competitive market is that the quantity of goods produced is also decided in an ideal manner from the point of view of the consumer. Each seller has the incentive to produce more units and sell them as long as the extra revenue (marginal revenue) received is larger than the cost of the additional units (marginal cost). If one seller fails to produce and sell extra units from which a profit could be

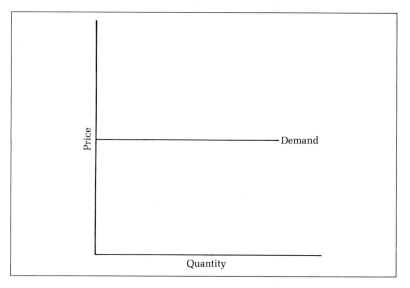

FIGURE 10.1   The Perfectly Competitive Firm's Demand Curve.   The demand curve for a perfectly competitive firm is a horizontal line at the current market price; thus, it is perfectly elastic. If the firm tries to sell at a higher price, sales will drop to 0 as buyers go to other producers. The firm has no incentive to sell at a lower price, since all that is produced can be sold at the market price.

made, another seller will seize the opportunity. Thus, the consumer will have available as many units as can be produced profitably by the sellers.

Supply, Demand, and the Perfectly Competitive Market

Perfectly competitive markets are composed of many buyers and sellers; actual competitors and potential competitors (those who are ready to enter the market given a particular condition) are both part of real world markets. Let us assume for a moment a *perfectly* competitive market—one that is unlikely to exist in the real world. Nevertheless, by doing so, we can describe the limit to which a real-world competitive market might tend, known as the equilibrium point.

In a perfectly competitive market, complete freedom of entry and exit exists: anyone can enter the market and produce and sell a duplicate of what is already being sold. Each competitor produces but a small share of the industry's total output. The market supply and demand curves might appear like those in Figure 10.2.

The demand for the good, wheat, for example, is downward sloping to the right and thus follows the law of demand outlined in Chapter 5. This market demand curve represents the maximum quantities of wheat that

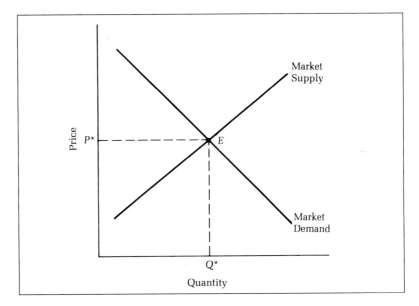

FIGURE 10.2   **Market Demand and Market Supply in a Perfectly Competitive Market.**   The equilibrium, or market, price is determined by the balance of supply and demand at point E. This price is shown as P^*. At P^*, producers (in total) produce Q^* units of product, and consumers (in total) purchase exactly Q^* units. Thus, the quantity supplied equals the quantity demanded at the price P^*. The market is in equilibrium.

would be purchased at various prices. In a perfectly competitive market, this curve would be known with certainty by all. The demand curve in Figure 10.2 is a *market demand curve* because all consumers are represented by the curve. The curve indicates what consumers will do when *all* producers change their prices.

The *market supply curve* represents production by all actual or potential producers, and its shape depends on how much each producer is willing to offer on the market at each price. This market supply curve, of course, is dependent on the cost functions of the individual firms in the industry. For reasons we will discuss later, the short-run supply curve for any individual perfectly competitive firm is that portion of the marginal cost curve lying above the average variable cost curve. If the price given to the individual firm falls *below* average variable cost, the firm would be better off not producing at all. Thus, if price falls below average variable cost *for a firm*, plant shutdown is a reasonable alternative. For this reason, the section of the marginal cost curve below the average variable cost curve is *not* part of the firm's supply curve.

The market supply curve is the horizontal summation of all the individual firm's supply curves, which are the marginal cost curves *above* average variable cost. Since the marginal cost curves are positively sloped in the relevant region, the market supply curve is also positively sloped, as shown in Figure 10.2.

Market price in the perfectly competitive market tends toward an equilibrium where the price is P^* and the quantity supplied is Q^*. This is shown at point E in Figure 10.2, where supply and demand cross, or are equal. Why does the market tend toward this point? To answer this question, let us see what happens if the price is not at the equilibrium price.

If the price charged is above the equilibrium price, say, at price P_1 in Figure 10.3, the amount of goods suppliers are willing to sell exceeds the amount purchasers are willing to buy. We could then say that there is excess supply equal to the distance between points A and B in Figure 10.3. There is now a downward pressure on prices because suppliers wish to reduce their now excess inventories. The many suppliers independently reducing their prices cause the market price to fall. As the market price falls, consumers increase the quantity they demand, and suppliers lower the amount they wish to produce. Prices continue to fall until supply equals demand at the equilibrium price P^* in Figure 10.3.

Now let us see what happens if the price charged is below the equilibrium price, say, at P_2. There will be excess demand equal to the distance between points C and D. Upward pressure on price results because some purchasers are willing to spend more than the current market price rather than forego consumption. Suppliers also find that they can raise price and continue to sell the product. As price increases, the quantities suppliers are willing to offer increase, while the quantity demanded by purchasers falls. This continues until supply equals demand at the equilibrium price P^*.

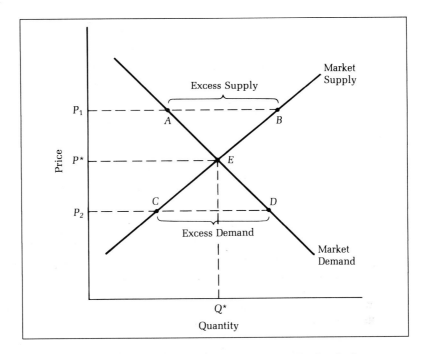

FIGURE 10.3 **Prices above and below the Equilibrium Price in a Perfectly Competitive Market.** The existence of high or low prices leads to economic decisions that in turn lead to the reestablishment of the equilibrium price P^*. At the high price, P_1, the excess supply causes producers to lower price, while at the low price, P_2, excess demand causes price to be pushed higher. Once the price is at P^*, however, no free market force will cause a change in price as long as supply and demand remain stable.

The Perfectly Competitive Firm: A General Example

Figure 10.4 represents the cost and revenue functions for a representative firm in a perfectly competitive market. Given that there are a large number of such firms all producing the homogeneous product, it follows that each of these firms will sell their output at the market equilibrium price, P^*. Consider what would happen if this individual firm decided *not* to sell at the market equilibrium price:

1. *If the firm sells at a lower price than P^**, any economic profit it currently enjoys would decrease (or their loss would increase). In Figure 10.4, the firm sells Q^* (we shall see why this particular quantity in a moment) at price P^* and earns the economic profit equal to the shaded area, which is $AR - ATC$ times the number sold. If the firm lowers price, the shaded area is reduced in size, and the firm loses economic profit.

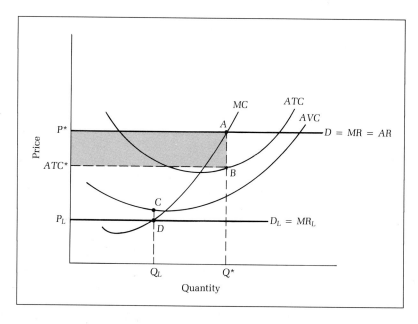

FIGURE 10.4   **A Representative Perfectly Competitive Firm: Short Run.** If the market price is P^*, the optimum level of production is Q^*, at which $MR = MC$. The profit per unit of production is A minus B (or P^* minus ATC^*). Total profit is the amount per unit times the number of units (Q^*). This is shown by the shaded area. If the market price falls below the minimum of the average variable cost (AVC), such as P_L, the firm minimizes its losses by shutting down. The per unit loss of C to D is thus avoided, and the loss is limited to the amount of fixed cost involved.

2.   *If the firm sells at a higher price then P^*, their sales would drop to 0* as customers would switch purchases to one of the many other sellers.

Again, you see that *in perfect competition, firms sell at the market equilibrium price and the demand curve is represented as a horizontal line*, such as the one labeled D in Figure 10.4. This same line also represents the marginal revenue (MR) to the firm, since the sale of each additional unit of product causes total revenue to increase by the price of the product (which is the same, P^*, at every level of output). This same curve is also the average revenue (AR) curve for the firm, since average revenue equals marginal revenue when the latter is a constant. These relationships can be shown most clearly as follows:

$$TR = (P^*)(Q)$$
$$MR = dTR/dQ$$

$$\boxed{MR = P^*}$$

$$AR = TR/Q$$
$$AR = [(P^*)(Q)]/Q$$

$$\boxed{AR = P^*}$$

Profit-maximizing competitive firms operate where marginal revenue equals marginal cost (point A in Figure 10.4). If a firm operates beyond this point and produces a quantity in excess of Q^*, the additional units of product add more to total cost than to total revenue. Note that to the right of Q^*, $MC > MR$.

If a firm operates below (to the left of) point A and produces less than Q^*, the production of more units increases total revenue more than the increase in total costs because to the left of point A, $MC < MR$.

Before looking at a specific example, let us investigate why a firm would shut down rather than produce if the market price fell below the minimum of average variable cost. Such a price is shown as P_L in Figure 10.4. At P_L, marginal revenue (MR_L) equals marginal cost at point D. The optimization rule that $MR = MC$ seems to call for an output of Q_L units, given the price P_L. But at Q_L units, the average *variable* cost is greater than the price, P_L. Thus, the firm does not earn enough revenue to cover even the variable cost of production. At this price, the firm is well advised to shut down and not produce. The fixed cost must still be paid and represents a loss to the firm, since revenues would be 0. But this loss is smaller than the loss of operating, given the P_L price, since the best that could be achieved at that price is an additional loss of C to D dollars per unit of production (Q_L).

At prices above the minimum average variable cost, a firm maximizes profit by producing the level of output at which $MR = MC$. And since $P = MR$ when the demand curve is horizontal, this means that $P = MC$ is the equivalent criterion for profit maximization. The collection of points at which $P = MC$ thus shows the quantities that a perfectly competitive firm would produce at each price. This is called the firm's supply function, and thus the marginal cost and supply curves are identical for a perfectly competitive firm (but only above the minimum of the average variable cost curve).

The Perfectly Competitive Firm: A Specific Example

For a specific numerical example of a perfectly competitive firm's short-run equilibrium, consider a firm with the following cost functions:

$$TC = 30 + 18Q - 2.7Q^2 + .15Q^3$$
$$MC = dTC/dQ = 18 - 5.4Q + .45Q^2$$
$$AC = TC/Q = 30Q^{-1} + 18 - 2.7Q + .15Q^2$$

Assume that price is determined by the market at $15. Then,

$$TR = 15Q$$
$$dTR/dQ = MR = 15$$

To find the quantity at which $MR = MC$, which is the firm's short-run equilibrium, we set MC and MR equal to one another and solve for Q^*:

$$MR = MC$$
$$15 = 18 - 5.4Q + .45Q^2$$
$$0 = 3 - 5.4Q + .45Q^2$$

Solving this equation for Q (using the quadratic formula from Chapter 3) yields two solutions:

$$Q^* = \frac{5.4 \pm \sqrt{(-5.4)^2 - 4(.45)(3)}}{(2)(.45)}$$
$$Q^* = .53 \text{ or } 11.42$$

Since the larger root is the profit-maximizing one, 11.42 units is the firm's optimum quantity, Q^*. (You could demonstrate for yourself that 11.42, rather than .53, yields a maximum by examining the second-order condition at each solution).

Figure 10.5 shows this perfectly competitive firm in graphic form. The intersection of MR and MC at point A determines the optimal quantity to sell, while the demand curve provides the selling price.

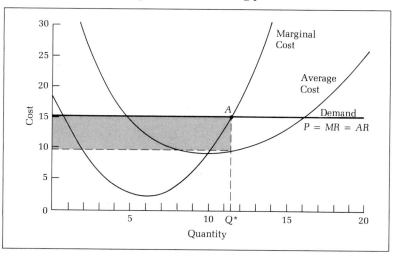

FIGURE 10.5   **A Specific Perfectly Competitive Firm: Short Run.**   In this example, the marginal and average cost curves are $MC = 18 - 5.4Q + .45Q^2$ and $AC = 30Q^{-1} + 18 - 2.7Q + .15Q^2$, and the market price is given as $P = 15$. We see that $MR = MC$ at point A, where $Q^* = 11.42$. Since price is greater than average cost at Q^*, a positive economic profit results. This is shown by the shaded area.

The single competitive firm pictured in Figure 10.5 and whose profit-maximizing optimum we found above is, however, earning positive economic (or excess) profits at Q^*. Recall that the cost curves already include normal profit; thus, the shaded area of Figure 10.5 must represent profit in excess of these normal profits. Figure 10.5 is labeled a short-run situation because these economic profits will not exist in perfect competition for a single firm in the long run. Why not?

The Long-Run Adjustment in Perfect Competition

In the long run, potential entrants to this market will know of the economic profits earned by the representative firm in the short run. Recall that such

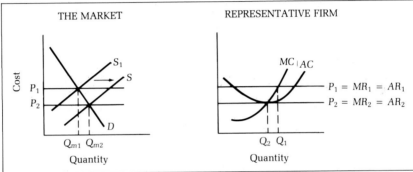

FIGURE 10.6
Long-Run Adjustment in Perfectly Competitive Markets. The market demand (D) and an original market supply (S_1) combine to determine a market price P_1 with Q_{m_1} units produced and sold. At the price P_1, the representative firm produces Q_1 units. Since price is greater than average cost, TR_1 is greater than TC, and a positive profit results. New firms enter the market because this profit shifts the market supply to S_2. The equilibrium price falls to P_2, and the slope of the firm's total revenue falls (see TR_2). The AC is tangent to the P_2 price line, and TC is tangent to TR_2; thus, there is 0 economic profit. Note also that under these conditions, the maximum for profit function 2 is at a profit of 0.

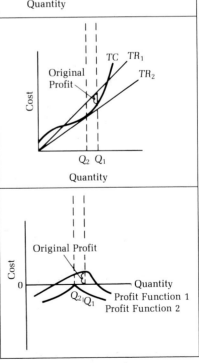

"perfect knowledge" is one of the characteristics of perfect competition. More firms will enter the industry, causing an increase in supply, which will drive the market equilibrium price down. This process will continue until all economic profit has been stripped from the market.

The market entry process and its effect on a representative firm are shown in Figure 10.6. We can see that the long-run equilibrium for the firm is where $MR_2 = MC = P_2 = AC$. Since price equals average cost after this long-run adjustment, the positive economic profits have disappeared.

If our original situation had been one for which $P = MR = MC$ at a point where price was less than AC, each firm would have made a negative economic profit (a loss). In such a situation, some firms would leave the industry, and the market supply function should shift to the left. Such a shift would be accompanied by an increase in the equilibrium price, and the amount of negative profit would be less for each firm. Ultimately, in a perfectly competitive market, the natural forces of firms entering and leaving the industry establish an equilibrium price at which each firm earns only a normal profit (i.e., no economic, or excess, profit).

10.4   MONOPOLY: A MARKET WITH A SINGLE SELLER

The market was described early in this chapter as a process in which rivals, in pursuit of their own interests, attempt to outdo one another. The perfectly competitive market we examined had the attractive feature that, in its long-run equilibrium, a firm earns only normal profits and sells its product only at the market-determined price. In that perfectly competitive system, no one firm could *significantly* influence the outcome of the market process.

Monopoly, however, is the opposite of perfect competition. In a monopoly, there is just one seller, and thus there is an absence of any attempt by market participants to outdo one another. As a result, there is also an absence of the perfectly competitive outcome. A monopolist does not have to compete because there are no rivals with whom the monopolist must share the market.

Barriers to Entry Help Maintain Monopoly Power

In order to explain how it is possible for a monopoly to exist, it is necessary to focus on what is required to make a market competitive. *The necessary condition for a competitive market is freedom of entry.* Since monopoly is the opposite of competition, *the necessary condition for a monopoly (or monopoly power) is a barrier to firms wishing to compete in the market.* A monopolist has what is called *monopoly power* to manipulate the price because it is protected from competition from firms who find it difficult to enter the market. There are several sources of barriers to entry:

1. The firm may have *sole ownership* of a strategic resource (e.g., the firm owns *all* the uranium in the world and thus bars others from entry into the uranium market).

2. The firm may have a *patent or copyright* on the product produced (e.g., only Academic Press may publish this textbook).

3. *Large scale production* may be required to enter the market, precluding many potential entrants from starting production (e.g., steel plants tend to require immense initial investment).

4. A *well-known brand name* can create a barrier by making it difficult for new firms to obtain customers (e.g., Apple Computer has high recognition among personal computer purchasers).

5. The *government may grant an exclusive franchise* to a firm, precluding any competition (e.g., television stations, utility companies, airlines, trucking firms).

By far the most important entry barrier is the last: the government franchise. The reason for this is that all monopoly power deriving from entry barriers is subject to decay in the long run — all except the exclusive government franchise. Note how various forms of entry barriers have withered away over time:

1. During World War II, the United States lost its supply of quinine because of the occupation by enemy troops of natural quinine–producing areas. In a short time, a substitute for quinine was found. This synthetic quinine continued to compete with natural quinine even after the war, breaking down the entry barrier due to sole ownership of a strategic resource.

2. Patents presumably protect a firm for 17 years from having another company produce a certain product, but both Polaroid and Eastman Kodak now produce instant picture film. Polaroid invented instant picture film and patented the process, but Kodak engineers "invented" a similar but "significantly" different process, in the eyes of the United States Patent Office.

3. Large-scale production often *appears* to preclude entry, but the appearance is often more than life-sized. When Federal Express sought to enter the small package air freight business, management realized they could not do it piecemeal (i.e., one route at a time). To be successful, they believed they had to begin service on day 1 with many routes and many planes. But that would require an immense investment before even one package was carried. Venture capitalists, firms in the business of lending money on very risky projects, loaned the money to Federal Express. Its success is history.

4. Brand names, too, are not effective barriers over the long run. While Apple Computer is well-known, many companies have done well by selling machines very similar to an Apple. Some of these firms even compare their machines to Apple computers in their advertising in order to take advantage of the high brand recognition Apple has achieved.

As we have mentioned, the one entry barrier that does not erode over time is the government franchise. It is true that the government may revoke the franchise at any time (as they did in the 1970s with the telephone companies' long lines division, allowing MCI, Sprint, and others to compete where competition was previously precluded). But it is also true that the government may choose to continue such a franchise for quite some time. A government franchise may give the monopolist complete monopoly power (such as the electric utility has in most towns), or the monopoly power granted may not be complete (as with radio and television stations, which receive government approval to use certain frequencies).

Many products now on the market were first sold by a short-run monopoly, but as time passed, their monopoly power eroded and the markets approached a more competitive situation. Only recipients of government franchises have been able to protect their monopoly power in the long run. For decades, some industries have been quite effective in enlisting the aid of the government: railroads, electric utilities, the medical profession (through licensing), and the broadcast industry. While almost all real-world markets lie somewhere between the polar cases of perfect competition and pure monopoly, these industries lie far closer to the monopoly end of the continuum.

The Monopolistic Firm: A General Example

The situation of a pure monopolist is pictured in Figure 10.7. The key difference between the market situation confronting a monopolist and that confronting a perfectly competitive firm is that the monopolist's demand curve is *not* horizontal. It slopes downward to the right because it coincides with the industry demand curve (if there is only one firm, its demand curve *is* the industry demand curve).

The monopolist is not a price taker but, rather, a *price maker* (or price searcher). While the monopolist is still subject to the law of demand (more units may only be sold at lower prices), the monopolist may choose the point on the demand curve at which to operate and thus sets price.

The upper frame in Figure 10.7 assumes a normal set of cost curves for this pure monopolist, and the corresponding total cost curve is shown in the middle frame. The monopolist's demand and average revenue curve coincide, but the marginal revenue curve is now a separate curve. The marginal revenue curve is now downward sloping because more units can only be

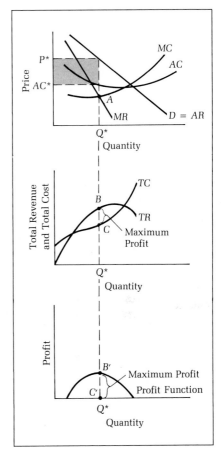

FIGURE 10.7

Equilibrium for a Monopolist. A monopolist maximizes profit by producing the rate of output for which $MR = MC$ (see point A). Since this quantity is Q^*, at which $P^* > AC^*$, a positive economic profit results (see shaded area). This profit is also shown in the middle graph by the distance between points B and C. Similarly, the maximum profit is illustrated by the distance between B' and C' in the lower graph.

sold by lowering prices and decreasing marginal revenue. Since the monopolist must decrease the product price to increase sales, the additional revenue (marginal revenue) from each successive unit of sales is less than the price at which the unit is sold.

To show that this is true, let us assume that the monopolist's demand curve is linear, with an intercept equal to a and a slope equal to $-b$. The demand curve is, then,

$$P = a - bQ$$

From this, we can find total revenue, which is equal to price times quantity.

$$TR = PQ$$
$$TR = (a - bQ)Q$$
$$TR = aQ - bQ^2$$

Marginal revenue can then be found as the rate of change in total revenue (i.e., the derivative of total revenue with respect to quantity):

$$MR = dTR/dQ$$
$$MR = a - 2bQ$$

Since the slope of marginal revenue $(-2b)$ is twice as steep as the slope of demand $(-b)$, while both functions have the same vertical intercept (a), marginal revenue is less than price for any quantity.

This can also be illustrated with a numerical example. Suppose the monopolist can sell 10 units of the product if price is set at $5 and 11 units if the price is set at $4.80. The marginal revenue from increasing the quantity sold by one unit is less than the $4.80 selling price because *each of the 11 units sell at the same price.* The first 10 units, therefore, each sell for $.20 less than they would have sold for at the $5 price. Thus, while the firm makes an additional $4.80 on the sale of the eleventh unit, it loses $.20 on each of the first 10 units. The change in total receipts is $2.80 [$4.80 − (10 units)($.20)]: this is the marginal revenue of the eleventh unit.

Short-run profits for the monopolist are determined in much the same way as for firms in competitive markets. In Figure 10.7, the profit-maximizing monopolist will choose to operate where $MR = MC$. The reasoning is precisely the same as for the competitive firm: as long as an additional unit of output adds more to the firm's revenues than it does to the firm's costs, profit on that unit will be positive and total profits will be increased (or losses decreased) by producing and selling the unit. This process of producing and selling extra units continues until MR equals MC. There is no incentive to move beyond that point (into the region where $MC > MR$) because producing and selling extra units then reduces profit (or increases losses). Thus, the monopoly firm in Figure 10.7 will choose to operate where $MR = MC$, produce the quantity of Q^*, and charge a price of P^* (found from the demand curve).

At price P^*, the monopolist is earning economic (or excess) profits equal to the size of the shaded rectangle. In the middle frame, this equilibrium can be seen to be at the quantity at which the vertical distance by which TR is above TC is the greatest. This is also the point where TR and TC have identical slopes. Since the slope of the total cost curve equals MC and the slope of the total revenue curve equals MR, MR must equal MC at exactly the output where TR exceeds TC by the greatest amount: at quantity Q^*.

The Monopolistic Firm: A Specific Example

For a specific numerical example of the monopolist's short-run equilibrium, consider a monopolist with the same total cost curve we used earlier for the competitive firm. Note that there is no reason to expect the cost curves of monopolists to be different from those of competitive firms:

$$TC = 30 + 18Q - 2.7Q^2 + .15Q^3$$
$$MC = dTC/dQ = 18 - 5.4Q + .45Q^2$$
$$AC = TC/Q = 30Q^{-1} + 18 - 2.7Q + .15Q^2$$

Since the monopolist is not "given" a price from the market, as is the competitive firm, we also need to know the firm's demand curve in order to calculate the short-run equilibrium. Let us assume that demand is given as

$$P = 20 - 1Q$$

It follows that total revenue and marginal revenue are

$$TR = 20Q - 1Q^2 \text{ and } MR = 20 - 2Q$$

To find the quantity at which $MR = MC$, the monopolist's short-run equilibrium, we set the equations for the marginal revenue and marginal cost functions equal to one another and solve for Q as follows:

$$MR = MC$$
$$20 - 2Q = 18 - 5.4Q + .45Q^2$$
$$0 = -2 - 3.4Q + .45Q^2$$

Solving this equation using the quadratic formula,

$$Q^* = \frac{3.4 \pm \sqrt{(-3.4)^2 - (4)(-2)(.45)}}{(2)(.45)}$$
$$Q^* = -.55 \text{ or } 8.10$$

Again, the largest root is the profit maximizing one, and thus the monopolist produces and sells 8.10 units. The monopolist's price can be found by substituting the output rate 8.10 units in the demand function and solving for P^*:

$$P^* = 20 - 1Q$$
$$P^* = 20 - 1(8.10)$$
$$P^* = \$11.90$$

This solution can be seen in graphic form in Figure 10.8. Marginal revenue (MR) is seen to equal marginal cost (MC) at point A. The quantity corresponding to this point is Q^* (8.1 units). By going up to the demand curve

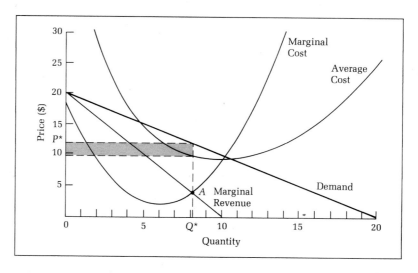

FIGURE 10.8   **A Profit-Maximizing Monopolist.** Like all firms, the monopolist maximizes profit by producing the level of output (Q^*) at which $MR = MC$ (see point A). The profit-maximizing price is then found from the demand curve as P^*. This monopolist's cost and revenue functions are

$$TC = 30 + 18Q - 2.7Q^2 + .15Q^3$$
$$MC = 18 - 5.4Q + .45Q^2$$
$$AC = 30Q^{-1} + 18 - 2.7Q + .15Q^2$$
$$P = 20 - Q$$
$$TR = 20Q - Q^2$$
$$MR = 20 - 2Q$$

from Q^* and then over to the vertical axis, we can find the price that should be set to maximize profit. It is $P^* = \$11.90$. We also can see that at Q^*, average cost (AC) is less than price. Thus, a positive economic profit exists and is shown by the area of the shaded rectangle in Figure 10.8.

The Monopolist in the Long Run

In the long run, the firm can continue to operate only as long as its price exceeds or equals its long-run average cost. For the firm pictured in Figure 10.8, the firm's short-run equilibrium is also its long-run equilibrium. The firm in Figure 10.8 is earning economic profit in each short-run period, but since no competitors are able to enter the market, the monopolist continues to produce 8.10 units per period. The firm in Figure 10.8 is a *natural monopolist* because its profit-maximizing output occurs at a production level at which long-run average costs are declining. This amounts to saying that a single firm can produce the entire supply of the product more cheaply than can two or more smaller firms. Natural monopolies have economies of scale that are large relative to the size of the market.

The government often grants an exclusive franchise to firms thought to be natural monopolies and then regulates the prices these firms charge in order to promote the passing of cost savings (from large-scale production) on to consumers. Most utilities (i.e., electric, water, natural gas, etc.) fall into this category, but there is considerable doubt among economists as to whether the natural-monopoly characteristics of some firms continue to exist over a long period of time.

Figure 10.8 is also useful for examining some conventional wisdom concerning corporations that are monopolies. Note that the point at which a monopolist maximizes profit *always* falls in the elastic range of the demand curve. Remember that straight-line demand curves are elastic in the upper left-hand half and inelastic in the lower right-hand half. The monopolist *always* operates in the elastic range because the firm will maximize profit where $MR = MC$, and MC is always positive. Further, when marginal revenue is positive, the price elasticity of demand is elastic. So it would be incorrect to say, as many do, that a monopolist's demand curve is inelastic—in fact, the monopolist always operates where the demand curve is elastic.

It is also clear from Figure 10.8 that a monopolist does not always charge the highest price the firm can command (that such firms do charge the highest price is perhaps the most common criticism of monopoly). Clearly, in Figure 10.8 there are many prices above the P^* that the monopolist could choose to charge, say, $16. But the monopolist will *not* choose to charge that price because the firm's profit would be decreased.

We can also see from Figure 10.8 that monopolists do not *always* make a profit. Suppose the AC curve was much higher. Then it would be possible that the monopoly could suffer a loss. If that short-run loss situation was predicted to be a continual problem, the firm might reasonably choose to exit the market. The firm pictured in 10.8 is, however, earning economic profit, and if this short-run situation was predicted to continue, the firm could be expected to remain in the market.

Price Regulation of a Monopolist

Monopolies are usually regulated by one or more government agencies "in the public interest." Although it is not our purpose in this chapter to provide an exhaustive discussion of regulation, we will look quickly at how a regulatory agency might determine the price a monopolist could charge. Often, the objective of the regulating agency is to make the industry operate in such a manner that the results are closer to those that would evolve if the industry was competitive. Generally, this means reducing monopoly profits and/or improving the allocation of resources.

To illustrate the concepts involved, let us use the diagram in Figure 10.9. The cost curves in that diagram could represent, for example, an electric power monopoly (see the electric power average cost function in

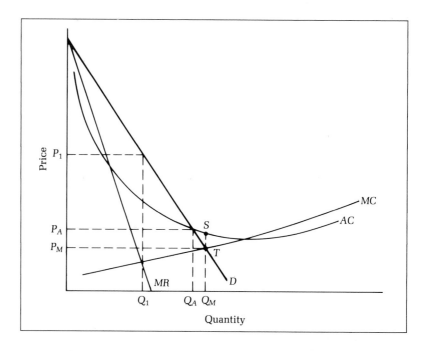

FIGURE 10.9   Price Regulation of a Monopolist.   The unregulated monopolist sets price at P_1 to maximize profits and sells Q_1 units. A regulatory agency that follows the "fair" rate of return criterion sets price at P_A, consumers purchase Q_A units, and the firm obtains 0 economic profit, since price equals average cost. For an optimal allocation of resources, it could be argued that the regulatory price should be P_M.

Chapter 9). Without regulation, the firm depicted would make the profit-maximizing decision to price at P_1 and sell Q_1 units (i.e., the price and quantity for which $MR = MC$).

Probably the most common approach to regulatory pricing is to establish a price that would allow the regulated firm a "fair rate of return" on a risk-adjusted basis (see Chapter 2 for a discussion of risk measurement and risk adjustments). This fair rate of return is an opportunity cost concept and is included in the cost functions. The fair rate of return price is, then, the price that equals average cost. This is shown as P_A in Figure 10.9. At the price P_A, consumers will purchase Q_A units, and the average cost of providing that many units is $AC_A = P_A$. Since average cost is equal to price, there is no positive or negative economic profit. The regulated firm obtains just the normal economic profit for a venture of equal risk. Comparing this result with the unregulated profit-maximizing monopolist, we see the following:

Price is lower: $P_A < P_1$
Quantity is greater: $Q_A > Q_1$

It is sometimes suggested that society would be best served if the regulatory decision makers would set price equal to marginal cost. Very briefly, the argument is that price is a measure of the marginal benefit people get from consuming a product. Thus, it follows that as long as price is greater than marginal cost, more of that good should be produced and consumed since the marginal benefit is greater than the marginal cost. The net benefit to society would rise up to the point at which price (marginal benefit) is equal to marginal cost. Following this reasoning, the best price for the regulatory agency to set would be P_M. At this price, consumers would purchase Q_m units. However, the firm would have a loss of S to T on each of the Q_m units, since average cost is that much greater than the price, P_M. In such a case, a subsidy would be required to keep the firm operating. Some mass transit systems are examples of this type of situation.

You might note that in a perfectly competitive market, both of these regulatory outcomes are obtained simultaneously through the natural workings of the free market. In a perfectly competitive long-run equilibrium, you have seen in Figure 10.6 that $P_2 = AC$ and $P_2 = MC$. There are 0 economic profits, and resources are optimally allocated.

10.5   PRICE DISCRIMINATION

In economic jargon, *price discrimination* is usually termed *monopoly price discrimination*. That label is appropriate because price discrimination cannot happen in a perfectly competitive industry in equilibrium. *Monopoly power must be present in a market for price discrimination to exist.* This seems a trivial point when you understand the definition of price discrimination: the practice of charging different prices to various consumers for a given product. In a competitive market, consumers would simply buy from the cheapest seller, and producers would sell to the highest bidders, and that would be that.

With monopoly power, however, the opportunity may exist for the firm to offer different terms (of which price is only one component) to different purchasers, thus dividing the market, a practice known as *market segmentation*. Or it may be possible for the firm to charge many prices to a single purchaser by creating a price schedule such that the consumer pays a different price for each block of purchases, a practice called *multipart pricing*. The ultimate in the ability to engage in price discrimination is termed *first-degree price discrimination*, in which a different price is charged for each unit sold to each customer. This form of pricing gets from the consumer the maximum amount he or she is willing to pay for each unit. What is the maxiumum you would pay for a soft drink right now? How about an appendectomy if you had acute appendicitis? While first-degree, or perfect, price discrimination is not common, milder forms of price discrimination abound.

For example, consider utilities, which in most areas of the United States charge a different kilowatt-hour price for different customers: households, farms, businesses, and so on. Consider also a theater that charges different prices for matinees and evening performances. A number of possible situations in which price discrimination may be practiced are presented in Table 10.1.

True price discrimination, however, is said to exist only when price differences are not supported by cost differences. For instance, an insurance company may require a medical examination of its prospective customers and, based on that examination, may charge people in poorer health higher rates than people in good health. Clearly, the insurance company is charging different prices, but as economists, we must be careful to be sure the goods sold at different prices are really identical in an economic sense. In order to do that, we must reference the marginal cost: if the marginal costs of providing insurance to the two customers differ, then the goods are not the same, and the situation is perhaps not a true case of price discrimination. However, if the difference in the marginal costs of provision is not proportional to the difference in prices charged (e.g., premiums), then it is a case of price discrimination. Note that charging different prices for two seemingly identical products may not be price discrimination. Therefore, some of the examples listed in Table 10.1 may not be true price discrimination. The test is whether the differences in the marginal costs of provision are in proportion to the differences in prices charged.

We should also be careful to note that not all price discrimination is necessarily undesirable. Price discrimination may perform a desirable service by allocating a scarce resource over some base, such as time or geographic location. The term *price discrimination*, then, has a neutral connotation when used in the present context.

We will discuss the three forms of price discrimination in turn: (1) market segmentation, or third-degree price discrimination, (2) multipart pricing, or second-degree price discrimination; and (3) perfect, or first-degree price discrimination.

Third-Degree Price Discrimination: A Graphic Model

Third-degree price discrimination, or market segmentation, requires that the seller be able to (1) segment, or separate, the market such that goods sold in one market cannot be resold by the buyers in another; and (2) identify distinct demand curves with different price elasticities for each market segment.

An example of such a market could be a campus bookstore. These stores often sell items to students at one price and the identical items to faculty at different (lower) prices. The individuals in each market segment are easily identified by an ID card, and their price elasticities are usually quite different (higher price elasticities for faculty). The price differential is not

TABLE 10.1
Representative Situations Conducive to Price Discrimination

Type	Basis for Discrimination	Examples
Individual or personal	Ability to pay in terms of income, wealth, or amount of insurance	Natural gas, electric, and telephone prices for residential versus corporate customers; senior citizen discounts at theaters, supermarkets, etc.; physicians' low fees for needy patients
	Relatives and friends of wealth and fame, trade classification	Jobber and wholesale discounts; club purchasing; lower credit and interest rates for friends
	Personal appearance, habits, mannerisms, health, size, weight, skill level	Conditions of purchase requiring a tie, shoes, cleanliness, no swimming or sports attire; different insurance premiums based on health
Group membership	Age, sex, race, religion, marital status, military status, employer, club	Group life insurance; special prices on student football and basketball tickets; "corporate days" at amusement parks; charter bus and airline trips; free senior citizen public transportation in off-peak hours; low video rental rates for members
	Geographic location	Higher prices for purchasers living outside the country, state, city limits, or zone; base-point pricing; out-of-state–in-state student tuition differences
	Use of product	Transportation rates based on size, weight, and value of goods shipped; use of milk for drinking, making ice cream, and processing cheese
Product classification	Qualities of product	Relatively higher prices for gourmet foods and drinks, stylish clothes, fine furniture, and deluxe models and accessories
	Labels and trademarks	Low prices on generic products
	Quantities of product	"Buy-two-get-one-free" type offers; quantity discounts
Time sequencing	Time of day	Lower electric rates during midnight to early morning hours; golf course greens fees
	Season of year	Low motel rates during the off-season; high costume rentals near Halloween

enough to make it worthwhile for faculty to buy at their lower price and then resell to students at a higher price. Providers of medical services (doctors, dentists, hospitals, etc.) commonly charge different prices to different customers, who would clearly find it difficult to resell the product (consider, for example, trying to resell a dental fluoride treatment). Theaters sell tickets to children at lower prices than they do to adults (and few adults try to enter on children's tickets).

The question confronting the seller when *market segmentation* is possible is how best to take advantage of the separate markets. The seller would like to maximize profits, but what price should be charged in each market in order to accomplish this?

If the seller had a certain quantity of output to sell and wanted to decide how to allocate it between two market segments, what information would be relevant? First, realize that this is a revenue maximization problem; maximizing revenue in this case is the equivalent of profit maximizing because the costs remain the same regardless of which market segment gets more product. Revenue can be maximized by dividing the output between the two markets in such a way that marginal revenue is the same in both markets. Let us look at a very simple example that involves just two markets.

In Figure 10.10, the separate demand curves for each market segment are labeled D_A for market segment A and D_B for market segment B. The marginal revenue functions, of course, are MR_A and MR_B. Since the two demand curves have different slopes, at each price, the elasticities differ in the two market segments.

The marginal revenue curve for the total market (MR_T) is shown in the right-hand frame of Figure 10.10 as the horizontal summation of the two market segment marginal revenue curves ($MR_A + MR_B$). Total output (Q^*) is set where this marginal revenue (MR_T) equals cost at point T. The marginal cost curve is simply the marginal cost curve for the entire firm regardless of where its output is sold.

The firm thus decides to produce and sell Q^* but must decide how to allocate Q^* between market segment A and market segment B. Now, at any level of Q, the seller would want to allocate that output in such a way that the marginal revenue was the same in both market segments ($MR_A = MR_B$). If this was not true, the seller could increase revenue by reallocating more units to the market segment with the higher marginal revenue and fewer units to the market segment with the lower marginal revenue. Thus, the optimality condition is

$$MR_A = MR_B$$

It is also the case that the seller would produce more units as long as $MC < MR_A = MR_B$. So the complete optimality condition is

$$MC = MR_A = MR_B$$

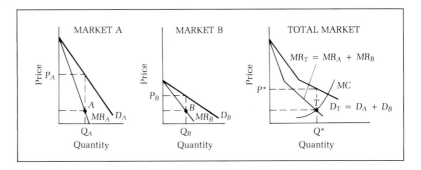

FIGURE 10.10   **Third-Degree Price Discrimination: Market Segmentation.**   In this model, the demand and marginal revenue functions for submarkets A and B are added horizontally to get the total market demand (D_T) and marginal revenue (MR_T). The optimum rate of output (Q^*) is found where $MC = MR_T$. Those Q^* units are allocated to the submarkets such that $MC = MR_T = MR_A = MR_B$, and the products are priced from the market segment demand curves $(D_A$ and $D_B)$. Thus, we find for markets A and B the price-quantity combinations P_A/Q_A and P_B/Q_B, respectively. If the firm simply aggregates the markets instead of segmenting them, the price P^* is charged for all Q^* units. Consumers in market A then buy more, and consumers in market B buy less. (Demonstrate this for yourself by drawing a horizontal line from P^* through each market segment and noting where that price line crosses each demand curve.)

The firm pictured in Figure 10.10 would then produce Q^* units in total and sell Q_A in market segment A and Q_B in market segment B. The prices in each market segment would be set with reference to the demand curve in that segment. Thus, price P_A would be charged in market segment A and price P_B in market segment B.

The key to Figure 10.10 is the curve labeled MR_T (the horizontal summation of the separate marginal revenue curves (i.e., $MR_A + MR_B$). It is the intersection of this curve with the marginal cost curve that determines the optimal output (i.e., $MR_T = MC$). The segmenting of the optimal output is then determined from the market segment marginal revenue curves (MR_A and MR_B) such that MR_A and MR_B both equal MC at the same level as $MR_T = MC$. This is found by drawing a horizontal line from the point T across to each submarket. Where this line intersects the MR_A and MR_B curves (points A and B, respectively) determines the appropriate allocation to each submarket (Q_A and Q_B, respectively).

Finally, prices are determined by reading up from the quantities Q_A and Q_B to their respective demand curves (D_A and D_B) and then over to the vertical axes where we find the prices P_A and P_B. In the example of Figure 10.10, market segment B has the greater price elasticity and so receives the lower price, P_B. The market segment with the more elastic demand always receives the lower price.

This characteristic of market segmentation explains the phenomenon of different college bookstore prices for students and faculty. The bookstore has considerable monopoly power with students on campus but much less power with faculty, who may do more shopping off campus. When many stores compete for the faculty members' purchases, demand tends to be much more elastic. If the bookstore is able to separate the students from the faculty, it is generally more profitable to charge a lower price to faculty than to students.

Third-Degree Price Discrimination: An Algebraic Example

Let us consider a mathematical formulation of third-degree price discrimination, since it is the most common type. We shall limit our discussion to the case of two submarkets, but the technique is entirely general and can be applied to any number of submarkets. Assume that demand in market 1 is

$$P_1 = 98 - 2Q_1$$

that demand in market 2 is

$$P_2 = 50 - .5Q_2$$

and that the firm has the following total cost function (we use a linear cost function only for ease in exposition, but any type of cost function could be used):

$$TC = 1500 + 2Q$$

where $Q = Q_1 + Q_2$, or total output. Profit is

$$\pi = TR_1 + TR_2 - TC$$

where TR_1 is revenue from submarket 1 (P_1Q_1), and TR_2 is revenue from submarket 2 (P_2Q_2).

Now we can express profit as a function of Q_1 and Q_2, recalling that $P_1 = 98 - 2Q_1$ and $P_2 = 50 - .5Q_2$. We have

$$\pi = (98 - 2Q_1)Q_1 + (50 - .5Q_2)Q_2 - [1500 + 2(Q_1 + Q_2)]$$
$$\pi = 98Q_1 - 2Q_1^2 + 50Q_2 - .5Q_2^2 - [1500 + 2Q_1 + 2Q_2]$$

Taking the first partial derivatives of profit with respect to Q_1 and Q_2, we can find the profit-maximizing quantities, and from them we can calculate P_1 and P_2:

$$\partial\pi/\partial Q_1 = 98 - 4Q_1 - 2 = 0$$
$$\partial\pi/\partial Q_2 = 50 - Q_2 - 2 = 0$$

and thus,

$$4Q_1 = 96$$
$$Q_1 = 24$$

and

$$Q_2 = 48$$

Substituting these values for Q_1 and Q_2 into their respective demand functions, we find

$$P_1 = 98 - 2(24) = 50$$
$$P_2 = 50 - .5(48) = 26$$

Thus, the firm should charge $50 in market 1 but only $26 in market 2. No other set of prices would bring the firm as much profit. Profit then is

$$\pi = 50(24) + 26(48) - [1500 + 2(24 + 48)]$$
$$\pi = 1200 + 1248 - 1644$$
$$\pi = 804$$

Thus, the maximum profit the firm could earn as a price discriminator is $804.

If the firm could not discriminate in pricing, the single price it would charge can be determined as follows. If price discrimination is not practiced, then

$$P_1 = P_2$$

and thus

$$(98 - 2Q_1) = (50 - .5Q_2)$$

which can be written

$$(48 - 2Q_1 + .5Q_2 = 0)$$

Adding this constraint to the profit function, the following Langragian function is obtained:

$$L = (98 - 2Q_1)Q_1 + (50 - .5Q_2)Q_2$$
$$- [1500 + 2(Q_1 + Q_2)] + \lambda(48 - 2Q_1 + .5Q_2)$$

To maximize profit subject to the constraint that prices be equal in the submarkets, we find the three first-order partials as follows:

$$\frac{\partial L}{\partial Q_1} = 98 - 4Q_1 - 2 - 2\lambda = 0$$

$$\frac{\partial L}{\partial Q_2} = 50 - Q_2 - 2 + .5\lambda = 0$$

$$\frac{\partial L}{\partial \lambda} = 48 - 2Q_1 + .5Q_2 = 0$$

Solving for Q_1 and Q_2, we obtain $Q_1 = 33.6$ and $Q_2 = 38.4$. From the demand equations for each market, we have

$$P_1 = 98 - 2Q_1 = 98 - 2(33.6) = 30.8$$
$$P_2 = 50 - .5Q_2 = 50 - .5(38.4) = 30.8$$

A price of $30.80 would be charged in both market 1 and market 2. We can now compare profit in the nondiscriminating case with the profit under conditions of price discrimination. We have determined above that in the latter case profit was $804. With equal prices, profit is

$$\pi = P_1Q_1 + P_2Q_2 - [1500 + 2(Q_1 + Q_2)]$$
$$\pi = 30.8(33.6) + 30.8(38.4) - [1500 + 2(33.6 + 38.4)]$$
$$\pi = 573.6$$

We see that this is less than the profit obtained by practicing third-degree price discrimination. Clearly, the firm is better off if it is allowed to price discriminate.

Second-Degree Price Discrimination

Second-degree price discrimination is also referred to as multipart pricing. It is a block, or step, type of pricing in which the first set of units is sold at one price, a second set at a lower price, a third set at a still lower price, and so on. Note that this is different from a quantity discount in which the lower (discounted) price applies to all units purchased. In second-degree price discrimination, the lower price applies only to units purchased in that block. The buyer must have already paid the higher price for the earlier units. Some familiar examples should make this clear:

1. *Electricity.* In many parts of the country, residential electricity users are billed at different rates for different blocks of consumption. For example, the first 100 kilowatt-hours may be priced at $.062 per kilowatt-hour, the next 100 kilowatt-hours may be priced at $.059 per kilowatt-hour, and everything over 200 kilowatt-hours may be priced at $.057 per kilowatt-hour. This is an example of three-block second-degree price discrimination. You can not buy the second 100 kilowatt-hours at the lower price until you have already purchased the first 100 at the higher price.

2. *Long distance phone calls.* When you make a long distance phone call, you are usually charged a higher rate for the first three minutes than for subsequent time. It is impossible to buy just the second three minutes of a phone call. You must first have used the initial three minutes. This is also an example of second-degree price discrimination.[2]

---

[2]You may have already thought to yourself that these same products are also sold using third-degree price discrimination based on different elasticities of demand. Electric rates to residential users (with relatively less elastic demands) are generally higher than those paid by commercial and industrial users (with relatively more elastic demand). Long-distance phone rates are generally higher during the 8:00 A.M. to 5:00 P.M. part of the day, when the demand is relatively less elastic, than in the evening and night hours, when rates are lower and demand is relatively more elastic.

Economic theory tells us that if demand curves are negatively sloped and if price is a reasonable measure of a consumer's marginal benefit from purchasing a good, there will be a *consumer's surplus* when all units of the product are priced the same. That is, we often get more than we pay for in terms of satisfaction.

This means, in turn, that we may have been willing to pay more than we are actually charged. Suppose, for example, that it is a hot summer day and you have just finished your daily three-mile run. You come upon a lemonade stand where you can buy a plastic glass of cold lemonade for $.25. You drink one, then another, then a third. And you have spent $.75. But you very well might have been willing to pay $.50 or $.60 for just one glass of that cold refreshment. If the seller knew something about your demand, he or she could have sold you the three glasses of lemonade at perhaps $.60, $.40, and $.25, respectively. After all, we do know that a third glass was worth at least $.25 to you. So perhaps the seller could have gotten revenues of $1.25 from you, rather than $.75, by capturing part of your consumer's surplus.

Let us now look at second-degree price discrimination in a more formal graphic model. In Figure 10.11, the seller faces the demand curve (D) of one typical consumer. While the cost function is not shown in the figure, assume that marginal revenue and marginal cost intersect and lead to an optimal price of P^*. The consumer would choose to buy the quantity Q^* at this price. The shaded area of the figure represents the consumer's surplus. It may be, however, that the firm uses multipart pricing to capture a portion of this surplus. Suppose the firm sets a price of P_1 for the first Q_1 units purchased and that additional units sell for P_2 (a two-stage pricing scheme). The consumer buys Q_1 units at price P_1 and Q_2 units at price P_2. That portion of the consumer surplus labeled P_1BCP_2 is now captured by the firm rather than by the consumer. This still leaves a rather large portion of the consumer surplus still in the consumer's hands. The firm's management would prefer to capture it all and could by using more parts in a multipart pricing strategy. However, to do so, management needs to know a great deal about the consumer's demand.

First-Degree Price Discrimination

Perfect, or first-degree, price discrimination can occur when a firm knows the maximum price the individual is willing to pay for each successive unit. The firm could then charge that highest price for each successive unit and capture the entire consumer surplus. Recall that all forms of price discrimination involve some monopoly power, but perfect price discrimination involves a degree of monopoly power rarely found in the real world. The fact that such a firm might be found in violation of the Clayton Antitrust Act or the Robinson Patman Act is probably much less important than the

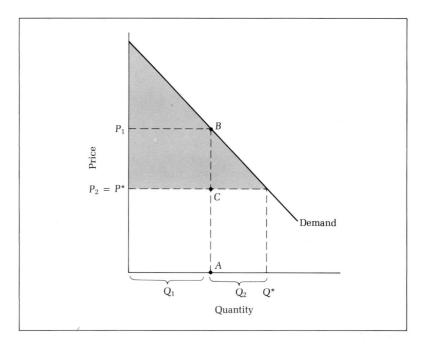

FIGURE 10.11   Second-Degree Price Discrimination.   In this example of second-degree price discrimination, or multipart pricing, the first block of units (Q_1 units) is sold at the price P_1, and the second block (Q_2 units) is sold at the price P_2. This allows the seller to capture that part of the consumer's surplus (the shaded part of the diagram), represented by the area $P_1 B C P_2$.

degree of monopoly power in determining whether such a situation could exist for any length of time.

10.6   PEAK LOAD PRICING

Peak load pricing is a type of third-degree price discrimination in which the discrimination base is temporal. We single out this particular form of price discrimination in part because of its widespread use. But remember that all forms of third-degree price discrimination, including peak load pricing, involve a seller attempting to capitalize on the fact that buyers' demand elasticities vary. In the case of peak load pricing, customer demand elasticities vary with time.

Very few, if any, business economic activities are characterized by an absolutely constant demand during all seasons of the year and at all times of day. For many, the variations, or fluctuations, are not large enough to be of concern, but for some activities, fluctuations in demand are significant. These variations are sometimes relatively stable and predictable. Electric utilities provide one good example.[3] During the hours from midnight to 7:00 A.M. demand is relatively low, but it reaches peaks in mid-morning and late afternoon–early evening. The demand for electricity is also fairly seasonal in many parts of the country because of heavy air conditioning in the summer months. Power companies must provide sufficient capacity for the peak demand periods and thus have considerable unused capacity much of the remainder of the time. If a higher price was charged for electricity during peak demand periods, perhaps less capacity would be needed and average rates could potentially be reduced. Figure 10.12 illustrates the nature of the peak load problem in comparing low, peak, and mean demand to capacity requirements.

Most other utilities are also subject to regular fluctuations in demand that create a peak load problem. Natural gas utilities must have sufficient capacity to meet the demand during cold winter months but need only a fraction of that capacity during the warmer summer months. City water departments are frequently pressed to capacity during warm and dry periods. The telephone communications industry also has a regular pattern of peak and low demand. During business hours, telephone

---

[3]See O.E. Williamson, "Peak Loading Pricing and Optimal Capacity under Indivisibility Constraints," *American Economic Review*, September 1966, pp. 810–827; Donald N. DeSalvia, "An Application of Peak Load Pricing," *The Journal of Business*, October 1969, pp. 458–476; and C.J. Cicchetti, "Electric Price Regulation," *Public Utilities Fortnightly*, August 29, 1974, pp. 13–18.

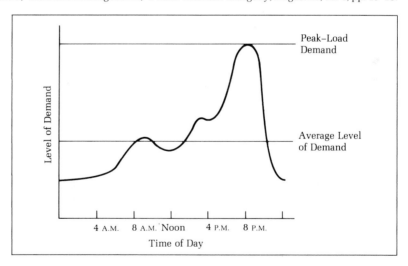

FIGURE 10.12   Peak Load Demand.   For many products, the demand has very wide fluctuations according to time of day or season of the year. This diagram illustrates a typical electric utility's demand for electric power.

lines and switchboards are very busy compared to the load during the rest of the day.

As mentioned in footnote 2, telephone companies and their competitors use a pricing scheme for long distance calls that encourages people to make such calls at slack times when equipment and personnel are less busy. Prices are the highest between 8:00 A.M. and 5:00 P.M., reduced between 5:00 P.M. and 11:00 P.M., and reduced still further from 11:00 P.M. to 8:00 A.M. The highest prices are charged during peak demand periods, and lower prices are charged at other times. This is an example of peak load pricing. Consumers are encouraged to shift demand from peak to slack periods through the price mechanism, and those who use the telephone system for long distance calls during peak periods pay a relatively greater share of the cost of providing and maintaining the phone system.

Whenever price discrimination is based on time differentials, the object of the selling firm is to charge a higher price for the product during the more inelastic period and a lower price during the more elastic interval. Electric utilities are usually required to have the necessary capacity to meet peak loads. Utilities argue that, given this requirement, they ought to be allowed to charge higher rates during peak periods. Utilities reason that failure to price discriminate will cause peak demand to be higher than it would otherwise be, forcing the utility to build bigger (and more expensive) electric generating facilities, making electricity more expensive for all customers.

The solution to the peak load pricing question—should we let the utility price discriminate with respect to time?—has been considered to be the following:[4] the price in each period should be its marginal cost of production. This solution is dependent on constant marginal cost (which is perhaps a good assumption in the electric utility industry). We also assume that the regulatory agency uses a fair rate of return criterion such that total revenues equals total costs.

Assume that there are two periods during the day: peak load time and off-peak time. These two periods are represented by the demand curves D_P and D_{OP} in Figure 10.13. In order to price at marginal cost in each time period, we would charge the relatively low price P_{OP} in the off-peak period. The price we would charge in the peak load period would have an additional capacity cost added in to correctly reflect the marginal cost at peak load. This capacity cost is considered part of the marginal cost in the peak load period because capacity must be added to meet demand during that period. The capacity costs (shown in Figure 10.13 as the difference between P_{OP} and P_P) is computed by dividing fixed costs at capacity output by the level of demand at capacity output.

---

[4]P.O. Steiner, "Peak Loads and Efficient Pricing," *Quarterly Journal of Economics*, November 1957, pp. 585–610.

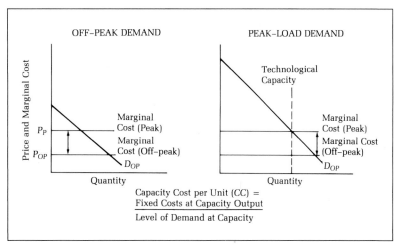

FIGURE 10.13   Peak Load Pricing Solution. The regulated utility facing a two-period (off-peak versus peak) demand should price so that the off-peak price (P_{OP}) is equal to the off-peak marginal cost. During the peak period, price should equal the off-peak marginal cost plus the capacity cost (CC).

The price to off-peak customers (P_{OP}) is set equal to the marginal cost (assumed constant) of providing the service at off-peak times. For peak load customers, the price is equal to this same marginal cost *plus* the capacity cost per unit (CC). Thus, the peak load price is P_P ($P_{OP} + CC$). Ideally, this will encourage consumers to shift demand to off-peak periods and thus help to level out demand overtime.

The solution depicted in Figure 10.13 can be thought of as a long-run equilibrium in which the shifting of demand from peak to off-peak periods has already taken place. In the short run, some varying of peak and off-peak prices would be expected as the utility converged on an optimum solution. Ultimately, a point would be reached, as in Figure 10.13, where the price charged in each separate time block equals the marginal costs of production. The revenues resulting from such a scheme will equal the costs of production.

The solution for a profit-maximizing firm is similar except that we add the marginal revenue functions to Figure 10.13 and set each marginal revenue equal to the respective marginal costs. Since marginal cost at the peak crosses marginal revenue for the peak period to the left of peak period demand, a lower capacity level is required.

SUMMARY

This chapter combined the demand and the production sides of the market in the framework of a firm's decisions regarding optimal price and output.

Discussion focused on the two extreme forms of market structures: perfect competition and monopoly.

Perfectly competitive firms were seen to have no control over the price at which products are sold. If the market price of wheat, for example, is $3.85 per bushel, the individual wheat farmer must sell at that price or not sell at all. This does not, however, mean that there are no managerial decisions to be made. In particular, the farm manager must decide how much wheat to produce, given the market price.

Because the output of one producer is identical to that of all the producers in perfectly competitive markets and because productive resources may freely enter and leave the industry, in addition to the existence of a great many buyers and sellers having perfect economic information, the market price is always driven toward a long-run equilibrium at which 0 economic profit is the rule. This 0 profit means that all resources are paid the opportunity cost value of their productive services.

In a perfectly competitive equilibrium, several results occur naturally that many people see as desirable:

P = AC: no excess economic profit or loss

P = MC: marginal social benefit = marginal cost of providing that good (optimal allocation of resources)

AC_{min}:   provision of goods at the lowest point on the average cost function

Only in perfectly competitive markets can we expect natural economic forces to lead to these results.

In a monopoly, there is a single seller of the product. This means that the firm's demand curve is identical to the market demand curve and as such has a negative slope. Thus, the management of a monopoly has significant control over the price that is set and thus indirect control over the quantity that is sold. For a monopolist, no natural economic forces push economic profit toward 0. In fact, it is likely that an unregulated monopolist could maintain positive economic profits in the long run.

Many monopolies are regulated "in the public interest," usually with the intent of limiting monopoly profits. Probably the most common regulatory criterion is the fair rate of return doctrine. This means that price should be set equal to average cost.

Firms with monopoly power are often able to discriminate in pricing and by doing so increase the revenue generated for a given level of sales. This, in turn, means greater profits than could be obtained by following a one-price policy. The most common form of price discrimination is third-degree price discrimination, in which markets are segmented according to price elasticities of demand. A higher price is charged in markets with the most inelastic demand. Thus, for example, residential users of electricity pay a higher price per kilowatt-hour than do commercial and industrial users of electric power.

Peak load pricing is a type of third-degree price discrimination, and in cases in which there is no marginal cost difference between peak and off-peak use, peak load pricing is an exact application of third-degree price discrimination.

SUGGESTED READINGS

Baumol, W.J. *Economic Theory and Operation Analysis*, 4th ed. Englewood Cliffs, NJ: Prentice-Hall, 1977.

Clark, J.M. *Competition as a Dynamic Process*. Washington, DC: The Brookings Institution, 1961, Chapters 2 and 3.

Cohen, K., and Cyert, R. *Theory of the Firm*. 2d ed. Englewood Cliffs, NJ: Prentice-Hall, 1975.

Henderson, J.M., and Quandt, R.E. *Microeconomic Theory: A Mathematical Approach*, 2d ed. New York: McGraw-Hill, 1971.

Kirzner, I.M. *Competition and Entrepreneurship*. Chicago: University of Chicago Press, 1973, Chapters 1 and 2.

Knight, F. *Risk, Uncertainty and Profit*. Chicago: University of Chicago Press, 1929.

Liebhafsky, H.H. *The Nature of Price Theory*, rev. ed. Homewood, IL: Dorsey Press, 1968.

Mansfield, E. *Microeconomics: Theory and Applications*, 3d ed. New York: W.W. Norton, 1983.

Scherer, F.M. *Industrial Market Structure and Economic Performance*, 2d ed. Boston: Houghton-Mifflin, 1980, Chapter 2.

Shepherd, W.G. "Causes of Increased Competition in the U.S. Economy." *Review of Economics and Statistics*, vol. 64, 1982, pp. 613–626.

Stigler, G.J. *Five Lectures on Economic Problems*. London: Longmans, Green, 1949.

Stigler, G.J. "Perfect Competition, Historically Contemplated." *Journal of Political Economy*, February 1957, pp. 1–17.

PROBLEMS

1. Explain why price (P), marginal revenue (MR), marginal cost (MC), and average cost (AC) are equal for a perfectly competitive firm in long-run equilibrium. Why do we say that the perfectly competitive firm is a "price taker"? Draw one graph showing P, MR, MC, and AC for a perfectly competitive firm that makes a positive economic profit, and draw another graph with these curves showing a negative economic profit. In each case, explain the adjustment process that will

lead to a 0 profit equilibrium. Draw the same four curves so as to illustrate this equilibrium.

2. Draw average revenue (demand), marginal revenue, average cost, and marginal cost curves for each of the following situations:
    a. Perfect competitor with a positive economic profit
    b. Perfect competitor with a negative economic profit
    c. Monopolist with a positive economic profit
    d. Monopolist with a negative economic profit
    Write a brief paragraph explaining each of the four graphs. Also explain what, if anything, might be expected to happen in each case that might alter the situation you have depicted (e.g., the existence of positive economic profit).

3. Which of the following firms is likely to be able to price discriminate? Explain why you answer as you do and indicate the basis for price discrimination in each case. Which consumers do you think would pay the higher price in each situation? Why?
    a. Barber
    b. Physician
    c. Soft drink producer
    d. Fine restaurant
    e. Concert promoter
    f. University bookstore

4. JVA Foodstuffs cans green beans for two distinct markets. JVA estimates the demand in each market to be

    $$\text{Market 1:} \quad Q_1 = 170 - 1.9P_1$$
    $$\text{Market 2:} \quad Q_2 = 65 - .45P_2$$

    The average total cost of producing the green beans is

    $$ATC = 9 + .11Q$$

    where

    Q_1 = amount sold in market 1
    Q_2 = amount sold in market 2
    P_1 = price in market 1
    P_2 = price in market 2
    Q = total amount produced

    a. If the markets are such that price discrimination is possible, what will be the price charged in each market?
    b. If the markets are such that price discrimination cannot be practiced, what price will the firm charge?
    c. Would the firm earn higher profits with or without price discrimination?

5. How is first-degree price discrimination similar to second-degree price discrimination, or multipart pricing? Physicians often charge older and younger patients smaller fees than the rest of their patients. Do you suspect this is because physicians wish to help these groups? What kind of price discrimination are physicians engaging in?

6. The allocation of mainframe computer resources in one university is accomplished by allocating to users a certain amount of "play money" each month. Users pay for jobs on the system according to a schedule of prices:

Overnight processing:	.2 × base rate
"When computer idle" processing:	.3 × base rate
"End of cue" processing:	1 × base rate
"Priority" processing:	2 × base rate
"Immediate" processing:	5 × base rate

   a. Could this be an efficient way to distribute mainframe resources even though no real money is used? Is there a market for mainframe services here?
   b. What type of pricing would you call this? What problems would be encountered in administering this system. What other resources could be allocated in a similar manner?

7. Electric utility rates are usually set by a utility after approval by some government body; requests for price increases and/or changes are often the subject of heated debate. The rate schedule given below is typical in many respects of utility rate schedules for residential users:

	Winter Rate	Summer Rate
Fixed charge	$1.50	$1.50
First 100 kilowatt-hours	.030	.030
101–500 kilowatt-hours	.025	.025
501–1000 kilowatt-hours	.022	.023
1001 + kilowatt-hours	.015	.020

   The difference between the winter and summer rates is a form of peak load pricing designed to discourage extensive use of electric air conditioning.
   a. What is the average price for a household that uses 1200 kilowatt-hours in the winter? In the summer?
   b. Plot the graph for the winter rate schedule (price per kilowatt-hour on the Y axis and kilowatt-hours used on the X axis). If a household purchases 1500 kilowatt-hours, how much would it pay in total? How much would the same household pay if all

kilowatt-hours were charged at the $.015 rate? Is price discrimination evident here?

8. Explain how the concept of price elasticity is related to peak load pricing. What are some examples of goods or services that you believe represent examples of this type of pricing policy?

9. Each of the questions below refers to the following table and graph:

Q	MC	ATC	TC	AVC
2	4.88	6.44	12.88	4.94
4	4.78	5.64	22.55	4.89
6	4.69	5.34	32.03	4.84
8	4.62	5.17	41.34	4.79
10	4.55	5.05	50.50	4.75
12	4.50	4.96	59.54	4.71
14	4.45	4.89	68.49	4.68
16	4.42	4.84	77.37	4.65
18	4.41	4.79	86.20	4.62
20	4.40	4.75	95.00	4.60
22	4.41	4.72	103.80	4.58
24	4.42	4.69	112.63	4.57
26	4.45	4.67	121.51	4.56
28	4.50	4.66	130.46	4.55
30	4.55	4.65	139.50	4.55
32	4.62	4.65	148.66	4.55
34	4.69	4.65	157.97	4.56
36	4.78	4.65	167.45	4.57
38	4.89	4.66	177.12	4.58
40	5.00	4.68	187.00	4.60
42	5.13	4.69	197.12	4.62
44	5.26	4.72	207.51	4.65
46	5.41	4.74	218.19	4.68
48	5.58	4.77	229.18	4.71
50	5.75	4.81	240.50	4.75

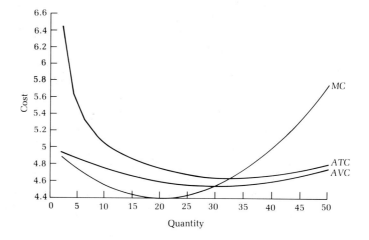

a. If this is a single firm in a competitive industry, what price must prevail for the industry to be in long-run equilibrium?
b. Suppose that there are 100 firms identical to the one depicted in the table and graph. Plot the supply curve for the entire industry.
c. For the industry, assume the demand function is

$$Q = 17571.43 - 2857.14P$$

Is the industry in long-run equilibrium? What might you expect to happen in this industry? Explain.
d. Assume now that the industry demand function is

$$Q = 29,000 - 5000P$$

What price will each of the 100 firms charge in the short run? What would you expect to happen in the industry in the long run?
e. Given the demand function of part d, graph the demand curve for one of the 100 firms in the industry on the graph.
f. Given the shape of the short-run cost curves, do you believe the production function would exhibit diminishing returns?
g. Given the firm's demand curve drawn in part e, approximately how much profit does the representative firm earn?

10. The manager of Keenan Foods has estimated the firm's average variable cost function to be

$$AVC = 9 - 3Q + .5Q^2$$

where AVC is in dollars and Q is in units. Keenan Foods operates in a perfectly competitive market. Assume fixed costs are $100.
a. Determine the marginal cost function.
b. At what output is average variable cost minimized? Does this point have any economic relevance?
c. Assume that the market price at which the firm can sell output is $50. How much output will Keenan produce if this is the case?
d. Will Keenan Foods earn a profit or a loss at the output level determined in part c? What is the dollar value of the profit or loss?
e. If the industry is made up of 10 firms identical to Keenan Foods, what output would be produced in the short run if the price was $50?
f. What would the equilibrium price be in the long run for this industry if all firms were identical?

11. Walsh Computer Products has recently been granted a patent covering their new "superchip." Final product manufacturers are expected to use the chip in a new generation of supercomputers. Consider that Walsh estimates the costs associated with superchip production to be

$$TC = 340 + 100Q - 12Q^2 + .5Q^3$$

Walsh has also estimated the demand for the chips to be

$$Q = 20 - .072P$$

a.   Compute Walsh's marginal cost curve, average total cost curve, and average variable cost curve. Plot these curves.
b.   Plot Walsh's demand curve on the same graph.
c.   If Walsh wishes to maximize profit, what quantity should it produce and what price should it charge?
d.   Compute Walsh's total dollar profits.
e.   Is this situation a long-run equilibrium for Walsh?

12.   You are employed by a hospital that has succeeded through some innovative contracts in dividing its market into three distinct segments; each segment is completely sealed off from the other. The demand curves for the hospital's output are

Customer group 1: $P_1 = 63 - 4Q_1$
Customer group 2: $P_2 = 105 - 5Q_2$
Customer group 3: $P_3 = 75 - 6Q_3$

where P_1, P_2, and P_3 are the prices charged in each market. Q_1, Q_2, and Q_3 are the amounts sold in each market. The hospital's total cost function is

$$TC = 21 + 16Q$$

where

$$Q = Q_1 + Q_2 + Q_3$$

Suggest what the hospital's pricing policy should be, assuming the hospital is a profit maximizer. How many units of output should be allocated to each market? What prices should be charged?

13.   Assume the hospital in problem 12 has a changed cost function:

$$TC = 21 + 16Q + Q^2$$

What quantities of product are now allocated to the three groups of customers?

14.   Compare the long-run equilibrium of competitive and monopoly firms. What are the differences in their long-run equilibrium positions?

15.   A "natural monopoly" usually exists only for some finite period of time; natural monopolies do not exist forever. Are there some real-world examples of this phenomenon? Does a government stifle the decay of a natural monopoly by granting a franchise to a particular group?

16. Assume that the market for wheat is perfectly competitive and that the government has limited the amount of land wheat can be grown on using various programs to 1 million acres. Current conditions are such that wheat is selling for $9 per bushel, but the government believes farmers should get $10 per bushel. The government could either buy enough wheat itself to bring up the competitive price to $10 per bushel, or it could simply subsidize farmers directly to bring their receipts up to $10 per bushel. Either plan will result in production of the same amount of wheat, since acreage is limited, but the government would like to implement the less expensive of the two alternatives. Should the government subsidize the farmers directly, or should the government buy wheat in the open market? Does your answer depend on any variable factors?

17. Recall that the long-run average cost curve for any firm is a U-shaped curve. Would a profit-maximizing monopolist ever operate on the downward-sloping portion of the curve? Would a profit-maximizing perfectly competitive firm ever operate on the downward-sloping portion of the curve?

18. A monopolist has no supply curve. The supply curve for a perfectly competitive firm shows the relationship between the price the firm receives for its output and the quantity of that output it is willing to supply; but no such curve can be drawn for a monopolist. How can this be explained?

19. A monopoly firm has the following total cost and demand functions:

   Total cost: $TC = 100 + Q^2$
   Demand: $Q = (600 - P)/4$

   What quantity of output will the firm produce? What price will it charge for the output? What profits will it earn? If the government limited this monopolist by imposing a $200 price ceiling on the product, how would the firm react? What would be its new price, output, and profit?

11

Market Structure and Pricing: Monopolistic Competition and Oligopoly

This chapter extends our discussion of market structure and pricing to the broad middle ground of industrial organization: monopolistic competition and oligopoly. The way of thinking inherent in the marginal analysis used throughout Chapter 10 will again be important as we look at these new market structures. The profit-maximizing rule that marginal revenue should equal marginal cost will continue to play an important role in our analysis.

11.1 MONOPOLISTIC COMPETITION

Most industries cannot be classified as either perfectly competitive or perfectly monopolistic because most industries are composed of firms producing similar, but not identical, products and because many industries clearly have more than a single firm but not nearly so many that we could expect perfect competition to result.

Monopolistic competition is the term used to signify a market in which there are many firms selling slightly different products. These non-homogeneous products are close but not perfect substitutes for one another. In addition, monopolistically competitive markets are characterized by the use of nonprice competition. The important characteristics shared by firms in this type of market are (1) differentiated products, (2) many firms from which customers may choose, (3) relatively easy entry and exit, and (4) independent decision making by the firms.

Product differentiation plays a key role in the economic model of monopolistically competitive firms. A product is differentiated from other products in the same group if it has some attribute or attributes that allow consumers to distinguish it from others in the market. The differences between products in a market may be either real or perceived. There is only one producer of Miller beer, only one manufacturer of Apple computers, and only one supplier of Big Macs, but each of these companies is in competition with others that produce very similar products. This is the meaning of the term *monopolistic competition:* there is only one producer of a particular item, but that firm faces more or less direct competition from many other firms producing very similar products. Like pure competition, monopolistic competition is characterized by the presence of a large enough number of firms producing similar products so that no one firm has the production capacity to supply a significant share of the industry's total output. Compared to other firms in the industry, a monopolistic competitor is a relatively small firm.

Monopolistic competitors are unlike pure competitors because the former may need advertising and product promotion to secure and maintain a reasonable share of the market. In this sense, a new firm wishing to enter a monopolistically competitive market may face a greater financial hurdle than a firm wishing to enter a purely competitive market.

The demand curve for any one firm under conditions of monopolistic competition is downward sloping and is generally highly price elastic (because there are many substitutes for the product). This is the fundamental difference between a single firm in a competitive market and a firm in a monopolistically competitive market; because products are differentiated in monopolistic competition, sellers have some discretion in their price setting. Price shaving to a price below the competitors' will attract some of the competitors' customers. The other side of this coin is that a single firm raising price may expect a significant (but not total) loss in sales as customers switch to close substitutes. So, in summary, the monopolistically competitive firm has a negatively sloped demand that is quite price elastic through a considerable range.

These characteristics of the monopolistic competitor's demand curve were reported on by Lester Telser in estimations of the price elasticity of demand in four markets considered to be monopolistically competitive:[1]

Product	Price Elasticity
Frozen orange juice	− 5.7
Margarine	− 3.0
Regular coffee	− 4.4
Instant coffee	− 5.5

The rather high elasticities for firms in these markets is caused by the presence of a large number of good substitutes in each industry. Apparently,

---

[1]Lester C. Telser, "The Demand for Branded Goods as Estimated from Consumer Panel Data," *Review of Economics and Statistics,* August 1963, pp. 300–324, and "Advertising and Cigarettes," *Journal of Political Economy,* October 1962, pp. 471–499.

even though manufacturers in these markets spend large sums of money differentiating their products, each individual firm's product remains a close substitute for the similar products produced by other firms.

Examples of other industries that might be thought of as monopolistically competitive are deodorants, frozen dinners, wood furniture, cardboard boxes, dog foods, shoes, restaurants, breakfast cereals, soaps, and many types of retail services, such as beauty parlors, barbers, accountants, and lawyers.

Monopolistic Competition Price-Quantity Decisions: A Graphic Model

If a firm can raise its price without sales falling to 0 (as it would if the firm were a pure competitor) and if when a firm lowers price, the sales of its product increases, it follows that the demand curve must be negatively sloped. Such is the case for the monopolistically competitive firm represented by the demand curve in Figure 11.1. The firm's demand curve is graphed along with the corresponding marginal revenue curve (MR) and the firm's marginal and average cost curves. Let us apply the logic of marginal analysis to the decisions this firm faces regarding the quantity to produce and the price to charge if the objective is to maximize profit.

In the top panel of Figure 11.1, we see a monopolistically competitive firm that is making a positive economic profit. This is true because at the selected output (Q^*), price is greater than average cost. Observe that the best output (Q^*) for the firm is determined by the equality of marginal revenue and marginal cost (see point A). To the left of Q^*, we see that $MR > MC$, which means that additional units of output in this region contribute more to revenue than to costs. It follows that a firm whose management is interested in increasing profit would expand throughout this region, since each additional unit produced and sold has a positive contribution to profit. On the other hand, in the region to the right of Q^*, $MR < MC$. Each unit of product in excess of Q^* actually increases cost more than revenue, and thus the firm would have less profit the farther to the right of Q^* it produces. The logic of marginal analysis therefore leads us to conclude that a monopolistically competitive firm will maximize profit by producing a level of output at which $MR = MC$. Note that this is the same profit-maximizing rule used by a perfectly competitive firm and a pure monopolist.

The price the firm will charge can also be determined from the top frame of Figure 11.1. The firm's demand function indicates the quantity individuals are willing to purchase at various prices. This relationship can be alternatively phrased to state that the demand function shows the price at which the firm is able to sell a given quantity of output. If the firm sets the price above P^*, the demand function indicates that it would be expected to sell less than the optimal output, Q^*. If the firm set the price below P^*, consumers would want to purchase more than Q^* units. Of course, if the firm

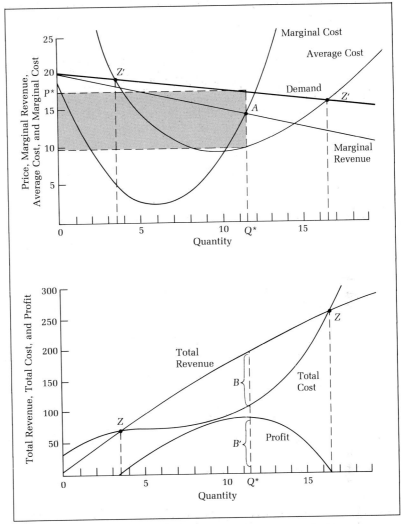

FIGURE 11.1 **A Monopolistically Competitive Firm with a Short-Run Profit.** The firm's optimal rate of output (Q^*) is at the level where $MR = MC$ (see point A). The resulting profit is shown by B and B' in the lower graph and by the shaded area in the top graph. Note that, while the total revenue curve looks nearly linear, it is actually increasing at a decreasing rate. You can demonstrate this by laying a straight edge along the TR curve. The TR curve shows only slightly above the straight edge because the TR curve is actually concave downward.

produces Q^* units and sets the price at P^*, the level of profit is seen to be at a maximum as shown in the bottom frame of Figure 11.1.

The profit function as well as total revenue and total cost are shown in the bottom part of Figure 11.1 so that you can easily see the relationship between these three functions. You see that at the quantities at which $TR = TC$ (at either point marked Z), profit is 0. As quantity increases from the left most Z, profit at first increases because total revenue is rising faster than total cost (i.e., $MR > MC$). Profit then reaches a peak at the quantity (Q^*) at which $MR = MC$, and then to the right of Q^* profit declines because total cost begins to rise faster than total revenue (i.e., $MC > MR$). Note also that at those quantities at which profit is 0, price is equal to average cost (see the points in the upper part of Figure 11.1 marked Z'). You should also see that for any level of quantity, the vertical distance between total revenue and total cost is equal to the height of the profit function. For example, at Q^*, the distance marked B is equal to the distance marked B'. Profit can also be represented by (price − average cost) × (quantity). This is shown by the shaded rectangle in the upper part of Figure 11.1.

Monopolist Competition Price-Quantity Decisions: An Algebraic Model

Let us now look at this same monopolistically competitive situation using an algebraic model. The firm's marginal revenue function in Figure 11.1 does not coincide with the demand curve as it would in perfect competition, but, rather, it lies below the demand curve. This is because the demand function has a negative slope, as described in the monopoly discussion in Chapter 10. The demand function for this representative firm can be written as

$$P = 20 - .25Q$$

and the total revenue function is

$$TR = PQ = (20 - .25Q)Q = 20Q - .25Q^2$$

You know that marginal revenue is the first derivative of total revenue with respect to quantity, and so marginal revenue may be written as

$$MR = dTR/dQ = 20 - .5Q$$

Let us again assume that the total cost function has the familiar cubic form and is

$$TC = 30 + 18Q - 2.7Q^2 + .15Q^3$$

Then MC is found as the derivative of total cost with respect to quantity as follows:

$$MC = dTC/dQ = 18 - 5.4Q + .45Q^2$$

Now, setting $MR = MC$ in order to find the profit-maximizing output, we have

$$MR = MC$$
$$20 - .5Q = 18 - 5.4Q + .45Q^2$$
$$0 = -2 - 4.9Q + .45Q^2$$

Solving this equation using the quadratic formula gives

$$Q^* = \frac{4.9 \pm \sqrt{(-4.9)^2 - 4(.45)(-2)}}{2(.45)}$$

$$Q^* = \frac{4.9 \pm \sqrt{27.61}}{.9}$$

$$Q^* = \frac{4.9 \pm 5.25}{.9}$$

$$Q^* = 11.28 \text{ or } -.39$$

The positive root is the profit-maximizing one, and so the monopolistic competitor will produce and sell 11.28 units. The profit-maximizing price is found by substituting the output rate of 11.28 in the demand function and solving for P. In terms of the example, we have

$$P = 20 - .25(11.28) = 17.18$$

We can also find the average cost of producing 11.28 units from the average cost function:

$$AC = TC/Q = 30Q^{-1} + 18 - 2.7Q + .15Q^2$$
$$AC = 30(11.28)^{-1} + 18 - 2.7(11.28) + .15(11.28)^2$$
$$AC = 9.29$$

Since the average cost is less than price, there is a positive economic profit, which can be found as follows:

$$\pi = TR - TC$$
$$\pi = (P)(Q) - (AC)(Q)$$
$$\pi = (P - AC)(Q)$$
$$\pi = (17.18 - 9.29)(11.28)$$
$$\pi = 89.00$$

You may want to refer to Figure 11.1 to see that these results are consistent with what is shown there for the same representative monopolistically competitive firm.

You will recall from Chapter 10 that if this type of positive economic profit existed for a perfectly competitive firm, new resources would enter the industry until the profits were eliminated. A similar long-run adjustment takes place in monopolistic competition.

Long-Run Adjustment in Monopolist Competition

When firms in a monopolistically competitive setting have a positive economic profit, there is incentive for other similar businesses to enter that industry. As new firms enter, each existing firm loses some sales to the new entrants. Thus, at each price, those preexisting firms find that fewer units can be sold.

In terms of the models presented above, this means that the demand curves for the preexisting firms move to the left (decrease). Whether this shift is parallel or includes a change in slope depends on the particulars of the given market. For purposes of illustration, we will assume that the demand curve shifts inward (toward the origin) in a parallel manner. The questions that we would like to answer are (1) How far will the demand curve shift?, (2) What new price will result?, (3) What quantity will maximize profits?, and (4) How much profit will result? To answer these questions, think carefully about what you would expect to happen in the industry.

Remember that entry is relatively easy. This means that new firms are likely to enter as long as there is a positive profit, such as shown by the shaded rectangle in the upper panel of Figure 11.1. Lay your pencil along the demand curve in that figure and then slide your pencil toward the origin, keeping it parallel to the original demand, until positive economic profits disappear. As long as the demand curve is above average cost at any point, positive profits exist. If you slide your pencil down far enough that it is below average cost at every point, then economic losses result and some firms leave the industry (causing the demand for remaining firms to shift upward).

You have probably reasoned correctly that the demand curve would shift until it is just tangent to the average cost curve. At that point of tangency, price would equal average cost, and so economic profit would be 0. At every other quantity, average cost would be greater than price and negative economic profits (losses) would result.

This long-run adjustment is shown in the top portion of Figure 11.2. The demand curve has shifted downward until it is just tangent to the average cost curve at the point E. The quantity associated with this point is Q^*, and we see that marginal revenue equals marginal cost at this rate of production and sales (see point A). The profit-maximizing price, P^*, can be read from the vertical axis and, of course, is equal to average cost. If $P = AC$, then profit must be 0.

In the lower panel of Figure 11.2, we see the total revenue, total cost, and profit functions. To the left of Q^*, where $AC > P$, we see that the total cost is greater than total revenue and that profit is below the horizontal 0 line (i.e., profits are negative). This is also true to the right of Q^*. Only at Q^* does total revenue equal total cost such that economic profit rises to the 0 level (see points B and B', respectively).

In addition to solving this long-run adjustment with a graphic model, we can use the algebraic functions behind the graph to find the exact solution. Where should we start? First, let us recognize that nothing occurs to change the cost functions, so they remain

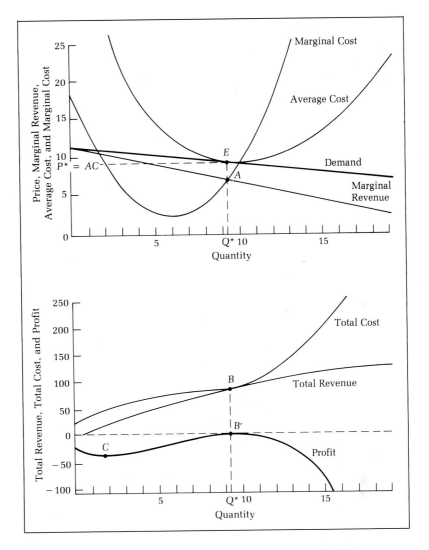

FIGURE 11.2 **A Monopolistically Competitive Firm in Long-Run Zero Profit Equilibrium.** Positive economic profit attracts new entrants to the market causing the demand curve for preexisting firms to shift to the left until it is tangent to the average cost curve. At this rate of output, TR = TC, and profit is 0. If demand is below average cost at every quantity, an economic loss results, and some firms leave the industry. The demand curves for remaining firms then shift up toward the 0 profit equilibrium.

$$TC = 30 + 18Q - 2.7Q^2 + .15Q^3$$
$$AC = 30Q^{-1} + 18 - 2.7Q + .15Q^2$$
$$MC = 18 - 5.4Q + .45Q^2$$

Second, we have assumed that the demand curve will shift in a parallel manner, so its slope will remain the same $(-.25)$. Thus, the equation for the demand curve is

$$P = a - .25Q$$

Total revenue and marginal revenue is, then,

$$TR = P \cdot Q = aQ - .25Q^2$$
$$MR = dTR/dQ = a - .5Q$$

Until we find the value for a, we cannot be more specific. Note, however, that if demand falls, we should expect this new value for a to be less than the 20 of the original demand function (recall that function was $P = 20 - .25Q$).

We know that the demand will shift down for this representative firm until it is just *tangent* to the average cost curve. That tangency is the key. *At a point of tangency, two curves have the same slope.* We can find those slopes as the first derivatives of the functions:

1. For average cost, the slope is

$$AC = 30Q^{-1} + 18 - 2.7Q + .15Q^2$$
$$dAC/dQ = -30Q^{-2} - 2.7 + .3Q$$

2. For the demand curve, the slope is

$$P = a - .25Q$$
$$dP/dQ = -.25$$

Setting these slopes equal to one another, we have

$$-30Q^{-2} - 2.7 + .3Q = -.25$$
$$-30Q^{-2} - 2.45 + .3Q = 0$$
$$.3Q^3 - 2.45Q^2 - 30 = 0$$

Solving this cubic (on a handy computer) we find

$$Q^* = 9.318$$

We can see that this is consistent with the graphs in Figure 11.2.

Given that $Q^* = 9.318$, we can find the value of average cost by substituting that value for Q in the average cost function:

$$AC = 30Q^{-1} + 18 - 2.7Q + .15Q^2$$
$$AC = 30(9.318)^{-1} + 18 - 2.7(9.318) + .15(9.318)^2$$
$$AC = 9.085$$

This value is also consistent with the graph in the top part of Figure 11.2. We know that if the demand curve is tangent to the average cost curve at Q^*, then price must equal average cost:

$$P = AC = 9.085$$

Then it follows from the demand function that

$$P = a - .25Q$$
$$9.085 = a - .25(9.318)$$
$$a = 11.414$$

And thus we now know the equation for the new demand function, the new total revenue function, and the new marginal revenue function:

$$P = 11.414 - .25Q$$
$$TR = 11.414Q - .25Q^2$$
$$MR = 11.414 - .5Q$$

These are also graphed in Figure 11.2.

As an exercise to help you understand that these functions do yield a 0 profit solution, use them to find the profit-maximizing output for a firm with the following total cost and demand functions:[2]

$$TC = 30 + 18Q - 2.7Q^2 + .15Q^3$$
$$P = 11.414 - .25Q$$

Let us now review the dynamics of monopolistic competition. In a monopolistically competitive environment, many firms produce very similar, but somewhat differentiated, products; there is relatively easy entry and exit; and the managers of the firms act independently of one another (there is little or no collusion among managers). You may think of local pizza firms as representative of such an industry. We often observe considerable fluidity in such situations as new firms enter when positive economic profits appear possible. Sometimes new entrants can so dilute the market that some (or all) firms make short-run economic losses until some firms close down and leave the industry. Because the products are very similar, it is likely that firms also have very similar cost functions. Those firms that are able to compete well on nonprice terms (such as quality) are more likely to be able to maintain their price above their average cost. But their profitability will always be a signal to other entrepreneurs that there is money to be made, and new entrants are likely. For this reason, it is often said that these industries are highly competitive, not competitive in the sense of a *perfectly competitive market*, but, rather, meaning a high degree of interfirm rivalry.

---

[2]You will find two possible solutions. That with the smaller Q (1.57) corresponds to a local minimum for profit rather than the maximum. See point C in Figure 11.2.

11.2 OLIGOPOLY: AN INTRODUCTION

Oligopoly is a market structure characterized by the presence of relatively few firms selling a particular type of product. The product may be differentiated, as in monopolistic competition, or it may be undifferentiated. Examples of industries that we might consider oligopolistic include the automobile industry, the computer industry, the aluminum industry, and the steel industry. In each of these industries, the number of firms producing the product is small relative to the size of the market for their output. With a small number of firms producing the entire supply of such products, it is not surprising that—much like monopolies and very unlike pure competitors—these firms may exercise considerable control over price.

The most significant characteristic of an oligopolistic market is that, because of the limited number of firms, actions by any individual firm in the market have perceptible repercussions on other firms in the industry. The interdependence of firms is the essence of oligopoly. If a single firm changes its price or introduces a new product, other firms in the industry must make note of the change and decide how to respond (if at all). Each firm must consider what possible reactions will be forthcoming from other firms when it considers a given strategy.

Consider a model of oligopoly in which the interdependence of firms is fully recognized. Each firm in the industry may recognize that the greatest industry profits can be obtained if, as a group, the firms produced the level of output that would be established if the industry were a pure monopoly. This quantity of output would then be sold at the monopoly price, as determined by the equality of the marginal revenue associated with the market demand curve and the monopolist's marginal cost. Each of the n oligopolistic firms would produce $1/n$ of the monopoly output (assuming identical cost curves). Thus, if the monopoly output in an industry would be 300,000 units and the monopoly price would be $10, then with a three-firm oligopolistic structure in that industry, each firm would produce 100,000 units and sell them at $10 each. Each firm would make one-third of the monopoly profit. It should be noted that in this model there is collusion between firms. Each firm would recognize that, due to the small number of producers, the action of any one firm would affect the others and that sharing the monopoly profit would be the optimal strategy for all. We will look at a formal model of such behavior shortly.

The Kinked Demand Curve Oligopoly Model

Probably the most famous model of oligopoly was developed in the 1930s by Paul Sweezy.[3] This model is particularly useful in explaining why prices

---

[3]Paul Sweezy, "Demand under Conditions of Oligopoly," *Journal of Political Economy*, August 1939, pp. 568–573.

tend to be rigid in many oligopolistic industries. Sweezy assumed that an oligopolistic firm would expect rivals to follow any price reduction but not a price increase. As a consequence, the firm would not be able to attract many customers away from its rivals by lowering price but would stand to lose considerable sales to rival firms if it was to increase price.

This line of reasoning indicates that the demand curve facing the firm would be steeper below the current price than above that level. Such a curve (DD'), called a *kinked demand curve*, is pictured in Figure 11.3. At the price P_1, an increase in price will cause the firm's sales to decrease rapidly. However, a price cut would result in only a slight increase in sales. That is, the demand function is considerably more elastic above P_1 than below.

The affect that a price change would have on the firm's total receipts can be evaluated by looking at the marginal revenue function (MR). The upper portion of the marginal revenue function (that part to the left of Q_1) corresponds to the relatively more elastic segment of the demand function.

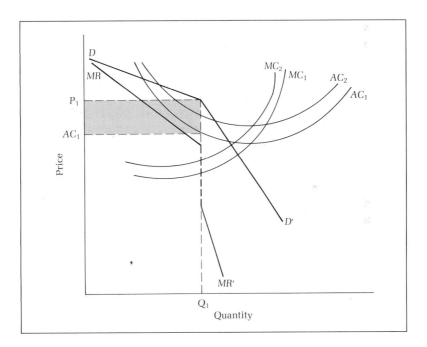

FIGURE 11.3   **The Kinked Demand Curve Model.**   The kinked demand curve model of oligopoly helps explain why prices may be resistant to change in oligopolistic industries. The kink always occurs at the existing price, indicating that demand function is relatively more elastic above than below the kink. The presence of the kink causes a discontinuity in the marginal revenue function. As long as the marginal cost curve passes through this gap in marginal revenue, there is no reason for a profit-maximizing manager to change price.

The lower and more steeply sloped portion (to the right of Q_1) corresponds to the relatively less elastic part of the demand curve. We see that the amount of change in total receipts for each unit change in sales is much greater to the left of Q_1 than to the right.

Recall that we have determined that any firm will maximize profit by producing that level of output at which marginal cost equals marginal revenue. If the oligopolist of Figure 11.3 is faced with the average and marginal cost curves AC_1 and MC_1, respectively, the optimum output would be Q_1 units, and the price would be P_1. Up to Q_1, marginal revenue exceeds marginal cost, and beyond Q_1, marginal revenue is less than marginal cost. Marginal cost, in fact, intersects marginal revenue in the discontinuous portion of the latter. Thus, the optimum output is Q_1 units. The firm would make an economic profit equal to the shaded portion of Figure 11.3.

Now consider what would happen if the firm's production costs were to change due to an increase or decrease in a factor price or a change in the cost of some intermediate good. In this event, the marginal cost function and the average cost function would either shift upward (cost increase) or downward (cost decrease). From Figure 11.3, we see that over some range of changes in the marginal cost function, it will continue to intersect marginal revenue at the same level of output. This is illustrated for the case of a cost increase to MC_2 and AC_2. Given that increase in cost, the firm faced with the demand curve DD' would have no incentive to change the existing price-quantity relationships. The effect would be a lower level of economic profit, but, nonetheless, the maximum profit possible, given the new cost functions.

One of the things this kinked demand curve model helps to explain about oligopolistic behavior is the relative stickiness of prices in some oligopolistic industries that Sweezy observed. While this is less true today than when the model was developed, it may still apply to such important industries as aluminum and steel.

11.3   COLLUSION AND CARTELS: AN INTRODUCTION

In oligopolistic market structures with relatively few firms, each of which recognizes the close interdependence among firms, we expect there to be considerable incentive for the firms to form collusive agreements. Some of the advantages to be gained from the formation of collusive agreements include greater industry profits, reduced uncertainty about the actions of rival firms, and greater ability to prevent entry by new firms. When a collusive agreement is made openly and in a formal manner, the agreement is called a *cartel*.

In the United States, most such formal agreements are illegal under the terms of the Sherman Antitrust Act. The famous case of collusion in the electrical equipment industry during the 1950s is sufficient evidence that such illegal arrangements can develop.[4] In some agricultural markets, notably milk and hops, cartellike structures do exist. International air travel is also controlled by a cartel known as the IATA (International Air Transport Association). Of course, the most publicized cartel in recent years has been OPEC (Organization of Petroleum Exporting Countries), which has set oil prices and allocated production among member countries.

In a centralized profit-maximizing cartel, all firms in the industry agree to yield decision-making power to a centralized committee, usually made up of representatives from each firm. This committee attempts to implement decisions designed to maximize profits by operating the collection of firms as if it was a monopoly. Thus, the industry is able to generate the monopoly profits. Each firm in the industry becomes analogous to an individual plant in a multiplant monopoly.

By now you are familiar with the rule that profits will be maximized by producing the level of output at which marginal revenue equals marginal cost. Let us look at how this rule can be applied to the cartel case in a situation involving just two firms. (A little later you will see that the general principles uncovered are applicable to a greater number of cartel members as well.)

Put yourself in the role of the czar of this cartel for a moment. You must decide how much should be produced in total, what price should be charged, and how much of the total output should be produced by each of the two firms. Let us put the total output and pricing decisions on hold for now. Consider this question: If you were just going to produce one unit, which firm would you have produce it? The logical answer would seem to be the firm that could do so at the lowest cost to the cartel. That is, the firm with the lowest marginal cost for that unit of production should produce it. Then, which firm would you have produce the second unit? Again, whichever firm has the lowest marginal cost would be the best choice. You would always allocate production to the firm that has the lowest cost of producing that additional unit.

Look at Table 11.1. The columns under "Marginal costs" show how much it costs each of the two firms to produce each additional unit of output. If you are going to produce just one unit, you would assign that unit to firm B since the cost would be lower than if that unit were given to firm A. To indicate this choice, a circle is drawn around the marginal cost of producing that unit and *1st* is written next to it.

---

[4] In this case, five major companies, including Westinghouse and General Electric, colluded to fix prices in the market for certain types of electrical equipment. According to the courts, fixing prices was a case of restricting free competition. The companies were fined and some top executives sentenced to prison. For a discussion of more of the details of this case, see Edwin Mansfield, *Monopoly Power and Economic Performance* (New York: Norton, 1968).

TABLE 11.1   **A Two-Firm Cartel**

| Quantity | Marginal Costs | | Quantity | Price and Marginal Revenue for the Industry | |
	Firm A	Firm B		Price	Marginal Revenue
1	② 3rd	① 1st	1	$14.50	$14
2	④ 6th	② 2nd	2	14.00	13
3	⑥ 8th	③ 4th	3	13.50	12
4	8	④ 5th	4	13.00	11
5	10	⑤ 7th	5	12.50	10
6	12	⑥ 9th	6	12.00	9
7	14	7	7	11.50	8
8	16	8	8	11.00	7
9	18	9	9	10.50	6
10	20	10	10	10.00	5

NOTE: Marginal costs for the firms are $MC_A = 2Q$, $MC_B = Q$. For the entire cartel demand is $P = 15 - .5Q$, and therefore $TR = 15Q - .5Q^2$. It follows that $MR = 15 - Q$ for the industry.

What about the production of a second unit? The second unit could be produced with equal efficiency by either firm A or firm B. We arbitrarily assigned it to firm B, as indicated by the circle and the notation that this is the *2nd* unit produced. Now let us consider the third unit of production a bit more fully. First, let us see if the cartel should even produce a third unit. The principles of marginal analysis you have learned suggest that it would be profitable for the cartel to produce any unit for which the marginal revenue to the cartel exceeds the marginal cost. What would the marginal revenue and marginal cost be for a third unit? From the "Industry Marginal Revenue" shown in the right side of Table 11.1, we see that the marginal revenue from selling a third unit would be $12. We also see that a third unit could be produced for $2 by firm A. Indeed it would be profitable to produce the third unit.

As the cartel's czar, would you go further and produce a fourth unit? Sure. The marginal revenue would be $11, and a fourth unit could be produced for $3 using firm B (note that this is the cartel's fourth unit of production, even though it is just the third unit for firm B). Continuing to evaluate the marginal revenue and marginal cost of producing successive units in this manner gives the production pattern shown by the circles and the unit notations in the marginal cost schedules.

As shown in the table, why does production stop with three units by firm A and six units by firm B (i.e., with the total output of nine units)?

Compare the marginal revenue from selling a tenth unit with the marginal cost of producing that unit. If it was produced by firm A, the marginal cost would be $8; and if it was produced by firm B, the marginal cost would be $7. However, the marginal revenue from selling a tenth unit would be only $5. Thus, the cartel's profit would be reduced if you decided to produce and sell a tenth unit.

Profit increases when production is expanded as long as $MR > MC$, but profit is reduced if production expands when $MR < MC$. So the cartel must maximize profit when $MR = MC$. This is true when nine units are produced. The marginal revenue from selling the ninth unit is $6, and the marginal cost of producing the ninth unit is also $6.

A Graphic Model of Cartel Behavior

The relationships shown in Table 11.1 are also illustrated in Figure 11.4. The two left-hand panels represent the marginal costs for firms A and B (MC_A and MC_B, respectively). These marginal cost curves are added horizontally to give the industry marginal cost (MC_I), shown in the right-hand graph. Marginal revenue for the industry or cartel is given by the line labeled MR_I. The optimum (profit-maximizing) output is $Q_I{}^*$, determined by the intersection of MC_I and MR_I. The level of marginal cost and marginal revenue at $Q_I{}^*$ is shown by the horizontal line drawn to the left from the point of intersection (E) through all three graphs. Where this line crosses the marginal cost curve for each firm determines each firm's allocation of the total production to maximize total cartel profits. These allocations are designated $Q_A{}^*$ and $Q_B{}^*$.

As czar of the cartel, you have answered two of the three questions we originally raised. You have determined the total level of production ($QI^* = 9$) and the allocation of those units between the two firms ($Q_A{}^* = 3$ and $Q_B{}^* = 6$). Now, what price should be charged? You know that the industry demand curve represents the quantities that consumers are willing and able to purchase at various prices. You want to produce and sell 9 units. So, you can go to the demand function to find out the price at which consumers would purchase 9 units. In this example the market, or industry, demand function is $P = 15 - .5Q$. Thus, the appropriate price is $10.50. The price can also be read from the demand curve in Figure 11.4 at P^* ($10.50).

What about profit for the cartel and each member firm? Let's assume that the firms have no fixed costs, to simplify the problem for now. The total cost for firms A and B must then be

$$TC_A = Q^2 \text{ and } MC_A = dTC_A/dQ = 2Q$$
$$TC_B = .5Q^2 \text{ and } MC_B = dTC_B/dQ = Q$$

You can see that these cost functions are consistent with the data shown for the marginal costs in Table 11.1 and with the graph in Figure 11.4. Total

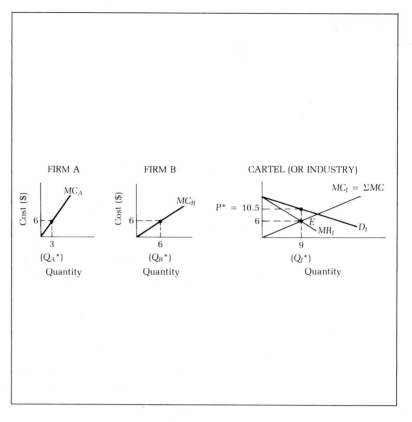

FIGURE 11.4   Graphic Cartel Model for Two Firms.   Cartel member firms combine to act as a monopoly. The industry marginal cost curve under such an arrangement is the horizontal sum of the marginal cost curves of the member firms (see MC_I). The demand curve for the cartel is the market demand curve (D_I) and is negatively sloped. The cartel's marginal revenue curve is MR_I. Cartel profits are maximized by producing where $MC_I = MR_I$ (see Q_I*). This rate of output can be sold at the price P*, as determined from the demand function. Production is allocated to cartel members such that each member's marginal cost is equal to the marginal revenue of the last unit sold (see Q_A* and Q_B*).

revenue for the cartel at nine units of production is P times Q, or $10.50 × 9 = 94.5$. For each individual firm, total revenue will be price (10.50) times the number of units of production allocated to each firm. That is,

$$TR_A = 10.5Q_A$$
$$TR_B = 10.5Q_B$$

Profit is always defined as total revenue minus total cost. So, for firms A and B;

$$\pi_A = TR_A - TC_A$$
$$\pi_A = 10.5Q_A - Q_A^2$$
$$\pi_A = 10.5(3) - (3)^2$$
$$\pi_A = 31.5 - 9$$
$$\pi_A = 22.5$$

$$\pi_B = TR_B - TC_B$$
$$\pi_B = 10.5Q_B - .5(Q_B)^2$$
$$\pi_B = 10.5(6) - .5(6)^2$$
$$\pi_B = 63 - 18$$
$$\pi_B = 45$$

Total profits for the cartel members would be 67.5. This industry profit is greater than could be obtained at any other level of production and/or other allocation of production.[5]

These principles can be applied to cartel arrangements with any number of firms. However, to do so in a graphic model would become increasingly difficult as the number of cartel members increased. Let us now look at an algebraic model that is about as easy to use for 15 or 20 firms as for 2, 3, or 4.

An Algebraic Model of Cartel Behavior

We will apply the logic developed above to an algebraic evaluation of a cartel that has four firms: $A, B, C,$ and D. The demand function for the industry and the total cost (TC) functions for all four firms are given below:

$$\text{Industry Demand:} \quad P = 100 - 0.1Q$$
$$\text{Total cost function for firm } A: \quad TC = 10Q_A + .1Q_A^2$$
$$\text{Total cost function for firm } B: \quad TC = .2Q_B^2$$
$$\text{Total cost function for firm } C: \quad TC = .2Q_C^2$$
$$\text{Total cost function for firm } D: \quad TC = 20Q_D + .05Q_D^2$$

From the cartel model we have developed, you know that the first thing we must find is the marginal cost curve for each firm. Remember that $MC = dTC/dQ$. Thus,

$$\text{Firm } A: \quad MC = 10 + .2Q_A$$
$$\text{Firm } B: \quad MC = .4Q_B$$
$$\text{Firm } C: \quad MC = .4Q_C$$
$$\text{Firm } D: \quad MC = 20 + .1Q_D$$

---

[5]Even if we put firm A out of business and keep just the relatively more efficient firm B, total industry profit would be less than 67.5. If firm B had the monopoly to itself, the highest possible profit would be

$$\pi = (15Q - .5Q^2) - (.5Q^2) = 15Q - Q^2$$
$$d\pi/dQ = 15 - 2Q = 0$$
$$Q = 7.5$$
$$\pi = 15(7.5) - (7.5)^2 = 56.25$$

In order to add these horizontally, we need to solve them each for Q as follows:

$$Q_A = -50 + 5MC$$
$$Q_B = 2.5MC$$
$$Q_C = 2.5MC$$
$$Q_D = -200 + 10MC$$

Adding $Q_A + Q_B + Q_C + Q_D$ to get the industry marginal cost curve, we get

$$Q = -250 + 20MC$$

Solving this function MC, we find

Industry marginal cost: $MC = 12.5 + .05Q$

All of these marginal cost curves are graphed in Figure 11.5.[6]

To maximize profit for the entire cartel, marginal cost for the industry must equal the industry's marginal revenue. So we must find the appropriate marginal revenue function. Industry demand is $P = 100 - 0.1Q$. Total revenue for the industry is then

$$TR = P \cdot Q$$
$$TR = (100 - 0.1Q)Q$$
$$TR = 100Q - 0.1Q^2$$

Remembering that $MR = dTR/dQ$, we find

Industry marginal revenue: $MR = 100 - 0.2Q$

The industry demand and marginal revenue curves are also graphed in Figure 11.5.

Setting marginal revenue equal to marginal cost and solving for Q yields

$$100 - 0.2Q = 12.5 + .05Q$$
$$-.25Q = -87.5$$
$$Q = 350$$

---

[6]Strictly speaking, the industry marginal cost curve derived from functions such as these will have a series of kinks in it due to the fact that the individual functions have different intercepts. The complete industry marginal cost for this problem is thus,

When Q is:	Industry MC is:
0 to 50	$MC = .2Q$
50 to 150	$MC = 5 + .1Q$
150 and above	$MC = 12.5 + .15Q$

Since, in the relevant range, only the last segment is appropriate, that is all we use in the algebraic solution and in the graph in Figure 11.5.

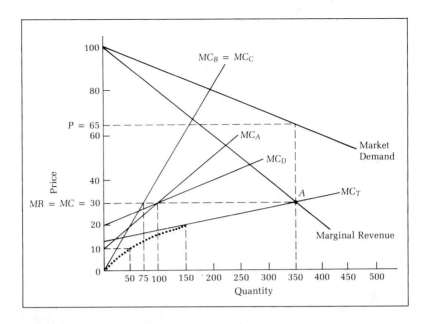

FIGURE 11.5   **Graphic Representation of a Four-Firm Cartel Example.**   The marginal cost for the entire cartel is MC_T, found as the horizontal sum of the four members' marginal cost curves (the dotted line shows the kinked marginal cost, as discussed in footnote 6). At point A ($Q = 350$), this marginal cost is equal to the marginal revenue associated with the market demand function. Since the marginal revenue of the three hundred fiftieth unit is $30, production should be allocated to each member until that member's marginal cost reaches $30. For members B and C, this point is reached at 75 units of production; for A and D, at 100 units.

Thus, the profit-maximizing level of output for the cartel is 350 units. We now need to determine how this total should be allocated among the four firms.

At the production level of 350 units, the cartel's marginal revenue is

$$MR = 100 - 0.2Q$$
$$MR = 100 - 0.2(350)$$
$$MR = 30$$

You would never allocate production to a member firm that had a marginal cost higher than this $30 level. However, cartel profits will be increased if you continue to add to production in member firms until their respective marginal costs rise to $30. So if you find the level of output for all four firms at which their marginal costs equal $30, you will have the best allocation of production among the four firms. Thus, using the equations found above for Q_A, Q_B, Q_C, and Q_D,

$$Q_A = -50 + 5MC = -50 + 5(30) = \boxed{100}$$

$$Q_B = 2.5MC = 2.5(30) = \boxed{75}$$

$$Q_C = 2.5MC = 2.5(30) = \boxed{75}$$

$$Q_D = -200 + 10MC = -200 + 10(30) = \boxed{100}$$

These outputs add up to 350, which is the level of output found to maximize the cartel's profit.

What price should the cartel set? The price should be the level at which consumers are willing and able to purchase 350 units. This can be found from the demand function, as shown graphically in Figure 11.5. Algebraically, we have

$$P = 100 - 0.1Q$$
$$P = 100 - 0.1(350)$$
$$P = 65$$

Thus, $65 is the price that all firms in the cartel should adopt to maximize total cartel profits.

Now let us look at profit for the four firms in the cartel. Total revenue for each firm will be equal to the price $65 times the number of units the firm sells. Their total costs will be determined from their individual cost functions. Thus, the profit for firm A is

$$\pi_A = TR_A - TC_A$$
$$\pi_A = (P \cdot Q_A) - (10Q_A + .1Q_A^2)$$
$$\pi_A = (65)(100) - [(10)(100) + .1(100)^2]$$
$$\pi_A = 6500 - 2000$$
$$\pi_A = 4500$$

Profit for firm B is

$$\pi_B = TR_B - TC_B$$
$$\pi_B = (P \cdot Q_B) - (.2Q_B^2)$$
$$\pi_B = (65)(75) - [.2(75)^2]$$
$$\pi_B = 4875 - 1125$$
$$\pi_B = 3750$$

Profit for firm C is

$$\pi_C = TR_C - TC_C$$
$$\pi_C = (P \cdot Q_C) - (.2Q_C^2)$$
$$\pi_C = (65)(75) - [.2(75)^2]$$
$$\pi_C = 4875 - 1125$$
$$\pi_C = 3750$$

Profit for firm D is

$$\pi_D = TR_D - TC_D$$
$$\pi_D = (P \cdot Q_D) - (20Q_D + .05Q_D^2)$$
$$\pi_D = (65)(100) - [(20)(100) + (.05)(100)^2]$$
$$\pi_D = 6500 - 2500$$
$$\pi_D = 4000$$

Total profits for the cartel can be found as the sum of the profits of the four firms:

$$\text{Total cartel profits} = 4500 + 3750 + 3750 + 4000$$
$$= 16,000$$

You may want to try to allocate production in some other way among the four firms (or any subset of the four) to see if greater profits can be generated.

Such cartel arrangements may appear very desirable, since total profits for the industry are indeed maximized. However, cartels are open to problems that can cause their dissolution. When a cartel follows the profit-maximizing equimarginal principle for allocating production, some firms may be allocated only a very small amount of production (or possibly none), leaving them with high average costs and low (or possibly negative) profit. Such firms then have incentive to break from the cartel, setting a price slightly below the cartel price to increase their own sales, thereby weakening the cartel. Some firms in the cartel, particularly the larger ones, may attempt to put pressure on the central committee (or governing board of the cartel) for preferential treatment in the allocation process. In addition, there is always incentive for firms to "cheat" in the cartel by offering lower prices (usually secretly), since each firm's demand under these conditions will be perceived as being very price elastic. Such price cutting reduces the level of overall cartel profit and can be expected to weaken the cartel, perhaps leading to its eventual breakup.

11.4 PRICE LEADERSHIP: AN INTRODUCTION

You have seen that the organization of cartels can lead to an equalization of prices within an industry. However, less formal arrangements may also lead to similar results. These are price leadership arrangements, two of which will be discussed here. In *barometric price leadership*, one firm acts as a price setter, and other firms follow its price. The leading firm is usually one that has developed successful pricing strategies in the past. Other firms are willing to follow that firm's lead rather than performing price analysis themselves because it saves time and expense. In addition, it reduces friction and uncertainty in the marketplace. The barometric price leader is not necessarily the largest firm in the industry. But the leader must have a proven record of successful operations in order to develop a following of other firms that respect its policies enough to continue to match the price signals emitted by the leader.

Some industries are characterized by having one large firm that dominates the industry. Such a firm often functions as the price leader for the entire industry. This is known as *dominant-firm price leadership*. The price leader sets the industry price and then allows the other, smaller firms to sell what they wish at that price. Thus, the smaller firms behave as though they were perfectly competitive: they become price takers.

This situation is illustrated in Figure 11.6, in which D_M represents the market demand for the product. Each individual following firm will have a supply function (S_i) that is the same as the firm's marginal cost curve (MC_i). This is because a price taker will maximize profit by producing the quantity at which price is equal to marginal cost. The total supply for all of the followers combined (S_f) is equal to the sum of the amounts supplied by the individual following firms. That is,

$$S_f = \Sigma MC_i = \Sigma S_i$$

Here again, we are adding the marginal cost curves horizontally.

The price leader's demand (D_L) is found by subtracting the quantity supplied by the following firms at each price (S_f) from the corresponding market demand (D_M). Thus,

$$D_L = D_M - S_f$$

From the leader's demand, it is possible to find its total revenue (TR_L) and marginal revenue (MR_L) functions:

$$TR_L = P_L \cdot Q_L$$
$$MR_L = dTR_L/dQ_L$$

The price leader equates its marginal revenue with its marginal cost to maximize its profit. This determines the quantity the leader should produce (Q_L). This quantity, at which $MR_L = MC_L$, is then used to determine the price the leader should set by referring to the *leader's demand function* (see point A in Figure 11.6). This price, P^*, is then taken as the follower's price. Since the followers are price takers, their marginal revenue (MR_f) equals price. That is,

$$MR_f = P_f = P^* = P_L$$

The following firms determine their profit-maximizing output by equating their price (or their marginal revenue) with their marginal costs. That is, each follower's output is determined by the condition that

$$P^* = MR_f = MC_i$$

For the sum of all followers, the quantity produced (Q_f) can be found from the followers' supply function (S_f) at the price P^*.

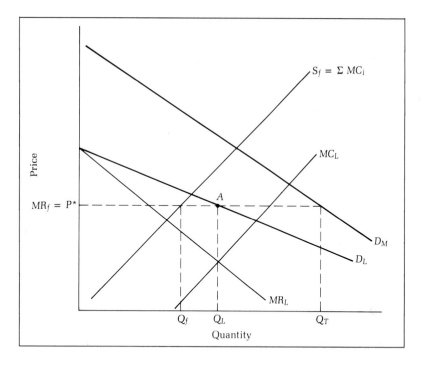

FIGURE 11.6   **Dominant Firm Price Leadership.**   The leader sets a price and allows the followers to produce and sell their profit-maximizing output at that price. Thus, the followers are price takers and behave much as do perfectly competitive firms, equating price with their marginal cost. The sum of the marginal cost curves for all the followers becomes the followers' supply (S_f). Subtracting this from the market demand (D_M) gives the leader's demand (D_L). The leader equates its marginal revenue and marginal cost to find the profit-maximizing quantity (Q_L), which is priced from the leader's demand curve at P^*. The followers take this price and produce where their marginal cost equals P^*. In total, the amount supplied by the followers is thus Q_f.

The total quantity purchased (Q_T) at the price P^* is found from the market demand function. This is also shown in Figure 11.6. As you would expect,

$$Q_f + Q_L = Q_T$$

This result can be seen more clearly in an algebraic example in which we have specific functions and actual numbers to work with.

Price Leadership: An Algebraic Example

Let us apply the logic of the dominant firm price leadership model developed above to a specific example involving three firms, one of which dominates the industry and acts as the price leader. The important total cost functions for these three firms are

$$
\begin{aligned}
\text{Leader:} & \quad TC_L = .015Q_L^2 \\
\text{Follower 1:} & \quad TC_1 = 0.1Q_1^2 \\
\text{Follower 2:} & \quad TC_2 = 0.2Q_2^2
\end{aligned}
$$

The market demand function is

$$P = 40 - 0.125Q_M$$

You know that the followers behave as price takers and so will equate price with their marginal costs. Thus, the supply of the followers will equal the sum of their individual marginal cost curves. Therefore, the first thing to do is to find the followers' marginal cost curves:

$$
\begin{aligned}
MC_1 &= dTC_1/dQ_1 = .2Q_1 \\
MC_2 &= dTC_2/dQ_2 = .4Q_2
\end{aligned}
$$

Solving each of these marginal cost equations for the quantity variable gives us

$$
\begin{aligned}
Q_1 &= 5MC_1 \\
Q_2 &= 2.5MC_2
\end{aligned}
$$

Remember that as price takers, these followers equate price with marginal costs. Thus, the equations

$$
\begin{aligned}
Q_1 &= 5P \\
Q_2 &= 2.5P
\end{aligned}
$$

represent the individual follower's supply functions. Adding these gives the supply function for all followers taken together (remember that $S_f = \Sigma MC_i$):

$$Q_f = Q_1 + Q_2 = 7.5P$$

To find the demand function for the leader, recall that we must subtract the supply of the followers from the market demand. To do so, we first must solve the market demand function for Q_m:

$$
\begin{aligned}
P &= 40 - 0.125Q_m \\
Q_m &= 320 - 8P
\end{aligned}
$$

Subtracting the followers' supply from this market demand gives the leader's demand:

$$
\begin{aligned}
Q_m &= 320 - 8P \\
-(Q_f &= 7.5P) \\
\hline
Q_L &= 320 - 15.5P
\end{aligned}
$$

This function is labeled D_L in Figure 11.7, which shows this problem in its graphic form.

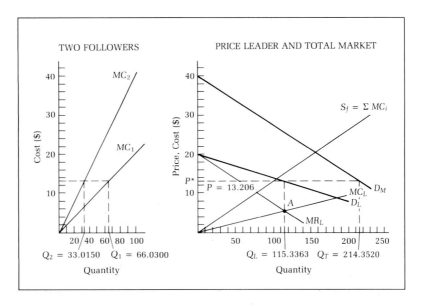

FIGURE 11.7   **Dominant-Firm Price Leadership: A Numerical Example.**   Because the followers behave as price takers, their marginal cost functions indicate how much they will supply at each possible price the leader may set. The best price for the leader is determined by the leader's demand at the quantity (Q_L) at which its marginal revenue and marginal cost are equal (point A). We see that the leader's demand is found by subtracting what the followers would supply at each price (S_f) from the market demand (D_M).

Solving Q_L for P sets the stage for us to find the leader's total and marginal revenue functions as follows:

$$Q_L = 320 - 15.5P$$
$$P = 20.6452 - .0645Q_L$$
$$TR_L = P \cdot Q_L$$
$$TR_L = (20.6452 - .0645Q_L)Q_L$$
$$TR_L = 20.6452Q_L - .0645Q_L^2$$
$$MR_L = dTR/dQ_L = 20.6452 - .129Q_L$$

The leader will maximize profit by producing the quantity at which $MR = MC$. The leader's total cost was given as

$$TC_L = .025Q_L^2$$

Thus,

$$MC_L = .05Q_L$$

Setting marginal revenue equal to marginal cost and solving for Q_L, we find

$$20.6452 - .129Q_L = .05Q_L$$
$$-.179Q_L = -20.6452$$
$$Q_L = 115.3363$$

So we now know how many units the leader should produce to maximize its profit. What price should the leader set? This is determined from the *leader's demand function* as

$$P = 20.6452 - .0645Q_L$$
$$P = 20.6452 - .0645(115.3363)$$
$$P = 13.206$$

Remembering that the followers take this price as given and equate it with their individual marginal costs, we can find the quantity produced by each follower as

$$Q_1 = 5MC = 5P = 5(13.206) = 66.030$$
$$Q_2 = 2.5MC = 2.5P = 2.5(13.206) = 33.015$$

The total output of all three firms is, then,

$$Q_1 = 66.0300$$
$$Q_2 = 33.0150$$
$$\underline{Q_L = 115.3363}$$
$$Q_T = 214.3813$$

Let us see how this compares with the amount consumers would be willing and able to purchase at the price of 13.206. From the market demand, we find

$$Q_M = 320 - 8(13.206)$$
$$Q_M = 214.3520$$

So, except for a slight rounding difference, the total produced equals the total demanded.

These results are summarized below. Be sure to compare them with the graphs in Figure 11.7:

$$\text{Price} = 13.206$$
$$\left.\begin{array}{l}\text{Leader's production} = 115.3363 \\ \text{Firm 1's production} = 66.03 \\ \text{Firm 2's production} = 33.01 \end{array}\right\} \quad \text{Total production} = 214.3813$$
$$\text{Market demand} = 214.3520$$

Before leaving this section, let us check the profit for each firm. For the leader,

$$\pi = TR - TC$$
$$\pi = 13.206(115.3363) - .025(115.3363)^2$$
$$\pi = \$1{,}190.57$$

For firm 1,

$$\pi = TR - TC$$
$$\pi = 13.206(66.03) - .1(66.03)^2$$
$$\pi = \$436.00$$

For firm 2,

$$\pi = TR - TC$$
$$\pi = 13.206(33.015) - .2(33.015)^2$$
$$\pi = \$218.00$$

The American automobile industry provides an example in which price leadership and possible collusion seem to exist. In a study of this industry by Boyle and Hogarty, examination of price announcements in the *Wall Street Journal* confirm the notion that General Motors is the price leader.[7] Boyle and Hogarty also report that "the overall results suggest that the three largest manufacturers in this industry collude in terms of quality adjusted prices."[8]

11.5   A SALES MAXIMIZATION MODEL

Thus far, our discussion of the economic models of market structure and firm behavior has been based on the assumption of profit maximization either by the individual firms or, in the case of collusion, by firms acting in concert. There is a class of oligopoly models that does not rely on this assumption but, rather, assumes that firms are more inclined to maximize sales revenue, perhaps subject to a profit constraint; these models are often referred to as *Baumol sales maximization models*. Such behavior would be quite rational if a high sales volume makes it easier for a firm to obtain capital, or if it produces a better image with consumers, employees, suppliers, or distributors. Also, there is some evidence that the compensation of executives seems to be more strongly correlated with sales than with profit.[9]

The determination of price and output under the alternative assumptions of profit maximization or sales-revenue maximization is illustrated in Figure 11.8. The price-output combination that maximizes profit is shown as P_1 and Q_1, as determined by the intersection of marginal revenue (MR)

[7]Stanley E. Boyle and Thomas F. Hogarty, "Pricing Behavior in the American Automobile Industry, 1957–71," *Journal of Industrial Economics*, December 1975, pp. 88–89.

[8]*Ibid*., p. 73.

[9]See C.L. Lackman and J.L. Craycraft, "Sales Maximization and Oligopoly: A Case Study," *Journal of Industrial Economics*, December 1974, pp. 81–95 and references cited therein (especially p. 86).

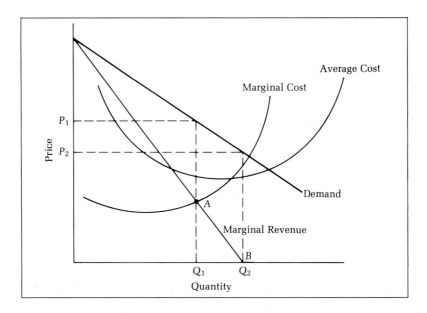

FIGURE 11.8   **Profit Maximization and Revenue Maximization.** The profit-maximizing firm produces the quantity (Q_1) at which $MR = MC$ (point A). This rate of output can be sold at price P_1, as determined from the demand curve. The revenue-maximizing firm's management want to produce and sell additional units as long as marginal revenue is positive. They decide to increase quantity up to Q_2, where marginal revenue falls to 0 (point B). From the demand curve, we can see that Q_2 units can be sold at the price P_2.

and marginal cost (MC). The price-output combination that would maximize sales revenue is determined by the level of output at which marginal revenue is 0 and is denoted P_2 and Q_2 in Figure 11.8.

Let us now consider a relatively simple numerical example. We will use unit cost functions that are linear just to keep from getting so entangled in the algebra that we forget the purpose of comparing profit maximization with sales maximization. Suppose that a firm has the linear demand function $P = 20 - Q$, and total cost is $TC = .5Q^2$. The unit cost functions will be $MC = Q$ and $AC = .5Q$. The price-output combination that would maximize profit can be determined as

$$\pi = TR - TC$$
$$\pi = P \cdot Q - TC$$
$$\pi = 20Q - Q^2 - .5Q^2$$
$$d\pi/dQ = 20 - 2Q - Q = 0$$
$$20 - 2Q = Q \quad (\text{i.e., } MR = MC)$$
$$3Q = 20$$
$$Q_1 = 6.67$$

And from the demand curve, we can now find P as

$$P = 20 - Q$$
$$P = 20 - 6.67$$
$$P_1 = 13.33$$

Profit may now be found as

$$\pi = (13.33)(6.67) - .5(6.67)^2$$
$$\pi_1 = 66.67$$

The price-output combination that maximizes sales revenue is found by simply taking the first derivative of total revenue (TR) with respect to output (Q) and solving for Q:

$$TR = P \cdot Q$$
$$TR = 20Q - Q^2$$
$$dTR/dQ = 20 - 2Q = 0$$
$$2Q = 20$$
$$Q_2 = 10$$

Price can again be found from the demand function:

$$P = 20 - Q$$
$$P = 20 - 10$$
$$P_2 = 10$$

Profit at this revenue maximizing price and quantity is

$$\pi = TR - TC$$
$$\pi = (10)(10) - .5(10)^2$$
$$\pi = 100 - 50$$
$$\pi_2 = 50$$

Note in particular that this sales-maximization solution is determined by finding where marginal revenue is 0 (see point B in Figure 11.8). At this point, the price elasticity of demand is unitary.

You should recall from the discussion in Chapter 5 that if demand is elastic, a decrease in price results in an increase in total revenue and that if demand is inelastic, a decrease in price causes a decrease in total revenue. Thus, revenue is maximized by setting price so that demand is unitarily elastic at that price. In Lackman and Craycraft's study of corrugated paper specialties products, it was found that the three-firm oligopoly studied did, in fact, price so that the elasticities of demand for the firms in 1969 were close to being unitary (1.09, 1.16, and 1.08). This result supports the notion that these firms seek to maximize sales revenue.[10]

---

[10]*Ibid*., pp. 83, 88.

It is entirely possible for pricing to maximize sales revenue to result in negative, 0, or otherwise unacceptable profits. Thus, we might want to maximize revenue subject to obtaining some minimum profit. The minimum required profit could be expressed as some total number of dollars, as a certain percentage of sales revenue, as a percentage of fixed or total cost, or in almost any other way that a given management team may want to express its profit requirement.

To illustrate how a required level of profit can be incorporated into the analysis, let us return briefly to the numerical example developed above. Demand was given as $P = 20 - Q$, and total cost was $TC = .5Q^2$. Suppose that the firm wants to maximize sales revenue subject to earning a profit equal to 140 percent of the total cost of production. This may be written as

$$\pi^* = 1.4TC$$

Where π^* is the desired profit objective. Since $TC = .5Q^2$, we have

$$\pi^* = 1.4(.5Q^2) = .7Q^2$$

But we know also that profit is defined as total revenue minus total cost ($\pi = TR - TC$). Thus, for our simple example,

$$
\begin{aligned}
TR - TC &= .7Q^2 \\
20Q - Q^2 - .5Q^2 &= .7Q^2 \\
20Q &= 2.2Q^2 \\
20 &= 2.2Q \\
Q &= 9.09
\end{aligned}
$$

From the demand function, we find price as

$$P = 20 - Q = 10.91$$

And the level of profit may be determined as follows:

$$
\begin{aligned}
\pi &= TR - TC \\
\pi &= (10.91)(9.09) - .5(9.09)^2 \\
\pi &= 57.86
\end{aligned}
$$

Note that this is less than the profit-maximizing profit (66.67) but more than the profit that resulted under the revenue-maximization objective (50).

SUMMARY

Most industries in our economy fall in the broad middle ground of market structures known as monopolistic competition and oligopoly. Monopolistic competition is nearer the perfectly competitive end of the spectrum of market structures, while oligopoly is nearer the monopoly end.

In monopolistically competitive industries, there are many sellers of products that are quite similar, yet differentiated, and entry is relatively easy. The product differentiation may be actual or just perceived by consumers.

The success of private-brand products illustrates how consumers may form brand preferences even though the physical products may be identical, with only the package or name differentiating them. It is the product differentiation and product preferences that result in a negatively sloped demand curve for monopolistically competitive firms. If the firm raises price, all sales will not be lost, as would be the case for a perfectly competitive firm. But, due to the large number of close substitute products available, the demand curves for monopolistically competitive firms tend to be quite elastic over a considerable range.

Monopolistically competitive industries tend toward a long-run equilibrium in which 0 economic profit is the rule. It is important to remember that this does not mean that such firms fail to obtain an accounting profit. That accounting profit is included in the cost functions as a normal, or opportunity cost, return. When there are excess, or economic, profits, new firms are likely to enter the industry, which causes some reduction in the demand curve for preexisting firms.

Oligopolistic industries have few firms relative to the size of the total market demand for the product. Because of the relatively small number of firms, it is not surprising to find a tendency for firms to recognize their mutual interdependence. Paul Sweezy first used the idea of a kinked demand curve to explain the price rigidity observed in oligopolies as a result of the interdependence of firms.

Cartels are a likely result in oligopolistic industries and probably would be much more common if such formal collusive arrangements were not illegal in most countries. When cartels are formed (legally or illegally), the objective is usually to impose monopoly control over the market. If the firms cooperate completely, they can generate the same profit that could be obtained by a monopolist. In such cases, each firm should produce up to the rate of output at which the marginal cost of the firm is equal to the cartel's marginal revenue from the last unit sold. For the entire cartel, the marginal cost curve is the horizontal sum of each participating firm's marginal cost. The cartel then equates this marginal cost with the marginal revenue associated with the market demand curve to determine the profit-maximizing rate of output. Price is then determined from the market demand curve at that rate of output.

SUGGESTED READINGS

Boyle, Stanley E., and Hogarty, Thomas F. "Pricing Behavior in the American Automobile Industry, 1957–71." Journal of Industrial Economics, December 1975, pp. 81–95.

Keating, Barry P., and Keating, Maryann O., "Network Television: A Synthetic Oligopoly." University of Michigan Business Review, July 1975, pp. 20–23.

Kirzner, I.M. *Competition and Entrepreneurship.* Chicago: University of Chicago Press, 1973, Chapters 1–4.

Marvel, Howard P. "Competition and Price Levels in the Retail Gasoline Market." *Review of Economics and Statistics,* May 1978, pp. 252–258.

Nightingale, John. "On the Definition of 'Industry' and 'Market'." *Journal of Industrial Economics,* September 1978, pp. 31–39.

Robinson, J. *The Economics of Imperfect Competition.* London: MacMillan, 1933.

Scherer, F.M. "Research and Development Resource Allocation under Rivalry." *Quarterly Journal of Economics,* August 1967, pp. 359–394.

Stigler, G.J. "Monopolistic Competition in Retrospect." In *The Organization of Industry.* Homewood, IL: Richard D. Irwin, 1968, pp. 71–94.

Stigler, G.J. "Price and Non-Price Competition." *Journal of Political Economy,* January-February 1968, pp. 149–154.

Telser, L.G. "Advertising and Competition." *Journal of Political Economy,* December 1964, pp. 537–562.

PROBLEMS

1. List five examples of product differentiation in a real world market. Does it matter that the differences in the product or service are actual or perceived?

2. Expenditures on advertising as a percentage of sales are larger for industries dominated by a few large firms. What are the possible reasons for such an observation?

3. One often hears the comment that there are "too many" brands of laundry detergent sold or "too many" gasoline stations in a town. Is there such a thing as "too many" of a particular type of business? What measures would you employ to gauge the appropriate numbers of businesses in a particular product line or market area?

4. A group of competing monopolistically competitive firms produces a slightly differentiated product, and so it is to be expected that they will not all have identical cost and revenue functions. When the firms attain equilibrium, will they necessarily charge identical prices? Will they necessarily produce the same output? Will they necessarily earn the same profits?

5. Draw average revenue (demand), marginal revenue, average cost, and marginal cost curves for each of the following situations:
   a. Oligopolist (kinked demand curve) with a positive economic profit
   b. Monopolistic competitor with a positive economic profit
   c. Monopolistic competitor with a negative economic profit
   Now write a brief paragraph explaining each of these graphs. Also explain what might be expected to happen, if anything, in each of these cases that might alter the situation you have depicted (i.e., the existence of a negative or positive economic profit).

6. There are four firms that produce ND-3 film for use in industrial applications. Top management of these firms have been meeting in the past several months to discuss forming a cartel arrangement to help stabilize the industry. They have agreed that the total industry demand for ND-3 film can be represented by the following function:

$$P = 100 - .1Q$$

The four firms that produce ND-3 film have the following cost functions:

Firm 1: $TC_1 = 100 + .05Q_1^2$
Firm 2: $TC_2 = .1Q_2 + .02Q_2^2$
Firm 3: $TC_3 = .04Q_3^2$
Firm 4: $TC_4 = 50 + .08Q_4^2$

William Leach, the chief executive officer of firm 1, has been authorized to perform the initial analysis of how the industry would operate as a profit-maximizing cartel. Assume that Mr. Leach has come to you for help in this analysis. Prepare answers to the following questions:
   a. What is the algebraic expression that represents the marginal cost function for the entire cartel?
   b. How many units of output should be produced by the cartel if the objective is to maximize total cartel profits?
   c. What price should that cartel set for the sale of the ND-3 film?
   d. How many units of output should be assigned to each of the four firms?
   e. In discussing the formation of the cartel, some concern has been expressed that firm 2 might dominate the other firms. All participants have agreed that ultimately the cartel should not be formed if one firm would get a market share of more than 50 percent or if any firm would have less than 10 percent of the total market. Does your solution satisfy these considerations? Calculate market shares based on your result and complete the table below:

Firm	Market Share
1	_____ %
2	_____ %
3	_____ %
4	_____ %

f.   Calculate the profit or loss for each firm and the percent of industry profits each firm has:

Firm	Profit	Share of Industry Profits
1	$ _____	_____ %
2	$ _____	_____ %
3	$ _____	_____ %
4	$ _____	_____ %

7.   An industry with 11 firms is characterized by price leadership by a single dominant firm. The 10 followers have the same cost structure, with the following marginal cost curve:

$$MC = .5Q$$

The leader's total cost function is

$$TC = 500 + .1Q^2$$

The market demand for the product is

$$P = 210 - Q$$

a.   What is the price the leader should set to maximize its profit?
b.   What quantity will the leader sell, and how much will be sold by all the followers combined?
c.   Using the market demand function, show that the quantity consumers would purchase at the price found in part a is equal to the total amount produced.

8.   Four firms in an industry have combined to form a cartel with the agreement that they will collectively price to achieve the profit that would result if the industry were fully monopolized and that they will allocate production in the most efficient manner. The firms have the following cost functions:

Firm 1: $TC = 10,000 + .1Q^2$
Firm 2: $TC = 10,000 + .1Q^2$
Firm 3: $TC = 10,000 + .1Q^2$
Firm 4. $TC = 10,000 + 5Q + .05Q^2$

The market demand function is

$$P = 100 - .03Q$$

a. What should the cartel price be?
b. How much should each firm produce?
c. Will total production match the quantity consumers would wish to purchase at the price determined in part a? Show why or why not.

9. An oligopolistic industry has a single dominant firm, which is the price leader, and several smaller firms. The smaller firms take the price determined by the price leader as given and attempt to maximize profit at that price. The leader's marginal cost function is

$$MC_L = 0.1Q_L$$

The *sum of all* of the followers' marginal cost functions is

$$MC_F = 0.25Q_F$$

The industry, or market, demand function is

$$P = 100 - Q_m$$

a. Find the profit-maximizing output for the leader.
b. Find the product price.
c. Find the quantity the followers would produce in total.

10. There are six printers in Red River Falls. The management of these firms have long cooperated on an informal basis to share the market and keep prices stable. They now plan to formalize their association into a formal cartel. The total cost functions for the six printers are given below:

Firm 1: $TC_1 = 10Q + .1Q^2$
Firm 2: $TC_2 = 10Q + .1Q^2$
Firm 3: $TC_3 = .2Q^2$
Firm 4: $TC_4 = .2Q^2$
Firm 5: $TC_5 = 20Q + .05Q^2$
Firm 6: $TC_6 = 20Q + .05Q^2$

The demand for printing services in Red River Falls has been estimated as

$$P = 150 - .1Q$$

a. Find the marginal cost function for this printing cartel:

$MC =$ _____ + _____ Q

b. What level of output will maximize total cartel profits?

Total $Q =$ _____

How should this output be allocated among the six individual firms?

$Q_1 =$ _____ $Q_2 =$ _____

$Q_3 =$ _____ $Q_4 =$ _____

$Q_5 =$ _____ $Q_6 =$ _____

c. What price should the cartel set?

$P =$ _____

d. Calculate the profit that each firm can expect, given the calculations you have made above:

	Profit	% of Total Industry Profit
Firm 1:	$ _____	_____ %
Firm 2:	$ _____	_____ %
Firm 3:	$ _____	_____ %
Firm 4:	$ _____	_____ %
Firm 5:	$ _____	_____ %
Firm 6:	$ _____	_____ %

e. Which firm or firms would you expect to be most likely to "cheat" on the cartel by lowering price? Why?

11. As presented in problem 6, there are four firms that produce ND-3 film for use in industrial applications. Suppose that a formal cartel agreement cannot be agreed upon, but that over time firm 2 becomes recognized as the price leader in the industry. The other three firms allow firm 2 to do all the pricing analysis and set prices, while they take that price as given and attempt to maximize their profits at firm 2's price. The four firms' cost functions are:

Firm 1: $TC_1 = 100 + .05Q_1^2$
Firm 2: $TC_2 = .1Q_2 + .02Q_2^2$
Firm 3: $TC_3 = .04Q_3^2$
Firm 4: $TC_4 = 50 + .08Q_4^2$

The market demand function has been estimated as follows:

$P = 100 - .1Q$

a. What is the algebraic equation for the leader's demand curve (i.e., firm 2's demand function):

$P =$ _____ $-$ _____

b. Find the quantity that firm 2 should produce and the price that should be set to maximize firm 2's profit:

$Q =$ _____ $P =$ _____

c. Given that firms 1, 3, and 4 take the price determined above and attempt to maximize their respective profits, find the quantity each of these firms should produce:

$Q_1 =$ _____

$Q_3 =$ _____

$Q_4 =$ _____

d. Show that the total quantity demanded at the price determined in part b is equal to the total amount produced.

e. Compare market shares and profitability under this price leadership scenario with the cartel arrangement evaluated in problem 6.

12. In a remote cross-country skiing region of northern Michigan, there are three motels that cater to skiers. Estimates of the marginal cost functions for these motels are

Northern Lodge (NL): $MC = .1Q$
Aspen Hotel (AH): $MC = .25Q$
Ski Hotel (SH): $MC = .15Q$

The market demand for rooms each week is estimated to be

$P = 40 - .1Q$

The management of Northern Lodge is generally recognized as having the most experience in the lodging industry, and they have become the price leader for this local industry.

a. Use the price leadership model to determine the quantity of rooms Northern Lodge should make available and the price they should charge:

$P =$ _____ $Q =$ _____

b. What quantity should each of the followers provide?

AH: Q = _____

SH: Q = _____

c. Calculate the market price elasticity of demand at the price determined above.

13. Students at SMSU have two bookstores at which they can buy textbooks and related supplies. The university-owned store is located in the Campus Center, while the privately owned store is in a shopping area just east of campus. The two stores have marginal cost functions as given below:

$$\text{University store:} \quad MC = .0002Q$$
$$\text{Private store:} \quad MC = 10 + .0001Q$$

The total market demand for books has been estimated as

$$P = 50 - .0001Q$$

You are to analyze this situation under the assumption that the two bookstores form a profit-maximizing cartel.

a. Determine the level of book sales that will allow the maximum profit for this two-firm cartel.
b. At what price should the two stores sell books?
c. Which store should be allocated the greatest volume of book sales? How many books should each store sell?
d. Find the amount of money each store will generate toward paying fixed cost and contributing to profit.

14. There are three outfitters that run white water raft trips on the Copper River's remote north fork. Wilderness Rafting (WR) was the first of these firms to use the Copper River and is now generally accepted as the price leader. WR has a marginal cost function that can be represented by

$$\text{WR:} \quad MC = .1Q$$

Mountain State Raft Company (MS) and Rafting Adventures (RA) are the other two outfitters offering trips on the Copper River. Their marginal cost functions are

$$\text{MS:} \quad MC = 10 + .1Q$$
$$\text{RA:} \quad MC = .2Q$$

The demand for raft trips has been estimated as

$$P = 80 - .2Q$$

a. What quantity of raft trips should the leader offer and at what price?

Leader's $Q =$ _____ $P =$ _____

b. How many trips should each of the two followers provide?

MS: $Q =$ _____

RA: $Q =$ _____

c. What is the total market demand at the price set by the leader? Is the total number of trips offered sufficient to meet this demand? Explain.

15. Two locally owned sandwich shops have been making sandwiches for sale in convenience stores, truck stops, and gas stations throughout the country. They have asked you to analyze their marginal cost data and sales data collected in ten representative markets with an eye toward forming a two-firm cartel. The data follow:

L & M Sandwiches		Sally's Sandwiches		Market Sales	
MC	Q	MC	Q	P	Q
.29	4,000	.45	4,200	1.13	13,000
.45	6,200	.52	6,200	1.12	14,900
.52	8,300	.51	10,100	1.03	15,000
.58	10,200	.63	9,300	.98	18,800
.64	9,200	.64	12,500	.82	20,900
.69	11,900	.68	13,900	.80	25,400
.90	14,000	.75	16,100	.75	27,000
.97	15,100	.76	18,000	.64	30,000
1.04	18,000	.84	19,100	.63	27,600
1.12	18,100	.86	16,900	.57	32,200

a. Use regression analysis to estimate each firm's marginal cost function as well as the market demand function. For marginal cost function:

L & M: $MC =$ _____ + _____ Q $R^2 =$ _____

(_____) t-ratio

Sally's: $MC =$ _____ + _____ Q $R^2 =$ _____

(_____) t-ratio

For market demand:

$P =$ _____ − _____ Q $R^2 =$ _____

(_____) t-ratio

Based on the functions you have estimated, determine the marginal cost function that is appropriate for the two-firm cartel:

$$MC = \underline{\hspace{3cm}} + \underline{\hspace{4cm}} Q$$

b. What is the algebraic function for the cartel's marginal revenue?

$$MR = \underline{\hspace{3cm}} - \underline{\hspace{4cm}} Q$$

c. Find the quantity that the cartel should produce to maximize total cartel profits.
d. How should this level of output be allocated between L & M Sandwiches and Sally's Sandwiches?
e. What price should each seller set?

16. The Pangborn Chair Company makes oak rocking chairs and sells them under conditions that approximate monopolistic competition. Product differentiation, however, is sufficient that Pangborn is able to make a positive economic profit. Economic analysis has been used to estimate the following demand function:

$$P = 1675 - 16Q$$

where P is in dollars and Q is in dozens of chairs sold per year. The owner's daughter, a recent MBA graduate, has estimated a cost function for chair production using regression analysis. Her results are

$$TC = 10,000 + 25Q^2 - 6Q + \tfrac{1}{3}Q^3$$

Using this information, answer the following questions:
a. Determine the rate of output that will maximize short-run profit and the price the firm should charge to sell that rate of output.
b. How much profit will the firm earn at this price and output rate?
c. Suppose that Pangborn Chair Company's total fixed costs decrease by 10 percent from the $10,000 indicated in the total cost function above. Calculate the impact this would have on the firm's price, output, and profits. How do you account for these results?
d. What is the point elasticity of demand at the price-output combination determined in part a?

17. The Armstrong Toy Company (ATCO) is a small toy manufacturer in the Midwest. ATCO cannot afford to have a full-time economist on the staff, but management is aware of the benefits that economic analysis can provide in decision making. The president of ATCO has kept some records on production costs and various prices that have been charged for one toy and is interested in determining an output rate and a price that will maximize ATCO's profits from that toy. The president knows little about economic analysis and so contacts the economics department at a nearby college and asks to hire a bright

economics major to help analyze the data that have been gathered. Suppose that you are that student and the president gives you the following information:

Quantity	Total Cost	Price
40	$110	$4.00
30	90	5.00
50	130	3.00
60	150	2.00
20	70	6.00

Assuming that the data are reliable for the range of production between, say, 10 and 70 units per period:

a. Estimate the total cost function (in linear form using simple linear regression; this can be done either by computer or by hand for this simple problem).

b. Estimate the demand function (in linear form using simple linear regression; again, this can be done by computer or by hand).

c. Graph the total revenue and total cost curves for ATCO.

d. Determine the equations for average cost, marginal cost, average revenue, and marginal revenue. Graph each of these functions. From this graph, determine the profit-maximizing price and output and shade the area representing profit.

e. Verify the results in part d using calculus to determine the profit-maximizing price and output.

12

Further Analysis of Pricing Decisions

This chapter discusses additional topics related to pricing that cross the bounds of market structures. First, we will consider cost-plus pricing and the important problems involved in determining the appropriate cost basis and the desired markup. We then discuss pricing when multiple products are produced, when more than one production facility is used, and when one division of a firm sells a product to another division of the same firm. Finally, we consider the potential use of pricing strategy as a barrier to entry into an industry.

12.1 COST-PLUS PRICING

In the day-to-day operations of many firms, the pricing practices actually used may not duplicate theoretically correct pricing practices. This is not to say that the pricing models you have reviewed thus far are not useful. Rather, it is a recognition that many simple rules of thumb are employed in the real world that are *similar* to theoretically correct practices. In practice, the cost of becoming "theoretically perfect" may outweigh the small enhancements to revenue that might result. One of the most widely used rules of thumb used in pricing is *cost-plus pricing*.

At first glance, this approach seems very simple. The firm needs only to determine the cost of producing a unit of output and then price it at that cost *plus* some markup. The actual process in use, however, is really much more complex. The firm must decide what costs should be included, at what volume of output the costs should be determined, and how large a markup is appropriate. These problem areas are addressed in this section.

For our discussion of cost-plus pricing, let us consider a container manufacturing company that is planning to market a new product, which we shall call cold pack. The product is a container for food products or beverages that are normally consumed at a temperature of 35° F to 45° F but are often consumed where refrigeration is unavailable. Such products include soft drinks and beer to be consumed on a fishing trip, apple sauce to be eaten on a picnic, and canned fruit to be taken on a camping trip. These products could be packaged in a cold pack, which is a double-walled container with a chemical mixture between the walls that provides an endothermic reaction (a reaction that causes a reduction in temperature) upon opening. Thus, when the product is opened, it is immediately (in less than one minute) cooled to the desired temperature, say 40° F.

Determining the Costs

In determining the relevant costs in pricing a given-sized cold pack (we shall simplify the problem by assuming that only one size is produced), the cost-plus method takes into account expenditures that go into a product before it is ready for the market. Examples of these expenditures include the cost of research and development, the investment in plant and equipment, the cost of special training for production personnel and the sales force, the cost of initial promotional activities, and the cost of obtaining related patent rights. These costs are summarized in Table 12.1.

How should the costs in Table 12.1 be incorporated in the determination of price? This is a question that can evoke some disagreement, particularly between economists and accountants, who follow standard accounting practices for reasons primarily related to their tax orientation. Both would agree that the cost of plant and equipment should be depreciated, but beyond this point, they often do not see eye to eye. Accountants argue that only tangible assets should be considered investments and thus that only plant and equipment should be capitalized. Economists, however, view the training of production and sales personnel as an investment in human capital that will also yield a stream of benefits to the firm over some period of years. The same is true of the investment in patent rights and the investment in good will established through preproduction promotional activities. These items are therefore just as appropriately depreciated as are tangible assets. Research and development expenditures have always been difficult to evaluate and allocate. However, in this case these expenditures were for research directed solely to the development of the cold pack

TABLE 12.1   Preproduction Investment Costs for Cold Pack

Research and development	$ 75,000
Plant and equipment	150,000
Preproduction promotion	50,000
Training of production personnel	12,000
Training of sales force	4,000
Patent rights	9,000
Total investment in cold pack	$300,000

container and thus should be considered a direct investment in the product. Therefore, all the costs in Table 12.1 should be capitalized.

The costs discussed thus far are of a fixed nature; that is, the expenses will not vary as the volume of output changes. Other fixed costs typically charged to the production of cold packs include the salaries of such supervisory personnel as the production manager assigned to this product; the salaries of the salespeople that will handle this product exclusively; the insurance on the building; equipment expenditures; the overhead charge to cover this product's share of other corporate expenses; and property taxes.

In addition to these fixed costs of producing and marketing the product, the firm also incurs direct variable costs for the cold pack project. The most important of these include the direct labor costs, the cost of materials used in production (primarily aluminum and the chemicals for the endothermic reaction), the carrying cost for inventory, the charges for general factory supplies, and utility costs. This group of expenses is directly related to the volume of output and is fairly constant on a per unit (average cost) of output basis.

Table 12.2 summarizes the firm's estimates for all of the costs discussed above (fixed and variable). Each of the columns represents a different projected annual sales volume. As we see from the bottom line, the average total cost per unit is different for each level of output. This

TABLE 12.2 **Unit Cost of Cold Packs for Three Projected Levels of Sales**

Costs	Sales (units)		
	80,000	100,000	120,000
Variable costs			
Labor	$ .15	$ .15	$ .15
Materials	.30	.30	.30
Inventory	.02	.02	.02
Supplies	.02	.02	.02
Utilities	.01	.01	.01
Total variable costs per unit	$ .50	$ .50	$ .50
Fixed costs			
Depreciation	$ .25	$ .20	$ .167
Salaries (production manager and sales)	.375	.30	.250
Insurance	.025	.02	.017
Taxes	.01	.008	.007
Overhead	.35	.35	.35
Total fixed cost per unit	$1.01	$ .878	$ .791
Average total cost	$1.51	$1.378	$1.291

illustrates one of the important difficulties in using costs to establish the product price: the unit cost changes as the quantity produced varies.[1]

Determining the Rate of Output

What quantity should the firm use in establishing the appropriate level of unit cost? Most firms use a "standard or normal" level of output set at 70 to 80 percent of capacity. In a situation such as this, the firm may have no historical data, so the decision is based either on subjective judgments concerning the most likely sales volume or on marketing forecasts of demand.

The depreciation costs in Table 12.2 are simplified somewhat for illustrative purposes. A straight-line depreciation of all the investments in Table 12.1 over a 15-year period has been applied. Overhead has been figured as 70 percent of unit variable costs. Using this method to determine the charge for general corporate overhead, we see that it acts like a variable cost. Nonetheless, showing this charge as a type of fixed cost is preferable since it represents a way of allocating fixed corporate costs that are not directly chargeable to any product (e.g., the president's salary).

Determining the Markup

Given that the most likely sales volume is judged to be 100,000 units per year, we can proceed with the cost-plus determination of price. Thus, we approach another critical problem: Plus what? Often the percentage markup is determined by industry tradition. That is, in many cases a standard markup is established outside the firm. If no standard is clearly appropriate for a given product, the firm must ask what return on investment is necessary to attract the funds needed for the project. The manufacturers of cold packs need an initial investment of $300,000, as indicated above.

For our present example, suppose that the standard markup in the metal container industry is 12 percent. For a sales level of 100,000 units, the average total cost is $1.378. The manufacturer's price would then be $1.378 times 1.12, or $1.54 per unit. If this firm wished to establish a markup designed to achieve a specific return on investment (i.e., a target rate), they would determine the desired rate of return and convert it to a dollar amount. That amount divided by the volume of output is the required dollar markup per unit. Assume, for example, that the firm desires to earn an average rate of return of 20 percent before taxes on its investment of $300,000. This implies a target profit rate of $60,000. With the expected output rate of 100,000 units, profit per unit must be $.60. Adding this to the average total cost per

---

[1]The problem is further complicated because the expected annual sales will be to some extent a function of the price charged; thus, to determine price from cost seems to be putting the cart before the horse.

unit at that level of output, the target rate of return price is $1.978 (or $1.98) per unit. A target price such as this may be used as a guide and adjusted up or down depending on demand conditions, other corporate objectives, extent of competition, and other factors.

Should Price Ever Be Below Cost?

Note carefully how important the determination of the *relevant costs* is for the pricing decision. To illustrate this importance, let us assume that cold packs are a commercial success and that the firm produces approximately 100,000 units per year, as anticipated. In addition, we shall assume that the factory was built to handle at least 120,000 units, and thus there is excess capacity available. Given these conditions, suppose that a food processing firm contacts the company with an offer to purchase 10,000 private-branded units per year at a price of $1.35? Should the firm accept this offer at a price that we have determined to be less than the cost-plus price and even below the average total cost?

The answer is yes as long as there is no effect on existing or future regular sales. The relevant costs now consist only of the variable production costs. The fixed costs have been fully allocated to the existing level of production and will not change. The desired rate of return on the capital investment is being achieved. Thus, if the added revenue from sales exceeds the additional cost of producing those 100,000 units, the firm will find the venture profitable. This variant of cost-plus pricing, based only on the additional revenue and costs, is called *incremental analysis* and is appropriate to any decision of this type.[2]

The incremental cost for the private branding contract is total variable cost per unit ($.50) times the number of units (10,000), or $5000. The incremental revenue is the price $1.35 times 10,000 units, or $13,500. The firm, therefore, increases its profit by $8500, even though the product is sold substantially below the original cost-plus price and even below average total cost.

Disadvantages of Cost-Plus Pricing

In whatever form it is used, cost-plus pricing has some clear shortcomings. First, the use of historic cost information rather than current cost data may cause price to be set lower than the price necessary to achieve the firm's objective. Furthermore, this method of pricing overstates the ability of most firms to accurately allocate fixed costs among various products. In the cold pack example, this is somewhat less of a problem, since most of the fixed

---

[2]An excellent example of the importance of incremental analysis to business decisions is found in "Airline Takes the Marginal Route," *Business Week* (April 20, 1963).

costs are directly attributable to just this product. The somewhat arbitrary allocation of corporate overhead is a manifestation of this problem.

In addition, this type of pricing strategy is virtually useless if variable costs fluctuate significantly. Unless the producing firm is confident that existing (or forecasted) prices for materials and supplies, as well as labor cost, will remain stable for its planning horizon, the use of cost-plus pricing can be very expensive. Many suppliers of industrial products have built escalators into their pricing structures so that the actual price is the price at the time of delivery rather than at the time of sale.

Finally, cost-plus pricing does not take into account possible changes in demand. Basing price on cost may have little relationship to what consumers are willing and able to pay. This can result in the firm's being unable to sell the "standard or normal" volume at the established price, or the firm may have set price too low to be able to keep up with consumer demand. In the latter case, ill will may accumulate, which could hurt long-run sales.

Advantages of Cost-Plus Pricing

As practiced in industry, cost-plus pricing does have advantages. First, cost-plus pricing leads to a relatively stable price. For industries in which the output is used by others as a material input, price stability may be very important.[3] In negotiating contracts, many corporate buyers prefer a stable price, since it reduces the time and expense they must exert in trying to get the best buy. Some managers may prefer a relatively high but stable price to a somewhat lower but fluctuating price because that stability makes their own planning a little easier.

Cost-plus pricing may also make price increases more acceptable to consumers. If the consumers can be convinced that an increase in price is simply a reflection of increased costs, they are less likely to develop feelings of ill will toward the seller. This rationale for price increases has been used when material and resource costs have pushed up the prices of consumer goods, as well as industrial goods, in periods of high inflation.

Also, cost-plus pricing is compatible with the objective of many firms to achieve a specified rate of return on investment. Obtaining a target return on investment is the dominant objective of many large corporations. This target rate of return can be incorporated in the determination of a cost-plus price, as we saw above.

Finally, once the methods to be used in determining the relevant costs and markup are established, this pricing strategy becomes fairly simple. This alone may account for the widespread use of cost-plus pricing at the retail level.

---

[3]Otto Wheeley, "Pricing Policy and Objectives," in Elizabeth Marting, ed., *Creative Pricing* (New York: American Management Association, 1968), p. 37.

Cost-Plus Pricing and Profit Maximization: A Reconciliation

Cost-plus pricing appears to violate the principles of marginal analysis behind an optimal profit-maximizing price determination because fixed costs are considered in the pricing decision. However, when per unit costs (average cost) are constant and when price elasticity is constant over a broad range, cost-plus pricing can lead the firm to make very nearly optimal decisions. We know that for profit maximization, marginal revenue should equal marginal cost. Furthermore, it can be shown that

$$MR = P[1 + (1/e)]$$

where MR is marginal revenue, P is price, and e is the price elasticity of demand.[4] Since marginal cost (MC) equals marginal revenue for profit maximization, we can substitute MC for MR:

$$MC = P[1 + (1/e)]$$

$$MC = P\left[\frac{e+1}{e}\right]$$

Solving this expression for price, we have

$$P = MC\left[\frac{e}{e+1}\right]$$

In many cases in which cost-plus pricing is practiced, unit costs are relatively constant over the relevant range of output, and thus marginal cost and average cost (AC) are equal. Thus, the profit-maximizing price may be determined as follows:

$$P = AC\left[\frac{e}{e+1}\right]$$

where the term $[e/(e + 1)]$ determines the profit-maximizing markup.

Let us illustrate with a simple numerical example. Suppose that $AC = \$1.50$ and $e = -2.0$. The profit-maximizing price is

---

[4]The proof for this relationship is not difficult. If we define total revenue as $TR = P \cdot Q$, marginal revenue is the derivative of total revenue with respect to quantity. Using the product rule, we find

$$MR = dTR/dQ = P(dQ/dQ) + Q(dP/dQ)$$
$$MR = P + Q(dP/dQ)$$
$$MR = P[1 + (Q/P)(dP/dQ)]$$

From Chapter 5, we know that price elasticity is equal to

$$e = (dQ/dP)(P/Q)$$

This is the reciprocal of the last term in brackets for MR, above. Thus,

$$MR = P[1 + (1/e)]$$

$$P = 1.5\left[\frac{-2}{(-2 + 1)}\right] = 3.00$$

The markup in this case is 100 percent (i.e., $[e/(e + 1)] = 2$; thus, the price equals AC plus 100 percent of AC). Now suppose that consumer tastes and preferences change such that demand becomes more elastic (more sensitive to price). If $e = -3$, we would have

$$P = 1.5\left[\frac{-3}{(-3 + 1)}\right] = 2.25$$

We see that a lower price would result if demand was more elastic. In this case, the percentage markup would fall to 50 percent.

These results are consistent with the pricing observed in many sectors of the economy in which cost-plus pricing is frequently used. Consider, for example, that retail food stores typically operate with a very low margin, or markup. We would expect the price elasticity of demand for any single food store to be fairly high because consumers generally have close substitutes (other similar stores) available. We have seen that a high price elasticity results in relatively low margins for the profit-maximizing firm. In this, as in other cases, we see that the action of businesspeople is often "consistent with classical theory" as expressed in economic models such as those you have been studying in this course.[5]

12.2   PRICING WHEN MORE THAN ONE PRODUCT IS PRODUCED

The pricing and output decisions considered so far have focused on firms that either produce one product or produce a set of products that are independent of one another. However, in many cases, the various products produced by a given firm are not independent of one another. The products may be related in the manner in which they are produced (e.g., beef and cattle hides, or automotive gasoline and heating oil), or in the market in which they are sold (e.g., tape recorders and tapes, or cameras and film), or in both (e.g., small cars and luxury cars, or denim jackets and denim jeans). Such situations call for special treatment in product pricing.

Establishing the best price-quantity configuration for multiple products can be a very complex problem. We shall only scratch the surface by considering two general cases: (1) two products produced in fixed proportions (e.g., beef and cattle hides), referred to as the joint products case; and (2) two products produced in variable proportions (e.g., denim jackets and denim jeans), referred to as the alternative products case.

---

[5]Readers may wish to refer to Gilbert Burck, "The Myths and Realities of Corporate Pricing," *Fortune*, April 1972, pp. 85–89, 125, 126 (especially p. 88).

The Joint Products Case

In the first case, the slaughter of beef cattle ultimately generates revenue from two sources: the sale of beef and the sale of hides. The relationship between the number of hides produced and the number of sides of beef processed is a technological constant. Therefore, rather than considering each product as a separate item, we ought to view them jointly as a product package.

The marginal cost of the product package is generally a positively sloped function (MC), as illustrated in Figure 12.1. Since the product package is sold in two components, the total revenue to the firm is the revenue from the sale of hides *plus* the revenue from the sale of beef. The marginal revenue to the firm (MR_f) is equal to the vertical sum of the marginal revenue from hides (MR_h) plus the marginal revenue from beef (MR_b).[6] The vertical sum is used here because the two products are produced in a package consisting of two fixed components. Note that the horizontal axis in Figure 12.1 is labeled "beef-hide packages" because output quantity is actually some combination of the fixed-proportion beef-hide package. The marginal revenue functions are depicted in Figure 12.1, along with the demand function for beef (D_b) and the demand function for hides (D_h).

Let us consider first the situation that exists when the relevant marginal cost function is MC_1. The firm will maximize profit at the output level Q_1. We can see from Figure 12.1 that Q_1 packages will be sold by the firm. In these packages, the beef portion will sell for P_b, and the hide portion will sell for P_h, as determined from the respective demand functions.

Consider what would happen if marginal cost happened to intersect the firm's marginal revenue function (MR_f) at a level of output greater than Q_2. The marginal cost curve MC_2 illustrates this possibility. The firm would certainly not want to sell more than Q_2 hides because this would necessitate lowering the price so much that the marginal revenue from hide sales would be negative. In this case, the firm should produce at the Q_3 level, where $MC_2 = MR_f$, but should destroy the $Q_3 - Q_2$ hides rather than reduce the price enough to sell them (because beyond Q_2 the marginal revenue of hides is negative).[7] In this case, Q_2 hides will be put on the market at a price of P'_h (from the demand function for hides, D_h). The quantity of beef offered for sale will be Q_3 units at a price of P'_b (from the demand function for beef, D_b).

---

[6]If the demand and marginal revenue curves for the jointly produced products have different horizontal intercepts, the combined total revenue function will not be a smooth curve. As a result, there will also be a kink in the firm's combined marginal revenue curve (see point A in Figure 12.1). Note that, in the example illustrated, this kink is at the output level where $MR_h = 0$.

[7]This assumes that the cost to destroy the excess hides is negligible. If there are important disposal costs, they would be added to the marginal cost function. This, of course, would have the effect of lowering the optimum rate of production.

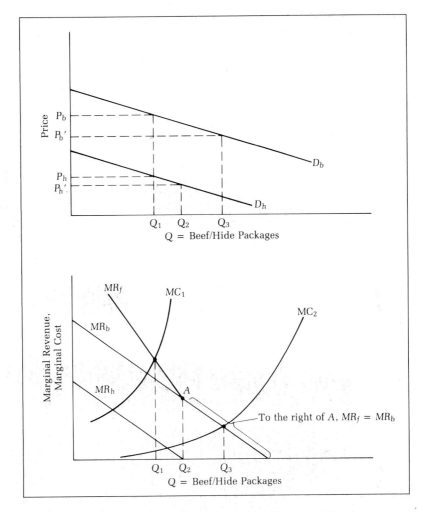

FIGURE 12.1 **Price Determination for Multiple Products: The Joint Products Case.** The marginal revenue to the firm (MR_f) from producing two products jointly is the vertical sum of the marginal revenue functions for each product (MR_b and MR_h). The optimum rate of output is the level at which $MR_f = MC$. The figure illustrates two possible levels of marginal cost and the resulting prices. For MC_2, the output rate Q_3 would mean negative marginal revenue for hides (MR_h), so only Q_2 units of hides would actually be sold, while Q_3 units of beef would be sold. The excess hides would be destroyed.

The Alternative Products Case

Let us turn to the case of two products that are jointly produced but in *variable proportions* (e.g., denim jeans and denim jackets). For any given amount of inputs, more jackets can be produced only if fewer jeans are made, and vice versa. This relationship between the output of the two products can be illustrated using a typical *product transformation curve* (sometimes referred to as a *production possibilities curve*). Several such curves are presented in Figure 12.2. Of the curves drawn, the one closest to the origin represents the various quantities of the two products that can be produced when the amount of inputs is lowest (and thus production costs are lowest). We note that as these successive product transformation curves move away from the origin, they represent greater resource use, more production of one or both of the products, and higher production costs. While only three such curves are shown in Figure 12.2, it is conceptually possible to have an infinite number, one for each level of input use.

Figure 12.3 illustrates three possible isorevenue curves for the sale of denim jeans and jackets. An isorevenue function shows the possible combinations of sales of the two products that will yield a given total revenue to the firm. For example, if jeans sell for $30 and jackets for $45, then $450 of total revenue could be generated by selling 10 jackets and 0 jeans, 15 pairs of jeans and 0 jackets, 3 pairs of jeans and 8 jackets, and so on. Again, there could be an infinite number of these curves, one for each level of total revenue. Isorevenue curves farther from the origin represent greater amounts of revenue than do curves closer to the origin. In Figure 12.3, the isorevenue

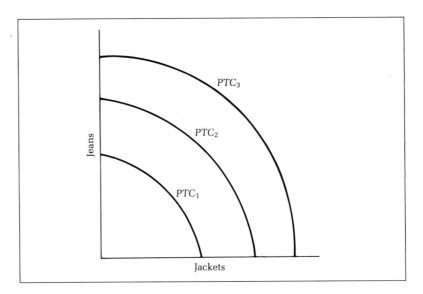

FIGURE 12.2   **Product Transformation Curves.**   For a given set of inputs, there is a trade-off between the amounts of two alternative products that can be produced. Each of these three product transformation curves (PTCs) represents a different level of available inputs: PTC_1, the lowest level; PTC_2, with somewhat more inputs; and PTC_3, the greatest level of inputs among the curves illustrated.

curves are drawn as linear functions. This assumes that the two products are sold in perfectly competitive markets. If they are sold in imperfectly competitive markets, the isorevenue functions will be convex to the origin. The analysis that follows is unaffected by that difference, and thus linear functions are used only for simplicity in illustration.

Figure 12.4 combines the elements of Figures 12.2 and 12.3 in one diagram. Product transformation curve PTC_2 represents greater input use (and therefore greater cost) than PTC_1. The isorevenue curves IR_1 and IR_2 are drawn for one set of product prices. The isorevenue curves IR_3 and IR_4 represent the same price for jeans but an increase in the price for jackets. Isorevenue curve IR_3 represents the same amount of revenue as IR_2 (note that both intersect the vertical axis at the same point).

If the level of resource used is that on which PTC_1 is based and with the original prices, the maximum revenue that could be generated by the firm would be IR_1. This amount of revenue would be forthcoming only if m_1 jackets and n_1 pairs of jeans were produced and sold. That is, the firm will

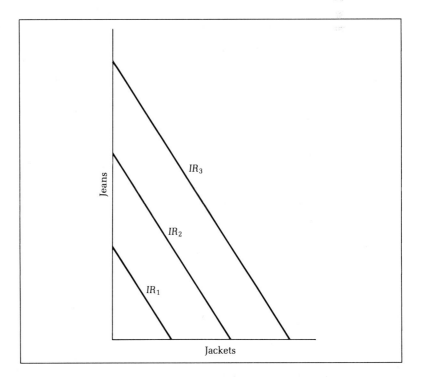

FIGURE 12.3   **Isorevenue Curves.**   Each isorevenue curve (IR) represents a constant amount of revenue and depicts the various combinations of products that could be sold to generate that level of revenue, given fixed product prices. The further an isorevenue curve is from the origin, the greater the revenue it represents. Thus, $IR_1 < IR_2 < IR_3$.

maximize profit (by maximizing revenue for a given cost) by producing the combination of outputs represented by point A. This is the point at which the product transformation curve is tangent to the isorevenue curve. If the firm uses more inputs (e.g., produces along PTC_2), the optimum combination of products would be determined by point B (assuming the original set of product prices).

Assume that the firm is producing at point B and that the price of jackets increases. The firm can now generate the same amount of revenue by selling any combination of products along IR_3. That is, the new isorevenue curve becomes IR_3. Note that, for example, this amount of revenue can be obtained by producing the combination of outputs represented by point E or by the combination represented by point C. Since the revenue is the same in

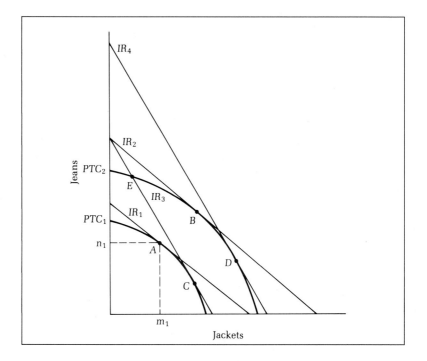

FIGURE 12.4   **Optimum Price Mix for Multiple Products: The Alternative Products Case.**   Given the set of resources associated with the lower product transformation curve (PTC_1) and the set of product prices that determines the first isorevenue line (IR_1), the optimum combination of outputs is determined at point A, where IR_1 is tangent to PTC_1. Similarly, with more resources (PTC_2) and the same set of product prices (see IR_2, which is parallel to IR_1), the optimum combination is determined at point B. Given PTC_2, if the price of jackets increases, the optimum combination of outputs would move to D. As expected, more jackets and fewer jeans would be in the optimum product mix.

each case, the firm would be wise to produce at point C because the amount of inputs used is less at C, and thus costs will be less as well, resulting in greater profits.

Given the increase in the price of denim jackets, another attractive alternative would be to maintain the original amount of input use (same cost, as well) but to switch to the combination of outputs represented by point D. With the new prices, the revenue generated at point D is indicated by IR_4 (which is parallel to IR_3). Clearly, $IR_4 > IR_3$; that is, it is farther from the origin and therefore represents a greater level of revenue. Since costs are the same at E and D, profits would be greater if the firm produced the combination of jackets and jeans represented by the point D.

Once the level of output for each product is determined using the approach outlined above, the firm will sell the product at the price determined by the demand curve for each product. In the case of perfectly competitive output markets (linear isorevenue functions), they simply set price equal to the market price. If the output market is imperfectly competitive, the price is determined by the firm's demand function for each of the products.

It should be noted that, while the models used in this section are applied to only two commodities, they can be generalized using mathematical functions to any number of multiple products.

Not only do many firms produce multiple products, but they also have multiple production facilities. So let us now turn our attention to the problem of how a firm should allocate production among alternative production facilities.

12.3 THE MULTIPLANT FIRM

The production manager of a multiplant firm faces the same type of allocation problem that faces a cartel (see Chapter 11). The firm should produce an additional unit as long as it can be produced at a marginal cost that is less than the marginal revenue from selling that unit. Further, in order to maximize profit for the entire firm, each additional unit should be produced at the plant that can produce the added unit most efficiently (i.e., at the lowest cost). Any number of plants could be used, but two are used here for ease of exposition. The algebraic problem that follows is shown in graphic form in Figure 12.5. You may find it helpful to refer to the graph as you follow the algebraic solution.

Assume that the firm in question faces the following demand for its product:

$$P = 15 - .5Q$$

Further, assume that the firm produces its product at two separate production facilities, A and B, with the following cost functions:

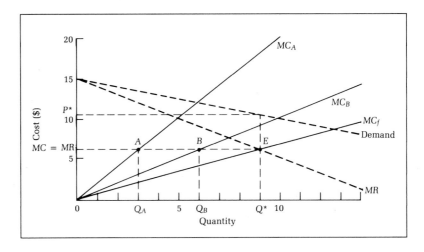

FIGURE 12.5   **Optimization for a Multiplant Firm.**   The manager of a multiplant firm would want to produce each successive unit in the plant that could produce the additional unit at a lower cost. This results in a marginal cost for the firm (MC_f) that is the horizontal sum of the marginal curves for the individual plants (i.e., $MC_A + MC_B$). The optimum output (Q^*) is determined by the intersection of MC_f and the firm's marginal revenue (MR). Price is then determined from the demand curve at P^*. The Q^* (9) units of output are allocated among plants so that the marginal cost in each plant is equal to the marginal revenue of the last unit produced ($MC = MR = \$6$). Thus, in this example, $Q_A = 3$ and $Q_B = 6$. We see that $Q_A + Q_B = Q^*$.

Plant A: $TC = Q_A^2$
Plant B: $TC = .5Q_B^2$

The marginal cost functions for the two plants are

Plant A: $MC = dTC/dQ_A = 2Q_A$
Plant B: $MC = dTC/dQ_B = Q_B$

Solving these for Q and adding, we get the firm's marginal cost curve allowing for production in plant A, plant B, or both:

$$Q_A = .5MC$$
plus
$$Q_B = MC$$
equals
$$Q = Q_A + Q_B = 1.5MC = \tfrac{3}{2}MC$$

Solving for MC, we have the marginal cost curve for the firm (including production at both plants):

$$MC_f = \tfrac{2}{3}Q$$

The firm's profit will be maximized by producing the level of output for which marginal cost is equal to marginal revenue (see point E in Figure 12.5). The latter can be found as follows:

$$TR = P \cdot Q$$
$$TR = (15 - .5Q)Q$$
$$TR = 15Q - .5Q^2$$
$$MR = dTR/dQ = 15 - Q$$

Setting marginal cost equal to marginal revenue, we solve for the profit-maximizing quantity:

$$\tfrac{2}{3}Q = 15 - Q$$
$$\tfrac{5}{3}Q = 15$$
$$Q^* = 9$$

If $Q^* = 9$, $MR = 6$. If we find the quantity for each plant at which that plant's marginal cost equals marginal revenue ($6), we will have the best allocation of the profit-maximizing output (9) among the plants (see points A and B in Figure 12.5). Algebraically, we can find the quantities from the marginal cost curves for each plant as expressed above as follows:

$$Q_A = .5MC = .5(6) = \boxed{3}$$
$$Q_B = MC = \boxed{6}$$

As we would expect, the total output of the two plants is equal to the profit-maximizing output for the firm.

Now, what price should the firm set? We know that $P = 15 - .5Q$, so $P^* = 15 - .5(9) = 10.5$. The firm's profit is equal to total revenue minus the total costs incurred in the two plants:

$$\pi = TR - TC_A - TC_B$$
$$\pi = P \cdot Q - Q_A^2 - .5Q_B^2$$
$$\pi = (10.5)(9) - 3^2 - .5(6)^2$$
$$\pi = 67.50$$

You may have noticed that this example of a multiplant firm is exactly the same as the two-firm cartel situation described in Chapter 11. The same functions have been used here to help you see that the allocation problem is really the same. It is just placed in a different context. The important point to realize is that decisions guided by marginal analysis will result in profit-maximizing outcomes regardless of the particular setting. In the following section, you will see yet another example of the usefulness of marginal analysis in an intrafirm decision situation.

12.4 TRANSFER PRICING

Many firms are faced with the problem of determining how much to charge for the transfer of a product from one division of the firm to another. This is most critical when each division is a separate profit center. As industry becomes more vertically integrated, this problem will be increasingly important. While a great deal can be said about transfer pricing, in a text on managerial economics only a limited amount of space can be allocated to this issue.[8] Our approach, therefore, will be to develop a general framework for analysis of the problem and to consider how some important market conditions influence the pricing policy established.

We shall focus our discussion in terms of an electric power company that owns a coal company. The power company can obtain coal from the mines it owns, from other coal-producing firms, or both. The coal company can sell coal to the parent company (the electric power firm), to other prospective buyers, or to both. The questions that must be answered are

1. How much coal should the power company buy in total?

2. How much of that coal should be purchased from the subsidiary, and how much should be purchased from other coal suppliers?

3. How much coal should the subsidiary produce?

4. How should the subsidiary's coal production be allocated between the parent company and other buyers?

5. At what price should the subsidiary sell coal to the parent company?

6. At what price should the subsidiary sell coal to other buyers?

The answers to these questions can be obtained by following the equimarginal principle that you have seen is so important to business-economic analysis. First, we must define the marginal relationships that impinge on this decision. Let us begin with the electric power company. It will demand more coal as long as the marginal net revenue from the electricity produced exceeds the added cost of purchasing coal. The marginal net revenue of the power company can be defined as the additional revenue from selling the added electricity minus the additional costs incurred for other (noncoal) factor inputs as the output level is expanded. We shall denote the marginal net revenue of the electric company *MNR*. To define *MNR*, we subtract a positively sloped function (marginal cost of noncoal

---

[8]For a classic discussion of transfer pricing, see Jack Hirschleifer, "On the Economics of Transfer Pricing," *Journal of Business*, July 1956, pp. 172–184.

inputs) from a negatively sloped function (marginal revenue); thus the *MNR* curve will be negatively sloped.

Now let us consider the coal-producing subsidiary. The marginal relationships for this firm will be influenced in part by the market conditions in the coal industry. In particular, we must consider whether the subsidiary sells coal in a perfectly or an imperfectly competitive market. One other possibility exists: it may not be in a position to sell any coal except to the parent company.[9] However, the marginal cost function for production will be the same regardless of the output market. The marginal cost function, *MC*, will be the typical positively sloped function.

No External Market for the Intermediate Good

In the simplest case, in which the coal-producing division has no outside market, the determination of the transfer price is straightforward. The relevant marginal relationships are shown in Figure 12.6. For the entire

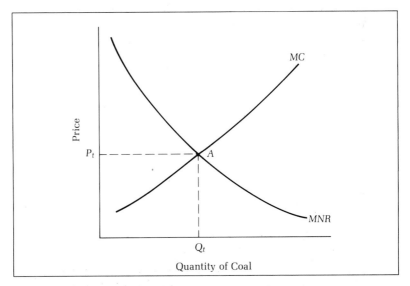

FIGURE 12.6 **Determination of the Transfer Price: No External Market for the Intermediate Good (Coal).** If the coal-producing division has no external market for its output, the entire corporation will maximize profit by transferring Q_T units of coal to the electric power division at a transfer price P_T. As long as *MNR* is greater than *MC*, profit will increase. As can be seen in the figure, this is true up to the output level associated with the point A, where $MNR = MC$.

---

[9]This situation may be unlikely for the current problem, but it may occur in cases in which there is no external market for the intermediate product. For this reason, it is prudent to discuss this possibility as well as the two more common cases.

corporation (including both divisions) profit will be maximized when the coal-producing division supplies the electric power division with Q_t units of coal at a price of P_t. At any quantity less than Q_t, the corporation adds more to marginal net revenue than to marginal cost and therefore makes a positive contribution to profit. For quantities greater than Q_t, the opposite is true. Thus, we reach an optimal solution using the equimarginal principle ($MNR = MC$, in this case).

Perfectly Competitive Market for the Intermediate Good

If we assume that the coal-producing division can sell coal in a perfectly competitive market as well as to the electric power division, the situation is only slightly more complex. Given the perfectly competitive nature of the output market, the coal division faces a horizontal demand curve, which is shown in Figure 12.7 as D. The marginal revenue for market sales of coal is shown as MR and, of course, equals the perfectly competitive price (P_m). Therefore, the marginal revenue function for the firm's coal division coincides with its demand curve.

For the electric power division, the optimum quantity of coal to purchase is again the amount at which MNR equals the subsidiary's marginal cost of producing the coal. Note, however, that since coal is produced in a perfectly competitive market, the effective marginal cost to the electric power company is the market price of coal.[10] If the marginal net revenue function is MNR, the power company should purchase Q_1 units of coal in order to maximize profit and should obtain the entire amount from the coal-producing division. The transfer price should be the market price P_m. It is important to recognize that the optimum transfer quantity is no longer where $MNR = MC$ (i.e., Q_2 in Figure 12.7) and that the optimum transfer price is not P_1, as was the case in the earlier example. The change is a result of the alternative possibility of selling coal at a higher price in the external market.

The coal-producing division will produce a total of Q_3 units because, up to that point, $MR > MC$ for that division. Of the total output (Q_3 units), Q_1 units will be transferred to the electric power division at a transfer price, P_m, and the remaining units ($Q_3 - Q_1$) will be sold in the external market at the same price.

Consider what would happen if the demand for electricity increased, causing the marginal net revenue function to shift to $MNR *$.[11] The coal-

---

[10]It is assumed that there is no monopsonistic influence in the market for coal. That is, the electric power division buys a very small fraction of the economy's total output of coal and thus has no effect on the market price.

[11]The same effect on the relationship between the functions illustrated in Figure 12.7 would occur if the market price of coal fell to a price less than P_1.

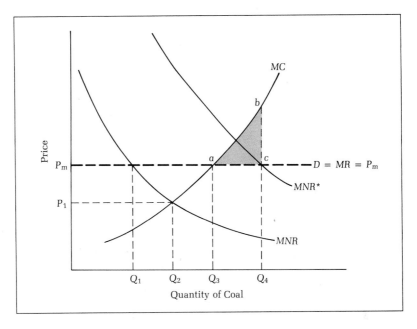

FIGURE 12.7   **Determination of the Market Transfer Price: Intermediate Good (Coal) Sold in a Perfectly Competitive Market.**   The coal-producing division can sell coal at the market price P_m, and the electric power division can buy coal in the market at that price. Given the lower MNR function, the electric power division will want to use more coal as long as $MNR > P_m$ and so would buy Q_1 units. All Q_1 units will be purchased from the coal-producing division at the transfer price P_m. The coal-producing division will produce Q_3 units (where $P_m = MC$), selling the extra production in the external market.

producing division would continue to produce Q^3 units, since that is the output level at which $MR = MC$. However, the power company would now want to purchase Q_4 units (where $MNR^* = P_m =$ the effective marginal cost of coal, as described above). It would get Q_3 units from the coal-producing division (its entire output) at a transfer price of P_m. The remaining $(Q_4 - Q_3)$ units would be purchased in the open market at a price of P_m. If the power company bought all its coal from the subsidiary in this case, the total cost of coal would be higher (by the amount of the triangle abc) than when it purchases some in the open market (assuming the firm continued to use Q_4 units).

Imperfectly Competitive Market for the Intermediate Good

The final case of transfer pricing involves the situation in which the division producing the intermediate product (coal) sells in an imperfectly competitive market as well as to another division of the same corporation (the electric power company). Under these circumstances, the coal-producing division faces a negatively sloped demand function (D) for sales in the external market and, correspondingly, a marginal revenue curve (MR) that has a negative slope and lies below the demand curve. These functions are illustrated in Figure 12.8.

For the entire corporation, additional revenue can be obtained either by selling coal in the external market or by transferring coal to the electric power division and selling the electricity produced. Thus, the effective marginal revenue function is the horizontal sum of the marginal revenue functions for the two separate markets in which the coal can be sold ($MNR + MR$). Furthermore, the corporation will maximize profit by producing coal up to the point at which the effective marginal revenue equals marginal cost, or up to Q_O units, in Figure 12.8.

Having determined the optimum quantity of coal to produce, we must determine how much should be transferred to the power company and at what transfer price, as well as how much should be sold and at what price in the external market. This can be accomplished by allocating the coal so that the marginal revenue from each market is equal to the marginal cost of producing the Q_O units. That is, MNR should equal MC, and MR should equal MC (i.e., $MNR = MR = MC$). If this was not true, some reallocation would be profitable.

The result of this method of allocation is shown in Figure 12.8. The quantity to be sold in the external market is Q_m, and the quantity to be transferred to the electric power division is Q_T. The optimum output, Q_O, of course, is equal to $Q_m + Q_T$. The external, or open market, demand function (D) indicates that the coal-producing division can sell Q_m units at a price of P_m. The quantity to be transferred (Q_T) will be sold at the transfer price P_T, and the transfer price will ensure that the electric power division will demand Q_T units. Note that, as in the other models of transfer pricing, the transfer price equals the marginal cost of producing the coal.

An Algebraic Example of Transfer Pricing

In this section, we will work through an example of a transfer pricing situation, first assuming that the intermediate product is sold in a perfectly competitive output market, and then assuming that the market for the intermediate good is imperfectly competitive.

The firm that produces the final product is Bio Industries (BI). Bio Industries purchases a major input Q from a subsidiary. The marginal net revenue (MNR) function for BI is[12]

---

[12]Recall that MNR is the marginal revenue minus the marginal cost of all other inputs. To simplify the algebra necessary, assume that each unit of Bio Industry's final product uses one unit of the transferred input.

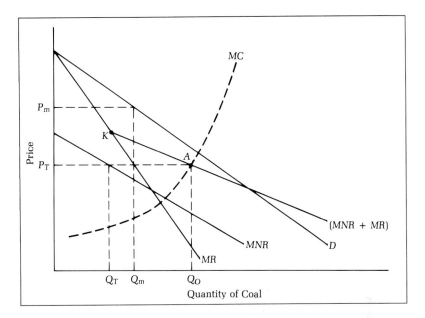

FIGURE 12.8   **Determination of the Transfer Price: Intermediate Good (Coal) Sold in an Imperfectly Competitive Market.**   The effective marginal revenue function for the firm in this case is the horizontal sum of the MNR function and the MR from sales to the external market. The optimum output Q_O units is found where $MNR + MR = MC$ (see point A). These Q_O should be allocated such that $MR = MC$ and $MNR = MC$. Doing this, we see that Q_T units should be transferred to the electric power division and that Q_m units should be sold in the external market. The transfer price will be P_T (which equals MC), and the units sold in the external market are priced from that demand curve (D) at the price P_m.

$$MNR = 200 - Q_T$$

where Q_T indicates units of the intermediate product to be used by BI. The subsidiary that produces the intermediate product (Q) has the following total cost function:

$$TC = .25Q^2$$

This information is important to both the cases we will evaluate.

In the first case, it is assumed that the intermediate product is sold in a perfectly competitive market. The basic model for this situation is described by Figure 12.7 and the related discussion in the text. Let us assume that the market price for the intermediate good is $8. The subsidiary should produce the good up to the point at which its marginal cost is equal to the $8 market price. The marginal cost is found as

$$TC = .25Q^2$$
$$MC = dTC/dQ$$
$$MC = .5Q$$

Setting $MC = P$, we have

$$MC = P$$
$$.5Q = 8$$
$$Q = 16$$

Thus, we find that the subsidiary should produce 16 units of the intermediate product.

To find how much BI should purchase, we equate its MNR with the market price. Thus,

$$MNR = \$8$$
$$200 - Q_T = \$8$$
$$Q_T = 192$$

We see that BI should purchase 192 units of the intermediate product, only 16 of which should come from its subsidiary. The transfer price should be equal to the $8 market price. This situation is the same as that in Figure 12.7, for which the operative marginal net revenue function is MNR^*.

Now let us turn to a case that is a bit more complex, but also more interesting and more realistic. We shall change our market structure assumption to one in which the subsidiary can sell the intermediate product either in an imperfectly competitive external market or to Bio Industries. We shall subscript the quantity variable to help keep track of what is sold in the external market (Q_m) and what is transferred to BI (Q_T).

From the model described in Figure 12.8, we know that we must find a composite marginal revenue curve (MR_c) by adding together the MNR and the marginal revenue from the external market (MR). We need, then, to know more about the external market. Assume that the external demand is

$$P_m = 400 - 2Q_m$$

Total revenue from sales to the external market is, then,

$$TR_m = P_m \cdot Q_m$$
$$TR_m = (400 - 2Q_m)Q_m$$
$$TR_m = 400Q_m - 2Q_m^2$$

Marginal revenue from the external market must be

$$MR_m = dTR_m/dQ_m$$
$$MR_m = 400 - 4Q_m$$

The marginal net revenue was given above as

$$MNR = 200 - Q_T$$

Solving these for Q_m and Q_T, respectively, we obtain

$$Q_m = 100 - .25MR_m$$
$$Q_T = 200 - MNR$$

Adding these functions, we get the composite marginal revenue curve (remember that MR_m, MNR, and MR are dollars per unit):

$$Q = Q_m + Q_T$$
$$Q = 300 - 1.25MR_c$$

Solving this for MR_c, we have[13]

$$MR_c = 240 - .8Q$$

Remember that the subsidiary's marginal cost was found above as

$$MC = dTC/dQ$$
$$MC = .5Q$$

Now we can equate the composite marginal revenue with the marginal cost to obtain the optimal quantity:

$$MR_c = MC$$
$$240 - .8Q = .5Q$$
$$-1.3Q = -240$$
$$Q = 184.62$$

This corresponds to Q_O in Figure 12.8 and represents the total amount of the intermediate product that the subsidiary should produce.

The marginal cost of production at the level found (i.e., at $Q = 184.62$) is

$$MC = .5(184.62)$$
$$MC = 92.31$$

The output of 184.62 units should be allocated to the external market (Q_m) and to the parent company (Q_T) according to the equimarginal principle that

$$MC = MR_m = MNR$$

This yields

$$Q_m = 100 - .25MR_m$$
$$Q_m = 100 - .25(92.31)$$
$$Q_m = 76.92$$

---

[13]While we show this composite marginal revenue as a single continuous equation for ease of exposition, there is actually a kink in the function, as illustrated in Figure 12.8, at point K. The equation used here is valid only to the right of the kink (for $Q \geqslant 50$, in this case). To the left of the kink, MR_c is equal to the marginal revenue for the external market (for $Q \leqslant 50$, $MR_c = 400 - 4Q$).

$$Q_T = 200 - MNR$$
$$Q_T = 200 - 92.31$$
$$Q_T = 107.69$$

The units transferred to BI ($Q_T = 107.69$) should be charged at a transfer price equal to the marginal cost of \$92.31 (see P_T in Figure 12.8). The 76.92 units sold in the external market (Q_m) should be priced from the external market's demand function. Thus,

$$P_m = 400 - 2Q_m$$
$$P_m = 400 - 2(76.92)$$
$$P_m = 246.16$$

12.5   LIMIT PRICING

In some situations, one or more existing firms in an industry may be in a position in which the profit-maximizing price would attract new entrants into the industry. This type of situation is probably most common in oligopolistic industries but is not limited to that market structure. In such cases, there may well be a lower price that would discourage entry but still yield a positive economic profit for existing firms.

Such a situation is illustrated by the graph in Figure 12.9. Suppose a given number of existing firms share the total market in roughly equal proportions and that each existing firm has a demand function such as D in Figure 12.9. Their marginal revenue curves would then be like MR.

We will assume that the industry is well represented by the long-run average cost curve $LRAC$. Further, we will assume that the existing firms are operating at a scale represented by the short-run average cost $SRAC_E$ and short-run marginal cost $SRMC_E$. Given this scenario, the profit-maximizing price and quantity would be P^* and Q^*, respectively.

If new firms could be expected to enter at the scale represented by $SRAC_N$, they could do so and earn a positive economic profit at the price established by the existing firms (P^*). However, existing firms may realize that the present value of their long-run profits may be greater if they lower price to prevent entry, even at the cost of some short-run profit.[14] Suppose, for example, that existing firms set price at P_L. They would still earn positive economic profit, since at the sales level Q_L average cost is less than the corresponding price (P_L). However, at this lower price (P_L, which lies below the short-run average cost of a potential entrant), entry is effectively blocked. Existing firms can limit entry in this way.

Even if existing firms are charging a price that is above $SRAC_N$ at some point or points, entry may not be advisable. If existing firms maintain

---

[14]The discount rate used in determining the present value of long-run profits will be instrumental in determining whether a limit pricing policy should be followed.

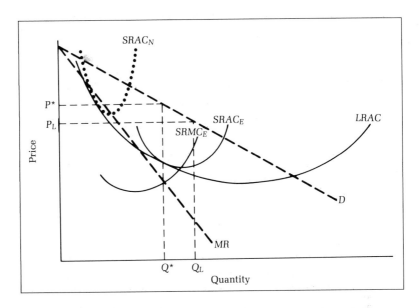

FIGURE 12.9   **Illustration of Limit Pricing.**   The profit-maximizing output for an existing firm is Q^*, where $MR = MC$, and the corresponding price is P^*. If a new firm could enter the industry at the scale represented by $SRAC_N$, it could also earn a profit at the existing price, P^*. However, if existing firms price at a level below the minimum of $SRAC_N$, profitable entry can be precluded. This reduces the short-run profits of existing firms but could increase long-run profits by preventing dilution of the product market.

current levels of production in the face of new competition, price can be expected to fall, since the total production would then surpass the total demand at that price. The demand curve for existing firms would shift to the left as the new entrant captured part of the market. In order to sell the Q^* units, price would have to be lowered. If this occurred and if price fell to below a minimum point on $SRAC_N$, the new entrant would again incur an economic loss.

SUMMARY

This chapter reviewed some pricing topics that cross the bounds of market structures. Cost-plus pricing was discussed as a common form of price determination based on the cost side of ledger, with little attention to the demand side. In many situations, it is difficult to determine exactly what costs should be included in the basis of a cost-plus price. It is essential to consider only the relevant costs, but all the relevant costs.

Once the appropriate cost basis is determined, the correct markup must be established. Sometimes an industry norm is followed, and sometimes the markup is determined to achieve a specified rate of return. The use of cost-plus pricing can be consistent with profit-maximizing behavior.

Many firms produce multiple products. In the type of situation described by the beef and hides example (i.e., jointly produced products), multiple products are considered as a product package consisting of two or more separate products. To determine the profit-maximizing quantity of product packages to produce, the firm's marginal revenue is equated with its marginal cost. But here, there is a different twist to finding the correct marginal revenue function. Since the products have separate demand curves but are jointly produced, the firm's marginal revenue is the vertical sum of the marginal revenue functions associated with the individual product demand curves.

Not only do many firms produce more than one product, many also produce in multiple production facilities. This adds another dimension to mangerial decision making: How should production be allocated among plants? This problem is like the problem of allocating production among cartel members discussed in Chapter 11. Output should be allocated among plants such that the marginal cost in each plant is equal to marginal revenue at the profit-maximizing rate of production. That level of production is determined by the familiar rule that MR = MC. For multiplant firms, the appropriate marginal cost is the horizontal sum of the marginal cost for each separate production facility.

With vertically integrated firms, yet another pricing-output decision must be made: What price should be charged when one division of a firm transfers a product to another division? The appropriate transfer price is always equal to the marginal cost of producing the transferred product (at the optimal rate of production). The number of units to be produced and the number of units to be transferred depend in part on the market structure involved. In some cases, there is no external market for the product; but usually there is an external market, and it is likely to be imperfectly competitive. Thus, the situation described by Figure 12.8 is particularly important. The product should be produced up to the point at which the effective marginal revenue function equals marginal cost. The effective marginal revenue is the horizontal sum of the marginal net revenue (MNR) function (for transferred products) and the marginal revenue (MR) function related to external sales. The amount to be transferred is found where MNR = MC and the transfer price is equal to that level of marginal cost. The amount to be sold externally is found where MR = MC, and it is priced from the external demand function.

Finally, this chapter discussed the concept of limit pricing. In some situations, it may be better to charge a price below the profit-maximizing price in order to discourage new entrants into the market. This reduces short-run profit but could, in fact, increase profit over the long-run.

SUGGESTED READINGS

Burck, Gilbert. "The Myths and Realities of Corporate Pricing." *Fortune*, April 1972, p. 85.

Clemens, E. "Price Discrimination and the Multiple Product Firm." *Review of Economics and Statistics*, vol. 19, 1950–1951.

Griffin, James M. "The Econometrics of Joint Production: Another Approach." *Review of Economics and Statistics*, vol. 59, 1977, pp. 389–397.

Hirshleifer, Jack. "On the Economics of Transfer Pricing." *Journal of Business*, July 1956, pp. 172–184.

Lovell, C.A.K., and Sicklen, R.C. "Testing Efficiency Hypotheses in Joint Production." *Review of Economics and Statistics*. vol. 65, 1983, pp. 51–58.

Silberston, Aubrey. "Surveys of Applied Economics: Price Behaviour of Firms." *The Economic Journal*, September 1970, pp. 511–582.

Weston, J. Fred. "Pricing Behavior of Large Firms." *Western Economic Journal*, March 1972, pp. 1–18.

Wheeley, Otto. "Pricing Policy and Objectives." In Elizabeth Marting, ed., *Creative Pricing*, New York: American Management Association, 1968, pp. 27–38.

PROBLEMS

1. Berman and Company produces a product that currently sells for $16. The unit costs for producing the product are:

Materials	$ 5.10
Direct labor	3.20
Overhead	4.00
Sales expense	2.10
	$14.40

   These unit costs are based on sales of $100,000 units per year. Berman's plant capacity is generally accepted to be 150,000 units per year. A foreign retail chain has contacted Berman with an offer to purchase 60,000 units on a short-term basis during the next year at a price of $13.00 each. Sales of these units in the foreign market would not have any effect on Berman's domestic market. Should the offer be accepted? Explain why or why not. Identify any assumptions you make in answering the question.

2. The Brown Pipe Company produces a product that has considerable competition in the marketplace, since there are a number of close substitutes and little substantive product differentiation. Brown has fixed

costs of $200,000 and average variable costs of $5. The total potential market is estimated at 1 million units. Mr Brown, president of the company, would like to maintain a 10-percent share of the market; and his plant has ample capacity.

    a. What price would enable Brown to break even at a sales volume representing 10 percent of the market (you may want to refer to the discussion of break-even analysis in Chapter 9)?

    b. Suppose that Brown wants to obtain a profit equal to 20 percent of fixed cost. Now what price should be charged?

3. A large plumbing supply wholesaler that usually produces its own pipe has run short due to a flood that curtailed production in its pipe factory. Mr. Callup, the purchasing agent for the wholesaler, calls Mr. Lavue, the sales manager for the Brown Pipe Company (see problem 2), and offers to buy 2000 units of pipe at $5.50 per unit. Mr. Lavue tells him that such a deal is out of the question, since their current average cost is $7 per unit. However, since Brown has excess capacity, Lavue makes a counteroffer to sell the 2000 units at $7.35, just 5 percent over cost. Mr. Callup refuses the offer and strikes a deal with another manufacturer. At a weekly staff meeting, Mr. Lavue relates the above to Mr. Brown and others. If you were Mr. Brown, what would you say about Lavue's actions? What would you have done in Mr. Lavue's position? Why?

4. The Yellow Bay Woolen Company (YBW) makes high-quality wool sweaters in three facilities, all of which are in the Yellow Bay area. The three production facilities are fairly similar except for the age of equipment used in each. The total cost functions for the three factories are given by the following:

$$\text{Factory 1:} \quad TC = 800 + .2Q^2$$
$$\text{Factory 2:} \quad TC = 1000 + .1Q^2$$
$$\text{Factory 3:} \quad TC = 900 + .15Q^2$$

Ann Folberg, founder and president of YBW, has hired an outside consultant to estimate the demand for the firm's sweaters. The consultant reports that the demand function is

$$P = 100 - .05Q$$

    a. Assume that Ann Folberg has hired you as the production manager. You are to report to her on the quantity of output that will maximize YBW's profit and the price that should be set to assure the corresponding level of sales:

$$Q = \underline{\hspace{6cm}}$$

$$P = \underline{\hspace{6cm}}$$

b. How many sweaters should be produced at each plant?

Q_1 = _____

Q_2 = _____

Q_3 = _____

c. Find the total profit for YBW, given your solution above:

Profit = _____

d. Calculate the point price elasticity of demand, given the price and quantity found above:

ep = _____

Based on this elasticity, what would happen to total revenue if price was increased? What if price were lowered? Would either raising or lowering price increase profits? Explain.

5. The Grownrite division of Glendale Company, a tomato canning company, grows tomatoes. The firm must determine the transfer price for tomatoes and the number of tomatoes Glendale should purchase from Grownrite as well as the total amount Grownrite should produce. The marginal net revenue (MNR) for Glendale has been estimated as

$$MNR = 100 - 2Q$$

and the marginal cost (MC) of producing tomatoes has been estimated as

$$MC = .5Q$$

Tomatoes are sold in what is essentially a perfectly competitive market, and the current market price is $10 per crate.

a. What should the transfer price be for tomatoes sold to Glendale by the Grownrite division?

b. What quantity of tomatoes should Grownrite produce?

c. What quantity of tomatoes should Glendale purchase in total?

d. If your answers to parts b and c are different, explain why. Also explain where Glendale should get any tomatoes it does not get from Grownrite (if $c > b$) and at what price; or if $b > c$, explain what Grownrite will do with the excess production not purchased by Glendale.

e. How would your answers to parts a, b, c, and d change if a late spring frost damaged the tomato crop such that the market price was pushed up to $30 per crate due to the shortfall in supply?

6. Zook Manufacturing (ZM) produces generators that are used primarily for backup power in hospitals and other health care facilities. The

copper wire used in these generators can be obtained from a subsidiary of ZM, the M & M Wire Company. The marginal net revenue function for Zook is

$$MNR = 210 - Q$$

where Q is measured in thousands of feet of copper wire used in manufacturing generators. M & M Wire Company has the following total cost function:

$$TC = .2Q^2$$

where, again, Q is in thousands of feet of copper wire.

a.   Assume that initially, since there is no other market available to M & M, they sell wire only to Zook and that M & M is the only supplier Zook has available. What should be the transfer price?

b.   How many thousand feet of wire should be transferred?

7.   Continuing the Zook Manufacturing example introduced in problem 6, assume that the market for copper wire is perfectly competitive. The market demand and supply functions are:

Market demand: $P = 20 - .00005Q$
Market supply: $P = 4 + .00005Q$

a.   What is the market price for copper wire?

Market price = $ _____

b.   What should be the transfer price between M & M and Zook?

Transfer price = $ _____

c.   How many units of copper wire should Zook purchase from M & M?

Quantity transferred = _____

d.   How many units should M & M produce?

M & M production = _____

8.   Continuing the example from problems 6 and 7, assume that M & M sells copper wire in an imperfectly competitive market and that M & M's external demand function has been estimated as

External demand: $P = 400 - Q$

a.   How many units of copper wire should M & M produce?

M & M production = _____

b. How many units should be transferred between M & M and Zook?

Quantity transferred = _____

c. At what price should these units be transferred?

Transfer price = $ _____

d. How many units will M & M sell to other buyers, and at what price?

M & M external sales = _____

External sales price = _____

9. Elk Stoves makes highly efficient wood-burning stoves and fireplace inserts that are marketed throughout the Northwest. Two production facilities are currently in use, one of which was opened six months ago. Data have been collected that provide the basis for the marginal cost estimates given below:

Q	MC	
	Old Plant	New Plant
40	180	60
60	255	120
80	300	150
100	390	180
120	510	260
140	595	300
160	650	320
180	700	355
200	810	410
220	880	450

a. Use these values to estimate linear marginal cost functions for both production facilities.

New plant: MC = _____ + _____ Q R^2 = _____

(   ) t-ratio

Old plant: MC = _____ + _____ Q R^2 = _____

(   ) t-ratio

b. The following 10 observations constitute a representative sample that can be used to estimate Elk Stoves' demand function:

P	Q	P	Q
570	60	440	220
529	120	430	280
555	160	420	340
550	210	405	380
500	200	400	390

Based on these observations, use regression analysis to estimate the linear demand function:

$$P = \underline{\hspace{2cm}} - \underline{\hspace{2cm}} Q \quad R^2 = \underline{\hspace{2cm}}$$
$$(\underline{\hspace{3cm}}) \, t\text{-ratio}$$

c. Using the marginal cost functions derived above, formulate Elk Stoves' combined marginal cost curve:

$$MC = \underline{\hspace{3cm}} + \underline{\hspace{3cm}} Q$$

d. Find the total number of units Elk Stoves should produce to maximize profits:

$$Q = \underline{\hspace{5cm}}$$

How should these units be allocated between the two plants?

Old plant: $Q = \underline{\hspace{4cm}}$

New plant: $Q = \underline{\hspace{4cm}}$

e. Plot the data and equations you have derived on the grid below:

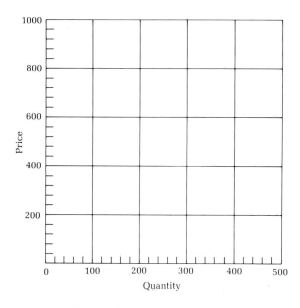

f. How would you respond to someone who suggested that the entire production take place in the new plant, since its marginal cost curve is lower than that of the old plant at every point?

10. Assume that Corby Corporation wishes to assign salespeople to each of its three markets. The salespeople can be hired from a pool of

persons with similar talents, but the salespeople are subject to diminishing returns as more are assigned to a given market area. The salespeople are paid a fixed salary of $11,500 regardless of where they work. Based on past data, Corby estimates the following sales, dependent on the number of salespeople assigned to the area:

Total Number of Salespeople in Area	Total Profit by Area ($ thousands)		
	1	2	3
0	0	0	0
1	15	12	14
2	29	23	27
3	42	33	39
4	54	42	50
5	65	50	60
6	75	57	69
7	83	63	77
8	88	65	83

a. What is the total number of salespeople Corby will hire?
b. How will the salespeople be allocated among the three sales regions? What is the economic basis of these allocations?
c. In a real-world situation, would you expect the assumption used here of diminishing returns to a factor (i.e., the salesperson) to hold? Explain.
d. What would the company do if the market wages of salespeople rose to $12,100 and the company was forced to pay this wage to hire them? How would the company react if the wage rate fell to $10,100?
e. Would it make sense for the firm to concentrate on a single market area in order to saturate the area with salespeople and capture all the sales in that one area? Why might market areas in the real world differ with respect to the marginal productivity of salespeople of similar ability?

11. A potato processor produces dehydrated instant mashed potatoes and starch (a by-product) from raw potatoes. The total cost function for the firm is

$$TC = 500 + 3Q + 3Q^2$$

where Q is the quantity of the instant potatoes–starch package. The demand functions for the two products are

$$Q_I = 800 - 1P_I$$
$$Q_S = 150 - 1P_S$$

Assume that the company produces one unit of mashed potatoes for each unit of starch.

a. What price per unit would be charged for instant mashed potatoes?

b. What price per unit would be charged for starch?

c. Assuming that the company produces two units of mashed potatoes for each unit of starch, what prices would be charged for each product?

12. Bigham Fabricating is currently the only producer of a new alloy that can be used to make exceptionally strong automotive bumpers of about 60 percent of the weight of conventional bumpers, but at roughly the same dollar cost per bumper as for the conventional product. From related production experiences, the industry long-run average cost has been estimated and is graphed below as $LRAC$. The current short-run marginal and average cost functions for Bigham are also graphed and are labeled $SRMC_B$ and $SRAC_B$, respectively. A new entrant into this industry could probably not enter at a scale greater than that represented by $SRAC_N$.

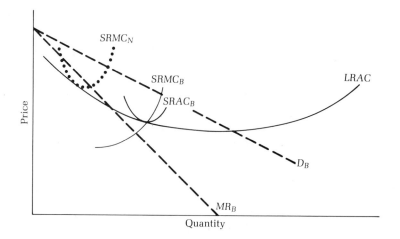

a. Based on these graphs, indicate on the graph the profit-maximizing level of output for Bigham and the corresponding price.

b. Could a new firm profitably enter the industry at this price? Why or why not?

c. Indicate on the graph a price that would allow Bigham to make a profit but that would prevent the new entrant from operating at a profit.

d. Suppose someone suggested that Bigham should operate with the objective of maximizing revenue rather than profit from the sale of this new alloy. Indicate the corresponding price and level of sales on the graph. What effect would this have on profit?

13. Blitzen Breweries produces its product at three locations. The marginal costs of producing the product at each of these locations and the demand schedule are given in the following table:

Output or Sales per Time Period	Price per Unit	MC of Plant 1	MC of Plant 2	MC of Plant 3
0	$1.60			
1	1.50	$.08	$.08	$.06
2	1.40	.10	.09	.10
3	1.30	.15	.10	.14
4	1.20	.20	.11	.18
5	1.10	CAPACITY	.13	CAPACITY
6	1.00		.16	
7	.90		CAPACITY	
8	.80			
9	.70			
10	.60			

a. What price will Blitzen use to maximize profits?
b. How will Blitzen allocate production among the three available plants in order to maximize profits? Explain the economic basis of these allocations.

14. Sounds-Right (S-R) is a major manufacturer of stereo equipment for the automotive market. S-R has three production facilities, each with somewhat different cost structures because of different distribution costs and varying ages of the production facilities. Carol Miller has recently been promoted to the position of production manager and is interested in allocating production among the three plants in such a way as to maximize Sounds-Right's profits. S-R's demand has been determined to be

$$P = 800 - .2Q$$

The three plants have the following marginal cost functions:

Plant 1: $MC = 20 + .2Q$
Plant 2: $MC = 10 + .4Q$
Plant 3: $MC = 20 + .4Q$

a. What is the appropriate marginal cost curve for S-R's production of automotive stereo equipment if the objective is to maximize S-R's profit?

$MC = $ _____ + _____ Q

b. What is the total level of output Sounds-Right should produce?

$Q =$ _____

c. What price should be charged?

$P =$ _____

d. Determine the quantity that should be produced at each of the three plants:

Plant 1: _____

Plant 2: _____

Plant 3: _____

e. Calculate the marginal cost of production at each plant, given the solution you found above:

$MC_1 =$ _____

$MC_2 =$ _____

$MC_3 =$ _____

Explain the importance of the relationship you observe in these marginal cost values.

13

Economic Regulation of Business

Virtually all industries and individual corporations in the United States today are subject to some regulations or regulatory agency of the federal government. This has not always been so; only in the last 50 years or so has government regulatory activity escalated to touch every nook and cranny of business activity. While any list of regulated industries is hardly complete—new ones are constantly on the horizon—the following is impressive because of its inclusiveness: drugs, airlines, railroads, trucking, communications, banking, utilities, medicine, automobiles, toys, farming, construction, and accounting. The objective of this chapter is not to offer a complete description and rationale of individual regulations and regulatory agencies, but, rather, to describe the theory of regulation and to examine a few of the more important regulatory areas in terms of their impact on business decisions.

13.1 WHY REGULATE? THE PUBLIC INTEREST RATIONALE

If you were to ask people involved with making and enforcing regulations about the reason for a particular regulation (which regulation makes little difference) you would likely be told that "this regulation is in the public interest: society is better off with the regulation than without it." This theory of regulation (the most commonly held theory or reason for regulation) could be called the *public interest theory* of regulation. According to this line of reasoning, the free market must be restrained or regulated in order to protect unwary consumers from unscrupulous producers and sellers and to protect us all in situations in which the market may affect people other than those directly involved.

Two assumptions are inherent in the public interest theory of regulation: (1) economic markets are extremely fragile, and most markets operate inefficiently and inequitably if left alone; and (2) government regulation is virtually costless.[1] If these assumptions are accepted, it is easy to argue that government interventions in markets are justified by public demand for efficiency and equity in those markets. Presumably, each regulation or regulatory agency comes about because of some market imperfection.

This critique of the market in which unwanted outcomes affect uninvolved parties seems valid. For example, if a paint factory is near a housing project and, in the process of making paint, emits fumes that discolor the houses in the neighborhood, we could say there is a *neighborhood effect*, or an *externality*. A neighborhood effect (or externality) is a situation in which uninvolved parties (the homeowners) are affected by the actions of some market participant (the paint factory). Most of us would agree that some adjustment of the market process might be in order in this situation, but the question remains whether any particular regulations or adjustments would produce a better result than the market itself.

In most cases, when you own a business, you make decisions about what to produce, what prices to charge, how many employees to hire, and other matters that determine the smooth operation of the firm. If you are a purchaser in a market, you decide whether to buy from any particular firm. Situations in which business owners and buyers are allowed to make independent decisions are called free markets. But price-output decisions often come under the control of such government regulatory agencies as the Civil Aeronautics Board (CAB), the Interstate Commerce Commission (ICC), and the Federal Communications Commission (FCC).

Why do we feel it necessary to have government intervene in the free market? Why can't anyone own a radio station? Why can't furniture be moved from state to state by anyone willing to do the job? Why can't all firms be allowed to choose the prices at which they attempt to sell their products? The common answer is that the market sometimes does not operate the way we would like it to, and adjustments are required. Government is thought to be able to do a better job than the unregulated interaction of market participants. Situations like the paint factory case above fall into a category of situations termed *market failure*. The public interest theory of regulation holds that market failure should be corrected by government regulatory action.

Why is it, however, that markets fail? Clearly, one type of failure is a case in which a desired good is not produced or not produced in sufficient quantity. Suppose a firm begins producing electronic digital watches. As the only seller of digital watches, the company commands a measure of monopoly power in the short run and is able to restrict output and charge higher than competitive prices. The existence of only a single firm in the

---

[1]You may wish to read the survey of regulation theory by Richard Posner, an article detailing many of the points made here: Richard A. Posner, "Theories of Economic Regulation," *Bell Journal of Economics and Management Science*, Autumn 1974, pp. 335–358.

market is an example of market failure because the firm is able to sell its watches at prices in excess of competitive market prices.

Is this a case in which the government ought to regulate the digital watch industry (which now, hypothetically, consists of only one company)? The need for any government intervention is dependent on the probability that competition and its resulting outcome will emerge from the market. With an absence of controls in the digital watch industry, will the single firm be the only seller of this popular product next year? This is the crucial question—it is not nearly as important that a situation deviates from the competitive optimum as it is whether the situation will or will not remain at wide variance with the competitive outcome. It is also quite important to analyze whether government regulation in the digital watch market is less costly than leaving the situation alone. Even though far from perfect, many markets might be even further from a competitive outcome with regulation.

If the public interest theory of regulation were a correct description of reality, we would find most regulatory effort in highly concentrated industries (to correct the inefficiencies of monopoly) and in industries in which externalities generate relatively large external costs or benefits. *We do not.* [2] Recent research indicates that regulation is *not* correlated positively with either monopolistic market structure or external economies or diseconomies. Do you believe, for instance, that in the airline industry there was some underlying reason that required prices and entry to be regulated by a government agency? Other heavily regulated industries beg the same question; consider taxi service, stock brokerages, ocean shipping, and massage parlors. The very term *market failure* has been questioned in regard to such industries as health care and the legal profession. Since government regulation is not actually costless, when costs of altering markets are examined, the term *government failure* may be more appropriate than market failure. [3] Government action is no longer thought of as a costless and dependable way of altering markets. The growing body of regulations cannot be explained by the simple public interest theory of regulation.

13.2   WHY REGULATE? THE ECONOMIC RATIONALE

The theory of regulation replacing the public interest theory is called the *economic theory of regulation*. The economic theory of regulation does not assume the legislative purpose of serving the public interest but admits that

---

[2] *Ibid.*, p. 336.

[3] J. Hirshleifer, J.C. DeHaven, and J. Millman, *Water Supply: Economics, Technology, and Policy* (Chicago: University of Chicago Press, 1960); and R.A. Posner, "Natural Monopoly and Its Regulation," *Stanford Law Review*, February 1969, pp. 548–643.

interest groups in society may effectively be served by economic regulation.[4] The economic theory of regulation is based on the strong assumption that individuals seek to advance their own self-interest. Two important insights distinguish this view of regulation from the public interest theory: (1) the coercive power of government can be used to give special consideration to individuals or industries, and these special considerations can be viewed as a product produced by the government; and (2) the theory of oligopoly and cartels may tell us how that product (special consideration) will be produced and distributed.

When special consideration is viewed as a product, as Richard Posner and George Stigler view it, we should expect the product to be supplied to those who value it the most. Oligopoly theory tells us that the less elastic the price elasticity of demand for the product, the greater the benefits of forming a cartel (see Chapter 11). But cartels are quite fragile or unstable *unless* members are unable to conceal their activities from one another. However, regulation provides the framework for industry members to agree openly on cartellike devices (e.g., entry control, minimum prices, and exemption from antitrust regulation). All the members of the industry must agree on the regulation (or, at least, obey the regulation); this ensures that there is a way of overcoming the inherent weakness of cartels, which nearly always have at least one member who would be better off cheating on the rules. In a regulatory setting, "cheating on the cartel" would be prohibited. Oligopoly-cartel theory is, then, at the heart of the economic theory of regulation. The growing body of economic evidence now suggests that the view of economic regulation as a product supplied to interest groups is a better mirror of reality than is the view of regulation as an expression of the social interest in efficiency or justice.[5]

The remainder of this chapter employs the economic theory of regulation to discuss the following three areas of regulation: antitrust theory, internalizing externalities (i.e., managing the environment), and consumer product regulation.

Action to regulate the hypothetical single-company digital watch industry mentioned above is an example of regulation to eliminate monopoly power and falls into a category of regulatory activity called *antitrust theory*. This area of regulation is the primary focus of the rest of this chapter.

Government action is also introduced into markets as a means of *internalizing externalities*. If government chose to regulate a paint factory

---

[4]The economic theory of regulation is expressed in these sources: G. Stigler, "The Theory of Economic Regulation," *Bell Journal of Economics and Management Science*, Spring 1971, pp. 3–21; J. Buchanan and G. Tullock, *The Calculus of Consent* (Ann Arbor: University of Michigan Press, 1962); M. Olson, Jr., *The Logic of Collective Action* (Cambridge, MA: Harvard University Press, 1965).

[5]Posner, "Theories of Economic Regulation," p. 350.

because the firm generated negative effects on local homeowners, the regulation would fall into the category of internalizing externalities. External effects (externalities), of course, may be positive as well as negative. For example, the production of hydroelectric power, expecially in the western United States, created reservoirs that have recreation potential.

The final regulatory situation discussed in this chapter concerns a movement started fewer than 20 years ago, spurred by such individuals as Ralph Nader (who criticized General Motor's Corvair automobile) and Rachel Carson (whose book *Silent Spring* pictured a polluted, silent end for earth). This type of regulation stems from a belief that responsibility for product safety, design, quality, and effectiveness is appropriately that of the seller-producer. This belief has led to the institution of some government agencies (such as the Consumer Products Safety Commission and the National Highway Traffic Safety Administration) as well as to a body of legislation loosely referred to as *consumer product regulation*.

13.3   ANTITRUST THEORY AND REGULATION

Antitrust regulation is enacted to deal with the monopolization problem: the problem that a few companies divide the market, restrict output, and raise prices or engage in price discrimination. Figure 13.1 shows one such monopoly (or a cartelized industry), where the output level Q_M is sold at price P_M when the firm maximizes profit by producing where $MR = MC$. But that level of output (Q_M) may be deemed inefficient in at least two dimensions: (1) it is a smaller output than could be produced within the constraints of the demand function and marginal cost function, and (2) the marginal benefit of the last unit produced is greater than the marginal cost of producing it. These two points amount to much the same conclusion we came to earlier when we compared the results of monopoly with those of perfect competition (see Chapter 10). In our discussion of price discrimination, we also saw that firms with monopoly power could extract at least a portion of the consumer's surplus from the market.

Oftentimes, as you also learned in Chapter 10, regulated monopoly firms are required to sell at lower prices and to produce and sell larger quantities than they would choose in the absence of regulation. The ideal situation would be to have costless regulators who were able to force monopolies and cartelized industries to produce Q_R units of product and sell that quantity at P_R, which, we note, is the price and quantity combination at which $P = MC$, as would be the natural result under perfect competition. Recall that it is at this combination of price and quantity that the marginal benefit from consuming the last unit equals the marginal cost of producing and selling the last unit.

But can we expect the ideal results outlined above to be enacted in real-world markets? The public interest theory of regulation indicates that

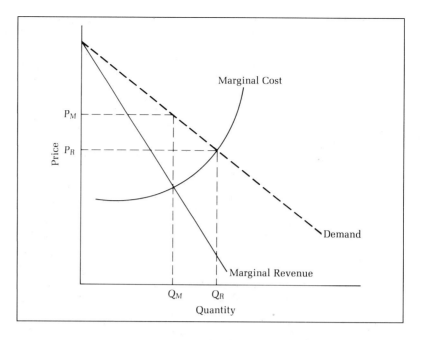

FIGURE 13.1   Regulation to Achieve an Optimal Level of Production and Consumption.   The unregulated firm with monopoly power would produce Q_M units (where $MR = MC$) and would sell those units at the profit-maximizing price P_M. From a societal perspective, the optimum level of output would be Q_R, with a corresponding price of P_R. If this price-quantity configuration was mandated through regulation, the marginal benefit of the last unit consumed (as measured by consumers' willingness to pay, i.e., by price) would equal the marginal cost of producing that unit.

there are real benefits to society to be gained by antitrust regulation, and so we might expect similar regulations in real life. The economic theory of regulation, on the other hand, does not predict these ideal results from the regulatory process. Regulators may not be able to accurately determine the optimal price-quantity relationship. However, to the extent that they move in the right direction, increases in market efficiency will result.

13.4   THE STRUCTURE-CONDUCT-PREFORMANCE PARADIGM

Most regulatory agencies are organized with the expressed purpose of dealing with the monopoly problem. It is argued that if an industry, such as trucking or the airlines, is concentrated in the hands of a few corporations, these firms are able to act as a monopoly by forming a workable cartel (having monopoly power with the unregulated result described in Figure 13.1).

It is sometimes helpful to look at the monopoly problem by using the structure-conduct-performance paradigm. A paradigm is a way of looking at a particular set of facts, a framework for analysis. The structure-conduct-performance paradigm provides a framwork for the study of anti-trust regulation.

The two people most commonly associated with the development of this paradigm are Edward S. Mason and Joe S. Bain.[6] The policy implications of the paradigm are of great importance. For example, if it is determined that the distribution of income should be equitable, above-normal profits that accrue to any monopoly will not be looked upon favorably. If concentrations of power are considered detrimental to the interests of society, explicit or implicit oligopolistic coordination or collusion may be deemed undesirable. An understanding of the perceived goals of society and their relationships to the structural characteristics, as well as daily operations, of firms may imply results that are contrary to the society's goals.

The structure-conduct-performance paradigm presupposes the existence of a casual relationship from structure to conduct to performance.[7] One facet of this framework that is of particular importance is the relationship, if any, between concentration and profits. Industries in which a few sellers account for a substantial fraction of output are often said to be concentrated. If the conduct of concentrated industries is similar to that of a monopolist, such industries would be expected to earn above normal profits. Therefore, it can be argued that the monopoly profits could be reduced by structural changes in the industry through regulation. This view of concentration is rather widely held.

13.5 CONCENTRATION: AN OVERVIEW

Aggregate concentration refers to the degree of control over economic activity exercised by the largest firms in the economy. Aggregate concentration is often loosely referred to as economic power. While this definition is imprecise, it has connotations of increasing control of the economy by large firms and a corresponding reduction in the role of the individual entrepreneur.[8] Regardless of the validity of these connotations, they have a significant

---

[6]For a discussion of the history of industrial organization, see Almarin Phillips and Rodney E. Stevenson, "The Historical Development of Industrial Organization," *History of Political Economy*, Fall 1974, pp. 324–342.

[7]There is by no means an uncritical acceptance of the paradigm. For a book of readings related to this topic, see Yale Brozen, ed., *The Competitive Economy: Selected Readings*, (Morristown, NJ: General Learning Press, 1975).

[8]The attention given to the Fortune 500 and 1000 may unwittingly reinforce feelings of uneasiness.

impact on the thinking of many individuals. Aggregate concentration can influence the pricing decision in two ways. First, to the extent that the interests of larger firms coincide, none of these firms will contemplate action that would harm the others. Next, changes in aggregate concentration may reflect changes that affect the firm's pricing decision, as will be demonstrated below. Before attempting to judge the validity of these statements, let us consider the trend of aggregate concentration.

The trend of aggregate concentration is difficult to determine because comparable and reliable data are not easily obtained. Before World War II, the evidence is contradictory. After World War II, however, both asset shares and value added of the 200 largest manufacturing firms have risen throughout the period.[9] The rate of increase in both series has been slow but persistent. Moreover, the data indicate that the largest corporations operate in a broad range of manufacturing industries. The largest firms are diversified into a number of markets that are themselves concentrated.[10] The implication of these trends remains to be established.

While the trend in aggregate concentration is clearly upward, the relationship between pure size and pricing behavior is tenuous at best. American Motors is absolutely large but possesses little independent pricing power. Any firm selling a differentiated product has a degree of monopoly power irrespective of its size. The degree of pricing discretion in the market depends not on absolute size, but, rather, on the number of competitors and the assumed pattern of reactions among them.

Empirical measures of market concentration provide the single most identifiable definition of the degree of monopoly power possessed by an industry. Market concentration refers to the number and/or size distribution of firms operating in a definable market.[11]

As shown in Chapters 10 and 11, the pricing decision is determined by both the number of competitors and the pattern of reaction among them. The monopolist has no other competitors and the market demand curve coincides with the monopolist's demand curve. On the other hand, the perfect competitor can only react to the exogenously determined price and correspondingly does not consider the reactions of the other perfectly competitive firms. Oligopoly and monopolistic competition lie between these extremes. Market concentration provides a summary measure of the

---

[9]John M. Blair, *Economic Concentration* (New York: Harcourt Brace Jovanovich, 1972) pp. 61–72. Reviews of Blair's book have indicated that while the wealth of statistics is excellent, the analysis is suspect. See the reviews by S.E. Boyle, (pp. 515–517), D.F. Green, (pp. 520–523) and W. Sichel (pp. 517–519) in *Journal of Economic Issues*, September 1975.

[10]Blair, op. cit., pp. 72–75.

[11]Douglas Needham, *Economic Analysis and Industrial Structure* (New York: Holt, Rinehart and Winston, 1969), pp. 83–85.

degree of monopoly power possessed by an industry and an indication of degree of pricing discretion available to the firm in that industry.

13.6 MEASURING CONCENTRATION

One commonly employed measure of market concentration is the *market concentration ratio*, defined as the percentage of the industry's size accounted for by the largest few firms. For example, concentration ratios, using sales data, are calculated by the Bureau of the Census for the leading 4, 8, 20, and 50 firms. Industries are usually defined using the Standard Industrial Classification (SIC) system also developed by the Bureau of the Census. Concentration ratios can be computed by using data on employment, assets, or value added. Concentration ratios suffer from an obvious defect: concentration ratios take a snapshot look at industrial structure for a given number of firms. While it is important to know the fraction of sales possessed by a given number of firms, the distribution of sales between the firms is also important. The strength or weakness of a competitive fringe can determine the effectiveness and type of price leadership that may exist. Concentration ratios may, nonetheless, be desirable as a summary measure of the overall concentration of a particular industry.

Some measure of concentration is necessary when describing the extent of market power in an oligopolistic market structure. Oligopolies are characterized by the interdependence of the decision-making processes of the firms in the industry. Summary concentration measures that emphasize the size distribution of firms are particularly applicable to oligopolies. Price determination differs in an industry consisting of five firms, each with 20 percent of the market, compared with that in an industry with one firm having 50 percent of the market and five firms with 10 percent each. While each industry would have a four-firm concentration ratio of 80 percent, the pricing behavior would be markedly different. The two most common summary measures of concentration that provide more information about the size distribution of firms are the *Gini coefficient* and the *Herfindahl concentration index.*

The Gini Coefficient

Table 13.1 provides illustrative data that we can use to illustrate the determination of a Gini coefficient. Column 1 gives firms by size class, and columns 2 and 3 provide the percentage of firms in each size class and the percentage of sales in each size class, respectively. Columns 4 and 5 give the cumulative percentage of firms and sales, respectively. Before calculating the Gini coefficient, it will be helpful to look at a graphic depiction of this information.

TABLE 13.1
Data for Evaluating Market Concentration Using a Lorenz Curve and Gini Coefficient

(1) Firm Size	(2) Percentage of Firms in Class	(3) Percentage of Sales	(4) Cumulative Percentage of Firms	(5) Cumulative Percentage of Sales
0–100,000	10	5	10	5
100,000–1,000,000	10	5	20	10
1,000,000–10,000,000	15	10	35	20
10,000,000–100,000,000	25	15	60	35
100,000,000–500,000,000	25	35	85	70
over 500,000,000	15	30	100	100

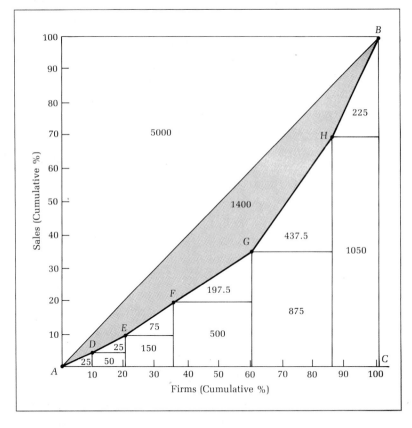

FIGURE 13.2   **Lorenz Curve for Data in Table 13.1.**   The shaded area between the 45-degree line and the line formed by connecting points, A, D, E, F, G, H, and B is called the area of concentration. The lower boundary of this area is the Lorenz curve. The Gini coefficient is the ratio of this area of concentration to the total area below line AB. The greater the degree of concentration, the larger the shaded area and the larger the Gini coefficient. In this example, the Gini coefficient is 1400/1500 = .28.

A Lorenz curve can be constructed from the data in columns 4 and 5 as shown in Figure 13.2. The 45-degree line *AB* represents the line of perfect equality. Along that line, the smallest 20 percent of firms account for 20 percent of sales, the smallest 60 percent of firms account for 60 percent of sales, and so forth. In this case, the Lorenz curve would coincide with the 45-degree line. However, for the data in Table 13.1, we see that this is not the case. The line segments connecting points *A, D, E, F, G, H,* and *B* depict the Lorenz curve for this set of data. The more the Lorenz curve bows away from the 45-degree line, the greater the degree of industrial concentration. In the case of a perfect monopoly, the Lorenz curve would be *ACB*. The extent to which the Lorenz curve deviates from the 45-degree line is usually designated the *area of concentration* and is measured by the area of the shaded polygon *ABHGFED*.

The Gini coefficient is a measure of concentration derived from these concepts. The Gini coefficient is the ratio of the area between the 45-degree line and the Lorenz curve (the area of concentration) to the area between the 45-degree line and the axes (the triangle *ABC*). The area of the triangle *ABC* is always 5000 (area $ABC = [.5][100][100] = 5000$). The area of concentration can be calculated as follows: (1) find the sum of the areas of the triangles and rectangles under the Lorenz curve (these are shown by the thin lines in Figure 13.2); and (2) subtract this sum from the total area under the Lorenz curve (5000) to determine the area of concentration.[12] For the data in Table 13.1 and Figure 13.2, we can then calculate the Gini coefficient as shown below:

1. Sum the areas below the Lorenz curve:

$$\text{Area under } AD = .5(5 \times 10) = \quad 25.0$$
$$\text{Area under } DE = .5(5 \times 10) + 5(10) = \quad 75.0$$
$$\text{Area under } EF = .5(10 \times 15) + 10(15) = \quad 225.0$$
$$\text{Area under } FG = .5(15 \times 25) + 20(25) = \quad 687.5$$
$$\text{Area under } GH = .5(35 \times 25) + 35(25) = 1312.5$$
$$\text{Area under } HB = .5(30 \times 15) + 70(15) = \underline{1275.0}$$
$$\text{Total area below Lorenz curve} = 3600.0$$

2. Determine the area of concentration:

$$5000 - 3600 = 1400$$

The Gini coefficient is, then, $1400/5000 = .28$ for this set of data.

The more concentrated an industry is, the more closely the Gini coefficient will be to its upper limit of 1.0 (for a monopoly the area of

---

[12]For a more complete discussion of the Lorenz curve and this method of calculating the Gini coefficient, see Eugene M. Singer, *Antitrust Economics: Selected Legal Cases and Economic Models* (Englewood Cliffs, NJ: Prentice-Hall, 1968) Chapter 13, "Concentration Indexes," pp. 136–155.

concentration is 5000). The lower limit for the Gini coefficient is 0.0, which would result if the area of concentration were zero, that is, if the Lorenz curve coincided with the 45-degree line of equality.

The Herfindahl Index

The Herfindahl index is computed by summing the squared ratios of firm size to industry size.[13] The Herfindahl index H is defined as

$$H = \Sigma \, (S_i/S)^2$$

where S_i is the size of the ith firm and S is total industry size. The Herfindahl index varies between 0 and 1. If a firm had a monopoly in a particular industry, we would have $S_i = S$ and $H = 1$. As the industry structure approximates perfect competition, H would approach 0.

The calculation of the Herfindahl index is relatively straightforward. For example, assume that an industry is composed of five firms with the following market shares: 1/20, 1/6, 1/5, 1/4, and 1/3. The Herfindahl index would then be

$$(1/20)^2 + (1/6)^2 + (1/5)^2 + (1/4)^2 + (1/3)^2 = .244.$$

Suppose that the industry became more concentrated through the merger of the last two firms. The Herfindahl index would then be

$$(1/20)^2 + (1/6)^2 + (1/5)^2 + (7/12)^2 = .411.$$

If, on the other hand, the firm with 1/3 of the market were split into two firms, each with 1/6 share of the market, the index would be

$$(1/20)^2 + 3(1/6)^2 + (1/5)^2 + (1/4)^2 = .188.$$

Snapshot and summary measures of concentration such as those illustrated above provide an indication of the degree of pricing discretion available to firms in a given industry. They also represent measures of structure that are watched closely by the appropriate government agencies. However, these indexes must be interpreted with care, considering other variables such as whether the industry is growing or declining, the extent of mergers, and the relative importance of substitute products.

The existence of some relationship between structure and conduct seems reasonable. We have observed that in the United States, aggregate concentration has changed very slowly. *Market concentration also has not exhibited any strong overall trends.*[14] We can say, however, that whether the relationship between structure and conduct is real or perceived, it exerts

---

[13]*Ibid.*, pp. 152–154.

[14]F.M. Scherer, *Industrial Market Structure and Economic Performance* (Chicago: Rand McNally, 1970), pp. 57–63.

an influence on policy and therefore may define the degree of correspondence between an industry's performance and the goals of society.

13.7   GOVERNMENT REGULATION OF MARKET STRUCTURE AND CONDUCT

Antitrust policy is either directed at industry structure or at industry conduct. Certain types of structure and some classes of mergers are considered anticompetitive and are dealt with severely. In many cases, such structural violations are illegal per se, and, if the offense is proved, guilt is thereby established. Certain types of conduct, such as price discrimination, tying contracts, and exclusive dealing, are deemed detrimental to competition and likely to lead to monopoly. These components of conduct are watched carefully, but it is recognized that they may be justified in certain cases. These components of conduct are therefore considered on a case-by-case basis. The following summary will highlight selected cases that illustrate the government's use of antitrust regulations.[15]

Antitrust Policy: Structure

While judicial decisions distinguish between monopoly and attempts to monopolize, we shall lump them together. The *Sherman Act,* passed in 1890, was the first piece of United States antitrust legislation. Section 2 prohibited monopolization or attempts to monopolize. However, the Sherman Act only provided for policies to combat existing monopolies. The *Clayton Act,* passed in 1914, made illegal certain practices that were deemed likely to lead to monopoly. In addition to various restrictions on conduct, section 7 of the Clayton Act prohibited mergers, the effect of which would be to substantially lessen competition in any line of commerce. In other words, the Sherman Act provided broad guidelines as to what was not acceptable market structure, while the Clayton Act more precisely defined and made illegal practices that might lead to Sherman Act violation.

Monopolization

A question basic to any analysis of cases of monopolization is whether monopoly as such is unlawful or if some sort of undesirable conduct is necessary to establish illegality. Such a distinction is basic, and, in fact, it is possible to divide opponents of monopoly into structuralists and

---

[15]For more detailed discussions of antitrust policy, see Clair Wilcox and William G. Shepherd, *Public Policies toward Business,* 5th ed. (Homewood, IL: Irwin, 1975); Roger Blair and David L. Kaserman, *Antitrust Economics* (Homewood, IL: Irwin, 1985); and Russell G. Warren, *Antitrust in Theory and Practice* (Columbus, OH: Grid, 1975).

behavioralists.[16] Structuralists argue that monopoly in and of itself is undesirable. Behavioralists, on the other hand, look at conduct and would require the existence of some business practice that fostered the monopoly. Not surprisingly, we shall find that there is a degree of inconsistency in interpretation.

In the 1911 Standard Oil case, the Supreme Court argued that Standard had exhibited both the intent to monopolize and, given its 90-percent control of both the refining and sale of petroleum products, clearly had the necessary market share. The Court argued that Standard had employed unreasonable measures to gain its monopoly position, and therefore intent to monopolize could be proven. It appeared that overt acts were required; that is, this was a behavioralist decision. Standard Oil was a landmark decision and the case against them was persuasive.[17]

The case against U.S. Steel, however, was not equally clear-cut. In 1911, the government began efforts to break up U.S. Steel. A subsequent 1920 decision of the Supreme Court established the principle that size was not an offense in and of itself and that there had to be some evidence of overt acts. The consequences of this ruling was to make monopoly contingent on overt illegal acts rather than on size alone.

This result made monopolization difficult to prove, since if firms avoided overt illegal action, absolute size, in and of itself, was no offense. This pattern was maintained until the Alcoa decision in 1945. By maintaining a low profit margin, Alcoa was able to exclude entry for several decades, and at the time of the decision, controlled by one definition 90 percent of the aluminum market.[18]

Let us look further at the evidence presented concerning Alcoa's intent to monopolize. In his opinion, Judge Learned Hand praised Alcoa for its technological efficiency, innovation, and expansion of capacity to meet anticipated demand. Hand, however, found Alcoa to be guilty of monopolizing the aluminum industry. He inferred the intent to monopolize from Alcoa's efficiency and the subsequent control of the market. Alcoa had not employed questionable tactics in maintaining its position of supremacy. By being efficient and earning profits such that entry by other firms was not profitable, Alcoa provided their product at a reasonable price. Hand's decision declared that efficiency was no defense against section 2 of the Sherman Act and that size alone, irrespective of illegal acts, was proof of violation.

---

[16]Warren, op. cit., pp. 71–79.

[17]For an excellent discussion of Standard Oil policies and a forceful argument that Standard Oil did not practice predatory pricing, see John S. McGee, "Predatory Price Cutting: The Standard Oil (N.J.) Case," *Journal of Law and Economics*, October 1958, pp. 137–169.

[18]The definition of the *market* was crucial to the decision in this case.

The decision appeared to indicate that monopolization could be attacked rather successfully; however, the results have been less dramatic. Soon after Alcoa, both United Shoe Machinery and Atlantic & Pacific (A & P) were convicted of monopolization and conspiracy to monopolize, respectively. While important, these decisions have not inspired further action, and from 1953 to 1968 there were few actions brought under section 2 of the Sherman Act. In 1969, a more activist stance concerning monopolization was developing. Actions against International Business Machines (IBM), American Telephone and Telegraph (AT&T), and the major cereal manufacturers were initiated. Ultimately, AT&T was forced to break up, with results that to date are mixed.

Mergers

Whereas few cases under section 2 of the Sherman Act have reached the Supreme Court in recent years, attacks on mergers under section 7 of the Clayton Act have been more numerous. As originally considered, section 7 prohibited mergers where the effect would be to substantially lessen competition in a line of commerce. However, only mergers achieved by acquisition of stock were subject to challenge under section 7. Mergers accomplished by the purchase of assets were legal until section 7 was modified in 1950 by the Celler-Kefauver Amendment. Section 7 can now be applied to horizontal, vertical, and conglomerate mergers. A *horizontal merger* is one between two firms that produce the same product. A *vertical merger* is one in which the merged firms form a buyer-seller relationship with respect to one or more inputs. A *conglomerate merger* can be defined simply as any merger that is not horizontal or vertical, or more precisely, a merger between firms in distinct markets.

The wording of section 7 is admittedly vague and correspondingly allows for substantial judicial interpretation. Two issues, however, demand attention. First, how is a "line of commerce" to be defined? Second, exactly what is meant by the phrase, "to substantially lessen competition"? Answers to these questions essentially define the limits for horizontal and vertical mergers.

Both the geographic and product markets are germane, when defining a market in a section 7 case. The geographic size of the market can be adjusted in order to give the accused firm either a substantial or minimal share of the total market. If the geographic product market is defined broadly, the market shares involved in a merger will be small, whereas a merger in a narrowly defined market will involve large market shares. Generally, it appears that in section 7 cases, markets are to be defined so as to be least favorable toward mergers. Two such examples were the Von's Grocery case, in which the merger of the third and sixth largest grocery chains in the Los Angeles area was found to be illegal; and a 1966 decision, in which a merger between Pabst and Blatz was disallowed when the market was defined as Wisconsin alone.

The definition of product markets can also be somewhat capricious. The question to be determined is whether the two products are, in fact, in competition with one another. Generally, all products are in competition with one another in that all compete for a fixed sum of dollars. Ideally, information on cross-elasticity of demand (for consumer goods) and technological substitutability (for inputs) could be used to determine when products are competitive. However, it is not possible to define the point at which the cross-elasticity of demand becomes sufficiently positive for goods to be in competition. No consistent approach to defining either geographic or product markets emerged in judicial opinion. It is unlikely that a consistent approach is possible, perhaps even desirable, for reasons of flexibility as well as the inability to consistently define markets correctly.

Some generalizations are possible on what is meant by "to substantially lessen competition." In the *Merger Guidelines* published by the Department of Justice, standards for acceptable horizontal, vertical, and conglomerate mergers are defined.[19] The result of these guidelines has been to severely restrict merger activity, particularly horizontal and vertical mergers. Generally, the phrase, "to substantially lessen competition" is interpreted in terms of increased market shares and/or reduction in the number of competitors.

The *Brown Shoe* decision was important for two reasons. First, the merger exhibited both horizontal and vertical dimensions. Therefore, the decision had to consider both these aspects. Discussion of both the proper geographic and product markets was evident as was what is meant by "to substantially lessen competition." Second, the Brown Shoe case was the first important merger case using the new section 7 of the Clayton Act.[20] For these reasons, this case merits a more detailed examination.

The merger in question in the Brown Shoe case[21] was one between Brown Shoe Company and the Kinney Shoe Company. Brown and Kinney both operated retail shoe outlets and manufactured shoes. At the time of the merger in 1955, Brown was the fourth largest domestic shoe manufacturer with about 4 percent of the national market. Brown had acquired 845 retail outlets between 1950 and 1955. Kinney's retail outlets accounted for approximately 1.6 percent of retail shoe sales. Kinney ranked twelfth in shoe manufacturing with 0.5 percent of the market. Throughout the opinion, the Court expressed concern over "two definite trends" in this industry. The first trend was the acquisition of retail outlets by manufacturers and the subsequent increase in purchases from the manufacturing unit of the parent

---

[19]U.S. Department of Justice, *Merger Guidelines* (mimeographed, May 30, 1968), p. 9.

[20]See Warren, op. cit., pp. 267–271; David D. Martin, "The Brown Shoe Case and the New Antimerge Policy," *American Economic Review*, June 1963, pp. 340–358.

[21]Brown Shoe Company, Inc. *vs* U.S. 370 U.S. 294 (1962).

company. The second trend was the decrease in the number of shoe manu-facturing plants.

The vertical aspect of the merger concerned the proper supplier-customer relationships between Brown and Kinney. That is, would there exist a foreclosure of competition since Brown could force shoes into Kinney retail outlets. The Court observed, however, that such a vertical arrangement would be illegal only if the affect "were to substantially lessen competition or tend to create a monopoly." The product markets were defined as men's, women's, and children's shoes, with the nation as the geographic market. The question then resolved to one of whether the vertical relationship would constitute a substantial lessening of com-petition.

The proportion of the market foreclosed, 1.6 percent of retail shoe sales, was not considered decisive. The Court supported its position that this vertical relationship would substantially lessen competition in several ways. The nature and purpose of the agreement was important. The Court voted that neither small nor failing firms were involved. Since Kinney oper-ated the largest independent chain of retail shoe stores, no possible larger foreclosure existed. The existence of trends toward concentration and verti-cal integration was cited, noting that the Clayton Act is a forward looking piece of legislation. The Court, seeking the economic way of life dictated by Congress, viewed the merger as one step in a chain of vertical mergers that would create an oligopoly if left unchecked.

The horizontal aspects of the merger concerned the effects of increased concentration of activity at both the manufacturing and retail level. The product market was defined as before. The geographic market was defined as "every city with a population exceeding 10,000 and its immediate contiguous surrounding territory" in which both Brown and Kinney had retail outlets, either owned or controlled. The Court considered the combined retail market share significant in light of the fragmented nature of the industry, the trend toward concentration, and the effect of any decision as precedent. That is, if this merger was allowed, others would also have to be allowed. The Court argued in favor of decentralization, indicating that potential offsetting circumstances such as a failing firm or increased ability to compete with larger firms were inapplicable.

This decision was extremely important in that it established as prece-dent a stringent position toward horizontal and vertical mergers. The cor-rectness of the decision is understandably open to dispute, but the significance of the decision is not. Little attention was paid to possible cost savings resulting from the merger. Issues concerning transfer pricing were raised but not adequately considered. The Court simply opted in favor of more rather than less competition. Perhaps it can be argued that the Court chose to err on the harsh side since they did not feel qualified to judge when the trend toward concentration had gone too far.

Antitrust Policy: Conduct

The two types of conduct we shall discuss are price discrimination and what has been called conscious parallelism (i.e., an inferred agreement to fix price when no visible evidence of agreement exists). The Clayton Act contains sections making modes of behavior such as tying clauses, exclusive dealing, and requirements contracts,[22] in addition to price discrimination, illegal when the effect may be substantially to lessen competition or to tend to create monopoly. However, the enforcement record was not impressive at all, and in response to pressure from lobbies representing small businesses, the *Robinson-Patman Act* was passed in 1936. The Robinson-Patman Act weakened the requirements necessary to prove that price discrimination was indeed harmful. Inferring price-fixing agreements in absence of explicit evidence is covered by section 1 of the Sherman Act, which prohibits conspiracies in the restraint of trade. These two aspects of conduct are discussed below.

Price Discrimination

The legal and economic definitions of price discrimination must first be distinguished. While it may be a slight oversimplification, judicial interpretation defines price discrimination as a difference in prices not justifiable by differences in cost. In the economic sense, price discrimination is defined as charging prices not related to cost differences. The economic definition includes as price discrimination, charging the same price for two commodities with different costs. The legal definition of price discrimination does not include this case. In Chapter 10, the conditions for maximizing profits with price discrimination were discussed, and we noted that price discrimination is not necessarily undesirable. While systematic price discrimination can entrench an existing monopoly position, selective price discrimination can chip away at joint monopoly power by causing firms to compete in terms of price, thereby reducing the effectiveness of any cartel arrangement.

If discrimination is defined among goods of "like grade and quality," we find ourselves in the difficult position of having to define industry boundaries. For example, are commodities that are perceived to be different by consumers, when in fact they are chemically identical, different commodities, or the same commodity? Such a question was raised in the Borden case, in which Borden sold canned milk with their own label at a higher price per case than the physically identical product in a private-label can. It is customary in economics to take consumer preferences at face value. Therefore, if the commodities are perceived by the consumer as being

---

[22]Tying clauses refer to requiring the purchase of one commodity as a condition of purchasing another. Exclusive dealing contracts give a supplier the exclusive right to sell to buyers for a given period of time. Requirements contracts are similar to exclusive dealing.

distinct, they are in fact different commodities. Moreover, to the extent that a trademark is the result of costly advertising, any price difference will be justifiable on the basis of the difference in cost. In this case, however, the Supreme Court stated that the two products were identical and the two-price scheme was declared illegal. This is but one example of otherwise competitive conduct outlawed by the Robinson-Patman Act.

Two defenses are available to the firm accused of price discrimination: cost justification and the good faith defense. From a strict economic point of view, a defense based on cost justification would be sufficient if the difference in prices could be explained by differences in marginal costs of production. Since marginal costs are not as readily observable, the Court has settled for a justification based on average costs. The evidence required is often voluminous and in more than one case, the defendant found it cheaper to modify the disputed pricing practice than to provide the requested cost information.[23]

The good faith defense refers to the practice of meeting, but not going below, the price of a competitor. As currently interpreted, the Robinson-Patman Act encourages price uniformity and penalizes price cutting by competitors. Generally, the Robinson-Patman Act is given low marks by economists. When passed in 1936, Robinson-Patman probably reflected the mood of a country still dealing with the Great Depression. It unabashedly protects competitors and not competition.[24] To that extent, it has a purpose counter to the other antitrust laws of the United States. If competition in the economic sense is to occur, someone gains and others may lose. To deny the losses and make them illegal is somewhat strange. Though all firms should, so to speak, play by the rules, those who lose should not be insulated from the consequences.

Conscious Parallelism

A discussion of conscious parallelism must be related to the indeterminant solution to the oligopoly pricing problem. The key concept in any discussion of oligopoly is interdependence and the methods by which the firms in the oligopoly attempt to resolve this interdependence. Three possible methods are (1) joint profit maximization, (2) full-cost or cost-plus pricing, and (3) either dominant firm or barometric price leadership. While the first is illegal under section 1 of the Sherman Act, the latter two methods are not and are reasonable methods of resolving the problem of oligopolistic interdependence. The doctrine of conscious parallelism states that an

---

[23]The firm referred to is General Electric. See F.M. Scherer, *Industrial Market Structure and Economic Performance* (Chicago: Rand McNally, 1970), p. 502.

[24]See Richard E. Low, *Modern Economic Organization* (Homewood, IL: Irwin, 1970), pp. 400–401.

agreement to fix prices can be inferred in the absence of an explicit agreement if the firms in the industry pursue courses of action, conscious of each other's actions. We shall examine this argument in the context of three antitrust cases.

Interstate Circuit dealt with the actions of a Texas theater chain that sent identical letters to all major motion picture distributors requesting forcefully that they be given exclusive rights to first-run showings and establishing minimum prices for admission. The question here was resolved to one of determining if the letter was sufficient to infer an agreement on the part of the theater chain and the distributor. While no formal agreement existed, the Supreme Court said the letter constituted an invitation not to compete, and therefore a conspiracy in restraint of trade was said to exist. This case set the framework for a crucial case in 1946 concerning the tobacco industry.

The big three tobacco companies were aptly characterized by a condition of dominant firm price leadership. While prices were not always identical, a set pattern of price differentials was maintained. The Supreme Court indicated that it was possible to infer an agreement to fix prices from the fact that prices moved in a parallel manner.[25] On reflection, this decision was extraordinarily significant. Had it been consistently applied, all forms of price leadership and full cost pricing would have been illegal under section 1 of the Sherman Act. From an economist's perspective, an alternative explanation for the parallel patterns of action of the big three tobacco firms is more likely than the Court's ruling. A cigarette is a standardized product, apart from any advertising expenditures. The cost of inputs would thus be approximately the same for all brands. If a cost-plus pricing policy was followed, prices would naturally follow a parallel pattern without any agreement to fix prices.

In the 1954 Theater Enterprises case, a suburban Baltimore theater brought suit against the downtown theaters and motion picture distributors, claiming that they had conspired to deny this theater first-run status for movies. The Supreme Court argued that parallel action was not evidence of a conspiracy, since each distributor could have independently reached the decision to deny the suburban theater first-run status on the basis of sound business judgment. That is, each distributor could independently ascertain that the suburban theater did not possess sufficient drawing power to warrant first-run status. This decision said that some sort of agreement, apart from parallel action, was necessary to establish the existence of a conspiracy in restraint of trade.

---

[25]William H. Nicholls, "The Tobacco Case of 1946," *American Economic Review*, May 1949, pp. 284–296. Reprinted in Richard B. Heflebower and George W. Stocking, eds., *Readings in Industrial Organization and Public Policy* (Homewood, IL: Irwin, 1958), pp. 105–117.

This discussion has provided at best a cursory glance at antitrust policy. We have emphasized the effects and consequences of antitrust policy for firms in several contexts. Antitrust policy provides a broad framework within which firms must operate. As we have seen, however, this framework is not necessarily consistent or logical. Economists studying antitrust regulation have tended to find that in a fair number of cases—in trucking, airlines, railroads, and many other industries—the effect of regulation has been to *increase* profitability in industries that otherwise would have been competitive.[26] These studies seem to support the economic view of regulation, which holds that economic regulation is a product supplied to interest groups rather than an expression of the goals of society.

13.8 REGULATION OF EXTERNALITIES

It is not uncommon to find that when two people enter into a contract, a third person may be affected by the contract. In most cases, this is because property rights are not clearly defined in the circumstance. Let us consider an example in which a man owns a factory that emits quite a bit of smoke. The factory is in a desolate area, and the only thing nearby is a house owned by a widow. The smoke from the factory has the unpleasant effect of peeling the paint from the widow's house.

If this situation exists in a country where the law says factories may emit as much smoke as they like (regardless of the consequences), we might expect the widow to try to bargain with the factory owner to secure the emission of less smoke. The widow would probably be required to pay the factory owner in order to convince him to reduce the smoke. The factory owner might be willing to enter such a bargain, since he would be paid for his trouble and thus would be better off by reducing emissions.

Now consider the same situation in a country where the law says factories may emit no smoke without the expressed permission of local residents. In this situation, it is the factory owner who would be willing to bargain with the widow by perhaps paying her for permission to emit some agreed-upon amount of smoke. The widow would have an incentive to at least listen to such an offer, since she might be better off with the extra money and a small amount of smoke.

---

[26]Richard A. Posner, *Economic Analysis of Law* (Boston: Little, Brown, 1973); W.F. Baxter, "NYSE Fixed Commission Rate: A Private Cartel Goes Public," *Stanford Law Review*, April 1970, pp. 675–712; R.H. Coase, "The Federal Communications Commission," *Journal of Law and Economics*, October 1959, pp. 1–4; P.W. MacAvoy, *The Economic Effects of Regulation: The Trunk-Line Railroad Cartels and the Interstate Commerce Commission before 1900* (Cambridge, MA: M.I.T. Press, 1965); S. Peltzman, "Entry into Commercial Banking," *Journal of Law and Economics*, October 1966, pp. 11–50.

Each situation described above involves an externality created by the factory that harms the widow, and in both cases, the suggested solution is a type of government regulation we commonly see today to handle situations in which externalities are important. Both laws are examples of a regulation fix to a free market system in order to account for what we see as undesirable outcomes of unhindered markets. In both cases, each party had the opportunity to be better off after a deal with the other only if property rights were clearly defined to begin with. With no clear property rights indicated at the outset, there is no incentive for an agreement and little chance such an agreement would ever emerge.

The real world, however, is far more complex than the world of the widow and the factory owner. There are many factories in the real world and many homeowners; the factories emit different quantities of numerous substances; the homeowners are scattered here and there; weather conditions change; and different governmental units may control the factories and homeowners. An optimal or near optimal solution may thus be quite difficult to reach in practice. It is possible that the government may not be able to produce a better outcome than the unhindered market may produce. It should also be clear that some situations, such as the smoke-emitting factory case, may produce a better outcome with intervention.

There is an estuary (the wide mouth of a river where it meets the tide of the ocean into which it flows) at the mouth of the Delaware River that is 86 miles long, running from Trenton, New Jersey, to Liston Point, Delaware. It is a densely populated area with a high concentration of heavy industry.

In 1957 the water quality in the Delaware River estuary was so bad that a study was requested by the federal government. A model of the river (a simulation) was built that allowed researchers to examine the particular effects downstream of pouring in a particular quantity of a certain pollutant at some point upstream. If, for instance, a certain factory were to dump a quantity of X into the river in Trenton, the model would predict (quite accurately) what condition this would cause downstream in Liston Point.

The model was constructed in order to allow the use of zone effluent charges, payment by polluters to the government based on the size and timing of the emission and its probable effects. Waste emitters in some zones were charged more than others if the effect of their pollutant was more pronounced on water quality. By clearly establishing the property rights to the estuary, the government set up a situation in which the externality was forced to be internalized by the polluters. While this particular situation was less complicated than many, its solution is illustrative of solutions of many similar cases.[27]

---

[27] Allen V. Kneese, and Blair T. Bower, *Managing Water Quality: Economics, Technology and Institutions* (Baltimore: Johns Hopkins University Press, 1968).

13.9   CONSUMER PROTECTION

Much recent government regulation has stressed protection of consumers, while the attitude for many decades had been caveat emptor: let the buyer beware. Consumer protection regulations are founded on the belief that consumer responsibility is unfair because businesspeople are thought to be in a superior position when dealing with individuals and so are able to take advantage of them. Consumer protection regulation is thus designed to protect consumers from the business sector; the legislation is designed to establish standards of business conduct in a number of areas. Many of the problems created by monopolies or externalities have encouraged various types of consumer protection regulation.

Most consumer protection regulation is based on an argument using either *external costs* or *external benefits*. We will review an industry involving possible external costs: tobacco products. The market for tobacco products includes cigarettes, cigars, pipe tobacco, and some specialty items (including chewing tobacco). More than a few firms have found a livelihood in producing these products for consumer use. However, during the 1960s and 1970s, researchers came to the conclusion (questioned by some) that tobacco products, especially cigarettes, impose rather high risks of permanent damage to users as well as individuals in proximity to heavy users. This would seem to be a clear-cut case of external costs: when smokers light up, they pay the price of the cigarettes and incur some individual risk of damaging their health; *but* the nonsmokers who find themselves in close proximity also run a risk of health damage (the external cost), and yet the nonsmokers are not paid or reimbursed for the deterioration in the quality of the air they must breathe. In other words, the smokers are not bearing the full economic costs of smoking. At the very least, the nonsmoking public incurs a risk cost.

This situation is depicted in Figure 13.3, which shows the consumers' market demand for cigarettes, D. S_1 is the marginal cost of producing the cigarettes with the exception of the effect on nonsmokers. In a competitive market, the quantity purchased will be Q_B because point B describes a market equilibrium where demand equals supply. If cigarette producers are somehow forced to pay the external cost imposed on the nonsmokers by the use of their product, the producers' new supply curve will be S_2, where the vertical distance between S_1 and S_2 represents the external cost of each pack of cigarettes sold. The new quantity purchased will be Q_A. While more packs of cigarettes would be purchased in a competitive market, that number (Q_B) is more than is socially desirable. We can think of social welfare as being increased by an amount equal to the shaded area in Figure 13.3.

When consumers buy Q_B, they do not pay the full cost of smoking Q_B packs of cigarettes because S_1 does not include the external costs. When S_2 is drawn to include the external costs, sales drop to Q_A. The cost that was being borne by nonsmokers is now seen to be the shaded area ABC.

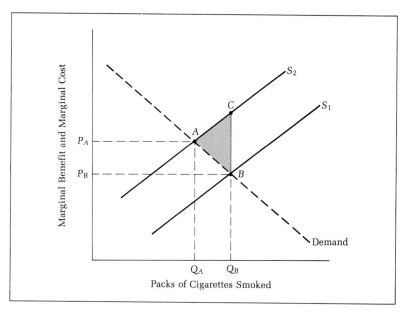

FIGURE 13.3 **Reduction of Consumption by Including External Costs.** The supply curve S_1 includes only the internal costs of supplying cigarettes. The intersection of S_1 with the demand curve, D, determines the free market price and quantity (P_B and Q_B). If the external costs to nonsmokers are included, the supply function shifts to the left, to S_2. The vertical distance between S_1 and S_2 is the amount of the external cost. If this external cost is included, the price would rise to P_A, and the quantity consumed would be reduced to Q_A.

Since those costs are now not incurred by anyone, social welfare has risen by that amount.

A symmetrical argument can be made on the basis of external benefits; there are situations in which the market underproduces a good because the benefits do not accrue directly to the purchaser of the good. Consider the case of energy-absorbing bumpers for automobiles. If you buy a car with these bumpers, I can benefit from your purchase. If I run into your car (or you run into my car), each of our cars will sustain less damage if one of us has energy-absorbing bumpers. We could make a case for consumer protection regulation regarding bumpers by pointing out that competitive markets will tend to underproduce items with significant external benefits.

Criticisms of competitive markets are valid; the real question is whether the regulations enacted to meet the criticisms are well devised or worse than the original problem. A key point to remember is that *signifi-cant* external costs or external benefits may reasonably trigger consumer protection regulation; however, in cases in which the external benefits and/or costs are small, the regulation may be worse than the disease. Many regulations promoted as being in the interest of consumers prevent products from being sold or require enormous sums of money to be spent on nonproductive processes or equipment; in many cases, the external benefits and costs involved are quite small with respect to the size of the cure. Consider, for example, Ralph Nader's crusade against the Chevrolet Corvair in the early 1960s. Nader's campaign discredited the product, caused its ultimate demise, and cost Chevrolet millions of dollars in lost revenue. Few people realize, however, that when the government finally got around to testing the automobile, it found that "the 1960-63 Corvair compared favorably with the other contemporary vehicles used in the tests."[28] Consumer protection regulation can be abused as well as used; the Corvair case was simply an abuse.

SUMMARY

The need for regulation of industry may be justified using either a public interest or an economic rationale. The latter is the more important from the perspective of managerial economics.

Market structure and the degree of concentration within an industry can influence the pricing decisions made by managers. The more concentrated an industry, the greater the chance of monopoly power's being used effectively. The concentration ratio is a measure of the percentage of total industry sales that is accounted for by the largest n firms (where n is often 4 or 8). A Gini coefficient can be used to measure the degree of inequality in the distribution of sales among firms. The closer the Gini coefficient is to 1, the greater the inequality and thus the higher the degree of concentration of sales. The Herfindahl index also can be used as a measure of concentration. As with the Gini coefficient, the upper limit of the Herfindahl index is 1, indicating complete concentration in a single monopolistic firm.

Three major forms of government regulation of business are antitrust regulation, regulation as a means of internalizing externalities, and consumer product regulation. The antitrust field has the longest history in our economy, dating to the Sherman Act of 1890. An understanding of the principles of managerial economics can help a person make better decisions regarding the impact and desirability of various government regulations.

SUGGESTED READINGS

Averch, H., and Johnson, L. "Behavior of the Firm under Regulatory Constraint." *American Economic Review*, December 1962, pp. 53–82.

---

[28]*Evaluation of the 1960–63 Corvair Handling and Stability* (Washington, DC: U.S. Department of Transportation, National Highway Traffic Safety Administration, July 1972), p. 2.

Bailey, E.E. "Contestability and the Design of Regulatory and Antitrust Policy." *American Economic Review*, May 1981, pp. 178–183.

Bain, J.S. *Essays on Price Theory and Industrial Organization*. Boston: Little, Brown, 1972.

Bator, F.M. "The Anatomy of Market Failure." *Quarterly Journal of Economics*, August 1958, pp. 351–379.

Bernstein, Peter W., et al. "The Antitrust Revolution." *Fortune*, July 11, 1983, p. 29.

Blair, Roger, and Kaserman, David L. *Antitrust Economics*, Homewood, IL: Irwin, 1985.

Keating, Barry P. "Direct and Indirect Impacts of the Matchbook Safety Standard of the Consumer Products Safety Commission." *The Quarterly Review of Economics and Business*, Autumn 1984, pp. 29–36.

Keating, Barry P. "Standards: Implicit, Explicit and Mandatory." *Economic Inquiry*, July 1981, pp. 449–458.

Scherer, F.M. *Industrial Market Structure and Economic Performance*, 2d ed. Skokie, IL: Rand McNally, 1980.

Shepherd, W.J. *Market Power and Economic Performance*, New York: Random House, 1970.

Stigler, G.J. "The Theory of Economic Regulation." *Bell Journal of Economics and Management Science*, Spring 1971, pp. 3–21.

Weiss, L.W. "Average Concentration Ratios and Industrial Performance." *Journal of Industrial Economics*, July 1963, pp. 12–29.

PROBLEMS

1. Distinguish clearly between the public interest theory of regulation and the economic theory of regulation.
   a. Are the two theories compatible, or must one be correct and the other incorrect?
   b. What do the terms *market failure* and *government failure* mean? How are these concepts related to each of the two theories of regulation?

2. Antipollution costs have been called by many politicians a cost of doing business, which it is proper to pass on to the consumer. Businesses have indicated, however, that the matter is not so simple; consumer purchases are affected by prices (which rise with increasing antipollution costs), which could result in lower corporate profits and less inclination by business to increase investment in plant. Furthermore, new efficient plants with antipollution devices are expensive, and if businesses choose less investment, unemployment, with accompanying outcries from local government, will result.
   a. Are antipollution costs a cost of doing business?

b. Can these costs be passed on to the consumer?

c. What will make companies pass these costs on: the market, government, conscience?

3. One method of limiting negative externalities caused by products is to prohibit the manufacture and/or sale of the product. Are there cases in which such a prohibition is reasonable and cases in which it is unreasonable? Consider the following:

a. Prohibit offshore drilling because oil spills are common in these situations and impose large negative externalities (considered by the California legislature).

b. Prohibit the use of plastic waste-drain-vent pipes in residential housing because it is not safe (this was illegal according to many building codes of the early 1970s).

c. Prohibit any company from competing with the United States Postal Service in the delivery of first class mail (this prohibition is currently effective).

d. Prohibit any company from competing with American Telephone and Telegraph in the provision of long distance service (this prohibition has been relaxed).

e. Prohibit builders from constructing buildings that are "too high" (this is a common provision of many local building codes).

f. Prohibit any particulate emissions from smokestacks in certain localities.

g. Prohibit the use of certain drugs (e.g., marijuana).

4. What insight would the economic theory of regulation give you into the following regulated industries:

a. Transportation (e.g., trucking, railroads, maritime shipping, and taxicabs)

b. Agriculture (e.g., dairy products and tobacco products)

c. Energy (e.g., natural gas, electricity, and coal)

Consider the regulations with which you are familiar in each of these situations. Are there interest groups that are effective in the regulated situations? Why has regulation not been introduced in other industries with less effective or less cohesive interest groups?

5. A salient feature of the medical system in the United States (which is stoutly defended by the American Medical Association) is fee-for-service pricing, which permits physicians to charge "reasonable and customary" fees as "set" by local boards of physicians. Is this a case of antitrust in reverse?

6. In 1973, there were 50 brewers in the United States. The 16 largest are listed below, along with their respective market shares:

Company	Market Share (%)
Anheuser-Busch	23.9
Schlitz	15.8
Pabst	10.6
Miller	8.7
Coors	8.1
Schaefer	4.0
Olympia	3.9
Stroh's	3.5
Carling	3.3
Heileman	3.1
General	3.0
Schmidt	2.2
Genessee	1.5
Rheingold	1.3
Pearl	0.9
Lonestar	0.7

a. Calculate the Herfindahl index for this industry. Is this index of concentration significantly affected by using just the largest 16 firms rather than all 50?

b. Since 1975, the brewing industry has become much more concentrated (perhaps you recognize some of the 16 firms as ones that are no longer in the industry). Will this greater concentration lead to monopoly power?

c. Since concentration has increased, should the antitrust laws be brought to bear on the brewing industry?

7. Another way of viewing the brewing industry in 1975 yields the following distribution of cumulative percentages of breweries and sales from smallest to largest:

Cumulative Percentage of Breweries	Cumulative Percentage of Sales
0	0
66	5.0
80	15.2
90	32.9
100	100

a. Graph the Lorenz curve for the brewing industry.

b. Calculate the Gini coefficient.

c. Compare the information conveyed by the Lorenz curve and Gini coefficient with that conveyed by the Herfindahl index calculated in problem 6.

8. Industries with four-firm concentration ratios in excess of 50 percent ought to be broken up by government action, according to Ralph Nader.

　a. Would consumers clearly be better off if we followed such a prescription? Explain.

　b. The beer industry, mentioned in problems 6 and 7, would clearly be subject to Mr. Nader's proposal. Would the industry be more efficient after such a breakup? Would the firms continue to operate as "small" firms after such a breakup?

9. Because many regulations promise a great deal but deliver very little, a number of alternatives or supplements to regulation have appeared. How does each compare to the public interest theory of regulation and the economic theory of regulation:[29]

　a. More and better regulation, including efforts to seek more qualified commissioners and staff, increase resources for regulatory commissions, and shift regulatory emphasis from profits to price structure

　b. Deregulation, including the withdrawal of regulations, either partially or entirely

　c. Hybrid, including reviews of monopoly franchises (e.g., utility franchises), renewal based on performance; changes in the incentive structure for regulated firms; and direct audits of regulated firms.

10. Considerable controversy has surrounded the deregulation of airlines. The government used to approve fares for various routes and to allocate routes to specific airlines. Recent deregulation has done away with much of the government's power. Many believe that the competitive forces will now allow airline prices to rise considerably. It is also argued that some airlines will be unable to compete in the new regulatory atmosphere and will perish.

　a. Evaluate these arguments in light of (1) the size of existing airlines precluding new competitors and (2) possible new restrictions placed on reservations (e.g., requiring consumers to purchase tickets one month early to ensure the fare).

　b. What would be the alternative to deregulation?

11. The United States cannot be said to be a free-trade country. Numerous regulations restrict, hinder, or threaten trade in certain items. The United States has entered into restrictive agreements covering rubber,

[29]Clair Wilcox and William G. Shepherd, *Public Policies toward Business* (Homewood, IL: Irwin 1975).

most interesting such restrictions involves *trigger prices* on steel, which levy penalties on foreign firms selling *below* the trigger price.

   a.   What would you suspect would be the announced reason for such a regulation?

   b.   Would such a regulation "reduce our trade deficit and slow down the export of American jobs"?

12.   Occupational licensing can be considered a form of government regulation. It is defended by proponents as a means of ensuring minimum standards of competency or quality. It is accused by its detractors of limiting competition, restricting entry, and preserving high wages of existing practitioners.[30] The following occupations received protection from California in 1984: auctioneers, dietitians, dog patrol operators, real estate agents, respiratory therapists, soil engineers, and tax preparers. In previous years, California protected manicurists, architects, barbers, pest control operators, geologists, plumbers, and employment agents, to name a few.

   a.   Who is protected by occupational licensure?

   b.   Does occupational licensure create monopoly power? Explain.

13.   Reuben Kessel notes that physicians have long had a practice of charging higher fees of well-to-do patients and accepting lower fees for similar services from poor patients. Such activity on the part of physicians is often explained by the notion that physicians are engaging in a sort of medical charity in which the fees of the well-to-do patients subsidize the lower fees of the poorer patients.[31]

   a.   Is this practice by physicians consistent with profit maximization? Explain.

   b.   What sort of price discrimination is exemplified by this practice?

   c.   What characteristics of physicians' services allow this type of pricing mechanism?

14.   "It is a fascinating exercise to look through the price quotations published daily in, say, the *Wall Street Journal*, not to mention the numerous more specialized trade publications. These prices mirror almost instantly what is happening all over the world.

"... Few readers even of the *Wall Street Journal* are interested in more than a few of the prices quoted. They can readily ignore the rest.

"... Anything that prevents prices from expressing freely the conditions of demand or supply interferes with the transmission of accurate information."[32]

---

[30] Dirk Yandell, "Occupational Licensure," *Freeman*, January 1985, pp. 56–59.

[31] John C. Goodman, *The Regulation of Medical Care* (San Francisco: Cato Institute, 1980), p. 24.

[32] Milton Freidman and Rose Friedman, *Free to Choose* (New York: Avon 1981) p. 8.

    a.   Do firms that have monopoly power either prevent the transmission of price information or distort the information transmitted? Explain.

    b.   When the price of oil quadrupled in 1973 (due in large part to the actions of OPEC), did that price increase signal a sudden reduction in the supply of crude oil? If not, what did the price change signal?

    c.   The United States Postal Service has long had a monopoly in first-class mail delivery, but it has not had a monopoly in parcel post–like delivery for some time. Which price (first-class mail rates or package delivery rates) more closely reflects the supply and demand conditions for the service? Does the United States Postal Service price discriminate in first-class service? Does it price discriminate in package delivery service?

15.   In 1976, the Federal Trade Commission found that there were numerous legal and private restraints on the freedom of optometrists, ophthalmologists, and opticians in advertising prices or the quality of their services.[33] At the same time, at both the manufacturing and the wholesaling levels, the price information was readily available. Some members of the industry argued that to allow advertising would increase concentration, create entry barriers, and lead to collusion and monopoly. Since that time, however, the restraints on the industry have eroded, and retail prices have dropped dramatically. It has also been the case, though, that retail sellers of eyeglasses and contact lenses have tended to be larger firms, often chains of retail stores.

    a.   With the advent of open advertising in the optical market, it appears that fewer firms are operating than in 1976. It also appears to be the case that concentration levels in the industry have risen; but it is also true that retail prices have fallen. Is a clear case of monopoly power benefiting consumers?

    b.   For many years, advertising the retail prices of prescription drugs was prohibited by some states. Prices in those states *with* a prohibition were found to be over 5 percent higher than in states that did not prohibit advertising.[34] Now large chain drugstores vigorously advertise generic prescription drugs, driving smaller "corner druggists" out of business. Would you expect the prices of drugs to skyrocket once the large chains have a virtual monopoly hold on the market? Explain.

---

[33]Federal Trade Commission, *Ophthalmic Goods and Services*, Staff Report to the Federal Trade Commission and Proposed Trade Regulation Rule, January 1976.

[34]John Cady, *Restricted Advertising and Competition: The Case of Retail Drugs* (Washington, DC: American Enterprise Institute, March 1976).

Appendix A   Algebra Review

The purpose of this appendix is to help you brush up on algebraic skills that are useful in solving algebraic equations. When we speak of "solving" an algebraic expression, our goal is to rearrange the terms so that the variable we are trying to find the value of is isolated on the left side of the equality sign, while all other terms are on the right side of the equality sign. We start with some basic algebraic operations and then review the rules that govern the use of exponents.

A.1   BASIC ALGEBRA

If you have not used algebraic relationships for some time, certain operations have probably become rusty and need to be polished up. The review provided here is basic and is intended primarily to bring back concepts you have already learned. Our approach is not mathematically formal. Rather, we use explanation through example to help you review these concepts.

We will begin by considering how to isolate one variable in an algebraic expression of two or more variables:

Case 1.   Suppose $Y = X + 5$, and you want to solve the expression for X. If you subtract 5 from each side of the equality sign, the equality would still be true. You would then have

$$Y - 5 = X + 5 - 5$$

and thus,

$$Y - 5 = X$$

or, alternatively,

$$X = Y - 5$$

Case 2. Suppose $Z = W - 200$, and you want to solve the expression for W. If you add 200 to both sides, the equality still holds and you would have

$$Z + 200 = W - 200 + 200$$

and thus,

$$Z + 200 = W$$

or, alternatively,

$$W = Z + 200$$

Case 3. Suppose $Y = 2X$, and you want to solve the expression for X. If you divide both sides of the equality by 2, the equality still holds, and you have

$$Y/2 = 2X/2$$

and thus,

$$Y/2 = X, \text{ or } X = Y/2 = \tfrac{1}{2}Y = .5Y$$

Note that all three ways of expressing the above equation for X are equivalent. They all mean that the value of X is one-half of the value of Y. If Y was 8, X would be 4 regardless of which of these expressions you used. This same result could have been obtained by multiplying both sides of the original expression ($Y = 2X$) by .5, where .5 is the reciprocal of 2. You would have

$$.5Y = (.5)(2X)$$
$$.5Y = X, \text{ or } X = .5Y$$

Case 4. Suppose $U = -4W$, and you want to solve the expression for W. If you divide both sides by -4, the equality would still hold, and you would have

$$U/-4 = -4W/-4$$

and thus,

$$U/-4 = 4W/4$$

The -4s on the right side cancel each other, so you have

$$U/-4 = W, \text{ or } W = U/-4 = -.25U$$

Again, this result could have been obtained directly by multiplying both sides of the original expression by $-.25$ (the reciprocal of -4). You would have

$$-.25U = (-.25)(-4W)$$
$$-.25U = W, \text{ or } W = -.25U$$

Case 5.   Suppose $2Y = 5X + 8$, and you want to solve the expression for X. You first subtract 8 from both sides and obtain

$$2Y - 8 = 5X + 8 - 8$$
$$2Y - 8 = 5X$$

Next, divide both sides of the expression by 5, yielding

$$(2Y - 8)/5 = 5X/5$$
$$(2Y - 8)/5 = X$$
$$X = (2Y - 8)/5$$

You may further simplify by dividing each term on the right-hand of the expression by 5:

$$X = (2Y/5) - (8/5)$$
$$X = .4Y - 1.6$$

It is important to remember that when you divide a complex term such as $2Y - 8$ by a number or a variable, each part of that term must be divided by the same divisor.

You will have a lot of opportunity to work with expressions such as the one in case 5, so let us see how such an algebraic statement could represent some economic relationship. Suppose that X represents the number of units of car sales for the United States in millions of units and that Y is personal income per capita in thousands of dollars. The algebraic statement $X = .4Y - 1.6$ could then be stated in a nonalgebraic way as follows: the number of millions of units of cars sold in the United States is four-tenths of the dollar value of personal income per capita expressed in thousands of dollars less one and six-tenths of a million units. It is certainly quicker and easier to state this relationship using the algebraic statement than using the longer, more conversational version. As you start to work with more complex models, the added simplicity of algebraic representations will become more and more useful to you.

Now suppose that you know that personal income per capita is $10,000. Then Y would be 10. Remember that Y is in thousands of dollars, so if $Y = 10$, income must be $10,000 (if $Y = 11.2$, income would be $11,200). Car sales can be calculated as follows:

$$X = .4Y - 1.6$$
$$X = .4(10) - 1.6$$
$$X = 4 - 1.6$$
$$X = 2.4$$

Since X represents car sales in millions of units, you would say that 2.4 million (2,400,000) cars could be expected to be sold if personal income per capita was $10,000.

A.2 RULES GOVERNING THE USE OF EXPONENTS

Of all algebraic relationships, the use of exponents is the area in which students often seem to need the most review. The rules and concepts discussed in this section will prepare you for future use of functions containing exponents and will give you confidence in using and interpreting such equations. We will begin by summarizing some basic rules and then illustrate their use in various examples. In an expression such as X^n, X is the *base* and n is the *exponent*. In stating the rules, we will use the letters m and n to represent any two exponents. They may be any real numbers. They can be positive or negative, integers or decimals. After each rule is presented, an example using specific numbers rather than m and n is given to illustrate the rule.

Rule 1. When multiplying like bases, the exponents are added:

$$(X^m)(X^n) = X^{m+n}$$

But if the bases are not the same, the exponents cannot be added. For example, using X and Y to represent different bases, we find that $(X^m)\,(Y^n)$ can only be rewritten as $X^m Y^n$, since the bases are not the same (X is not Y). Let us consider an example in which the bases are the same. Suppose you want to multiply X squared (X^2) by X cubed (X^3):

$$(X^2)(X^3) = X^{2+3} = X^5$$

Similarly, multiplying X cubed by X to the fifth power,

$$(X^3)(X^5) = X^{3+5} = X^8$$

Rule 2. When dividing like bases, the exponent of the denominator is subtracted from the exponent of the numerator. Again, this is true only if the base is the same. The rule is, then,

$$X^m/X^n = X^{m-n}$$

For example, suppose you want to divide X^5 by $X^{3.1}$:

$$(X^5)/(X^{3.1}) = X^5/X^{3.1} = X^{5 - 3.1} = X^{1.9}$$

Rule 3.   When raising a power to another power, the exponents are multiplied. This rule can be stated as

$$(X^m)^n = X^{mn}$$

For example, suppose you want to square X cubed:

$$(X^3)^2 = X^{3 \cdot 2} = X^6$$

Remember that $X^3 = (X \cdot X \cdot X)$, so $(X^3)^2 = (X \cdot X \cdot X)^2$, which is $(X \cdot X \cdot X)$ times $(X \cdot X \cdot X)$, or X to the sixth power (X^6).

Rule 4.   Rule 4 is really an extension of rule 3 to the situation in which the product of unlike bases (X and W) is raised to a power. We will again use m and n to represent powers for the now unlike bases, and we will use k for the other power. The rule can be stated as

$$(X^m W^n)^k = X^{km} W^{kn}$$

For example, suppose you have X squared (X^2) times W cubed (W^3) and want to square that product (raise it to the second power). You would have

$$(X^2 W^3)^2 = X^{(2)(2)} W^{(2)(3)} = X^4 W^6$$

What would UV squared equal? The implied power for both U and V is 1, but we normally do not write the first power. So $(UV)^2 = U^2 V^2$.

Rule 5.   When moving any term from numerator to denominator, and vice versa, the sign of the exponent is reversed. This rule can be written as

$$1/X^n = X^{-n}$$

It might be useful to look at this rule in three other general forms as well before looking at some examples. These forms are

$$Y^m = 1/Y^{-m}$$
$$1/Y^{-m} = Y^m$$
$$X^m/Y^n = X^m Y^{-n}$$

The following four examples illustrate each of these forms of rule 5:

$$1/X = X^{-1}$$
$$Y^3 = 1/Y^{-3}$$
$$1/Y^{-2} = Y^2$$
$$X^2/Y^3 = X^2Y^{-3}$$

Rule 6. Anything raised to the 0 power is equal to 1. In general, this can be written as

$$X^0 = 1$$

So,

$$(15)^0 = 1$$

as does

$$(10X + X^2)^0 = 1$$

Let us review these algebraic relationships by looking at two examples:

Example 1. Suppose $X = 10 - 2Y^2$ and you want to solve the equation for Y. First add $2Y^2$ to both sides:

$$X + 2Y^2 = 10 - 2Y^2 + 2Y^2$$
$$X + 2Y^2 = 10$$

Now subtract X from both sides:

$$X + 2Y^2 - X = 10 - X$$
$$2Y^2 = 10 - X$$

Dividing both sides by 2 gives

$$2Y^2/2 = (10 - X)/2$$
$$Y^2 = 5 - .5X$$

Now raise both sides to the .5 power to get Y to the first power on the left side:

$$(Y^2)^{.5} = (5 - .5X)^{.5}$$
$$Y^{(2)(.5)} = (5 - .5X)^{.5}$$
$$Y = (5 - .5X)^{.5}$$

Note here that raising something to the .5 power is the same as finding its square root. That is, we could also write the above result as

$$Y = \sqrt{5 - .5X}$$

Example 2. Suppose $2X^8Y = 8X^3Y^5$ and you want to solve this expression for Y. You would first multiply both sides by $Y^{-.5}$ to get rid of the Y term on the right side:

$$(2X^{.8}Y)Y^{-.5} = (8X^{.3}Y^{.5})Y^{-.5}$$
$$2X^{.8}Y^{1-.5} = 8X^{.3}Y^{.5-.5}$$
$$2X^{.8}Y^{.5} = 8X^{.3}Y^{0}$$
$$2X^{.8}Y^{.5} = 8X^{.3}$$

Now you can get rid of the X term on the left side by multiplying both sides by $X^{-.8}$:

$$(2X^{.8}Y^{.5})X^{-.8} = (8X^{.3})X^{-.8}$$
$$2X^{.8-.8}Y^{.5} = 8X^{.3-.8}$$
$$2X^{0}Y^{.5} = 8X^{-.5}$$
$$2Y^{.5} = 8X^{-.5}$$

Now divide both sides by 2 to get just a Y term on the left side:

$$2Y^{.5}/2 = 8X^{-.5}/2$$
$$Y^{.5} = 4X^{-.5}$$

You must now raise both sides to a power that will leave you with Y to the first power on the left side. From rule 3 of using exponents, you know that when raising one power to another, the powers are multiplied. So you need only ask yourself: What number do I need to multiply .5 by to get 1? The answer is obviously 2. So square both sides:

$$(Y^{.5})^2 = (4X^{-.5})^2$$
$$Y^{(.5)(2)} = 4^2 X^{(-.5)(2)}$$
$$Y = 16X^{-1}$$

Remember that this result can also be written

$$Y = 16/X$$

Appendix B   Differentiation

This appendix expands the discussion of differentiation provided in Chapter 3 to review some additional rules that are helpful in finding derivatives of more complex functions and to include a more formal development of the concept of a derivative.

B.1   FIVE ADDITIONAL RULES FOR FINDING DERIVATIVES

The rules discussed here build on the more basic rules covered in the text. These rules are used less frequently but can save a great deal of time in finding derivatives when complex functions are involved. As in the text, examples are provided to illustrate the use of each of these rules.

The Product Rule

Suppose that Y is a function of the product of two separate functions of X: $f(X)$ and $g(X)$. That is, $Y = f(X) \cdot g(X)$. The derivative of Y with respect to X is the first term, $f(X)$, times the derivative of the second term, $g'(X)$, plus the second term, $g(X)$, times the derivative of the first term, $f'(X)$. Thus, for $Y = f(X) \cdot g(X)$,

$$dY/dX = f(X) \cdot g'(X) + g(X) \cdot f'(X)$$

Example 1.   Let $f(X) = X^2$, and $g(X) = 4X^3$:

$$Y = (X^2)(4X^3)$$
$$y' = (X^2)[(3)(4X^{3-1})] + 4X^3(2X^{2-1})$$
$$y' = X^2(12X^2) + 4X^3(2X)$$
$$y' = 12X^4 + 8X^4$$
$$y' = 20X^4$$

You can check this first by multiplying $f(X)$ times $g(X)$ and then finding the derivative.

Example 2.   Let $f(X) = (3X + X^2)$, and $g(X) = 12X^3$:

$$Y = (3X + X^2)(12X^3)$$
$$dY/dX = (3X + X^2)[(3)(12X^{3-1})]$$
$$+ (12X^3)(3X^{1-1} + 2X^{2-1})$$
$$dY/dX = (3X + X^2)(36X^2) + (12X^3)(3 + 2X)$$
$$dY/dX = 108X^3 + 36X^4 + 36X^3 + 24X^4$$
$$dY/dX = 144X^3 + 60X^4$$

You can again check this result by doing the multiplication first.

Example 3.   Let $f(X) = X^{-2}$, and $g(X) = 4X^3$,

$$Y = (X^{-2})(4X^3)$$
$$y' = (X^{-2})[(3)(4X^{3-1})] + (4X^3)(-2X^{-2-1})$$
$$y' = (X^{-2})(12X^2) + (4X^3)(-2X^{-3})$$
$$y' = 12X^0 - 8X^0 = 4X^0 = 4$$

Check this by doing the multiplication first. Remember that $(X^{-2})(4X^3) = 4X^{-2+3} = 4X$, which is a linear function with a constant slope equal to four.

The Quotient Rule

Suppose that Y is a function of the quotient of two separate functions, $f(X)$ and $g(X)$. That is, $Y = f(X)/g(X)$. The derivative of Y with respect to X is the denominator, $g(X)$, times the derivative of the numerator, $f'(X)$, minus the numerator, $f(X)$, times the derivative of the denominator, $g'(X)$, all divided by the denominator squared, $[g(X)]^2$. That is,

$$dY/dX = \frac{g(X) \cdot f'(X) - f(X) \cdot g'(X)}{[g(X)]^2}$$

Let us look at some examples of this complicated sounding rule. Once you do it a few times, it becomes much easier than it sounds.

Example 1.   Let $f(X) = X^2$, and $g(X) = 4X^3$:

$$Y = X^2/4X^3$$
$$y' = \frac{(4X^3)(2X^{2-1}) - (X^2)(3)(4X^{3-1})}{(4X^3)^2}$$
$$y' = \frac{(4X^3)(2X) - (X^2)(12X^2)}{16X^6}$$
$$y' = \frac{8X^4 - 12X^4}{16X^6} = \frac{-4X^4}{16X^6}$$
$$y' = -.25X^{-2}$$

You should try doing the division first to verify the result.

Example 2. Let $f(X) = 3X + X^2$, and $g(X) = 6X^4$:

$$Y = \frac{3X + X^2}{6X^4}$$

$$dY/dX = \frac{(6X^4)(3 + 2X) - (3X + X^2)(24X^3)}{(6X^4)^2}$$

$$dY/dX = \frac{18X^4 + 12X^5 - 72X^4 - 24X^5}{36X^8}$$

$$dY/dX = \frac{-54X^4 - 12X^5}{36X^8}$$

The Function of a Function, or Chain, Rule

Let us assume that Y is a function of $Z\,[Y = f(Z)]$, and that Z is a function of $X\,[Z = g(X)]$. Suppose that you would like to know the rate of change in Y as X changes. We can find this by multiplying the derivative of Y with respect to Z by the derivative of Z with respect to X:

$$dY/dX = \frac{dY}{dZ} \cdot \frac{dZ}{dX}$$

Example 1. Let $Y = 2Z^4$, and $Z = X^2 + 3X$:

$$dY/dZ = 8Z^3$$
$$dZ/dX = 2X + 3$$
$$dY/dX = (8Z^3)(2X + 3)$$

and since $Z = X^2 + 3X$,

$$dY/dX = 8(X^2 + 3X)^3(2X + 3)$$

Example 2. Let $Y = Z^{.5}$, and $Z = X^2 + 2X + 1$:

$$dY/dZ = .5Z^{-.5}$$
$$dZ/dX = 2X + 2$$
$$dY/dX = (.5Z^{-.5})(2X + 2)$$
$$dY/dX = \frac{.5(2X + 2)}{Z^{.5}}$$
$$dY/dX = \frac{.5(2X + 2)}{(X^2 + 2X + 1)^{.5}}$$

But

$$X^2 + 2X + 1 = (X + 1)^2$$

and

$$[(X + 1)^2]^{.5} = (X + 1)$$

Therefore,

$$dY/dX = \frac{.5(2X + 2)}{X + 1} = \frac{X + 1}{X + 1} = 1$$

See if you can show this to be true by making the substitutions first. Do you find that $Y = X + 1$?

Example 3. Suppose that

$$Y = (X^2 - 3X + X^{-1})^{50}$$

To raise $(X^2 - 3X + X^{-1})$ to the fiftieth power would take a long time, and even then the process of finding dY/dX would be cumbersome. However, a problem such as this is easily handled using the function of a function rule. If we let $Z = X^2 - 3X + X^{-1}$, we have the following set of relationships:

$$Y = f(Z) = Z^{50}$$
$$Z = g(X) = X^2 - 3X + X^{-1}$$

and using this rule, we find the rate of change in Y as X changes as

$$dY/dX = \frac{dY}{dZ} \cdot \frac{dZ}{dX}$$
$$dY/dX = (50Z^{49})(2X - 3 - X^{-2})$$

Since $Z = X^2 - 3X + X^{-1}$, we can write the derivative as

$$dY/dX = 50(X^2 - 3X + X^{-1})^{49}(2X - 3 - X^{-2})$$

Derivatives of Logarithmic Functions

If Y is equal to the natural logarithm of a function of X, we would have[1]

$$Y = \ln U \text{ and } U = f(X)$$

The derivative of Y with respect to X is, then,

---

[1] A natural logarithm has the base e, where e is approximately 2.71828. Formally,

$$e = \lim_{n \to 0} (1 + \tfrac{1}{n})^n$$

The $\ln W = N$ means that W is the value we get when e is raised to the N power. For example,

$$\ln 100 = 4.6052$$

and

$$e^{4.60529} = 2.71828^{4.6052} = 100$$

$$dY/dX = \frac{1}{U} \cdot \frac{dU}{dX}$$

Example 1.   Let $Y = \ln U$, and $U = X^2 + X$:

$$y' = \frac{1}{U}(2X + 1)$$

$$y' = \left(\frac{1}{X^2 + X}\right)(2X + 1) = \frac{2X + 1}{X^2 + X}$$

Example 2.   Let $Y = \ln(2X^3 - 4X)$:

$$dY/dX = \left(\frac{1}{2X^3 - 4X}\right)(6X^2 - 4)$$

$$dY/dX = \frac{6X^2 - 4}{2X^3 - 4X}$$

$$dY/dX = \frac{3X^2 - 2}{X^3 - 2X}$$

Derivatives of Exponential Functions

If $Y = a^U$, where $U = f(X)$, the derivative of Y with respect to X is defined as

$$dY/dX = a^U(\ln a)\frac{dU}{dX}$$

In many situations, $a = e$, where e is the base used for natural logarithms. When this is the case, the rule is simplified, since $\ln e = 1$. We then have

$$Y = eU \text{ and } U = f(X)$$

$$dY/dX = e^U\frac{dU}{dX}$$

Example 1.   Let $Y = 8^U$, and $U = 2X^2 + X$:

$$y' = (8^{2X^2 + X})(\ln 8)(4X + 1)$$

Example 2.   Let $Y = e^{6X + 1}$:

$$dY/dX = (e^{6X + 1})(6)$$

Example 3.   Let $Y = e^X$:

$$y' = e^X(1) = e^X$$

B.2   AN ALGEBRAIC DEVELOPMENT OF DERIVATIVES

The relationship between the average rate of change of a function and the derivative of the function is shown graphically in Figure B.1. The average

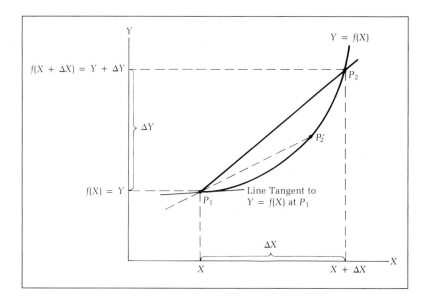

FIGURE B.1   **A General Nonlinear Function: Y = f(X).**   As X becomes less (i.e., as P_2 moves closer to P_1), the average slope of the line between P_1 and P_2 comes closer to being the same as the slope of the line tangent to the curve at P_1.

rate of change of the function $Y = f(X)$ between P_1 (coordinates X, Y) and P_2 (coordinates $X + \Delta X$, $Y + \Delta Y$) is the slope of the straight line through the two points. If you now hold P_1 fixed and allow P_2 to move down the curve of the function toward P_1 (such as to P'_2), you note that ΔY and ΔX become smaller. Also, the slope of the line through the fixed point P_1 and the moving point P'_2 becomes less as ΔX becomes smaller. As ΔX decreases and approaches 0, P'_2 approaches P_1 and finally, at the limit ($\Delta X \rightarrow 0$), the line "through" P_1 and P'_2 becomes the tangent to the curve of the function at point P_1. The slope of this tangent at P_1 is called the derivative of the function at P_1.

Let us now look at Figure B.2, which shows the function $Y = 2X$. You can write the slope of that function in a more formal way that is helpful in understanding the concept of a derivative. If $Y = f(X)$, it follows that $Y + \Delta Y = f(X + \Delta X)$. For example, if $Y = f(X) = 2X$, then $Y + \Delta Y = f(X + \Delta X) = 2(X + \Delta X)$. Suppose that in the case of this function $X = 2$, and we wish to know the value of Y. It would be found as

$$Y = f(X) = 2X = 2(2) = 4$$

If we increase X by ΔX, Y will change by some amount ΔY. For example, if $\Delta X = 1$, then we know that

$$Y + \Delta Y = f(X + \Delta X) = 2(X + \Delta X)$$
$$Y + \Delta Y = 2(2 + 1) = 2(3) = 6$$

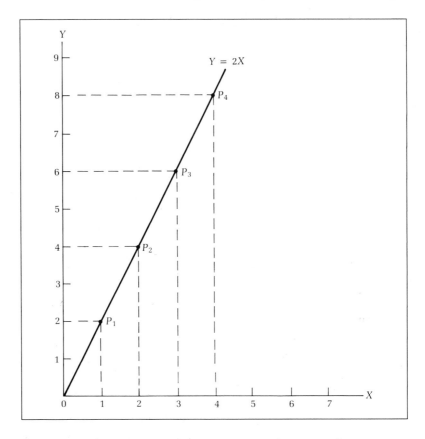

FIGURE B.2   **Graphic Representation of the Linear Function Y = 2X.**   The slope
of this function is constant: it is always 2.

Since $Y = 4$ when $X = 2$, if X is increased by $\Delta X = 1$, ΔY must be 2 because
$Y + \Delta Y = 6$. The slope of this function is, thus,

$$\Delta Y/\Delta X = 2/1 = 2$$

or

$$\Delta Y/\Delta X = \frac{f(X + \Delta X) - f(X)}{\Delta X} = \frac{6 - 4}{1} = \frac{2}{1} = 2$$

The latter form of expressing the slope of a function lies at the heart of
the branch of mathematics referred to as calculus (a term that tends to scare
people but, as you will see, unnecessarily so). A *derivative* of a function is
defined as the rate of change in the function as the change in the
independent variable becomes very small (i.e., as ΔX approaches 0, often
written as $\Delta X \rightarrow 0$). Thus, the derivative of $Y = f(X)$ may be written as

$$y' = f'(X) = dY/dX = \lim_{X \to 0} \Delta Y/\Delta X$$

or, alternatively, as

$$y' = f'(X) = dY/dX = \lim_{X \to 0} \frac{f(X + \Delta X) - f(X)}{\Delta X}$$

The latter form is a mathematical definition of a derivative.

The notations y', $f'(X)$, and dY/dX are equivalent but alternative forms of denoting a derivative. The derivative of any continuous function can be found using this mathematical definition, but the process is cumbersome. To further illustrate this, let us use the simple functions graphed in Figures B.2 and B.3 as examples.

The function graphed in Figure B.2 is $Y = 2X$. Since $Y = f(X)$, the following two relationships must be true:

$$f(X) = 2X$$
$$f(X + \Delta X) = 2(X + \Delta X)$$

You simply replace X in the function with $(X + \Delta X)$ to find $f(X + \Delta X)$.

You can now find the derivative of $Y = 2X$ using the definition of a derivative given above and repeated below:

$$dY/dX = \lim_{\Delta X \to 0} \frac{f(X + \Delta X) - f(X)}{\Delta X}$$

which for $Y = f(X) = 2X$ becomes:

$$dY/dX = \lim_{\Delta X \to 0} \frac{2(X + \Delta X) - 2X}{\Delta X}$$

Multiplying $(X + \Delta X)$ by 2, we get

$$dY/dX = \lim_{\Delta X \to 0} \frac{2X + 2\Delta X - 2X}{\Delta X}$$

The $2X$ and $-2X$ cancel one another, and thus,

$$dY/dX = \lim_{\Delta X \to 0} 2\Delta X / \Delta X$$
$$dY/dX = \lim_{\Delta X \to 0} 2$$

Since there is no X or ΔX on the right-hand side of this equation, $dY/dX = 2$ for any value of X or ΔX. So the slope of $Y = 2X$ is always equal to 2 regardless of the point on the function you want to evaluate.

Now let us turn our attention to the nonlinear function shown in Figure B.3. That function is $Y = f(X) = X^2$. Thus,

$$f(X) = X^2$$
$$f(X + \Delta X) = (X + \Delta X)^2$$

The derivative of this function may be expressed as

$$dY/dX = \lim_{\Delta X \to 0} \frac{f(X + \Delta X) - f(X)}{\Delta X}$$

$$dY/dX = \lim_{\Delta X \to 0} \frac{(X + \Delta X)^2 - X^2}{\Delta X}$$

By squaring the $(X + \Delta X)$ term, we get

$$dY/dX = \lim_{\Delta X \to 0} \frac{X^2 + 2X\Delta X + (\Delta X)^2 - X^2}{\Delta X}$$

The X^2 and $-X^2$ terms cancel one another, and thus,

$$dY/dX = \lim_{\Delta X \to 0} \frac{2X\Delta X + (\Delta X)^2}{\Delta X}$$

Now we can divide through on the right-hand side by ΔX to obtain

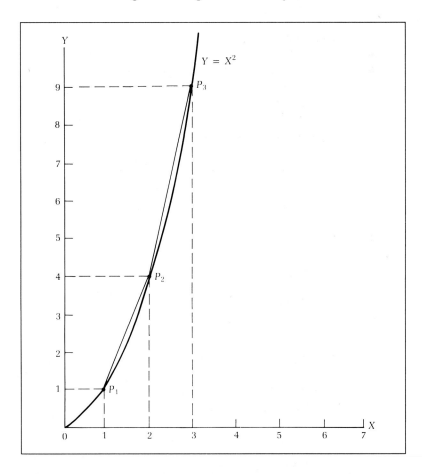

FIGURE B.3   **Graphic Representation of the Quadratic Function $Y = X^2$.**   The
slope of this function increases from P_1 to P_2 to P_3.

$$dY/dX = \lim_{\Delta X \to 0} (2X + \Delta X)$$

But as $\Delta X \to 0$ (i.e., ΔX becomes very small),

$$\lim_{\Delta X \to 0} (2X + \Delta X) = 2X$$

Thus,

$$dY/dX = 2X$$

So we see that the slope of the function $Y = X^2$ at any point is 2X. Since the slope is itself a function of X, the slope varies at different points along the function $Y = X^2$. This can be seen by inspection of Figure B.3. As we move from left to right along the function (i.e., as X increases), the slope of the function becomes greater.

From the derivative of the function, we can evaluate its slope at various points. At $X = 1$, $y' = 2X = 2$; at $X = 3$, $y' = 2X = 6$; and at $X = 10$, $y' = 2X = 20$. We see that as X increases, the slope of this function does indeed increase.

As you work with derivatives in this course and others, the following two points should always be kept in mind: (1) a derivative is the slope of a function at a point on the function; and (2) a derivative should always be thought of as a rate of change; thus, dY/dX is the rate of change in Y as X changes (for very small changes in X).

Appendix C
Sources of Information and Data

The purpose of this appendix is to provide a reasonably comprehensive, although not complete, set of information and data sources that may be of value to a business economist. A number of bibliographies covering business and economic data are available. Some of the most useful of these are Comen's *Sources of Business Information* (University of California Press, 1964); the American Marketing Association's *Basic Bibliography on Marketing Research*; *Statistical Sources of the U.S. Government* (Bureau of the Budget, Government Printing Office); the U.S. Department of Commerce's *Marketing Information Guide*; Paul Wasserman et al., eds., *Statistical Sources* (Gale Research Company, Detroit, 1965); the Public Affairs Information Service's *Bulletin*; and the *Monthly Catalog of U.S. Government Publications* (U.S. Government Printing Office).

Available guides to information sources include McGraw-Hill's *How and Where to Look It Up*; the American Marketing Association's *Current Sources of Marketing Information*; the U.S. Department of Commerce's *Catalog of United States Census Publications*; John L. Androit's *Guide to U.S. Government Statistics* (Arlington, VA: Documents Index); and the Bureau of the Budget's *Statistical Services of the United States Government*.

Other useful indexes and directories include the *Reader's Guide to Periodical Literature*, the *Business Periodicals Index*, the *Index of Economic Journals*, the *New York Times Index*, the *Wall Street Journal Index*, the *Index of Publications of Bureaus of Business and Economic Research*, the *Journal of Economic Literature*, the *Directory of Trade Associations: Fact Book* (U.S. Department of Commerce), the Special Libraries Association's *Directory of Business and Financial Services*, the *Fortune Directory* (Time, Inc.), the *Economic Almanac* (National Industrial Conference Board), and the *Reference Book of Dun and Bradstreet*.

The following list is composed of specific publications that contain extensive data related to the major subject under which they appear. Many of these publications contain data on several or many subject categories and thus appear more than once. To simplify the listing the following abbreviations are used:

AMA American Medical Association
BC Bureau of the Census
BLS Bureau of Labor Statistics
BM Bureau of Mines
CSC Civil Service Commission
DA Department of Agriculture
DB Dun and Bradstreet
DD Department of Defense
FAA Federal Aviation Administration
FPC Federal Power Commission
FRB Federal Reserve Board
FTC Federal Trade Commission
IRS Internal Revenue Service
NBER National Bureau of Economic Research
NEA National Education Association
NSF National Science Foundation
OBE Office of Business Economics
OE Office of Education
OMB Office of Management and Budget
PHS Public Health Service
SEC Securities and Exchange Commission
SRC Survey Research Center, University of Michigan
SSA Social Security Administration

AGRICULTURE

Census of Agriculture. BC, every five years.
Commodity Futures Statistics. Commodity Exchange Authority, annual.
Agriculture Statistics. DA, annual.
Changes in Farm Production and Efficiency: Summary Report. DA, Economic Research Service, annual.
Crop Production: Acreage, Yield, and Production by States. DA, Statistical Reporting Service, monthly with annual summary.
Statistics of Farmer Cooperatives. Farmer Cooperative Service, annual.
The Role of Agriculture in Economic Development. NBER, Erik Thorbecke, ed. 1969.
Resources in America's Future: Patterns of Requirements and Availabilities, 1960 – 2000. Resources for the Future, 1963.
Agricultural Finance Review. U.S. Economic Research Service, annual.

BUSINESS, GENERAL

Table of Bankruptcy Statistics. Administrative Office of the U.S. Courts, annual.

Federal Reserve Bulletin. FRB, monthly.
Business Conditions Digest. BC, monthly.
Census of Business. BC, most recent (every five years).
County Business Patterns. BC, annual.
Current Business Reports. BC, monthly, quarterly, annual.
Economic Indicators. Council of Economic Advisors, monthly.
Economic Report on Corporate Merger Activity. FTC, annual.
Statistics on Income. IRS, annual.
Survey of Current Business. OBE, monthly.
Economic Reports of the President. Office of the President, annual.
Monthly Failure Report. DB, monthly.
Monthly New Business Incorporation Report. DB, monthly.
The Fortune *Directory of the 500 Largest Industrial Corporations.* Fortune (Time, Inc.), annual.
The Behavior of Industrial Prices. NBER, Stigler and Kindahl, 1970.
The Business Cycle in a Changing World. NBER, Burns, 1969.
Executive Compensation in Large Industrial Corporations. NBER, Lewellen, 1968.
Industrial Composition of Income and Product. NBER, 1968.
The Dollars and Cents of Shipping Centers. Urban Land Institute, triennial.
Survey of Buying Power. Sales & Marketing Management, annual.

COMMODITY PRICES

Federal Reserve Bulletin. FRB, monthly.
Consumer Price Index. BLS, monthly.
Estimated Retail Food Prices by Cities. BLS, monthly.
Handbook of Labor Statistics. BLS, annual.
Relative Importance of Items in the CPI. BLS, annual.
Retail Prices and Indexes of Fuels and Electricity. BLS, monthly.
Wholesale Prices and Price Indexes. BLS, monthly.
Agricultural Statistics. DA, annual.
Agricultural Prices. DA, monthly and annual.
Commodity Yearbook. Commodity Research Bureau, annual.
The Morgan Guaranty Survey: Wholesale Prices. Morgan Guaranty Trust, monthly.
The Behavior of Industrial Prices. NBER, Stigler and Kindahl, 1970.

CONSTRUCTION, HOUSING, AND REAL ESTATE

Federal Reserve Bulletin. FRB, monthly.
Census of Construction Industries. BD, decennial.
Housing Construction Statistics. BC, monthly.

Vacant Housing Units in the United States. BC, quarterly.

Construction Review. Bureau of Domestic Commerce, monthly.

Union Wages and Hours: Building Trades. BLS, annual with quarterly releases.

Saving and Home Financing Source Book. Federal Home Loan Bank Board, annual.

Survey of Current Business. OBE, monthly.

Dodge Construction Contract Statistics Service. Dodge Division, McGraw-Hill Information Systems, monthly.

Source Book of Statistics Relating to Constructions. NBER, Lipsey and Preston, 1966.

Census of Housing. BC, every ten years.

CONSUMER INCOME EXPENDITURES

Bank Credit-Card and Check-Credit Plans. FRB, 1968.

Volume and Composition of Individual's Savings. FRB, quarterly.

Monthly Labor Review. BLS, monthly.

Three Budgets for a Retired Couple in Urban Areas of the United States. BLS.

Three Standards of Living for an Urban Family of Four Persons. BLS.

Statistics of Income. IRS, annual.

Income Distribution in the United States, by Size. OBE, annual.

Survey of Current Business. OBE, monthly.

Statistical Bulletin. SEC, monthly.

Economic Behavior of the Affluent. The Brookings Institution, Barlow, Brazer, and Morgan, November 1966.

Survey of Consumer Finances. SRC, annual.

Finance Facts Yearbook. National Consumer Finance Association, annual.

Survey of Buying Power. Sales & Marketing Management, annual.

ECONOMIC INDEXES

Federal Reserve Bulletin. FRB, monthly.

Federal Reserve Chart Book on Financial and Business Statistics. FRB, monthly.

Business Conditions Digest. BC, monthly.

Monthly Labor Review. BLS, monthly.

Economic Indicators. Council of Economic Advisors, monthly.

Survey of Current Business. OBE, monthly.

Economic Report of the President. Office of the President, annual.

Across the Board. The Conference Board, monthly.

Monthly Review. FRB, monthly.

Survey of Consumer Finances. SRC, annual.

Forecasting and Recognizing Business Cycle Turning Points. NBER, Fels and Hinshaw, 1968.

EDUCATION

Census of Population. BC, every ten years.

Statistics Concerning Indian Education. Bureau of Indian Affairs, annual.

Monthly Labor Review. BLS, monthly.

The Directory of Public Elementary and Secondary Schools in Selected Districts. Office for Civil Rights, 1968.

Undergraduate Enrollment by Ethnic Group in Federally Funded Institutions of Higher Education. Office for Civil Rights, 1968.

Bond Sales for Public School Purposes. OE, 1970.

Digest of Educational Statistics. OE, annual.

Earned Degrees Conferred. OE, annual.

Fall Statistics of Public Schools. OI, annual.

Preprimary Enrollment of Children under Six. OE, annual.

Opening Fall Enrollment in Higher Education. OE, annual.

Projections of Educational Statistics. OE, annual.

Statistics of State School Systems. OE, biennial.

Vocational and Technical Education. OE, annual.

A Fact Book on Higher Education. American Council on Education, quarterly.

National Norms for Entering College Freshman. American Council on Education, annual.

A Statistical Report on Catholic Elementary and Secondary Schools for the Years 1967–68 to 1969–70. National Catholic Educational Association.

Economic Status of the Teaching Profession. NEA, annual.

Estimates of School Statistics. NEA, annual.

Salaries in Higher Education. NEA, biennial.

Salary Schedules for Principals. NEA, annual.

Salary Schedules for Teachers. NEA, annual.

Teacher Supply and Demand in Public Schools. NEA, annual.

Teacher Supply and Demand in Universities, Colleges, and Junior Colleges. NEA, biennial.

FEDERAL GOVERNMENT FINANCES AND EMPLOYMENT

Federal Reserve Bulletin. FRB, monthly.

Annual Report. Civil Service Commission, annual.

Federal Civilian Employment in the United States by Geographic Area. CSC, annual.

Occupations of Federal Blue-Collar Workers. CSC, biennial.

Occupations of Federal White-Collar Workers. CSC, annual.

Pay Structure of the Federal Civil Service. CSC, annual.

Environmental Quality. Council on Environmental Quality, annual.

Combined Statement of Receipts, Expenditures, and Balances of the U.S. Government. Department of Treasury, annual.

Federal Funds for Research, Development and Other Scientific Activities. NSF, annual.

Survey of Current Business. OBE, monthly.

Poverty Program Information. Office of Economic Opportunity, quarterly.

The Budget of the U.S. Government. OMB, annual.

The U.S. Budget in Brief. OMB, annual.

Economic Report of the President. Office of the President, annual.

Moody's Municipal and Government Manual. Moody's Investors Service, annual.

Census of Governments. BC, every five years.

Manpower Report of the President. Office of the President, annual.

FOOD

Canned Food Report. BC, five times a year.

Retail Food Prices by Cities. BLS, monthly and annual.

Family Economic Review. DA, Agriculture Research Service, quarterly.

National Food Situation. DA, Economic Research Service, quarterly.

National School Lunch Program. DA, Economic Research Service, annual.

Frozen Food Pack Statistics. American Frozen Food Institution, annual.

Canned Food Pack Statistics. National Canners Associations, annual.

Survey of Buying Power. Sales & Marketing Management, annual.

FOREIGN COMMERCE

U.S. Commodity Exports and Imports as Related to Output. BC, annual.

U.S. Exports, Schedule B Commodity Groupings, World Area, Country, and Method of Transportation. BC, annual.

U.S. Exports, Schedule B Commodity and Country. BC, monthly.

Foreign Agricultural Trade of the U.S. DA, Economic Research Service, monthly.

World Agricultural Production and Trade. Foreign Agricultural Service, monthly.

Survey of Current Business. OBE, monthly.

International Financial Statistics. International Monetary Fund, monthly.

Trade Yearbook. Food and Agricultural Organization of the United Nations, annual.

Balance of Payments Yearbook. International Monetary Fund, annual.

Commerce America. Department of Commerce, biweekly.

FORESTS AND LUMBER

Census of Manufacturers. BC, every five years.

Current Industrial Reports. BC, monthly, quarterly, and annual.

Construction Review. Bureau of Domestic Commerce, monthly.

Monthly Labor Review. BLS, monthly.

The Demand and Price Situation for Forest Products. Forest Service, annual.

Wildfire Statistics. Forest Service, annual.

Wood Pulp Statistics. American Paper Institute, annual.

Fingertip Facts and Figures. National Forest Products Association, monthly.

HEALTH AND MEDICAL CARE

Annual Report. Department of Health and Human Services, annual.

A Report to the President on Medical Care Prices. Department of Health and Human Services, 1967.

Clean Waters for the 1970's. Federal Water Quality Administration, 1970.

Air Quality Data. PHS, annual.

Mental Health Statistics: Current Facility Reports and Reference Tables on Patients in Mental Health Facilities, Age, Sex, and Diagnoses. PHS, 1968.

Outpatient Psychiatric Clinics. PHS, annual.

Reported Tuberculosis Data. PHS, biennial.

Residents in Public Institutions for the Mentally Retarded. Social and Rehabilitation Service, annual.

The Benefit Structure of Private Health Insurance. SSA, 1970.

Financial Experience of Health Insurance Organizations in the U.S. SSA, 1966.

Medicare Statistical Reports. SSA, annual.

Prescription Drug Data Summary. SSA, annual.

Social Security Bulletin. SSA, monthly.

Annual Report of Administrator of Veterans Affairs. SSA, annual.

Distribution of Dentists in the U.S. by State, Region, District, and County. American Dental Association, annual.

Hospitals: Guide Issue. American Hospital Association, annual.

Distribution of Physicians, Hospitals and Hospital Beds in the U.S. AMA, annual.

Facts about Nursing: A Statistical Summary. American Nurses' Association, annual.

Statistical Study of the Osteopathic Profession. American Osteopathic Association, annual.

Physician's Earnings and Expenses. Medical Economics, annual.

INSURANCE

Survey of Current Business. OBE, monthly.

The Extent of Health Insurance Coverage in the U.S. SSA, 1965.

Health Insurance Plans Other than Blue Cross, Blue Shield Plans, or Insurance Companies. SSA, 1969.

Health Insurance Statistics. SSA.

Charts and Graphs: Statistical Data on Voluntary Prepayment Medical Benefit Plans. AMA, annual.

Voluntary Prepayment Medical Benefit Plans. AMA, biennial.

Best's Insurance Publications. Best Company, monthly.

The Extent of Voluntary Health Insurance Coverage in the U.S. Health Insurance Council, annual.

Source Book of Health Insurance Data. Health Insurance Institute, annual.

Insurance Facts. Insurance Informational Institute, annual.

Health Insurance Review. The Spectators, annual.

Life Insurance Review. The Spectators, annual.

INVESTMENTS AND SECURITIES

Survey of Changes in Family Finances. FRB, 1968.

Commodity Figures Statistics. Commodity Exchange Authority, annual.

Annual Report. SEC, annual.

Office Summary of Security Transactions and Holdings. SEC, monthly.

Securities Traded on Exchanges under the Securities Exchange Act. SEC, annual. with quarterly supplement.

Statistical Bulletin. SEC, monthly.

Stock Transactions of Financial Institutions. SEC, quarterly.

The Investment Outlook. Bankers Trust Company, annual.

Survey of Consumer Finances. SRC, annual.

Moody's Manual. Moody's Investors' Service, annual.

Fact Book. New York Stock Exchange, annual.

Analyst's Handbook. Standard and Poor's, annual.

Security Owner's Stock Guide. Standard and Poor's, monthly.

Value Line Investment Survey. Weekly.

LABOR

Federal Reserve Bulletin. FRB, monthly.

Census of Population. BC, every ten years.

City Employment. BC, annual.

Public Employment. BC, annual.

Analysis of Work Stoppages. BLS, annual.

Area Wage Surveys: Metropolitan Areas, U.S. and Regional Summaries. BLS, annual.

Employee Compensation in the Private Nonfarm Economy. BLS, biennial.

Employment and Earnings. BLS, monthly.

Handbook of Labor Statistics. BLS, annual.

Indexes of Output per Man-Hour, Hourly Compensation and Unit Labor Costs in the Private Economy. BLS, annual.

Monthly Labor Review. BLS, monthly.

National Survey of Professional, Administrative, Technical and Clerical Pay. BLS, annual.

Review of Productivity, Wages and Prices. BLS, quarterly.

Farm Labor. Department of Agriculture, Statistical Reporting Service, monthly.

Area Trends in Employment and Unemployment. Manpower Administration, monthly.

Manpower Report of the President by the U.S. Department of Labor. Office of the President, annual.

MANUFACTURERS

Federal Reserve Bulletin. FRB, monthly.

Annual Survey of Manufacturers. BC, annual.

Census of Manufacturers. BC, 1972.

Concentration Ratios in Manufacturing Industry. BC, 1966.

Current Industrial Reports. BC, monthly, quarterly, and annually.

The U.S. Industrial Outlook. Bureau of Domestic Commerce, annual.

Survey of Current Business. OBE, monthly.

Frozen Food Pack Statistics. American Frozen Food Institute, annual.

Annual Statistical Report. American Iron and Steel Institute, annual.

Commodity Yearbook. Commodity Research Bureau, annual.

Canned Food Pack Statistics. National Canners Association, annual.

Industry Survey. Standard & Poor.

MINERALS

Census of Mineral Industries. BC, every five years.

Commodity Data Summaries. BM, annual.

International Coal Trade. BM, monthly.

International Petroleum. BM, annual.

Minerals Yearbook. BM, annual.

Treasury Bulletin. Department of Treasury, monthly.

Year Book. American Bureau of Metal Statistics, annual.

Metal Statistics. American Metal Market, annual.

Petroleum Facts and Figures. American Petroleum Institute.

Commodity Yearbook. Commodity Research Bureau, annual.

The Oil Producing Industry in Your State. Independent Petroleum Association of American, annual.

Bituminous Coal Facts. National Coal Association, biennial.

The Oil and Gas Journal. Petroleum Publishing Company, weekly.

MONEY AND BANKING

Assets and Liabilities of Member Banks. FRB, semiannual.

Federal Reserve Bulletin. FRB, monthly.

Federal Reserve Chart Book on Financial and Business Statistics. FRB, monthly.

Assets, Liabilities, and Capital Accounts: Commercial and Mutual Savings Banks. FRB, Comptroller of the Currency and FDIC, semiannual.

Treasury Bulletin. Department of Treasury, monthly.

Report to the Federal Land Bank Association. Farm Credit Administration, annual.

Bank Operating Statistics. Federal Deposit Insurance Corporation, annual.

Savings and Home Financing Source Book. Federal Home Loan Bank Board, annual.

Trends in the Savings and Loan Field. Federal Home Loan Bank Board, annual.

Annual Report of the Administration: National Credit Union Administration, Federal Credit Union Program. SSA, annual.

The Investment Outlook. Bankers Trust Company, annual.

National Fact Book: Mutual Savings Banking. National Association of Mutual Savings Bank, annual.

Annual Report. U.S. Comptroller of the Currency, annual.

Annual Report. Federal Deposit Insurance Corporation, annual.

NATIONAL DEFENSE

Defense Indicators. BC, monthly.

Military Assistance and Foreign Military Sales Facts. DD, annual.

Prime Contract Awards by State. DD, quarterly.

Real and Personal Property of the Department of Defense. DD, annual.

Selected Manpower Statistics. DD, annual.
Annual Statistical Report. Office of Civil Defense, annual.

POPULATION AND POPULATION CHARACTERISTICS

Census of Agriculture. BC, every five years.
Census of Population. BC, every ten years.
Statistical Bulletin. Metropolitan Life Insurance Company, monthly.
Demography. Population Association of American, annual.
Survey of Buying Power. Sales & Marketing Management, annual.
Statistical Yearbook. (UNESCO), 1981.

POWER

Annual Report to Congress. Atomic Energy Commission, annual.
Financial Report. Atomic Energy Commission, annual.
All-Electric Homes: Annual Bill. Federal Power Commission, annual.
Annual Report. Federal Power Commission, annual.
Electric Power Statistics: Production of Energy and Capacity of Plants, Fuel
    Consumption of Electric Power Plants, Electric Utility System Loads,
    Sales of Electric Energy, Financial Statistics of Private Utilities. Fed-
    eral Power Commission, monthly.
Statistics for Interstate Natural Gas Pipeline Company. FPC, annual.
Statistics of Privately Owned Electric Utilities in the U.S. FPC, annual.
Statistics of Publicly Owned Electric Utilities in the U.S. FPC, annual.
Annual Statistical Report: Rural Electrification Borrowers. Rural Electrifi-
    cation Administration, annual.
Annual Report. Tennessee Valley Authority, annual.
Gas Facts. American Gas Association, annual.
Monthly Bulletin of Utility Gas Sales. American Gas Association, monthly.
Statistical Year Book of the Electric Utility Industry for the Year. Edison
    Electric Institute, annual.
The Handy-Whitman Index of Public Utility Construction Costs. Whitman,
    Requardt and Association, semiannual.
The Handy-Whitman Index of Water Utility Construction Costs. Whitman,
    Requardt and Association, semiannual.

RECREATION

Census of Transportation. BC, every five years.
Boating Statistics. Coast Guard, annual.

Federal Aid in Fish and Wildlife Restoration. Fish and Wildlife Service, annual.

Camper Days in Areas Administered by the National Park Service. National Park Service, annual.

Public Use of the National Parks. National Park Service, monthly.

Annual Market Research Notebook: The Marine Market. Boating Industry Association, annual.

Statistical Reports on Horse Racing in the U.S. National Association of State Racing Commissioners, annual.

Recreation and Park Yearbook. National Recreation and Park Association, every five years.

SCIENTIFIC RESOURCES, RESEARCH, AND EDUCATION

American Science Manpower. National Science Foundation, biennial.

Federal Funds for Research, Development and Other Scientific Activities. NSF, annual.

Research and Development in State Government Agencies. NSF, biennial.

Research and Development in Local Government. NSF, biennial.

Research and Development in Industry. NSF, annual.

Enrollment for Masters and Higher Degrees. OE, annual.

Annual Report of the Commissioner of Patents. Patent Office, annual.

Summary Report. National Academy of Sciences, annual.

Digest of Educational Statistics. U.S. Office of Education, annual.

SERVICE ESTABLISHMENTS

Census of Business. BC, most recent (every five years).

Monthly Selected Services Receipts. BC, monthly.

Trends in the Hotel-Motel Business. Harris, Kerr, Forster, and Company, annual.

Production and Productivity in the Service Industries. NBER, Fuchs, ed., 1967.

The Service Economy. NBER, Fuchs, ed., 1968.

Survey of Buying Power. Sales & Marketing Management, annual.

TRANSPORTATION AND PUBLIC UTILITIES

Waterborne Commerce of the U.S. Army Corp of Engineers, annual.

Census of Transportation. BC, every five years.

Handbook of Airline Statistics. Civil Aeronautics Board, annual.

Census of U.S. Civil Aircraft. FAA, annual.

FAA Statistical Handbook of Aviation. FAA, annual.

Highway Statistics. Federal Highway Administration, annual.

Transport Economics. Interstate Commerce Commission, monthly.

Maritime Manpower Report. Maritime Administration, monthly.

Air Transport Facts and Figures. Air Transport Association of America, annual.

Transit Fact Book. American Transit Association, annual.

Cars of Revenue Freight Loaded. Association of American Railroads, weekly.

Yearbook of Railroad Facts. Association of American Railroads, annual.

Automobile Facts and Figures. Automobile Manufacturers Association, annual.

Motor Truck Facts. Automobile Manufacturers Associaton, annual.

Annual Statistical Issue. Automotive Industries, Chilton Company, annual.

Survey of Consumer Finances. SRC, annual.

Survey of Buying Power. Sales & Marketing Management, annual.

Statistics of Communications Common Carriers. Federal Communications Commission, annual.

Statistical Services FPC's. FPC, annual.

Annual Statistical Report. Rural Electrification Administration, annual.

Transport Statistics in the U.S. Interstate Commerce Commission, annual.

WHOLESALE AND RETAIL TRADE

Federal Reserve Bulletin. FRB, monthly.

Census of Business. BC, every five years.

County Business Patterns. BC, annual.

Monthly Retail Trade Report. BC, monthly.

Monthly Wholesale Trade Report. BC, monthly.

Retail Sales. BC, annual.

Employment and Earnings. BLS, monthly.

Monthly Labor Review. BLS, monthly.

Survey of Current Business. OBE, monthly.

Survey of Buying Power. Sales & Marketing Management, annual.

INDEX

674

Durbin-Watson Statistic
(95-Percent Confidence Level)

n	K = 1		K = 2		K = 3		K = 4		K = 5	
	d_l	d_u	d_l	d_u	d_l	d_u	d_l	d_u	d_l	d_u
15	0.95	1.23	0.83	1.40	0.71	1.61	0.59	1.84	0.48	2.09
16	0.98	1.24	0.86	1.40	0.75	1.59	0.64	1.80	0.53	2.03
17	1.01	1.25	0.90	1.40	0.79	1.58	0.68	1.77	0.57	1.98
18	1.03	1.26	0.93	1.40	0.82	1.56	0.72	1.74	0.62	1.93
19	1.06	1.28	0.96	1.41	0.86	1.55	0.76	1.72	0.66	1.90
20	1.08	1.28	0.99	1.41	0.89	1.55	0.79	1.70	0.70	1.87
21	1.10	1.30	1.01	1.41	0.92	1.54	0.83	1.69	0.73	1.84
22	1.12	1.31	1.04	1.42	0.95	1.54	0.86	1.68	0.77	1.82
23	1.14	1.32	1.06	1.42	0.97	1.54	0.89	1.67	0.80	1.80
24	1.16	1.33	1.08	1.43	1.00	1.54	0.91	1.66	0.83	1.79
25	1.18	1.34	1.10	1.43	1.02	1.54	0.94	1.65	0.86	1.77
26	1.19	1.35	1.12	1.44	1.04	1.54	0.96	1.65	0.88	1.76
27	1.21	1.36	1.13	1.44	1.06	1.54	0.99	1.64	0.91	1.75
28	1.22	1.37	1.15	1.45	1.08	1.54	1.01	1.64	0.93	1.74
29	1.24	1.38	1.17	1.45	1.10	1.54	1.03	1.63	0.96	1.73
30	1.25	1.38	1.18	1.46	1.12	1.54	1.05	1.63	0.98	1.73
31	1.26	1.39	1.20	1.47	1.13	1.55	1.07	1.63	1.00	1.72
32	1.27	1.40	1.21	1.47	1.15	1.55	1.08	1.63	1.02	1.71
33	1.28	1.41	1.22	1.48	1.16	1.55	1.10	1.63	1.04	1.71
34	1.29	1.41	1.24	1.48	1.17	1.55	1.12	1.63	1.06	1.70
35	1.30	1.42	1.25	1.48	1.19	1.55	1.13	1.63	1.07	1.70
36	1.31	1.43	1.26	1.49	1.20	1.56	1.15	1.63	1.09	1.70
37	1.32	1.43	1.27	1.49	1.21	1.56	1.16	1.62	1.10	1.70
38	1.33	1.44	1.28	1.50	1.23	1.56	1.17	1.62	1.12	1.70
39	1.34	1.44	1.29	1.50	1.24	1.56	1.19	1.63	1.13	1.69
40	1.35	1.45	1.30	1.51	1.25	1.57	1.20	1.63	1.15	1.69
45	1.39	1.48	1.34	1.53	1.30	1.58	1.25	1.63	1.21	1.69
50	1.42	1.50	1.38	1.54	1.34	1.59	1.30	1.64	1.26	1.69
55	1.45	1.52	1.41	1.56	1.37	1.60	1.33	1.64	1.30	1.69
60	1.47	1.54	1.44	1.57	1.40	1.61	1.37	1.65	1.33	1.69
65	1.49	1.55	1.46	1.59	1.43	1.62	1.40	1.66	1.36	1.69
70	1.51	1.57	1.48	1.60	1.45	1.63	1.42	1.66	1.39	1.70
75	1.53	1.58	1.50	1.61	1.47	1.64	1.45	1.67	1.42	1.70
80	1.54	1.59	1.52	1.62	1.49	1.65	1.47	1.67	1.44	1.70
85	1.56	1.60	1.53	1.63	1.51	1.65	1.49	1.68	1.46	1.71
90	1.57	1.61	1.55	1.64	1.53	1.66	1.50	1.69	1.48	1.71
95	1.58	1.62	1.56	1.65	1.54	1.67	1.52	1.69	1.50	1.71
100	1.59	1.63	1.57	1.65	1.55	1.67	1.53	1.70	1.51	1.72

SOURCE: From J. Durbin and G.S. Watson, "Testing for Serial Correlation in Least Squares Regression," *Biometrika*, 38 (1951): 159–177. Reprinted with the permission of the authors and the trustees of *Biometrika*.

NOTE: K = number of independent variables
n = number of observations